BIRTH OF A REPUBLIC

The Republican Thrust for Liberty in Ireland, 1798 - 1923

Eoin Neeson is the author of ten plays and fourteen books, some of them pioneering works on aspects of Irish history notably THE CIVIL WAR 1922-23, THE LIFE AND DEATH of MICHAEL COLLINS and A HISTORY of IRISH FORESTRY. His lifelong interest in mythology resulted in four books, the most recent, DEIRDRE AND OTHER GREAT STORIES FROM CELTIC MYTHOLOGY, (1997), is a re-telling for adults of myths from the Irish cycles with a comparative Introduction. Under the pseudonyms Desmond O Neill and Donal O Neill he has had historical novels and thrillers published world-wide and translated into several languages.

i

By the same author:

The Civil War
The Life and Death of Michael Collins
A History of Irish Forestry
Deirdre and Other Great Stories from Celtic Mythology
Irish Myths and Legends
Poems from the Irish
The Book of Irish Saints
Aspects of Parallelism in Japanese and Irish Character and Culture

Fiction

Life Has No Price (Desmond O'Neill)
Red Diamonds (Desmond O'Neill)
Crucible (Donal O'Neill)
Of Gods and Men (Donal O'Neill)
Sons of Death (Donal O'Neill)

Drama

The Earth a Trinket
Public Enemy
The Face of Treason (in collaboration)
Various radio and TV plays

Eoin Neeson was born in Cork and had a privileged upbringing in a home where visits from national and international figures in the arts and politics were the norm. He has memories of many distinguished and diverse people as regular visitors in his home, amongst them Jussi Bjorling, Frank O'Connor, Arnold Bax, Fritz Kreisler, Mac Liammoir and Edwards, Erwin Schroedinger, de Valera, Eoin MacNeill, Lord Monteagle, Ernie O'Malley, Carl Hardebeck, Tom Barry. His first school was St. Ita's, Cork, founded by Terence Mac Swiney. As a child he lived in Gougane Barra, went to school in Keighmaneigh and knew the Tailor and Anstey well. He served in the Army Air Corps during the Emergency. During his career as a journalist, he held senior positions with national papers and was also editor of *The Kerryman* and managing editor of *The Munster Tribune*. He spent eight years with RTE where he edited the station's first public affairs programme, *Broadsheet*. For several years he presented *Newsview* on Television and *City Newsreel* on radio. He wrote and co-directed RTE's first two full-length documentary films. He wrote RTE's first full-length play, *Public Enemy*. In 1968 he was appointed Director of the Government Information Bureau, which he upgraded and reorganised. He retired early from the Civil Service in 1991 having served as Assistant Secretary in the Departments of Foreign Affairs, Agriculture and Energy. He was founder and first chairman of the airline EI-Air Exports/Ireland Airways.

Birth of a Republic

Eoin Neeson

PRESTIGE

DUBLIN

First published in Ireland in 1998 by
PRESTIGE BOOKS, DUBLIN

ISBN 0 9533788 0 2

All trade and other enquiries to
Columba Mercier Distribution
55a Spruce Avenue
Stillorgan Industrial Park
Blackrock
Co. Dublin
Ireland
Telephone: 2942560, Fax: 2942564

Typeset 11 on 12 point Times
Printed and Bound in Ireland by Mount Salus Press

CONTENTS

Acknowledgements

I OWE A LOT OF GRATITUDE to many people who, over the years during which this book was researched and written, were generous of their time, knowledge and patience and who helped with personal information and comments; in listening to and discussing with me the book and its progress, and in helping avoid some significant pitfalls.

My particular thanks are due to those who read and commented on various drafts and excerpts and whose interest and encouragement kept both the book and myself going – J.P. McGuinness; Darach Connolly; T.L. Sudway; Ruairi and Maire Brugha and my late friend and cousin Derry MacCarthy.

To Andrew Boyd, unfailing and generous source of information on the North of Ireland; to Jonathan Williams, my agent, whose conviction and encouragement helped crest many a difficult hill; to Bill Murphy, Jim O'Connor and all those who contributed in any way to the production of the book; and to those who offered help, advice, encouragement and tolerence in a long gestation, I am grateful.

I must also thank Sgt. Terry Hudson of An Cosantóir and, my late friend Capt. Dick O'Shea for helping locate elusive material.

A special word of appreciation to a number of old military friends, An Corneil Eoghan O Neil, the late Maj. Gen. P. Hally for putting their knowledge at my disposal, and to the one with whom I had the longest and closest association over many years, the late Lt. Gen. M. J. Costello, who was generous of time and expertise over many years to help illuminate much that went into the later part of this book.

I owe a debt of gratitude to the late Sean MacBride who, over several evenings with me, discussed many of the lesser known aspects of the War of Independence and the Civil War. Fr. J. Anthony Gaughan kindly gave his permission to cite the Kelleher document we had both been given access to, and Jack Moylett helped focus my attention on Casement. My thanks to Helen Litton for her editing.

To them all my heartfelt thanks which comes with the assurance that the opinions, mistakes and shortcomings are mine alone.

Eoin Neeson, 1998.

What is that in your hand?   *It is a branch.*
Of what   *Of the Tree of Liberty.*
Where did it first grow?   *In America.*
Where does it bloom?   *In France.*
Where did the seeds fall?   *In Ireland.*
(United Irishmen, Cork, December 1797)

Introduction

IN THIS BICENTENERY YEAR OF THE RISING by the oppressed Dissenter and Catholic majority population of Ireland in 1798, the objective of which was to establish an Irish republic, and with momentous events of statesmanship and the formulation of new and the farsighted principles of constitutional democracy (which may well set precedents for developments elsewhere), taking place, it is appropriate to look again at, and take some account of, what lay between the beginning of this effloresence and the proclamation of the Republic at Easter, 1916, the War of Independence that followed, the Treaty with Great Britain in 1921 and the Civil War that ended in 1923.

The events leading to the foundation of an independent Irish nation-state took place — mainly in this country — between 1910 and 1923. In themselves these events, while extraordinary and phenomenal, also belong to a progression that began in the decade before the Rising of 1798 with the introduction of a new and dynamic political philosophy to Ireland — republicanism.

Since we know, if with some little surprise, that republicanism was not of Irish origin - indeed might almost be said to have been alien to the traditional Irish political climate - how did this concept, in such a deep and profound manner, capture the imaginations of a people by nature conservative, whose country was occupied and who were oppressed by an alien power and riven by sectarian dissent?

Why, moreover, did it survive and strenghten throughout the nineteenth century to culminate in the 1916 Rising eighty-two years ago?

The American War of Independence (1774 to 1781), in which many Irishmen fought with the Americans, and the French Revolution of 1789, were beacons of hope for oppressed peoples everywhere. Nowhere was that beacon seen more clearly than from Ireland. Tom Paine's *The Rights of Man* sold 40,000 copies in Ireland alone between 1791 when it was published and 1798 — a sale few authors achieve today. The American and French challenges to monarchical misrule, opened up for the people of Ireland the prospect of liberty for themselves with a self-image and identity undreamed of for two hundred years. When, therefore, the republican idea took root towards the close of the eighteenth century, it was really the first assertion of a political philosophy by the people since before the Flight of the Earls in 1607. When, in 1793, war broke out between revolutionary France and Great Britain, France offered assistance to countries seeking freedom. For the republican Society of United Irishmen, founded in Belfast only two years earlier, this offer must have sounded like a clarion call. When the Society was suppressed the following year (1794) it became 'a secret, oath-bound organisation, dedicated to the achievement of an Irish republic with French military assistance' (Thomas Bartlett, *The Invasion that Never Was*, THE FRENCH ARE IN THE BAY, ed. John A. Murphy, p. 49). The republican flame spread through the substantial oppressed and dissident population, Catholic and Dissenter, uniting them in the first truly national political endeavour since the collapse, in 1601, of the so-called Gaelic Order under the Tudor Conquest by an England haunted by the prospect of a strong, possibly hostile, Ireland. A glow of positive expectation, the reflection of shimmering and world-shattering changes in the decadent monarchical systems elsewhere, for the first time in hundreds of years, fell, like a mantle of promise, across the land.

True, there had been wars, hardship and political growth since the Tudor Conquest, but the wars of the seventeenth and eighteenth centuries, though fought in Ireland and often based on religious and legal grievances, were not wars for an Irish cause; nor were they fought under traditional Gaelic leadership. They were wars of religion and/or for an English cause and an English (or Scottish) king and the Irish leaders came, in the main, from Old English Catholic stock. Hardship came with coercion and oppression while all but the privileged Anglican Church few were excluded from political activity.

For almost two hundred years the people, overruled and coerced by those they perceived as tyrants, alien both as to race and religion, had had little to say in the ordering of their own lives. That may not have been all that unusual in the eighteenth century, but the background circumstances on which the republican dynamic impinged, were. From the mid sixteenth century onwards, religion and religious bigotry played an increasingly, and in many ways bizarre, part in Irish/English relationships. To try to leave them and persecution out of the equation would be like trying to leave eggs out of an omelette.

That seventeenth and eighteenth century leadership came dominantly from Old English Catholic sources serving a foreign monarchical cause with strong religious overtones, was also instrumental in fostering a strange idea that would have lasting effects. Gradually, the Catholic masses adopted the curious notion that political freedom and religious freedom were synonymous; that if one was achieved, so would the other be. This was also an idea encouraged, even if sometimes ironically, by the Anglican overlords (and also by the Dissenter oppressed), both of whom saw 'Popery' as treasonable and superstition-ridden. But this idea had a rude awakening when, in response to the French Threat and in a spectacularly successful stroke of political strategy, the British administration in 1795 accorded some recognition to the Catholic Church and funded the foundation of Maynooth seminary — thus incorporating, to some extent, the Catholic Church into the status quo Establishment. By strengthening the Church's position against atheistic France, the source of much separatist and republican support, this move had the confusing consequence of restoring the concept of separation between religious and political freedom. Thus the Church's opposition to republicanism became institutionalised. To a considerable extent this policy sowed doubt and confusion in the minds of the Catholic masses, its effects enduring long after the French threat had disappeared, although it did not outlast the republican thrust — except in an unforeseen way in Northern Ireland.

Reinforced by successes in America and in France the idea and principles of a modern republic — imported or not — fell in Ireland on fertile soil amongst Dissenter and Catholic alike. They were seen as the route to the rights of liberty. The spirit of republicanism grew so quickly that, in the space of eighteen months, the French sent two major (and one smaller) invasion fleets to Ireland with the strong hope that a nationwide uprising against the British would follow when the French troops landed. As we know the two great fleets — like the Spanish Armada before them — were wrecked and scattered by Atlantic storms.

Encouraged by the expectation of yet another major French invasion fleet (which did not materialise), the republican inspired 1798 rising nonetheless took place. A smaller French force did land (in the wrong place for maximum effectiveness, and too late). The rising was suppressed, but it lasted for over five weeks[1]. In assessing these events and their aftermath it should not be overlooked that, by 1798, the Establishment, particularly the landed classes, were motivated largely by fear of the emergence in a republican Ireland of a terror similar to that which had decimated their counterparts in France a mere eight or nine years earlier. In fact the wholesale slaughter in Ireland after 1798 — estimated at 30,000 plus — outdid the French death rate under the Terror by almost ten to one.

What is less evident is the profound influence that outside events continued to have on the course of Irish republicanism over the next century and a quarter. For instance the almost continuous struggles of small nations all over Europe; that of reunification in Italy; the Munroe Doctrine; South America — off of these, and others, deeply affected — and confused — the course of Irish republicanism, especially — so far as Ireland was concerned — the Papacy,. On the one hand was the concept and aspiration of freedom and independence in modern terms, on the other was the condemnation of the source of that concept of freedom — France — as atheistic by the Pope and the refusal, for that reason, of most Irish bishops to endorse republicanism at home (in fact a far cry from the 'Home Rule, Rome Rule' catchword of Unionists).

The 1848 revolution in France, which brought the tricolour that is the national flag of Ireland to-day, had a profound influence on the perhaps over idealistically minded Young Irelanders, who rose though all unprepared to do so.

The Fenian movement was powerfully influenced by America and former American Civil War Irish officers. The Fenian invasion of Canada — startlingly successful until the United States authorities prohibited further Fenian reinforcements across the border — coincided with and to some extent aided Louis Riel's bid for republican independence in Canada.

The influence of the Hungarian revolt against the Austrian Empire was observed with great interest in Ireland and the social and industrial revolutions that swept Europe and Britain in the years before the First World War were of immeasurable importance in bringing many of the working people of the country to the climate of opinion that made, first, the 1913 Strike and secondly the 1916 Rising practicable.

The moral and practical assistance offered by Germany during the Rising, though limited, were critical — particularly the guarantee that at the peace conference after the war (which in 1916 looked as if it would be ended in Germany's favour), Ireland would have a republican voice. This was the only objective of the three objectives of the Easter Rising that was not fulfilled. But the flame of republicanism, though it flickered and faltered from time to time, and though it was sometimes dimmed by the light of constitutional progress (which, curiously, might be said to have developed at least in part from the same dynamic and was eventually absorbed by the republican movement), was never subsequently extinguished in Ireland. The events of the early twentieth century, therefore, were part of a continuum and belonged to a process — were, indeed, intended to be their end result — both older and more abiding than the events themselves.

The Act of Union at the turn of the eighteenth century polarized the republican thrust, and in so doing emphasised it. In 1856 the secret revolutionary organisation, the Irish Republican Brotherhood (IRB), was founded and dedicated itself to the establishment of a free republic in Ireland. Yet by the end of the nineteenth century it seemed as if some form of constitutional Home Rule within the Union was most likely to prevail.

But the IRB, taking advantage of the Great War (1914-1918) and the fact that Home Rule had been diluted and suspended, eliminated that prospect with the Easter Rising of 1916, followed within three years by the outbreak of the War of Independence.

There is a view that between 1798 and the end of the Civil War a century and a quarter later the republican movement remained essentially unaltered in form, structure and objective. This may be the case so far as objective is concerned (and even that was so only in a general way as is demonstrated below). So far as form and structure are concerned it was certainly not the case. Wolfe Tone's objective: 'To subvert the tyranny of our execrable Government, to break the connection with England, the never-failing source of all our political evils, and to assert the independence of my country — these were my objects. To unite the whole people of Ireland, to abolish the memory of all past dissentions, and substitute the common name of Irishman, in place of the denominations of Protestant, Catholic and Dissenter — these were my means' (*Life of Tone*, Washington, 1826, Vol. 1. pp 51-2. Speech from the dock), was modified only slightly.

But, in common with the rest of humankind, the leaders of the republican movement were, during these hundred and twenty-five years, children of their own times, subject to and influenced by the changes taking place over several generations. It follows that the forms and structures — and no doubt too the perception — of the objective — also changed. Even revolutionary movements, if they have any hope or vision of success, are, like politics, bound by what is possible.

During the nineteenth century and the first part of the twentieth there were a number of marked changes in the dynamics of the republican movement itself. One can argue that it moved from the pragmatism of the '98 leadership and of Emmet, to the, perhaps reactive, endeavour of the Young Irelanders, which might be characterised as being more romantic, to the equally reactive and perhaps less centralised Fenian movement, then to a decline and to renewed vitality allied, I believe and contrary to much popular opinion, to another bout of selfless pragmatism which gave rise to the powerful outburst of republican sentiment and activity between 1917 and 1923.

The Easter Rising of 1916 is a prime example of how the republican objective itself was calculatedly modified to accommodate the tumultuous times, to become at once a means and an end. And it was that inspired combination that made possible what followed. While the Rising achieved two of its three purposes — namely the proclamation of the Republic and a profound stirring of the national consciousness, allied to the one it did not achieve, a voice at the post-war peace conference which had been guaranteed by Germany — the Rising was not conceived as something that could, of itself, bring about either a significant victory over the British, or independence.

But the 1916 Rising, The War of Independence, the Civil War and individuals connected with them are, today, frequently confused and taken out of proper context, with resulting distortion. As a result there is the likelihood of overlooking that the painful emergence of a separate nation-state in 1922 was as much the end of one epoch as the beginning of another.

C. Desmond Greaves in his important booklet 1916 as *History; the Myth of the Blood Sacrifice*, wrote:

> How then are we to look at 1916? Not surely in isolation from the events which followed. One way of viewing its history is to regard the entire period from 1912 to 1923 as the Irish revolution, and the Home Rule crisis, the distortion of its development through the war, the Rising and aftermath, the national resurgence, declaration of independence, Anglo-Irish war, truce and civil war, as the concrete forms the struggle took in its successive phases.

Between 1910 and 1923 trauma followed trauma in Ireland. In a time when, for four years, great nations were involved in a war that changed the face of the world that is, perhaps, not startling. But there is a difference. For most of those countries involved in the Great War of 1914-1918 there was always a central and cohesive factor — namely clearly defined parameters of war to link a succession of experience. That was not the case in Ireland, where there was no such visible linkage (certainly at the outset). The peoples of Ireland were struggling to regain (or, in the case of the Northern unionists, to maintain) a sense of identity no less than national freedom.

The Rising of 1916 was the end of every separatist movement preceding it and the inspiration of much that followed. Yet over the past thirty years younger people seem to know less and less about the Rising, the events that gave rise to it or about the War of Independence and the Treaty with Great Britain that resulted from it. One wonders if they are being taught about these formative events in school, or to what extent national commemoration of this epochal period in the life of the nation has been, to say the least of it, muted. Indeed it is not uncommon to hear people actually sneer at the 1916 Rising, because — even if indirectly or by omission — they *are* being encouraged from some quarters to do that.

Awareness of dearly-won national heritage was raised by the events of 1969 and after in the North of Ireland, but, ironically, indifference then accelerated in part as revulsion against terrorist activities, rightly rejected by the people as a whole. In a misguided attempt to prevent the neo-IRA from capitalising on their claim to be the <u>only</u> legitimate descendants of the men and women of 1916 and the War of Independence, successive Irish governments sought to dissociate official ceremonies of remembrance of the Easter Rising — up to then marked by a military parade and a march-past at the GPO — from a military presence. In much the same way — in a curious pointless palliative gesture — it was also ordained that a ceremony would be held to celebrate <u>all</u> Irishmen and women who died in war anywhere. In practice this came to mean those who died serving with the forces of Britain and has all but ignored the much greater contribution by Irishmen to the fighting forces of France, Spain, Austria, Russia, Argentina, Bolivia, the United States and other countries.

Predictably, instead of obtructing the neo-IRA from capitalising on their unwarranted claim, these actions allowed them to effectively hijack the people's heritage of 1916 to the point where younger generations, ignorant of the facts, often maintain that they see no difference between the neo-IRA and those who proclaimed the Republic and fought the War of Independence, as if they saw republicanism and terrorism as being identical — which is precisely what the clumsy prohibitions on traditional commemoration ceremonies of 1916 sought to prevent. In short, successive governments are themselves to some extent responsible for diminishing the opportunities for younger generations to understand and appreciate their rightful and proper national heritage — even to the point of depriving them of that opportunity. For where government leads, others follow; and it is now commonplace to hear not only younger generations, but those who should know better, claim that they 'were never taught about it [the period 1916 to 1923], in school'.

On the one hand, young people not only know little about the formative history of the state of which they are citizens, but are ashamed of, or indifferent to, their national heritage and identity. On the other hand there was, for instance, a proposal — by, of all things, a minister for Education — to abolish history as a 'core' (that is compulsory) subject in junior high school. A thankfully sustained public outcry caused the abandonment of this lamentable notion. Such shallow and simplistic attitudes have substituted for normal pride in, and honour for, what in the United States would be called 'the Founding Fathers', and what in other countries are celebrated with dignity and without excessive jingoism or xenophobia, namely their national heroes and heroines, honoured on a daily, and natural, basis.

Much of the indifference might lie at the door of the so-called 'liberal agenda' (more correctly, perhaps, the 'phoney liberal agenda', seeming to personify

Goldsmith's observation on 'doctrines fashioned to the varying hour —') that 'knows and has an instant answer for all things'. Perhaps partly as a result of this influence, some sort of limp and insipid national outlook evidently dedicated to the proposition of making a virtue of an irresponsible tolerance devoid of any corresponding sense of duty, is not uncommon. This view requires awkward facts — such as the big picture heritage of national identity and self-image — to be suppressed virtually out of existence in the name of tolerance, a 'virtue' which simultaneously enables the sham and the ignorant to bestride a docile and undemanding moral high horse. From that saddle the sometimes misjudged, sometimes bloody, frequently heroic, always idealistic deeds and values of previous generations can be castigated and condemned as 'unacceptable' in current terms. This abandonment of the values and identity which were fought for and clung to so tenaciously and valiantly for generations is a strange phenomenon, prompting the question: Can a people become so self-deluded that they willingly reject their birthright simply from fear of acknowledging it?

Developing National Outlook

Between the first Home Rule Bill of 1886 and the third in 1912, two specific climates of opinion dominated Irish nationalism, that of constitutional Home Rule and that of Separatism. They differed significantly in one important respect from the repeal and separatist movements of the first two-thirds of the 19th century. Once Gladstone's first Home Rule Bill (1886) had passed the House of Commons, *some form* of domestic parliament for Ireland was inevitable sooner or later. In effect, whatever else might occur, the writing was on the wall so far as the Union of 1801 was concerned. Until 1913 matters turned essentially on two things, both of which accepted — albeit with ill-grace — the inevitability of some form of Home Rule. These were the struggle between Conservatives and Liberals in England (a death-struggle for the Liberals) and an incitement to frenzy, by the Conservatives, of Unionist temper and fantasy in opposition to Home Rule, which they saw as a means of destroying the Liberals [2]. The climate of opinion thus created encouraged the view that while Home Rule was an achievable — if not the most desirable — objective, a price must be paid for it. The price became partition.

Accordingly, during the first years of this century, the common view was that Home Rule was home and dry, but that it would drag some form of partition with it. Hence a growing apathy amongst the general public and the increasing tenacity and boldness of the separatists.

During the sittings (18 and 19 May, 1916) of the Royal Commission on the Rebellion in Ireland, Augustine Birrell, former Chief Secretary for Ireland, set the public attitude to Home Rule in place:

> If the Home Rule Bill had *not* been placed on the Statute Book there must have been in Ireland and the United States a great and dangerous explosion of rage and disppointment which when the war broke out would have assumed the most alarming proportions. In Ireland all (outside parts of Ulster) would have joined hands, whilst our reports from Washington tell us what the effect on America would have been.

Still, even with Home Rule on the Statute Book the chance of its ever becoming a fact was so uncertain, the outstanding difficulty about Ulster was so obvious, and the details of the measure itself were so unattractive, and difficult to transmute into telling platform phrases, that Home Rule as an emotional flag fell out of daily use in current Irish life.

Roger Casement came close to a prophetic summary of the wave of public opinion which was about to sweep the country when, in his remarkable speech from the dock, he said: 'Home Rule when it comes, if come it does, will find an Ireland drained of all that is vital to its very existence — unless it be that unquenchable hope we build on the graves of the dead ... Self government is our right, a thing born in us at birth; a thing no more to be doled out to us by another people or withheld from us by another people than the right to life itself ...'

An argument commonly heard since the mid-sixties states that the Rising did not fit the political climate of the times and was, therefore, not justified. By extension it is sometimes additionally argued that the Rising should not have taken place. There is little argument that the Rising did not fit the political climate of the times — provided the phrase 'political climate' is restricted to mean constitutional activity *only*. But throughout the nineteenth century the Irish political see-saw had swung indecisively between constitutional and activist means of achieving political self-determination. It is, accordingly, unrealistic to exclude separatist activity from any general assessment of contemporary public perceptions. The risings of 1803, 1848, 1867 were not supported by 'the mass of the people' either. Were they, therefore, equally unjustified? The argument is selectively one-sided. While neither argument — for constitutional progress or for separatist action — has exclusive claim to represent the 'political climate of the times', neither are they mutually exclusive.

Indeed it was the 'exclusivity' of these movements that had seriously impeded them. It was with their finding common cause in 1917 that the vital progress to the fundamental cause they both stood for came about. It was, in the main, the constitutionalists who, until the 1918 general election, demonstrated the extent of change that had taken place up to then. However they would have been satisfied with an independent Irish parliament, whereas the separatists wanted an independent country. Both by definition and historically, uprisings seldom have popular support before the event, whether they are against domestic or alien governments. Ireland is no different to anywhere else in this respect. Nevertheless, by 1916 it was increasingly evident to the mass of the Irish people that the means at the disposal of their constitutional leaders, no less than the constitutional leaders themselves, were inadequate if not discredited. The see-saw was again on the tilt towards activism. It is therefore incorrect and unhelpful to judge an activist/separatist movement, such as led to the Easter Rising, by the standards relevant only to a constitutional movement, particularly when the latter is already in decline.

Hard on one another's heels came the general strike of 1913 (which stirred in the urban working-classes a spirit of social revolt that spilled over into nationalist revolt), the Larne gun-running, and, at Bachelor's Walk, the killings that roused the country as had nothing else for many years. Thousands flocked to the Volunteers after these killings, only to have their national wrath sabotaged a year later when John Redmond, instead of conserving it for the opportunity visibly imminent, tried to present it to an England marching to a war fuelled by commercial concerns.

The war itself, the indefinite suspension of the Home Rule Bill together with a statement of intent about partition, coupled with the split in the Volunteers brought about by Redmond's incitement to the members to go to war for England, all helped to extend public apathy. One wonders if it was an indifference resulting from confusion? But then came the Rising at Easter, 1916. The barbaric response from London and Dublin Castle of executions, martial law, exile and internment, the attitudes of the Establishment and the Press were countered by a virtual explosion of nationalist fervour in the public — virtually what the French call a *bouleversement du mystique*. This unequivocally demonstrated the achievement of one of the second of the three purposes of the leaders of the Rising. Now the public mind became closely attuned to the drumbeat of separatism and, within a year of the Rising, was to demonstrate as much at the polls.

The War of Independence was very different from the Rising of 1916. It was a protracted campaign of incident and purpose, but unlike the Rising, it had little discernible strategic pattern. It had a specific political object, part of which was to continue striving for a hearing at the peace conference — a hope, though diminished by the victory of the Allies, that nonethless placed unfulfilled confidence in President Woodrow Wilson's pledges to principles of national sovereignty. Unlike 1916 the War of Independence was supported by an overwhelming majority of the people — the second objective of the Rising.

In contrast to the Rising it was, to a considerable extent, militarily successful, becoming a 20th century prototype for guerilla warfare. The volunteer Irish army of the time shook the edifice of the British Empire which had already seen the empires of Turkey, Austria, Germany, Russia and China shattered in a few short years. During the war and the subsequent Treaty negotiations this fact, together with the (as it had been from the sixteenth century onwards) strategically significant proximity of Ireland to the British Isles, greatly influenced British attitudes.

Martial law, coercion, arrests and brutality contributed as much to the Irish efflorescence of national spirit as did principles of freedom. The hypocrisy in the claim of Britain to be 'fighting for the rights of small nations' when she herself occupied and suppressed the oldest nation in Europe, stuck in the throats of Irish men and women up and down the country. They showed this at both the local elections of 1917 and at the general election of 1918, before committing themselves to taking decisive steps against their oppressors.

The War of Independence and an attempt to crush the Irish movement by terror were the result. By now the idea of Home Rule was well and truly dead in Ireland — but not, as became evident, in England. The demand in Ireland was for the republic proclaimed in 1916, summarised in the phrase of William Conyngham Plunket speaking about *The Nation* newspaper eighty years earlier: 'The tone is that of Wolfe Tone'.

Suddenly came Truce: Peace out of nowhere. Three months later peace negotiations began. Two months after that the ensuing Treaty, signed as Michael Collins put it, under duress, divided the cabinet of the Dail, the Dail itself, the Army and, finally the people, and led to civil war six months later.

Before the civil war broke out haggard and distressed men and women on both sides sought for reconciliation and some means of compromising their differences of principle. The proposed Constitution and the Collins/de Valera Pact promised some hope of accommodation, only to have that recede at the last minute. Then followed civil war. Six months after the outbreak, and while the war still defaced the heart and hopes of the country, Saorstat Eireann, the new Irish Free State, came into being on 6 December 1922.

Some of the strongest support for the Treaty came from the rump of the, by then, defunct Irish Parliamentary Party. As matters developed these experienced politicians and their supporters, who had been in a political wilderness for over two years, were enabled to return to active politics and bring to bear in support of the Treaty all their accumulated influence and expertise.

In any realistic consideration of this period it must be remembered that the Irish people, following two years of war, had then known peace for nearly six months. The anxiety to continue this peace was, understandably, strong; the fear of further war great. Both sides were well aware of this.

This 'Peace even at a Price' feeling swayed many dismayed and bewildered people to support of the Treaty. When the establishment as a whole, the Churches, the professions, the middle-classes, those in trade and commerce, the Press, home and domestic, massively came out in support of the Agreement, the people in general found little to disagree with in their opinions.

The Sinn Fein Dail Eireann was a single-party, republican administration which now divided. For de Valera and his supporters, the delay at Christmas 1921 before the next cabinet meeting was disastrous. Public opinion, under pressure from the Churches, the Press and vested interest pressure groups, hardened against them.

Griffith, a principal architect of the Treaty, was elected President of the Republic he was committed to abolishing, while the Opposition in the Dail were those committed to its preservation. Five ministers of the Dail were also ministers in a Provisional Government formed by the new Dail cabinet to administer the Treaty. Every pro-Treaty member of the Dail was also a member of the Provisional Government.

The anti-Treatyites claimed that the Executive of the Dail was in revolt against the Legislature and Judiciary. Pro-Treaty supporters claimed that their opponents were acting contrary to the wishes of a majority of the people.

Collins remained republican in outlook — though that outlook was now, to coin a phrase that meets the case, 'republican gradualism', expressed in his well-known 'Stepping-Stone' formula.

In the power-struggle that then existed civil war was clearly a possibility. But the anti-Treaty leaders, claiming to be guarding the rights of the people as vested in the Republic, made a major error of judgement at this time.

The situation required coordinated and practial political and military activity. But the anti-Treaty military leadership rejected all political authority so that it became the Army Executive, not the politicians, who, on the anti-Treaty side, directed the civil war.

Accordingly the charge may be fairly made that if they believed they carried responsibility for the Republic then they did not protect it adequately.

Collins and de Valera were the two outstanding figures of the period and they were close in thinking in many ways. But there were important differences between them. Collins never relinquished his dominance of either the Provisional Government or the Irish Republican Brotherhood. De Valera, on the other hand, had no influence whatever over the anti-Treaty forces once hostilities began. Indeed, because of his anxiety to make peace, he was considered by the anti-Treaty military leadership to be an embarrassment.

Moreover what divided the anti- and pro- Treaty elements was not acceptance or rejection of the Treaty, but how what had been signed might be brought to accomodate the republican point of view (hence, for instance, both the Pact and Document Number Two).

That is the main sequence of events during those thirteen years. They could not have occurred as they did outside the context of the events of 1798, and onwards, which helped form them. The forces which produced them were annealed and hammered on the anvils of Emmet and O'Connell, Davis and Stephens; honed under Parnell, Griffith and Pearse and driven home by such as Collins and de Valera.

The Truce had a greater, and in a sense more expectantly enduring, impact on the people than the Treaty which followed. After the Truce everyone believed that some kind of Treaty would emerge from the negotiations. But before July, 1921, they did not know that or that a Truce was about to materialise. But the reality was that no matter what treaty came back from London it would generate opposition. Of that there could have been no doubt.

Clearly the British would seek a treaty favourable to them; equally the Irish would seek one favourable to themselves. Since no treaty could accommodate both extremes compromise was inevitable. And compromise would, equally inevitably, mean dissent. That fact — together with the long-standing, and what should have been clearly understood, British position on partition and how to deal with it — does not seem to have received in advance the consideration it deserved from those Irish leaders in a position to provide it. 'So far it [Dail Eireann] had been a parliament without an opposition, now an opposition was being created, in the worst manner' (P.S.O'Hegarty, *A History of Ireland Under the Union*, London, 1952, p. 760).

Oddly enough the Home Rule movement is a good indicator of popular national outlook in the eventful thirty-five years between 1886 and 1921. It provide a clear example of the essential weakness of the nationalist constitutional movement under British rule. During those thirty-five years Home Rule progressed from being a new and exciting conception, to becoming, in turn, a wished-for expectation, a perceived solution, a right to be defended, a limited concession, an inadequate promise, to a diluted, discredited and no longer acceptable resolution of 'the Irish question'. In the last twelve of those thirty-five years, especially from 1912 onward, the increasingly perceived limitations of Home Rule were counterpointed to some extent by a growing social militancy and a renewed perception of revived republicanism. It is ironic that this progress of Home Rule should serve so clearly to show that **any** attempted solution to the so-called 'Irish question' that did not provide for full sovereignty would, sooner or later, be seen as only an interim measure — as events subsequent to 1916 and to the foundation of Saorstat Eireann in 1922 amply verify.

Judicious and prudent reassessment of accepted and standard versions of historical events is a very proper and desirable thing. Ever since the late 1960s there has been a growing volume of (mainly academic) criticism directed at the period from 1910 to 1923, in particular at the 1916 Rising and the War of Independence. It seems important to distinguish between 'revision' and 'revisionism'. Revision — the proper reassessment of history essential in seeking the determination of its true course insofar as that is possible given the human conflicts that are its common base — is an integral feature of the process of historical perception. Revisionism — that is revision for its own sake become an end in itself - is an entirely different matter.

It may well be that what we know as 'revisionism' set out with a critically contributory purpose. The results have been different. Baby and bathwater have often both been thrown aside. The simple, straightforward facts and examples of courage and tenacity in the service of a clear ideal of which we, the inheritors, can be rightly proud, have been rejected by tortuous, sometimes egregious, arguments usually secondary to the rejected superior and simpler narrative. There can be no objection to proper historical reassessment. In a sense it is what history is about. But 'revision' for its own sake, become an end in itself that would change the building-blocks of history to try to force facts out of their time so that they may seem to agree with contemporary mores, is a different matter. It has then, itself, become the error it purports to correct. There is an analogous attitude of mind which purports to judge the past by the standards of today, as if those who lived before us should have had precisely the values of our self-determined and so-called 'enlightened liberalism' and *'autre temps, autre moeurs'* was meaningless.

No doubt those who set out to 'revise' the history of the period had no such intention. But they must bear much of the responsibility for the bizarre outcome that to-day two, perhaps three, generations are confused about the sequence of events which brought into being the State of which they are the citizens. They have learned, or been taught, to reject — or are afraid, even ashamed of — the republicanism which brought it about, or any pride in it and the men and women who achieved it.

In part this is because — if I may borrow a phrase — 'things fell into the hands of lesser men'. The purpose of the post-1966 revisionists may have been contributory, and they may have known where it would fit in with, and be appropriate to, the superior theme. Some of their students, however — some of whom would themselves become teachers or disseminators of the 'new' history — were a different matter.

Part of the problem seems to be that the 'revisionist' idea took hold as a result of the 1966 anniversary celebrations of 1916. Ironically it appears to have become a protest against the 1916 portrayed in the celebrations, rather than a just assessment of what was being celebrated. Part of the problem, also, is that the movement began at roughly the same time as did an enduring campaign of IRA violence in the north. While universally condemning the second, no satisfactory distinction was made by the revisionists between the Easter Rising and the War of Independence, fought by men under the title IRA, and contemporary acts of terrorism in the north by those claiming the same title. This failure was particularly confusing for younger generations who were thus not only deprived of expert guidance in that respect, but were fed false judgements and inferences masquerading as fact about the superior issue.

It is, of course, important to appreciate that facets less dramatic than central ones also had a contributory role. But it is idiotic to give them the central place and to assert that they were as important as — if not more important than — the fundamental facts.

Sometimes we come across observations that, in the light of the facts, are simply incorrect. Hence we unfortunately find Foster (p.495) dismissing the guerrilla classic as 'a rigorous adherence to pieties of language, enshrined in determinedly epic accounts like Tom Barry's *Guerrilla Days in Ireland*', and Lawlor asserting that, when the first Dail, in 1919, claimed that it and the army were 'acting on behalf of the Irish people', [it] 'was, to say the least, an exaggeration. Sinn Fein's strength and development owed little to 1916 except in that it was mistakenly implicated retrospectively in the rising.'

These two observations from respected historians, one of them deprecatory, the other — since it takes no account of the 1918 election results — simply wrong, are seriously misleading. It is difficult to understand how such comments can be made in the face of the available facts. If the intent is to excise what is perceived as the romanticism of older accounts of the period, that is hardly to be achieved by denigration of first-hand accounts by participants (perhaps, it may be, unskilled in the precise and skilful employment of pointed syntax), or by 'rearrangement' of the facts to fit a new theory or point-of-view. Both examples simply do precisely what revision is supposed to correct.

Put another way; It may well be that there are mixed apples in a barrel of apples. Different species; large ones, small ones, sweet ones and sour ones; red ones and green ones — even, perhaps, the occasional bad one. Categorising them as to species, size, shape, colour and condition is, no doubt, a useful thing to do. But it is not more important than the barrel of apples, which remains the central fact. The true purpose of reassessment, or revision, is to add hidden, overlooked, lost, forgotten or even new, perspectives to the fundamentally correct view of history, not to obliterate it. It is reckless and irresponsible to distort the fundamentally correct understanding of historical events. The late Bryan McMahon in his autobiography[3] wrote: 'The greatest mistake a commentator can make is to pass judgement on "then" in the context of "now". To do so is to ignore either the prevailing atmosphere of a particular era and hold it up to an unjust scrutiny or ridicule by applying to it standards that now prevail in a completely altered set of circumstances ... historians of the shallower kind are dab hands at this shabby practice...' — a statement properly reinforced by Caitriona Clear (*Irish Times*, 4 May 1998), who observed: 'It is depressing to live in a culture where memories of the past have to conform to pre-set agendas before they are treated with respect.'

Obviously in dealing in narrative form with a long and complicated period it is necessary to condense. Here the attempt is made to correlate essential information and place it in context. In so doing two things are important; retention of the essential dominant thrust and sufficient flexibility to include some reappraisal.

The following points have been given particular attention in the narrative context, and some new, or under-emphasised, aspects are presented.

1. In the late eighteenth century, in the minds and hearts of the ordinary people, the long-vanished Gaelic Order, to the ideals of which they had clung through music and oral tradition, was reinforced if not replaced by the vibrant political philosophy from across the Atlantic called republicanism.

2. A question fundamental to any appreciation of Protestant extremism in the late 19th and early 20th centuries — and indeed today — is why the Ulster Dissenters, particularly the Presbyterians (large numbers of whom had been avid republicans a mere two years earlier), became enduring and extreme unionists when the Act of Union was passed in 1800? The answer is clear enough. The Union conferred on them the very rights and liberties they'd been previously denied and which, as republicans, they had sought and fought for. In addition the Union preserved them in positions of power and privilege in Ulster over the despised Catholic neighbours whom they had dispossessed. For the first time in their history the Union gave the Ulster Dissenters full British citizenship with more or less the same rights and entitlements, at least on paper, as any other British citizen. And, of course, it secured their Protestantism, Dissenters though they were. Their objective was achieved with Union — indeed, because of the privileges and protectionism from which they benefitted locally, it might fairly be said that it was more than achieved — and the Crown became for them a bulwark for Protestant identity and self-image, with only the proviso that the Crown remain Protestant. No other Irish group, political or religious, gained from the Union. Both Catholics and Anglicans lost economically, and *de jure*, lost their Irish identity as well.

3. Throughout the 19th century — the century of Union — nationalist political leadership in Ireland see-sawed between the twin, but dialectically opposed, constitutional and separatist movements. In general the majority supported constitutionalism, while the sporadic bursts of separatist violence were always maintained by a nucleus of dedicated support with an enduring republican content. This 'see-saw' became a powerful factor affecting later events.

4. Between about 1890 and 1910, the development of the so-called Gaelic Renaissance provided significant cultural, artistic and intellectual stimulus for political activists in both constitutional and separatist camps. More significantly it helped to promote and cultivate an awareness of Irishness and of a separate Irish identity in the population as a whole, at that time being encouraged to think of themselves as British. Thus was created a vital climate of national thought and feeling.

5. The tremendous importance of influences, direct and indirect from outside, the struggles of small nations all over the world in the nineteenth century, and the pan-European social and workers' movements between 1910 and 1914

(culminating in Ireland in the 1913 general strike), and the violence and strikes associated with them, also contributed importantly to the creation of the revolutionary climate of thought which made a struggle for independence a realistic prospect.

6. The Rising is held to be a 'romantic', militarily poorly planned, 'blood sacrifice', cobbled together by impractical idealists and poets. The argument appears to rest on the notion that there was a so-called 'blood-sacrifice', and that it and military competence were mutually exclusive — a view very likely the result of British counter-propaganda and misinformation. Insofar as there was a 'blood-sacrifice' it was not a wild, romantically impossible gesture, but the result of a series of misadventures, most notably the failure of the arms ship Aud to deliver her vital cargo. The actual battle-plan was sound and practical as to timing, strategy and tactics. The purpose of the Rising was three-fold: a/ to proclaim Ireland as an independent republic; b/ to achieve what might be achieved militarily and by so doing secure a place at the post-war peace talks, and c/ to arouse the Irish people's national self-awareness. Its success in achieving the first and third was as dramatic as the limited, but extraordinary, achievements of those who actually fought.

7. The hi-jacking by the Irish Republican Brotherhood (IRB), of the entire Volunteer organisation in 1916 is of vital importance. Although it is possible that some volunteer organisation might have developed without the encouragement of the IRB (Casement, Childers and others were actively concerned in this regard), it was, in fact, the IRB that promoted and organised the movement from the outset. They had been waiting to do precisely that when the opportunity presented itself, and any movement such as the Volunteers would certainly have been infiltrated by the IRB precisely as they did the Volunteers. In fact the Volunteer leadership was essentially Redmondite — that is to say supporters of the constitutional Irish Party — and left to their own devices would hardly have precipitated a Rising. The IRB was a secret insurrectionist movement; it brought the Volunteers about, and brought the rebellion about through the aegis of the Volunteers. Because the Citizen Army[4] was strictly a trades-union militia, the IRB did not infiltrate or have access to it in the same way.

8. The importance of the 1918 general election is usually held to be the overwhelming electoral victory of Sinn Fein. But the general election had another significance no less important. For the first time in more than one hundred and twenty years the constitutional and separatist national movements which, throughout the 19th century, had been in sporadic conflict on the question of which course the nation should follow, had come forward as a unified and homogeneous movement sharing not only the common goal of national independence, but common accord as to how this should be achieved. The mandate given by the people in the general election dramatically emphasised this conjunction.

9. The virtual obliteration of the Irish Party in the 1918 election was an extraordinary phenomenon which needs to be placed in context. Mere months before, John Redmond, its leader, had been acknowledged in Britain — and in much of Ireland — as **the** Irish political leader. In 1914 he was sufficiently powerful to all but take over the Volunteers, thousands of whom he provided as canon-fodder for

the British war-effort. But by June, 1918, the Irish Party, for all practical purposes, no longer existed. A renewed sense of national identity and separateness, the revival of which was a major objective of the 1916 Rising, had been decisively achieved. Nothing in Ireland would ever be the same again. Not just the visionaries and the leaders, but the people as a nation, were on the move towards independence and a republic.

10. The predictable division in Sinn Fein following the Treaty negotiations need not have led — though lead it did — to civil war. Irrespective of what Treaty came back from London, constitutional opposition to it would have split the hitherto unified Sinn Fein, homogeneous only in that the array of political outlooks represented in it had one common and overriding purpose — a free and independent nation. Once that purpose was achieved to the greater or lesser satisfaction of its members, Sinn Fein would certainly have fractured into normal democratic political groupings. That this particular Treaty, manipulated as it was, brought civil war in its wake is the bitter capstone to this period of recent Irish history.

11. Casement's story is of significance, particularly because of the importance attached to him by the British. His own character and motives have been so grotesquely distorted by enemy propaganda and misinformation that, even today, it is extremely difficult to get at the reality. However, as I have attempted to show, a/ he was accorded a role by the British of far more importance than he actually had, and, b/ because of that, but more especially because of his high international reputation and his public repudiation of Britain at the outbreak of the First World War, he became the object of a campaign of sustained and ruthless character assassination.

12. As Chairman and Head Centre of the IRB Michael Collins was also, according to a specific resolution of that organisation, *ex officio* President of the Republic — a position, according to General Sean MacEoin, that the IRB did not relinquish even with the formation of the Dail in 1919. How this secret role may have coloured Collins's relationship with Brugha, de Valera, Griffith and others is of particular interest.

A clear narrative of the main events and the reasons for them as they evolved and focused throughout the period is the basic purpose of this book. The number of important cognate events and personalities — all fascinating in themselves — is enormous. Any one of them taken in isolation can provide — and has done — enough material for a study on its own. The temptation to overemphasise and present any such an aspect as an explication of the whole is sometimes too strong to resist, and distorts the main picture. Was it not Huxley who wrote: 'There is an intrinsic plausibility in any explanation of the diverse in terms of a single principle'?

Some of the events related here may seem remote and of a different world. In particular the continuity of republican purpose may seem hard to grasp — *autres temps, autres moeurs*. But it is too easy to fall into such a facile error. A simple example will illustrate this; in 1997 there are men and women who can effortlessly and with understanding bridge the gap between those whose ideals and motives were moulded between the early and middle years of this century and those whose outlook is of now, and relate comfortably to both. Yet that is a span of almost a century. Similarly, those who were active at the beginning of the twentieth century had direct — and in some ways even more specific — links with the activists of the earlier republican movement; for instance Michael Collins's father was born in 1815.

Those who wish to reassess history must bear in mind that the Second World War was a transition. In real, rather than merely chronological, terms it brought about the effective end of 19th century outlooks and values, and ushered in a radical set of concepts vividly offset by the fact that war now involved civilians in the 'front line', and by the consequences of nuclear power and the prospect of destruction on an unimaginable scale, with the horrors of genetic mutation thrown in. There is a vast distance between the image of a galloping hussar with drawn sabre amidst the shot and shell of the 19th century battlefield, and that of the officer in a bunker, or the pilot twenty miles off and nine miles high, who presses a little button and annihilates half a million people with one bomb. It is absurd to try to refashion the history of one age because it seems 'politically incorrect' according to the values of a later age.

To the Ireland of the late eighteenth century republicanism represented freedom in modern terms as established in France and America, with both of which there were powerful links; it was a political system with which, through their well-established connections with these countries, the people were familiar, and, above all, it was one with which they could identify and, so, be clearly and unequivocally independent of British monarchism.

Constitutional progress and reverses notwithstanding, it is all but incontrovertible that after 1798 and 1803, the only form of independence which would have been both acceptable to, and enduring for, a majority of the Irish people was a republic. This is powerfully illustrated several times during the nineteenth century, nowhere more clearly and incisively than by Thomas Francis Meagher ('Meagher of the Sword', U.S. brigadier-general and commander of the 'Irish Brigade' in the War between the States), when he wrote:- 'The Republic that gave us an asylum and an honourable career — is threatened with disruption. It is the duty of every liberty-loving [Irish] citizen, who aspires to establish a similar form of government in our native land — to prevent such a calamity at all hazards. . . We could not hope to succeed in our effort to make Ireland a Republic without the moral and material aid of the liberty-loving citizens of these United States...'(Michael Cavanagh, *Memoirs of General Thomas Francis Meagher*, Massachusetts, 1892, p. 365).

The intention is to present in this book, in broad outline and in a balanced narrative not distorted by either over-emphasis or selectivity, the republican thrust and sequence from 1798, leading, inevitably, to the foundation of the State, making it as comprehensive, informative and accurate as possible consistent with readability and length. There are bound to be subjects which some readers might feel should have been given greater attention. There will also be errors. These are regretted where they are significant.

This narrative ends with the 1923 Cease Fire of the Civil War and, as mentioned above, the entry into the Government of the Irish Free State in 1927 of the new republican party, Fianna Fail (consisting of, and in the main supported by, those who were anti-Treaty during the Civil War). Many people, including the author who was the first to document it, have written about the tragedy of the Civil War. But what is truly remarkable — and quite possibly unique — is how the bitterness and divisions resulting from it were largely overcome, especially in the Army, and were effectively not just subordinated, but effaced, when, during the Second World War (1939-1945), the State faced threat from outside. In the main leaders, civil and military, many of whom a mere sixteen years before fought harshly against one another, responded to serve together with unity of mind and purpose in the national interest.

An old friend and colleague, to whom I described the compass, if not the purpose, of this book, once asked me if it included what happened in the republican movement between the end of the Civil War to date. When I said 'No', he answered 'coward'.

Cowardice has nothing to do with it. If I believed that an account of the activities of militant and unconstitutional republican splinter groups, with no electoral mandate after the state came into being, was relevant to this overview of the mainstream republican thrust for independence from 1798 to the foundation of the State, I would certainly have included it. However there is no relevancy here.

The activities of such groups, acting without civil authority as the Executive Forces had during the Civil War, but, unlike the Executive Forces, doing so in continued defiance of the clear will of the people expressed in several elections, were — at least until after 1969 — at best peripheral to the progress of republican democracy, and at worst inimical to it.

The State, albeit incomplete and still partly occupied, was established and had a democratic electoral system. The splinter groups were rejected by the electorate and, outside the northern six counties, perhaps, had very limited constitutional support, even from those of deep republican beliefs.

In post 1969 Northern Ireland the republican military did emerge as the only effective means of defence available to the beleaguered Nationalist/Catholic minority and succeeded in providing an element of essential protection for that minority, especially amongst the working classes.

Regrettably the militants, possibly as a result of guerilla principles taught elsewhere, North Africa and the Middle East for instance, adopted terrorism which they then — unsuccessfully — sought, with inadequate propaganda, to legitimise as a valid war tactic, the whole being significantly counter-productive of their stated (and traditional) purpose - an all-Ireland republic. The result was a dilution of idealism and a dissipation of the moral status which had been one of the (old) IRA's greatest strengths.

Equally regrettably they engaged in, or tolerated the engagement by supporters in, certain criminal activities for fund-raising purposes, which also had a significant corrupting influence.

From the mid 1980s onwards the Sinn Fein political party (which in a sense stood in relation to the <u>old</u> Sinn Fein much as the IRA stood in relation to the <u>old</u>

IRA, and in relation to the IRA as the old Sinn Fein stood in relation to the old IRA), more and more asserted its independence of, and influence over, the republican military. It was in some ways a repetition of the process that obtained (1917 to 1922) between old Sinn Fein and the Volunteer (old IRA) Army Executive (in 1919 the Army placed itself under the authority of Dail Eireann; in 1922, following the [Sinn Fein] one-party Dail Eireann split over the terms of the Treaty, the Army rescinded that and resumed its independent Executive and conducted the Civil War on the anti-Treaty side).

By the 1990s Sinn Fein had sufficient political authority to encourage the IRA to cease fire in the interests of constitutional progress. This later fell due to extraordinary attempts by the British Government to alter the terms of the agreement on which it was based.

But a second cease fire was important in enabling the peace process referenda to be held in both parts of the country with the intention of introducing, for the first time in its history, a visible process of democracy in Northern Ireland.

This was due in no small measure to a reaffirmation by the IRA of its basic moral strength and ideals in backing the Peace Agreement. This clearly involved the political wisdom to adopt difficult (and for some insuperable), if significant, constitutional principles.

PART ONE

History to the defeated
May say Alas but cannot help nor pardon . . . W.H Auden

Chapter 1

The Background
1600 to 1800

THE SEQUENCE OF EVENTS LEADING TO THE EVENTUAL RECOVERY — at least in part — of national independence in 1922 began, as an element of the process that laid the foundations of modern Europe, with the struggle against the Tudor conquest and the Reformation in the last quarter of the 16th century. The Irish nation, with its language, laws, traditions, learning and culture, was one of the oldest in Europe. Hugh O'Neill and his allies envisaged an Ireland independent and incorporated (in some form) into the European mainstream of development. That this vision, at the time, was sometimes held to lie within, or closely allied to, the ambit of Spain may be taken as elementary statesmanship. There was in reality little definition except that of religious freedom and political independence.

Although this ideal was overwhelmed by the unexpected defeat of the combined Irish and Spanish forces by the English at Kinsale in 1601, it endured; reviving and being set back, adapting to the climate and conditions of the times. The risings of 1803, 1848, 1867, 1916 belong to a continuum which began with the resistance to the Tudor Conquest and received its modern definition with the Rising of 1798. Between 1798 and the War of Independence a number of political and social imperatives influenced, and sometimes affected, that process without altering it fundamentally.

Ireland's involvement with Britain is very old, stretching back to long before the period of recorded history. But, so far as we know, from in or about the 2nd/3rd century BC to the 8th/9th century AD, there were significant differences in the character and make-up of the inhabitants of both islands, who also appear to have had different origins[5]. The people inhabiting England were, and continue to be, a polyglot group, consisting of many races and tribes of different origins — Celtic, Pictish, Germanic and, of course, Roman. To that mix were added Northumbrian, Angle, Saxon, Jute, Friesian, Norse (both Norwegian and

Dane) Irish, Norman and others. The Irish, on the other hand, remained largely homogeneous. They spoke a common tongue and, in the main — certainly so far as the dominant Celtic peoples are concerned — came from a common source bringing with them a specific culture that endured for many centuries. Such admixture as occurred in later years with Dane, Norman and English was limited and did not approach the scale of what had continuously occurred in England for millennia. Any importance these things have is the extent to which they may have coloured respective aspects of enduring national character, behaviour, cultural patterns and self-image.

Roman and later Britain were rich targets for Irish kings such as Nial Noigiallach (Niall of the Nine Hostages). As far as the Ictian Sea (St George's Channel) and Glevum (Gloucester), the power of the Irish kings was felt in Britain. Welsh chieftains were Irish, or owed allegiance to Irish overlords, and Argyle in Scotland was colonised by the Dalriada who later extended their holding over the entire country, ultimately giving it its name — Scotland, Scotia Minor; Ireland, homeland of the Scots, Scotia Major.

An interregnum between the eighth and eleventh centuries, when the Norse held much of England and built a number of Irish coastal towns, was a period of transition, from a pastoral/agricultural society to an almost feudal and more centralised trading structure.

Normans to Tudor Conquest

The Norman invasion from Wales in 1169 introduced an entirely new element to Ireland which would lead to a fundamental change of relationship between Ireland and Britain. The element in question, the idea of a foreign king (originally Henry II of England and Normandy) claiming title in Ireland, was a novel and unheralded development in the Irish experience.

Part of the initial problem lay in differences between Irish and Norman laws and in their respective interpretations. This is a critical point bearing in mind that the Normans did not come either as conquerors or invaders.

They were 'invited' to come to the aid of a friendly power in Ireland, much as the United States and the USSR were, respectively, invited to come to the aid of friendly powers in Vietnam and Afghanistan — though, of course, the political morality of the times (such as it ever is) was different. It is important to recognise that the Normans adapted primarily as settlers and that they were neither perceived, nor treated, as conquerors by the Gaelic society on which they impinged. But to imagine that either the Irish or the Normans were unaware of the political realities of their times would be foolish.

When the Normans arrived in 1169 they brought with them the concept... 'of possession of the land and what stood upon it. This concept, which was not only valid in Norman law, but was the foundation on which it rested, was, in the twelfth century, as alien to Irish law and to Irish leadership as it could possibly be... The Norman settlers were accepted by some Irish rulers and obtained land from them. Each side, naturally, assumed that in such transactions the law with which they were familiar would prevail...The conflict of legal and economic systems that followed the Norman settlements in Ireland encouraged political confusion and contributed largely to the decline of the already demoralized Gaelic order. Kings and chiefs countered the castles and baileys of the Normans knights with their own and, in order to minimise the effects of the Norman heavy cavalry and Flemish bowmen, began to 'plash' and entrench the forests (Neeson, Eoin *A History of Irish Forestry*, Dublin, 1991, pp. 32, 38/9).

When an Irish lord, such as Mael Mordha, granted land to a Norman he could do so only subject to certain 'prudential limitations', as Eoin MacNeill[6] expressed it (MacNeill, Eoin *Celtic Ireland*, p. 145 et seq.). The idea of donating land to a foreigner who could then in turn 'give' it to his king in England was unimaginable under Irish law. Such an Irish lord was not conferring ownership as would have been the case under the Norman concept of title, but granting a dominion in trust with rights of reversion. The land was not his to donate. It was the trust of the *tuath*, or tribal grouping. It could not be *given* in perpetuity to anyone; that was a concept totally outside any notion of title in Ireland. Accordingly, for many years throughout the period of Norman settlement, there was much confusion of rights and loyalties between Norman and Irish. The situation was additionally confused because of shifting local allegiances in a period when feudalism and the developing principle of centralised authority were also in constant opposition.

This uneasy relationship between Irish and Norman Irish was to be the pivot on which the relationship between Ireland and England turned. From time to time the Normans ruling England became alarmed by how much the Normans in Ireland were being assimilated by their adopted country and took intermittent steps to try to check this tendency. On occasion, too, Norman Irish lords developed symptoms of separatism and ambition and England took more drastic steps to curb this.

The Norman settlers, like the later English colonists, lived in a legislative, social and judicial world separate from and different to that of the native Irish whom they grew to regard as 'a slave, and had treated him as a slave and was in the habit of unctuously reproaching him for the faults and vices in him for which he [himself] was largely responsible (O'Hegarty, p. 130). The differences were, perhaps, best synthesised in the Statutes of Kilkenny (1366) which themselves synthesised what has been called 'a policy of apartheid' (*The Course of Irish History*, Moody and Martin) in Ireland. These laid down a pattern which dogged the fortunes of Ireland for centuries and the vestiges of which may be seen even today.

The Irish, already chronically afflicted socially and politically as a result of powerful and conflicting loyalties, struggled to retain a national culture and self-image that had sunk very low. In this they were successful, but at the price of a species of recidivist isolationism that now trapped a people once at the forefront of European progress, in a feudal vacuum, while the rest of the world sought new political, social and economic horizons. This enabled the Norman settlements to resemble colonies and the English royal claim to Ireland to be strengthened.

This tripartite relationship changed, utterly, with the Tudor Conquest of Ireland in the 16th century. This conquest was for purely strategic reasons.

As the sixteenth century opened England was on the threshold of that explosion into piracy (at several levels — trade, colonization and statecraft), which gave her such a powerful influence on world events for the next four hundred years. It was a time when sail moved the goods of empires on the oceans of the world, and Ireland occupied a dominant geographical position. The prevailing winds were westerly, from the Atlantic. Whoever held Ireland had England open before them. As a jumping-off ground for an invasion of England Ireland could not be bettered; it was close, it was self-sufficient, it possessed troops and, above all, it was for long hostile to England in both religion and politics.

The strategic factors for Tudor consideration of a conquest of Ireland were obvious. At that period in Europe religion and religious allegiances were causes of war and battle; across the civilized world (and parts of it not so civilized) world-shaking religious and political events were shaping the destinies of nations. Almost by accident England became allied to the north European Protestant cause rather than to the south European Catholic one at a time when religion and colonization dominated European events. An alliance between Ireland and Spain would threaten English ambitions, perhaps decisively. The war with Spain was expensive; if one includes the colonization and planting of Ireland, the cost was enormous.

After the Battle of Kinsale (1601) and Hugh O'Neill's submission in 1603, the English rapidly established control over the country in a way never hitherto possible. In accordance with the spirit of the times in England, once the conquest was complete, the superior strategic impulse rapidly degenerated into commercial exploitation. This left a fearful legacy, reaching its nadir in the 18th century, when Ireland and its people became virtually destitute. But the fruits of conquest, if initially incredibly profitable, became increasingly bitter.

The process of conquest, which at times became a policy of virtual genocide (to be boasted about in the English press)[7], accelerated. Three elements were involved:– a) strategic; b) mercantile, the pursuit of wealth and to that end the exploitation of the country's resources — mainly timber — in a manner and on a scale comparable to the devastation occurring in the world's rain-forests to-day; and, c) an associated policy of protectionism for English goods and manufacture, ensured by prohibiting any Irish enterprise which might compete either in domestic or overseas markets. The means used to secure all three were 'planting', dispossession and coercion. These methods were strengthened by a deliberate policy of fomenting religious bigotry and hatreds. Within a century the Irish forests were gone and her indigenous population was reduced to a state of leader-less and illiterate subsistence.

The Irish were now a conquered people in their own land, ruled by conquerors who exercised more or less unfettered rule over them. And, with the conquest, a second and more emotive element became a major factor in the relationship between the two countries. Since the Reformation, religion had played an increas-ingly major part in that relationship. With the conquest it became dominant. Moreover, leadership of the Irish national cause — or what remained of it — passed resoundingly, and virtually simultaneously, from the hands of the native aristocracy to those of the Norman Irish, or Old English as they came to be called. They, while

Catholic, were also royalist. In them was found, in mind and faith, the energetic spirit of the Counter Reformation. To them came the support and attention of Rome.

But the Old English were a relative minority. They were politically removed from the Gaelic people. Insofar as the Irish and the Old English sympathised with one another it was because they were both Catholic, not because they were both nationalist. But the Old Irish were at that time leaderless and without visible national purpose. Thus the Old English picked up the reins of leadership in Ireland and redirected the Gaelic people from being Catholic, nationalist and separatist, strongly linked with Spain, to being Catholic and royalist, strongly linked to the House of Stuart. This goes some way to explaining the symbiotic relationship between notions of political and religious freedom that, until the end of the eighteenth century, filled the minds and fuelled the aspirations of the ordinary people.

In a curious way the Old English may be compared with — and in a sense were forerunners of — the constitutional nationalists of the 19th and 20th centuries, in particular the Home Rulers. They put loyalty to the Stuarts (and, indeed, to other foreign monarchs) above loyalty to their own country. Later they raised regiments of 'Wild Geese' which took hundreds of thousands of Ireland's young men to fight abroad[8]. There was no illogicality or disloyalty involved in the Old English supporting an English Catholic dynasty based on primogeniture. That the Old Irish were leaderless and a source of raw manpower was a bonus. The Old English would have considered the old Irish system of elective kingship archaic, as they did the Gaelic system of monastic Catholicism.

The New — Protestant — English and the new, Dissenter, settlers also formed a curious relationship which had a political/religious base and which received but one major jolt two hundred years later — in 1798.

In Ireland anti-Catholicism and the material insecurity regarding landholding that was inextricably woven into it, were more important than doctrinal differences within Protestantism. Already friendly to Calvinist influence, the Church of Ireland could even put up with Presbyterianism (Roy Foster, *Modern Ireland 1600-1972*, p. 57).

Foster also points out that, with the onset of virulent anti-Catholicism in Reformed England 'the fate of the Old English was intrinsically linked to Stuart fortunes and the exercise of the royal prerogative on their behalf...with the rapid increase of Protestant settlement, anti-Catholic feeling was growing [in Ireland]'(Foster, Ibid. pp. 52/3).

The position the Old English were in was equivocal. As Catholics they were alienated from English domestic policy and politics, but remained Anglo-royalist. In Ireland they were subject to persecution and dispossession and had no political rights. They were in political, and to some extent religious, opposition to the leaderless Old Irish Catholic masses. Yet the latter provided a power-base which enabled them to strengthen their position with the Stuarts. With the Flight of the Earls (1601-1608) went much of the essence of the old Gaelic Order. The Flight of the Wild Geese eighty-three years later denuded the country of most of the remaining Old English leadership and of many of its young Gaelic Irish active manhood, to become cannon-fodder for regiments abroad.

England's expansion could not have been made without a secure Ireland to the west. From the viewpoint of the English Privy Council, secure did not necessarily — or at all — mean a friendly Ireland. Herein lay the prime and continuing error of English diplomacy in relation to Ireland. It was an error compounded by the religious confrontations of the Reformation. A friendly Ireland might have strengthened England's position. But perhaps as much could be said of the relationships between Austria/Hungary, Austria/Italy, Spain/Portugal, Russia/ Poland and so on.

On the resumption of the Stuart dynasty in 1601 England was an established European power, though nowhere near as powerful as Spain, France and Austria. By conquering Ireland she closed her vulnerable back door — or at least put a bush in the gap. But Ireland remained England's weak spot — a fact that explains much of that country's attitude and subsequent policy towards Ireland.

The Seventeenth Century

In 17th-century Ireland the roles of Catholicism and nationalism were thoroughly confused in a way that had at least as much to do with events in Europe as with anything that was happening in Ireland. Because of James II's reversion to Catholicism religious issues came to the fore in England. James relaxed discrimination against Catholics, both in England and Ireland, and encouraged Catholics to join the army and professions, hitherto prohibited. This liberalization of restrictions on Catholics in both countries caused the English establishment to coalesce against James. There were fears of another civil war. James brought in Irish troops to maintain order and, eventually, to defend himself against the Protestant William of Orange, a Dutch princeling (who also happened to be both James's nephew and his son-in-law). This exacerbated the already delicate situation. English Protestant leaders, alarmed by Louis XIV's discrimination against Protestants in France, but more especially by his annexation of Orange, William's fief, offered William the throne of England — after he had landed there ostensibly to rally the English to the Protestant cause. James fled to France, and thence to Ireland, where was the only army at his disposal. William accepted the throne of England more for European than for English reasons, and ultimately the religious/political issues which were the cause of the differences between these two monarchs came to a head in Ireland. The ensuing war was fought largely in Ireland, with Old English commanders leading Gaelic Irish troops for James, and William leading a mixed army of Dutch, Danes, English and Dissenter settlers from the north. Ireland became a sort of off-beat microcosm of the Counter-Reformation (an aspect that was to continue through the 30 Years' War and beyond). The confrontation was no simplistic one of conqueror v. conquered, Catholic v. Protestant, but was extremely confused and obscure. It is worthwhile getting the main thrusts, at all events, into perspective.

The complexities — and paradoxes — of European politics were to continue to harass Irish nationalist aspirations and their relationship with the Catholic Church. Eventually the Irish hierarchy condemned nationalist separatists thereby giving the impression that they supported the British establishment in Ireland, which would be an incorrect inference. The Irish Church was protecting its own position by supporting the *status quo*. But the idea of separate Irish nationhood in its Gaelic form was virtually extinguished with the exile of its leaders and aristocracy in the early seventeenth century and the exile of its fighting men at the end of that century. The Gaelic religious — and also, to an extent, political — mantle was then draped shapelessly on the lean and unready shoulders of the leaderless and barely subsisting masses. The Irish had been Catholic — but this Catholicism was largely monastic, individualistic, ascetic (sometimes even dissolute) and was generally in disfavour with Rome. This accounts in part, then and later, for some Papal want of enthusiasm for Ireland's case against England, although in the seventeenth century this was related more to friction between the pope and Louis XIV, who became James's ally and protector.

There were now two basic religious groupings in Ireland, each sub-divided into mutually distrustful, if not hostile, elements. There were two political groups, synonymous with these, which were also divided and which held conflicting loyalties, allegiances and expectations. These groupings were:

1. The Old English — royalist and Catholic (orthodox).
2. The New English — ascendancy, Protestant.
3. Settlers, often Scots — privileged but deprived of some rights (Dissenters).
4. The Old Irish (Gaelic) — leaderless, nationalist, Gaelic, Catholic (unorthodox).

* * * * *

There is a popular tendency to see Irish history and the events which shaped it from a purely local — that is to say Irish — standpoint, as if the influences that affected political and historical development here were concerned with this country only. That is far from being the case. The lingering effect (amongst northern unionists in particular) of the Counter-Reformation and the Thirty Years war is a typical — if rather extreme — example of the reality. In 1691 Ireland was an isolated, conquered Catholic country in what was essentially a north European Protestant sphere of influence. The conquest was seen as being both a political and religious victory. Attitudes and patterns of behaviour in Ireland were also, and with enduring results, shaped in the 18th century when the effects of great and lengthy religious wars in all their intensity, still disrupted the European continent.

The puritanism that took hold of England under Elizabeth I and the Commonwealth primed the cannon that ripped Ireland to shreds. To secure her strategic interests, England set Catholic and Protestant at each other's throats in the classic manner of the conquistador, but was unable to contain the consequences when they went out of control. The religious wars and oppressions in Ireland reflected attitudes that racked much of Europe until the end of the 18th century. In Ireland religious and political confrontation, and bigotry, lasted longer because they were manipulated into so doing as a means of controlling and subduing **both** the old, Catholic, Irish and the new Protestant Irish who purported to govern them and were themselves governed from Whitehall.

Within the space of one hundred years, three major changes in Ireland's fortunes reversed the political/religious dominance. These were i/ the Tudor

Conquest, ending in 1601; ii/ the Stuart revival during the seventeenth century and, iii/ the Williamite victory in 1691, ending with the Treaty of Limerick. The main effect was to lock Catholic Ireland into mainstream north European Protestant reformationism, where it became isolated and subject to enduring conflict at several levels. The 150-year 'Wild Geese' syndrome complicated the situation; because of the continual drain of young men to the 'Wild Geese' regiments[9] there was limited 'nationalist' resistance capability left in the country. The Irish in general were suspect, persecuted and seen by the British/Protestant powers-that-be as untrustworthy, inferior and servile. Throughout the 18th century the people perceived religious freedom and political freedom as being synonymous. This was not such a curious outlook as may at first appear. It was into this atmosphere and under the influence of the European Enlightenment (through Voltaire, Hume, Rousseau and Diderot, for instance), that the dynamic which was, literally, to revolutionize Ireland and become its enduring, if sometimes idiosyncratically interpreted, ideal, now spread. After the Flight of the Wild Geese, and the many young women who followed them, what remained was, largely, a peasant people subjected to hardship and privation by a foreign administration and governing class. In such circumstances they found leadership in the persecuted priests who, sometimes at risk of their lives, often linked the people and their undefined hopes. It was an idea, moreover, reinforced by the attitude of the Anglican Reformists and, to a lesser extent, the Dissenter settler, population which portrayed the Catholic peasant population as 'priest-ridden' and superstitious.

From the seventeenth century onwards there were essentially two separate races in Ireland, polarised as to religion and politics (with internal divisions and alignments in both) — namely the Catholic native Irish (the large majority) whose heritage, language, laws and customs were, collectively, proscribed and prohibited by the second — the Protestant Anglo-Irish. These, a tiny colonial class in the main, at the direction of London, supported a subservient and dependent kingdom. The remnants of the Old English fell somewhere between the two. The Dissenters fell into a bizarre category of their own. Ethnically similar to the native Irish, they were politically dependent on the Anglo-Irish. They were also opposed, religiously, to both, but were marginally more hostile to Catholicism than to the established Protestant Church — a good, if somewhat complicated, example of all Christians being equal, but some being more equal than others[10]. The Anglo-Irish (planters and Cromwell's soldier-settlers, paid off with land seized from the Irish) retained privilege and authority. The Dissenters came unsteadily somewhere in between. One of the curious features of this curious relationship is that even the better-minded among the settlers refused to acknowledge, save as a repellent curiosity, the separate identity of the Irish people, who were merely dependent serfs.

They were, in their own 'kingdom', themselves deprived — by England — of the most elementary legislative and other rights. '... Nearly all the Irish poetry of the sixteenth, seventeenth and eighteenth centuries is, looked at broadly, one impassioned outcry against England' (Daniel Corkery, *The Hidden Ireland, 1924*, p. 157).

The Eighteenth Century

The final conquest in 1691 was followed by 'the starved and savage eighteenth century' (George Dangerfield, *The Strange Death of Liberal England*, London, 1935; New York, 1961, p.321). The national spirit was all but extinguished; native leaders gone or subdued; the Catholic Church and its clergy outlawed. The people were enslaved. The resources of the country — especially the woods and forests — were exploited on an unbelievable scale. It is interesting that amongst the casualties was the very building material of the Gaelic Irish, hazel wattling, which was virtually wiped out, presumably as industrial fuel.

Between 1680 and 1700, or thereabouts, there was a remarkable nationwide decline in hazel growth. Pollen analysis by Professor Frank Mitchell at Littleton Bog near Thurles shows that before 1700 hazel formed 30-40 per cent. of all pollen grains, but afterwards it formed less than 5 per cent (Neeson, op. cit., citing Frank Mitchell, *Littleton Bog, Tipperary, the Geological Society of America, 1945*).

From about 1700 onwards the people were at such a low ebb that it was not their own voices, but those of generous and open-hearted members of the alien society such as Molyneaux and Swift, that were raised in wrath at their plight. The people had little but their faith to reassure them — '"Gan triáth ach Dia na Glóire (Without leader save the Glory of God) is a commonplace in their verse' (Corkery, op. cit., p.130). Then, towards the middle of the century, the people's self-awareness and self-image started to revive. Ideas and knowledge of events from America and elsewhere began to stimulate like ideas in Ireland. Just as it was the voices of liberal Protestants that were raised loudest in protest at the condition to which the people were reduced, now it was the Protestant Dissenters who first responded quickly to the republican doctrines of America and France.

The Dissenters were rightly dissatisfied with their own condition under the so-called 'Irish' parliament of the Protestant Ascendancy. While this parliament had existed 300 years before the Tudor Conquest and continued, with hiccups, until the Act of Union in 1800, it was no parliament of the people, but rather an assembly for the settlers and the Anglo-Irish, those who — from time to time — governed the Pale, that flexible area around Dublin, always the administrative capital of English or Anglo-Irish authority. But this Irish parliament was, in its own right, an important institution. It was independent of the English Parliament and it was the only political forum — albeit a partisan and selective one — in Ireland. Both Catholic and Dissenter were excluded from it; it represented, there-fore, only the dominant Protestant class.

The Protestant ruling classes — the so-called Ascendancy — were in a position of almost total power. Both Catholics and Dissenters (mainly presbyterians almost entirely confined to Ulster), were subject to penal laws, though not to the same degree. In order to maintain the Protestant position, Dissenters were given powers and privileges specifically denied to Catholics. These included the opportunity to become 'planters' in Ulster, taking land from dispossessed Catholics — who were looked upon, and treated, as 'white niggers' in a racist environment[11]. As Dardis[12] pointed out the Dissenters were given power, protection and privilege, but were, nevertheless, denied equality — especially legislative equality — with the Protestant ascendancy. From the beginning of the 18th century they proceeded to agitate for full equality. In the face of persistent refusals from Dublin and London, many left for America where, together with Catholic fellow Irishmen, some achieved positions of importance in the American War of Independence, providing many of George Washington's foremost supporters and leaders.

Meantime, the reduced and oppressed Catholics also aspired to some basic rights — not, as yet, Catholic emancipation, but relief from religious persecution. A Catholic Association was formed as a debating group which would synthesise and formulate a method of appeal. This led to a Catholic Relief Act in 1793 which alleviated, but did not remove, the grossest abuses.

So two elements of the disaffected Irish population, Irish and planted Dissenter, set about relieving their distress and seeking reform at about the same time. It was likely that, of their own momentum, these two movements would have sought support from one another. The precedents in America and France made it inevitable. The long gone Gaelic national spirit began to be replaced with a republican ideal that exploded in separatist nationalism in 1798, in the common name of 'Irishman'. 'Though the penal laws were becoming less rigorous the condition of the people was worsening rather than improving; they were growing poorer and poorer. The peasants, almost all Catholics, were increasing rapidly, while the political and social economy of the country was still working towards their extinction, a tug-of-war that led to widespread brutality and wretchedness' (Corkery, op.cit.). The movement for civil and political rights in the eighteenth century could not be limited to Dissenters only. Otherwise it was not, by definition, a movement for right and justice. The Catholic Relief Act of 1793, a gesture by the authorities, was dictated more by a desire to suborn the populace after the French Revolution than by any humanitarian considerations. The groundswell continued. Dissenter and Catholic intellectuals and merchant/professional classes, which had been growing in number, espoused the cause of Liberty. Amongst them were those who envisaged this in terms of freedom and independence. Wolfe Tone, a young Dublin lawyer, was later to become general of brigade in the French Army and one of the leaders of the great attempted French invasions of 1796 and 1798[13]. He, and others like him brought with them from France the republicanism that strengthened the minds and hearts of the people and that filled the vacuum left by the collapse of the old, vanquished Gaelic Order.

This new republicanism was recognised as a threat to British interests. Nowhere within England's sphere of influence was more vulnerable to that most heady and fierce of weapons, ideas, than was Ireland. With a remarkable ability to identify and offset a threat that occasionally flared like a flame in a mire of corruption and inefficiency, the English administration speedily took steps to offset this one of ideas. For the first time they recognised the Catholic Church, and in 1795 founded, 'the national seminary of Maynooth, endowing it as a royal college' (Liam Swords, *The Green Cockade, the Irish in the French Revolution, 1798-1815*). They repealed some of the penal legislation. The results were complex and often contradictory.

The leadership from a persecuted clergy (and it should be remembered that there was scarcely a family in the country, however humble, that did not have relatives abroad, in Europe or America) was thrown into confusion both by Maynooth and by Church condemnation of republicanism. Unfortunately this was seen, not always without justification, as condemnation by the Church of the Rising of 1798 and its republican separatist aftermath[14]. In that traumatic fashion were the ideas of religious and political liberty again separated[15].

The Union of England and Scotland had taken place in 1707, and in 1782 England tried, by Act of Parliament, to abolish the Irish parliament. The attempt was illegal and unconstitutional, and was unsuccessful. England was forced to withdraw its claim of superiority over the Irish Parliament in the Renunciation Act of 1783.

Also in 1782 a strange and, from England's point of view, undesirable development took place in Ireland; a group of gentlemen soldiers — what in England might have been classed 'yeomen' — was formed called the (mainly Protestant) Volunteers. They operated in close association with Grattan's Irish parliament, and offered to defend the country and hold it for Britain in the face of the French threat. In other words, they, and the parliament to which they gave allegiance, were establishing a Home Rule mind-set. In practical terms they helped to found Grattan's independent parliament, and paved the way for the country's prosperity. This succeeded so well that Ireland was soon in active competition with Britain on the world's markets. That more than anything spelled its doom; England would not, and her merchants and producers could not, tolerate competition from a country able to produce more and better, and sell cheaper. 'The Union', wrote his permanent Under-Secretary to Pitt in 1799, 'is the only means of preventing Ireland from becoming too great and too powerful.' Thus was the foundation for Union laid.

During the Union debates in the Irish Parliament, such as they were, John Foster, the Speaker, in one of his anti-Union speeches appealed 'to every man who heard him, whether, since the free Parliament was established, the country had not risen in every respect of trade, wealth, and manufactures, more than any other country in the world in the same given time...'(Report of the Union Debates, Dublin, 1800, p.35). The Irish economy — thanks in some measure to the rise of a Catholic merchant class — was flourishing and Irish goods were rivalling British products on the international market. This growth and development alarmed the English Government, uneasy at the prospect of finding an energetic and capable commercial rival on its doorstep. Something had to be done. British manufacturers, producers and exporters were complaining.

After the 1798 Rising it had become clear to the British establishment that, with an increasing population and in a climate of economic strength and political liberalism, even an Irish parliament composed of Protestants only must, sooner or later, find common cause with an increasingly vocal Dissenter and Catholic population in pursuit of the liberties and equalities that all Europe resounded to. In such circumstances the flourishing Irish economy would be an even greater threat to the British home market. It was decided to thwart any such possibility. Hence the

Union which at a blow abolished the Irish parliament, made self-interest the principal concern of the bought sycophants who had voted it out of existence (a remarkable example of constitutional sleight-of-hand), re-established the gap between a Protestant minority and the Catholic majority, and provided the means of securing both Britain's strategic and economic interests in this matter. With the Union a concerted campaign, disguised by selective legislation favouring Britain, wrecked Irish commercial enterprises that competed with those of Britain, and limited Irish agriculture by forcing its produce to the English market at manipulated rates. Because of the real or potential threat to English economic interests, the Irish parliament was coerced into 'dissolving' itself in favour of Union with England.

But the collective national spirit was never again allowed to become as destitute as it had been in the early part of that century. Edmund Burke[16], for instance, speaking against the Union, said:

> You are called upon to give up your independence — and to whom are you called upon to give it up? To a Nation which for six hundred years has treated you with uniform oppression and injustice...For centuries the British Parliament and Nation kept you (the Irish) down — shackled your commerce, and paralysed your exertions; despised your characters and ridiculed your pretensions to any privileges, commercial or constitutional. She has never conceded a point to you which she could avoid, or granted a favour which was not reluctantly distilled[17].

Robert Emmet's declamation from the dock remains one of the great testaments of republicanism and of modern Irish history. In 1799, the year before the Union, Edward Cooke, Under-Secretary at Dublin Castle, wrote to Lord Castlereagh with the following observations: '...we are in a disadvantageous situation, we must of course look to those causes which have brought us into that situation. What are they?
1st. The local independent acting of the Legislature.
2nd. The general prosperity of the country, which has produced great activity and energy.
3rd. The emancipation of the Catholics (He refers to the Relief Act of 1793, not Catholic emancipation as pursued by O'Connell).
4th. The encouragement given to the reform principles of the Presbyterians.
5th. The want of number in the Protestants.
Throughout the eighteenth century the Irish people, Dissenter and Catholic alike, had been kept in a conveniently servile condition, and the nation was exploited — until the liberal Dissenters and Catholics found, nourished and shaped a new dynamic called republicanism that revived and gave pride to an all but eclipsed national self-image.

The impact of this republicanism was magical. It revived the soul of the people and provided an ideal to fill the place of that which had fled with the earls in 1608. The Rising of 1798 was the most important and powerful since the time of Cromwell and it was national, not royalist, in spirit, if not in fact.

Millions of leaflets were let loose in the land picturing Ireland as a country which would be given over to a combination of the Inquisition and Saint Bartholomew were the strong hand of England removed'. . . P. S. O'Hegarty.

Chapter 2

The Nineteenth Century

THE IMPACT ON IRELAND OF THE UNION IN 1800 can scarcely now be imagined. Once again the relationship between the two countries was altered significantly — but this time by a constitutional perversion. This attempt by the British to extinguish the 'dangerous idea' of republicanism and to control Ireland did not succeed. The eliminated parliament was not of the people, but, even so, the Union did deprive the country of such basic electoral and parliamentary rights as there were, and it brought ruin to an expanding economy. The destruction was deliberately enforced to the anticipated benefit of England, but it proved to be counterproductive in many ways, requiring continuing force and coercion throughout the century. The first resistance came within a couple of years.

Contrary to the commonly held view, Emmet's rising of 1803 was well-planned and carefully organised and, had it not been for a catalogue of unforeseen mishaps, might have been of greater, rather than of less, significance than 1798. 'The secrecy and professionalism of his preparations, and the extent of the organization among tradesmen and artisans in Dublin and provincial towns, are striking'(Foster, op.cit., p 286). Byrne (Miles Byrne, *Memoirs*), who was one of the leaders in Dublin and later a chef de brigade in Napoleon's Irish Legion, wrote:

Had all the leaders who promised to be at their posts assigned them, been exact and done their duty, or even had they come to the depot to assist Mr. Emmet in the first bustle, their presence then would have caused more discipline, and in spite of mistakes and accidents, we should have taken the Castle; and once in possession of it, the English had not sufficient forces to retake it, and make head against the thousand armed citizens who would meet in the morning, and the thousands of armed men pouring in from all parts of the country.

After union, a struggle between two aspects of national endeavour also developed. The constitutional movement can — tenuously — be linked to the Old English, certainly to the 'Old English' parliament. The physical force separatist element may be linked directly to republican 1798. Interestingly both movements — one seeking constitutional reform under British dominion, the other seeking complete separatism — from 1798 onwards followed parallel, but fluctuating, paths of public interest, awareness and support culminating on the one hand in the rise of the Home Rule movement and, on the other, in the emergence of the IRB and Sinn Fein.

O'Hegarty summarises the attitude of Irish Protestants in 1843 to O'Connell's agitation for Repeal of the Act of Union:

> The Irish Protestant had for a century and a half regarded the Irish Catholic as a slave, and had treated him as a slave; he was in the habit of unctuously reproaching him for the faults and vices in him for which the Irish Protestant was largely responsible . . . and he could not contemplate being placed on an equality with him . . . one finds difficulty in understanding the Protestant mentality of that age, its devastating and ignorant religious bigotry, its assumption of the superiority of everything Protestant and everything British. Even . . . men like Plunket and Grattan, did not contemplate the Irish Catholic as proper to be placed on an equality with the Irish Protestant . . . Small wonder was it then that the Irish Protestant minority grew alarmed, and held aloof from Repeal... (op.cit., 130/1).

O'Hegarty continued, describing the post-Union position as nothing but an Ascendancy that was 'England's Jackal', with the crumbs of office as reward. (ibid. p.133).

England was determined to preserve the Union, even if that meant war in Ireland. In 1843 Peel said in the English House of Commons:

> There is no influence, no power, no authority, which the prerogatives of the Crown and the existing law give to the Government which shall not be exercised for the purpose of maintaining the Union, the demolition of which would involve not merely the repeal of an Act of Parliament but the dismemberment of this great Empire ... I am prepared to make the declaration which was made, and nobly made, by my predecessor, Lord Althorp, that deprecating as I do all war, but above all civil war, yet there is no alternative which I do not think preferable to the dismemberment of this Empire ... [18].

Lecky's comment is: 'He [Peel] clearly intimated that he would not concede Repeal even if the whole representation of Ireland demanded it...'(Lecky, *Leaders of Public Opinion in Ireland, 1903*, vol. 11, p.246).

Dublin ceased to be a capital city and all that that implied. Events from 1800 onwards reveal a pattern of continuous struggle between the people and the English administration. On the same tapestry may be seen lesser, perhaps more intricate and often more subtle, struggles, but the former is the dominant theme throughout. One should not fall into the error of imagining that there were not considerable periods when the everyday business of making a living, irrespective of the regime, occupied the minds and thoughts of most of the population. But, if the people were at times apathetic or indifferent, the administration itself would not let them be.

At all levels sectarianism was evident. The unity of purpose that had existed briefly a few years earlier between Dissenter and Catholic was gone. Under the

Union the Dissenter minority acquired certain civil and political rights and, more significantly, an identity. In addition they realised that to support Catholics was not only supporting 'blasphemous' papists, but would encourage the exchange of the old ascendancy parliament for a Catholic-dominated one. This thought helped persuade them that the devil they knew was a better bet. Meantime they were pleased enough to be acknowledged 'British'.

There were struggles between sectional interests and government; between the Protestant ascendancy and their fellow (Dissenting) Protestants, and with the Catholics. But, within the Irish national movement, above all is to be seen evidence of the fluctuating struggle by the two main elements, constitutionalist and separatist. The increasing Catholic middle-class became quickly identified with the constitutionalists, while the numerically smaller separatists, deriving directly from Wolfe Tone's republicanism, drew on a broader cross-section of the population. They were frequently in opposition, and it was not until the 1880s that they became purposefully united for the first time.

As the century advanced it became evident that the national spirit was alive and active when the people were adequately led. Minor protests of a more restricted momentum contributed to and helped stimulate this spirit. An increase in the popularity of separatism invariably followed an attempted rising. The star of constitutionalism generally waxed as the result of public political action. The thrust of this 'national' movement swung to and fro between both strands until, in 1885, they resolved some of their philosophical differences in support of the Land League. From then they moved forward, ultimately as Sinn Fein.

The nineteenth century was a time when imperialism, the most powerful political and social order of the era, was still expanding. Rival colonial powers carved up a divided world in the face of widespread cries for independence. Like much else ingrained in the tempestuous determination that marked much of the century in Ireland, the *means* by which independence might be achieved, rather than any *form* it might eventually take, were, amongst nationalists, the main issues of disagreement, for a majority of whom a republic was the bench-mark of freedom.

Perhaps the most significant binding factor was the recognition that *the Irish people as a whole had not lost their sense of separate and independent identity*, even though, as O'Hegarty commented, the Union remained constant to the principle established by Castlereagh and Pitt of giving Irish Protestants all power and patronage in Ireland and so governing through them, (O'Hegarty, op.cit., p 106).

Thus, as modern Ireland begins to take shape we find two polarised and subject people, in an undivided land — a land occupied by a foreign power. The Protestant population — Dissenter and 'landed gentry' alike — reinforced and strengthened their position under British rule.

Daniel O'Connell's phenomenal political accomplishments and Catholic emancipation saw his personal stature reach heights unknown by any Irishman since Hugh O'Neill. But, in some ways — although it was not successful, precipitated his decline and failed — his contribution to the Repeal Movement in the 1830s was an equally remarkable phenomenon. With emancipation achieved, repeal of the Union became for O'Connell the Great Objective. But he rejected violence and wished to operate within the existing constitutional framework[19]. The structure O'Connell created was developed by the Young Irelanders, particularly Thomas Davis and John Mitchel. It became a blue-print less than a hundred years afterwards for action by Sinn Fein and the separatist movement. '... The policy of appealing to the Englishman's sense of justice and fair play, an entirely non-existent sense so far as Ireland is concerned, this policy, initiated by O'Connell, was developing on the characteristic lines it retained until it was swept away in 1918' (O'Hegarty, op.cit., 72). The policy referred to was the policy of parliamentarianism — influencing the British Parliament favourably by action in that parliament towards reducing abuses in Ireland.

Catholic emancipation had consequences which went beyond religious liberty. In effect, while conferring freedom on the majority to practice their religion, emancipation also indirectly encouraged the divorce of the Catholic Church, now part of the Establishment, from nationalist political leadership. O'Connell committed himself to Repeal only by means within the *status quo*, which meant striving to do so through the British Parliament at Westminster, which was impossible at that time.

Lecky[20] points out that the people 'were now on the verge of revolution. The vast majority had been organised like a regular army and taught to act with the most perfect unanimity'(*Leaders of Public Opinion*, 1903, vol. II, p.62). Sir Thomas Wyse (one of O'Connell's lieutenants), wrote in 1829: 'The delay [in granting emancipation] has created a feeling of discontent and speculation, and this speculation a spirit of republicanism ...'(*History of the Late Catholic Association*, cited O'Hegarty, op.cit., p.54).

In spite of hostility from the Catholic hierarchy and disassociation from it by the Catholic leadership, the republican spirit of independence, according to Lecky, writing in the 1880s 'affected the whole population'.

When the Young Irelanders preached republicanism in the first quarter of the nineteenth century they were articulating an ideal already existing in the hearts and minds of many. The foreign government they knew did not express the will of the people, but rather the tyranny of alien privilege supported by coercion.

It is probable that after 1798 no form of government other than a republic could have emerged by popular acclaim in Ireland. Alternative possibilities certainly existed, but the likelihood that one of them might have won sufficient popular support to overwhelm the republican ideal is small. Home Rule was never seen as more than an interim measure, and by the time a Home Rule Bill reached the Statute Book of the British Parliament in September, 1914 — to be, in any case, accompanied by a Bill suspending its operation indefinitely — it was effectively dead so far as nationalists were concerned.

Education and Climate of Thought

One of the weapons in the armoury of a ruling conqueror is the successful promotion of a feeling of inferiority in the conquered people. It helps to persuade them, of their own volition, to perversely reject their own heritage and culture, and seek to emulate those of the conqueror. Accordingly, after the Treaty of Limerick, every Irish custom and institution, from religion to revelry — language, dress, housing, sports, behaviour and manners — was labelled 'inferior', fit only to be rejected and exchanged for something better. In order to give visible credence to this the ordinary people were reduced to — and maintained in — a state of abysmal poverty and beggary which 'justified' the claim of inferiority. Education became therefore of prime importance, and was pursued vigorously by the Catholic heirarchy and especially men and women such as Ignatius Rice, founder of the Christian and Presentation Brothers, and Mother Mary Aikenhead.

But the official educational thrust for the masses in the early 19th century Ireland was to produce docile, willing helots. In the main such formal schooling as was provided was through Protestant schools and they 'were all, to a greater or lesser degree, carried on with the object of converting Catholic children to Protestantism, so that the people did not avail themselves of them to any great extent' (O'Hegarty, op. cit. p.390). Thus proselytism, even if not officially encouraged, was given a relatively free hand.

In 1831 A Board of National Education was established by Lord Edward Stanley to provide general undenominational education for young children. But the programme of teaching as conducted by the Board was directed against Irishness of any sort and towards 'something better'.

The 'something better' was to become a shining example of that ardent, but improbable, juvenile depicted in reading books prescribed by the 1831 Irish National Board of Education and used in Irish schools into the twentieth century:

> *I thank the goodness and the grace*
> *Which on my birth has smiled*
> *And made me in these Christian days*
> *A happy English child.*

In this context Christian meant Protestant. The ultimate humiliation was that no Irish child would ever be accepted as English anyway, aspire though he might, giving rise to such terms as '*seoinín*', '*slíbhín*', '*castle-Catholic*' and so on. He could never presume to parity with an English Protestant gentleman, and was despised by most fellow Irishmen if he tried. However, in spite of these things, the limited elementary formal education that resulted from the establishment of the Board facilitated the spread of both old and new ideas about republicanism and nationalism. In the main the people's religious faith and fervour and the enduring sense of an independent Irish identity persisted tenaciously. It was, of course, established government policy that education should be through the medium of English, a fact which may also have facilitated proselytising. But in the nineteenth century, too, began that process of transition from an Irish-speaking to an English-speaking nation, so that by the beginning of the twentieth century Ireland was the only English-speaking Catholic country in the world — a uniqueness that would have a significant impact on its people and their development.

Ironically, through this very policy of education through English the republican separatism the authorities were so anxious to destroy received the very means essential to its survival, namely universal literacy in a powerful and influential international language.

The process of so-called 'unification' was carried out in parallel with the basic administrative policy of divide and conquer. With the doctrine of *'inferiority-ness'* and the penal laws, by establishing the Protestant ascendancy as superior in all respects (but depriving them of the right to self-government), the British created not one, but several conflicting divisions. To control them all with a common policy was impossible.

At the root lay religious differences. In his important work, *Ireland Since the Famine*, F. S. L. Lyons observes that throughout the period religion was central to the personal lives of most people, and was a formidable divisive barrier: that these religious divides closely coincided with the division between native and settler, conquered and conqueror and had complicated Irish history since the Restoration. He goes on to point out that these rivalries altered significantly in the nineteenth century.

Following Union the power of the established Anglican Church of Ireland, while still enormous, was changed. From being autocratic it became something less. Anglicans remained the smallest element of the population and accounted for most of the so-called gentry and aristocracy, though a few Old English and Irish remained among the latter. Before the century was over the Anglican Church would be disestablished and the tithe system, under which Catholics were obliged to support it, was abolished (but not without alternative financial assistance).

The Catholic position also changed enormously in two particular respects. Emancipation and education gave encouragement to an emerging Catholic middle-class, and this led to a corresponding development in organization and influence. Catholics represented over three-quarters of the Irish population; the Presbyterians and other Dissenters comprised about thirteen per cent, and the Anglicans rather less (1861 census). The Union diminished the role of the Anglicans, but the Dissenters of the north achieved not just social and political equality, but a collective identity with which they were well satisfied. Where not so long before the Presbyterians and Catholics had united in libertarian purpose, the demographic facts now brought Anglican and Presbyterian populations to uneasy common cause. They realised that in the view of the Catholic majority they were all seen as oppressive aliens and that their hold in the country and its people was precarious. To maintain their status in the face of growing nationalist activity and a slightly more liberal political climate, they must either change or stand together.

The Catholic Church was reluctant to offend the Establishment, and was opposed to republicanism (especially the French variety) and the anti-clericalism associated with it. (The curious and unanticipated conflict between religious and political freedom and loyalties, which had up to 1798 seemed much the same thing, was sharpened in the early part of the nineteenth century[21]). The failure of Emmet's Rising in 1803 to carry forward Tone's republican flag widened this ideological/spiritual division. With the advent of O'Connell a *via media* was achieved which seemed to offer the prospect of some joint progress. But it was not to be. Following the success of Catholic emancipation, O'Connell led the movement for repeal of the Union. But he became old, out of touch and discredited and the movement failed. The failure of Repeal, followed by the Great Famine, and the failure, at a time when the Church was under 'republican' onslaught in Europe, of the 'Young Irelanders' rising in 1848, reinforced the conservative anti-republican outlook of the Irish Church. From then onwards — with individual exceptions — it consistently opposed republican separatism.

Curiously enough, it also showed opposition to constitutional nationalism. That is not to say that it was entirely anti-national, but throughout the nineteenth century it certainly remained pro-Establishment. O'Hegarty took the view that the Church saw the future evolution of Ireland as 'necessarily conditioned by whatever could be accomplished by an acceptance of English domination and English civilization' (op.cit., p.400).

This confusing relationship between separatists and the Catholic Church was not helped by the publication of Pope Pius IX's Syllabus of Errors in 1864, which was inspired largely by the rise of Italian nationalism. The Syllabus of Errors condemned Socialism, Freemasonry and Liberalism as well as secret societies and stopped short, but only just, of condemning republicanism. Of significance is the fact that the rise of nationalism in Italy had not only united that country, it threatened the existence — and the revenues — of the Papal states.

The position of middle-class Irish Catholics was strengthened by the appointment as Archbishop of Dublin of Paul Cullen (later cardinal), conservatively European in education and outlook and, as a consequence, unsympathetic to nationalism.

Cullen had been Rector of the Irish College at Rome and was more than simply a conservative Irish priest. He had first-hand knowledge of the Papal attitude to nationalism, which in Europe was sometimes accompanied by anti-clericalism and a sort of spiritual mysticism, which alienated the populace from orthodoxy in a manner considered to be deeply sinister. Although that was not the case in Ireland, Cullen nevertheless denounced and continued to denounce the Fenians and any activities against the existing order of things, political no less than clerical, in the most violent terms. This hostility from the Church in Ireland towards what the Fenians believed was a legitimate 'Catholic doctrine of the right of revolution' provoked a strong response, especially from the writer Charles Kickham, and also from some priests. Kickham, a Catholic, again and again belaboured the point that priests 'sympathetic or unsympathetic had no place in politics'(Lyons, op. cit., p. 131). It was a far cry from the situation of little more than a hundred years earlier when, by and large, the only leaders available to the people were the priests and religious and political liberty seemed to amount to the same thing.

This quarrel between 'the Fenians and the Church went far beyond the immediate issues of the day and was to have a permanent importance in the history of Irish nationalism'(ibid, p 132). Clearly, clerical influence on Irish nationalist politics has been overstated and distorted. As Kickham expressed it (*The Irish People*, June 1864):

We may safely affirm that, as a general rule, ecclesiastics are not to be coveted as political guides. It is natural that we should expect to find in them a knowledge of all essential truths of theology. But it is ludicrously illogical to infer that because they are acquainted with theology, they must necessarily be political adepts ... So far from priests being infallible in politics, they are, generally speaking, the most unsafe and fallible of all political teachers. This truth has been illuminated over and over again in Irish affairs. Their electioneering blundering and divisions have shocked all persons possessed of unprejudiced minds ... No, the vast majority of the bishops and parish priests will never cordially support the cause of Irish Independence. The best that can be expected from them is neutrality ...

And of the 'Castle-Catholics' Thomas Clarke Luby, the Fenian historian, wrote: '...they are, for the most part... more English than the English themselves; they are a foreign garrison, whose existence is an obstacle to our prosperity, second only to that of British rule itself; in short, any attempt to make Irish nationalists out of them at this time of day would be as rational and practicable as to attempt to induce hyenas to play the part of lap-dogs...'

In a telling and perhaps prefigurative sentence O'Hegarty summarised the attitudes of the people of the country to coercion from England. 'The declarations of Wellington and Peel that England would fight a civil war, if necessary, rather than concede Repeal, even though all Ireland wanted it, moved Ireland profoundly, moved it to anger' (op. cit., p.136).

The struggle between constitutionalists, such as O'Connell, Gavan Duffy and Smith O'Brien, who shunned physical force and those who, like Davis, Mitchel and Stephens, saw it as the essential tool without which freedom was impossible, continued throughout the nineteenth century. O'Connell's decline lost him the authority which the Young Irelanders had been eroding. For the rest of the century, the see-saw between constitutionalists and separatists favoured one or the other in turn. Events such as the Famine, the land agitations of the '50s, '60s and '80s and political events overseas — especially in France, Italy, Hungary and America — affected the fortunes of both sides. It was essentially a struggle to win the wholehearted support of the people. The institutions, the merchants and the Church, mainly supported constitutionalism. But until Home Rule the constitutionalists did not have a clear, sustained policy and, with the exception of the ageing O'Connell (and, much farther down the road, Parnell), they did not have the leadership capable of providing one — as those who came after Parnell amply demonstrated. The physical force movement, on the other hand, had a clear vision and, from Davis onwards, produced adequate — if not always inspired — leadership (including, it can be argued, the later Parnell). But, whatever about enthusiasm, besides essentials such as money and other vital resources, they frequently seemed wanting in good judgement.

In any revolutionary movement the importance of creating the necessary climate of thought is paramount. Without it the prospect of success is minimal. A successful revolution is, first and foremost, a popular revolution. In Ireland, where the spirit of national independence manifested itself, almost uniquely, over centuries, and had been reinforced by republicanism, it was less a matter of initiating such a climate of thought as of reviving and restimulating an existing one.

In 1842 Thomas Davis, a Protestant, and John Blake Dillon started *The Nation* newspaper. It encouraged the idea of separatist republicanism and helped to build the climate of thought that sustained the movement throughout the remainder of the century. They were joined by Charles Gavan Duffy, an experienced and able journalist, who provided the professional knowledge and energy that made *The Nation* into the powerful influence it became. Its philosophy, as described by Davis himself, was to offer 'a nationality of the spirit as well as of the letter' ... which would establish internal union and external independence' (*Prospectus for The Nation included in Thomas Davis: Essays and Poems, with a Centenary Memoir*, Dublin 1945, p.13). This philosophy would, as Lyons remarks 'embrace all creeds, races and classes within the island'(op.cit., 105) in the same spirit as that of Wolfe Tone.

The impact these men quickly made was almost entirely confined to a small intellectual minority, mostly in Dublin. They at first subscribed to O'Connell's Repeal Association, but their outlook was radically different and the inevitable split ensued. O'Connell sought constitutional improvement, while retaining the link with Britain. Davis and his followers — derisively dubbed 'Young Irelanders' by O'Connellites (a name which stuck and became popular) — were separatist and republican. O'Connell had been capable of dominating the masses whereas the appeal of Davis and *The Nation* was, as yet, to a limited audience. Following Davis's death (of scarlet fever in 1846 when he was 31) the breach between O'Connell and the Young Irelanders came to a head over the question of third-level education and Peel's proposal for universities in Cork, Belfast and Galway. O'Connell absolutely opposed the principle of mixed education at any level. For the republican Young Irelanders, no doubt in the contemporary spirit of liberalism then sweeping Europe, it was a vital principle of religious freedom and tolerance. But the sectarian polarisation that had characterised Irish society and politics for 150 years was too strong a mix and a majority opposed Peel's Bill. The Catholic Church's newly won recognition had been too dearly bought to put its consolidation at risk through broad tolerance. And Rome itself was under threat from liberal and republican forces.

The work of *The Nation* in cultivating and disseminating nationalist and republican separatist ideas was continued by Gavan Duffy after Mitchel's exile. He revived the paper in 1849. After his own emigration the theme of *The Nation* was continued by the secretive and monumental James Stephens, a founder and Head Centre of the IRB, in his paper, *The Irish People*. In the third issue he coined the phrase 'Felon-setting' to describe those who claimed and supported national feelings, but condemned violence against the British administration.

After Davis died the British determined to 'get' Gavan Duffy knowing that he and Mitchel, because of the influence of *The Nation*, were their most dangerous opponents in Ireland. *The Nation*, according to O'Hegarty '... raised up in Ireland the spirit of Nationality which was never again to be wholly quiescent' (op.cit., p. 376). This statement should be read carefully and in context. In no sense can it be said that *The Nation* **created** the spirit of nationality. That is not O'Hegarty's intent. But the phrasing is open to misinterpretation. The correct reading is that *The Nation* **revived** a flagging spirit of nationality.

John O'Leary, one of the almost legendary Fenians, was a Protestant, and one of the most formidable writers of his time on nationalism. The following extract from *The Irish People* of January 1864, in its directness and forcefulness, indicates a prelude to Parnell. 'Twenty years ago Thomas Davis appealed to the aristocracy to save the people with their own hands. [By 'aristocracy' he means the Protestant ascendancy class who had turned their backs on nationalism after the Union]. We make no appeal to the aristocracy. For we know that, though we spoke with the tongues of men and angels, our appeal would be in vain... The people must save themselves. Without counting then who belong to, or who have gone over to, the enemy, or the more numerous section of Irish-born men who see their country bleeding to death, and, dastards as they are, will make no real effort to save her — the Irish people still count by millions. And millions, if properly instructed, can defeat the most cunningly devised scheme of the most powerful tyrant for their destruction. The question is, can our people be properly instructed? ... We have the best reason for believing that they can; and to this task we call upon all true men to bend their energies...It is the *people* who have kept the national faith alive; and whatever of that faith exists among the 'higher orders' is derived from the people. Instead of being imbued with the spirit of patriotism by the upper classes, the people impart to them the little of patriotism these upper classes possess. The well-spring of nationality is in the heart of the people. So long as this is so, it would be just as rational to expect that the sun ought to revolve around the earth as to say that the '*elite* of property' are the 'natural leaders' of the people.'

Rise Of Sectarianism
Few of the Church of Ireland Protestants gained from the Union. On the contrary. In the main it was their industries and exports that were most grievously affected by ensuing economic restrictions, and their taxes (bolstered, of course, by rack-rents) also went to shore up England's war debts. The Catholics and nationalists continued their struggle. But the Dissenters, mainly Presbyterians, gained enormously, materially and psychologically, from the Union. They did not, *en masse*, adopt Orangeism until after the Union, when it was an obvious source of organised defence against a strengthening Catholic majority, a perceived threat to their recently acquired status[22]. Moreover, as is clear from contemporary accounts, the dreaded Orangemen of the pre-Union period were neither essentially confined to Ulster nor to Dissenters, with whom they later became closely associated. The northern Presbyterians were republican, generally speaking, at the time of the 1798 rebellion. Like their fellow southern united men, large numbers of Presbyterians were waiting for the word that the French had landed before they, too, rose. As for the Orangemen, they tended to belong to the middle- and lower-class Protestant established church element who lacked the security and power of their wealthier co-religionists — land owners, professional classes, merchants etc.[23]

There were multiple effects of this ancient continuation of sectarian division'. Both the Orange order and presbyterianism changed to the extent that they became perceived as one and the same; Orangeism became concentrated in the north and received a dominant (loyalist) focus. Nationalist opinion shifted to include loyalist Dissenters in its anti-government outlook, and presbyterian opinion shifted from being republican to being loyalist/anti-Catholic. A further question, namely what is meant by 'loyalist', arises. The answer takes us back to the Union and what was achieved under it by the Dissenters — namely a sense of place and identity. That was not — and is not — simply 'Britishness', whatever that may be. Their Protestantism/presbyterianism came first, anything else afterwards. A Catholic British monarchy, for instance, would lose their 'loyalty' overnight. As Shepherd says:

> The original Orange oath enjoined its adherents 'to support the king and his heirs as long as he or they support the Protestant ascendancy'. The Orangeman's loyalty is thus conditional ... the conditionality of Ulster Loyalism has remained a consistent strand in the Orange tradition, and has baffled successive generations of British politicians and officials as they try to come to terms with self-professed 'loyalists' whose loyalty attaches to a Protestant monarchy, not to the modern symbol of authority in the British state, the Crown-in-Parliament (Robert Shepherd, *Ireland's Fate*, the Boyne and After, p 209).

A characteristically acute passage by Lyons (op.cit. p.287) begins: 'The historical factors which separated Unionists from other Irishmen of course went back centuries rather than decades' (See footnote 11). In case we overlook the fact — and it is easy to do so — Unionists, by definition, did not exist before 1800 and the Act of Union of that year. What the Union did for the Northern settlers, Presbyterians in particular, was to provide them with the kind of political focus and identity they had been so forcefully seeking when so many of them sought freedom through the republicanism they had adopted a few years earlier. A mere two years after the defeat of '98 came the opportunity for more or less equal citizenship, and a specific British identity. *Equality,* not *liberty,* was what they had sought. Whether it was achieved with or without independence was irrelevant. The Union offered a considerable degree of religious, economic and political equality, as well as protection of those rights. Overnight the hard-won republican common-ground between Presbyterian and Catholic Irishmen evaporated.

In adopting a protective stance over Union the presbyterians, who so readily abandoned republicanism, adopted a defensive role that would lock them into ferocious anti-Catholic, anti-national bitterness and prejudice. They adopted Orangeism, which hitherto had been largely a society for poor and disgruntled established church Protestants. It followed that they and their Catholic nationalist fellow-citizens, who outnumbered them perhaps twenty-to-one, were on a collision course. In a sense it can be argued that the Unionists themselves were, by default, major contributors to Irish nationalism. Their reaction to the groundswell of public opinion that led to Emmet's Rising (1803), to Catholic emancipation and to the separatist movements was to support and encourage coercion and force by the government against the vast majority of the population. Willy-nilly the government responded. It followed that the possibility of, as Plunkett put it, a reconciliation of the people to the Union receded more and more as the nineteenth century advanced. On the contrary, the minds and mood of the people moved in the opposite direction.

To assume, as is often done, that all landlords and unionists were endemically anti-Irish — as distinct from being opposed to nationalism — is wrong. While most Unionists remained so, some notable individuals of unionist background were nationalist. A considerable and influential body were also concerned at the gross inequities in Irish society and in the Irish economy, and were anxious for improvement — but within the political *status quo*. Lyons says:

> ... the differences of origin, of religion and of social and economic develop-
> ment which produced this fundamental cleavage in Irish society were focussed
> more sharply than ever before by Parnell's success in bringing Home Rule into
> the realm of practical politics in 1885-6.

Lyons points out that Parnell's success had the effect of pushing 'Irish Unionism as an entity' into Ulster. Moreover, he says, since the 1885 election was perceived as being about the fall or survival of the Union, 'a process of polarisa-tion almost inevitably set in, constituency after constituency being won by representatives of either of the two extremes' (*op. cit.* p. 287).

As today, Northern Unionists refused, in Lyons's phrase, 'to distinguish between degrees of nationalism'. They were galvanised into hostile action no less by Gladstone's proposed Home Rule Bill in the 1880s than they were in the 1980s by the Anglo-Irish Agreement. But the seat of power of Unionism at that time in Ireland continued to lie in the south, not in the North. Here were the enormously wealthy landowners like Lords Lansdowne and Midleton who, besides being powerful influences within the Irish Unionist party, also had enormous influence in the English Conservative party. And here, if anywhere, is the origin of that metamorphosis from Conservative to Unionist that overtook the British Tory party at that time. Here, also, is the genesis of Randolph Churchill's 'playing the Orange card'[24]. Although Gladstone was committed — and committed his party — to Home Rule, his successors, particularly Asquith, were cut from a different and more politically expedient cloth. True, Asquith did not abandon Home Rule; he could not abandon Home Rule because it was nailed firmly to the Liberal party's masthead, but he sought to dilute it with partition and thereby created more problems than he could solve. Although it was not always clearly seen from the beginning — except instinctively by Unionists — Home Rule and the Union were, in fact, mutually exclusive.

The effect that the French Revolution of 1848 had on Ireland was considerable. In its own way it was as stimulating to Irish nationalists of the mid nineteenth century as the revolution of 1789 had been to their fathers and grandfathers almost sixty years earlier. Men who, a few weeks before, had denounced physical force and preached caution, spoke very differently in the aftermath of the revolution. In common with an explosion of nationalistic and republican fervour across Europe, the heady belief that Ireland's opportunity was NOW provoked calls to arms and to the barricades to a totally unprepared and unorganised public. In *The Nation* (March 1848), Gavan Duffy trumpeted:

> Ireland's opportunity, thank God and France, has come at last! Its challenge
> rings in our ears like a call to battle and warms our blood like wine... We must
> answer if we would not be slaves forever... if needs be we must die, rather than
> let this providential hour pass over us unliberated.

Though the Rising when it came was disorganised and easily put down — indeed its peculiar timing during the course of the Great Famine brings into question the judgement of the Young Ireland leadership — it was Gavan Duffy's revolutionary policy, drafted for the Confederate programme, that, later on, provided a blue-print for Parnell.

The Great Famine

The famine of 1845-1849 was so destructive that its effects are still felt. John Mitchel, who lived through it, believed that it was deliberate British government policy to reduce Ireland's population by starvation. According to O'Hegarty (op. cit., p.328)

... there is justification for the view that government policy, under which over a million died, and over a million emigrated in five years, was a deliberate policy of extermination, in pursuance of English political advantage, so as to ensure Ireland remaining indefinitely and powerlessly under England's control[25].

Gallagher (Thomas Gallagher *Paddy's Lament; Ireland 1846-47, Prelude to Hatred*, Dublin 1982, p. 85), in his detailed study of the famine and famine consequences in Ireland and America, writes: 'There is no historical evidence implicating the British Government in a conspiracy to exterminate the population of Ireland, but many Government officials, as well as those advising them, looked upon the famine as a God-sent solution to the so-called Irish question.' He continues with the following:

The idea that the peasantry had become superfluous in Ireland, that more attention should henceforth be given to ridding the land of people and stocking it with cattle, gained more and more adherents among Ireland's landlords as the famine's ravages continued (Ibid. pp. 112.145).

Here may be discerned the attitude, on the part of both government and landowner, which led to the later Land Wars. Even in 'Black '47' there was still in the country enough wheat, oats, barley, butter, eggs, beef, pork and lamb to feed the entire population of the country for a year. Not only was all this produce exported, relief ships from America and elsewhere were stopped by the British Navy from coming into Irish ports which, in the interests of 'free' trade were closed to all but English vessels.

Isaac Butt wrote (*The Famine in the Land*, 1847), 'Can we wonder if the Irish people believe — **and believe it they do** — that the lives of those who have perished, and who will perish, have been sacrificed by a deliberate compact to the gain of English merchants?' O'Hegarty (ibid, p.299) elaborates with the view that the United Kingdom parliament was, in effect, the parliament of Great Britain only and legislated solely from that point of view.

The famine all but extirpated the very soul of the country. 'It didn't matter who was related to you' wrote one woman, 'your friend was whoever would give you a bite to put in your mouth. Sport and pastimes disappeared. Poetry, music and dancing stopped. They lost and forgot them all ... The famine killed everything'(Gallagher,op. cit. p. 27). It also halved the population, killing more than a quarter and exiling another quarter.

But the establishment of considerable Irish populations in the United States, Canada, Argentina, Britain itself, and Australia helped to bring Ireland's condition to world attention, and it became no longer possible for England to treat the appalling circumstances in Ireland as simply a domestic issue. The involvement of Irish emigrants and those of Irish descent in the affairs of the mother country 'remained deep and continuous, leading them both to give the large-scale financial support without which the development of vigorous Irish nationalism would have been impossible in the seventy years after the Famine, and also, at certain crucial moments, to affect directly and decisively the maintenance and development of the revolutionary movement which worked secretly but tirelessly for the violent overthrow of British rule in Ireland and its replacement by a republic' (Lyons,op. cit., p.16).

The effects of the Famine[26] were decisive so far as militant separatist action was concerned, and limited the scope of '48. After the Famine the country was — or seemed to be — again leaderless and apathetic. The failure of the 1848 rising and the exile of most of the leaders stultified national activity for almost a decade. During that decade the British policy of depopulating Ireland became clearer. It was to exile, or otherwise dispose of, as many Irish as possible thus making the country easier for England to exploit — as a source of cheap labour and food, on the economic side, and as a strategic buttress to her own back door on the other.

One of the strangest weapons of the **entire** movement for national independence in its various aspects throughout was that it was grounded in principles of moral justice. This enabled the Irish leaders to speak and act with the force of innate conviction. In all of this, of course, the everyday life of the people continued within the confines of contemporary circumstances. Life went on and if, now and then, it did so with a red coat or in the company of a peeler; under the flag of the Union and the eye of the resident magistrate, it is simply because that is how it was. Forward movement at national level was a slow business. But it was sustained and deep. After the Young Irelanders it took time, and a new generation, for the national spirit to recover sufficiently to, again, take up, plan and carry forward the 'heroic enterprise' of the separatist ideal. But,

> though the Irish people had exhibited a constancy of purpose which have few parallels in history, it was certain that they were sunk in a torpor from which it was hopeless to lead them to heroic enterprises ... all that could be done directly for Nationality was to recommence teaching its principles and duties to the young...(Gavan Duffy, *The League of North and South*, 1886, pp 29/30).

This observation was written 36 years after Duffy had restarted *The Nation*, and the key word is 'nationality'. Its use a generation later, after an appalling interim, indicates how deeply the continuity of ideal and purpose was felt.

John Mitchel's insistence upon the need to achieve a republic entirely independent of England, was not of course a new idea ...but his enunciation of it struck with particular force upon a generation that had grown up under the shadow of O'Connell and his very different programme of constitutional nationalism.

The Young Ireland Rising lit the fire that produced a powerful and enduring movement, Fenianism. It seems appropriate that the phoenix, the mythical bird which, through its own self-immolation, gives birth to its solitary young became from that time the symbol of resurgent separatist Ireland. That is how the Young Irelanders were born from the embers left after Tone and Emmet; it was from the ashes of their pathetic rising that the Fenians, and the IRB emerged.

The influence of the Irish in America on events in Ireland, particularly the Fenian movement can hardly be exaggerated.

In 1854 a new organisation was formed, jointly, in Ireland and America, by veterans of the 1848 rising. It synthesized, in terms both contemporary and persistent, the principles that had promoted nationalist, republican and separatist action since 1798, and became instrumental in pursuing that synthesis to the foundation of the new state sixty-eight years later. That organisation adopted the name the Irish Republican Brotherhood (IRB) in 1873. 'The organisation of the IRB was in Circles, each with a Centre, Secretary and Treasurer, District Centres and County Centres. The Supreme Council was elected by representatives of these District and County Centres. A committee of five from County or District Centres in each of the divisions elected the members of the S.C. for their respective divisions under a strict pledge of secrecy. The Executive of the IRB consisted of the President, Secretary and Treasurer of the Supreme Council'... (Desmond Ryan, *The Rising*, Dublin, 1949, p. 9).

Another Irish/American organisation, the Fenian movement, also fuelled by resurgent nationalism (not least from the Irish in America), was stimulated by the availability of experienced soldiers and officers, thousands of whom were unemployed after the American civil war. They possessed vital qualities, including a love of their homeland, a desire, stimulated by civil war propaganda, for freedom, and the experience and trade of soldiering. It was an explosive mix needing only leadership for a fuse. And it was all, so far as England was concerned, a safe and happy three thousand miles away across an ocean. Then General John J. O'Neill, formerly of the famous U.S. 2nd Cavalry, in 1866 led a thousand armed veteran Irishmen across the Niagara river into Canada, where he defeated a force of Canadian troops under Lt. Col. John Stoughton Dennis and captured Fort Erie. O'Neill had 10,000 reinforcements in the United States waiting to join him in Canada, but at that stage the United States Government, responding to British pressure, intervened and prevented the movement. O'Neill's small force was forced to withdraw. There were a number of other attacks on Canada by Fenian troops and then, in 1871, William B. O'Donoghue, in conjunction with Louis Riel's French/Canadian war of independence, planned a grand assault on Manitoba. Internal disputes between the Fenians, the IRB and the French Canadians resulted in a fiasco. But the republican spirit, nevertheless, remained alive and well in the United States.

In Ireland during the same period republicanism was also reaffirmed and expanded and it is interesting to consider the effect that O'Neill's invasion of Canada must have had on the planning of the 1867 rising. In 1865 James Stephens (known as *An Seabhac* — the hawk) wrote a letter, intended for the Fenians of

Clonmel, in which he powerfully affirmed the republican position: 'I speak with a knowledge and authority to which no other man could pretend, and I repeat the flag of Ireland — the flag of the Irish Republic — must this year be raised'. The letter came to the attention of the British through the activities of a spy called Nagle, who worked in Stephens' office.

Although as an insurrection the Fenian rising of 1867 was totally inadequate, as a phase in the evolution of Irish nationalism it was of central importance. Not merely was it a link in the chain connecting the men of 1848 with the men of 1916, but in its brief high noon it established and clarified certain fundamentals of the separatist ideal. By its resistance to ecclesiastical censure and its rigorous attempt to separate Church and State it proclaimed that the independence for which it fought was intellectual, even spiritual, as well as political...

> Fenianism, by its call to arms, reiterated for its own generation the old, harsh maxim that freedom had to be fought for, while by their integrity and bravery in hopeless circumstances its champions passed on to their successors like a living flame the lesson that to sacrifice himself for his country was the highest good to which a man might aspire. Fifty years later the full meaning of that lesson would be made plain (Lyons, op. cit. pp.138)

In spite of the failure of the rising, the republican Fenian spirit, whatever name it used, became the dominant separatist spirit in Ireland. On St. Patrick's day, 1873, at a convention in Dublin the IRB adopted a written constitution in which it was stated, *inter alia*:-

> the IRB shall await the decision of the Irish Nation as expressed by a majority of the Irish people, *as to the fit hour for inaugurating a war against England, and shall, pending such an emergency, lend its support to every movement calculated to advance the cause of Irish independence consistently with the preservation of its own integrity.*

At that convention a further vital decision, and one which was to have the most far-reaching and profound effects, was taken. The IRB Supreme Council was declared to be 'the sole Government of the Irish Republic'.

Simultaneously with this Fenian/IRB move occurred a burst of constitutional activity under the leadership of a great, but overshadowed Irishman, Isaac Butt. An MP who was also a lecturer in political economy at Trinity College, Butt had been in politics for over 25 years and had supported Repeal. Like Mitchel he had lived through the famine and had been deeply affected by it. He, too, believed it to have been deliberately manipulated — if not worse — by the British Government as part of their policy to reduce the population of Ireland. He became leader of the Irish Parliamentary Party at Westminster, and threw the gauntlet of Home Rule into the Anglo-Irish ring. A lawyer and, to begin with, a conservative unionist, Butt's outlook modified and changed during the Famine and when he defended some of the Young Irelanders. In a pamphlet — *The Famine in the Land* (1847) — he demanded that the authorities act to relieve distress and warned of the danger of profound reaction to neglect by even moderate classes in Ireland.

The perspicacity and implications of that warning were noteworthy. Following this Butt proposed a form of federalism which would give Ireland a separate and subordinate parliament within the Union. For the next twenty years he sojourned in England as a member of parliament, but returned in 1870 to propose and found the Home Government Association, the forerunner of the powerful Home Rule movement, with the object of achieving an Irish parliament in federation with Britain. It was Butt's hope and ideal to weld together within his association Protestant, Catholic, Liberal, Unionist and Fenian and move forward on a basis of limited nationalism within the Union, but the conflicting interests proved too much for the idea. Conservative Ascendancy Protestants were reluctant to have anything to do with a movement that proposed to loosen the economic ties with Britain that maintained them in their privileged positions and, at the other end of the scale, Fenians were not prepared to accept Butt's federal ideas as satisfactory. Other factions had their own reservations. However, Butt persisted, and out of his idea grew the Home Rule movement that won its first electoral success the following year, if with a modified platform. 'It was significant that when, during 1871, Home Rule began to register its first electoral success, the demand for simple legislative independence to be substituted for federalism began immediately to be heard' (Ibid, p.151). None of this was lost on Gladstone.

The key to Home Rule was fashioned by Butt in 1873 when he changed the Home Government Association to the Home Rule League which anyone could join for one pound a year. The aims and objects were the same, but there was one critical difference so far as elected members were concerned. Hitherto, as we have seen, there were Irish Liberals, Irish Conservatives and so on. But by now there were enough MPs on a Home Rule ticket in the League to make it feasible for them to consider voting with strength and in concert.

In 1874 fifty-nine members were elected on a Home Rule platform out-numbering by 14% the combined numbers elected as Conservative (33) and Liberal (10). That was the genesis of the Home Rule movement which, thanks to Parnell's political genius, was, within a few years, powerful enough to persuade Gladstone to introduce his first Home Rule Bill. But Home Rule as the goal of the Irish constitutional movement in the nineteenth century, was never subscribed to by the separatist republicans[27].

At the time of the 1867 rising Butt was an old man. Nevertheless he again shifted national political emphasis, this time away from physical force — with which, for the constitutionalists, there was not, as yet, a *rapprochement* — back to constitutional methods. Constitutional reform within the *status quo*, rather than republican separatism, reasserted itself as the dominant vehicle of national aspiration. Then the election of 1875 brought to the British Parliament an element that would infuse the Irish national aspiration and the means of achieving it with extraordinary dynamism. Charles Stewart Parnell took his seat with the Irish Parliamentary Party at Westminster, and soon succeeded Butt as leader.

Parnell was an unlikely nationalist. He was a Protestant and a landowner and had been educated in England. But he quickly showed a talent for leadership and love of country and of justice, traits perhaps acquired from his American mother.

He claimed that it 'was Fenianism that had first turned him towards politics —
that, and memories of the 1798 rebellion which still lived in the Wicklow countryside around his home' (Avondale, Co. Wicklow). He also acquired a deep and
abiding loathing of England and Englishmen. '...We must stand up to them. That's
the only way to treat an Englishman — stand up to him'.

Another powerful figure to come on the national scene in the 1870s, Michael
Davitt, was concerned with and involved in the land issue, which he believed
would provide the bridge linking separatists and constitutionalists. There was,
however, a problematic social factor involved — to which O'Leary and Kickham
referred and which only O'Connell and Parnell seemed able to surmount. All,
from the humblest starving peasant to the professional member of parliament,
were, at that time to some extent conditioned by what is now, often derisively,
termed 'Victorian attitudes', amongst them powerful notions of place and status.
These attitudes pandered to social and sectarian snobbery, facilitating the implementation of the 'Divide and Conquer' policy of the British. Generally speaking, the
physical force supporters were of peasant, small farmer, working class and intellectual
background, whereas constitutional support came, in the main, from the professional
and middle-classes. It is, of course, commonplace in any revolutionary situation that
those with most to lose tend to take the route of least risk, if they become involved at
all. And it is to the credit of many of the Irish professional and middle classes
throughout the nineteenth century that, on the whole, they remained supporters of
constitutional nationalism — indeed, were its main support.

Clearly, it would be foolish to assume that no separatists came from the middle
and professional classes, or that there were no constitutionalists amongst the
others. Equally it would be wrong, like Stephens, to dismiss all those who
supported the constitutionalist movement as mere time-servers. The contribution
of the constitutional movement to sustaining progress towards self-determination
was, until the fall of Parnell — and possibly to 1912 — very important. All the
concessions won in the 19th century following Union were, without exception —
though often under the additional influence of physical action of some sort —
achieved by the constitutionalists. More than once a major break-through, such
as Parnell's near achievement of Home Rule in 1882, was frustrated by unco-
ordinated and ill-considered physical action (in that case the Phoenix Park
murders). But neither should it be overlooked that the principle underlying
physical force movements throughout the nineteenth century — namely that no
country had achieved rightful and full independence without the use of force —
was entirely valid and correct and consistent with historical fact. All other matters
notwithstanding, here lay the essential difference between these two elements; the
constitutionalists saw their objective in terms of an Irish parliament subordinate to
Britain and within the British sphere of influence. The physical force element
stood for completely separate national identity and independence.

James Fintan Lalor, son of an O'Connellite member of parliament, virtually 'discovered' the land issue and made of it one that would, for a decade or more, come
to occupy much of the social and political energies of the nation. It is a good example of what might be called 'The myopia of history', which is particularly prevalent

in Ireland. It is often the case that events — even historic events of considerable moment — are perceived as happening here in isolation, which is often far from being the case. To confuse this myopia with insularity is a mistake; it is more an intensity of focus occupying the energies and talents of the people which absorbs universal movements into a national one. Ideas of social and political revolution stirred and surfaced in Ireland in the 19th century no less than elsewhere in Europe. If they were absorbed by more spectacular events, that should not be allowed either to diminish or exaggerate their importance — not only as of right in themselves, but because they very often helped create the climate of thought and feeling that made later achievements possible.

Initial resistance to Davitt's Land League idea came from both sides. The republicans feared that it would dilute their purpose, and the constitutionalists' fear was expressed by Parnell: 'Mr. Davitt was very anxious that the Land League should be formed, and that the tenants should be supported by an agrarian movement. I had in my mind advice given to me by Mr. Butt once, two years previously, when I pressed upon him the extension of the Home Rule Movement by the formation of branches throughout the country. He said, looking at it from the lawyer's point of view, that we should be made responsible for every foolish thing done by the members of the branches. I was rather disinclined to entertain the idea of the formation of an extensive agrarian movement on account of that caution which I received from Mr. Butt'[28].

Significantly Butt's definition of Home Rule, with dramatic consequences for both nations, coincided with the accession to the English premiership of a vigorous, honest and high-minded individual — W.E. Gladstone (first in 1868, again in 1880, in 1886 — losing again the same year — and in 1892). Gladstone's advent as prime minister of a Liberal Government in England, and his concern for Ireland, had dramatic consequences. It is hardly going too far to say that Gladstone did as much for Ireland in the second half of the 19th century as any Irishman of the period. He did not, of course, support separatism, but his motives and principles were of the highest, and were striking and unusual in a politician in so lofty and vulnerable a situation. They led him to disestablish the Church of Ireland and to introduce the first of the several Home Rule Bills on which his government, and eventually his party, was to founder.

It may well be asked why Gladstone put his government at risk on foot of a measure for Irish constitutional self-sufficiency. He was leader of a great and powerful popular political party (it disappeared, almost without a trace, in the turbulent years of the First World War). He was a man of immense popularity and prestige; he had no need to take such political risks. Why, then, did he do so? It is well to remember the period to which he belonged in which manners, morals and principles (irrespective of what seethed beneath) occupied a notable position in the conduct of affairs in general; that these were also often generally abused and corrupted in private and seclusion was a concomitant fact. And it was the nobility of one and the hypocrisy of the other that, to a very considerable extent, motivated Gladstone. He was not a self-seeker, but rather that unusual man, a seeker after justice. He pinned his political reputation on this and was rewarded with understanding and acceptance from the popular electorate, particularly in response to the doctrine that property has its duties as well as its rights.

In 1882 the Irish National League was formed, with Home Rule as its primary objective. It immediately began to organise along party and constituency lines. The result was that in the 1885 election it won almost every seat in Ireland except for some in Ulster, and one in Trinity College. Now, for the first time, there was a united and more or less homogenous Irish party going to Westminster, with a total of eighty-six seats, which would, under a party undertaking, sit vote and act together. A formidable force at a critical time, the Irish Party now held the balance of power in the English Parliament and, by acting in concert, could determine whether it stood or fell.

Without Gladstone it is unlikely that there would have been a Liberal Party with a Home Rule policy. Equally, and as importantly, without Gladstone's Home Rule policy, there would have been no Unionist party. In the absence of Gladstone's Home Rule proposals it is inconceivable that the Conservatives would have considered Unionism as the platform to which to harness their resources against the Liberal Party in England. They had conceded the principle of domestic legislation for Ireland and would have had little reason to woo and make use of sectarian violence there[29]. Had it not been for Home Rule that platform would simply not have existed. As a matter of principle Gladstone was determined to see Home Rule through for the good of both Ireland and England. It was this determination that enabled the Conservatives, in 1886, to identify Unionism as the plank — shaky though it might have been — from which to fight for re-election.

To the increasing alarm of the Anglican community in Ireland, the disestablishment of the Anglican Church (in 1869) had been signalled for years before it actually occurred. But when it did it was not as painful as anticipated. Though its status as the 'official' church was removed, it retained most of its wealth and social privileges while its educational dominance in the country was protected. (See O'Hegarty, *op. cit.*, p.620).

In other words, when the Anglican Church of Ireland heaved a sigh of relief that disestablishment was not as calamitous as expected, it did so for all the wrong reasons; the real threat lay ahead.

By 1885 Gladstone had reached the conclusion that Home Rule for Ireland was a matter of right and justice. Nevertheless it would be Home Rule with limitations. It would provide Ireland with a legislature of its own, but, unlike the Dominions, (Canada became a Dominion in 1867), it would have no fiscal independence. This was to ensure that there would be no possibility of Irish enterprise becoming a danger to British production. Both sides in the British Commons agreed on that.

Modern historians take the view, probably correctly, that Parnell saw Home Rule as the first major step towards full freedom. Davitt quotes him as saying of Gladstone: 'I don't care who leads when I am gone, but I am anxious the old country should get some kind of parliament as a result of our struggles, and unless Mr. Gladstone can do this for us, no other living Englishman can' (Davitt, *The Fall of Feudalism*, p.518/9).

In spite of the earlier reservations of Irish nationalists from both sides, the Land League came into being in 1879, following a rent protest meeting in Claremorris. It won immediate general support. The Claremorris meeting was followed by an important one at Westport at which Parnell associated himself and the Irish Party with the Land League. The alliance was directed in the first instance against the inhuman landlord system which was of a feudal and unjust kind long since dispensed with in other civilised countries, even Czarist Russia.

In 1879 the potato crop had again failed and famine threatened. This was prevented when the Land League persuaded tenants to withold their rents so that they could survive the threat[30]. It is salutary to remember that this was relatively recently, in the lifetime of the grandparents of some still living. In that year also Parnell was elected president of the new Irish National Land League. The collective energies of the Land League and of Home Rulers were harnessed under his leadership to become the first powerful mass movement since Catholic emancipation (the Repeal movement never acquired the same momentum). It provided Parnell with a power-base, and the whole-hearted support of the people such as no national leader had obtained since O'Connell. An election in 1880 brought yet another significant change. Not since the time of the Young Irelanders and O'Connell had both elements of national endeavour been on the verge of joining forces (and that was less a conjunction than a splitting-off). Now, in what was the first visible indication of the long-anticipated coming together of these hitherto often opposed national elements, in an unprecedented move, a number of candidates with Fenian background offered themselves as, and became successful, national candidates for election. The effect was electric. Until the advent of Parnell Irish constitutionalists would certainly have been satisfied with a return to a Grattan-style parliament, but these republican separatists sought complete independence. Parnell succeeded in marrying the two and when seeking the 'plank of National Independence', stated:

> We cannot ask for less than the restitution of Grattan's Parliament, with its important privileges and far-reaching constitution. *We cannot under the British Constitution* ask for more than the restitution of Grattan's Parliament, *but no man has the right to fix the boundary to the march of a nation* (author's italics).

The 1881 Land Act gave tenants some rights and, though it was strongly opposed as inadequate, led to what was perhaps the greatest social change in Ireland between the Famine and the 1916 Rising. The 1881 Act, although it left a great deal to be achieved in terms of justice, had secured the 'Three Fs' — fixity of tenure, fair rent and freedom of sale. It was called, and with reason, the *Magna Carta* of the Irish tenant. It was supplemented by subsequent Acts, notably the Wyndham Act of 1903, which enabled transferance to the tenant of actual ownership of the land and created a peasant proprietorship. But it was the Act of 1881 that first gave the tenant a foothold in the soil and thus began the process of diminishing the autocratic power of the landlord.

Land agitation by peasant secret societies continued after the 1881 Act. The British government reacted with renewed coercion. *Habeas corpus* was suspended; the Land League was declared an illegal organisation. Parnell, together with other Irish leaders and parliamentarians, was arrested and jailed without trial. These steps proved ineffective. When Parnell had been in jail for six months (October 1881 — April 1882), negotiations were begun. The Irish intermediaries were Frank Hugh O'Donnell, described (by O'Hegarty, op.cit., p.509) as one 'whose self-conceit and arrogance far exceeded his ability', and one Captain W.H. O'Shea, who was to play a vital role in a drama then unfolding. O'Shea, at the time a colleague (and to some extent under the political patronage) of Parnell, was just as pretentious as O'Donnell. Why these men were selected has been questioned ever since. The simple fact is that they were there and were available. O'Donnell, at least, was a man capable of imposing his personality and, were it not for Parnell, might, and expected to, have been leader of the Irish party. O'Shea was still ingratiating himself with and — literally — pandering to Parnell.

Parnell was released on 2 May 1882. A few days later (6 May), as O'Hegarty wrote: 'Ireland was rejoicing and optimistic. Home Rule, Arrears Bill (to alleviate tenants in arrears of rent), no coercion, were all in the air'(p.515). En route to London Parnell was jubilant. 'We are on the eve of something like Home Rule', he said to Davitt. 'Mr. Gladstone has thrown over coercion and Mr. Forster [former] (Chief Secretary at Dublin Castle), and the government will legislate further on the land question. The Tory party are going to advocate land purchase, almost on the lines of the Land League programme, and I see no reason why we should not soon obtain all we are looking for in the League movement' (Michael Davitt, *The Fall of Feudalism*, 1904, p.356).

This jubilant mood was shattered that same day. In the Phoenix Park, Lord Henry Cavendish, the new Chief Secretary and T.H. Burke, Under-Secretary, were assassinated by a tiny group called The Invincibles, formed the previous year with the sole purpose of assassinating members of the ruling establishment in Dublin[31]. It is a measure of their stature that the assassins were later betrayed by their leader, a man called James Carey. But the damage done that fatal May day was disastrous from the point of view of the national movement. Not only did it halt progress towards limited self-government within the United Kingdom, it set the face of the Conservative Party against Irish interests for many years to come. From then until long after the foundation of the Irish State the Conservative party was a ruthless, implacable and doctrinaire opponent of Irish independence of any sort[32]. When Parnell learned of the murders he issued a statement on behalf of the Irish Party.

> On the eve of what seemed a bright future for our country, that evil destiny which has apparently pursued us for centuries has struck another blow at our hopes, which cannot be exaggerated in its disastrous consequences. In this hour of sorrowful gloom we venture to give an expression of our profoundest sympathy with the people of Ireland, in the calamity that has befallen our cause, through a horrible deed, and to those who had determined at the last hour that a policy of conciliation should supplant that of terrorism and national distrust...We feel that no act has been perpetrated in our country during the exciting struggles for social and political rights of the past fifty years, that has so strained the name of hospitable Ireland as this cowardly and unprovoked assassination of a friendly stranger ...

Parnell's reference to struggles of the past fifty years is particularly revealing in the context of a continuing process, however haphazard from time to time.

The 1885 (December) election increased the Irish Nationalists' return at Westminster to 86 seats. A few months later, in April 1886, (following another change of government in February), Gladstone moved his first Home Rule Bill. However, the issue was so divisive that it resulted in a Liberal Party split. Austen Chamberlain, who saw himself as Liberal leader after Gladstone, and who was one of his most powerful supporters, broke with him on the Home Rule issue. He believed it would not work and 'would infallibly lead to a demand for entire separation'. He crossed the floor of the House and voted with the Conservatives against the Bill to help defeat it. It was then that the Conservative anti-Irish attitude hardened and they selected the Irish question as their platform. 'Conservative' and 'unionist' began to be interchangeable terms.

Yet, paradoxically, when the Conservatives rattled the Orange drum it was not the Irish question that was uppermost in their minds. What brought them to bed with the Ulster Unionists was a fury with, and a determination to bring down, the Liberal Party in England. In spite of the fact that they, too, had conceded the principle of a limited legislature for Ireland, the fact was that in England the Conservatives had lost government to the Liberals, who looked as if they might hang on to it for some time. In a do-or-die classic of political cynicism the Conservatives determined to prevent this at all costs — even, as it turned out, to the verge of treason, some might say to the fact of it. It became a sustained and increasingly bitter campaign.

The Ulster Unionists, evidently, did not realise — nor, one supposes, would they have much cared if they had — that the Conservatives were merely making use of them and of their barbaric bigotry for their own cynical ends. On the other hand the Conservatives do not appear to have realised that what they had taken to bed was no compliant professional, but a raging termagant from another century who would hang in deadly and disgraceful embrace about the neck and honour of England and all decent Englishmen for many decades to come; or that from this strange union would issue a politically manipulated sectarian monstrosity that still exerts a grotesque — and disproportionate — influence on both countries.

Sectarian rioting had occurred sporadically in Belfast since the mid 1800s. Belfast, originally an essentially Protestant town ('in 1787 the Catholics numbered a mere 1,300 in a total population of about 15,000'- Boyd, Andrew, *Holy War in Belfast*, Belfast, p.3.) became the focus of this sectarian 'warfare'. It reached its nineteenth century nadir after the introduction of the first Home Rule Bill, particularly after the intervention of the English Conservative party (especially in the person of the unstable Randolph Churchill) fomenting religious bigotry in the name of Unionism. As Randolph's son, Winston Churchill, wrote:

From that moment the excitement in Belfast did not subside. Eventually dangerous riots, increasing in fury until they almost amounted to warfare, occurred in the streets between the factions of Orange and Green. Firearms were freely used by the police and combatants. Houses were sacked and men and women killed. The disturbances were savage, repeated and prolonged... (Churchill, W., *Life of Lord Randolph Churchill*).

The reasons for the Ulster Dissenter opposition to Home Rule are many and complex. In the popular and obvious conception as elucidated by Lee (op. cit., pp.

6-14), they boil down to three, all very high in emotional voltage with hardly a shred of applied common-sense between them; namely religion, politics and economics. But the core of intense Ulster Dissenter opposition was the threat that Home Rule implied to the hard-won sense of identity they had acquired with Union. Indeed, as events proved, they had no objection to Home, or any other sort of non-British, Rule at all — so long as it guaranteed their own power and dominance, which was precisely what democratically-based Home Rule would not do.

As far as Home Rule was concerned the limited self-government it offered was more appropriate to a local authority (more like the powers of the subsequent Stormont Parliament of Northern Ireland than to any kind of national parliament). Relations with the crown, foreign policy, defence, customs and excise and land control were reserved to the British parliament at Westminster. Lyons says (op. cit., p.186) 'So modest do these proposals appear, that it requires an effort of the imagination to understand the uproar they caused at the time'. The fears of the Ulster unionists 'were brilliantly exploited by Randolph Churchill and his slogan, "Ulster will fight, and Ulster will be right" was no mere catchphrase. Already in that year (1886) symptoms were appearing of what would become a raging fever between 1912 and 1914'.

Fearful sectarian riots took place in Belfast with Catholics — by association identified as Home Rulers — as the targets. Andrew Boyd writes: 'A wave of terror, arson and murder swept through Belfast in the summer of 1886 — the worst sectarian disturbances the town had ever experienced'. Attacks by armed Protestant mobs on Catholic areas became commonplace. Pitched battles occurred and there were many deaths and murders. The Dissenter perception was; since the Union which conferred on them a status and protected their Protestantism was under attack, then so were they. Deeper still went — and still goes — the conviction that they were Protestant (Dissenter) first and Unionist (loyalist) second.

At the same time English public opinion was also subjected to a barrage of anti-Irish and anti-Catholic propaganda. Randolph Churchill, in particular, manipulated English public opinion with the most blatant political sectarianism:

> A great struggle is hanging over the Protestants of Ireland. It is likely before long to be precipitated in an acute form. England cannot leave the Protestants of Ireland in the lurch. England is bound to the Protestants of Ireland; you ... are bound to the Protestants of Ireland by every conceivable tie. [They] on an occasion such as this, and in a national crisis such as this, are the only **Nation** which is known to the English people in Ireland. On four ... occasions they have conquered Ireland ... at the request of England. During 680 years the Protestants of Ireland have held Ireland mainly for the benefit of England ...

(Irrespective of which political interpretation one puts on it, this reflects on his historical perception. The Reformation took place in England some 350 years earlier. In the course of this speech he also incited the Ulster Protestants to civil war to prevent Home Rule, and, about the same time, coined his sonorous and bellicose slogan).

In a speech later that year Parnell replied to these and similar distortions.
There are twelve hundred thousand Protestants of all denominations in Ireland, including those who have no religion at all. I am a Protestant myself. I know them very well. I believe from experience that the truth of the matter about the feeling of the Protestant minority is this, that the great majority of them do not feel strongly about the question, one way or the other. They would rather, I think, of the two, that things were left as they are, but certainly they have no fear of the Catholics of Ireland. There is a small minority of Protestants strongly in favour of Mr. Gladstone's settlement; and there is another small minority of Protestants or Orangemen[33] in the North of Ireland, who are strongly opposed to Mr. Gladstone's settlement. That is how the matter stands. It is the small minority who are strongly opposed to Mr. Gladstone's settlement who have raised the question of the Protestant minority, and they ask you either to reject the Bill altogether or insert provisions in the Bill which give special protection to what they call the Protestant minority[34].

What, in fact, Parnell was identifying was the gap between the Ulster Dissenter/Presbyterian whose self-image was tied to the Union, and the southern Anglican who had been diminished by it. But reason, logic and fact were of no concern to a raging conservative lion, not alone seeking the defeat, but hell-bent on the destruction, of the British Liberal party, and intent on whipping the emotional British public to whatever xenophobic heights it could. 'The Conservatives appealed to feelings which were fundamental in the majority of the English people, to anti-Catholicism and anti-Irishism, and millions of leaflets were let loose in the land picturing Ireland as a country which would be given over to a combination of the Inquisition and Saint Bartholomew were the strong hand of England removed' (O'Hegarty, op.cit., p.571).

Coercion and arrests without trial, strong elements of British rule in the past, became wholesale and commonplace between 1885 and 1900 during the reign of A.J. 'Bloody' Balfour as Chief Secretary. 'Balfour was aiming at the crushing of the Irish spirit, at the destruction of the national organization and the discrediting of Parnell. Force, he thought, could do everything', (Ibid., p.574). The political balance in England could be tipped by a mere 100,000 votes, and the Irish party controlled many of these.

As the flag of Home Rule began to flutter more strongly at the masthead of Irish constitutional nationalism, that of land agitation began to suffer set-backs. Parnell was not as committed to the Land League as were William O'Brien and Michael Davitt. For him it was a means to another political end. With Gladstone's Home Rule Bill — defeated though it was — clearly marking the trail forward, he concentrated on this.

Unfortunately, in 1886 an economic depression more severe than usual struck the country and there were renewed, and very real, fears of famine. Tenants were unable to pay rents and evictions multiplied — giving, for instance, a black cast which has lingered to this day to the name Clanrickarde. John Dillon and William O'Brien were instrumental in organising resistance. They published a 'Plan of Campaign' in *United Ireland* advising tenants to organise to combat rent demands and evictions. It looked as if matters were going to return to the dreadful days of the previous decade. In a new strategy, the British sought support from Rome and, as a measure of their success in doing so, in 1888 Pope Leo X111 issued a 'rescript' condemning both the Plan of Campaign and 'Boycotting' as illegal. To this John Dillon responded characteristically in a speech at Drogheda: '... if tomorrow, in asserting the freedom of Ireland, we were to exchange for servitude in Westminster servitude to ... any body of cardinals in Rome, then I would say good-bye for ever to the struggle for Irish freedom'. It is a fact still evident that it is not, in general, Catholics who in Ireland are a priest-ridden (at least in the political sense) people, but, ironically, the very ones who accuse them of being so — Ulster Protestants.

Now Conservative determination to bring Parnell down — at any price — became obsessive. One Richard Pigott, a rag-tag journalist and blackmailer, was approached in that year (1886) by Edward Houston, secretary of the virulent unionist organisation the Irish Loyal and Patriotic Union, and asked 'if he could find any evidence which would be discreditable to Parnell' (O'Hegarty, p.575). Pigott assured him that he could and, after an all-expenses-paid trip to Paris, resurfaced with forged letters purporting to implicate Parnell in the Phoenix Park murders. *The Times* of London (then, and later, not only the voice of the English Establishment, but a centre of British intelligence, especially disinformation), published a series of articles the next year based on these letters. The same Captain O'Shea who had helped to negotiate Parnell's release from prison had broken with him when it became clear that he would neither succeed Parnell as leader of the Irish Party, nor obtain any high office under him (ironically, this egregious time-server threw in his lot with Austen Chamberlain who had earlier broken with Gladstone and become a dedicated conservative). Now O'Shea rounded on Parnell with venom and swore the letters were true. The allegations were investigated by a parliamentary judicial commission and thrown out when the letters were proved to be forgeries. Pigott fled to Spain and committed suicide. However, while this plot was unsuccessful, Parnell was well and truly laid low in 1890 by a combination of ill-health and a plot that had a more substantial foundation.

Given the climate of the times, and his position, to say that Parnell had been indiscreet in his private life is an understatement. Mrs. Kitty — or Kate, as she preferred — O'Shea was the estranged wife of Captain O'Shea. Parnell met her in 1880 when she had been married to O'Shea for thirteen years. The O'Sheas were already living much of the time in separate establishments and both were dependent on Mrs. O'Shea's wealthy aunt, Mrs. Wood. Parnell and Kitty O'Shea fell in love — certainly he did, with all the commitment and passion of a man who had hitherto lived a lonely and dedicated life. Whether, as has been suggested, Mrs O'Shea was an adventuress bored with or tired of her marriage is difficult to say. But she seemed to give to Parnell much that was missing in his life and enrich in it that which had been barren. By 1882 they were living together intermittently and in 1883 and 1884 she bore him children. In 1886 they decided to live together permanently. There is little doubt that O'Shea knew what the situation was between Parnell and his wife, and connived at it.[35] Having political ambitions his intention was to try to gain by doing so. 'Up to 1885 [he] had been able to cut something of a figure as the principal (and almost wholly unreliable) intermediary between Parnell and Chamberlain. Even as late as February Parnell took an enormous risk in forcing O'Shea as an 'unpledged' candidate on Galway City in the teeth of a virtual mutiny by J.G. Bigger and T.M. Healy, which very nearly blew the lid off the scandal'.

But O'Shea had another and equally unsavoury motive. Kitty O'Shea stood to inherit a considerable fortune from her aunt when she died — provided, of course, that she did nothing to bring disgrace the family name beforehand. O'Shea had his eye on this. (See Lyons, op. cit., p.196).

In 1881 the aunt was eighty-eight. It seemed likely that it would be quite a short while only until her fortune was left to Mrs. O'Shea — and, of course, her husband. But the old lady did not die until 1889, when the fortune was, in fact, left to Mrs. O'Shea — but in such a way that the Captain could not get his hands on it.

Whether O'Shea's antipathy in '86 was fuelled by the relationship between Parnell and his wife is an open question. The financial considerations involved were probably of more importance to him. But when, in what was probably the only accurate political decision of his life, he decided that a divorce action would bring Parnell down, he succeeded beyond any expectation he might have had. The aunt died in May, O'Shea took his action in December the same year. He also joined forces with other aggrieved relatives who proposed to contest the will. Lyons puts it like this: — 'Obviously he had a strong card to play for if, in divorcing his wife, he could demonstrate that Mrs. O'Shea had for years been deceiving the aunt who left her all her money, then the case for overturning the will might be strengthened. Or if not this, then at least the threat of divorce might be used as blackmail to extort a handsome sum in settlement....This Mrs. O'Shea could not do — her inheritance being in jeopardy — and so the case went to court'.

Obviously Parnell does not emerge from this entirely untarnished. He had clearly tried to temporise with O'Shea by offering him political inducements and favours when he was already living with Kate and had fathered two of her children. But O'Shea's conduct is equally clearly that of an unscrupulous blackguard. The outcome of the divorce was political disaster for Parnell.

Gladstone, his own party and much of the Irish establishment — including the Catholic hierarchy (though neither Parnell nor Mrs. O'Shea were Catholic), condemned Parnell. Gladstone, standard-bearer of Home Rule in England, being the man he was, would not countenance further negotiations with a party led by Parnell, saying he would resign unless Parnell did so.

Notwithstanding the splendid services rendered by Mr. Parnell to his country, his continuance at the present moment in the leadership would be productive of consequences disastrous in the highest degree to the cause of Ireland. ...(His) continuance ... would render my retention of the leadership of the Liberal Party, *based as it has been on the prosecution of the Irish cause*, almost a nullity...(John Morley, *Life of Gladstone*, 1908, p.507).

Although the Irish Party initially reaffirmed its support for Parnell, it became clear that the choice was between Parnell and Home Rule. Parnell did not resign, but the Party split, leaving Parnell with a minority. It was announced that Parnell had been removed from office and that Justin McCarthy was the new leader. However McCarthy and his lieutenants, Tim Healy, Thomas Sexton and Michael Davitt, followed later by William O'Brien and John Dillon, had — with the exception of Davitt — reached political maturity in the shadow of Parnell and were not equivalent leadership material. They now, with little sure seating, tried to ride the shaky and spinous back of a moral sow. The important support of the Catholic bishops was summarised thus:— 'Without hesitation, or doubt, and in the plainest possible terms, we give it as our unanimous judgement that whoever else is fit to fill that highly responsible post, Mr. Parnell decidedly is not. As pastors of this Catholic Nation we do not base this our judgement on political grounds, but simply and solely on the facts and circumstances revealed in the London Divorce Court ... (Bishop's Manifesto, cited A.M. Sullivan, *Recollections of Troubled Times in Irish Politics*, p.298).

Irresponsible though this manifesto was, its effect was decisive. As intended it drove support from Parnell, but it also reinforced the curious Unionist — particularly the Ulster Presbyterian Unionist — view of the rest of the country as a priest-ridden community under the domination of idolatrous Rome. In general clerical opposition to Parnell demonstrated the Irish Catholic Church's general view of the time that the 'evolution of Ireland must be within the sphere of English domination and "civilisation"'. When Gladstone asked the Pope to intervene against nationalist activity the result was a letter from the Cardinal Prefect of Propaganda in Rome condemning Parnell and his followers. But it proved counter-productive, merely serving to reinforce the loyalty of Parnell's supporters. Gavan Duffy wrote: 'The Roman policy towards this country has undergone a complete change, and one hostile to its nationality' (Gavan Duffy, *The League of North and South*, 1886, pp 308/9).

Though Parnell and Kate married the political breach in the Irish Party was not healed. Broken in heart, spirit and health, Parnell died in the arms of his wife at Brighton, England, on 6 October, 1891, only two years after the divorce. His achievements were enormous, the greatest for his country of any man since O'Connell. Both secretive and expedient, he was a consummate politician and he hated the English and things English with vehemence. For him to have had the long-term objective of a separate and independent Ireland is entirely consistent with what we know of him and of how he operated. If, as is thought, it was his intention to go further and carry on towards full independence, the fact that there is no absolute proof of this is not sufficient to dismiss the idea.

Home Rule After Parnell
Two things of profound importance to the future of Ireland took shape in the years following 1885. The first of these was the development of the Home Rule idea. The second was the use and development by the British Conservative party of Ulster Protestant loyalism as a political weapon with which to oppose it. The consequences of both developments bedevilled relations between the communities in Ireland and between Ireland and Great Britain for generations. In 1886

the Home Rule Bill was carried in the House of Commons, but the House of Lords rejected by a huge majority (419 votes to 41). The second Home Rule Bill (1893) also fell and Gladstone, old, blind and tired, retired from politics soon after. The third Home Rule Bill was introduced in 1912 by the new Liberal leader, H.H. Asquith and was to prove as contentious and equivocal as its two predecessors. Meantime important social, cultural and semi-political activities, both at home and abroad, helped to prepare the way for a swing from constitutionalism to a more active phase.

It was clear that, in whatever form independence from Britain was to be won, whether by constitutional or revolutionary means, major social and political changes would also occur. That some of them were already underway is impossible to ignore. From the early 19th century — almost as soon as the Union was effected — the nationalist thrust demonstrated that fact. If the actual social changes at independence were less than they might have been a hundred years earlier, it is partly because many of them had occurred in the interim, especially in the last twenty years of the century when the feudal structure in Ireland gave way to a semblance, at least, of a democratic, agricultural colony.

Ironically, the split that occurred, further shattering in the public mind any lingering image of synonimity so far as political and religious liberty were concerned, was to some extent restored with the establishment of the Irish Free State. Lyons says:—

> . . .the Irish presented to the twentieth century world the strange and paradoxical spectacle of a people who, having pursued with immense tenacity and a great measure of success the goal of independence, were content to rear upon the foundations of that independence one of the most conservative states in Europe (op. cit).

This is a picture which is, simultaneously, accurate and misleading[36]. While it was the Sinn Fein republican movement that brought the Irish Free State about, once it was achieved, the old constitutional rump, the scattering of the parliamentary party — conservative, Catholic and constitutionalist by inheritance; now republican *malgre lui* — emerged from the political limbo in which it had languished for four years, to give the support and provide much of the vital state infrastructure a nation-state required.

PART TWO

The moment the very name of Ireland is mentioned, the English seem to bid adieu to common feeling, common prudence and common sense, and to act with the barbarity of tyrants and the fatuity of idiots — Sidney Smith.

Chapter 3

1900 to 1910

THE UNION LAID THE FOUNDATIONS FOR profound social and economic changes which, in turn, brought about the political upheaval that was to dethrone the Union for more than three-quarters of the country. But no such turbulent events as those of the years leading up to and immediately following Union marked, in Ireland, the beginning of the twentieth century. Nevertheless great — if sometimes disparate — forces began, with apparently unrelated momentum, to converge on as yet unperceived revolutions which would bring about even more profound changes. By 1885 both English political parties had come to terms with the fact that some measure of Irish self-government was unavoidable[37].

There are three essential phases in a successful revolution or rebellion. The first is creating the necessary supportive climate of opinion in the masses. This does not need to be overwhelming, but it must have solid intellectual and some popular support. The second is the active phase and, third, is the establishment of the offices and machinery of a new regime — the new *status quo*. By 1900 the first phase (though vague, uncoordinated and in marked contrast to the increasingly relaxed and anglicised life-style of the middle classes), was virtually complete. Phase two was waiting in the wings for its cue as defined by the IRB at its 1867 convention.

Two streams of mutually exclusive strategic thinking dominated Irish political developments in the 19th century. One was that of the governing authorities whose method was to pacify the Irish people through coercion followed by modest concessions in order to control rebellious tendencies and maintain the connection with Britain. The second stream embraced all those movement which might be termed national. At times they overlapped — increasingly so with the emergence of a Catholic middle-class and the Protestant/Unionist liberalism. By the early 1900s there was some ambiguity in a country where Home Rule satisfied many, yet was nowhere near the nationalist *desideratum*. Living standards and incomes, while still considerably below those in the rest of the United Kingdom, had improved; and modest economic, national and cultural progress was taking place.

Between 1900 and 1910 events moved slowly and, on the whole, undramatically. In England government roller-coasted from Conservative to Liberal and was not interested in — indeed, was exasperated with — Ireland except insofar as it gave the Tory (Conservative) Party an Orange stick with which to beat the Liberals. On the constitutional level the Irish Party was not in full fighting trim and on the physical front the IRB seemed to have retreated into a state of inactive hibernation. Onto this scene, in 1900, stepped a new figure and a new force, both of which would have dramatic effects on future events. In 1899 Arthur Griffith, a fluent and persuasive journalist, founded a nationalist weekly paper, *The United Irishman*, and, in the following year, a political/social organisation, Cumann na nGael (later to be called *Sinn Fein*)[38]. Its object was 'To advance the cause of Ireland's National Independence by:–

1. Cultivating a fraternal spirit among Irishmen.
2. Diffusing knowledge of Ireland's resources and supporting Irish industries.
3. The study and teaching of Irish history, literature, language, music and art.
4. The assiduous cultivation and encouragement of Irish National games, pastimes and characteristics.
5. The discountenancing of everything tending towards the Anglicization of Ireland.
6. The physical and intellectual training of the young.
7. The development of an Irish foreign policy.
8. Extending to each other friendly advice and aid, socially and politically.
9. The Nationalising of Public Boards.

Together with industrial development in Ireland, abstention from Westminster was a basic principle of Sinn Fein policy. It will be noted that the objects of the organisation were not in any sense revolutionary, yet Sinn Fein was destined to become the symbol of separatist and nationalist Ireland.

Griffith put forward Sinn Fein as the inclusive compound of all Irish traditions. 'It is,' he wrote, 'the declaration of the Irish Protestant Parliament and Protestant Volunteers of 1782, it is the Declaration of the Irish Catholic Parliament and Catholic Army of 1698, and the meaning and justification of every Nationalist movement in Ireland since 1172..we ask nothing of England except her departure from our house' (Sean O Luing, *Arthur Griffith and Sinn Fein, Leaders and Men of the Easter Rising: Dublin 1916*, ed Martin, p.57).

But, as was so often the case throughout this period, more than one thread ran through the shuttle. While *The United Irishman* and Cumann na nGael may not have been overtly activist, they provided the IRB with, as Hobson put it (op. cit. p. 14) 'an organ in the Press, and the ablest paper at that time in Ireland, to support and propagate its views' ...[and]... 'an open political organisation in which members of the IRB could work without reserve'.

To judge from general contemporary accounts, the Ireland of 1900 was a more or less tranquil and complacent part of the United Kingdom, politically concerned only with the prospect of a benign Home Rule. Such accounts reflect the opinions of 'people who mattered' (for whom, and by whom, they were largely written). And the people who mattered were of two kinds; the so-called 'upper-crust', a tiny and alien minority; and a more substantial and growing middle and professional class, referred to disdainfully by the so-called Ascendancy, many of them descended from Cromwell's troopers, as 'the Prof. classes'. These now included considerable numbers of Catholics — merchants, civil servants, shop-keepers, clerks — mostly outside the 'Castle -Catholic' category. After the Parnell split many of them continued to support the United Irish League, the Irish Party and Home Rule in a not very vigorous way. Sectarianism still marked community, caste, social, status and political boundaries. But that was changing, and not for the better. The sectarian caste system was modifying, it is true, but, especially in the North, it was giving way to politically manoeuvred sectarianism. Most of the industries in the country, again particularly in the north, were owned and controlled by Protestants. So were the large estates and commercial enterprises. The better and more secure jobs therefore tended to be held by, or in the gift of, Protestants, and, also especially in the north, these often tended to be presbyterian, Unionist and rabidly anti-Catholic and Home Rule.

> The Protestant Ascendancy, though it essentially had been a profitable union of landlords and clergymen, had always smiled upon the Northern Orangeman; he was part of it in the sense that he had been spared by it, and he was part of it in the sense that he had learned from it. He utterly despised his Catholic neighbours, they were no countrymen of his: they were a lower order of human being...
> The Orange population of Ulster was thrifty and industrious but not lovable. And it had no love for England. It was quite alone; it owed no allegiance to anyone but itself and the grim God it had fashioned in its own likeness. England was a convenience, England existed to see that no Catholic Irish Parliament ever controlled affairs in Ulster (Dangerfield, op. cit., pp. 76/7)[39].

At professional and merchant level Catholics had made substantial inroads and it was clear that social change was in the offing. Naturally Protestants, whether Church of Ireland or Dissenter, did not view with any pleasure a prospect, however distant, that would further diminish their position of privilege, power and authority. But that is what Home Rule (to say nothing of the unthinkable, separatism), would mean. That it also meant a more equitable distribution of power, privilege and authority does not seem to have occurred to many of them, since any infringement of the burden they so willingly bore would be evil and wrong-headed because (as everyone except Home Rulers and Liberals knew), the Irish were not [yet] fit to govern themselves.

But, as even the administration itself was soon forced to concede, that British colonial viewpoint was not even an arguable case. Education for Catholics had been prohibited up to the 1790s and, thereafter, until the Christian Brothers began to teach in the early 1820s, was confined to illegal 'hedge-schools', classes given by itinerant schoolteachers wherever they could, usually in the open (hence the name), in elementary classics and 'the three Rs' — (reading, (w)riting and (a)rithmetic. Towards the end of the 19th century, and certainly by the beginning of the 20th, universal education for males (and increasing literacy for females) was established. Following recognition of the Catholic church education became for it a matter of prime importance. After Catholic emancipation mass education was quickly allied to the strategic purposes directing the energies of the people. Education meant ideas, and ideas when uncontrolled were dangerous. At first such formal and government-promoted schools as there were were Protestant and proselytism was not simply commonplace, it was policy. By the turn of the century 'almost all the national schools in Ireland were under denominational control, being managed, in the great majority of cases, by clergymen of the various churches'(O'Hegarty, op. cit., p.84). By 1911 the proportion of those who could read but not write was four per cent, 'and the proportion of those who could both read and write had risen from thirty-three (in 1851) to eighty-four per cent. Without this revolution, the foundations of a modern Irish state could not have been laid' (ibid.). Undoubtedly this observation is correct. But, of equal significance is the part played by *The Nation* and other publications and by men such as Davis, Mitchel and Kickham — and, of course, the Christian Brothers — who preached the republican and nationalist tradition and created the vehicle, and in turn the climate of thought, which maintained it.

Towards the end of the 19th century — inspired, perhaps, as much by Gladstone's Home Rule Bill as by '67, the dynamism of Parnell, and the Land League movement; as much by the revelations of people like Kuno Meyer and others about Irish literature and in other cultural and economic fields; a vibrant and high-minded national outlook began to filter through the country. It is easy and enticing to see in this growing enthusiasm the raw power and energy that was to lead to the Rising of 1916 and subsequent events. To do so — as some have — is wrong. The two were expressions of a different kind and with different — though not necessarily opposed — objects. The cultural revival was, in part, a response to similar romantic cultural expression elsewhere and, in part, a search for an elusive national identity. The movement towards a rising was, as yet, not only secret, but — until the rejuvenation of the IRB Supreme Council in 1908 — lacking in vigour. The Gaelic League, under Douglas Hyde, was (with the exception of the distinctive Keating Branch which was, intentionally, taken over by the IRB later on) simply an Irish language and cultural organisation and was part — perhaps the most evident part — of the thrust for a cultural self-image. Except for the Keating Branch, and some individual members, it had nothing to do with the militant nationalist movements, except insofar as there were those who were members of both organisations. That 'Sinn Fein' was a Gaelic League catchphrase probably confused the distinction.

The fact is that Ireland, with perhaps more right than most, was affected no less by the 'rebellious dynamic' that swept European society in the early years of this century than by its own innate propulsion towards freedom. While the Gaelic League and the separatists were aspects of this lively dynamic, they did not necessarily share all its principles. An important distinction must be made between an active revolutionary body, such as the IRB, and other groups with a national outlook, such as the Gaelic League — and even the early Sinn Fein — which were essentially concerned with the self-image of the people, rather than with how that self-image was expressed in political terms.

Nevertheless the overall contribution made by such organisations as the Gaelic League, the Celtic Literary Society, the Gaelic Athletic Association and Sinn Fein to the national movement as a whole was incalculable, even though immediate results may have been visibly meagre. As Murphy (Brian Murphy, *Patrick Pearse and the Lost Republican Ideal*, Dublin, 1991), expresses it (p.24)

> The pro-Boer resolution of the Celtic Literary Society, made in October 1899 with Maud Gonne acting as president, 'that we heartily approve of the action of the Irishmen who have taken up arms to assist the country of their adoption', reflects accurately the militant spirit of the more advanced nationalists.

By definition these societies contained many members with differing political outlooks. A majority would have supported the constitutional Irish Party, others supported radicals like Griffith and McBride, taking a moderately separatist view, while others would, more circumspectly, have been out-and-out republicans and, perhaps members of the IRB, as in the case of the members of the Keating Branch of the Gaelic League. But they were in a minority. And, of course, there was cross-membership of many such organisations. It is, perhaps, ironic that Patrick Pearse was, at this time, a moderate[40]. Had Stephens been then alive he might even have accused Pearse of being a felon-setter. Pearse joined the IRB in July, 1913, five months *before* the Volunteers were founded.

> There can be no doubt...that thoughts of a republic were far from the mind of Pearse, the [Gaelic] League executive and the vast majority of the League members in the early years of the century. Their actions in rejecting the Sinn Fein ideal ... leave no doubt on that score (Murphy, op.cit.,p.25).

The Gaelic League and what became Sinn Fein, amongst other organisations, did share the common object of stimulating in the people a sense of national pride and self-respect. That this would be realised politically with independence was a purpose confined to a limited few in the IRB. But, notwithstanding, 'The burgeoning of this new nationalism, its grafting onto the old republican stock, and the subsequent withering of constitutionalism' (Lyons, op.cit., p.30) became the common purpose in the years between 1916 and 1921. The question of self-image was also an ingredient of the Rising. If the Union had provided the Ulster Presbyterians with the sense of identity they coveted, it diminished even further that of the mass of the Irish people. The quest for rediscovery of this sense of Irishness was, accordingly, a considerable part of the political, social and cultural movements between 1900 and 1917.

This umbrella of Irish 'self-image', covering the Gaelic League and other groups, was more potent than may have been realised. Referring to the Gaelic

League, Casement wrote: 'I got back to Ireland early in 1904 — got to find the Gaelic League at once — and all the old hopes and longings of my boyhood have sprung to life again. What we are now fighting for in Ireland more than anything else, is the continuity of our national character. If we do not preserve that (or restore it rather) we shall cease to be Irish. We must recapture many other things England, or contact with her, has filched from us.' His outlook was crystallised and reinforced by Pearse when he wrote (*The Irish Volunteer*, February, 1914): 'What has happened is that this aged people had renewed its youth ... we are about to attempt impossible things, for we know that it is only impossible things that are worth doing', and by Tom Clarke in a letter to John Devoy, when he simply wrote : 'The change that has come over the young men of the country ... 'Tis good to be alive in Ireland these times.'

This cultural resurgence thrived even in the north and in the face of Orangeism. It was aided by extensive literacy in English, one of its foremost objectives (the supreme irony) being the restoration and preservation of the Irish language. The Gaelic League, the GAA, the Abbey Theatre and other literary and cultural clubs and societies flourished throughout the country and attracted, if with differing objectives, revivalists, separatists and nationalists alike. The most important of them was the Gaelic League. Its popular success, and the fact that, for obvious reasons it attracted political activists, caused some confusion as a result of which the Gaelic League has often, incorrectly, been understood to have been a hot-bed of revolutionary thinking and teaching. By and large the Gaelic League — while stimulating the Irish cultural revival, and encouraging a positive national (as distinct from nationalist) self-image — was, until 1916, run by people who were basically constitutional and Home Rule in outlook.

Additional impetus was given to this flowering in the English language of Irish culture by scholarly interest in Irish mythology and music from such authorities as Meyer[41], Ernest Windisch, Rudolf Thurneysen, Carl Hardebeck, taken up by English and Irish scholars alike. These people helped to unleash a flood of creative interest which found, in this rediscovered heritage, a great wealth of material. A new cultural awareness allied itself to the established political awareness and helped to provide dignity to the people's convalescent self-image. During the abysmal eighteenth century, for the first time in Irish history, the English language supplanted Irish completely in the administration and running of the country. Government, commerce and administration were increasingly conducted through English as part of the policy to eliminate all things Irish.

I wish to show you that in Anglicising ourselves wholesale we have thrown away with a light heart the best claim which we have upon the world's recognition of us as a separate nationality. What did Mazzini say? What did The Spectator and *The Saturday Review* harp on? That we ought to be content as an integral part of the United Kingdom because we have lost the notes of our nationality, our language and customs... What ... the wile of the Saxon (was) unable to perform we have accomplished ourselves (Douglas Hyde, addressing the National Literary Society of Dublin, 1892)[42].

Two events between 1907 and 1910 reactivated respectively the IRB and the Irish Party. The first of these was the return from America, in 1907, of Tom

Clarke. The Keating branch of the Gaelic League, the exception to the rule that the Gaelic League in general supported constitutionalism and Home Rule, was located in Parnell square, Dublin, not far from Tom Clarke's shop. Clarke had come back

> with the declared intention of putting the IRB back on its revolutionary Fenian lines. From his tobacco shop at 75a Great Britain (Parnell) street, he began to fashion the new IRB organisation (Murphy, op.cit., p.38).

The extent of change in attitude between 1904 and 1914 of earnest and dedicated men such as Pearse is an indication of how powerfully the force of principles of freedom affected them. That they were also influenced by the mass movement for civil rights and justice sweeping Europe must be taken into account. But it would be foolish to claim that they were other than a small minority.

The Keating branch attracted a number of individuals with strong republican views, many of whom became leaders of the 1916 Rising and its aftermath. Among them were Tom Clarke himself, Sean MacDermott[43], Richard Mulcahy[44], Thomas MacDonagh[45], Michael Collins, Fionan Lynch, Eamonn Ceannt[46], Cathal Brugha, Con Colbert, Tom Ashe and many others. The branch had founded the Teachers' Training College in Ballingeary, Co. Cork, in 1905, and had a strong Munster connection. In 1909 Cathal Brugha became president and encouraged the separatist outlook. The National Council which Griffith developed from Cumann na nGael, Cumann na nGael itself, and the northern Dungannon Clubs, united to become Sinn Fein and 'influenced an important segment of nationalist, mainly separatist, thought throughout Ireland' (O Luing, ibid.).

An insensible complacency enervated much of the remaining, mainly middle-class, population. The poor, whether urban or rural, were so poor that complacency of any sort was beyond them and their enervation was a purely physical matter[47]. The complacency reached such a point in the first years of the century that the Conservative Prime Minister, Lord Salisbury, could taunt the Irish members of parliament in Westminister that he could 'withdraw from Ireland every able-bodied soldier and hold the country with cripples'(O'Hegarty, op.cit., p.634).

The suggestion has been made (Lyons, op.cit. p. 247) that during the split following Parnell's death young people disheartened by it turned 'again' to the idea of a nationalist independent Ireland '— Young people did not cease to be interested in politics simply because Parnell was no more, or because his lieutenants seemed bent on mutual extermination. They simply turned in a different direction... the time had come to think again of self-reliance'. He refers to the proliferation of 'little clubs and societies' practically all of which 'looked back to the political tradition which owed far more to Wolfe Tone and the Fenians than it did to Isaac Butt and Parnell'. This may be so. It seems likely that such a reversion would have occurred anyway. Even Parnell seems to have been moving in that direction.

It is also likely that the return swing of the national pendulum towards sepa-ratism following a strong, but inconclusive, period of devotion to constitutional procedure, played its part. Moreover challenging intellectual, cultural and social debate and activity are an integral part of any dissenting — and the word is used here in its secular sense — movement, and the 19th century in particular was a period of splendid creative and revolutionary activity throughout Europe. It would have been a very strange thing if the revolutionary energy in Ireland had failed to produce an intellectual and artistic surge which, in the stagnation of the 'split' period, did not interact and cross-fertilise with dormant political energy, especially as the struggle for identity and self-image was of such concern to all of the groups involved. From to-day's standpoint the activities of such political and cultural groups in the period from 1900 to 1914 were — in the otherwise apparently settled times — startling. It is not enough to say that the mass of the people were not involved. The mass of the people are seldom involved in events affecting their future. Nor is it appropriate to dismiss it as the activities of the kind of small pressure groups always capable of exerting a disproportionate influence on any period, let alone one that, as we have seen, was in many respects lethargic to the point of apathy. Nonetheless the sheer intellectual energy generated by the Gaelic League, Sinn Fein, the literary revivalists, the Unionists, Sir Horace Plunkett[48] and his co-operatives during these first years of the 20th century, was astonishing and, a *posteriori*, clearly presaged something of magnitude.

It is as if those involved were endeavouring, each in his own way, to define a concept of Ireland which would express their separate individuality. But was to be separate also to be free and independent? That was the great question that, like some barely submerged colossus, kept thrusting its unavoidable visage into view. Only the Unionists were satisfied with the existing structure, which provided them with an identity of sorts, even if they were dissatisfied with their place in it. Common to most, if not all, of these groups was the desire to identify with an undefined 'sense of Irish nationality'(Lyons, op.cit., p.247).

Since thought precedes action it was inevitable that the IRB would sooner or later tap into the cultural dynamism spreading through the country. Gradually the movement to clarify national identity and self-image became important to more and more people — if in different ways. The proliferation of specifically Irish — Gaelic — clubs and organisations in the balmy, Anglicised atmosphere of the early 1900s was extraordinary by any standard. That it was largely a movement by intellectuals and social and cultural activists is neither here nor there. They were establishing a popular climate of thought. Side-by-side with these more or less non-political activities (though it is important to bear in mind the considerable cross-fertilisation between the Gaelic League, Sinn Fein, the Irish Party, the IRB and later, in much greater numbers, the Volunteers) existed the political dynamism both of the Irish Party, striving for Home Rule, and of the Unionists, bitterly opposed to it.

Towards the end of the 19th century there had also emerged a new, unexpected and now largely forgotten phenomenon. This was the genuine efforts of some — mainly southern unionist — individuals to harness, within the *status quo*, the resources of the country for its betterment and that of the people. The leading light in this activity — it never had the commonalty to be a movement — was Sir

Horace Plunkett. Like most of the others who involved themselves in what was primarily a loose programme for social progress, he was unionist. It is probably correct to assume that the common purpose of these individuals was to copper-fasten the Union by encouraging the support of the people through social progress and development rather than by coercion and repressive measures. That they were moved to take this course as a result of an understanding of, and sympathy for, those suffering most from the lamentable plight of the country is admirable, but almost incidental. But it was after the turn of the century, in the period between 1904 (when the Wyndham Land Act of the previous year had begun to take effect), and the outbreak of the Great European War in 1914, that the stage was set and the props came to hand for the momentous events ahead.

Nationalists had come to view Home Rule as a staging post on the road to something else — constitutional independence, perhaps. Unionists, as Carson put it, saw: '...as Irish ministers saw in 1800, that there can be no permanent resting place between complete union and total separation'. Out of this belief — which is probably correct — emerged the first crude concept of partition. It boiled down to an attitude by the Ulster Unionists which can be summarised as: 'No Home Rule at all; but if there is to be Home Rule, it will not be in Ulster because we will oppose it by force if necessary'. Financial independence was as critical an issue as was political independence. Neither was complete without the other. Yet Gladstone never conceded financial independence for Ireland under his Home Rule proposals. Clearly, therefore, and in spite of all the *furore* they caused, the Home Rule proposals were far less than full constitutional independence and in reality amounted to little more than suggestions for a provisional settlement which would, inevitably, prove inadequate and lead to further demands for full independence.

The reluctance to afford financial independence was based on a well-established British policy, namely that of preventing Ireland, by whatever means, from competing on the open market with British trade and trade goods. Financial independence would have enabled Ireland to revive, develop and protect its own industries, which had been destroyed for that very reason; it would have made it possible to raise tariffs against British goods and, in competition with Britain, to enter into trade agreements with other countries. The Unionist industries, mostly in northern Ireland and developed as part of the British industrial base and which did not compete against other British enterprises, depended on the British market and therefore opposed financial independence even more emphatically than political independence. In a situation of financial independence, that assured marketplace could become less certain.

The new century stimulated new thinking on old ideas and new ideas. In Germany, where the young Polish firebrand Rosa Luxemburg and her colleague Karl Liebknecht were hard at work undermining the established order, socialism was making great strides. Aware of this lively social, cultural and political ethos, Arthur Griffith wrote for his paper *The United Irishman* an article called *A National Organization*. It concerned the need for a nationally co-ordinated effort in the cultural field, and included:

It is not a new organization that is wanted, but a federation of existing ones ... Beyond the adoption of such a programme ... the discountenancing of English ideas, manners and customs — not because they are foreign (there are many things which it would benefit us to learn and assimilate from the foreigners) but because they are English and, therefore, under the political circumstances, a menace to our national individuality — beyond the adoption of such a programme no affiliated body should be in any way bound or tied by the central authority ...'

He also drew, firmly, the distinction between nationalists and Home Rulers: 'Let it be clearly understood that Home Ruler and Nationalist mean wholly opposite and irreconcilable things. The Home Ruler acknowledges the right of England to govern this country, while he demands facilities for purely local Irish matters in Ireland, and for that purpose seeks the erection of a legislative body in Dublin. In return for this concession, he guarantees the loyalty and devotion of the Irish people to England and their readiness to share in the turpitude of the British Empire. The Nationalist, on the other hand, totally rejects the claim of England or any other country to rule over or interfere with the destinies of Ireland...'.

In 1903/4 Griffith wrote a detailed exposition of the illegality of the Act of Union in which he compared Ireland's constitutional position vis-a-vis England with that of Hungary and Austria, concentrating on Austria's illegal suspension, in 1848, of Hungary's Constitution (Hungary continued to assert its constitutional independence until this was, again, recognised by Austria). 'The Act of Union is illegal and unconstitutional', wrote Griffith, continuing that 'an alliance, or co-operation, with men willing to accept a statutory and emasculated legislature as a "settlement of the Irish question" was an abandonment of the principles of Irish Nationalism, and could never be entertained by any Irish Nationalist' (*United Irishman*, July, 1904). This theme was developed in 1905 in a series of articles which, when published as a pamphlet, and at least a year before Sinn Fein was formally inaugurated in 1906, became known as 'The Sinn Fein policy'. By 1907 the movement was nationwide and had a constitution which made clear how far Griffith's ideas had moved since he put forward the objects of Cumann na nGael in 1900 (p. 69 supra). The constitution began, bluntly: 'The object of *Sinn Fein* is the reestablishment of the independence of Ireland'. It continued:

The aim of the *Sinn Fein Policy* is to unite Ireland on this broad platform: (1st), That we are a distinct nation. (2nd) That we will not make any voluntary compact with Great Britain until Great Britain keeps her own compact which she made with the Renunciation Act of 1783, which enacted 'that the right claimed by the people of Ireland to be bound only by laws enacted by His Majesty and the Parliament of that Kingdom is hereby declared to be established and ascertained forever, and shall, at no time hereafter, be questioned or questionable'. (3rd) That we are determined to make use of any powers we have, or may have at any time in the future, to work for our own advancement and for the creation of a prosperous, virile and independent nation.
That the people of Ireland are a free people, and that no law made without their authority or consent is, or ever can be, binding on their conscience.

That the General Council of County Councils presents the nucleus of a National authority, and we urge upon it to extend the scope of their deliberation and action; To take within its purview every question of national interest, and to formulate lines of procedure for the nation.

That National development, through the recognition of the duties and rights of citizenship on the part of the individual, and by the aid and support of all the movements originating from within Ireland, instinct with national tradition, and not looking outside Ireland for the accomplishment of their aims, is vital to Ireland.

Clearly this document fell short of advocating complete separation. But what was proposed was a considerable advance on the emasculated Home Rule proposal, and envisaged a settlement as a subordinate kingdom within the British Empire[49]. Nevertheless it was, at the time, a bold clarion call that, so far as its authors — who anticipated a long and gradual process of development — were concerned, had a dramatic and unexpected result. In spite of some setbacks such as failing to gain a seat at the Leitrim by-election of 1908, by the end of that year *Sinn Fein* had established branches all over the country and looked as if it would be a serious political contender against the Irish Party for the Irish electorate.

Another important event took place in 1910 and enabled the Irish Party to regain — though only temporarily — the parliamentary balance of power. The parliamentary structure of the time differed from the present in a number of ways, one of the most important being the power vested in the House of Lords which could — and when their interests seemed threatened as with the previous Home Rule Bills, sometimes did — veto by majority a parliamentary Bill. Since the Lords was almost entirely Conservative, the passage of controversial Bills could be a lengthy process. As the year 1909 drew to a close the mood of the Liberal Government was optimistic. The Liberal victory of 1906 was not the boon to Irish parliamentary hopes it might have been; the Liberal majority was enough for them not to have to rely on Irish support. Accordingly the previous strong position of the Irish Party, when they had held the balance of power and could play Liberal off against Conservative and *vice versa*, was seriously weakened. Moreover, on Gladstone's death (1898) the Irish question had, so far as the British parliament was concerned, undeniably lost any moral highground with which he might have invested it. Home Rule became, for Britain, no more than a simple matter of expediency and, as a result, was moving steadily towards the back boiler.

Perhaps the Irish Party had for too long been associated in too many ways with the Liberal Party so that, when the latter returned in 1906 with what was a stunning, if twilight, victory, the relationship acquired a more realistic political colour. And perhaps here also may be discerned the beginning of the slide of the Irish Parliamentary Party from being the representative voice of the Irish people. As brokers holding the balance of power, they had wielded a somewhat false authority. With a substantial Liberal majority, that authority and influence evaporated and the inherent weakness of the party began to show. At the same time the energetic Gaelic cultural revival and Sinn Fein established themselves.

With a substantial majority the reins of office seemed to be comfortably in the Liberal grasp without need of favours or concessions. But when the Liberal government introduced a Budget proposal, essentially to finance some badly-needed welfare reforms and which included new taxes on the wealthy, the House of Lords threw out the Budget and, in January 1910, the country went to the polls in small and unenthusiastic numbers. To everyone's surprise (not least that of Mr. Arthur Balfour, leader of the Conservative Party), the Liberal majority was so reduced, and the Conservative minority so increased, that they were very closely represented in Westminster. An astonished and unprepared Irish Party, together with the neophyte Labour Party, found itself once again holding the balance of power.

It was only too clear to Asquith that if the Liberals were to remain in power they could only do so with Irish help. 'The Act of Union between England and Ireland, so disreputable in its origins, so lamentable in its history, had at last revealed its great constitutional weakness. It had bestowed the control of Parliament upon a handful of men to whom England was an enemy...' (Dangerfield, op. cit., p.25).

Making full use of the situation Redmond immediately brought pressure to bear on Asquith to introduce Home Rule. And Asquith, faced with the choice of complying or losing his government, agreed to bring in a Home Rule Bill — which he would afterwards dilute with suspension and the spectre of partition. Once again Home Rule was off the back boiler. From then until the outbreak of the Great European War in 1914 the question of Home Rule became increasingly strident in English council chambers and on English public platforms.

The period between 1910 and 1914 was, in both countries, one of social turbulence and drama and yet, on the middle-class surface, there remained apparent calm and tranquillity. But in the lodges, clubs and party headquarters of the Tory party; in the trade-union meeting halls; in suffragette gatherings and, of course, at the cutting edge, on the streets of Belfast, London and other cities throughout the United Kingdom of Great Britain and Ireland, the violence showed itself. Yet, extraordinarily, the trundling juggernaut of approaching war was something not even all members of the government seemed aware of.

Social revolution was in the air, and was being quietly, but powerfully and vigorously, resisted. The suffragette movement under the Pankhursts militantly swept aside criticism and opposition; the workers — miners, dockers, transport workers and many others — organised themselves and went on prolonged strikes for better conditions; words and phrases like 'grievance' and 'social-justice' brought people in their thousands and tens of thousands onto the streets of cities across England to fight in an industrial struggle, as had the peasant farmers in Ireland thirty years earlier for fairness and fixity of tenure. England was felt to be in decline, seized, as it were, with 'the decadence of a great democracy'(Dangerfield, op.cit, p 367). But the blazers and boaters still stereotyped those who 'affected' not to be affected, and the banjos still played. The republican movement for independent self-determination in Ireland was — even in Ireland — seen by most citizens as simply another expression of minority dissatisfaction. If it touched a deeper chord, the response was muted or cloaked with the pabulum of Home Rule.

But before the period was half over treason against the British crown was being preached throughout the United Kingdom and, before Easter, 1914, was openly undertaken by, of all people, the officer corps of elite cavalry regiments in Ireland supported by many generals, the Tory party and members of the House of Lords. However one looks at it this was a situation unprecedented since the civil war in England three hundred and fifty years earlier. But happen it did, and it happened because of the possibility that the people of Ireland might, after a hundred and fourteen years, have an opportunity — not of independence — but of limited self-government.

No less than Ireland, England seemed to be moving in a direction that could lead only to violent upheaval, both social and political. One wonders what might have been the outcome had the Great War not come along as the greater crisis.

It is often, mistakenly, thought that the question of partition for Ireland (all, or part, of the province of Ulster to be excluded from any Home Rule provision granted to the country); was introduced, slyly, by the British during the Treaty negotiations in 1921 to force a conclusion favourable to themselves. But partition had been a very live issue off and on from the moment Gladstone's first Home Rule Bill was introduced in 1886. It flared and receded, from time to time, but never became dormant. It is, therefore, a gross mistake to think that the idea of partition sprang suddenly and fully fledged into existence with the Treaty, or, indeed, with the 1920 Government of Ireland Act. The latter merely provided a vehicle on which it might legally travel.

Having selected Unionism as their platform, the Conservatives floated the partition fire-ship to sink the Home Rule brig. As a direct result the elusive idea of partition, in a sinister way, began to dominate the superior issue of Home Rule. When the third Home Rule Bill was introduced in 1912, even the Liberals took the view that some form of 'optional partition' — by which was meant giving counties a choice in the matter — was the only alternative to, at best, severe rioting and, at worst, civil war. Accordingly, in the inimitably earnest way the British have in such 'colonial' matters, they took what they convinced themselves were well-intentioned, but idiotic, steps which ensured only that the outcome in Ireland would be as unsatisfactorily bad all round as it could be. With Gladstone dead there was no one left in government with the vision, power and integrity to pursue a form of Home Rule for Ireland that would benefit and honour both countries. Instead Asquith's Liberal government decided to exclude **some** Ulster counties from Home Rule, thus ensuring a legacy of division, injustice and outrage.

When the Home Rule Bill passed its second reading in 1912, and so, under new legislation, had only two years before becoming law, the Ulster Unionists intensified their campaign of subversion and treason. In that year Casement wrote from the Canaries the following, which, allowing for the present constitutionally different context, might as easily have been written to-day:

If the British people clearly and finally asserted their intention of re-establishing an Irish Parliament then Belfast and 'Ulster' will, after splutters and protests, be forced into passive acceptance (See Mackey, Herbert O., *The Life and Times of Roger Casement*, p. 31).

The initial government reaction was to outface them with military confrontation. But that constitutionally correct decision was treasonably thwarted.

By 1911 two things were clear; firstly, there was no constitutional way to now prevent the Home Rule Bill passing, and, secondly, the intense emotions that had accumulated on the issue were almost out of hand. As Lyons expresses it: 'the real pressure would come from outside parliament and [that] the crisis would take the form, not of reasoned argument in the constitutional mode, but of a gigantic war of nerves carried on in an atmosphere of mounting hysteria and bitterness'. Given the fears and commitments of the Unionists such was all but inevitable. But when, due to the deliberate tactical choice of the leaders of the British Tories, the entire Unionist cause became identified with — and, for a considerable time subsumed by — the cause of the Dissenting Protestant Unionists of Ulster, it underwent a subtle and sinister change. Now the Ulster Unionist Protestant tail began to wag the Tory dog in a manner which, while in the short term it provided a political victory (the destruction of the Liberal party), in the longer term was to become the cause of international embarrassment for successive British governments.

The Liberal Government itself felt threatened, both if Home Rule were introduced and if it were not. For them it was no longer simply a matter, as Gladstone saw it, of political morality, right or wrong. Political expediency was now the critical factor, and, the emotional climate having escalated alarmingly, expediency was no longer just a matter of politics; the threat of war within the United Kingdom and in Europe existed independently. Certainly the Protestants in Ireland were a small enough minority, in total perhaps twenty per cent. of the population. But not all Protestants were Unionists, and a surprisingly large number of them were nationalists, even separatists. But the point was that those who were Unionist controlled enormous power both in Ireland and in England; they commanded the support of a majority of the British Conservative party and, not least, they shared with the vast majority of the British people, the north-European Protestant ethic. The anti-Catholic bias of north-European countries was, in Britain, tied to an anti-Irish one that was almost endemic.

The old question was raised; are these people [the Irish] fit to govern themselves? And, even if they are, the question of their being fit to govern a strong, industrious, Protestant minority was quite another matter. On the other hand, in the event of war with Germany, a fractious and rebellious Ireland was a threat. Appeasement was clearly called for, but it needed to be appeasement with two hands. How to achieve it? In spite of his statement in 1912 (in Dublin, shortly before the introduction of the Home Rule Bill) that 'Ireland is ... not two nations, but one nation' (See; R.Jenkins, *Asquith*, London, 1964, p.279), Asquith informed John Redmond that the government would feel free to make concessions to Ulster if it became necessary to do so. The partition embryo was growing healthily. A few months later it was proposed in parliament that Antrim, Armagh, Derry and Down be excluded from Home Rule. Carson, though committed to securing the whole of Ulster, voted for this proposal as a step forward and on the grounds that: 'If Ulster succeeds, Home Rule is dead'. It might be noted that Griffith, whose view it was that Ireland must have control of its own finances, rejected the Home Rule Bill on the grounds that it did not provide financial independence, which he saw as the key to national independence.

In spite of the destructive split in the Irish Party that had followed his disgrace, some of those who supported Parnell were, by 1900, raising their own voices in a somewhat different refrain, notably John Redmond, leader of the Parnellite rump, and William O'Brien. Redmond had united the splintered parliamentary party, becoming an increasingly controversial figure who remained leader until his death in 1918. In the intervening years he established his position as national constitu-tional leader, rebuilt the party and saw it wilt mortally. Within two years of his death the party — but not its great influence, which was to revive, phoenix-like, during the Treaty split — was no more. Dangerfield (op. cit. p.174) expresses an unflattering view of Redmond, but one which seems to carry a ring of truth when he says that Redmond was never touched by the 'cold flame' that burned in Parnell. He says that Redmond was fond of Parliament, its rituals, devices, subter-fuges, and intrigues, which meant more to him than they should have to an Irish leader. He cites what was often said of Redmond, that he had been so long in Westminster that he had forgotten what Ireland was like.

During the fretful year of 1910, with the king's prerogative anxiously sought by the government to assent to the restriction of the Lords' veto, Home Rule hovered in the background like Banquo's ghost. At the end of the year yet another election resulted in a tie, 272 seats each for Liberals and Conservatives. Now the Liberals were dependent more than ever on the support of the Irish Party to retain power. Home Rule climbed higher on the political agenda.

But who, except the Irish, really gave a damn about Home Rule? It was a 'thing' that did not, to any significant extent, affect the Empire or the public purse of England. It would happen and that would be an end to it. No doubts remained about that. How it would happen and what form it would take were all that needed to be agreed. The Liberal government's confrontation with the House of Lords, during which Asquith threatened to create sufficient peers to outvote the Conservative lords, brought an acceptance of The Parliament Bill (a restriction of the Lord's veto) of 1911. 'The Irish Party as good as held Mr. Asquith's I.O.U. A Home Rule Bill was to be one of the first pieces of legislation which, passing through the Commons on three consecutive sessions, would become law, however the Lords voted' (Dangerfield, op.cit., p.37).

The Third Home Rule Bill was introduced in 1912. It was much the same as the previous Bills — with one important difference; it had a very good chance of becoming law.

... built on the old Gladstonian formula of transferring purely Irish matters to the Irish Parliament, while it reserved for the Imperial Parliament at Westminster all questions touching the Crown, the making of peace or war, treaties and foreign relations, new customs duties and certain other services... If ever a nation was huddled into perpetual swaddling clothes by a piece of legislation, Ireland was so huddled by Mr. Asquith's Home Rule Bill... (Ibid.,p.100).

But an amendment that was to raise a new spectre was moved by Sir Edward Carson[50], the Dublin lawyer (who, with Randolph Churchill, had taken up Unionism as the means of defeating the Liberals). Carson's proposed amendment was to exclude the whole of Ulster from the Home Rule Bill, but he was defeated at that time. The Bill gave to Ireland its own parliament, with limited autonomy. Griffith made the point convincingly that 'not altruism but the menace of Germany compelled the offer of Home Rule. Ireland placated was a sword brandished against Germany'. In a letter written by Winston Churchill to Redmond in 1913, he made the revealing statement: 'I do not believe that there is any real feeling against Home Rule in the Tory Party apart from the Ulster question, but they hate the Government, are bitterly desirous of turning it out, *and see in the resistance of Ulster an extra-Parliamentary force which they will not hesitate to use to the full*'.

> Everything they [the Conservatives] did in the next two years (from 1912 on) was aimed, not against Home Rule, but against the very existence of Parliament ... their conscious aim was to destroy Liberalism ... An utterly constitutional party, they set out to wreck the Constitution; and they very nearly succeeded (Dangerfield, op. cit., p.96).

The Irish Party accepted this Bill, further diluted to the point of being meaningless before it went, virtually automatically, on the statute book two years later, as a great and victorious settlement of 'the Irish question'. That it represented an achievement in the long constitutional struggle for Home Rule there is no denying. But it was a long way from the independent Irish Parliament that had been bribed and coerced into voting itself, illegally, out of existence in 1800; a longer way from colonial self-government, and nowhere at all close to independence. Yet it would probably have met the expectations of most of the people. Nonetheless the House of Lords rejected the Bill, which was accordingly delayed a further two years. By then, when war had broken out, both the Ulster and Irish Volunteers had been formed, the Bachelor's Walk shootings and the 'Curragh Mutiny' by the British officer corps in the Curragh had taken place, it was too little and too late.

> Ireland remained the only question on which the Conservatives could hope to turn the Liberals out [of government in England], and therefore they opposed the Home Rule Bill with their full force, and let loose on England the bigotry and pre-judice which had on previous occasions been so effective. And not in England alone, they loosed it in Ireland too... For centuries the Unionists on both sides of the Irish Sea had been preaching to the Irish people that it was their duty to accept the decrees of that [United Kingdom] parliament, but now that that parliament, in the name of the people and with the assent of the people, threatened their class and property privileges, it was another matter. They threw overboard both the parliament and the people. Mr. Bonar Law, speaking for the English Unionists, of whom he was the leader, and Sir Edward Carson, speaking for the Irish Unionists, of whom he was the leader, threatened physical resistance to the Home Rule Act, if and when it passed into law, as it would, by the automatic operation of the Parliament Act, in the spring of 1914'(O'Hegarty, op. cit. pp. 658/660).

Unionist Resistance

Andrew Bonar Law, the Tory leader, was one of the greatest demagogues of Ulster Unionism. This Canadian-born Ulster Orangeman made his political career in England and successfully managed to hold the British Government to ransom on behalf of the northern Unionists on a number of occasions. During the critical years of 1911/1912 he made it clear that if Home Rule were introduced in Ireland — thus 'depriving' as he expressed it, Ulster Protestants of their 'birthright' — 'they would be justified in resisting such an attempt by all the means in their power, including force ... I can imagine no length of resistance to which Ulster can go in which I should not be prepared to support them, and in which, in my belief, they would not be supported by the overwhelming majority of the British people' (R. Blake, *The Unknown Prime Minister*, London, 1955, p.130).

The reckless and despotic attitude of the Unionists and the lords is clear. On 20 July, 1911, Lord Londonderry in the House of Lords trumpeted the essence of the anarchy that had been accumulating in his circle since the previous year. 'I warn your lordships', he said, 'that if a Home Rule parliament is established there will be lawlessness, serious disorder and bloodshed'. He went on to say that if blood was shed it would be the fault of His Majesty's Government. Those were strong words to use, he conceded, but he wanted to warn the Government what would occur. They would ... bring about civil war. They [the Unionists] declared 'that if the worst came to the worst they would fight'. Seven months later, in February 1912, his fellow peer, Lord Robert Cecil, developed the bloody theme: 'If Home Rule is persisted in it will lead to civil war. If I lived in Belfast I would seriously consider whether rebellion were not better than Home Rule'.

The 'Orange card' so cynically played fifteen years earlier by Randolph Churchill and his colleagues to unseat the Liberals was on its way home to roost with a vengeance. The Ulster termagant the Conservatives had bedded turned out to be a slavering war-goddess. Perhaps it was because they were English that these Tory manipulators mis-read their 'Orange card' and failed to realise the forces they let loose. More likely, being politicians, the short-term gain was all they considered. Yet Carson was different. Carson was not opposed to Home Rule for political reasons only. He was opposed to it because he was a fanatic. He was Irish, a Dubliner, and as much a product of the tensions and stresses of 19th century Ireland as were Parnell, Griffith or Redmond. He had seen the rise of a people crawling from their mud cabins to their knees; from their knees to stand up and see the world for what it was and from there to begin to take their proper place in it, and he knew that, once those places became firm, the unjust privileges of his kind were not just threatened, but doomed. If that cold man feared anything, it was the break-up of the Union. And Home Rule, in whatever limited form, would be the first blow.

Events, many of them seemingly disparate, but all in one way or another connected to the comprehensive surge of movement impelling the people and their leaders towards a new Rubicon, came into closer focus in 1913.

The year 1913 was an eventful one in Irish politics. Twenty years of political agitation conducted upon the most constitutional lines conceivable, had followed upon the more virile Parnell period, and after huge labour had produced an emaciated measure of Home Rule supported in a half-hearted and insincere manner by the Liberal Party and Government in England. This measure passed the English House of Commons in January, 1913, and was thrown out by the House of Lords a few weeks later. Under the leisurely operations of the Parliament Act it might hope to outlive the power of the House of Lords to prevent its passage, if the Liberal Government lasted long enough, and if it could be made to fulfil its oft-repeated promises to the Irish people.

Such was the state of affairs when a new factor, introduced into Irish politics by Sir Edward Carson, began to have important results both in Ireland and in England, The opposition of a section of the people of Ulster to Irish self-government was nothing new, but the organisation of that section into a military force, armed, trained and officered, claiming to dictate to both Ireland and the English Government, and declaring its readiness to enforce its dictation by military measures, was a departure that has already had momentous results, and which may have yet more momentous results in the future. (Hobson, *A short History of the Irish Volunteers, 1918, from The Irish Volunteers 1913-1915*, ed. F.X.Martin, p.3).

Why, one might well ask, and how, did a Dubliner, Edward Carson, become leader of the Ulster Orangemen? Nearly fifty years ago George Dangerfield provided a reasonable answer in his book when he said that Carson was a fanatic, particularly on the question of the union. Carson, he said, believed in union between England and Ireland, not just as a constitutional system, 'but as a religious man might believe in the marriage between his parents which, if annulled, would turn him into a bastard'. Carson, he said, hated Home Rule, so blindly 'that he had not bothered to inquire into its nature'.

Dangerfield went on to point out that it was one of the contradictions of Carson's nature that 'he could turn his principles against themselves, and attempt to overthrow the Constitution in the name of the Constitution, and discredit the Crown in the Crown's honour...' In September, 1911, when Home Rule was certain to become law, 'Sir Edward felt that his place was in Ulster. On 23 September, therefore ... he [told] a vast audience of inquisitive Ulstermen . . . We must be prepared ... and time is precious in these things — the morning Home Rule is passed, ourselves to become responsible for the government of the Protestant Province of Ulster' (See Dangerfield op.cit., pp. 82-85).

In July/August 1912 Carson and his fellow leaders of the Conservative Party decided it was necessary to bind the Orangemen to them more firmly. They came up with the idea of a 'Solemn League and Covenant'. The 28 September was nominated 'Ulster Day', the day on which this covenant would be pledged. It was drafted initially by Captain James Craig, and Mr. B.W.D. Montgomery, secretary of the Belfast Unionist Club. Between them they decided that the perfect model was the old Scots Covenant which

breathed a harsh, militant Protestancy very congenial to the modern Orangeman. Some modifications were necessary, of course, and then it was adopted by the Protestant Churches. The Presbyterian Moderator insisted on an amendment which would not bind the signatory forever as did the original, and the phrase 'throughout this our time of threatened calamity' was substituted. (Dangerfield, op. cit., p.108).

This Ulster Covenant, known as 'the sacramentum', was sworn and signed by 471,444 men and women, some in their own blood[51] on 28 September, 1912. And, as we shall see, the military, too, were prepared for treason.

With no apparent indication that they were aware of any contradiction the Ulster unionists pledged themselves to opposing the government and to 'defeat the present conspiracy to set up a Home Rule parliament in Ireland. And in the event of such a parliament being forced upon us we further solemnly and mutually pledge ourselves to refuse to recognise its authority'. In support of this pledge and, as Lyons (p.305) puts it, 'what gave this tribal ritual its real menace was the fact, insufficiently appreciated either by the government or the nationalists, that the Ulstermen were beginning to drill and to organise in support of their threats.'

The Unionists also needed to consolidate their position in case of the need for powerful unilateral action, should that become necessary. The first steps towards forming a provisional government had been taken: A conference of Unionist clubs and Orange lodges in Belfast on 25 September, 1911, had passed a resolution stating: — 'We have again and again expressed our intention not to submit to Home Rule; the time has now come when we consider it our imperative duty to make arrangements for a Provisional Government for Ulster... to take immediate steps in consultation with Sir Edward Carson to frame and submit a constitution for a Provisional Government for Ulster ... to come into operation on the day of the passage of any Home Rule Bill ...'.

Almost exactly a year later, in Coleraine, following twelve months of extreme rabble-rousing, Carson said: 'In the event of this proposed parliament (Home Rule) being thrust upon us, we solemnly and mutually pledge ourselves not to recognise its authority ... *I do not care twopence whether it is treason or not*' (21 September 1912). And almost exactly a further turbulent twelve months on the Ulster Provisional Government was established when, on 24 September 1913, in Belfast, the Unionist Council decreed itself the central authority of the provisional government and its standing committee the executive committee of the provisional government. Carson was appointed head of the central authority, or president of the provisional government (See Horgan, J.J., *The Complete Grammar of Anarchy*, London, 1918, p. 27).

In November of that year the influential *Irish Churchman* coyly reassured many of its readers as follows:

It may not be known to the rank and file of Unionists that we have the offer of aid from a powerful continental monarch who, if Home Rule is forced on the Protestants of Ireland, is prepared to send an army sufficient to release England of any further trouble in Ireland by attaching it to his dominion, believing, as he does, that if our king breaks his coronation oath by signing the Home Rule Bill he will, by so doing, have forfeited any claim to rule Ireland. And should our king sign the Home Rule Bill, the Protestants of Ireland will welcome this continental deliverer as their forefathers, under similar circumstances, did once before.'

Major Crawford, who later became notorious for the gun-running at Larne, had already signalled the above message when he said at Bangor in April, 1912, 'If we are put out of the Union ... I would infinitely prefer to change my allegiance right over to the Emperor of Germany'.

Fear and bigotry had taken hold of the Unionist masses in the north of Ireland who were being manipulated by the Tory leadership. It was, at first, made easy, for their audience was only too willing to listen to the Tory's message, believing already that no statement could, when it came to Catholics and Home Rulers, be as outrageous as the truth they knew 'in their hearts'.

There is no bigotry anywhere quite so bad as the narrow Protestant bigot, who has been reared upon Protestant fables and has never found them out. Bonar Law was a combination of two things of extreme narrowness, he was a Canadian and an Orangeman, wrote O'Hegarty (op. cit., p. 660.).

The change of allegiance suggested by Major Crawford very nearly came about, as we will see. A manifesto was issued which contained the following: 'If the Home Rule Bill is passed, we shall consider ourselves absolutely justified in asking and rendering every assistance at the first opportunity to the greatest Protestant nation on earth, Germany, to come over and help us'.

To give strength and substance to what up to that time had been essential groundwork, an Ulster Volunteer Force[52] was formed from Unionist and Orange clubs. In order to oppose Home Rule on the ground it began to organize along military lines. The coordinator of the UVF was Gen. Lord Frederick Roberts (a former British commander who had achieved distinction against African tribesmen, and Boers). He nominated Lieut. Gen. Sir George Richardson, another retired British warrior, to be its commanding officer. Other than the British army, the UVF was the first organised military force to be raised in Ireland since 1867 and it was, of course, raised in defiance of the law[53]. In August Carson went to Germany where he lunched with Kaiser Wilhelm. The results of this meeting were not long in following.

The UVF acquired a substantial number of weapons and ammunition from Germany. The Tory MP, Col. T.E. Hickman, was already involved in gunrunning: You may be quite certain that those men are not going to fight with dummy muskets. They are going to use modern rifles and ammunition, and they are being taught to shoot. I know, because I buy the rifles myself... (at Wolverhampton, 24 November 1913, when the UVF was formed).

Proclamations had been issued forbidding the importation of arms into Ireland and prohibiting assembly as well as the possession of arms. But the authorities ignored such breaches by the Ulster Volunteer Force and, even if they had not, Sir Edward Carson and others put matters into perspective for them; for instance with the following, at Blenheim, in July, 1913:

We will shortly challenge the government to interfere with us if they dare, and we will with equanimity await the result. We will do this regardless of all consequences, of all personal loss, of all inconvenience. They may tell us if they like that this is treason. It is not for men who have such stakes as we have at issue to trouble about the cost. We are prepared to take the consequences, and in the struggle we will not be alone, because we will have all the best in England-with us.

Or this from Lord Alington the following September:–

If there is any blood spilled in Ireland through the government trying to force Home Rule upon Ulster, the people of this country will be so enraged that they will require some blood of the members of the Cabinet to make up for the loss of the blood in Ireland. If an Irishman is killed he could hardly be spared. But if it was a couple of Cabinet Ministers we should say, 'Good riddance'.[54]

Also in 1913, acting evidently on the principle 'if treason prosper none dare call it treason', Carson, Bonar Law and F.E. Smith[55] established a framework for setting up a provisional government of Ulster if the Home Rule Bill became law. These practical steps, as we have noted, were followed by the establishment of the Provisional Government of Ulster that year with Carson as its president.

. . . through the foul womb of night
The hum of either army stilly sounds — Shakespeare, Henry V.

Chapter 4

The Arms Race
1913 — to The First World War

THE UNIONISTS WERE CLEARLY READY FOR civil war[56]. Funded with donations from a Conservative-promoted 'Defence Fund', a large quantity of arms and ammunition were landed a Larne, Co. Antrim[57] in April, 1914, for the Ulster Volunteers. The password used by the UVF on the night of the landing was 'Gough', the significance of which becomes evident in this chapter.

The founding of the Ulster Volunteers prompted the formation of a similar nationalist volunteer movement in Dublin, known as the Irish Volunteers. It quickly became nationwide, though for want of funds it functioned on a less well-equipped military scale. Initially it was ignored or derided by the nationalist constitutional establishment, particularly the Irish Party.

'The effect of the arming of Ulster on the rest of Ireland was not immediate, but as Carson's movement gathered momentum a growing alarm spread through the country. Instead of realising that a new portent had appeared in the Irish skies the Parliamentary Party emitted a few gibes about wooden guns and buried their heads still deeper in the sands of English politics' — (Bulmer Hobson[58]; Foundation and Growth of the Irish Volunteers, *The Irish Volunteers 1913-1915*, Ed. Martin, p.17).

This threatening situation was aggravated by other events, some domestic, some not: — the suffragette movement with its associated and distressing violence; the Dublin general strike of 1913, a culmination of two years of industrial unrest in the United Kingdom which totalled 1,497 strikes in 1913 alone; the Volunteer movements, including the gun-running at Larne and the killings at Bachelor's Walk; the treasonable activities of senior officers of the British Army, culminating in the so-called Curragh Mutiny the following year; all these events helped to create, to the external eye, the picture of a United Kingdom very disunited indeed[59].

From 1912 onwards the pressure for partition, from both outside and within parliament, increased, to the point where it looked like a choice between either some such mutilation, or civil war. Throughout 1912 and 1913 clamour for this grim choice became more insistent, with accompanying intrigue and rivalry. In January, in an attempt to reconcile the Conservatives to Home Rule, Asquith secretly offered to Bonar Law the temporary exclusion of such counties of Ulster as preferred it for a period of six years. Asquith 'selected a six-year period because this should permit at least two general elections in the interval' (Lee. p. 13 citing D. Gwynn, *The Life of John Redmond*, London, 1932, p.208; see also Stephen Gwynns, *John Redmond's Last Years*, 1919). Bonar Law refused this offer.

Asquith eventually conceded that the government would reserve its right to make concessions to the Ulster Unionists, and introduced the 'exclusion' option in the form of an Amendment to the Home Rule Bill. This provided for six of the Ulster counties to opt out of Home Rule for a period of six years on a county by county basis, after which they would become subject to an all-Ireland parliament. This typically British compromise was intended to i/ offset the threat of civil war in Ireland, ii/ counter Carson's total opposition to any breach of the Union and iii/ satisfy, to some extent, both constitutional Nationalists and the Unionists. None of these objects were achieved. Casement wrote: 'The game now, I see, is this. Under cover of "an offer to Ulster" they are going to strip all the flesh off the Home Rule Bill — if we let them ... I am convinced the right and patriotic thing for all Irishmen to do is to go on with the Volunteers; volunteers in every county, city, town, and voilage in Ireland. Don't despair of arms. I think we can get them ... the English are going to surrender to Carson...'(letter to a friend, cited Mackey, op. cit. p. 43)

The so-called Curragh Mutiny in March 1914 by elements of the British Army remains one of the most extraordinary events of the entire period. In effect the Conservative Opposition, the highest levels in the British Army and the House of Lords became involved in a conspiracy against the government that was an archetype of self-seeking treason. 'The elderly lawyers who for the most part governed England had great veneration for blue blood, and they were considerably startled at the prospect of an insurrection of peers, led by field-marshals and admirals, all pledged to sacrifice their lives in the cause of Ulster' (Hobson, op. cit.).

A considerable number of officers in the British Army came from Anglo-Irish Unionist families who, because of their position, politics and religious affiliations, exercised an influence out of all proportion to their numbers. Rumours of dis-affection over Ulster and Home Rule in the officer corps of the British Army in Ireland were common throughout 1913. By the following year it had spread to England — perhaps not so surprisingly when it is understood that one of the main conspirators was the Director of Military Operations, [the then] Major-General Henry Wilson, a bigoted Ulster Unionist of deep conviction, and an accomplished intriguer. It should also be borne in mind that the officer corps of the British Army, in particular of the elite regiments like the Lancers, were almost without excep-tion of the landed or upper middle-classes with, virtually to a man, deep Tory backgrounds.

'The British League for the Support of Ulster' was organised 'for the purpose of organising those of our fellow countrymen who will reinforce the Ulstermen in their armed resistance to the *tyranny of the Government...*' (author's italics).

Men were openly recruited in England, Scotland, and the English colonies for the purpose of levying war on the Nationalists of Ireland. . . Field Marshal Lord Wolseley stated that to use the army against the threatened Ulster insurrection 'would be the ruin of the British army' (Hobson, op. cit. p.9).
Lyons draws attention to another important aspect of Conservative tactics.

> The Unionist leaders were at this time seriously considering whether they might not cause the House of Lords to refuse to pass the annual Army Act, without which no government could exist, since in the absence of an Army Act the army itself could not be paid or even kept in being as a regular force.

He comments, correctly, that it was 'a staggering indication of how far the Irish crisis corroded all the ordinary decencies and conventions' of constitutional government, that the Conservative party threatened this with such profound inter-national tension existing in Europe (See Lyons, op. cit. p.308).

However, a group of Army officers stationed at the Curragh acted first, pre-empting the necessity. An estimated 60 officers stationed there resigned rather than, as they expressed it, be 'forced' to 'coerce' Ulster. In this they were led and encouraged by some of their superiors, including Brigadier Sir Hubert Gough, another Ulster Unionist, who conspired with Wilson in London to use the situation to their advantage.

The crisis arose when, alarmed by such declarations as 'civil war was the path of danger, but it was also the path of duty; and I am convinced that no other alternative is left to the loyalists of Ulster' (Sir James Campbell, MP[60] at Swansea, March 1914); and by the sabre-rattling of Carson and Bonar Law, perilously reinforced by the rampant Unionist gun-running in Ulster, the govern-ment sent orders to General Sir Arthur Paget, GOC British forces in Ireland, to move troops to Armagh, Omagh, Enniskillen and Carrickfergus — the four strategic bases for military containment of Ulster[61].

Clearly the threat was perceived in London as coming from the UVF and its belligerent political supporters such as Bonar Law and Carson. Nowhere outside Ulster is mentioned. Clearly, also, these 'orders' are so vague as to be — dis-ingenuously — capable of more than one interpretation. By now the officer corps of the British Army had, in England as well as in Ireland, become seriously dis-affected with the Government's Irish policy[62]. Deliberately or otherwise, Paget affected to misunderstand his orders. Overlooking, or ignoring, the possibility that his government may well have wished to bring about a confrontation with the Unionists on the issue of Home Rule, instead of moving troops, he moved stores. He then weakened his credibility by sending a signal to London saying that any other manoeuvre would 'create intense excitement in Ulster and possibly precipitate a crisis' and compounded this by following his signal to London himself. The orders were then repeated to General L.B.Friend, Paget's deputy. He, too, prevaricated. He replied that he 'greatly feared' the Great Northern Railway would refuse to transport his troops northward! Clearly the Army 'top brass' was not well disposed to taking part in what Ulster Loyalists called 'a horrible plot to subdue them by force of arms'.

The real plot had been hatching since 1911. In October, 1912, for instance, in Glasgow — another hot-bed of Orangeism — Carson said: 'The Attorney General says that my doctrines and the course I am taking lead to anarchy. *Does he not think I know that?* Does he think that after coming to my time of life and passing through the various offices and responsibilities I have accepted, I did this like a baby, without knowing the consequences?' In his moving and dignified speech from the dock in 1916, Casement condemned those who had allowed such an attitude to develop: 'While one English party was responsible for preaching a doctrine of hatred designed to bring about civil war in Ireland, the other, and that the party in power, took no active steps to restrain a propaganda that found its advocates in the army, navy and privy council — in the Houses of Parliament and in the State Church — a propaganda the methods of whose expression were so "grossly illegal and utterly unconstitutional" that even the Lord Chancellor of England could only give words and no repressive action to apply to them.'(Casement's speech from the dock, July 1916).

The army had been specifically targetted for over a year in a sustained campaign of subversion, of which the following is but one example:

> It must be evident to everyone in Ireland, as it has become evident to everyone in England, that the present Bill [the Home Rule Bill] was not going to be forced through under the Parliament Act without bringing about the risk, which I think amounts to a certainty, of civil war... Perhaps no one could strike a more tremendous blow against the very foundations of society than to compel the military forces of the Crown into such a position that there was grave doubt as to whether the officers and men would obey the orders given to them in the event of civil war taking place, (Alfred Lyttleton, M.P., Cork, May, 1913).

Carson's statement the following September that 'They had pledges and promises from some of the greatest generals in the army that ...they would come over to help us', was part of the the same campaign. Now came the full fruiting. Accordingly the responses of Paget and Friend to their orders to make protective troop dispositions in Ulster, while astonishing, were the result of an orchestrated campaign that had gone on for over two years.

When he learned of the prevarication of the generals in Ireland, Churchill, then First Sea Lord, who invariably responded with gallons of adrenalin at the first whiff of grapeshot, said:

> If Ulstermen extend the hand of friendship it will be clasped by Liberals and by their Nationalist countrymen in all good faith and in all good will; but if there is no wish for peace; if every concession that is made is spurned and exploited; if every effort to meet their views is only to be used as a means of breaking down Home Rule and of barring the way to the rest of Ireland... if all the loose and, wanton and reckless chatter we have been forced to listen to these many months is in the end to disclose a sinister and revolutionary purpose; then I can only say to you 'Let us go forward together and put these grave matters to the proof'.

He then ordered two cruisers to Dublin Bay, two destroyers to Belfast Lough, and a flotilla to the west coast of Scotland.

Meantime Generals Paget and Friend had neither received clear orders to act, nor been dismissed for refusing to carry out their vague original ones. Instead Paget sat in the War Office with the Secretary for War — an ex-colleague, one Colonel Seely — with whom he reached the extraordinary agreement that all officers domiciled in Ulster would be allowed to 'disappear.... Which, in the circumstances, was about the most lunatic concession that could possibly have been made'(Dangerfield, op. cit., p.342).

The likelihood is that the generals — with some reason — felt themselves to be almost invulnerable at that time because of developments in Europe and the probability of a Conservative government soon (what else, after all, but a Conservative government could pursue a war for Britain?). Then Brigadier Hubert Gough, KCB, entered the picture.

With his guarantee from the Secretary for War in his pocket Paget returned to his command in Ireland and called a conference. His ability to communicate appears to have been little better than his ability to interpret orders. Making allowance for his somewhat disdainful view of things in general, Dangerfield's account of what happened seems to catch the flavour:

> In the conference with his general officers, on the afternoon of 19 March, he [Paget] gave those gentlemen the distinct impression that he was offering them a choice between 'active operations against Ulster' and 'dismissal with loss of pension'. Now the picture which immediately leaped to the mind of the generals was one which a series of Orange orators had for some time been impressing upon the public imagination: it was a picture of English soldiers conscientiously annihilating a citizen army which advanced against them under the Union Jack, singing 'God Save the King'; and this rhetorical oleograph, with its several qualities of farce and tragedy, of cheap theatre and overwhelming fact, was not merely ridiculous, but bewildering and beastly. The generals went away to their own officers, and, before midnight of the 19th, two telegrams reached the War Office from General Paget.

The first of these ran: 'Officer commanding the 5th Lancers [Gough] states that all officers except two, and one doubtful, are resigning their commissions to-day. I much fear same conditions in 16th Lancers. Fear men will refuse to move.'

Said the second: 'Regret to report, Brigadier and fifty-seven officers Third Cavalry Brigade prefer to accept dismissal if ordered North.' This was mutiny. General Gough, who commanded the Third Cavalry Brigade knew it was mutiny. After the war, he saw fit to explain that his orders were either to undertake active operations or to leave the army, and that, in obedience to these orders, he decided to leave the army. The explanation is ingenious; but one cannot help inquiring whether an officer can be given orders to disobey orders? His Majesty's Government, for the first time since the Revolution of 1688, had lost the allegiance of His Majesty's forces; it was powerless.

If a crisis was what the government had sought, that was what they had on their hands. But it was far from the one they might have wished for. In spite of what nationalists, Home Rulers and separatists alike, thought (and have apparently, continued to think), there is some evidence that, in the spring of 1914, the government were prepared to outface the Ulster Unionists on the issue of violence, if not on Home Rule. In order to do so, however, they needed the support of the army. Not only was that support mutinously withheld, it was withheld at a time and in circumstances (the increasing unrest in Europe) that placed the United Kingdom, indeed the entire British Empire, in serious peril, thus initiating a crisis far more sinister than the bellicose threats of Carson and his Orangemen.[63]

It was clear by mid-1914 that Ulster would have to be coerced into Home Rule, but that the British Army could not be relied upon to do it (Foster, op. cit., p.469).

`Gough, having resigned, hastened to London and went straight to see General Wilson (at his home, not his office). Wilson was in constant consultation with his army colleagues. Somewhat later the two men met Seely (Secretary for War) at the War Office, where they held a lengthy conference. The dilemma now facing the cabinet was as much a result of Wilson's behind-the-scenes activities as anything else. And it was this: if they disciplined Gough, (and/or Paget and Friend), they would almost certainly, thanks to the orchestrated campaign over the past two years and to Wilson's control of military affairs, invite the resignation of most of the ranking generals in the army. With war looming closer every day such a development, whatever the calibre of these officers, was not to be considered. At the same time they could not permit Gough to be seen, unscathed, to get away with mutiny. A compromise, about as weak as any a government could reach, was formulated. It ended in a farce truly Gilbertian and of its time, lacking only the background music to: 'I am the very model of a modern major-general...'

A document (in the preparation of which Seely was not involved), requiring an undertaking from Gough that he would assist in the maintenance of law and order in Ulster, was drawn up by the cabinet. However, at his earlier meeting with them, without consulting or informing his government colleagues, Seely had promised Wilson and Gough that the latter would **never** be required to move his cavalry against Ulster. Accordingly when, in his capacity as Secretary for War, Seely received this cabinet document, what did he do? It seems that he simply added two paragraphs of his own to the cabinet document which, in the blithe and all but incomprehensible spirit of his class, i/ justified the mutiny and, ii/ included the undertaking he had already given verbally to Wilson and Gough. He then had the amended document initialled by Generals French and Ewart. This he gave to Gough who returned, happily, to the Curragh, once more a soldier of the king, with in his pocket a guarantee that his regiment of officers and gentlemen would never have to operate against Ulster, *even if ordered to do so*[64]. When this was discovered the resulting uproar was resolved only when Asquith sacked Seely, Ewart and French (a cosmetic exercise if ever there was one; the latter two were rapidly reinstated when England declared war on Germany soon afterwards).

Hobson (op. cit., p.11) wrote: 'It became apparent at this time that the sincerity of the English Liberals about Home Rule was as suspect as their courage in the face of the Carsonite campaign ...'   Casement was even more damning; 'Redmond's mistake for 20 years' he wrote to Sir Horace Plunkett, 'has been to trust the Liberals. They will assuredly betray him in the end. Of that I have an entire conviction. The Bill is now such an attenuated and wretched thing — an abortion from the day it was born — that I doubt the possibility of its doing any good. Even the principle of Home Rule, however cribbed and cabined, I'd accept at a high price — but we do not get the principle of Home Rule here at all.' He goes on to make a vital point, one that influenced the minds and attitudes of many thoughtful people. 'The Imperial Parliament with its members from Ireland will be just as it is now — supreme and constantly on the spot. The *Government* of Ireland — the important thing of all — will still be at Westminster'.

Later in the same lengthy letter Casement illustrates the clarity of thinking which made him so feared by the British. 'They have allowed Ulster to arm, to act, not merely to preach rebellion and open sedition; and when the first glimmer of manhood begins to show on the side of the unhappy people they and their long line of predecessors have reduced to moral, material and economic servitude, they at once, within a week, pervert the law of the UK to prohibit the "import" of arms from abroad — from Great Britain! What liars! ... Remember all I told you — for two years now — that *this* Home Rule Bill will not go through ... British rule in Ireland is an iniquity — a thing to be fought and driven out of the island. If it remains it corrupts, destroys and -' in a prophetic word ' — debauches the people to their final destruction ... The function of the army is not to defend Ireland but to hold it down in the interests of "England" ... the army declines to enforce the law. It says, quite truly, it is not here for that. It is not here to coerce any but Irish "rebels" — that is its time honoured function and it will not lift a finger except to hold Ireland as a subjugated land. General Gough and company have torn down the sham veil of Constitutional rights of the Irish people and have waved the sabre over our heads as in '98. (Letter to H.P. — Horace Plunkett — cited Mackey, op. cit., p.47).

For the moment Asquith seemed to have saved his government, if not his face, but at what a cost? It was seen as a situation in which the army dictated policy to the government. Furthermore, and of particular concern to Ireland, it raised partition to an acceptable level of consideration. There was now no question in the collective cabinet mind of Home Rule without 'special provisions' for all, or part, of Ulster. The Unionist minority was 'successful' — to use Churchill's words — 'in barring the way to the rest of Ireland'.

So ended March, 1914, and the 'Curragh Mutiny'. While it bore traces of 'Blimpism' it was, nonetheless, a real crisis for the British Government facing the threat of a European war, no less than it was for Ireland. For Ireland it provided a clear message, as Mackey (p. 55) points out: 'The lesson of the Curragh affair was not lost on the Orangemen for they now realised that they had a free hand to do as they liked, and that there was no effective power to resist or to control them.' The Larne gun-running, at which the password was 'Gough', took place on 24 April.

Interestingly in the light of subsequent events, in March, during the 'British Army mutiny' crisis, Griffith wrote condemning the proposal for partitioning the country, prophetically using the phrase 'six years hence':

Ireland has paid for the Home Rule Bill in eight years' slavish support of the Liberal Party, in meek acquiescence in increased taxation and prohibited trade. Now at the eleventh hour she is jockeyed and told she must add to the price the sacrifice of national principle and renounce her claim to be sole mistress of her own soil. The excuse of the jockeyers is that Ulster is armed and will shed blood. Who was it connived at the arming of Ulster? And six years hence if Ulster were still to decline to come under the operation of the so-called Home Rule Act would the English government then not have the same reason it has to-day? *Who on this side of sanity believes that England six years hence would use force to compel Ulster to do what it will not compel it to do now?* National principle has been sacrificed by those who accepted the proposal to alienate Irish soil whether it be for a day or for eternity. Let Ireland not sacrifice its commonsense also. This Bill if passed into law as it stood would in our judgement, though a wretched thing in itself, have helped Ireland's foot to the stirrup. This Bill if passed into law on the basis of the exclusion of part of the island will accentuate those fatal divisions which have kept Ireland poor and impotent (*Sinn Fein*, March, 1914).

In May, two months after the 'Curragh Mutiny', the Home Rule Bill passed its third reading in the House of Commons. Under the new legislation it would become law as soon as it received the king's assent. But the glare from the fires that enveloped the upper echelons of the army officer corps still glowed warningly. And war was uncomfortably close.

Britain was in a state of social unrest. For Asquith the major domestic threat in this time of crisis — the prospect of civil war in Ireland between Nationalists and Unionists in the north, followed by clashes between the two sets of Volunteer armies — had been averted for the moment. The Liberal Party itself was under serious attack by the Conservative Opposition, who had gone so far as to provoke and defend those who participated in treasonable mutiny. But Asquith was unable to act against any of them with determination, largely because of the impending danger of war in Europe.

His instructions to General Macready, new GOC in Ireland, were that if fighting broke out there between the Nationalists and the Unionists, British troops were not to intervene. They were to isolate the areas of combat until reinforcements arrived. In particular it should be noted that his instructions were that *if* Carson set up his provisional government, Macready 'was to remain on the defensive and do nothing ... with notes of these heroic instructions in my pocket I returned to Ulster', wrote Macready (General Sir Nevil Macready, *Annals of an Active Life*, Hutchinson, London, 1924).

The treasonable activities in which the House of Lords, the British Army and the Ulster Unionists had been involved provided a reactive fillip to the recently formed Irish Volunteers. Soon afterwards, another 'incident' galvanised recruitment. But, as it turned out, it was all counter-productive. The events prompting the boost also stimulated a take-over bid by Redmond. This, for public consumption, was presented as an attempt to organise the Volunteers on a nationally representative scale. At the time Redmond wrote for the Press:

Up to two months ago I felt that the Volunteer movement was somewhat premature, but the effect of Sir Edward Carson's threats upon public opinion in England, the House of Commons, and the Government; the occurrences at the Curragh Camp, and the successful gun-running in Ulster, have vitally altered the position, and the Irish Party took steps about six weeks ago to inform their friends and supporters in the country that, in their opinion, it was desirable to support the Volunteer movement...

The political reality was that Redmond could not afford the presence of such a powerful armed force that was not under his control[65].

The Irish Volunteers were the result of the activity in Ulster, particularly the formation of the Ulster Volunteer Force, attracting the attention of the IRB. In their view it was time the rest of the country also took arms in self-defence. But, without risk to themselves and their plans, the IRB could not act openly.

> The IRB believed rightly that the Liberal Government would not disarm the Orangemen in Ulster, and that the way would therefore be open for the foundation of an armed nationalist body also. It was Hobson, however, who took the initiative ... In July 1913 he suggested to the Dublin IRB Centres that active preparations for an Irish volunteer body should be undertaken. Drilling of IRB members began secretly in the National Foresters' Hall, Parnell Square, under instructions from Fianna Eireann. The crucial questions now were — Who would begin the movement publicly? when? and where? (F.X.Martin, *McCullough, Hobson and republican Ulster* — Leaders and Men of the Easter Rising, Dublin, 1916, p. 102).

Bulmer Hobson (pp.23-24) writes:
> In the middle of July, 1913, I told the Dublin Centres Board of the I.R.B., of which I was chairman — I was then a member of the Supreme Council — that in my opinion the time was rapidly approaching when it would be possible to start an Irish Volunteer organisation. As a preparation, I suggested, and it was decided, that the members of the I.R.B. in Dublin should commence drilling immediately...

The formation of the Ulster Volunteers had stirred the minds and political souls of more than the IRB. Hobson noted that it was in October of 1913 that it was decided the time had come to start the Volunteers, but, equally '*that the I.R.B. must not show its hand*'. He outlined the quest for someone of prominence who 'would become the focal point of a public movement' and how that quest seemed resolved when, on 1 November 1913, an article by Eoin Mac Neill, 'The North Began', appeared in *An Claidheamh Soluis* [The Sword of Light], the official organ of the Gaelic League. MacNeill was Professor of Early and Medieval Irish History in University College, Dublin, and was noted for his advanced views on the independence of the country.

'This article of MacNeill's was certainly not inspired by the I.R.B. MacNeill, who was an avowed adherent of John Redmond, leader of the Irish Parliamentary Party, was never a member of the I.R.B. and was not in any way in touch with them. *His article was for that very reason providential.*

'I went immediately to the O'Rahilly, who was then manager of *An Claidheamh Soluis*, and proposed the formation of a National Volunteer Force. O'Rahilly said that if I could get fifty reliable men he would join them. I said I could guarantee five hundred, and although he, like MacNeill, was not a member of the I.R.B., he realised what I had in mind and at once consented.'

MacNeill's article (See Appendix One) pointed out that the Unionists had created a precedent in four north-eastern counties which might be followed in the remainder of the country. This exactly suited the IRB. MacNeill was also a vice-president of the Gaelic League and was a prominent and formidable individual, the ideal figurehead (willing or unwilling) for what the IRB sorely needed in order to render its plans viable — a source of trained manpower. He was persuaded[66] to convene a meeting to consider the idea. A committee was formed with MacNeill in the chair and, according to O'Hegarty, 'twelve other members, of whom eight were members of the IRB, most of them unlikely to be publicly known as such'(op. cit. p.669)[67]. This committee met at Wynn's Hotel. Within weeks a meeting was called for the Rotunda in Dublin to form the Irish Volunteers. It was chaired by MacNeill.

So many — an estimated 5,000-6,000 — attended the inaugural meeting on 25 November that a sub-meeting, chaired by Sean T. O Ceallaigh (later two-term President of Ireland) had to be held in the adjoining Rotunda large Concert Hall. Something over 3,000 men were sworn in that night. All of this had, to some extent, been engineered by the IRB. Hobson's men were already drilling with a view to controlling a force which he, too, anticipated as being inevitable following the formation of the Ulster Volunteers (Hobson, op.cit, p.39). 'The Brotherhood knew that MacNeill was in no way a separatist and that he would have been satisfied with the goal of the parliamentarians' (See T. Desmond Williams *Eoin Mac Neill and the Irish Volunteers*, Leaders and Men of the Easter Rising, ed. Martin p. 140). From then on the IRB, either covertly or in some cases in rural areas, overtly, controlled the Volunteers so that they would become the IRB's instrument when the time was judged right. It is essential to appreciate this point, which has become obscured by time and argument — namely the IRB's control of the Volunteers from the outset.

And so, on 25 November 1913, the Irish Volunteer Force was launched. It adopted as its motto 'Defence, not Defiance' and quickly expanded. By the end of the year there were 10,000 members. The stated object of the Volunteers was 'to secure and maintain the rights and liberties common to the whole people of Ireland. The movement grew, patriotic and unselfish, its moving force patriotism, its object the defence of their country'.

A short while before the establishment of the Volunteers a third, smaller, para-military organization had been formed[68]. It was organized by a former British officer, Captain J.R.White, DSO, who had become disillusioned with colonialism and turned republican as a result of what he had seen of the treatment of the Boers in South Africa. This force was essentially a labour self-defence movement, with its base in Liberty Hall, and it was called the Irish Citizen Army. It came into being partly because of White's enthusiasm and partly because of Jim Larkin's[69] exhortations[70]. The General Strike, started at the beginning of Horse Show Week when it would be most inconvenient, had begun in August 1913, and after day one Larkin ordered the workers to arm to protect themselves. 'My advice to you is to be round the doors and corners, and whenever any of your men are shot, shoot two of them'.

The Citizen Army, of which James Connolly[71] was the commander, was a small force of about 200 men. It provided the workers with a means of protecting themselves and gave them a sense of purpose. Sean O'Casey was a member.

The General Strike of 1913 has not always, recently, been accorded the recognition that is its due in helping to mould the climate of public opinion that made not only the Rising of 1916 a possibility, but helped to ensure the subsequent popular support for the movement for self-determination and the War of Independence. Yet hardly a writer or commentator who lived through the period has failed to emphasise its importance. It was not simply an industrial dispute on a grand scale, it was a social revolt — class warfare — in an age of entrenched capitalism and gross exploitation of workers. As surely as the IRB did so at an intellectual and patriotic level, the strike stimulated amongst the workers of the country — especially in Dublin — a popular spirit of rebellion for human rights, for freedom and justice, without which the conditions which made the Rising possible would have been significantly less promising. An inquiry by inspectors of the Local Government Board showed that Dublin housing conditions were 'the worst in Europe'. There were 21,000 *families* each living in only one room. Wages ranged from 5/= a week to 25/= (25p to 105p in today's money: roughly £8.00 to £40.00 in purchasing power) at the top. Workers were unorganised and trade union power was limited.

The strike was brought about when a Dublin federation of some 400 employers, organised by William Martin Murphy, a powerful Dublin-based industrial magnate, refused to employ anyone who was a union member and fired anyone who joined a union. There was no security of tenure and benefits simply did not exist. It is extremely difficult today to imagine these conditions and their effects. Lock-outs, evictions, extreme distress were, for months, the order of the day for many Dublin families. Nevertheless there were sympathetic strikes in both Ireland and England. Food ships and funds were sent to Dublin from England and the Continent. George Russell (AE) accused the employers of deliberately deciding to starve out one third of the population of the city, 'to break the manhood of the men by the sight of the suffering of their wives and the hunger of their children... Blind Samsons, pulling down the pillars of social order' he called them (See Macardle, op. cit., p.93).

Initially, in 1913, the Citizen Army attracted large numbers. But, when after ten months the employers employed a 'lock-out' policy, the strike was finally broken, and starvation and general deprivation suborned the initial enthusiasm, if not the will. 'Here was confederated capital deliberately setting out to starve into surrender, not a few hundreds, but the whole working class of a city' (Brian O'Neill, *Easter Week*, London, 1936, p. 12).

The Volunteer movement did not, at first, unduly upset the rather complacent Dublin Castle authorities, who were much more exercised by the Ulster Volunteer Force and its treasonable activities. Nathan's view of the Volunteers was typically bureaucratic, at once dismissive and admonitory, as a letter to John Dillon in

November, 1914, illustrates. It also, by implication, underlines the fact that government anxiety was really concerned with the UVF. Nathan describes the Volunteers as: 'Armed mobs which assembled to hear hatred-reviving speeches that no government could allow at that time of national peril and paramountcy of military interests',(See O Broin, *Dublin Castle and the 1916 Rising*, citing a letter from Nathan to John Dillon).

The passing of the Home Rule Bill could not be now more than a matter of months. The British Government were much vexed by the situation presented by Carson and his Ulster Unionists. They had tried to take steps, if necessary military intervention, to control the threat presented by the Unionists and their army, but with disastrous consequences. For Redmond, as the generally acknowledged leader of the Irish people, the Irish Volunteers represented a different kind of threat. 'They had come into being without his consent. He could not forgive that' (Dangerfield, op. cit., p. 360). At this point, therefore, he went to considerable lengths to bring them under his control.

If it is true that de Valera, as he was to say himself later on, found himself in the strait-jacket of the Republic, it is equally the case that in 1914 that curious enigma, John Redmond, found himself in the strait-jacket of an already discredited Home Rule on behalf of an Ireland with which he was largely out of touch and which had significantly passed him by. His attempt to hijack the Volunteers and its extra-ordinary aftermath, is a good example both of how out of touch he really was with Irish public opinion, and the extent to which the so-called Irish renaissance had left him behind. That he had, in constitutional terms and outlook, become more English than the English themselves is hard to deny. As Eoin O Caoimh expresses it in his important article **Redmond's Change of Policy, August-September 1914** (*The Irish Volunteers 1913-1915*, ed. Martin):

> Whatever about his Parnellite days he [Redmond] was now convinced that Ireland's interests lay in being a self-governing state of the Empire or Commonwealth similar to Australia. His first wife was an Australian, his second wife an Englishwoman. Of necessity he lived a good deal in England, and while, of course, he observed the Party rule against entertainment by British political circles he had no doubt become affected by English life and he was somewhat out of touch with the Irish renaissance. His position as The Irish Leader was however unquestioned, and he felt no doubt that if the heads of the new movement did not accede to his demands he was in a position to effectively compel them ... The enactment of Home Rule depended on the Liberal Government. With or without pressure from that Government he must show publicly that he was The Leader. Otherwise, on the plea that they had introduced it [Home Rule] as a final settlement the Government could with justification drop it. And if this chance of Home Rule were lost when would another come?

Also to be taken into account is the fact that he felt himself close to becoming the first prime minister of an Irish parliament in over a hundred years.

The existence of the Irish Volunteers was central to much that followed. They became a catalyst and pivotal point for nationalist attitudes, hitherto focussed, insofar as they were focussed at all, on Home Rule. But, once formed, the Volunteers inevitably brought the question of physical force and separatism for Ireland again to centre stage. The purpose of the Volunteers, as MacNeill stated at the inaugural meeting, would be 'defensive and protective...towards safeguarding the rights of the (Irish) nation'. But the fact behind the rhetoric — of which MacNeill's was one of the more moderate, if more influential, voices — was that an additional and formidable private army now openly paraded the streets and roadways of Ireland. And this time it was a nationalist army. Even today it is a concept it takes some time to grasp. What other purpose does an army have but, in certain given circumstances, to fight?

In spite of its own command structure, it was, as we know, planned by the IRB that this army would be under its own secret control, and so, like itself, be dedicated to fighting for the full freedom of the country. Following the successful Larne gun-running, the Volunteer leaders, including MacNeill, decided that they, too, must acquire arms[72]. The problem was that they had neither the money nor the other resources available to the Unionists. Nevertheless, arrangements were made to procure rifles and ammunition from Germany[73].

> The problem posed for John Redmond by the formation and development of the Volunteers was considerable. His initial contempt for them quickly evaporated. Ireland was changing and it was changing without his (Redmond's) consent; he knew that if he was to get Home Rule in a constitutional manner, he would have to hurry, for — with events hurtling onwards at their present speed and towards what unthinkable destination! — the Parliament at Westminster would very soon be helpless, (Dangerfield, op.cit.p.133).

> Hobson (Ibid. p.44) writes: 'The Irish Volunteers was a new national organisation and MacNeill and others thought it important that it should have the benediction of the country's leader [Redmond], or at least that it should not have his opposition'.

MacNeill was a supporter of Redmond and, on his own initiative, he got in touch with Redmond with a view to getting his cooperation in the development of the Volunteers. He did not, however, consult the Volunteer Committee beforehand. Unfortunately these contacts may have given Redmond the impression that MacNeill was acting with the authority of the Volunteer Committee. Hobson writes:

> MacNeill was a straight-forward honourable man, incapable of deliberately deceiving anybody, whether his own committee or John Redmond. But it is possible that John Redmond believed that Eoin MacNeill, who was Chairman of the Provisional Committee, was acting with the full approval of that Committee, and that MacNeill failed to make the true position clear.

When the combined threat to their plans presented by Redmond and MacNeill was recognised by the IRB, a National Convention of the Volunteers was summoned and companies were instructed to affiliate with the Provisional Committee on or before 10 June, 1914. The intention was to create a National

Executive which would forestall any attempt by Redmond to gain control. But Redmond, well aware of this proposal, sabotaged it by publishing an ultimatum in the Press on 9 June.

He had decided that, as an organised and military body, the Volunteers must come under the control of the Irish Parliamentary Party. From his point of view as the leader of the constitutional movement, this was sound logic. But neither the Volunteer executive nor, in particular, the hidden IRB controlling group, agreed with or welcomed his intervention, which was to have regrettable consequences for all three.

In May, 1914, Redmond, John Dillon and Joseph Devlin — the leaders of the Irish Party — put intense pressure on MacNeill and, through the press, on the Volunteers in general, with the intention of bringing the Volunteers under Irish Party control. From their point of view this was an entirely correct step and one that justified — within reason — the use of whatever political manoeuvring was needed to bring it about. And, in the Ireland of 1914, there were few political manoeuvrers in the same class as these three. They were approaching, they thought, the actual realisation of Home Rule. Then they might expect to govern Ireland. They could not permit an independent armed body such as the Volunteers to exist.

'...I suggest' wrote Redmond, 'that the present Provisional Committee should be immediately strengthened by the addition of twenty-five representative men from different parts of the country, nominated at the instance of the Irish Party, and in sympathy with its policy and aims ...' (letter to the national Press, June, 1914). Because of who he was this letter received wide publicity, creating exactly the impression Redmond wished for; namely that he simply wanted to contribute his great influence and authority to the Volunteer movement[74].

Clearly MacNeill was in a fearsome dilemma. On the one hand, Redmond still possessed the allegiance of the vast majority of nationalists and could very probably ruin the whole Volunteer movement if he chose to instruct his followers to boycott it. On the other hand, if the movement were handed over to him lock, stock and barrel, the more advanced nationalists would move out at the precise point when, unknown to them, the weapons which were to give the Volunteers real power and authority were still on the high seas.

Naturally enough MacNeill temporised. Naturally enough, the parliamentarians grew impatient. They thought him vain, confused and unbusinesslike. He was none of these things, but was simply playing a waiting game. Yet time was running out...

Redmond's demand that the provisional committee of the Volunteers should be expanded by twenty-five of his own nominees was initially rejected. His proposal was, of course, condemned by the IRB in their paper, *Irish Freedom*. But, in order to prevent a disastrous split at a critical time the committee later voted, by a small majority, to accept Redmond's ultimatum. The IRB group were furious, particularly because Hobson, one of themselves, voted in favour and several of them, including Tom Clarke, never spoke to Hobson again. In fact this vote to include Redmond's nominees was a serious blow to the IRB. About it Hobson writes:

I was as much opposed to this action on the part of Redmond as those who disapproved of my attitude. I recognised even then that Redmond's aim was the destroying or curbing of a growing national organisation which he had hitherto bitterly opposed; but I realised equally that if his request, which was in fact an ultimatum, were not acceded to, it would lead to a disastrous and, indeed, fatal split in the Volunteers and in the country as a whole. (op. cit., p.47)

Those months between March and the outbreak of war in August, 1914, were important in shaping what would happen in Ireland over the next two years, culminating in the Rising of 1916. Although they were effectively burying the Home Rule Act, which was the essential prop supporting him, the British Government (and the Opposition), saw Redmond as the leader of Ireland and, therefore, of the Volunteers. It was a misconception that was to colour much of their attitude to dealing with Ireland in general[75].

In the meantime the Volunteers had armed themselves to a limited extent. After his call for twenty-five seats for his nominees on the Volunteer committee had been rejected, Redmond threw down the gauntlet to the Volunteer Executive by calling publicly on the Volunteers and new recruits to form, in defiance of their own Committee, a new organisation led by himself. Ten days later, on 26 June, arms for the Volunteers were landed at Howth from Erskine Childers' yacht, *Asgard*. It was in these circumstances that the Volunteer executive, as a matter of expediency, accepted Redmond's proposal, but   at great cost to itself — especially to the IRB element.

The resulting divisive tensions lingered and may have made their own con-tribution to what happened in 1922-23. In the event, had they been blessed with premonition, the divisiveness need not have happened for, within a few months, Redmond made his extraordinary speeches in Westminster and Woodenbridge, the effects of which were to remove again from the Volunteers all those his participation in the expanded committee had introduced. The additional irony was that Redmond's intervention not only precipitated the very split in the Volunteers Hobson feared, but also caused a split in the IRB.

When Redmond urged every Volunteer to don the khaki and 'fight for Catholic Belgium', the IRB struck back. In September [in fact on 25 October E.N.] a Volunteer convention was called, the headquarters seized, and Redmond and his clique were expelled. One section followed Redmond and became the National Volunteers ... The anti-war section became the Irish Volunteers, about 12,000 strong, with all their leaders IRB men except MacNeill and The O'Rahilly. And the IRB began to plan for definite insur-rection and to investigate the possibility of German assistance. (O'Neill, op.cit., p.25).

The entire Volunteer gun-running episode, with its romantic overtones of yachts, shady arms dealers, the imminence of war and — to crown it — a passage through the might of the imperial fleet at Spithead by one of the yachts loaded with contraband rifles and ammunition and crewed by an Englishman and two Anglo-Irish women, is redolent of the romantic view of the period, and of the whole extraordinary, high-minded idealism which was an essential ingredient of the ethos that motivated so many of those involved. While this is true and while it was, perhaps, as Foster (op. cit., pp. 468/9) says 'more reminiscent of a John Buchan novel than of intransigent Gaelic republicanism', Foster nevertheless distorts the reality both by omission and commission, firstly by contrasting the Larne and Howth gun-runnings to the organisational and quantitative detriment of the latter. The simple facts are that the Larne gun-running was subvented and organised by powerful Tory backers from Britain who funded it to the extent of being able to provide a steamship and a huge quantity of rifles, machine-guns and ammunition without significantly contravening the law. The Howth gun-running, on the other hand, was not organised by 'intransigent Gaelic republicanism', but by a group of Anglo sympathisers, who provided limited funds (to be repaid) and their yachts as a means of transport, both because they felt it to be unjust that the Volunteers were without funds and/or weapons in the face of the UVF armed threat and, in the interval between the two gun-running events, because they had been further constricted by the introduction of a ban on the importation of guns. The Volunteers and the IRB were involved in a *post-factum* arrangement of events.

What had happened throws an interesting light on one aspect of the Howth gun-running, namely the question of raising the funds necessary to buy the arms and make the operation possible. Roger Casement[76] — who was a member of the Volunteer Provisional Committee, but not of the IRB — went to London in early 1914 and, together with his friends Alice Stopford Green, Erskine Childers and his wife Mary Spring Rice (Lord Monteagle's daughter), and a Captain Berkeley, raised £1,500. Mrs. Stopford Green put up half the money and the others put up the remainder. Casement, although never a member of the IRB, was the only one of the group connected with the Volunteers, but all five had a passionate belief in right and justice, particularly so far as Ireland was concerned. 'The idea was that the money should be used to purchase arms, to bring them to Ireland, to sell the arms to the Irish Volunteers and to reimburse the subscribers. The subscribers took a very uncommercial risk, and I think they must have been very astonished when they did subsequently get their money back' (Hobson, op. cit., p.33).

This group selected Darrell Figgis, now a somewhat shadowy figure, but then soon to be prominent amongst the Volunteers, to go to the Continent to purchase the guns and ammunition[77]. Erskine Childers was an English writer who had served in South Africa during the Boer War and had worked with the British Foreign Office. His yacht, *Asgard* and that of Conor O'Brien[78], an international yachtsman, were to be used to bring the guns and ammunition to Ireland. Since the Volunteers had little money or resources, this was a considerable bonus. It did not, of course, compare with the ability of the Ulster Volunteer Force to land a huge quantity of rifles and ammunition from a steamer chartered with Unionist money.

After some difficulty a couple of German arms-dealers, brothers named Magus, were located in Hamburg. They undertook to provide 1,500 rifles and ammunition, then in Liege[79]. The consignment was brought from Liege to Hamburg, where, in order to evade the authorities, a tug was chartered for a short journey and a date, 26 July, set for the landing. Off the Scheldt on 12 July — the irony of which date was hardly lost on the conspirators — the guns and ammunition were transferred to the two yachts. O'Brien set sail for Kilcoole, Co. Wicklow, and safely landed his cargo there. *Asgard* made sail for Howth, en route passing through the might of the British Grand Fleet at Spithead. The British patrol destroyer *HMS Panther* was lured away from Dublin Bay by rumours that guns were to be landed in Wexford. *Asgard* was crewed by Childers, his wife and Mary Spring-Rice. At Howth seven hundred Volunteers under Bulmer Hobson were on the pier as the yacht came alongside with its cargo of 1,000 rifles.

Hobson was anxious to get the ammunition away as soon as possible and to this end had instructed a number of the IRB to 'invite their lady friends out for the day. They were to go by taxi to Howth and order lunch at the hotel ... When they saw the yacht coming in they were to abandon both the ladies and the lunch and bring their taxis to the harbour ready to carry their appointed loads to their appointed destination' (Ibid, p.35). Having unloaded the cargo the Volunteers proceeded to march with the balance of the rifles to Dublin, but were halted by police and military *en route*.

When they realised what was happening the police in Howth telephoned David Harrell, second in command of the DMP (later dismissed from office for 'provocatively' calling out the military to deal with the landings at Howth). He in turn phoned the Under-Secretary at Dublin Castle, Sir James Dougherty. Dougherty ordered out a battalion of the King's Own Scottish Borderers to meet and disarm the Volunteers. This action, which was not in accordance with the law, is said to have been the result of a misunderstanding between Harrell and Dougherty. The troops, with Dougherty and Harrell, met the Volunteers at the Malahide road. Harrell ordered his men to disarm the Volunteers and there was a short, bloody fight lasting about a minute, after which the police withdrew. Hobson attempted to negotiate with Harrell. While this was going on Tomas MacDonagh and Darrell Figgis joined them. Seeing that 'either of them could have talked him [Harrell] blind... I ran to the back of the column and ordered the men to disperse across the fields' (Ibid.). MacDonagh and Figgis talked so well that all except a few Volunteers escaped with the rifles across what were then open fields, bringing the guns safely to Dublin. The remainder were allowed to march off. There were a few more minor incidents involving the Volunteers at Howth road and Fairview, but nothing of significance. But it was all in marked contrast to the attitude of the authorities to the arms landing at Larne for the Ulster Volunteers where there was no official interference of any kind. The remainder of the guns were landed at Kilcoole, Co. Wicklow, on the night of August first/ second where Hobson had a charabanc, later supplemented with taxis and lorries, to bring them to Dublin.

But tragedy did ensue indirectly from the Howth landing. Conflicting with the common view that the populace were pro-British and anti-Volunteer, on their way back to barracks the military, who had only been onlookers in the attempts to disarm the Volunteers, fired on an unarmed crowd of civilians who jeered at them near O'Connell (then Sackville) street. A large crowd, thus justifiably enraged, armed themselves with stones and brick-bats and followed the soldiers on the quays. The troops were ordered to fix bayonets and the rearguard was constantly changed in an efforts to prevent trouble. In Bachelor's Walk, Major Haig ordered his bruised rearguard to block the road, but instead they fired, indiscriminately, killing three people and wounding thirty-eight.

> ... The soldiers had fired hastily and without orders; but if ever a slipshod killing deserved to be called 'massacre', the killing in Bachelor's Walk deserves that name. For comparisons between Larne and Howth are odious and revealing. At Larne 30,000 Orange rifles were landed while the police and coastguards and the soldiers slept: At Howth, the landing of 1,500 Nationalist rifles could only be expiated in blood. And the Army, which refused to march against Ulster, had shown no unwillingness to meet the Nationalist Volunteers. Under these circumstances, it matters very little whether three thousand civilians were slaughtered, or three hundred, or thirty, or three: there are stains in Bachelor's Walk which nothing will ever quite wash away...(Dangerfield, op. cit., pp.420/1).

The reaction throughout the country was one of shock and outrage. Recruits flocked to join the Irish Volunteers, many of the new Volunteers being ex-soldiers, both officer and other-rank.   Nationalist fervour, whether constitutional or separatist, burgeoned like an explosion of spring growth. The enlarged Volunteer movement, however, shrank just as quickly after Redmond's speech at Woodenbridge a few weeks later split their ranks[80].

Before The War

Notwithstanding such atrocities and the intense events which gave rise to them, the months before the outbreak of war were a time of measured and deliberate blindness. In spite of impending war and social unrest, it was a comfortable, not to say comforting, time; one when the writings of men like Kipling and Saki sold in their hundreds of thousands of copies and trumpeted (or tootled, if you prefer) abroad the honour and heroic doings of the vast British Empire 'upon which the sun never set', and those who served it. It was a time when those who read these grandiose accounts of Britain's role as preceptor of the world and bearer of 'the white man's burden' often believed and tried to emulate what they read — despairing reality notwithstanding. It was a time when it was self-evident, not to say undeniable, that the supreme privilege in this life was to be born an English gentleman (even an English gentlewoman would do, so long as she wasn't a suffragette); particularly to be born an Englishman endowed with the manners and (if possible) the mannerisms exemplified by such striking examples of idiosyncrasy as Lord Curzon, neatly caricatured:- 'My name is George Nathaniel Curzon, I am a most superior person'. It was a station to which all proper men of other nations should aspire — without, of course, the slightest prospect of ever being able to achieve it. So powerful was this propaganda that its decadent aroma lingers with marginal effect, even today.

In Ireland the Catholic middle-class of substantial merchants and professionals could entertain thoughts of a wider culture and, amongst their children, even ones of frivolity. The new, asymmetric harmonies of Stravinsky and Bartok, the raw tones of Gauguin and Cezanne, and the images of Shaw and Turgeniev, jostled with the rhythms of New Orleans, striped blazers, boaters and banjos. Politics occurred in Westminster where Redmond and his cohorts performed their unsteady pavane to small effect. For 'comfortable' people at home in that comfortable time, all seemed for the best; and, for the best, it seemed best to do nothing that would 'rock the boat'.

A kind of political exhaustion accompanied by an atmosphere compounded of suspended menace and euphoric xenophobia gave a frentic fillip to middle-class social activities right across Europe that summer. In Ireland, in spite of the accompanying Suspension Bill, Unionist sabre-rattling and, indeed, the prospect of war, a kind of delusion that all-resolving Home Rule was imminent had settled on the country. But instead of joy, this seemed to sap people of their critical faculties. The wished-for was about to happen; all would be for the best 'in this best of all possible worlds'. Yet the question often heard was 'What's the difference? Is it worth it?'

While still much below comparable levels in England, Scotland and Wales, living standards in Ireland had improved marginally in the pre-war years, though poverty was still appalling and on a scale unimaginable to-day. Things were considerably better than they had been, especially in rural areas. Ironically this improvement in living standards contributed in no small measure to stimulating amongst workers the will for further improvements, carrying through the general strike of 1913. The Irish merchant and middle classes were strong, and the professional classes, everywhere, were penetrated by the people. It was no more an encouraging milieu for physical force separatists than when Griffith, responding to a call for him to lead a constitutional movement similar to that led in Hungary by Francis Deak in the 1860s, had written in the *United Irishman* of July, 1904 that, while agreeing that it was what the mood of the country approved and wanted, he could not lead such a movement as *he was a separatist*. But, he went on to say, he would support it. The Irish Party, led by Redmond, was the epicentre of this inaction. Of the period O'Hegarty wrote 'Outside the young men of the various sections of the Sinn Fein movement the land was politically asleep' (O'Hegarty, op. cit., p.675).

The Volunteers

On 28 June, 1914 the Archduke Ferdinand of Austria was assassinated in Sarajevo. European nations which had, more or less earnestly, been trying to avoid war, now rattled their sabres and found themselves locked in a passage to arms. The situation affected English parliamentary deliberations, not least those concerning Ireland. The outcome was a typical Westminster attempt to evade the issue. In June, therefore, the government introduced an Amending Bill which was virtually the same as the offer·made by Asquith in January to Bonar Law. Characteristically the House of Lords amended 'such counties as preferred it, for six years' to 'the permanent exclusion of the whole of Ulster'.

Now, over everything, hung the darkening shadow of the vast crisis looming in Europe. No doubt, too, this tension contributed to the quickening of Irish blood. But, however it might be with England (and the threat of civil war in Ireland — perhaps England too — had not dissipated), for Ireland a European war was of secondary importance to events at home. When, on 4 August, England declared war on Germany, that was not the matter of primary political concern to most Irish people.

When the Amending Home Rule Bill came back from the Lords to the Commons, Asquith abandoned it because of the European crisis. This, in turn, raised the question of the Home Rule Bill itself. Would it also be abandoned? If not, what would the Unionists do? In this emotional and political tumult Redmond made what was, perhaps, the greatest error of judgement of his career. Home Rule had been the end goal of his political life. He would not, could not, see it abandoned when it — and all it promised — was almost within his grasp.

Committed to support Britain in the war, within weeks Redmond stated in the House of Commons that Britain could withdraw its troops from Ireland, which, he maintained, would be defended 'from foreign invasion by her sons, and for this purpose armed Nationalist Catholics in the south will be only too glad to join arms with the armed Protestant Ulstermen in the North ... We offer to the Government of the day that they may take their troops away, and that, if it is allowed us, in comradeship with our brethren in the North, we will ourselves defend the coasts of our country'. As Dangerfield (op. cit., p.424) put it: '... he had just rendered an enormous service to the British Empire and ruined his own career'[81].

Even at the time this was was seen as an absurd statement, and one which Redmond had no mandate from the Volunteers to make[82]. The genesis of Redmond's gratuitous intervention (which is what it was; he spoke to a speech of Sir Edward Grey on the Order Paper) lay in a note he had received the previous Saturday from the wife of the prime minister, the great beauty and political hostess, Margot Asquith. In it she suggested that he should make a 'great speech' offering the Volunteers to the Government. Whether Mrs. Asquith had been prompted by her husband to provide Redmond with an opening, it is impossible to say. Redmond's subsequent offer in the House of Commons gave Asquith more than he could possibly have hoped. Why he did so is unknown; perhaps he feared that he had already burned his boats; perhaps he sensed a growing hostile public reaction in Ireland and did so in order to strengthen his position with the British. Asquith, in turn, gave an empty — and qualified — promise. He agreed to place the Government of Ireland Act — the Third Home Rule Bill — on the statute book. But he also introduced two provisos: i/ it would not come into operation until **after** the end of the war and ii/ it would not come into operation until after parliament had provided for Ulster by special amending legislation. Home Rule was dead.

Redmond then went even further. In a speech at Woodenbridge, County Wicklow, on 20 September, he permitted himself to be wildly carried away:

The duty of the manhood of Ireland is twofold. Its duty is at all costs to defend the shores of Ireland from foreign invasion —' so far, so good. But he went on; 'It has a duty more than that, of taking care that Irish valour proves itself on the field of war as it has always proved itself in the past. The interests of Ireland, of the whole of Ireland, are at stake in this war.'

After this refractory statement, which may be understood only in the light that Redmond hoped for some kind of preferment by offering the Volunteers as cannon-fodder for Britain, he offered the following nonsense: 'This war is undertaken in defence of the highest principles of religion and morality and right, and it would be a disgrace forever to our country, a reproach to her manhood, and a denial of the lessons of her history' (*sic*!), 'if young Ireland confined her efforts to remaining at home to defend the shores of Ireland from an unlikely invasion, or should shrink from the duty of proving on the field of battle that gallantry and courage which have distinguished her race all through its history. I say to you, therefore, your duty is twofold ... go on drilling and make yourselves efficient for the work, and then account for yourselves as men, not only in Ireland itself, but wherever the fighting line extends in defence of right and freedom and religion in this war' (Gwynn, *John Redmond's Last Years*, pp. 154-5). This plain exhortation to go to war for England, which threw away the young lives of thousands of Irish soldiers, was made a mere six weeks after Britain had entered the war[83].

The Provisional Committee had accepted Redmond's twenty-five nominees only from a strong sense of public duty, and every week since his actions and his speeches had strained the frail unity of that body. The Woodenbridge speech might have been made at a public meeting without breaking that unity, but it was made to a body of Volunteers, and purported to lay down a duty which was inconsistent with the Constitution and objects of the Volunteers and which revolted the inmost feelings of the active members of that body. (O'Hegarty, op.cit. p.688).

Following this speech, members of the original Volunteer council issued a statement repudiating Redmond and his nominees. The Volunteers at once split, and the majority — mainly those who had joined since Bachelor's Walk and Redmond's take-over, and numbering about 170,000 — stayed with Redmond and formed the National Volunteers. The remainder, about 11,000/12,000, representing in the main the original group, retained the name Irish Volunteers and proceeded to form a general council with a central executive. It was to be organised on more military lines; MacNeill became Chief of Staff, Bulmer Hobson QMG, O'Rahilly Director of Arms. 'But, as it turned out, it was the holders of three other posts who were to exercise supreme authority at the critical moment. These were Patrick Pearse[84], Director of Military Organisation, Thomas MacDonagh, Director of Training and Joseph Plunkett[85], Director of Military Operations' (Lyons, op. cit., p. 330); all three were members of the IRB which controlled the General Council.

In the Volunteer newspaper, *The Irish Volunteers*, MacNeill wrote (in December, 1914):'The European war has not merely complicated, it has annihilated the ordinary political forces of Ireland as a factor in British politics. At this moment the Irish members of Parliament are as helpless in British politics as so many babies ... Trust yourselves, Irishmen. If you are asked to trust British politicians, excuse yourselves from being fools. For two years before last March, the Asquith government was pledged to the Irish Party and their supporters in Ireland to give Ireland a certain measure of Home Rule. That was their treaty with their Irish allies... They broke that treaty...'

Connolly followed up with:

The action of the Provisional Committee of the Irish Volunteers in repudiating the nominees of Mr. Redmond and proceeding to take that control, which they ought never to have abandoned, sent a thrill of joy through the heart of every true man and woman in the country. It was felt that the ground was at last being cleared for action, and that the insidious attempt to betray the Volunteers into the clutches of the Empire had received a staggering blow at the very outset of the campaign.

Never was the peril of Irish Nationality greater, never were the forces of national and social freedom more in danger of death from moral asphyxiation than at the outset of this Asquith-Redmond conspiracy...'(*The Irish Worker*, October, 1914).

The argument is sometimes heard that Pearse, MacDonagh and Plunkett usurped — and, in some undefined manner, betrayed — the Volunteers in organising the Rising. There is a certain *prima facie* plausibility about the argument, but only on the basis that the Volunteers were not a revolutionary army, but some kind of democratic society to be consulted at all times and at all levels about important matters. There could be no surer formula for betrayal. It was, and remained, IRB policy to act and this is what MacDonagh, Pearse, Plunkett and the other IRB members planned and did[86].

Contrary to the fears expressed when the Amending Bill had been abandoned a few weeks earlier, the Home Rule Bill received the Royal Assent on 18 September, but it was in the foregoing feeble form that it was put on the Statute Book (Suspensory Act 1914, Worthington Evans papers, C.903.3', together with a *Bill suspending its operation indefinitely*). With these conflicting Bills safely shelved and on the Statute Book, by which they became law, Asquith further emasculated Home Rule. In the House of Commons — no doubt bearing in mind the defunct Amending Bill — he gave an undertaking that *when* the Home Rule Act became operative at some future date after the war, a new Amending Bill dealing with Ulster *would* simultaneously be introduced — yet there was no such qualification in the suspending Act.

That summer and early autumn of 1914 saw the general public, apart from the committed, caught up in a curious, paradoxical, indifferent mood, the antithesis of that animating *Sinn Fein*, the Volunteers, and the cultural activists of the Gaelic League and the GAA. It is sometimes suggested that if the British had suppressed Sinn Fein in 1913 or 1914 they would have prevented the Rising. This ignores the fact that it was the IRB and the Citizen Army, not Sinn Fein (which was neither politically nor conspiratorially active at that time), that planned the Rising. So potent, widespread and profoundly imbued with a sense of 'Irishness' were its members, the reality is that the suppression of the Gaelic League, in spite of the fact that it was non-political, might have been a more practical step.

Even moreso in England than in Ireland, Redmond was perceived as 'the Irish leader'. He spent much (too much, according to many commentators) of his time in England[87]. He was a first-class parliamentarian. At all events, instead of rejecting outright any question of partition, he began a series of discussions with the government, the Opposition and Unionists themselves, not on 'the question of meeting the Ulster Unionists within the framework of an Irish State, but on the question of what Counties should be excluded, that is to say they accepted the principle of partition'[88].

Redmond's actions were confused and confusing. Instead of acting as a strong, decisive leader, he sought to compromise with the British on the question of partition. At home, evidently uneasy at the erosion of his party's popularity and the rise of the Volunteer movement, he, inexplicably, turned the first sod of what was to prove the grave of his own party.

These extraordinary discussions, undermining the principle of nationhood central not only to the separatist movement, but to the Home Rule movement itself, were to have appalling consequences. They:-

> turned mainly on the question of the area to be excluded. Enormous trouble had been taken and Redmond told me later that a great map in relief had been constructed showing the distribution of Protestant and Catholic populations (in Ulster). This brought out with astonishing vividness the contrast; the Catholics were on the mountains and hilltops, the Protestants down along the valley lands, (Gwynn, Stephen, *John Redmond's Last Years,* London, 1919 p.122).

King George V called a conference to consider the situation. The vital question, as Dangerfield wrote (op. cit. p 412) was: '— should Ulster be excluded simply for a period of years, or should it be excluded forever?' It was discussed in several aspects for days. Clearly Ulster in its entirety could not be excluded, but what remained? Four counties, five counties, or what? And how were they to be decided? Instead of rejecting the partition proposal out-of-hand Redmond proposed a county by county option. Under that system, he believed, four counties and Belfast would be all that would remain in the United Kingdom. In that sense, not simply because of his acceptance of it in principle but also because it was the formula picked up and advanced at a crucial stage of the Treaty negotiations later on, some blame for partition may be said to rest with him.

For the modern student the point is that the question of excluding all or part of Ulster was a vital, compelling and already enduring issue years before the treaty negotiations with Britain took place. Thus we have the real prospect of partition of Ireland beginning to loom in Britain with Carson's proposal of 1912 until, by 1914, it was a virtually entrenched, and repeatedly advanced, feature of policy. It did not, as some historians seem to suggest, spring to life with the 1920 Government of Ireland Act; that simply provided the mechanism by which partition was effected. The principle, which was adhered to assiduously and enduringly by different British administrations, was already eight years old in 1920.

Even though the real and perceived threat of war and revolt came from the Unionists and their provisional government, there was an important element which would have been closely perceived in Whitehall and which would have coloured the British attitudes. It was that in spite of their threats and bluster, even to the quixotic extent of treason against Britain and possible civil war, the Unionists stood for, indeed visibly and vociferously represented, matters of internal British concern. 'Wrong-headed, but their hearts are in the right place, eh?' and all that. They were stupid; annoying; treasonable, if you like, but they hadn't actually **done** anything yet — except for those idiots in the Army, and they'd come to heel pretty dam' quick when the chips were down — and one could reach an accommodation with them. They simply didn't want Home Rule. It simply meant the Home Rulers would get less. It just needed to be worked out.

The Irish Volunteers and Sinn Fein were another and a different matter. That was also clear. The peasants were restless. As yet they were no threat, but what they stood for was disturbing. They wanted independence, of all ridiculous things. Should **they** become a threat it would be a very different matter; the security of the United Kingdom *might* then be at risk, and there could be no compromise on that. They were, after all, offered Home Rule — well, most of them. What more could they seriously want? Yet that didn't satisfy them. There could never be any question of accommodation on a possible threat to the United Kingdom itself. That was *sine qua non*.

That is how it was seen. It was on that basis that the British Government — as always in the spirit of Lord Palmerston's dictum — responded. Just now it was not, after all, the natives who were actually protesting. It was the colons. If and when the natives did so, well, that would be dealt with *vi et armis*. The Home Rule Bill was, in any case, as O'Hegarty puts it 'dead and out of date. The political situation had changed materially both in Ireland and in England. In Ireland the Bill itself and the political theory behind it, that Irish self-government was something which England was entitled to give or to withhold, no longer commanded any support' (O'Hegarty, op.cit. p. 744).

In November, 1913 Pearse had written in *An Claidheamh Soluis*: 'Whether Home Rule means a loosening or a tightening of England's grip on Ireland remains yet to be seen. But the coming of Home Rule, if come it does, will make no material difference in the nature of the work that lies before us: it will affect only the means we are to employ, our plan of campaign. There remains, under Home Rule as in its absence, the substantial task of achieving the Irish Nation.'

This political *danse macabre* raised temperatures in Ireland, where two things became very clear. First, that Home Rule (if it ever materialised) would be so watered down as to be little more than a local authority with, moreover, partition as a *de facto* inclusion and, secondly, that because of this Home Rule was now as unacceptable to the people in general, as it was to Unionists, if for vastly different reasons[89]. Separatism, which had been subordinate to constitutionalism since the Land Wars gave the rural population reality rather than image to fight for, began again to find both tongue and acceptance.

Give dreadful note of preparation. . . Shakespeare, Henry IV

Chapter 5

Outbreak of War to Easter 1916
Preparations for Action

W ITHIN DAYS OF THE 4 AUGUST DECLARATION of war by England against Germany the Supreme Council of the IRB met in the Gaelic League building 25 Parnell Square, Dublin, and took three crucial decisions[90]. The first was that preparations should be made for a rising i/ should a German Army invade Ireland; ii/ should England attempt to enforce conscription on Ireland and, iii/ if the war *looked like ending and a rising had not yet taken place* (author's italics), and which, as we will see was crucial. In any event 'we should rise in revolt, declare war on England and, when the conference was held to settle the terms of peace, we should claim to be represented as a belligerent nation'[91]. A Provisional Government was to be established with the outbreak of hostilities.

The second decision was to seek whatever help was possible from Germany, and the third was to create a military council to plan the rising. This was the fourth such IRB military council, and it was charged to 'prepare an insurrection *and secure control of the Volunteers*'(author's italics). Its first members were Pearse, Plunkett and Eamonn Ceannt[92]. Special purpose committees of the IRB were not unusual and it was not the Supreme Council of the IRB that appointed the military committee but the officer board of the IRB Executive, which consisted of the President, Denis McCullough, Tom Clarke, treasurer, and Diarmuid Lynch, acting secretary. Lynch, in the absence of McCullough (in Belfast) proposed and nominated the military committee.

'*To secure control of the Volunteers —*'. That statement of purpose is clear and specific. As we know the IRB was already not just involved with the Volunteers, it had been instrumental in forming and organising the entire Volunteer movement to its own agenda. For more than fifty years the IRB had waited to kindle the torch that now seemed almost ready.

So much was happening in Ireland, so many new movements were competing for a share of the limelight, in the decade before the First World War that it is hardly surprising that what in the end was to be the most significant of all these developments escaped the attention of most contemporaries. Admittedly, it was designed to escape their attention, for it was nothing less than the revival of the old, secret, separatist movement, the awakening into life once more of that phoenix which had been the emblem of the Fenians fifty years earlier. At the beginning of the twentieth century such a resurgence seemed, on the face of it, impossibly remote (O'Hegarty, op. cit. p.315).

The IRB decision to go to war with England **does not** mean that there was any prospect of military victory, but the existence of the Volunteers gave to a possible rising some prospect of its being a serious endeavour. Because of England's involvement in the war, the time was 'right' for the IRB to strike. The deliberate infiltration of the senior ranks of the Volunteers throughout the country was an important and valid tactical step essential if the IRB was to be in a position to control the Volunteers when the time came for action. Insofar as there was deception of the Volunteer command, it was limited to this. The IRB strategy already dominated the command structure of the Volunteers. The Volunteers numbered about 16,000 in all, the IRB about 2,000. That is not a total of 18,000, since virtually all IRB members were also Volunteers; the IRB represented about 12% of the total. With that kind of representation, particularly since most of the IRB members tended to be officers, control was by no means impossible.

That the Rising was a *coup de main* by the IRB over unsuspecting Volunteers, especially at Headquarters, is incontrovertible. That is not to say that, outside the IRB, there were not in the Volunteers those who expected and looked for a rising at some future date. There were. But they did not affect IRB policy-making. In fact in Dublin there were two policies; the apparent, Volunteer one and the real IRB one. Both emanated from Volunteer HQ, but one was planned in the closest secrecy, unknown to non-IRB Volunteer officers often sharing HQ duties, responsibilities and directorates with the planners. O'Hegarty emphasises that the IRB decision to use the equipment, organization and training of the Irish Volunteers was done without the knowledge of its Executive.

From the late twentieth century security of a comfortable place in a sovereign state, it is not easy to recreate the temper of the times. There are those who try, with myopic hindsight, to look back and argue that 1916 was wrong and unnecessary because its motivation and action do not conform with their own, contemporary, 'liberalistic' views. This nonsensical attempt to impose later values on an earlier period serves no purpose except to confuse. The fact is that (not counting the Unionist UVF) there were three organisations preparing one way or another for military action, namely the Volunteers, the IRB and the Irish Citizen Army — the last two for immediate action. There is no doubt, from Connolly's writings, that if the IRB — or the Volunteers — had not moved, then Connolly and his 200 men of the Citizen Army would have done so. Since the Citizen Army had no hope of even a sustained fight, they would have gone out in precisely the same spirit in which the Rising, in fact, occurred — that is to provide a catalyst for the recovery of national pride and spirit, and to seek international recognition for the nation's independence. It can hardly be doubted that if that had happened,

German arms or no, statements to the contrary notwithstanding, the IRB and many of the Volunteers would have come to their aid.

While arms and ammunition were critical, for the Volunteers shortage of ammunition was more critical than shortage of weapons.

German Plot

The 'German conspiracy' theory, later trumpeted by the British in an extra-ordinary way when the reality was long gone, did have some substance. But it can hardly be argued that the Germans took the question of a rising in Ireland as seriously, or supported it as strongly, as the Irish conspirators hoped — or, indeed, as their plans justified. The question is not whether or not there **was** a 'German conspiracy', the answer to which is clearly 'Yes, there was'. The really important questions are i/ who were involved; ii/ how was it seen in terms of military significance; iii/ what were its prospects of success; iv/ what was its extent and its respective motivations and objectives, v/ did it achieve its objectives and if not, why not? Up to the present most considerations have concentrated on question i/, a distorted version of v/ and, purely from the Irish point of view, ii/.

It involved, on the Irish side, the IRB, in particular its military committee (more usually called the military council), who were also all ranking Volunteer officers. Roger Casement, who was instrumental in organising the Howth gun-running expedition, was the archetypal romantic hero — so much so that he was distrusted and discounted by some of those he came in contact with in this connection, a notable exception being his experienced military advisor Robert Monteith. But, in turn, the IRB, Devoy[93] and the Germans appear to have decided that he was over-romantic and unreliable, to the detriment, it must be said, of Irish/German relations at a critical time, and the effect that this had on the plans for the Rising. (It is interesting to contrast the different responses to Casement and to Plunkett who also had a certain romantic air about him, but who was held in high esteem by his colleagues as a pragmatic and skilful military expert.)

In America were Clan na Gael, in particular John Devoy, and, on the German side there, Count von Bernstorff and Wolff von Igel, respectively Imperial German Ambassador and first secretary in Washington.

In Germany, initially, the Foreign Office in Berlin was involved, especially Count Bethmann Hollweg with whom Plunkett had dealings in 1915, as well as the German Admiralty, especially Captain Heydel of the Admiralty Staff, the German General Staff, including Count Nadolny, and the War Ministry. And last, but by no means least, Captain Karl Spindler of the *Aud*.

As to how the Rising was seen in terms of military significance, the views of the Irish and the Germans were, to say the least of it, poles apart — and widening from the beginning. At one point the German General Staff, initially enthusiastic, became quite the reverse. This is alleged to have been due to their loss of faith in Casement, but there may have been other factors that affected their outlook: for instance, the enormous demands on German resources when the French held their great — and expressly decisive — onslaught at Verdun, and then unexpectedly counterattacked. But there is no doubt that Casement's attempt to recruit an Irish

Brigade from prisoners of war in Germany was unsuccessful, no more than about a hundred being recruited.

The Irish view has been examined at length and was, essentially, in accordance with the IRB decisions mentioned above (p. 109). The timing, with Germany on the offensive and looking as if she could impose peace on her own terms, was more opportune than it had been, or was likely to be, for years. The German view was based on different considerations: a major rising in Ireland would tie down British troops; on sufficiently large a scale it might draw British troops from the Western front; it could cause unrest and expense on a large scale within the United Kingdom; it might be possible to construct submarine stations along the Irish coast; and, finally, the German General Staff 'reckoned on the possibility of a timely end being put to the war as the outcome of a successful uprising' (Spindler, Karl, *The Mystery of the Casement Ship*, Berlin, 1931 — originally an abridged edition, *Das Geheimnisvolle Schiff*, Berlin, 1920 — p. 265).

These considerations did not exist all the time between 1914 and 1916, and they were not all held with the same degree of confidence; nor were they all there, or in agreement, or held with maximum confidence at the same time. But essentially two factors determined the German attitude — firstly a strategic one, the extent, if any, to which an Irish uprising would benefit the German war effort; and, secondly, their confidence in the Irish to conduct a successful uprising. Of these the first was by far the more important to German interests. In that age of imperialism their concern for the rights of subject peoples was limited. They were themselves an imperial power with subject peoples and had little sympathy with suffragettes, nationalists and other 'dissidents'; they were experiencing problems in Poland not dissimilar to those of England in Ireland.

It should be remembered that the First World War altered the established tactics, strategy and philosophy of warfare in a way that not even the American civil war had done. A drawn-out war of attrition, unconditional surrender and national humiliation on a vast scale was not foreseen in 1914, and was, even in 1916, as yet uncertain. Both sides entered the war in the summer of 1914 expecting it to 'be over by Christmas' with, perhaps, economic and territorial gains for one side and war reparations on a more or less acceptable scale from the other. That it would result in the destruction of empires, nations and cultures was beyond comprehension and was to lead to a burgeoning belief (not to flower until after Hiroshima and Nagasaki thirty-one years later), in the 'destruction of civilisation'. German support for the Irish enterprise was, therefore, initially enthusiastic. It was based on the view that, once the balance had been decisively tipped in their favour, a speedy end to the war by negotiation was still possible. As matters developed that enthusiasm waned for the reasons mentioned and the General Staff were more relieved than anything else when the Admiralty Staff took over a much modified proposal.

As to its prospect of success, this was always governed by two contradictory factors. The first was the secrecy of the IRB regarding their plans (both as to the Rising itself and to the hijacking of the Volunteers to implement it). This not only gave rise to confusion, it also unsettled their methodical military allies. The second was the effect of this, and other apparent military inadequacies, on German confidence in the enterprise. A plan on the scale originally sought — 50,000 men with appropriate ancillary support — required detailed organisation, method and planning, in particular with regard to elementary logistics. What occurred was a conflict of systems. The professional military mind is notoriously wary of the amateur, usually for sound reasons. Lives and sometimes great enterprises are at stake. Evident inadequacies and uncertainty, even when added to a national *flair* for improvisation however well-intentioned, do not inspire confidence in the trained military mind at the best of times, let alone when battle is the subject.

That is not to suggest that the military mind is incapable of error in its own field, or that the amateur cannot produce a brilliant *coup*. The IRB secrecy, while obviously vital in itself and in Ireland, ensured a suspect confusion. But, equally, more detailed consideration by the Germans of the strategic and military merits of the Irish proposals was well justified, but did not occur. In short it should have been possible to overcome the apparent shortcomings on both sides, but that did not happen. If it had, coordination and adequate support in terms of men and munitions could have resulted in a different immediate outcome[94].

As to whether or not the Rising achieved its objectives; the answer, so far as the Irish are concerned, must be that it did — that is to say the Irish Republic was declared and broadcast to the world, it aroused separatist national fervour to the pitch where, within a short time, a war supported by the population in general was successfully undertaken against the British in the name of the Republic declared in 1916 with the object of national self determination. The only one of the three Irish objectives not achieved was a place at the post war peace conference, which was for reasons over which they had no control. So far as the Germans are concerned it had little effect on the course of the war . Almost all the troops used by the British to quell the Rising were — with the exception of some battalions on leave from the front — second-line troops. In the post-Rising period it did tie down a number of troops in Ireland for some time.

Critically and conveniently, the personnel of the IRB military committee also constituted the Military Committee of the Volunteers, without their dual role becoming known to the non-IRB members of the Volunteer general staff. The IRB plan envisaged using the 16,000 Irish Volunteers in the country together with the 200 or so Citizen Army men. These were to be the strike force of the insurrection. MacNeill, Chief-of-Staff of the Volunteers, was *not* in the confidence of the IRB. Supported by Hobson and O'Rahilly he favoured a strategy of reserving the Volunteers as a well-disciplined, but essentially protective, fighting force which would become a pressure-group **after the war** in seeking Home Rule, or something more; what, was unclear. But the Volunteers were to maintain a military role and be prepared for hostilities in the event of certain things — an attempt to impose conscription, for instance — happening. Then they would resort to *guerrilla* warfare[95].

The Citizen Army, much smaller than the Volunteers, was openly more rebellious. Connolly taunted the Volunteers in his paper, and wrote that if the

German army landed in Ireland men of the working class would be perfectly entitled to join it: 'if by so doing we could rid this country once and for all from its connection with the Brigand Empire that drags us unwillingly into this war'(*Irish Worker*). Towards the end of 1915 and the beginning of 1916 it looked to the IRB as if Connolly, unaware of IRB plans and, presumably, of their influence in the Volunteers, intended to precipitate a Rising with his little Citizen Army on the presumption that he would 'shame' the Volunteers into following suit. In fact he was putting the IRB plans in jeopardy. Consequently the IRB arranged a meeting between Connolly, MacNeill and Pearse at which MacNeill urged Connolly to be cautious. But 'Connolly was completely impervious to argument and pressed for an immediate insurrection, repeating his by now well-worn theme that whether or not the Volunteers came out, the Citizen Army would fight in Dublin. "I said" MacNeill recalled some months later, "that if he counted in that event on compelling us to fight rather than stand by and see his men destroyed, he was mistaken. We came to no agreement"'(Lyons, op.cit., p.346, citing *Eoin MacNeill on the 1914 (sic.) Rising*, ed. F.X.Martin, IHS, xii, 246, Memorandum II)[96].

Even though Home Rule was all but a dead issue after the split brought about by Redmond, the Volunteers still saw themselves as a counter-balance to the Ulster Volunteers. Gradually the view that they might have a role in a separatist context became 'an unspecified — sometimes speculative —' idea. That such speculation was encouraged by the IRB goes without saying. Clearly, even if there had been no Rising in 1916 there would, in accordance with the IRB's 1914 decisions (see p. 109), undoubtedly have been one soon afterwards, probably before the war was over and certainly before 1920.

Pearse, who became a member of the IRB in July, 1913, and who was a member of both military committees, was Volunteer Director of Organization, a position which made it possible for him to exercise very considerable control over that organisation — probably more than that of MacNeill himself. Other leading IRB members at this time were Bulmer Hobson, Tom Clarke, Sean McDermott, P.S.O'Hegarty, Tomas MacDonagh, Joseph Plunkett, Eamonn Ceannt and Denis McCullough. MacDonagh and Ceannt were also senior Volunteer officers in key positions. And, of course, Connolly's Citizen Army was also making military preparations.

O'Hegarty has an interesting comment to make about the preparations for the Rising; how dependable his remarks are is impossible to judge. He may be assuming, because he was unaware of certain developments, that others were also unaware of them, but it should be borne in mind that, although he was a highly placed member of the IRB, the IRB and its various cells were highly secret in all their activities and as a matter of policy did not unnecessarily disclose information — in particular sensitive information — except on a 'need to know' basis. O'Hegarty claims that since the Military Committee was set up by the IRB Supreme Council it was subordinate to that body, and was bound to report its proceedings to it, but that, instead, it reported only in a general way, and only as much as it chose. He goes further and makes the point that it is not clear if the entire military committee were involved in the decision-making process.

O'Hegarty suggests that Clarke, MacDermott, Pearse and Plunkett may have worked together as a group, with MacDonagh and others kept outside this inner circle. He also contends that even this inner body had a further core consisting of MacDermott and Plunkett who 'did things on their own, and possibly in association with Connolly after the latter had agreed to come behind the IRB'.

> There is, however, no doubt that the insurrection was prepared, date fixed and carried through without any sanction for an offensive, as distinct from a defensive, insurrection, from the Citizen Army, the Volunteers, or the IRB, these bodies being committed to it by Connolly, Pearse, Clarke and MacDermott. The last meeting of the IRB Supreme Council to be held before the Insurrection was held early in January, 1916, and it decided that there was to be no insurrection unless and until there had been another meeting by the Supreme Council and it should find an insurrection warranted and should sanction it. They were not, in fact, in January 1916, convinced that an offensive insurrection was warranted', (O'Hegarty, op. cit., p.699).

O'Hegarty does not offer any supporting source for these statements. In any case the points are now essentially academic. That an insurrection must take place before the end of the war was already agreed and sanctioned. Preparations obviously had to be in secret and a number of people who might have felt they *ought to have been in the know* would equally obviously have been kept in the dark for fear of jeopardising the plan. As events moved towards the decisive year 1916, 'it was becoming steadily clearer that the whole struggle was passing out of the sphere of peaceful argument and into the sphere of physical force' (Lyons, op.cit., p.319).

At the beginning of the century the key figures of the IRB and of the Rising, Clarke, McDermott, Ceannt, Pearse, were unknown to each other and widely scattered. Yet they were vital ingredients which, when brought together, provided the essential compound which made the rising possible and without which it probably would not have occurred — at least at that time. The critical year was 1907, when Clarke returned from the United States and McCullough and McDermott — already gaining an ascendancy in the declining IRB in Belfast — began, with the declaration of 1885 in mind, to look at the broader picture.

While Spain had been the ancient traditional ally and friendly neighbour of Ireland, its role in and influence on Irish affairs had been reduced, and since the 18th century two other countries had exercised an important and continuing effect on the course of events in Ireland — France and the United States. In the United States especially there was a huge pool of emigrants to provide both stimulus and money for political and physical-force activity at home, and, as we have seen, within the United States itself. But it was from Paris, the hot-house of European revolution, socialism, even anarchy, that, in the mid 19th century, there came two of the most dynamic Irishmen of their generation. These were James Stephens and John O'Mahoney, who had become close friends there. Inspired by their inherited ideals and principles (both came from prosperous nationalist backgrounds), they resolved to move towards independence. Since they were both able men of powerful conviction and determination and were both possessed of leadership qualities — virtually demagogic in the case of Stephens — they pursued this course with great energy. O'Mahoney went to the United States to organize the Irish there and Stephens returned to Ireland to organize at home, launching on St. Patrick's Day 1858, a new secret society with — as Lyons puts it (op. cit., p.125) — 'the old aim, "to make Ireland an independent democratic republic"'. It was highly secret and secretive and, although it was at the beginning — understandably and for that reason, perhaps — known by different names to different people in different countries, in 1873 these minor problems of definition were resolved and from the conference that resolved them the movement emerged as the Irish Republican Brotherhood, the IRB[97]. Clan na Gael, the American Fenian organisation, later became closely linked with it.

Between 1900 and 1907 the IRB, though quiescent, was, like the phoenix-egg, very much alive and waiting. Its Supreme Council was dominated by three men, Fred Allen, P.T.Daly and John Hanlon. But between 1907 and 1910 it had been taken over by young tigers, including Denis McCullough, Bulmer Hobson, Sean MacDermott, Sean MacBride, Dr. Patrick MacCartan, P.S.O'Hegarty and by one old, but vital, tiger Thomas Clarke[98]. It should be borne in mind that at the time they took over there was no thought of war in Europe.

Rumours of Rebellion

In November 1915 Sir Mathew Nathan and Augustine Birrell, respectively Permanent Under-Secretary to the Lord Lieutenant (Wimborne) and Chief Secretary, met Lord Midleton and Mr. Evelyn Cecil, two leading unionists. Nathan offered his views on the state of the country: he 'told them Ireland was going down the hill. Sinn Fein was edging out Mr. Redmond, the Volunteers were doing much mischief, and the young priests who supported them were very extreme' (O Broin, op. cit., p.54/55). Much of Nathan's intelligence was inadequate, and this observation contained more inaccuracies than accuracies. His information on the Rising, both before and after, is proof of the extraordinary inefficiency of British intelligence in Ireland at that time — perhaps because they believed that Home Rule was the acceptable answer to nationalist aspirations, just as they believed Redmond to be the national leader. They looked on themselves as a 'caretaker' administration. On the other hand, when they **were** provided in advance with accurate information regarding the proposed Rising, they ignored it.

By March 1916 Sir John French, GOC British Home forces (sacked, one recalls, after the Curragh Mutiny) was summarising for the adjutant general RIC reports on Ireland in this fashion: 'Certain parts of Ireland were in a very disturbed state and insurrection had been openly suggested in the public press' (O Broin, op.cit. p.70). As a result the adjutant general offered to apply for reserve infantry brigade(s) to be sent to Ireland if General Friend (Major-General Lovick Bransby Friend, GOC Ireland), wanted this. Friend replied that 'in the event of having to take serious action in support of the Royal Irish Constabulary against the disloyal organisations, I should be glad to have one or two brigades from England, and I would then, if all went well, ask for such troops to be left here for some months ...but at the present moment these anxieties are not quite so great as they were. Under these circumstances ... I do not propose to put forward an official application for additional troops...' (See O Broin op.cit., p.72/3).

This letter was dated 7 April, barely two weeks before the Rising and four weeks after information had been passed to the GOC Southern command at Queenstown (Cobh), Brigadier William Francis Howard Stafford, about plans for a German arms-landing in Kerry on 22 April. This was information which Stafford had obtained from Admiral Sir Lewis Bayly, also based at Queenstown, which in turn had been reported to him by Captain H.C.Hall, head of British naval intelligence. Coincidentally, several weeks earlier on 22 March Major Gen. G.M.W. MacDonagh, Director of Military Intelligence, had told French that 'he had received information from "an absolutely reliable source" that a Rising in Ireland was contemplated at an early date, and that the Irish extremists were in communication with Germany with a view to obtaining German assistance' (Ibid., p. 144)[99]. Yet on 10 April Nathan told the Adjutant General 'that he did not believe that the Sinn Fein leaders meant insurrection or that the Volunteers had sufficient arms if the leaders did mean it...' It was these words that may have finished Nathan. In point of time they were later than the latest statement of Birrell's and ... they prevented the military from taking the action that they considered necessary'(Ibid.).

On the very same day Major Ivor H. Price, Inspector-General of the RIC and Irish Command intelligence officer, told Nathan that 'There was undoubted proof that Sinn Fein Irish Volunteers were working up for a rebellion and revolution, if ever it got a good opportunity....' Informers whom the Government had placed in the Volunteer ranks reported regularly and similarly, one, in mid-April, to the effect that 'the young men of the Irish Volunteers were very anxious to start business (a rising) at once and they were being backed up strongly by Connolly and the Citizen Army, but that the heads of the Irish Volunteers were against a rising at present' (O Broin op.cit., p.75).

All of this was quite accurate, so far as it went. It confirms the success of the IRB's policy of secrecy. But that policy was so complete that it became, in the end, self-defeating. 'Secrecy was undoubtedly indispensable if surprise was to be achieved, but it was pushed to such extremes that it ultimately defeated its purpose. With a few exceptions the key figures in the Volunteer movement were only alerted in Holy Week, and their instructions were so rigid that they were left with no possibility of improvising when, as in Kerry, the basic plan went wrong'. This very strong statement by O Broin (p.153) goes, perhaps, too far. But, up to Spy Wednesday, the extraordinary fact is that not more than a handful of men, including Casement (who, although not a member of the IRB, was in Germany trying to secure help) and Devoy knew when the Rising was to take place, and until the day of the Rising itself only the Military Committee and three or four other Volunteer officers knew what the operational plans were. The confusion resulting from orders and countermanding orders, rather than inflexible instructions, was the principal reason that the Rising was not more widespread. In point of fact it seems clear that if IRB orders were as inflexible as suggested by O Brion, the countermanding order of MacNeill (who was not an IRB member) should not have affected them.[100]

By the beginning of 1916 Connolly's taunts were a serious threat to the plans of the Military Council who feared that they might attract the attention of the British authorities (as indeed they appear to have done). It was to offset this threat that Pearse persuaded MacNeill to intervene with Connolly on the grounds that Connolly's ridicule was diminishing the position and prestige of the Volunteers. But, as we saw, to no avail. *Connolly was adamant that a Rising should take place soon and that if the Volunteers would not participate, then the Citizen Army would do so alone.*

At that stage neither Connolly nor MacNeill knew of the IRB's military council, or its plans. Connolly continued to heap scorn on the Volunteers, on whom the military council depended for a successful rising. Suddenly and mysteriously, on 19 January 1916, Connolly disappeared for three days. Equally suddenly, after he reappeared, the scornful references also stopped and all reference to the Volunteers, other than in neutral terms, vanished from his columns. What had happened?

There are contradictory opinions. Some argue that Connolly was kidnapped by the IRB and held prisoner until he was convinced to 'lay-off'. He was released just before Connolly's second-in-command, Michael Mallin, was about to confront the Volunteer Executive. And yet Connolly was in the habit of disappearing unannounced, therefore such a disappearance should not, in the normal course, have caused undue alarm. It is equally plausible that the IRB simply asked Connolly for discussions. This would explain Mallin's otherwise odd proposed action — odd in the sense that if it were a secret 'kidnap', where would Mallin know where to look? Certainly, the kidnap theory makes a better story. Connolly himself never spoke or wrote of his disappearance in any detail.

Several writers, including O'Neill (op. cit. p.29), accept the 'kidnap' theory. It is argued that Connolly was brought before the Military Council and told he'd be held prisoner unless he agreed not to take action before they were ready; that he held out for three days but finally agreed to await the Committee's decision. In return, it is held, the Military Council agreed to act, and fixed Easter Sunday as the date for the Rising.

These melodramatic accounts, though they follow the general 'kidnap' outline, don't ring correct. Their obvious weaknesses are i/ Connolly was demanding action; the IRB were already planning action; ii/ that being so there was no need to hold him for three days on that score. It makes more sense to assume (which is all one can now do) that the three days were spent largely in reconciling plans and fixing dates. What is beyond question is that during those three days he and the Military Committee exchanged frank views and reconciled their differences. Connolly was sworn into the IRB shortly afterwards. He did not attack the Volunteers in his paper again.

In an Appendix (p. 268) to the second (1949) edition of **his** book, Ryan has this to say about Connolly's alleged kidnapping:

Joseph Plunkett told his sister, Mrs. Gertrude Dillon, in January, 1916, that Connolly had been decoyed into a taxi and driven to a house outside Dublin. Plunkett, Pearse, MacDermott were also in the car. They informed Connolly at once of their plans for insurrection, and insisted he must discuss their differences once and for all. The discussions lasted three nights and the Rising plans, based on Plunkett's scheme, were adopted in outline. Connolly, at first angry, became so enthusiastic that his captors *could hardly persuade him to leave*. A Volunteer on duty in the house informed the writer that no attempt to detain Connolly was made. The house was near Chapelizod.

During the three days the Military Committee convinced Connolly that their way was best. When he was released he was a *de facto* member of the council, and his lips (and pen) were tight shut.

In January, too, Asquith reluctantly indicated that he would consider some form of compulsory recruitment. Conscription became a factor that affected attitudes right across the spectrum of society, not just in Ireland, but in Britain as well. Up to then — indeed until later that year — the British military contribution to the war was through its small (by European battle standards) volunteer army. By April conscription was no longer a question of 'if' or 'maybe' and, together with the executions following Easter week and the imposition of martial law, later became one of the the the main factors in persuading the general public to support what came to be called 'the Sinn Fein movement'.

Politically in Britain the war, more than anything else, popularised the Conservatives — or at least their policies — and damned the Liberals. The Conservatives were blatantly what today would be called hawks in a 'gung-ho' war-party, while the Liberals were being very cautious doves, even half-hearted and nervous. This nervousness was, of course, political, and the big issue was conscription. But the Liberals dithered so much that they got the mood of Britain wrong, whereas aggressive Conservative war policies carried much more popular appeal. The Liberals alone had provided a reluctant war-cabinet. It was not until May, 1915, that Asquith included Opposition members in Government. Then there was an almost immediate split in Government between the Conservative 'Hawks' and the Liberal 'Doves'. Kitchener demanded an army of 3,000,000 and this, and how to achieve it, became the essential political questions in Britain. The Liberals, by and large, were opposed both to the idea of so large an army and to conscription, which was proposed as a means of achieving it. Conscription, therefore, became a second club with which the Torys might beat the Liberal Party.

In April 1916, Asquith — then virtually at the end of his political career — wrote: 'In the circumstances the Government have no alternative but to proceed with legislation for general compulsion' (Asquith to King George V, 29/4/1916, Asquith MS — cited Sheila Lawlor, *Britain and Ireland, 1914-23*, London, 1983). Redmond, too, wrong-footed himself over conscription. With the exception of the Unionists and some of his own party, there was almost universal opposition to the idea in Ireland. Between January and April bishops and clergy came out in opposition to it — a fact which separatists latched onto avidly — and by mid April, with the Rising just a week away, public opinion was vigorously anti-conscription. Nonetheless Redmond supported it.

It is commonplace now, in an era when nationalism is both misunderstood and unfashionable, to attribute to Pearse, especially, the doctrine of blood-sacrifice which has become almost ineradicably associated with 1916, as if the event and its motivation occurred in isolation.[101]

The leaders of 'the secret movement within the secret movement'; and those of the Volunteers who, like MacNeill, were not members of the IRB, were not of one mind when it came to what circumstances justified a rising. It was MacNeill's view that, with one important qualification, a rising — or war to give it its proper name — was not justified unless it had 'a reasonably calculated' prospect of success. The qualification he allowed to this was: 'if the destruction of our nationality was in sight and if we came to the conclusion that at least the vital principal of nationality was to be saved by laying down our lives then we should make that sacrifice without hesitation'. The view of Pearse, Plunkett and McDonagh was, in effect, that the point had been reached where the destruction of the Irish nationality was at least in question, and only an action as grave and dramatic as an armed uprising would be enough to stir the people to a reassertion of their independence as a nation.

It is clear that there was a basic difference of opinion at another level between MacNeill and the IRB military planners on the kind of campaign the Irish might conduct in the event of war. MacNeill speaks in terms of 'the prospect of success', meaning military success — hence his plan for guerrilla warfare given the appropriate provocation. But neither a sustained guerrilla campaign nor military victory were envisaged by the IRB military planners. Moreover, the prospect of waging such a campaign in 1916, or at any time during the war *in the absence of a catalyst such as the Rising*, was much less than it became in 1919 -1921.

As for justification, the facts were sufficient justification. The argument which holds that rebellion is only justified when the evils of the existing regime are intolerable and can be removed in no other way, and when there is a real prospect of success, does not apply (although it was what restrained MacNeill). It does not apply because it is relevant only to a domestic 'regime' and not to a foreign conqueror. To maintain otherwise is to accept the principle of *force majeur* and, in this case, the Act of Union.

The theology of Rebellion has been argued *ad nauseam* and with prolific hindsight — in connection with the 1916 Rising. F. X. Martin expressed it (**1916 — Revolution or Evolution**, *Leaders and Men of the Easter Rising: Dublin 1916*, London, 1966, p.248): 'Many have wrestled with the problem of formulating a justification for the Easter Rising, but they have not found it an easy task'. It is doubtful if those involved in planning the Rising would agree. For them the justification was self-evident and inherited. Action was a matter of means and opportunity. If the Rising had not taken place when it did, it would have taken place soon afterwards. Of that there can be no doubt. The moral validity of the struggle of 1916 and the moral fibre of those who were engaged in it were inextricably bound together, giving to those involved an almost unassailable moral position. They took the moral high ground, and held it, forcing the British into the invidious position that no matter what they did (and some of it was appalling) it would reflect badly on themselves and force them into contravening essential and basic human rights and principles. The Rising reawakened the sense of a separate Irish identity, which had been eroded, in the people.

The Easter Rising established permanently, as the dominant tradition in the country, the Irish way of looking at the most vital interests of its own citizens (Martin, op. cit., p.252).

Nevertheless MacNeill's dilemma was shared by many, both Volunteers and other separatists. There were two other points of concern. The first was the Catholic Church's condemnation of secret societies; the second was a nervousness of having anything to do with the Germans, who were at war with a traditional Irish ally, France. 'On these ...two points the Proclamation of the Republic was explicit: Ireland's manhood had been organised and trained primarily through the secret revolutionary organisation, the Irish Republican Brotherhood, and was seizing an opportunity to strike, supported "by gallant allies in Europe"'(O Broin op. cit., p.154). The claim that Ireland's manhood was organised and trained by the IRB holds good **only** if it is accepted that a majority of the Volunteer officers were also IRB officers. If that is accepted, then the possibility for a more wide-spread and more lasting Rising is, by that very fact, increased.

The relative available strengths before the Rising are really of academic interest since only a fraction of the available Volunteers and Citizen Army were actually involved (although it is interesting and suggestive that, in proportion to their overall numbers, and due one assumes to the fact that they were not affected by MacNeill's countermanding order, there were far more Citizen Army men involved than Volunteers)[102].

According to Lyons the conclusion Mac Neill drew was 'eminently sensible, but psychologically unsound'. Mac Neill pointed out that the British troops could overpower the Volunteers at any time and that, accordingly, the Volunteers should not give provocation, but should build up their strength and, above all, hold on to their arms. It was only on this last point (or given definite major German military assistance) that Mac Neill conceded that the Volunteers might fight — a point to become of some significance (if only academically) later on. 'I have not the slightest doubt ...'Mac Neill wrote, ' that we are morally and in every way justified in keeping by all necessary force such arms as we have got or can get. I hold myself entitled to resist to death any attempt to deprive me of any arms or ammunition or other military material that I have or can protect for the Irish Volunteers'(See Lyons, op.cit., p.349). .

Yet this argument, which remained throughout the basis of his whole position was, for two reasons, much more dangerous than he seems to have realised. One was that by stating so clearly that the seizure of arms would be the signal for fighting to begin, he put himself at the mercy of every rumour or false alarm, deliberately contrived or not, that this was about to happen, and thus committed the Volunteers in advance to a battle of which he would have chosen neither the time nor the place. But the second danger was even greater. It came from the fact that he was asking desperate and excitable men to observe *indefinitely* an unnatural restraint. In asking this he was underestimating the amount of tension and aggression that the mere possession of arms by a justly motivated force can engender.

The valid point emphasised by Lyons is that the Volunteers were an amateur body led by amateur military leaders. It follows that they possessed that curious combination of considerable moral discipline with a corresponding lack of routine — and often boring — military experience, often common to such forces. But the risk, as MacNeill would have seen it, of precipitate action by the Volunteers was less real than the possibility of precipitate action by the Citizen Army. About the influence of the IRB he was evidently less aware.

The Howth and Wicklow gun-running had produced a mere 1,500 old rifles and, as Lyons points out, most of the Volunteers were unarmed and many of those who were lacked ammunition. The build-up of arms was therefore, clearly and properly, an important priority. Any attempt to seize Volunteer weapons would, of necessity, have been localised (unless the authorities either a/ made a sweep or b/ attacked the Volunteers *en masse*). Such action seemed unlikely, as the authorities were both complacent and unprepared. When they finally reacted to the warnings they'd been receiving, the plan, based it is thought on existing contingency Army plans and proposed by Lt. Col. W. Edgeworth at a meeting in the vice-regal lodge on Easter Sunday night, was to arrest the Volunteer leaders in Dublin, and round up others on succeeding days. The Volunteer leadership would, of course, have understood that some such contingency plan existed. Taken in this general context MacNeill's policy was, on the whole, a cautiously pragmatic one of building up his logistical base before any attack. But control of events was, by this time, out of his hands.

Clearly one of the major questions relating to the Rising is: Why did MacNeill, the Chief-of-Staff of the Volunteers, try to cancel the Rising at the last minute? Even though he was a not a military man, he should have realised the confusion that must surely follow. He must also have understood that any rising was, to say the very least, problematical. He had been misled by Pearse, McDonagh and Plunkett and, to a lesser extent, by Connolly with regard to the nature and extent of help from Germany. Was it, therefore, because he felt the Rising would fail for want of German help? Because he felt it would fail anyway? Because he was aggrieved that it had been organised without his knowledge? For some other reason? In fact the plans for the Rising, while far from offering any prospect of a military success, did outline a strategy which provided for a nationwide uprising, concentrated on Dublin, from which there would in due time be an orderly withdrawal westward and then, perhaps, guerrilla fighting before any surrender. The idea was that sufficient international attention would have been generated in the meantime to ensure two essentials: — 1/ that the Irish people's will was for independence and 2/ that Ireland would be recognised as a belligerent nation at the post-war Peace Conference.

With regard to the second of these essentials, it is important to emphasise two points. Firstly, in 1916 it was an even bet that Germany would win the war or force an advantageous peace. Secondly, America had not entered the war on the side of the Allies *and* showed no intention whatever of doing so on either side. Accordingly the Irish strategy, German help or no, was hardly as doom-laden as is often postulated.

But, as is a matter of historical record, many of the essential parts of the plan went awry at the critical moment, in particular the landing in Tralee Bay of 20,000 rifles and ten machine-guns, with adequate ammunition from Germany. This was due to a forlorn chain of events, but mainly to inadequate planning by both the

Irish and German authorities. The failure to land the German arms had a profound affect on the essential dynamic, philosophy and extent of the Rising and it is in that context that MacNeill's decision must be judged.

MacNeill changed his mind twice between Good Friday and Easter Saturday. From being opposed, he gave his reluctant consent when he first heard of *Aud*. When he learned it had been captured he changed his mind again. For him the arms were clearly the critical factor. But the arms were never destined for Dublin. They were to be used in the south and west to enable Volunteers to hold the line of the Shannon, where they would meet the Dublin Volunteers when they withdrew. The original plan called for a nationwide rising with its main first strike in Dublin. Evidently, then, MacNeill must have been — even if reluctantly — satisfied that the men and weapons in Dublin were sufficient for their task. Had he not changed his mind on the second occasion, upwards of 3,000 men would have been available in Dublin.

MacNeill felt that not only himself, but the Volunteers as a body, had been deceived by the 'war-party', and so they had. The Volunteers were the only body in any position to render a rising feasible[103]. The ordinary Volunteers were well aware of this and the argument that a majority of them did not anticipate such an event *at some stage or another* is unrealistic. But the Volunteers were not the IRB. The secrecy and confusion resulting from the intense intrigue, plus the need to reassure (falsely) MacNeill and others from time to time, caused uncertainty and ill-will between IRB members and non-members, some of it to linger for decades. Indeed this foundation is thought to have contributed to the colouring of some attitudes during the civil war. While the IRB were aware of the cause — essential secrecy — of this uncertainty, the vast bulk of the Volunteers were not. It was, therefore, for the IRB, a calculated risk based both on experience and sound principle. The experience was of informers wrecking plans in the past; the principle was that of need-to-know, and if some confusion resulted, it was the lesser of two evils. The initiative that Easter week-end 1916 was, at all times, with the IRB.

At Volunteer headquarters a tense and somewhat unreal situation developed. On the one side were MacNeill, Hobson and O'Rahilly, whose view was that the Volunteers should gradually accumulate strength and fight only if an attempt were made to suppress them, or if conscription were attempted, or in the event of a German landing. On the other side were Pearse, Plunkett, McDermott, McDonagh and Ceannt, supported by Connolly, who were planning a rising proclaiming Ireland's independent status which would win domestic and international approval.

From late 1915 and through the winter and spring of 1916 MacNeill seems to have suspected that there was a plot but, apart from seeking assurances from Pearse — which he received — he does not seem to have taken any steps to verify the suspicions for which he had sound reason.

By the beginning of April, despite all the disclaimers he had received, MacNeill was again becoming anxious about the rumours of an impending outbreak and on the fifth of that month he secured the consent of the headquarters staff that, apart from routine matters, no order would be issued to the Volunteers without being countersigned by him. It appears that once again he received an assurance from Pearse that no independent action was being contemplated (F.X.Martin, ed., *Eoin MacNeill on the 1916 Rising; Memorandum II*, pp. 247 — 255/6).

Then, on 19 April, into the picture arrives a mysterious paper which came to be known as 'The Castle Document'. Some authorities maintain that it is a forgery by Plunkett and/or MacDonagh intended to provoke the Volunteers (particularly MacNeill) into action. Others hold that, in view of the Castle plans to round up 'Sinn Fein' leaders, the document was genuine. There is no reason to suppose it wasn't both. It is inconceivable that the military authorities (the document was signed by General Friend) did not have contingency plans to round up and arrest Volunteer and Sinn Fein leaders. That plan, proposed by Col. Edgeworth at the vice-regal lodge on Easter Sunday (23 April), followed the broad outline of 'The Castle Document'. It is also not unlikely that Plunkett, having seen or obtained details of the genuine article, 'modified' and made use of it to suit IRB intentions. The two situations are far from being mutually exclusive.

On the other hand it must be borne in mind that the provenance of this paper has never been verified. The British military were long in favour of some such action and had only been prevented from taking it by Nathan's veto (See O Broin, op. cit.). In view of this veto it would have been quite natural for the subsequent denial when the document was published. It is clearly an 'either/or' situation. It was undoubtedly useful to Plunkett and the others in bringing pressure to bear on MacNeill at the proper time. It may have been a product, or adaptation, by Plunkett or McDermott, or it may have been a fortuitous out-fall from a genuine memorandum prepared by Friend, but halted or postponed by Nathan. It is one of the eventful aspects of the run-up to 1916 that is likely to remain a mystery. In this case, as with much else to do with 1916, the provenance of this document is not the superior issue, which it tends to overshadow. The issue is the effect which publication of the document might have had on the Volunteers.

On 19 April, Spy Wednesday, a few days before the Rising was due to take place Alderman Tom Kelly read to Dublin Corporation a document described as a decipher of a paper on the official files of the Castle, giving details of an order that General Friend had signed for large-scale raids on buildings in the city, as part of a plan for disarming the Volunteers. The Government, it was alleged by Patrick J.Little, the editor of *New Ireland*, had embarked on this course with the intention of provoking armed resistance and deliberately causing bloodshed. It was officially denied that any such document existed or ever existed; and some people saw through it immediately.

Whether it was forged or genuine the timing of its public release was right, as MacNeill's response shows. Although, according to Lyons (page 354), he later came to regard the document as false, immediately on discovering the document MacNeill held a meeting at headquarters and issued a general order instructing the Volunteers to be prepared to resist suppression.

The document may have been a *ruse de guerre* by Plunkett and McDermott, calculated to create the atmosphere they wanted. But that it was based on a genuine Castle plan is equally likely. There can be little doubt that the British military had contingency plans to arrest the Irish leaders, nor can there be any doubt that these plans existed in written form.

After the Rising Nathan stated that 'no such document nor any similar document was or had been in existence in the files of Dublin Castle or elsewhere. 'I find that what purported to be a decipher of this imaginary document was circulated to many people of position in Irish affairs. You may be able to judge what was the wicked purpose of this'. In reading this one must bear in mind that Nathan, for all that he was a civil servant, was a very political animal, who, within a few weeks, would be held by a Royal Commission of Inquiry to share responsibility for the rising by 'not having impressed on the Chief Secretary... the necessity for more active measures ... which he had described as "most serious and menacing"' before the rising. It is also the case that at the very moment the Rising broke out he had, in fact, plans to arrest and intern upwards of 100 leaders of the Volunteers, as arranged at the Viceregal Lodge on Easter Sunday night. Therefore, while the document may, or may not, be a forgery; while Nathan may well make the claim above, it is highly likely that some documentation of such a nature existed. And the Castle Document, or some version of it, is as good a candidate as any.

Late on Holy Thursday night Bulmer Hobson discovered from J.J. (Ginger) O'Connell (who later figured in the events leading to the outbreak of the civil war in 1922), that general command orders had been issued for a rising to take place on Easter Sunday. He immediately went to MacNeill's house to inform him. MacNeill was in bed, but when he heard the news he went with Hobson and O'Connell to St. Enda's to confront Pearse, who only a short time before, had reassured him on this very point.

'Then for the first time I learned by Pearse's admission what was intended' wrote MacNeill. A confrontation between the two men ensued, MacNeill declaring that he would do everything possible — 'short of informing the government' — to stop the insurrection. Pearse answered that MacNeill was powerless to do so and added, reasonably and accurately enough in the circumstances, that interference now would only cause confusion. MacNeill left and prepared orders countermanding those issued by Pearse for a general muster of the Volunteers on Sunday. O'Connell was sent to Cork to take control of the situation in the south. However, before he issued new orders on Good Friday, MacNeill was visited by the three IRB men who had issued the mobilisation orders — namely Pearse, McDonagh and MacDermott. They persuaded him that new countermanding orders would not only be counter-productive, but extremely dangerous. They would, they argued, create confusion, would be ignored in many areas and would not, therefore, prevent but significantly weaken the rising. MacNeill remained unmoved until he learned that a German arms shipment was *en route*, and then agreed to let the mobilisation orders stand. He went further and drafted a 'circular', presumably based on what he'd learned from the 'Castle Document', to be distributed to the Volunteers in general warning them that government action to suppress them was inevitable and might begin at any moment. But the plans for the arms shipment — and, indeed, the shipment itself — had gone completely awry.

The Arms Ship

The full story is as romantic as one could wish and is — or at least much of it is — told by Spindler (*The Mystery of the Casement Ship*. But see also *The Sea and the Easter Rising*, John de Courcy Ireland, National Maritime Museum, Dun Laoghaire). Spindler was a Leutnant of the Kaiserlich Kriegsmarine. Negotiations between the Irish and the German authorities had been continuous, if intermittently intensive, since Casement landed in Germany in 1914. The Germans eventually took Casement's representations — and, consequently those of other Irish sources — much less seriously either than the Irish wished or than the situation might have warranted. It was a time when it looked as if the Central Powers — Germany, Austro-Hungary, Turkey — might achieve a satisfactory peace settlement; a time also when the German High Command would not have been anxious for military resources to be diverted from the Western front where the critical battle of Verdun was being planned. It was France, after all, which was its principal adversary, not the relatively small British Expeditionary Force. Consequently Casement's demand for 50,000 troops with naval and air support fell on deaf ears, and the more it was made the deafer those ears became. A German suggestion that men of Casement's Irish Brigade be sent for the Rising was turned down on the grounds, as Monteith expressed it: 'even should they have had the good fortune to get through the blockade, every man would have gone into action with a rope around his neck.'

Before Casement left for Germany he wrote an open letter to the Press from New York dated September 17, 1914, two days after Asquith had given his pledge that the Home Rule Bill would not come into operation without an Amending Bill. It was probably this letter, as much as anything else, that roused the vicious hostility of the English Establishment he spurned so powerfully against him (See Appendix Two).

Coming as it did from someone who had been honoured by the British Government for his humanity, integrity and allied sense of purpose, this statement, redolent of burning anger, must certainly have moved Casement to the very top of the British 'Black List' — a by no means mythical catalogue. The plan to send arms to Ireland had been initiated six months beforehand. In October, 1915, the Military Attache of the German Embassy in Washington forwarded to Berlin a letter which reached the General Staff in November. That letter from John Devoy outlined Irish plans for a rising, based on Irish resistance to proposed conscription, and suggested that arms be sent to help, Fenit being a suitable landing point (Spindler, op. cit., p.238). Apart from the request for assistance, two things are noteworthy about this letter; firstly that it was sent seven months before the Rising occurred, and, secondly that several non-IRB people knew of it. It is possible that Devoy's communication was on the basis of a rising 'in principle', which did not conflict with Volunteer attitudes.

In February 1916, the Military Council of the IRB told Devoy in New York that a rising was intended for Easter Sunday, just over a month ahead. It was ludicrously inadequate notice, given the state of communications at the time, bearing in mind that messages to Berlin had to go from Ireland to New York and thence to Germany, often by way of South America and Madrid. In transmitting the message, on 17 February, however, either Devoy or the Imperial German Ambassador in Washington, Count Bernstorff, altered the date of the proposed arms landing, suggesting instead of Easter Sunday that the arms should be landed *between Good Friday and Easter Sunday* — 'Irish leader Devoy tells me that revolution begins Ireland Easter Sunday stop Request deliver arms between Good Friday and Easter Sunday Limerick Westcoast Ireland stop protracted waiting impossible comma desire cabled answer whether may promise help from Germany — Bernstorff', (Imperial German Embassy, New York, telegram No. 675). If this was an attempt to ease the timing schedule, or confuse the enemy, it failed on both counts.

The British had already broken the German secret code and were monitoring all wireless traffic to and from German sources. They accordingly picked up Devoy's message from New York to Berlin and alerted British naval and military authorities in Ireland — which, with the exception of Naval HQ at Queenstown (Cobh), added a touch of farce to the situation by paying the alert no attention whatsoever.

The German response to Devoy's cable was also picked up by the British and passed on. It was that they would land 20,000 rifles and ten machine guns with 4,000,000 rounds of ammunition, besides 400 kilograms of explosives, at Tralee Bay 'between April 20th and April 23rd' — thus moving the time-table back yet another day. Alarmed by this, Devoy answered specifically that the arms should be landed on Easter Sunday, 23 April. By the time his response reached Berlin the arms ship had sailed.

The arms were loaded aboard the captured English steamer *Castro*, renamed *Libau*, which sailed on Sunday, 9 April. It was a modern steamer, highly suitable for the purpose, but it had no wireless. This question had come up for consideration at a meeting at the headquarters of the German admiralty staff on 17 March but was deferred, as no ship had been selected at that stage, and it was agreed that the question 'could only come up for discussion if the steamer carried electric plant on board — this was subsequently not the case, unfortunately' (Spindler, op.cit., p.253).

Libau sailed from Luebeck with a cargo of pit-props, tin baths, enamelled steelware, wooden doors, window-frames and other building materials besides the main cargo, which was carefully concealed. The ship was also booby-trapped and was disguised at sea as the Norwegian trader, the *Aud*, with the words AUD-NORGE painted in large letters on its sides. After a horrendous voyage which took them above the Arctic Circle, Spindler made the correct landfall in accordance with his instructions on the afternoon of 20 April, three days too early. He lay between Inishtooshkert and the mainland, signalling the shore as instructed, expecting an answering signal and a pilot boat to guide him to Fenit pier. But neither came. What had happened?

Firstly, of course, the times were truly out of joint. The Irish were not expecting the arms ship until Saturday night at the earliest, preferably Sunday; the

Germans understood that any time between Thursday and Sunday was suitable, while either von Bernstorff or Devoy — who did re-emphasise Sunday, but too late — had indicated a time between Friday and Sunday.

Secondly, The British were aware of the possibility of an attempted landing of arms on a large scale, and of a threatened rising, and the admiral at Queenstown (the only British officer to actively heed the intelligence about an arms landing from Germany) had patrols watching the western approaches ready to intercept such an attempt. The American secret service had raided a German mission in New York where they found messages from Dublin about the rising, together with one already sent to Berlin (too late) with the specific demand that the arms-landing should not take place until the night of Easter Sunday, 23 April. The Americans immediately passed these messages to the British, who did not, evidently, act on them with the same degree of urgency.

Thirdly, the local Volunteer commander, vice-Commandant Patrick Cahill of the Tralee battalion, had obtained the two green fishing lamps which were the signal agreed to be shown *between Easter Saturday evening and the early hours of Easter Monday*. On Easter Thursday, the day *Aud* hove to, or steamed between the Blaskets and the mainland in 90 fathoms of water. Spindler, congratulating himself on his precise timing, sought in vain for the signal from the mainland. That same Thursday the pilot, Mort O'Leary of Castlegregory, was on his way home after meeting vice-commandant Cahill who had, for security reasons, waited until then before finalising arrangements. As he walked towards his house he spotted *Aud* lying off Inishtooskert: 'however, he had been told that the German ship would be a small one and that she would not arrive before Easter Sunday at the earliest, so he presumed that she was a British decoy ship and went home and forgot about it' (Max Caulfield, *The Easter Rebellion*, London, 1964, p.49).

Fourthly, Roger Casement had left Germany to be in Ireland when the rising took place. Because the Germans were not going to send the expeditionary force of (50,000 men, with artillery), that he had asked for, Casement had reached the conclusion that a rising should be postponed. Because of this an erroneous assumption that he sailed with the intention of 'stopping' the Rising is common, in spite of all the evidence to the contrary, and has been spread by some historians (including Roger McHugh and T.P. Coogan), of which the following is an example:

> Though he became a republican and endeavoured to secure German support for the 1916 Rising, he too was never a member of the IRB and ultimately like MacNeill did his best to stop the Rising (T. Desmond Williams, *Eoin MacNeill and the Irish Volunteers* Martin — ed — op. cit, p. 142).

There is nothing in Casement's own writings, or those of his companions, to support this view; on the contrary. Because of the limited nature of the proposed German help Casement **had** reached the **conclusion** that a rising should not take place. But he did not return to do 'his best to' try to stop the Rising. He returned to take part in it. It was he, after all, who was largely responsible for arranging that the arms shipment from Germany. The theory that he came from Germany to 'stop' the Rising may have originated with Eva Gore-Booth (Countess Markievicz's sister), who wrote a letter during Casement's trial making this allegation — presumably in an attempt to moderate the case against him (see extract from Sir Basil Thompson's diaries for 22 July, 1916, cited by Alfred Noyes *The Accusing Ghost or Justice for Casement*, London, 1957, p. 17). Thomson interrogated Casement and, with Captain Reginald Hall of Naval intelligence, was largely responsible for the circulation of the so-called 'extracts' from Casement's diary[104].

The idea that Casement returned to 'stop' the Rising (which he was in no position to do), may be a misinterpretation of his anxiety to *postpone* it if possible[105]. There is no doubt that Casement was not in favour of a rising which was not backed by a powerful force of men and arms from Germany (or elsewhere) and he had little faith in a successful military outcome for the Rising as planned. There is no doubt, from his own writings, that he believed he was going to his death. Nor is there any doubt that he insisted — for weeks before, so the question of its being a late, hurried decision does not arise — on returning to Ireland in spite of express orders from both Ireland and America to remain in Germany. But to conclude from this that he came to Ireland to 'stop' the Rising contradicts the obvious:

1/. He was in no position to do so.
2/. Even if he were, he would not have had the time. So far as he knew the Rising would take place at any time between Good Friday and Easter Sunday night — he landed, weak and extremely ill, on Good Friday.
3/. Casement himself had negotiated the German arms which sailed in *Aud*.
4/. Captain Robert Monteith, who was with him, expressly denies the allegation.
5/. The decision to send Casement to Ireland by submarine was made on 7 April only, two days before *Aud* sailed.
6/. And (though Casement did not know this), the conduct of the Rising was not in the hands of the Volunteers, but in those of the IRB and the Citizen Army[106].

It may be in this context that confusion arises. Casement thought of a rising in terms of possible military success, but this, as we know, was not what the IRB contemplated. Of course if a massive German landing occurred that could alter the picture, but such was never really on the cards; even without such assistance a rising was contemplated anyway. It was elementary common sense to indicate to Germany that a military victory was a major option.

In April, 1915, Plunkett had gone to Germany from Switzerland, where he was being treated for thyroid tuberculosis. There he met the Imperial Chancellor, von Bethmann-Hollweg, representatives of the General Staff and Casement[107]. It is interesting that throughout, in spite of the work he was entrusted with in both the United States and Germany, and in spite of the fact that he knew a rising was about to take place, Casement was evidently under the impression that it was planned by Volunteer, not IRB, leadership. This view was apparently encouraged by

Joseph Plunkett whose father, Count Plunkett, contacted Casement in Germany in April, 1916, from Berne. He told him, amongst other matters, that he was 'sent here as a delegate by the President and Supreme Council of the Irish Volunteers (a non-existent body), to confirm the date of the rising. The letter was dated 5 April and Casement received it on the sixth, just over two weeks before the chosen date[108]. Obviously it was not considered possible that he would inadvertently alert MacNeill or Hobson.

Casement, who travelled to Ireland by U-boat and landed, extremely ill, from a small canvas boat at Banna strand, was discovered and arrested while his companions (Monteith and Sergeant Beverly[109]) had gone to Tralee in search of help.

The theory of his returning to stop the Rising is, apparently, reinforced by a request he made to a Dominican priest, Fr. Ryan, O.P. while being held in Tralee. Casement asked Fr. Ryan to keep his identity secret until after he was taken out of Tralee. The reason he gave was to prevent any rescue attempt, and that he had come to stop the impending rebellion (See Ryan, op. cit., p. 241). This has been adduced as additional evidence that he had come to 'stop' the Rising. In fact this was to gain time, and to deny to his captors confirmation of his identity, which they only suspected. It was designed to mislead and confuse. Casement understood that confirmation of his identity might alert the authorities — who believed Casement to be the ringleader — to the imminence of a rising. They evidently believed that the *Aud* was merely an attempt at gun-running.

Major Price prevented the press from publishing any account of what had happened in Kerry and Cork in regard to Casement and the *Aud*, and this helped to isolate the IRB plotters. According to O'Neill, Monteith learned of Casement's arrest on Good Friday night and immediately sent an urgent message to Volunteer HQ in Dublin. Like Casement, Monteith was not an IRB man and did not know that the rising was an IRB, not a Volunteer, plan. The men who brought the despatch to Dublin — and this is some measure of the successful infiltration of the Volunteers — were IRB men and brought Monteith's message to Connolly at Liberty Hall.

On 11 April Casement sailed from Wilhelmshaven in the U-20 in the command of Kapitan Oberleutnant Walther Schwieger. When the U-20 developed engine-trouble Casement and his companions, Captain Robert Monteith and Sergeant Beverly (Bailey) were transferred at Heligoland to another boat, the U-19, Oberleutnant Raimond Weisbach. Possibly, and not untypically, because he was an ex-British consular official, and had been knighted, the British attributed to Casement far more responsibility and involvement in Irish plots than he had. The fact appears to be that he was at this time emotionally overwrought and, in the opinion of the Germans, a possible source of danger rather than anything else. That his physical health was very poor is in no doubt. Casement, as is notoriously well-known, was an inveterate diarist. His account of what occurred when he, Monteith and Beverly landed includes the following: 'Sometimes he [Monteith] urged me to stop the whole shipment — to stop the steamer. I said "that can't be done. Don't you see — these men in Ireland say they will rise on 23 April *in any case, guns or no guns, steamer or no steamer*; if I do anything to stop the ship I shall betray them and leave them in the lurch. No — the ship must go and I must go — there is nothing else for it'" (cited, Mackey *The Life and Times of Roger Casement*, p.89). Casement, Monteith and Beverly rowed ashore from the U-19 on Good Friday morning at Banna strand and Casement was captured close by next day while Monteith and Beverly were looking for help.

Meanwhile four Volunteers, one of them a wireless expert, were sent by car from Dublin to Kerry to disable the government wireless station at Cahirciveen and set up their own transmitter instead. Tragically they took a wrong turning at Ballykissane, onto the pier, and drove off it. There was only one survivor, Colm O Lochlainn, the driver, who was one of MacNeill's students. It was he who, on his return to Dublin, inadvertently informed MacNeill on Saturday of what had happened to *Aud*.

The Aud

And what had happened to *Aud* was this: Spindler's orders had been — 'if, after half an hour's wait, none of the aforesaid vessels or persons [a pilot boat with a green flag at the masthead and a man with a green jersey in the bows] are at the rendezvous, and there does not appear to be any possibility of communicating with them, you are to use your own judgement as to whether to proceed or turn back'. After steaming or lying-to in the narrows between the Blaskets and the mainland all Thursday and throughout the night until 0500 on Good Friday morning — during which time he had sailed to within six hundred yards of Fenit pier — Spindler's luck finally ran out and after two burlesque encounters with the British navy *Aud* was, late on Good Friday, escorted to Cork harbour where Spindler successfully scuppered his ship, 20,000 rifles, ten machine guns, 400 kilograms of explosives, 4,000,000 rounds of ammunition and sundry pit-props, tin baths, enamelled steel-ware, wooden doors, window-frames and other building materials, together with the IRB's hopes of help from Germany for the rising[110].

A certain amount of confusion has tended to linger about the entire incident, in particular two aspects — namely the timing and Casement's motives. As we have seen the confusion about the timing resulted either with Devoy or with the German embassy in Washington, one of which, unknown to Dublin, inserted a degree of flexibility regarding the date of arrival of the arms ship. On the whole the question might be approached in the knowledge that two or three days flexibility in timing would have suited the German Admiralty, but would have been disastrous for the Irish. The error was not discovered until after *Aud* had sailed, without wireless. Regarding Casement's motives, Mackey deals with them peremptorily: 'It is curious that the notion has been spread that Casement came to Ireland to stop the Easter Rebellion. He did nothing of the sort' (op. cit. p. 93). Robert Monteith, Casement's lieutenant who landed with him at Banna, is equally categoric: 'Another error into which some writers have fallen is the assumption that Casement tried to stop the Rising. This is not even half-truth', (Robert Monteith *Casement's Last Adventure*). However, Lyons accepts unequivocally that he did: 'The Irish government (the British administration in Ireland, is what is referred to) would have been considerably taken aback to learn that he had come to stop the outbreak, not to lead one' (op. cit., p.365).

The part played by the British Navy in frustrating the plans for the Rising has received inadequate attention. British Naval Intelligence, under the famous (or infamous) Captain Reginald Hall, first received information about the Rising through its interception of German radio correspondence between the Embassy in Washington and the Foreign Office in Berlin [111]. Hall was also the man allegedly responsible for 'manufacturing' the diaries and was largely responsible for the character assassination of Casement by dissemination of the alleged copies of the diaries. He was clearly at the centre of a knowledgeable conspiracy of character assassination and misinformation directed against Casement. It may well be that Admiral Bayly, in accordance with the discretion imposed on him by Hall, passed the 'absolutely reliable' information on to General Stafford in a less emphatic manner than the circumstances warranted. Nor did Stafford, in his turn, evidently attach to the information he received sufficient importance when he forwarded it to General Friend, who did not inform Nathan until 17 April, almost a month after the information had been received and five days before the Rising. As we know neither Nathan nor Friend placed much reliance on this information. Operations between the various branches of the British forces were, in those days, in their infancy and were marked more by 'cap-badge' rivalry than by co-operation. There is also the fact that von Igel's offices (in New York) were raided on 18 April by US authorities during which a copy of the following telegram was discovered: 'From Ambassador in United States of America; No 7. of April 15th. 'Recalling telegram No. 1 of February 2nd,[112]. Delivery of arms must occur precisely on April 23rd in the evening, this is most important, as smuggling impossible, unloading must occur promptly'. This information, as noted above, was immediately passed to the English.

Admiral Bayly in Queenstown, on the other hand, acted decisively within his own remit. He organised tight surveillance of the western approaches to the Irish coast, with trawlers, sloops and a light cruiser, *Gloucester*, with four destroyer escorts on detachment from the Grand Fleet to augment his own complement. This resulted in *HMS Zinnia* and *HMS Bluebell* intercepting *Aud* and receiving orders that if she resisted to sink her. It is interesting that, even as late as 1931, Spindler does not appear to have been aware of the comprehensive interception by British Naval Intelligence of German Kriegsmarine signals. Commenting on the fact that the above captured telegram was also reported (by Cearrbhail O Dalaigh[113] in an article in *An Phoblacht*, 27 September, 1930) as being 'intercepted', he makes no reference to any other interceptions. But continues: ' — it follows that the British Government was fully informed, by 18 April at the latest, that an uprising in Ireland was imminent and that Germany was to participate in it by a delivery of arms!'

'In my own opinion, it is quite within the realm of possibility that the English got wind of how things were shaping at a still earlier date' (Spindler, op.cit., 263/4). Spindler does not elaborate. But the effective British intercepts do raise another significant point, which is:— even if *Aud* had carried wireless, and it was used to pin-point for Spindler a precise time and landfall, and even allowing for the alert precautions of Hall and Bayly, the failure of the Castle authorities to act on their intelligence does not suggest that they would have acted any more vigorously on any such additional information. Bayly with his screen might have presented a problem, but, in the event, *Aud* was in the Blasket roads for nearly twenty-four hours before being intercepted — plenty of time to offload and distribute if the timing was synchronised. In that case the landing would seem to have had a reasonable prospect of success[114].

On receiving the fatal news about *Aud* MacNeill went immediately to see Pearse. According to some writers Pearse said to him: "We have used your name and influence for what they were worth, but we have done with you now. It is no use trying to stop us: our plans are all made and will be carried out"[115]. MacNeill replied that he was still Chief-of-Staff and would forbid the mobilisation. Pearse told him the men would not obey him, whereupon MacNeill replied that if they did not the responsibility would be Pearse's.

These exchanges make painful reading in retrospect. Here were two good and honourable men caught in a web of distrust and mutual recrimination at the most critical moment in the modern history of their country. Each was intensely, selflessly, patriotic, yet the gulf between them was unbridgeable. The deception of MacNeill cannot have been other than distasteful to Pearse and his friends, but they had learnt quickly in the hard school of conspiracy that devotion to the cause cancels friendships, old loyalties, and all the ordinary ties that bind men to one another. Given that they honestly believed a rising to be necessary, and believed also that MacNeill was the chief obstacle in their path, they easily convinced themselves that to deceive him became a revolutionary duty... Although his countermanding orders struck a fearful blow at their plans, Pearse, McDermott and MacDonagh all in their last hours were careful to exonerate him from any charge of disloyalty or lack of patriotism. Indeed Pearse's doing so also incorporates his final assertion on the rising: 'If we accomplish no more than we have accomplished, I am satisfied. I am satisfied that we have saved Ireland's honour. I am satisfied that we should have accomplished the task of enthroning, as well as proclaiming, the Irish Republic as a Sovereign State had our arrangements for a simultaneous rising of the whole country, with a combined plan as sound as the Dublin plan has proved to be, been allowed to go through on Easter Sunday. Of the fatal countermanding order which prevented those plans from being carried out, I shall not speak further. Both Eoin MacNeill and we have acted in the best interests of Ireland...'(P.H.Pearse, *Manifesto, Collected Works*). But, as Brian O'Neill points out (op.cit) 1936, p.72):

> Neither Connolly nor Tom Clarke would agree to the exoneration of Professor MacNeill...Connolly the revolutionary Socialist could not reduce the countermanding order to a question of personal integrity only... Tom Clarke's rugged Fenian instinct made him equally implacable.

As for MacNeill: '... deeply injured though he was at the moment when he faced his crisis of confidence, [he] steadfastly defended the honour of his former comrades at his own courtmartial and in later life.'(Lyons, op. cit., p.356/7). On Good Friday Hobson was arrested by Pearse and the other revolutionaries. This, coupled with what he learned from Colm O Lochlainn, alerted MacNeill and he sent Volunteer officers through the country with the message:— 'Volunteers completely deceived. All orders for special action are hereby cancelled, and on no account will action be taken'. He followed this up with a countermanding notice in the *Sunday Independent* 'which had to be drafted with greater care — because MacNeill did not want to help the Government to any understanding of what had gone on behind the scenes. It referred to the "very critical position", which might have been an allusion to any or all of the things that had happened in recent days, and rescinded all orders for parades, marches or other movements of the Irish Volunteers. This notice ... had an effect that was not intended. It ensured its object, that the Rising that was planned for 4 o'clock on Easter Sunday afternoon did not take place, but it led MacNeill and the Government alike into believing that that was the end of the affair ... the Military Council decided to go ahead at midday on the following day, Easter Monday, despite everything that had happened, and sent out their own officers in an endeavour to undo the effects of MacNeill's counter-action. In order, however, to cloak the decision to rise on the Monday ... they confirmed MacNeill's cancellation of the Easter Sunday manoeuvres, and Pearse told MacNeill in a note that this had been done because, as he said, the leading men would not have obeyed MacNeill's countermand without his, Pearse's, confirmation'(O Broin op. cit. p.161). This involves Pearse in the responsibility for the fatal confusion of countermanding orders.

In view of the undoubted ruthlessness with which the IRB pursued its object to this momentous point, and in view of the kidnapping on Good Friday of Bulmer Hobson (the officer responsible for sending out orders from HQ and who could, therefore, disrupt their plans), the astonishing thing is that MacNeill was not, himself, kidnapped and held prisoner on Friday and Saturday, after which any intervention by him would have been too late. The most likely reason is that Pearse and the others were satisfied, after their Good Friday meeting with him — when they all anticipated the landing of the German arms — that MacNeill was sufficiently, if reluctantly, persuaded to allow the Rising to proceed and was no further threat to their plans.

Of Hobson, who had been an IRB man but had voted for compromise with Redmond during the latter's attempted take-over of the Volunteers, the Council was less sure. This explains his kidnapping. When MacNeill learned from O Lochlainn about the scuttling of *Aud*, the capture of Casement and the drowning of O Lochlainn's three companions at Ballykissane — together with 'evidence' that the 'Castle Document' was a forgery — he was completely shaken. Not alone had he been deceived by the IRB Military Committee, if the 'Castle Document' was a forgery then the authorities had not decided to round up the Volunteer leadership, which meant that his own alert to the Volunteers was a false alarm — in which reasoning, if that is what it was, he was, of course, mistaken. The Castle authorities had decided to do just that.

On that Holy Saturday evening, 22 April, 1916, MacNeill sent his messengers hurrying to all Volunteer headquarters with the aforementioned message. Since the mobilisation for the intended rising was not due to occur until late Sunday afternoon (4 pm) there seemed to be time to contact all units. As a safeguard he also published in the next day's *Sunday Independent* (the only Irish Sunday newspaper at that time), the order cancelling all Volunteer movement that day. That same Saturday night the men of the Citizen Army were interviewed one by one in Liberty Hall and told that there was going to be a rising. Each was given the opportunity to withdraw. None did. But, unlike most of the Volunteers, they knew the purpose of the forthcoming Easter Monday parade.

That Easter Sunday night another order went out to all Volunteer battalion commands in Dublin. It read:

GENERAL HEADQUARTERS,

April 24, 1916.

The four city battalions will parade for inspection and route march at 10 a.m. to-day. Commandants will arrange centres. Full arms and equipment, and one day's rations.

Thomas MacDonagh,
Commandant.

Dieu n'est pas pour le gros bataillons, mais pour ceux qui tirent le mieux — Voltaire.

Chapter 6

The 1916 Rising

IN TERMS OF OVERALL POPULATION (about five million people) the Ireland of 1916 was not dissimilar to that of the 1990s, but demographically and in terms of population distribution it was — as in other matters — very different. The majority of the population lived in the country. Dublin — and other principal cities — were between one-third and one-fourth their present size. Rural values were much stronger and exercised a much greater influence on life in general. The land agitation of the previous forty years had left in the rural heart of Ireland not only a powerful dynamic of justice and independence, but also an alert awareness of any infringement of these rights. Along with the urban rebelliousness typified by the Dublin Strike of 1913, this provided fertile ground for the IRB.

From 1910 or thereabouts, a sense of impending change — envisaged as some form of Home Rule — encouraged an attitude throughout the British administration in Ireland that they were simply an interim, caretaker, government. A consequent casuallness was almost unavoidable. But, in fact, Home Rule was no longer a credible proposition.

On the threshold of war the British Government suddenly found itself face to face with a 'new and unexpected' Irish problem, one that had been moving inexorably to the point of inevitability for years, and we can discern the first perceptible shift by the people as a whole in the twentieth century away from constitutional methods, if not yet quite towards separatism. But there existed, stretching backwards through the different revolts of nineteenth century to the Union and the Rising of 1798, a sustained background of support and justification for a rising, without which one could not have succeeded.

As in the case of Emmet's rising (1803), the 1916 planners realised that an essential weakness of 1798 was that the Irish had neither taken nor assaulted Dublin which, psychologically, was important to successful achievement. Even if it was not possible to hold Dublin, more than any similar action elsewhere a major rising in the capital would be of immense moral significance so far as the rest of the country was concerned. In short, a rising confined to rural areas was not considered to be a satisfactory strategic option.

The military object was to seize and hold Dublin City; to hold it openly as the army of the Irish people; to hold it in such a manner that the British would be forced to attack; on such a scale that that it would be obvious that the capital city, and not a few back streets, were held; and for sufficient length of time to ensure it could not be written off as just a riot or a street brawl ... The occupation of the city had a strategic as well as a tactical significance. A battle for its possession had a strategic as well as a tactical aim. (Col. Eoghan O Neill, *The Battle of Dublin 1916, An Cosantoir,* May, 1966, p. 215.

But the authorities did not anticipate trouble from 'the Sinn Feiners'. The rather portly Sir Mathew Nathan, Permanent Under-Secretary for Ireland and — in the absence (in London) of his political boss, Augustine Birrell, Chief Secretary for Ireland — a key figure in the administration of the country, was complacent[116]. Such trouble as might have been expected would have come from the well-armed, well-organised and bellicose northern unionists — and that threat had been defused by the outbreak of war. With the shelving of Home Rule and the promise of partition, the Orangemen, encouraged by Wilson and others, had forgotten their recent attachment to the Kaiser and formed the Ulster Division, with its own standard and colours. As late as 10 April 1916, Major Price[117] had written in a memorandum: 'The general state of Ireland, apart from recruiting and apart from the activities of the pro-German Sinn Fein minority, is thoroughly satisfactory' (Greaves, op. cit, p.19).

With the Home Rule issue and all that related to it comfortably shelved for the duration, a point of crucial significance between March 1914 and the Rising was — and to some extent still is — obscured. The accumulating evidenced to the contrary, the unwillingness of the Castle authorities to consider seriously the possibility of a rising until it was too late, smacks of wishful thinking. But why? What possible reason could there have been for such complacency in wartime? The answer surely lies in the manner in which they interpreted their roles. Birrell and Nathan, in particular, saw themselves merely in a temporary capacity. When Home Rule did come it would bring with it Redmond as head of government with Dillon as his right hand man. Accordingly Redmond saw himself, was seen, and behaved as a prime-minister-in-waiting. This also helps explain some of his otherwise inexplicable actions. In that capacity he *had* to control the Volunteers; he *had* to placate the British and he *had* to dominate the separatists without provoking an outbreak. That seems to have been the logic behind the thinking. But there was a major flaw. If, because of the proposed transfer of power, Redmond and Dillon were anxious to placate the administration and not to take, or encourage, an offensive against republicanism, it did not follow that republicanism would not take the offensive against the British.

The grand design behind the Rising was, of course, for a free republic. But, even in those 'heady' days there was the clear realisation that a rising would be a means to an end and would not of itself achieve that objective. It is on this point that pragmatism — as opposed to a romantic notion of a blood-sacrifice — is evident. The objective of the planners was to bring about a situation which would establish Ireland's right to independence, proclaim a republic and which could

lead to a hearing as a belligerent nation before the post-war peace conference[118].
Moreover it was an objective also supported to one extent or another by the
Citizen Army, the Volunteers and Sinn Fein. But it would not be possible to
achieve the required status of 'belligerent nation' unless, under recognised 'international law', Ireland was in a position to claim it. Only a rising would make that
possible. This was the point at which the IRB, the Volunteers and the Citizen
Army diverged, but, in the main, it was only the leadership of the IRB and the
Volunteers which differed, and the officer ranks of the Volunteers were by now so
significantly infiltrated by the IRB that it was accepted that the bulk of the
Volunteers would carry out their orders to rise. By then bearing in mind the IRB
position, they were, in any case, probably more attuned to the drumbeat of the IRB
than to that of the Volunteer leaders. Accordingly the differences, which
concerned tactical policy and policy *per se*, were virtually confined to regional
headquarters and to central HQ in Dublin where both sides — one wearing
blinkers — came together.

Even today there is considerable disagreement and confusion about the purpose
and merit of the Rising. There are those, clearly unfamiliar both with the virtual
collapse of Home Rule as an option and with British policy regarding Ireland,
who argue that it was not necessary at all. There is conflicting speculation as to
whether it was a success, or not; whether it was a military or a political protest;
and what its purpose was.

The question of self-image was a major ingredient of the Rising. If the Union
had provided the Ulster presbyterians with the sense of identity they coveted, it
diminished even further that of the mass of the Irish people. The quest for
Irishness was, therefore, a not inconsiderable and potent ingredient of the entire
political, cultural movement between 1900 and 1922. There was, in a sense, an
unspecific 'gut feeling', that had an unspecified primary focal point in a rising[119].

The European war has brought about a crisis which may contain, as yet
hidden within it, the moment for which the generations have been waiting. It
remains to be seen whether, if that moment reveals itself, we shall have the
sight to see and the courage to do; or whether it shall be written of this generation, alone of all the generations of Ireland, that it had none among it who
dared make the ultimate sacrifice (Pearse).

The Rising was a means, not an end. But a means to what? That is one of the
questions around which considerable confusion hovers. If, for instance, it was
purely a military venture it was clearly doomed from the outset. If, on the other
hand, it was a political protest by military means, what was the point? Or was it,
as the cultivated popular denigratory view has it, merely a species of 'mystical
blood sacrifice'?

Curiously, although it is most commonly believed, it is the last theory that has
least substance. These were, on the whole, hard-headed practical patriots with
little time for making a grand gesture simply for its own sake, particularly if it cost
lives. This theory is grounded mainly on extracts, taken out of context, from some
of the writings of Pearse and the other leaders. There is little doubt that selected
lines from the poems of individuals might be used to attribute to him, or her,

almost any theory you like. Criticisms that the Rising was unnecessary because the Home Rule Bill was on the statute book; that it was militarily impractical; that it did not have the support of a majority of the people; that it was morally and theologically unsound and that, as an IRB plot, it was grounded in deception of the nation in general and of the Volunteers in particular; that matters should have been left to Redmond and the Parliamentary Party who would have achieved Home Rule; these are essentially intellectual value-judgements based on myopic hindsight. Home Rule had been finally discredited in 1914; it had been suspended indefinitely and if and when it was brought forward it involved partition. For obvious reasons few, if any, secret rebellions enjoy the open support of a majority of the people before the event. The agonising about the 'morality' of the Rising is an intellectual exercise; a rising against an alien and coercive invader is manifestly just. The IRB adopted 'the end justifies the means' technique, but it should not be overlooked that the Volunteers were essentially an IRB creation. As to matters being left to Redmond, his marching the Volunteers to be Britain's cannon-fodder may have pleased Kitchener, but it damned him at home. Nor was 1916, as is often depicted, simply a revolution or rebellion implying disobedience to, or action against, lawful authority.

The fact is that the Rising went much further than having a simple military or political purpose. The 1916 Rising was a *revendication*, that is a claim to indefeasible right — which cannot be forfeited — of the sovereign nature of the land and people. Its secondary purpose was to proclaim, and to create an awareness of, that claim, to both demonstrate it and to create a situation in international law where it would be acknowledged and sustained. The claim to an indefeasible right, the right itself and the Rising which demonstrated it, are bound together.

One of the problems is that the leaders of the Rising were not, as they are sometimes portrayed, extraordinary people. They were ordinary people who did extraordinary things. That they were high-minded, idealistic, chivalrous and, in some ways, romantic may be something of a curiosity to eyes focused on contemporary consumerist values, but it in no way precluded them from being pragmatic and practical as well.

The Arguments

The four usual arguments against the Rising are: Firstly, that it shouldn't have taken place because Home Rule would bring all that was expected anyway. (The curious point has even been made that it was wrong because the values that inspired it are out of kilter with today's so-called liberal ethic.) P.S.O'Hegarty wrote: 'The Home Rule Act was dead and out of date and the political theory behind it that Irish self-government was something that England was entitled to give or withhold, no longer commanded any support...'

The argument that the Rising should not have taken place, that it was a waste of life and purpose, is an entirely academic exercise. Both the Irish Citizen Army and the IRB had determined on a rising before the end of the war; if the Rising had not taken place at Easter, 1916, it would certainly have occurred soon afterwards. In the event, as we shall see, 1916 seemed the most propitious time. The facts are that the Rising took place, it had purpose and that purpose was largely achieved. Somehow it was seen and felt — intuitively if you like — by the men and women of the period that it was essential to act decisively and cooperatively before it was too late. Perhaps Roger Casement perceived and expressed it best: '... The case of Ireland ... is desperate; it is now or never. Ireland can wait less than any other country in the world. If she is not helped now all the help of Christendom a few years hence cannot restore her as Ireland ... an Irish Party might very credibly be in existence 30 years hence ... attending just as regularly at Westminster — but there will be no Ireland' (Mackey, op.cit., pps. 11, 17, 18).

Secondly the Rising is held to have been a 'blood-sacrifice' cobbled together by impractical, romantic idealists and poets. This theory has no merit. The inapt phrase, suggestive of mindless immolation, smacks of 'Black propaganda', which is probably what it is. As we know much of the zeitgeist of the period 1880-1915 romanticised war. To diminish and belittle one of the few genuinely idealistic and honourable events of that period seems contemptible. The idea is as preposterous as the suggestion that poetry and military ability are mutually exclusive, all evidence to the contrary — from Xenophon onwards — notwithstanding. The late Major General P.J. Halley wrote: 'There is a widely held opinion that the Rising ... was organised and led by impracticable intellectuals and dreamers who impulsively led their followers into an unplanned and impossible military situation which could only have one end, the destruction of those taking part ... [that they] were incapable of clear military planning ... I must disagree.'

Desmond Greaves (*1916 as History*) says 'reams of cant have been poured over a few rhetorical phrases of Pearse's' such as 'There are many things more horrible than bloodshed; and slavery is one of them'. This is often used out of context to support the 'blood-sacrifice' theory. In context it is in fact a condemnation of national servitude *'The tree of liberty must continually be watered with the blood of martyrs and tyrants'* is a similar phrase.... Of course, it wasn't written by Pearse, but by Thomas Jefferson. Is it then the case that the American war of Independence was also a 'blood-sacrifice'? The poets among the executed were Padraic Pearse, Thomas MacDonagh and Joseph Mary Plunkett — three of the key IRB planners. The survivors of 1916 were tough, pragmatic men and women who led the nation in war and peace thereafter. Are we supposed to believe that all the poets and romantics died in 1916 and that only the pragmatists survived? Pearse and his associates made possible the freedom in which such nonsense could be articulated and written. We might consider in whose interests it is to diminish the Rising and those who led it. Perhaps ideals and pragmatism are mutually exclusive only in one's enemies. The attitude of the 1916 leaders is more accurately expressed: 'I am prepared to sacrifice myself so that the people may have liberty with justice'. It is hardly an attitude to be sneered at.

But it is true that there was also a dimension deriving from the age-old tradition of Irish independence inspiring the aspirations of the Rising.

It is argued that the Rising did not reflect the current mood of a majority of the people and should not have taken place because it wasn't part of a popular revolutionary movement. Of all the nonsensical arguments it is the strangest. Is it really necessary to point out that the number of secret rebellions that enjoy the open support of a majority of the people before the event is very few? Indeed one of the aims of the Rising was to revive a sense of separate national identity in the people. To argue that the Rising did not have the support of a majority of the people in advance is absurd.

Revolutions and uprisings seldom reflect the mood of a majority of the people before the event. Except for 1798 — and there is room for doubt about that — the separatist republicans had never, when they rose, had the substantial support of public opinion in advance. The apathy of the population in 1916 was no more than a kind of imposed, uneasy *status quo Brittanicum*. But that was already changing. That the *status quo* required a shock to restore national dignity, events confirm. The IRB would sooner or later have launched a Rising, as had been decided in 1914.

One criticism is that the Rising should not have occurred because it could not result in military victory. It is the only criticism of any substance, but not much. It is based on a misunderstanding of what the Rising was about. Military victory was <u>not</u> one of its objectives. It is not a question of whether or not a rising had, or did not have, military merit, but whether the rising that took place was adequate as to purpose, timing and effect.

Clausewitz's third aim of war (the winning of public opinion) was the main military achievement of the Rising. This became quickly clear. And that achievement was spectacularly demonstrated a few years later with the establishment of Dail Eireann, ratification by it of the Republic, and by the War of Independence — the second aim of the Rising.

Eamon Ceannt was one of the most important leaders of the Rising. A 'clerical worker who strongly supported the workers in the 1913 strike' (Greaves, op.cit., p.31), he was also an IRB officer and, from the outset, was a member of the Military Council that planned the Rising. As a summary of motivation for the rising, his last message is worthy of note:

> I leave for the guidance of other Irish revolutionaries who may tread the path which I have trod, this advice: never to treat with the enemy, never to surrender to his mercy, but to fight to a finish. I see nothing gained but grave disaster caused by the surrender which marked the end of the Irish Insurrection of 1916 — so far as Dublin is concerned. The enemy has not cherished one generous thought for those who with little hope, with poor equipment and weak in numbers, withstood his forces for one glorious week. Ireland has shown that she is a nation. This generation can claim to have raised sons as brave as any that went before; and in years to come Ireland will honour those who risked their all for her honour at Easter 1916.

As Greaves points out 'there is no trace of a death wish here, except perhaps for a few more of his enemies.'

Pearse and his motives have been roughly handled in prejudiced excursions into the aesthetics of the phoney-liberal ethic by careless or ill-informed commentators.

At the time of the Rising Pearse, the clear-headed educationalist, was thirty-seven. He was no spring chicken. More importantly, and especially in the context of the lines often quoted to portray him in the ridiculous light referred to, he had gone through an important crisis of conscience before the outbreak of the World

War and the decisive IRB meeting in 1914. Up until then Pearse had been a Home Ruler and, as late as 1913, had appeared on the same platform as Redmond speaking for Home Rule. His poetry of the period reflects the crisis of conscience that brought about the change. He rejected constitutionalism as the appropriate path for the country to follow to freedom, and adopted separatism and all that it implied. But it was not done without a severe inner struggle. It is in that context that the lines often cited as evidence of his 'blood-bath' outlook should be seen. Moreover his views were shared by other hard-headed, practical, men like Connolly and MacDermott (See also David Thornley in Martin's *Leaders and Men of the Easter Rising: Dublin 1916*, pp. 159-162). In fact Pearse was a man of such capability and efficiency that, within a year of joining the Volunteers and the IRB, he held vital positions in both organisations over older and more experienced colleagues. Even then in those days it would have been difficult for an impractical romantic to achieve such pre-eminence over his tough, practical fellows. He quipped: 'If we do nothing else, we will rid Ireland of three bad poets' (Ryan. Introduction, *The 1916 Poets,* Allen Figgis, 1963).

A rising was certain before the end of the war. Its three objectives were clear, and two of these were achieved quite remarkably.

Some writers (See Lyons p.359) argue that the conditions necessary for a successful rising did not exist. That is to argue with hindsight. Clearly if the conditions for a national insurrection were evident, then they would have been evident to the authorities who would take steps to prevent an insurrection taking place. In the paradox at the heart of insurrection, it is precisely because the conditions for a rising were not evident, that the conditions existed. The other is a view, however, reflected in the opinion of MacNeill: 'I do not know at this moment whether the time and the circumstances will yet justify distinct revolutionary action, but of this I am certain, that the only possible basis for successful revolutionary action is deep and widespread popular discontent. We have only to look around us in the streets to realise that no such condition exists in Ireland. A few of us, a small proportion, who think about the evils of the English government in Ireland are always discontented. We should be downright fools if we were to measure many others by the standard of our own thoughts.'

Here is a clearer statement and one that is not only contemporary, but also that of a committed nationalist. The underlying philosophy, however, is not — and never was — revolutionary. MacNeill was pledged to a **defensive** role for the Volunteers unless one of a limited number of things happened i.e., an attempt to enforce conscription on the country, **or**, if the Volunteers were attacked or in some other fashion restrained by the authorities. He placed his faith, primarily, in the post-war peace conference. He was not committed, come hell or high water, to an insurrection **in order to rouse the people's national conscience** as were the IRB and Connolly. The war itself was not, in general, considered to be Ireland's business. Some British authorities, aware of the expansion and outlook of the Volunteers and of their drilling and arming, took the view that extremism was on the increase and that, even, as early as March 1916 if not before, an insurrection was contemplated with assistance from Germany. But these views were based on the unconfirmed rumour and intercepts, already mentioned, of German code messages and were neither widely circulated nor accepted. 'Normal' sources, loose talk and spies within the Volunteer organisation, simply didn't exist, since the Volunteers themselves knew nothing. Those who did, the military council of the IRB, were neither spies not loose talkers.

The essential facts are that on Easter Monday, 1916, Ireland was a country occupied and governed by a foreign power, and a small group of men and some women went out to demonstrate in arms, in the spirit of the highest ideals and of a tradition at least as old as the occupation itself, against this enforced and coercive alien rule. Their intent was to reactivate a temper of militant national separatism in pursuit of national liberty. That intent was successful, if in a shocking manner. But it could not have been other than shocking. Even if the Rising had been on the largest possible scale the outcome, without massive German intervention, would have been similar. The spirit these men and women sought to revive in the people had been suppressed by, and become subordinate to, the then discredited mechanisms of constitutionalism. That the people were awaiting a lead to go in another — more active — direction, events proved. The issue was independence.

The Irish Rising of 1916 . . . [is complicated] . . . because . . . the complexity of the situation was increased by the fact that affairs moved towards their climax in the midst of a great war and were at certain vital moments influenced by events far beyond the frontiers of Ireland (Lyons, op. cit., p. 339).

The outbreak of the war resulted in the diluting and shelving of the Home Rule Bill. By March, 1916, the war that when it began was 'to be over by Christmas' was 18 months old and it looked as if it might, indeed, end soon — on a negotiated basis, with Germany the stronger protagonist. The possibility of a rising in Ireland was, nonetheless, unforeseen by all but the conspirators. The question of deception must be put in the context of the superior issue[120].

The international context in which the Rising, and the decision for it, took place requires to be put in context. Firstly was the anxiety that the war might end before a rising was possible. In 1916 the pressure on the belligerents from the United States to end hostilities was considerable, and in the early part of the year the British cabinet were giving serious consideration to a negotiated peace. 'Serious consideration of peace terms in Britain started in 1916 with the growing US pressure on the belligerents to end the war,' (Greaves, op. cit., p. 41 And see, for example, C.J.Lowe and M.L.Dockrill, *British Foreign Policy, 1914-1922*, vol 2; *The Mirage of Power*, London, 1972, p.238 et seq). In March General Erich von Falkenhayn (German chief-of-staff) had launched the battle of Verdun, the great German *putsch* intended to capture Paris and end the war. For a number of reasons 1916 seemed most advantageous and the IRB did not want to lose what seemed to be an opportunity at the optimum time.

It was Sinn Fein's intention to try to secure a hearing for Ireland as a belligerent nation at the post-war peace conference. Since the Union still existed, *de jure*, that meant an armed rising, holding out long enough to generate sufficient national and international attention to ensure recognition as a belligerent nation. Pearse said (Ryan p. 42) that Germany had promised that if there was a rising during the war Ireland would come into the peace terms as a belligerent.

A second objective of the Rising was to gain public opinion. The successful achievement of this aim was dramatic. And the third objective was to proclaim the Irish Republic and, if possible — as Pearse expressed it — 'enthrone it' as a sovereign state[121].

The aims and objectives of the IRB battle-plan were excellent. It was in execution, not in terms of purpose, strategy, timing, planning, tactics and opportunity, that it did not fully succeed, and that was not because of failure on the part of its leaders. So far as timing is concerned, had the Rising been attempted earlier it would almost certainly have failed in its purpose; later and the likelihood of overseas support would have diminished. In 1916 Germany was on the crest of the war-wave. Russia, though nominally still at war with Germany, was defeated, Italy was on the retreat.

The Allied victory in 1918 was not a victory of superior military force or tactics. Nor was it, strictly speaking, a strategic victory. Germany's army was still intact and on foreign soil at nearly every point. But the entry of the United States in the war on the Allied side in 1917 was decisive. Germany's 'means of waging war, physical and psychological, had been exhausted' (*Strategy and Tactics of War*, Wilmore and Pimlott, p.12). The military effort had become only part of the strength that could not survive when hope had gone and these other important ingredients, financial, industrial, economic, agricultural and psychological had been bankrupted. 'In the end Britain and France almost broke before the Germans. But for the Americans they might have' (Ibid.).

Subject probably only to a successful outcome of the Battle of Verdun, then raging, it looked as if in 1916 the Central Powers would reach a satisfactory negotiated peace settlement without the intervention of the United States. The Dardanelles had been a disaster for England and the German U-Boat campaign reduced her to near starvation. There was pressure from the United States on the belligerents to end hostilities, which the British cabinet were seriously considering.

The Allied victory in 1918 has been read as meaning that the Allies were likely victors throughout. In fact it was a victory 'against the run of play'. Therefore speculation about the Easter Rising in Ireland that relies for its validity on any optimistic prospect of an Allied victory before 1917 is — to say the least of it — highly speculative.

Towards the end of 1915 the British war situation was not good. 'The year 1915', wrote the French Marshal Joseph Joffre, (*Life of*, by G.Hanotaux and J.G.A. Fabry, 1921; See also *The Great War*, Corelli Bartnett, London, 1976), 'was dragging to a close under conditions that brought small comfort to the Allies. Our armies had everywhere been checked or beaten — the enemy appeared to have succeeded in all his undertakings'. Indeed the Germans had been victorious on most fronts and had inflicted very heavy losses. 'The withdrawal from the Dardanelles was a particularly heavy blow to British prestige...it was inevitable that there would be some form of conscription'. (O Broin, *Dublin Castle and the 1916 Rising*, p.60). The battle of Verdun was still underway at the time of the Easter Rising[122]. But, though victory looked likely, Germany was also still engaged in the war on two fronts her military chiefs had dreaded. Although militarily it seemed as if Germany could at the time, with decisive action, force a favourable conclusion, the odds were against her in a protracted total war involving the harnessing and utilisation of national resources, in which she was considerably exceeded by France, Britain, Italy and Russia. In these circumstances it was unrealistic for Irish leaders to a/ expect any sizeable army from Germany in support of a rising, let alone 50,000 men (four to five divisions), and b/ postpone a rising indefinitely.

Plan Of The Rising

A major military difficulty of those who led the Rising lay in trying to hold isolated positions with small garrisons. Inevitably this led to a series of sieges. The plan as originally conceived did not envisage this siege development, which was a result of the small numbers who in fact mustered. There was no way of knowing how many would be affected by MacNeill's countermand, nor any time to change or modify the original plan to accord with much reduced manpower on the day. Hence the occupation of a reduced number of strongpoints with inadequate troops and without effective communications. Disruption of the enemy's own communications by taking the telephone exchange, occupation of other vital strong points, e.g. the Castle and Trinity, or the securing of adequate or any means of withdrawal, proved impossible. All of these had been provided for in the original plan. In effect, as the plan itself became telescoped, so did the Rising.

Given the objective of national liberty, there were even those who considered the possibility of an Irish monarchy[123]. On the whole, and with one notable exception — Arthur Griffith — it seems to have been an idea of expediency rather than of principle. But there was another element in Ireland which had been far more serious about the question of a foreign king. Underlining the fact that Ulster Unionist loyalty is essentially to themselves, their spokesman, Bonar Law, declared in the House of Commons, in 1913: 'These people in the Northeast of Ireland, from old prejudices perhaps more than from anything else, from the whole of their past history, would prefer, I believe, to accept the government of a foreign country rather than submit to be governed by the honourable gentlemen (The Irish Party) below the gangway', (Dangerfield, op. cit.,p.117/8).

The events of the Easter Rising are well documented and it is not necessary here to go into greater detail than is warranted by the overall narrative. It is, however, important to emphasise that the Rising was the focus of all preceding republican activity and the pivot on which subsequent separatist activity turned. Because of MacNeill's countermanding order, what was to have been a countrywide national uprising became, instead, concentrated in Dublin. With inadequate troops at the disposal of the leaders, it soon became a siege, or series of sieges, of the buildings and outposts held, with inevitable consequences. The plan for Dublin alone required more than four times the number who mustered (700-800). Because of this limited turnout the Volunteer posts either did not have, or were unable to adequately utilise, effective lines of withdrawal.

The original battle-plan provided tactics and a strategy for a nationwide uprising focussed on Dublin. From there a withdrawal westward to the line of the Shannon and a link-up with troops from the west, south and north would take place. Limited guerilla fighting might follow before surrender. The plan was defensive in concept, but no less valid for that. (Col. O'Neill refers to von Moltke's observation that: 'a clever military leader will succeed in many cases in choosing defensive positions of such an offensive nature from the strategic point of view that the enemy is compelled to attack')[124].

In a city, as in mountainous terrain, a small force, well deployed, can exert pressure on a much larger force out of all proportion to its size. This is particularly the case if the larger force is untrained in street fighting and/or is badly led. The general military plan for Dublin in 1916 was based on this principle. The basic plan included three important factors; first, that a majority of the 16,000 Volunteers in the country — 4,000 or so of them in Dublin — would deploy and draw off possible British reinforcements from Dublin; secondly, that the city would be held for a period and the planned withdrawal take place;[125] thirdly, that the German arms shipment would be landed and distributed successfully. Even allowing for the advantages to smaller units of street and guerrilla fighting, it was clear that there could be no successful military outcome. Victory would be political and moral.

In Dublin the plan was that a number of strategically placed buildings would be taken during the Easter holiday, when they might be expected to be relatively lightly manned, or empty. These buildings were so selected as to dominate the approaches i/ to and from the military barracks in the city; ii/ those to the city itself, and iii/ to hold open a corridor of withdrawal westward when, inevitably, withdrawal became necessary. The buildings were selected so that communication between them should have been good. The minumum force needed to put this plan into effective operation was 3,000 men[126].

The arms from Germany were to be landed at Fenit in Kerry, and from there distributed by rail to Limerick and Galway, where the strongest body of unarmed volunteers was, by the Cork, Kerry and Limerick commands. It was planned to take over the requisite railway junctions and stations to ensure the safe passage of the train and the distribution of arms. Road, rail and telegraph communications were to be disrupted throughout the country to hinder British troop movements. The western Volunteers would move eastwards, attacking or isolating police barracks *en route*, and hold the line of the Shannon where they would eventually be joined by the Volunteers from Dublin withdrawing westwards. Together and reasonably armed they would constitute a formidable fighting force which would then, as deemed appropriate, disperse and form guerila units for as long as possible. But a prolonged guerila war was not part of the IRB's military strategy. Nevertheless, while the outcome must have been inevitable surrender, a prolonged rising in Dublin with a break-out to link up with western Volunteers at the Shannon could have resulted in a longer struggle between the rival forces — with, of course, many more casualties.

The other provincial centres, Cork, Belfast, Waterford, would act in support. The Northern Volunteers were to mobilise at Dungannon and then move south-west to link up with those from the west along the line of the Shannon/Erne. Because of the strength of the UVF, and Unionist strength of feeling, mobilisation in most of the Ulster counties was considered impractical. All were to be moved into position under the guise of a routine training exercise, but officers would have received orders for general action from Pearse. (In fact they received a series of contradictory orders over the weekend, not all delivered everywhere, or in correct sequence, with resulting confusion.) Had the arms and munitions from *Aud* been landed and distributed that would have made a major difference, particularly in Cork and Kerry and the line west of the Shannon.

Half of the headquarters staff of the Volunteers, unknown to MacNeill, consisted, not just of IRB officers, but of IRB military council members, all of them in vital positions. Pearse was the Director of Organisation, McDonagh the Director of Training, Ceannt the Director of Communications and Plunkett, the key man, was Director of Military Operations. Their power to use the chain of command of the Volunteers to their own ends, with the intention of doing the same with the Volunteers themselves, was all but absolute. Only the accidental discovery of their plans by Bulmer Hobson and MacNeill two days before the Rising was scheduled prevented it being as widespread as intended. What the consequences might have been if they had not been uncovered, if MacNeill had not issued his countermanding order and if the Rising had not been delayed by twenty-four hours, is impossible to say. A great deal turns on whether the Rising began on Sunday, as planned, or on the Monday, as occurred. The twenty-four hour delay was caused by the IRB military Council of Pearse, Plunkett, Ceannt, Clarke and McDermott deceiving MacNeill, for the second time that week-end, and giving him an assurance that they would accept his counter-manding order for Sunday's 'maneouvres'. They did not tell him they had simply moved the time-table back twenty-four hours.

So far as arms were concerned, the Volunteers were not well supplied[127]. The Dublin in which the Rising took place was a city of some 400,000 people, a majority of them living in the horror of what had become 'the worst slums in Europe'. Productive work, in the sense of producing a marketable product, was almost non-existent if one discounts Guinness's brewery and Jacobs' biscuit factory. In general the only work available for men and women was utterly servile — transport and other unskilled labour, washing and shop-keeping at the huckster level, domestic service. '... Its vast masses of unskilled labour without organisation or shield, condemned to casual jobs at coolie wages, herded into slum tenements, living eight, ten, and more to a room...'(O'Neill, op.cit., p.6).

The *Irish Times*, which was later to savagely condemn the Rising and its leaders, spoke out trenchantly in February, 1914 following the publication of a government enquiry into housing in Dublin:

We knew that Dublin had a far larger percentage of single room tenements than any other city in the Kingdom. We did not know that nearly twenty-eight thousand of our fellow-citizens live in dwellings which even the Corporation admits to be unfit for human habitation. We had suspected the difficulty of decent living in the slums; this report proves the impossibility of it. Nearly a third of our population so lives that from dawn to dark and from dark to dawn it is without cleanliness, privacy or self-respect. The sanitary conditions are revolting, even the ordinary standards of savage morality can hardly be maintained.

Wages for those living under such conditions averaged between 15 shillings and 20 shillings a week, with no security of tenure. And it is worth bearing in mind that this was after the Dublin Strike. The city no less than the country had been reduced to a wretched and non-productive dependency useful to and serving only the interests of imperial Britain. It was a situation that could not be expected to last.

Public Attitudes Prior To The Rising

i/ the IRB were (in secrecy) moving heaven and earth to ensure that a rising would occur as planned[128].

ii/ The Volunteer leadership did not know of the IRB plans until the last minute and would have opposed them, but when they were explained to MacNeill he gave the IRB what might be called the unavoidable support a *fait accompli* required — until he realised the German arms would not materialise.

iii/ The public at large were confused and in ignorance, subject to rumour and propaganda from various sources. They were probably less favourably disposed towards a rising than the IRB hoped, but, thanks to a revived cultural national outlook, opposition to conscription, and what was generally seen as 'the betrayal' of the Home Rule principle, amongst other factors, they were better disposed than they might have been a few years earlier.

iv/ The British, in spite of having been warned in advance by naval intercepts of German code messages (rather like the USA 25 years later before the Japanese attack on Pearl Harbour), ignored the warnings and did not convert the information received into intelligence. When Casement and *Aud* were captured it reinforced their view that a rising was not possible — largely because of their attribution to Casement of an importance he did not have in any possible insurrection. Nathan went to see the Lord Lieutenant, Wimborne, on that Saturday morning and they both agreed that since the threat of a rising had probably been contingent on the successful landing of arms and on Casement's leadership, that threat could be considered over (O Broin 84).

On seeing in the *Sunday Independent* the following day that the mobilisation of the Volunteers for that day had been cancelled, the British military, holding the view they did on Casement, not unnaturally, appear to have concluded that any threat of an immediate rising was cancelled too. A point worth bearing in mind is that their plans to suppress the Volunteers — after the Easter holidays — still stood, although these were mildly complicated because of a cabinet crisis, brought about by England's unsatisfactory war position, that was shaking the English government at that time. Lloyd George became war secretary and a precariously balanced prime minister.

Up to Easter Sunday night Nathan took no decisive steps to quell any plans the 'Sinn Feiners' may have had by way of seizure of arms, arrests or deportations of known leaders on any appropriate scale. In the already disturbed state of the country — there had been many armed incidents involving loosely termed 'Sinn Feiners' and the Ulster Volunteer Force, including confrontations at Tullamore, Portadown and shots fired in Dublin at Grafton street and College Green — foremost in Nathan's mind was to preserve some sort of balance which would not inhibit the desperately-needed recruiting for the British Army — which was then, as described by General Haig in his diary in March 'not an Army in France really, but a collection of divisions untrained in the field'. However few and untrained though these divisions were, they, and additional recruits, would have been of great assistance to the embattled French facing at Verdun 1,500,000 men, the largest attack force ever assembled in Europe. At the same time Nathan saw no point in trying to provide recruits for the British forces if it meant having to reinforce the Irish garrison with seasoned British soldiers in brigade strength or better to maintain order in Ireland. Lastly, he did not think a rising could get underway without German help.

* * *

THE RISING OF EASTER WEEK
Easter Monday, 24 April.

According to all accounts Easter Monday, 24 April 1916, was a beautiful spring day, with brilliant sunshine and small, fleece-like cumulus clouds dotting a blue sky. In Dublin people headed for the beaches at Sandymount, Dollymount and Bray, or into the shimmering countryside, where a majority of the Irish people still lived. It is easy to imagine the half-deserted cobbled streets of the city devoid of commercial traffic and shoppers. A major attraction was the races at Fairyhouse, which attracted punters of all classes, including many officers of the British garrison.

But in spite of the sunshine and the unwarlike holiday atmosphere, three determined men sat in serious conference in an office in an almost deserted Dublin Castle. The meeting had been summoned by Sir Matthew Nathan. The others present were Major Price and Mr. Arthur Hamilton Norway, Secretary of the Post Office. They had been summoned by Nathan to finalise arrangements to arrest and intern or deport the leaders of Irish Volunteers, the Irish Citizen Army and Sinn Fein following the decision taken the previous night at the meeting with the Lord Lieutenant, Lord Wimborne, in the vice-regal lodge (now Aras an Uachtarain) in Phoenix Park. That decision had followed a week of rumour and event, notably the arrest of Casement, the scuttling of the German arms ship, and the almost simultaneous cancelling by Eoin MacNeill of 'maneouvres' by the Volunteers scheduled for that week-end. Taken together these events were sufficient indication to Wimborne — a recent appointment — and his military advisors that something seditious, whatever it might be, was afoot in Ireland.   The authorities believed that, even if something had been contemplated, it was now out of the question. When the German arms ship had been captured and was scuttled with its cargo, MacNeill had publicly cancelled whatever arrangements the Volunteers might have been contemplating that Easter weekend (on such an important matter there was small likelihood of the advertisement being a hoax), Casement — the arch-traitor and ring-leader, as they believed — had been captured and, finally, as Nathan had written to Birrell, there was 'no indication' of a rising. Nevertheless the decision was taken to arrest Sinn Fein and Volunteer leaders as a precautionary measure before anything did have a chance of getting started.

Nathan, who up to this had opposed any direct action against the Volunteers, was persuaded to act, less because he felt the situation now justified it than because the opportunity presented itself. As permanent under-secretary and the man on the spot it was his responsibility. The proximate cause of the previous night's decision was the robbery that day (Easter Sunday) by Citizen Army men from a Dublin quarry of a quantity of gelignite, which they brought to Liberty Hall. When he learned of this Wimborne was all for an immediate raid that night, to arrest, and if necessary deport, the leaders and disarm the remainder. While it was agreed that it was necessary to disarm 600 or 700 Irish leaders, it was pointed out that it would be impossible to mount such a large operation that night. It would have been possible to arrest the men the following day, but it was also agreed that Easter Monday would be a bad day on which to do so. It was therefore decided to postpone action, but only until Nathan had clarified the position with Birrel in London. A list of those to be arrested was already prepared. It was, perhaps, this list that had provided the origin for the so-called 'Castle Document' the previous Thursday. It must also be understood that, irrespective of IRB and Citizen Army intentions, the putting into effect of this British plan would, in any case, have been the signal for the Volunteers to fight.

Birrell wired his agreement, which reached Dublin Castle that Easter Monday morning. It is, perhaps, some measure of the new urgency being felt by the authorities that, holiday or not, Nathan went at once to his office to make the necessary arrangements. He alerted Price, who had been with him at the vice-regal lodge meeting the previous night and who was vital to the programme of arrests. He also summoned Norway, who had served with him previously, and when he arrived Nathan gave him instructions 'to take immediate steps for denying the use of the telephone and telegraphic services over large areas of southern Ireland to all but military and naval use' (O Broin, op. cit. p. 92). He outlined the plan to arrest, disarm and, where necessary, intern and deport the leaders of the Volunteers, the Citizen Army and Sinn Fein and began to issue the necessary orders. He was interrupted by the first shots of the Rising, fired by the Citizen Army contingent detailed to attack the Castle.

Less than a mile away, in Liberty Hall, another equally decisive meeting had just ended. It began at nine o'clock, and when it ended the seven men who attended had elected Padraic Pearse 'who has been mindlessly revered and mindlessly reviled' (Lee, op.cit., p. 37) President of the Provisional Government of Ireland and Commandant-General of the Army of the Irish Republic. James Connolly was chosen vice-President and Commandant-General of the Dublin Division[129]. Since, because of MacNeill's counter-order, they did not know what their final muster would be, the remainder of the conference concentrated on what essential modifications it was necessary to make to the military plan. The plan called for more than three thousand troops, but that sunny April Monday morning they mustered seven hundred Volunteers, one hundred and eighteen Citizen Army men (later joined, surprisingly, by twelve Hibernian Rifles, unexpected Redmondite — and sectarian — allies, with twelve guns); in all, less than one-third of the minimum considered essential to make the plan effective. This tiny force was, from then on, to be known collectively by the old term, the Irish Republican Army. 'The fusion of Irish Volunteers and Citizen Army on Easter Monday morning expressed dramatically the alliance that made the Uprising possible — the alliance between the revolutionary workers and the best of the middle class nationalists against their common enemy' (O'Neill, op. cit., p. 5).

The original intention was to hold the line of the canals and their bridges, essential military targets for both sides. As it turned out the Irish did not have enough manpower to defend them all. But, to the south, the old Ringsend bridge was raised, Fenian street and Mount street bridges were covered by de Valera's third battalion, Portobello bridge by outposts from Stephen's green and Rialto bridge from the South Dublin Union. Baggot street bridge was to have been defended by C Coy., 3rd Btn., but it mustered barely a quarter of its parade strength. Leeson street bridge was also covered for a while from what later became the HQ of the Blood Transfusion Service. Harold's Cross, at Donore Avenue, and Dolphin's Barn bridges would also have been covered had there been enough men.

Street-fighting, or fighting in a built-up area, was clearly the most favourable to the Irish. It is — or was — an accepted principle that an attacker needs, at a minimum, a force three times that of a defender for a reasonable chance of success, and an attacker moving in through defended streets is vulnerable and has poor observation. But in defence the ability for all round defence, and having a reserve force to deploy quickly as required against any successful enemy attack, are vital. Fire is one of the quickest and most effective means of dislodging a defending force in a built up area. Clearly, then, if only one side has artillery it will eventually become decisive in street fighting, particularly the use of incendiary shells.

The IRA[130] had initial successes, taking most of the intended strongpoints with little difficulty with, what would prove to be the disastrous exception of Trinity College. By Monday afternoon they'd made their dispositions and effectively held the city. The success was, of course, temporary.

Apart from the GPO Headquarters, quickly identified by the British, and which came under constant sniper attack from early Monday, followed by machine-gun fire on Tuesday and artillery bombardment from Wednesday, there were six principal actions in Dublin city during the course of the Rising, one major one in each battalion area, and one in County Dublin. These were at the City Hall, at the Mendicity Institute, at the South Dublin Union, at St. Stephen's Green, at North King street and at Mount street Bridge in the city (there were, of course, other smaller, if not less significant, actions), and at Ashbourne in County Meath, where Commandant Thomas Ashe and vice-Commandant Richard Mulcahy mounted what in effect became a prototype for the kind of engagement that became common during the later War of Independence.

Generally, the scheme adopted was sound. It followed a logical estimate of the situation. It was carried out with courage and determination. In holding the city for a week against such odds the small force accomplished a task which might dismay a much stronger one '... the British were manoeuvred into the position that almost any course they could adopt would rebound upon themselves, and force them into contravening some of the principles of war' (Eoghan O Neill, op. cit., pp.220/221).

Shortly before noon a group of about thirty boys of Countess Markievicz's Fianna Eireann, a paramilitary boy scout movement, began to play football near the gate of the Magazine Fort in Phoenix Park. When the ball landed near the sentry a number of them rushed forward to retrieve it and instead grabbed the sentry, tied him up and gagged him. Their object was to blow up the munitions stored in the fort. The explosion was to be both a major psychological boost for the Rising, and the signal that it had begun. But the officer commanding the fort had gone to the races and, unexpectedly and against orders, had taken the key to the magazine with him. The best the boys could do was explode the small arms magazine, which they did.

Because of the small turnout, all the designated battalion areas were too big for the troops available. All four city battalions occupied their now restricted positions, establishing outposts and securing their flanks without much trouble, though with protests here and there, notably at the Four Courts and St. Stephen's Green (where one of the park attendants, having made his dutiful protest, decided to join them). The First Battalion under Eamon (Ned) Daly was based at the Four Courts area, blocking the quays and approaches from the Phoenix Park and Royal and Marlborough barracks. His area included Church street and North King street. Estimates of his strength vary from 120 to 180 men. The battalion plan — to occupy the city from the Mendicity Institute to Cabra, Broadstone and the North Dublin Union was sensibly modified; nonetheless a large British force was tied up until Wednesday. The Second Battalion under Thomas MacDonagh occupied Jacobs' biscuit factory with some 150 men, in Kevin street and Camden street, covering the approaches from Rathmines (Portobello barracks), and linked up with the Fourth Battalion to block troops from Wellington Barracks, holding the centre. The Third Battalion under Eamon de Valera, who was also Brigade adjutant, took Boland's Mills and Westland Row station with a slightly smaller force (about 130 men), covering Grand Canal and Mount street, Northumberland road and commanding Beggar's Bush Barracks and the road and rail approaches from Kingstown (Dun Laoghaire). It was also intended that this force would help to hold open the neck of a retreat corridor to the west, possibly by rail. The Fourth Battalion under Eamon Ceannt and his vice-Commandant, Cathal Brugha, who was to carve a *niche* for himself in the annals of Irish history before the week was out as 'the bravest of the brave', occupied the enormous South Dublin Union (now St. James's hospital), a network of buildings covering most of the fifty-two acres they stood in, as well as Marrowbone Lane, Roe's Distillery and Watkins

Brewery, with some hundred and fifty men. A headquarters battalion, formed by taking a unit from each of the other battalions and the Citizen Army, took the GPO, the political and military HQ of the Irish; initially with about 70 Volunteers. These were augmented to something like 180 as news of the Rising spread. A predominantly Citizen Army contingent of about 150 under Michael Mallin and the Countess Markievicz[131] occupied the City Hall area and St. Stephen's Green — a vital junction. But occupation of the park itself was the only major tactical blunder by the Irish forces. It should not — contrary to what Connolly emphasised — have been occupied unless the strongest of the surrounding buildings, including the Shelbourne Hotel which dominated it, were first taken. As it was the garrison wasted time digging useless trenches and were driven out by machine-gun fire on the second day to the Royal College of Surgeons. This was enfiladed from the Shelbourne, and by the British machine-guns that had driven them from the park.[132] But their outposts were good in Harcourt street station, covering the South Circular road (from the railway bridge over the canal) and Portobello. In addition there were the twelve men of the Hibernian Rifles and the Fifth Battalion in North County Dublin under Thomas Ashe, which fought a significant encounter that was a prototype of things to come a few years later. 'Fringing out from each of the chief commands were small squads to maintain contact and act as mobile units', (O'Neill, op. cit.,pp.39/40). In fact each commandant secured his flanks and established outposts along the expected line of attack. Some of these critical outposts fought the most significant engagements with the enemy. The Irish were further handicapped by having no supply or support systems and by having to rely on their first line ammunition only.

If they were to hold the city centre for any significant period, there were a number of tactical and strategic positions to be taken. Included were Dublin Castle, Trinity College, the deep-water quays at the North Wall and Kingstown and Amiens street (Connolly), Westland Row (Pearse), Kingsbridge (Heuston) and Broadstone stations. Because less than a third of the forces mustered and all but Trinity and Kingsbridge were occupied, each of these important positions had to be again abandoned in favour of immediate tactical ones. As events proved Trinity was a severe loss.

Since the quays were covered from the Mendicity Institute, the South Dublin Union and the Four Courts and their outposts, Dame street became a critical artery for the British assault. Had it been possible for the Irish to take and hold the Castle and Trinity College it might have been different. With a full complement of the Dublin Brigade the Irish might have held an extended perimeter and maintained lines of communication within it, holding railway stations and keeping open their line of withdrawal and protecting their vulnerable rear at the quays and Dun Laoghaire.

By Monday afternoon the Irish effectively held the city centre. At noon 'One group marched through the principal street — O'Connell street (then Sackville street) — and swung into the General Post Office. The staff was ordered out at gun point, windows were barricaded and the Tricolour — the green, white and Orange standard of the Republic about to be proclaimed — was raised on the flag pole on top of the building...' The Proclamation, then posted up outside the building for the public to read, is one of the great documents of Irish history...' (Neeson, *The Civil War*, 1922-23, p.15).

Other positions in Sackville (O'Connell) street were occupied, including a wireless school beside the Dublin Bread Company. From here the news that 'Ireland Proclaims a Republic' was flashed abroad, being received in New York and Germany before the British learned of it. Because of the shortage of manpower the Irish were unable to take the telephone exchange in Crown Alley[133], Trinity College and the Castle itself. Here the first shots, and the first casualty — a policeman — occurred. The force sent to attack the Castle (nineteen in all, nine men, nine women and a boy), was a Citizen Army contingent under Sean Connolly (no relation of James). Six of them seized the guard-room and the English guard (tying them up with their own puttees). Having occupied the guard room for a short while, they withdrew with the remainder of the small force, as it was believed they could not hope to hold the Castle itself.

The castle was not taken. Only about a score of men assembled in the unit detailed for the attempt; they were *ordered*, therefore, not to try to take the castle, but to prevent troops from leaving it (Dorothy Macardle, *The Irish Republic*, pp. 169/70).

The moral effect of capturing the Castle — one of the strongest points in the city — was lost. Failure to destroy the major telephone junction point outside Crown Alley telephone exchange meant that the British could maintain communications, both internal and with England[134]. All this was due to shortage of manpower. The unit attacking the Castle was ordered to deploy to occupy the City Hall. Strategic buildings in nearby Parliament street and Cork Hill were occupied by other units, amounting to a total of about forty.

Sniping from the Castle began almost at once and was reinforced by machine-gun fire late on Monday afternoon. The firing, from troops which had successfully filtered down from Richmond barracks, crossed one of the Liffey Bridges, and reinforced the Castle, continued throughout the night. At Portobello bridge a republican outpost from Jacobs covered the nearby Portobello barracks and held up troops from there for some hours before withdrawing under machine-gun fire towards Earlsfort Terrace.

Demonstrating that Dublin was the capital of an occupied country, the British held a semi-circle of nine barracks around Dublin from the Bull Island in the north to Merrion in the south, confining the city between them and the sea. At either extremity were a Bombing School at Elm Park (now a golf club), and a Musketry school at Dollymount (also now a golf club) on the Bull Island. In between were Beggars Bush Barracks, between Northumberland and Shelbourne roads; Portobello (now Cathal Brugha) Barracks near the canal in lower Rathmines; Wellington (now Griffith) Barracks on the South Circular Road; Richmond Barracks, at Islandbridge; The Royal Hospital, Kilmainham; Islandbridge Barracks; Military Headquarters at Parkgate; Marlborough Barracks (now McKee); Arbour Hill; Royal Barracks (now Collins); Ship Street Barracks beside the Castle and the RIC Barracks in Phoenix Park (now Garda Headquarters). Of these, four were strongly garrisoned, and dominated approaches to the city centre.

At the outbreak of the Rising the British had about 2,500 troops stationed in Dublin, and roughly 6,000 mobile combat troops in the remainder of the country. The 6th Cavalry regiment was in Marlborough Barracks, (McKee), eight hundred and fifty men and thirty-five officers; the 3rd Royal Irish regiment in Richmond Barracks (Keogh, never formally taken over by the Irish Army), three hundred and eighty-five men, eighteen officers; the 3rd Royal Irish Rifles, an Ulster, presumably loyalist, regiment, Portobello, (Cathal Brugha) six hundred and fifty men, twenty-one officers. The 10th Royal Dublin Fusiliers were in the Royal (Collins) Barracks, four hundred and thirty men, thirty seven officers, a total of 2,265 officers and men. In addition were Beggars' Bush Barracks (later HQ of the Auxiliaries), Wellington (Griffith) Barracks, the Royal Hospital at Kilmainham and HQ at Parkgate street together with the RIC Depot in the Phoenix Park. It can be seen from the titles of these regiments that internecine complications lay ahead.

From Belfast and the Curragh additional British troops were being rushed to Dublin. But no one on the British side had any idea yet of what they faced. The GOC Irish Command, Major-General Lovick Bransby Friend, was on leave in England; Brigadier W.H.M. Lowe was in the Curragh. Colonel Cowan was acting O/C in Dublin and the Castle was in the command of Colonel Kennard, who was also on leave, with Major Lewis, his adjutant, in acting command.

Unable to take and hold Kingsbridge (Heuston) station, twenty-five-year-old Sean Heuston of Ned Daly's 1st Battalion occupied the Mendicity Institute with twenty men and orders to delay British troops from the Royal and Phoenix Park barracks for three hours. He did so under continuous bombardment for three days, beginning shortly after 1 p.m. on Monday when they fired on a regiment marching along the quays from Royal Barracks towards the Four Courts. 'This was ... the opening of one of the hardest-fought and most persistent sieges of Easter Week' (Ryan, op. cit., p. 159). At 1330 (1.30 p.m.) Heuston's position came under machine-gun fire. From then on he and his party were subjected to attack, during which they developed a technique of catching Mills grenades before they exploded and throwing them back at the enemy.

Once the Irish had occupied and strengthened their positions, more or less continuous rifle-fire between Irish and British forces was heard throughout the city for the remainder of Monday. From Tuesday onwards the rifle-fire was supported by machine-gun and artillery fire as the British closed in. Barricades were thrown across roads and in front of fortified positions. These often consisted of overturned trams and other commandeered vehicles. To facilitate communications with advance defence positions and eventual withdrawal, the Irish also tunnelled through from one building to the next wherever they established headquarters or outposts. Criticism has been levelled at the Irish leaders for not 'appreciating' the importance of communications in war and allowing the Telephone Exchange in Crown Alley and the nearby Telegraph Exchange to remain in British hands. As we have seen it was lack of manpower that was responsible for this. There was a well-organised system of Cumann na mBan (the women's auxiliary volunteer force) scouts on bicycles touring the city. These began to report back to the GPO in the early afternoon, and from then on, throughout the Rising members of the Cumann na mBan, and individuals like Dr. Kathleen Lynn who was in the City Hall throughout its occupation, performed as heroically as their male companions.

A troop of British lancers, who had (if the Irish but knew it when they saw them earlier on the quays) been escorting munitions wagons to the magazine in the Phoenix Park, were fired on at Ormond quay and eight were hit or dismounted. Two lancers returned fire, killing a young girl before being killed themselves. Shortly afterwards another troop of lancers, under orders from Colonel Cowan, acting British O/C in Dublin in the absence of General Friend, took up position in Sackville street at the Parnell monument end, proposing to 'rout' the Irish from the GPO and outposts. According to Ryan they had come from Marlborough barracks as part of a move against the Irish by troops from Richmond, Portobello and Royal barracks. In what must surely have been one of the most extraordinary and inept actions of the week, the lancers, under a Colonel Hammond, charged the GPO, and would, had the Volunteers been more experienced, certainly have galloped into another 'valley of death'. As it was some of the excited Volunteers fired too early, bringing down four lancers in 'a ragged volley'[135]. The lancers wheeled and galloped back to the Parnell monument to the jeers of a crowd of onlookers, who promptly christened this gallop 'the Leopardstown races'. The first ambulances of the week retrieved the bodies of the dead lancers. Pearse sent to the nearby pro-Cathedral for a priest so that his troops could receive absolution. The British response when it came was capable and effective. By 12.30 on Monday the O/C the Curragh had been ordered to send his 1,600-man stand-to mobile column (25th Irish Reserve Infantry Brigade) to Dublin, where they arrived at about 16.45 that afternoon. A thousand men from the 3rd Reserve Cavalry Brigade were also ordered in from the Curragh, arriving at 03.45 Tuesday with Brigadier W.H.M. Lowe. From Belfast and the Curragh additional British troops were rushed to Dublin, bringing the British fighting strength by Tuesday to 6,627 officers and men. A battery of 18-pounder field-guns was ordered up from Athlone.

Within days they had more than 12,000 active troops in the city, and quickly identified and isolated the main Irish strongpoints. They mounted sustained attacks to get freedom of movement, especially from Kingsbridge to the North Wall, dividing the Irish forces. By Friday they had the Irish position encircled. The GPO Headquarters came under constant fire from early Monday. As Gen. Halley put it: 'The British had made up their minds to blot out the headquarters as quickly as possible and it was sound tactics to do so'. By Tuesday rifle-fire was supported by machine-gun and field artillery bombardment as the British closed in.

In the afternoon Lt. Colonel R.L. Owens attacked the South Dublin Union where Eamon Ceannt and his garrison had taken up position. So began another of the extraordinary actions which, night and day, lasted until Thursday. Sometimes soldiers from either side were shooting at each other in the same room, or separated by no more than interior doors and panel walls.

In the afternoon, too, looting began, almost entirely in Sackville street, which fronted the most appalling slums in Europe. In the circumstances, it was both understandable and moderate. An eccentric figure, about to become a tragic one, Francis Sheehy-Skeffington, attempted to stop the looters to no avail, and also called a meeting to set up a voluntary constabulary in the conspicuous absence of both the Dublin Metropolitan Police and the Royal Irish Constabulary. These had been recalled to barracks on the outbreak of the Rising, thus facilitating looting[136].

Towards evening a company of British reserve militia which had been on a route march in Kingstown were returning when, at the junction of Haddington and Northumberland roads, they came under fire from the small outpost of the 3rd Battalion. They were the First Dublin Battalion Associated Volunteer Corps, a body of professional men over military age, known as the *Georgius Rex* (freely translated by Dubliners as 'Gorgeous Wrecks'). Five were killed and seven wounded before the two attackers in No. 25 Haddington road realised that the column had no ammunition for their weapons, and stopped shooting. The militia ran to their depot, nearby Beggar's Bush Barracks, where they helped the British garrison.

Colonel Cowan spent much of Monday on the telephone. He made urgent requests for the 1,600-man strong mobile column of the 3rd Cavalry Brigade from the Curragh; from Templemore he demanded the 4th Battalion, the Royal Fusiliers; from Belfast whatever they could send — initially 300 troops — and from Athlone, artillery. He was promised that these would be available as soon as possible. Brigadier Lowe, himself an experienced field general officer, would come to Dublin to take command. When Field-Marshal Lord French, GOC the British Home Forces, received news of the Rising he immediately ordered the remaining two brigades (177th and 178th) of the 59th division, to join the first brigade in Ireland. One brigade was in Liverpool, the other, a cavalry brigade, was in Aldershot. They were units of the 6th and 7th Sherwood Foresters, the 5th North Staffordshire Rgt., the 6th South Staffordshire Rgt., 4th and 5th Leicestershire Rgts. and the 4th and 5th Lincolnshire Rgts., with support troops, bringing the British strength in Dublin to 16,000 effectives. A battery of field guns and 10,000 hand grenades were also despatched. The 60th division at Salisbury was brought to stand-to.

Having made the above dispositions French consulted the Imperial General Staff. It was his view that the Rising was prompted by the Germans 'to prevent us from sending reinforcements to France or to delay their despatch. I do not want to play into their hands more than we can help' (Asquith Papers, cited O Broin, op. cit., p.114). The Chief of the Imperial General Staff, General Sir William Robertson, agreed. French also arranged a meeting with Redmond, who briefed him as best he could. Redmond must have been acutely aware that his star, such as it was, was rapidly setting. Control of the loyalty of the people of Ireland was visibly at risk, and was soon to pass from his hands forever. French's final move at this time was to appoint a general to take command in Ireland. The man he selected was Major General Sir John Grenfell Maxwell. Like, Kitchener, Maxwell had served much of his career in Egypt, but had also served in Ireland on the staff of the Duke of Connaught in 1902.

By evening Colonel Cowan had some reason to feel pleased with himself. He had fairly good intelligence by this time and he had occupied, or held, the Castle, the Custom House, Kingstown, the telephone and telegraph exchanges and Trinity College. He was pinning the Irish outposts and headquarters down with sustained fire. And he was expecting reinforcements and a general officer. At 1900 hours (7 p.m.) a concerted attack was mounted with rifle and machine-gun fire on the City Hall from reinforced Dublin Castle, where there were now more than 300 troops. An Irish outpost from Jacobs covered Portobello barracks and bridge, holding up troops from there for some hours before withdrawing under machine-gun fire towards Earlsfort Terrace. Preferably they should have been reinforced to hold the position, but it was impossible. Westland Row and Broadstone — the Great Western Terminus — were briefly occupied. In Trinity eight members of the university Officer Training Corps decided to hold this vital post at all costs. It was a correct decision and the failure of the Irish planners to take Trinity was to cost them dear.

In the GPO there was a mood of jubilation. They had done well, so far. The Irish Republic had been proclaimed to the world. They had inflicted casualties on the enemy, receiving few themselves. They held the positions they'd occupied and, surely, the rest of the country was 'out' by now too. But here was a major weakness — communications outside of Dublin were virtually nil.

So ended Monday, the first day of the Rising. During the night British forces under Major H.F. Sommerville of the Musketry school at Dollymount filtered along the railway lines from the north and occupied Amiens street (Connolly) station and the North Wall, securing the docks. During Monday, as a diversionary gesture, the Germans sent a flotilla of zeppelins to bomb the east coast of England. They followed this on Tuesday with units of the High Seas Fleet which shelled areas of the same coast.

Tuesday, 25 April.

In contrast to the glorious weather of the previous day, Tuesday was wet, with a heavy drizzle falling. The morning was quite cold. About 0345 Brigadier Lowe, Commanding the Reserve Cavalry Brigade, arrived in Dublin with 1,000 dismounted cavalry of the Curragh Mobile Column (25th Irish Reserve Infantry Brigade) to take command[137]. Lowe's first priority was to assess the situation and formulate a battle-plan.

The Irish were spread out in a vague circle around the centre of the city. Their central axis was a line from the GPO to Jacobs and east and west of that line they held the battalion strongpoints at the Four Courts, the South Dublin Union, Bolands and St. Stephen's Green with outposts. Lowe was uncertain of the Irish strength, but could be reasonably confident that he both outnumbered and outgunned them. The Irish axis was a line, north to south, from the GPO in Sackville street to Jacobs in Whitefriar street; east and west of that line they held battalion strongpoints, with outposts, at the Four Courts, the South Dublin Union, Bolands and St. Stephen's Green. The Irish forces were divided by the River Liffey. Lowe made the obvious decision to extend that division and split the Irish force, isolate the strong points and take them one by one, throw a cordon around the GPO, and, in an encircling action, tighten the perimeter and destroy the Irish

HQ. He thus hoped to keep his own casualties to a minimum. The GPO HQ and the Four Courts were north of the River Liffey; Jacobs biscuit factory, Bolands Mills, St. Stephen's Green, the South Dublin Union and the Mendicity Institutue south of it. Lowe's first objective was to secure a line from the Richmond Barracks to the North Wall via the Castle, Dame street and Trinity College, where he would set up his operations headquarters[138], and which, like Dublin Castle, became a troop deployment area. General Friend returned from London to take command. But the plan was Lowe's, and when Maxwell arrived on Friday with plenary powers to proclaim Martial Law, Friend was relieved and Lowe was con-firmed in his command.

Before light on Tuesday machine-guns had been established with good fields of fire in the Shelbourne Hotel, the United Services Club, Trinity College, Amien's street railway station, and other points covering the Irish positions. Early that Tuesday morning an assault was mounted by a detachment of the 5th Royal Dublin Fusiliers (filtered in from Royal Barracks via Watling street Bridge to reinforce the Castle during the night), on the City Hall and the *Daily Express* building dominating Dame street and preventing Lowe from establishing his line between Trinity College and the Castle. Supported by machine-guns and grenades they carried the City Hall, and were astonished to find that it was defended by only nine men, with Dr. Kathleen Lynn, Helena Moloney and a few other Cumann na mBan girls in support. The *Daily Express* building was then attacked, but it became a fierce, sometimes hand-to-hand, fire-fight before 'the weight of numbers succeeded. The dead bodies of 26 rebels were then found on the premises' (Brian O'Neill, op. cit., p. 44.)[139]. Other outposts in the area fell during the day after considerable fighting. This success effectively divided the Irish force in two. Lowe now had a secure line of advance to extend operations, and a protected line of communications across his command area. Telephone, but especially telegraph, lines were commandeered from private sources by the British, and rerouted, to re-establish communications where they had been disrupted.

Under withering machine-gun fire from the Shelbourne Hotel and the United Service Club which began at first light, the St. Stephen's Green garrison withdrew first to the meagre shelter provided by small hillocks in the north-east corner of the park and then to the Royal College of Surgeons, perhaps the strongest, if not the loftiest, building on the square.

The artillery from Athlone arrived but had to detrain at Blanchardstown because the rails were torn up. They advanced on Dublin and fired on the Irish positions as they approached, enabling the Broadstone railway station to be recaptured from Daly's men[140]. At the Inchicore railway yards, locomotive boilers were hurriedly adapted by the British and fitted to lorry chassis as make-shift armoured cars with slits in the sides. They could carry up to thirty men in safety.

By nightfall on Tuesday Lowe had established his position and was waiting for reinforcements to tighten the cordon. Martial Law had been declared and curfew was in operation throughout the city. As night fell a small body of men from the north of the city made it to the GPO and joined the Irish garrison. In England the 59th Division was entrained, the first troops leaving their depot before dawn.

So far as the Irish were concerned, 'no weakness or false step of a purely military character was as disastrous as the insurgents chief omission' wrote O'Neill (op. cit. p. 46). This, according to that writer, was their failure to adequately publicise the Rising[141]. That same evening Wimborne wrote to Asquith, enclosing for his attention a copy of the proclamation of the Republic.

Wednesday, 26 April.

After Tuesday's drizzle, Wednesday was again a bright, sunny day. Two field-guns had been brought to Trinity and, after some initial difficulties, shelling began from just outside its Great Brunswick (now Pearse) street gate straight down Tara street at Liberty Hall, the trades-union headquarters. In the main incendiary shells were used. The coastal defence vessel, *Helga* (later renamed *Muirchu* — Seahound — the first ship of the infant Irish marine service), was brought up the River Liffey to berth at Sir John Rogerson's Quay on the northern bank. From here she also began to shell Liberty Hall— ineffectively at first, hitting Butt Bridge with its first shot. Machine-gun emplacements were established on the roof of the Custom House, in the tower of Tara street fire station and on a roof in Trinity College, and a steady stream of fire was directed at Irish positions. *Helga* bombarded Liberty Hall and its environs for over an hour while machine-gun fire also poured in. Liberty Hall, empty except for its caretaker Peter Ennis, who escaped miracu-lously under a hail of machine-gun bullets, was eventually destroyed.

At one stage the British, who brought up a one-pounder naval gun to shell de Valera's position, missed and sent shells screaming over the intervening houses to land near *Helga*. The captain, thinking he was coming under Irish fire, res-ponded, shelling Ringsend in the mistaken belief that it was an enemy stronghold, and for a while the British were busy shelling themselves. That evening, too, two companies of the mauled and jittery Sherwood Foresters opened fire, blazing away at each other for over ten minutes in the belief that they were fighting the enemy before realising the truth. It did not augur well for what was to happen later, as events in North King street would demonstrate.

Lieutenant Michael Malone of de Valera's 3rd Battalion held the position at Mount street bridge with thirteen men, of whom four were withdrawn early on. He posted seven men in Clanwilliam House (now gone), facing Northumberland road across the bridge, four more in the nearby school and parochial hall a hundred yards on the Balls Bridge side of the the canal bridge and two, one being himself, in number 25 Haddington road, a hundred and fifty yards further on at the junction of Haddington and Northumberland roads. About nine o'clock in the morning Malone received a despatch telling him that over 2,000 British reinforcements were advancing towards his position from Kingstown. He was to hold them as long as possible. Here, before the day was out, 'nine men cut up two full battalions, killing or wounding over two hundred soldiers' (O'Neill, op.cit., p.61). They were armed with four Lee-Enfield British service rifles, two Howth Mausers, two Martini-Henry rifles, two .38 and two .45 revolvers, with some 2,000 rounds of ammunition.

Advance elements of the British reinforcements, two battalions of the Sherwood Foresters (2/5th, 2/6th, 2/7th and 2/8th), with other units of the 176th and 178th brigades of the 59th Division, reached Balls Bridge at noon, where the brigadier, Colonel Maconchy, established his HQ in the Town Hall. Their destination was the Royal Hospital, Kilmainham. Their intelligence was that the Irish were holding a *school* at Mount street Bridge. An advance guard under Lt. Col. Fane went forward towards Mount street bridge where, as he was informed, the 'rebels' were waiting. Fane's men advanced in file on either side of the road with fixed bayonets to clear these Irish positions and came under a deadly triangular cross-fire from Malone and his men. The battle lasted until late that night, with heavy British casualties.

Malone and his small unit of nine men held up the advance of two full British battalions in attack and inflicted two hundred and thirty-four casualties before the survivors — nine men — were forced to abandon their positions under intense fire and, in the case of Clanwilliam House, with the building itself a blazing inferno. Malone and his companion, Seamus Grace, in No. 25. Northumberland road held up the British for five hours under continuous fire. At the end of that time the house was in flames, and Malone died under a hail of bullets as the British eventually burst in.

When the British pushed on to take Mount Street Bridge they came under a cross-fire from Clanwilliam House and the Parochial Hall. They were sent into attack in waves, and were cut down as they did so[142]. Bombs and machine-guns eventually took their toll against rifles, parabellums and pistols — but not until the defenders were virtually out of ammunition and the attackers had, literally, penetrated the ruins of the buildings they were attacking. For what it is worth Caulfield presents a dramatic account of casualties in one British company:-

the fire from Clanwilliam House had been extremely fierce and accurate. To the desperate military, trying to carry the narrow pass, it seemed as though a whole army of men had ensconced themselves in the house — trained riflemen whose every bullet seemed to claim a victim. Some were convinced that the rebels were using a machine-gun, the casualties were so appalling. Lieutenant Hewitt's platoon [perhap 30 men, give or take a few], had been reduced to two men. Lieutenant C.P.Elliot's had been cut to ribbons and Elliot himself severely wounded. All officers and the sergeant-major and NCOs of B Company (a normal company, about 200 men) had been either killed or wounded...(Caulfield, op. cit., p.262).

Over at the Mendicity Institute, Sean Heuston and his little garrison had been under non-stop attack since Monday. They were suffering from sleeplessness, the effects of continuous fire and little food and drink. They were almost out of ammunition. Their rifles had become so hot — as was the case in most of the outposts under attack — that they had to use precious water to cool them down. When there was no ammunition left, surrender became inevitable. They had been asked to hold out for three hours; they had done so for three days. When Heuston and his tiny force marched out under a white flag,[143] they were beaten up by the enraged troops they had been opposing. As they stood to attention before their captors, one of them was shot dead.

In Sackville street incendiary shells started the fires which were to roar uncontrollably through parts of the city during the next four days. The heat became so intense that glass in the shop-fronts melted and flowed in a translucent river, reflecting the very flames that caused it, along the gutters. In the GPO the soldiers used oil from sardine tins to cool their rifles (See Macardle, p. 172)

Perhaps because they felt that they were dealing with 'mere rebels' the British ignored ordinary war protocol (if there is such a thing) and established machine-gun posts in some hospitals, including Jervis street Hospital, which opened up on the GPO, and Sir Patrick Duns, which attacked both de Valera's position at Bolands and Malone's at Mount street bridge.

In Britain the Government decision to send General Maxwell to Ireland with plenary power to proclaim martial law over the whole country to 'sort things out' was implemented. Maxwell was given a free hand 'in regard to such measures as may seem to him advisable under the proclamation (Martial Law) dated 26 April issued under the Defence of the Realm Act'. It was a decision that would have far-reaching consequences.

Thursday, 27 April.

Thursday, another truly beautiful day, was remembered as 'the day of the fires' and the day of the main British assault. Maxwell sailed to take command. Machine-guns, incendiary and high-explosive artillery shells, improvised armoured cars and infantry reinforcements began to close the net on the tiny Irish force. It was also the day that Connolly was wounded, twice, once in the arm and once when a ricochetting bullet smashed his ankle. The British had a firm military grip on the city. With ample troops, more on the way, and further reinforcements if needed, they also had information on the Irish positions and could make a reasonable estimate of what opposed them. The ring was closed on Thursday night and Friday. The great, hidden dynamo that powers the unseen wheels of a great city had stopped, and the city itself had followed. There were severe food shortages. The streets were deserted and without traffic; inside the British cordon there was neither bread nor milk. Entertainment houses, factories and banks were shut. There were no newspapers; social and public services were at a standstill; the port and docks were empty. In the midst of the ruin and gunfire was the strange and unnatural silence of a city no longer functioning.

In Westminster prime minister Asquith announced: 'The Cabinet have decided to-day that the Irish Executive must at once proclaim martial law over the whole of Ireland. General Sir John Maxwell left this afternoon for Ireland ... and the Irish Executive have placed themselves at his disposal to carry out his instructions. There are indications of the movement spreading, especially in the West. The rebels continue to hold important public buildings in Dublin'. During the morning Pearse issued a manifesto which included:

If we accomplish no more than we have accomplished, I am satisfied. I am satisfied that we have saved Ireland's honour. I am satisfied that we would have accomplished more, that we should have accomplished the task of enthroning, as well as proclaiming, the Irish Republic as a Sovereign State, had our arrangements for a simultaneous rising for the whole country, with as sound a plan as the Dublin plan has been proved to be, been allowed to go through on Easter Sunday. Of the fatal countermanding order which prevented these plans from being carried out, I shall not speak further. Both Eoin MacNeill and we have acted in the best interests of Ireland.

During the afternoon fire, which had destroyed a number of buildings in and near Sackville street, spread from one end to the other of this fine boulevard. Flames crackled round and through the Irish GPO headquarters like a tornado, sucking what little air there was into a vortex and literally exploding from one part of the building to another. The heat and smoke were almost unendurable and hoses were in constant use. When the sand-bags were doused they gave off steam.

In the South Dublin Union the battle that had continued since Monday, with soldiers from either side fighting desperately — sometimes within feet of one another — neared its climax. The overwhelming British odds eventually told and they penetrated Ceannt's Nurses' Home headquarters, breaking in through a tunnel. The attack began at 3 p.m. with men literally dropping bombs and hand-grenades over barricades, only to have them thrown back again before they exploded. 'Now opened six hours of the most fantastic, unnerving fighting, with men chasing each other from room to room, small parties of both sides being cut off in buildings held by their enemies, with each wall and door threatening death' (O'Neill, op. cit., p.59). The British were held up and their advance stopped for over two hours by one man. Cathal Brugha, entrenched behind a barricade, and wounded repeatedly by bullet and shrapnel, kept the British back with his Mauser parabellum until he was rescued by his comrades towards seven o'clock in the evening. He was wounded more than twenty-five times and was given up for dead when brought to hospital. The battle raged well into nightfall. Towards the closing stages two British battalions launched attacks from different points, coming under fire from each other. At 9.30 p.m. the attack was called off.

By nightfall, too, the GPO was isolated from the other posts and any hope the besieged had of breaking out to join those in the Four Courts vanished. All hope of a break-out to the west in accordance with the original plan had long since gone. De Valera's outposts, of which Clanwilliam House had been one, were overrun. In one sense he and his men were fortunate — they had food in the bakery, but ammunition was almost gone.

Throughout the night the centre of the city was lit up with lurid flames visible twenty-miles or more away. Clery's was blazing, as was the Imperial Hotel above it and the buildings to the right and left. Oil drums exploded and flew into the air like giant fireworks, sending cascades of flame showering down on the stricken streets. The GPO was surrounded by a sea of flame.

On Thursday, also, Ned Daly's positions around the Four Courts were attacked by the still jittery Sherwood Foresters and their companion regiments of the 59th Division, the North and South Staffords, who assaulted North King street. It took them nearly two days, using the improvised armoured-cars to deploy men forward from house to house, to capture that 150 yards long street, during which they lost five officers and forty-two men. During the night the British troops took vengeance on the people of the area. The members of the 2nd battalion 6th South Staffs ran amok with bayonets and shootings. In one block of houses nine men and boys, none with any connection with the Rising, were murdered in their homes. At the opposite side of the street four men were dragged from their firesides and bayoneted. Sworn statements exist regarding these murders. In all fifteen innocent men and boys, taking shelter with their families and friends in their own homes, were murdered out of hand. Some were also tortured.

Friday, April 28.

Maxwell landed with his chief-of-staff, General Hutchinson, and aide-de-camp, Prince Alexander of Battenberg. He now had 12,000 men at his disposal. He confirmed Lowe as GOC operations in Dublin and issued a proclamation, which was published in *The Weekly Irish Times*, Saturday, 29 April, 1916.

Most vigorous measures will be taken by me to stop the loss of life and damage to property which certain misguided persons are causing by their armed resistance to the law. If necessary, I shall not hesitate to destroy all buildings within any area occupied by rebels, and I warn all persons within the area specified below, and now surrounded by His Majesty's troops, forth-with to leave such areas under the following conditions: — (a) Women and children may leave the area from any of the examining posts set up for the purpose, and will be allowed to go away free; (b) men may leave by the same examining posts, and will be allowed to go away free, provided the examining officer is satisfied they have taken no part whatever in the present disturbance; (c) all other men who present themselves at the said examining post must surrender unconditionally, together with any arms and ammunition in their possession.

Having issued this proclamation, which did not appear in the newspapers until the Rising was over, Maxwell had a pit capable of accommodating 100 corpses dug in the grounds of Kilmainham jail with, as events were to show, the firm resolve to fill it.

The British placed a field gun in Great Britain (now Parnell) street to cover any attempted escape by the Irish in the GPO via Henry street. Fire now became the chief and most successful weapon of the British attackers. By mid-morning the GPO, itself a flaming island, was at the centre of a sea of fire as incendiary shells rained on the area. The efforts of the garrison were directed more to trying to contain the fires than to engaging the enemy. By 6. 30 p.m. the building was ablaze everywhere and was doomed. There was no alternative to surrender or a break-out. It was decided to try to break out and establish new HQ in Williams and Woods jam factory in Great Britain street. From there it was hoped to link up with the Four Courts garrison. There were, at this stage, about 200 men left[144]. This number was to be reduced further before the end. The withdrawal began at 8 p.m. and the initial party, intended to draw fire and see what the British positions were like, was led by Michael Joseph O'Rahilly, The O'Rahilly, who together with several of his men, died in the attempt. The British had a barricade across the northern end of Moore street and it was into Moore street, at the southern end, that the Irish hoped to withdraw en route to Williams and Woods — by then a forlorn hope indeed.

There was no other option, as withdrawal down Henry street was cut off and impossible. Eventually the main body reached houses in Moore street and began to tunnel through them towards Great Britain street, setting up HQ in O'Hanlon's fish market.

Pearse addressed the girls and women who had helped in the defence and were now ordered to leave. He told them that without the inspiration of their courage the Volunteers could not have held out so long. They deserved, he said, a foremost place in the nation's history. He shook hands with each one before they left (Dorothy Macardle, *The Irish Republic*, p. 175).

On Friday, too, the British closed their assault on North King street where they had suffered many casualties and where resistance was as stubborn as any they had experienced during the week.

Saturday, 29 April.

At noon on Saturday, Pearse and his colleagues decided that it was time to surrender. Their struggle had lasted longer than they had any right to expect. They were satisfied that it had served its purpose. Any further loss of life would not be justified.

Elizabeth O'Farrell was one of the brave women who refused to leave the garrison and had accompanied them in their dash from the GPO to Moore street the previous evening. On the Saturday, in Moore street, she was asked by Pearse if, under a flag of truce, she would contact the British commander and tell him that they wished to discuss surrender terms. It was a dangerous mission; Not long before, they had seen a local family of four, parents and two daughters, shot down by the enemy as they fled their burning home and approached the British barricade carrying white flags. One of her companions, Julia Grennan, said: 'Elizabeth, there are too many people shot down with white flags'. But Miss O'Farrell, though nervous, was determined to do as she had been asked.

A white flag was held out of O'Hanlon's. Immediately there was a burst of fire, and it was withdrawn. At the second or third attempt there was no fire on the flag and Miss O'Farrell, holding it, ventured into the street. Her verbal message was that 'The Commandant-General of the Irish Republican Army wishes to treat with the Commander of the British forces in Ireland' (Ryan, op. cit., p. 253). She walked towards the British barricade. It was about 12.45 p.m. There she was taken into custody and held in, of all places, Tom Clarke's shop at 75 Great Britain street, where she was eventually interviewed by Brigadier Lowe. Initially Miss O'Farrell was treated as a spy by 'a very truculent and panicky colonel' (Ryan). But after he had searched and interrogated her he sent a message to Brigadier Lowe, who arrived from his HQ in Trinity after an hour or so. Lowe was courteous, but refused to treat except on the basis of an unconditional surrender, failing which hostilities would recommence within half an hour. Miss O'Farrell returned with this message.

Finally, at 3.30 p.m. she and Pearse met Lowe at the Great Britain street barricade where Pearse handed his sword to Lowe in surrender. The genuine religious ardour of these volunteer Irish soldiers and representatives of the people was demonstrated when, before marching out from number 16 Moore street to far from ignominious surrender, the garrison knelt and said the Rosary. It is even more interesting, and certainly an indication of their moral integrity at the end of a week's fierce fighting, that in all the posts and before marching out to surrender, the men voluntarily knelt for the same purpose.

Brigadier Lowe suggested that Miss O'Farrell should bring a surrender order from Pearse to the battalion commandants in the other positions. Pearse and Miss O'Farrell agreed to this and Pearse wrote out an order:

In order to prevent the further slaughter of Dublin citizens, and in the hope of saving the lives of our followers now surrounded and hopelessly outnumbered, the members of the Provisional Government present at Headquarters have agreed to an unconditonal surrender, and the Commandants of the various districts in the City and Country will order their commands to lay down arms.

P.H.PEARSE
29 April 1916,
3.45 p.m.

Connolly, who was brought to Dublin Castle on a stretcher, added 'I agree to these conditions for the men only under my own command in the Moore street district and for the men in the Stephen's Green command'.

Sunday, 30 April.

Throughout Saturday afternoon and Sunday, Miss O'Farrell brought the order to surrender to the various Irish commands. She was accompanied on many of these journeys by Captain de Courcy-Wheeler, a Dubliner and an aide-de-camp of Lowe's. Occasional shots could be heard, but a curious quiet hung over the city. A huge pall of smoke rose from the rubble that had been Sackville street. The Rising was all but over. The last outposts to surrender were those of MacDonagh in Jacobs and de Valera in Bolands. De Valera marched his men to Mount street before finding any British, although he had earlier contacted a Dr. Keogh — the first civilian he saw in the vicinity of Sir Patrick Duns' Hospital — and asked him to contact the British in order to receive his surrender. It was when handing over their arms to the British in Mount street that de Valera, looking at the onlookers, made the remark which has sometimes been distorted: 'Oh, if only you had come out with knives and forks'.

Those who surrendered in Sackville street on Saturday were kept overnight in the open and marched to Richmond Barracks next day. Those who surrendered on Saturday were marched first to the Royal Dublin Society grounds at Balls Bridge. There is a story that as they were marched through the streets the citizens of Dublin reviled and spat at them. Let the words of a Canadian journalist, F. A. McKenzie, no lover of the Irish, who witnessed the surrender, speak for themselves:

I have read many accounts of public feeling in Dublin in these days. They are all agreed that the open and strong sympathy of the mass of the population was with the British troops. That this was so in the better parts of the city, I have no doubt, but certainly what I myself saw in the poorer districts did not confirm this. It rather indicated that there was a vast amount of sympathy with the Rebels, particularly after the Rebels were defeated'(McKenzie, *The Irish Rebellion*, London, 1916, p.92 et seq.)[145].

McKenzie also describes people cheering a column of arrested Irish, some of them women, marching between lines of British soldiers near Dublin Castle on the Sunday evening following surrender and singing a Irish song.

There was one important action not mentioned above which took place in County Dublin on Friday. That was the Battle of Ashbourne, as it came to be called. It was a precursor of the type of guerilla action which was to prove so effective during the War of Independence a few years later, but the situation was very different in 1916 to what it became in 1918-21 when the populace as a whole, moved by events between the Rising and the following year, provided the support without which a guerrilla army cannot function for long. In 1916 it is questionable if that support would have been forthcoming on a sufficient scale to sustain a prolonged guerrilla war even if that had been part of the original plan.

On Friday, 28 April, [Thomas] Ashe with less than fifty men overran north County Dublin, captured four police barracks, and decisively defeated the R.I.C. with heavy casualties in a stand-up fight[146]. The capture of Ashbourne Barracks and the accompanying action at Rath Cross near-by crowned a bold sweep through the Counties of Meath and Dublin (Ryan op. cit., p.218).

Ashe and his men also captured a relief column more than fifty strong and in all took over ninety prisoners. The Volunteer casualties were two killed, five wounded. The R.I.C. lost eleven dead and forty to fifty wounded, of which ten were later also said to have died.

Ashe and his men had been so successful that when the order to surrender reached him at his camp in County Dublin (at Newbarn near Kilsallaghan) on Monday, 1 May, he refused to believe it. He was offered safe-conduct to Kilmainham Jail to see Pearse in person and not until his second-in-command, Richard Mulcahy, had been brought under safe conduct to consult with Pearse and returned with confirmation, was he convinced[147]. Ashe and his men marched into Swords under lancer escort, where they laid down their arms and were taken to Richmond Barracks by lorry.

The confusion of orders and counter-orders that had gone out from Dublin headquarters to the provincial commands resulted in indecision and perplexity in all areas. Nonetheless in Wexford and Galway mobilisation did take place and, in Wexford particularly, with some success. Under Robert Brennan, Sean Etchingham, Seamus Doyle, Seamus Rafter and Michael de Lacy and acting on verbal orders from Dublin 600 Volunteers established headquarters in Enniscorthy on Thursday and seized the town. Railway communications were cut and Gorey and Ferns were occupied briefly.

The British dispatched a crude armoured train with a 15-pounder gun, and a force of 1,000 infantry and 70 cavalry against Enniscorthy...News of the surrender in Dublin arrived before hostilities began, and Pearse's message was brought to the Volunteer leaders by a messenger whom they trusted (Ryan, op. cit. p.249).

Again the message was not believed and safe conduct was sought, and obtained from Col. F.A.French (himself a Wexford man) to visit Pearse and have the surrender confirmed. Pearse wrote the surrender order for the Wexford men when they arrived and whispered to them to dump their arms in a safe place 'as they will be needed later' (Seamus Doyle, *With Pearse in Arbour Hill, Irish Press*, 3 May, 1932 — cited Ryan, op. cit., p. 249).

For most of the provincial commands on Easter Monday Dublin was suddenly shut off in a 'fog of rumour and silence' (Ryan). MacNeill's order in the *Sunday Independent* was uncompromising, but nevertheless uncertainty and expectancy crackled in the atmosphere like electricity. The experience of the Limerick Brigade (Commandant Liam Manahan) was typical. He issued orders for a mobilisation with arms for Sunday (at which some of his officers protested). His full battalion was mobilised and ready to move off when the *Sunday Independent* appeared, followed by a verbal order from Mitchelstown issued by The O'Rahilly. In spite of this Manahan conducted manoeuvres throughout the day until confirmation of MacNeill's order reached him from Cork at about 7 p.m., when he stood the battalion down. But early the following morning rumours filtered through of fighting in Dublin and Manahan tried throughout Monday and Tuesday to obtain confirmation of this, ordering his battalion to stand-to the meanwhile. Late on Wednesday night he was visited by Sean Treacy, later to make his mark in the War of Independence, who confirmed that there was fighting in Dublin. Manahan decided to mobilise and take action. But by now rumour and counter-rumour, dispersal and re-dumping of weapons, had taken their toll. By the time a full company of the battalion had been brought together, news came that Cork and Limerick had definitely demobilised. It was clear that isolated and unsupported company action would be pointless and demoralising, and Manahan stood his men down again.

In Galway the brigade, under a remarkable man, Liam Mellowes, having mobilised on Sunday only to disband in accordance with MacNeill's order at about 2 p.m., took the field again with 1,200 men at about 8 pm on Monday when a message from Pearse was received — 'Dublin has acted 12 noon to-day, P.H.Pearse'. Headquarters were at Athenry. They remained in the field until Saturday, attacking RIC barracks in the county and capturing RIC and weapons. During the week a number of skirmishes with police and British army units occurred. A British destroyer attempted to shell their positions on Wednesday, to no effect other than some more holes in Conemara. On Saturday, having already disbanded more than half his force, Mellowes decided to stand-down the rest, in view of news from Dublin, as a large force of military and marines were marching against him. He and two companions took to the hills. There were some other small mobilisations in the provinces, including Louth and Kildare in Leinster. In Munster there was mobilisation in Clare. In Kerry mobilisation was aborted, largely because of Casement's arrest. In Cork, a city surrounded by hills on which the British hurriedly placed artillery commanding it, mobilisation was stifled when The O'Rahilly arrived to reinforce MacNeill's order before returning to Dublin to join the Rising. The Bishop, Dr. Cohalan (locally known as 'Danny Boy'), arranged an agreement under which the Volunteers would hand over their arms to the British, under the muzzles of whose field-pieces they were trapped. When they did so there was a military swoop in breach of the terms of the agreement. One of the houses included was that of the Ceannts, near Fermoy, a family that had been prominent during the Land League struggle. A pitched battle lasting three hours followed, in which one of the four brothers who lived there with their mother was mortally wounded. Several police were wounded and the Head Constable was killed.

Terence MacSwiney carried the burden of the Cork failure to mobilise to his famous death-bed four years later. He had, perhaps prophetically, written in his *Principles of Freedom* what may be considered to be the essential summation of the ideology of the Rising:

> We fight for freedom, not for the vanity of the world, not to have a fine conceit of ourselves, not to be as bad — or if we prefer to put it so — as big as our neighbours. The inspiration is drawn from a deeper element of our being. We stifle for self-development individually and as a nation. If we don't go forward we must go down. It is a matter of life or death; it is our soul's salvation. If the whole nation stand for it, we are happy; we shall be grandly victorious. If only a few are faithfully found, they must be the more steadfast for being but a few.

* * * * *

During the week some British troops were guilty of atrocities against civilians, mainly in the North King street area and the battle for the Four Courts. As already mentioned, fifteen civilian men and boys were murdered. A number of people were shot while carrying white flags. A very high number of civilians were killed and wounded by sniper fire, many in their own homes. But, whatever the want of discrimination, the latter, in the absence of proof to the contrary, could not really be classified atrocities.

But the cases of the fifteen men and boys murdered in North King street and elsewhere could. Some were tortured and their bodies were looted or mutilated after death. None of the soldiers involved was charged with an offence.

The most notorious, if not necessarily the worst, examples of atrocity were those committed by Captain J.C.Bowen-Colthurst, who most authorities agree was deranged. He shot, or caused to be shot, in cold blood, four men and a boy, all of them his innocent prisoners. One of his victims was Francis Sheehy Skeffington, or 'Skeff', as he was known, the noted pacifist and eccentric. He was shot with two other men by Colthurst's orders while being held as a prisoner, on no grounds, after he had seen Colthurst murder one of the boys, J.J. Coade, shot as he was coming from Rathmines Church on Tuesday. Colthurst first ordered one of his soldiers to 'bash' the youth. The soldier struck Coade with his rifle-butt. Then Colthurst shouted at him that there was a curfew and that he could be 'shot like a dog'. The youngster replied that he did not know of the curfew, imposed only an hour earlier while he was in the church. After he was struck on the head again with a rifle butt and had fallen senseless to the ground, Colthurst drew his revolver and shot him in the stomach, leaving him to die in the gutter. Coade was later taken by ambulance to the nearby Portobello barracks hospital, but was dead on arrival.

During the Monday attack on the Castle Sheehy-Skeffington, in a gruesome irony, made an heroic dash to drag a wounded British officer to safety. When reproached afterwards by his wife for taking such a risk he answered: 'I could not let anyone bleed to death while I could help' (Ryan, op. cit., p. 168). On Wednesday Sheehy-Skeffington and two other men (both staunch Redmondites as it happens), were taken — illegally — by Colthurst from their cells in Portobello and shot without ceremony in a small enclosed yard. Colthurst afterwards tried to fabricate evidence to justify these murders. An official attempt was made to brush the matter under the carpet, and would probably have succeeded were it not for another British officer, Major Sir Francis Vane, who sacrificed his career in order to pursue justice in these cases. Later General Macready (who succeeded Maxwell) issued an 'explanation' in the *Daily Mail* on 18 May: 'Possibly unfortunate incidents, which we should regret now, may have occurred ... it is even possible that under the horrors of this peculiar (*sic!*) attack some of them '[British troops]' "saw red"...That is the inevitable consequence of a rebellion of this kind'. His predecessor, Maxwell, was equally clear. 'A revolt of this kind' he stated' could not be suppressed with velvet gloves.'

The verdict of the inquest jury on one of the North King street victims is of interest. It reads:

We find that the said Patrick Bealen died from shock and haemorrhage, resulting from bullet wounds inflicted by a soldier, or soldiers, in whose custody he was, an unarmed and unoffending prisoner. We consider that the explanation given by the military authorities is very unsatisfactory, and we believe that if the military authorities had any inclination they could produce the officer in charge.

The officer in charge was Lt.Col. Henry Taylor.

* * * * *

The official figures for those killed or wounded in the Rising is 1,351. The number of Irish soldiers killed has not been determined, but Macardle gives it as fifty-six and Ryan as sixty-one, and says it is incomplete. He puts the number of wounded at between 100 and 120. Caulfield refers to two British snipers (pps. 238 and 239) who between them accounted for more than seventy hits. Clearly many of the civilian casualties were the result of such 'snipers'. The remainder were British casualties. Dorothy Macardle states (p. 181) that British casualty estimates were 'just over three thousand'. She states that in Glasnevin cemetery 'alone' there were four hundred and fifteen burials between 27 April and 4 May and that 'it was said that two hundred and sixteen of these were burials of people who had died of wounds'. The *Irish Independent* listed twenty-eight unidentified civilians and one hundred and twelve men and twenty women who were identified.

The third aim of war is to gain public opinion — Karl von Clausewitz

Chapter 7

The Achievement

CLAUSEWITZ'S THIRD AIM OF WAR WAS ONE of the primary objectives of the Rising (the others being to proclaim the Republic and seek its international recognition) and it became quickly clear that this third aim was achieved. The achievement was spectacularly demonstrated a few years later with the establishment of Dail Eireann, ratification by it of the Republic, and the War of Independence.

Favoured now by its association with the rising, the name Sinn Fein took on a magic ring and Griffith found a nationwide audience. The Sinn Fein organization expanded and became militant, O Luing (*Arthur Griffith and Sinn Fein*, Leaders and Men of the Easter Rising, ed. Martin, p. 63).

O Luing's observation encapsulates one of the most curious — and curiously enduring — aspects of the Rising, which still has a resonance today. For the British the expressions 'Sinn Feiners' or 'Shinners' were universal labels for anyone and anything in Ireland not obviously loyalist, including the Irish Party and Home Rulers. They indicated anything vaguely national — even, at opposite ends of the spectrum, the Abbey Theatre and the Volunteers. Naturally this outlook was transferred to the Rising, immediately dubbed 'The Sinn Fein Rebellion', thus creating a label — and a platform for Griffith — that became identified with Irish nationalist separatism The reason is undoubtedly (See Lyons op. cit. p.381) because Sinn Fein was a known separatist movement, whereas the IRB moved in the deepest secrecy. Even before the Rising the Volunteers were sometimes referred to derogatorily as 'Shinners'. Clearly the coincidental involvement of Sinn Fein cannot be overlooked, and Sinn Fein members undoubtedly fought in the Rising, but they did so as members of the IRB, the Volunteers and the Citizen Army, not as members of Sinn Fein.

For Griffith, however, the consequences of this misnomer were dramatic and fortuitous. The misconception catapulted him to the forefront of public affairs in a manner hitherto unattained. To this mantle of revolt may also be attributed a change in the Sinn Fein constitution, tranforming that organisation from a nationalist pacifist one to one that accepted the use of force when necessary. The

Rising and the executions that followed triggered an immense public response which found in 'Sinn Fein' a focus for its indignation. Under false colours or no, the unexpected development could not be ignored by the Volunteers or the IRB. It was, therefore, adopted — and adapted — by them too, to bring about the 'new' Sinn Fein.

After the Rising all, was indeed, changed utterly. But it was not, as is most usually thought, a change in the attitude of the Irish alone. The change in British administration was total, fundamental and nation-wide.

The Easter Rising was the essential pivot on which the whole movement for national sovereignty swung. The people suffered, but increasingly the realisation that their suffering was in a cause for which they were prepared to continue to suffer took hold. From a more-or-less comfortable, complacent, rather mindless, society with agitating fringes, the country was hurled into a painful rebirth. From the civil, more-or-less benign, 'caretaker administration' of Birrell and Nathan that had meandered along carelessly in the years before 1916, it became, in a matter of days, strict martial law with curfew across most of the country, with coercion, intimidation and seizure of the general populace its most obvious public features. This was later coupled to naked terrorism, murder and torture by crown forces, for which, eventually, no established authority wanted to accept reponsibility. The more or less caretaker administration had been supplanted by a repressive and coercive military administration under a military governor. That situation modified little during 1917 and 1918. From 1919 to 1921 it was war. It quickly became evident that the Irish Party were not only discredited, they had lost even their own support.

The Irish Party were slowly augmented by an ever increasing awareness that Pearse was right and the Irish Party was wrong (Murphy, op. cit., p. 65).

But, in fact, the realisation was neither slow nor very small. 'When the captured survivors of the Easter Week war marched away to exile and imprisonment through a silent, smoke-clouded Dublin in the first days following the surrender, they felt that hope was dead for at least another generation; but before the last batch of them had been taken out of Ireland there was a miraculous change' (*Wolfe Tone Annual*, 1946, p. 22).

And, within a few weeks of the Rising, Maxwell himself with unusual accuracy recorded ....

Censored correpondence of interned prisoners ... shows a decided turn for the worse. Whereas at first their letters were humble and apologetic, now the tone has become defiant, and shows that they think themselves national heroes ... There is a growing feeling that out of rebellion more has been got than by constitutional methods, hence Mr. Redmond's power is on the wane ... It is becoming increasingly difficult to differentiate between a Nationalist [Irish Party] and a Sinn Feiner. Recruiting in Ireland has practically ceased ... If there was a general election very few, if any, of existing Nationalist M.Ps. would be re-elected so there is a danger that Mr.Redmond's party would be replaced by others perhaps less amenable to reason ...' (Asquith papers, Maxwell to French, 16.6.1916).

What had wrought this complete reversal of attitude on the part of so many people? In effect the Rising had, in accordance with von Clausewitz's dictum and with spectacular success, achieved the second of its three aims. The vengeful policy of executions spread out over two weeks is an obvious factor. But there were others. It is possible, even had the executions not taken place or been limited to a smaller number, that the change in national attitude would have taken place anyway. The movement in that direction was already discernible before the Rising. What the Rising and the executions did was give it vital emphasis and impetus.

Except for the quite small number of separatists and some of those in Sinn Fein, the initial reaction in Ireland to the Rising had generally been one of shock. That in England was one of fury at what was seen as absolute and treasonable betrayal. The Unionists, of course, managed to forget their own treason of a couple of years earlier and now shouted 'I told you so', to the accompanying, though slightly less hysterical, indignation of loyalists. Both were supported by the Irish Parliamentary Party which reacted with great hostility.

Initially, too, there were, throughout the country, many calls from the 'secure' classes for the most rigorous measures against the men and women of 'Sinn Fein'. So hostile were certain sections of the influential Dublin establishment that they took active steps to counteract the appeals for mercy made to the authorities. A petition was signed by the extraordinary number of 763 people, all Unionists, 'protesting against any interference with the discretion of the Commander-in-Chief of the forces in Ireland and the operation of martial law'.

The principal Dublin media, *The Irish Times* and the *Irish Independent*, verged on the hysterical in their demands for execution, not just of the leaders of the Rising, but of many more. In its first edition after the Rising, *The Irish Times* declared:

We know now, beyond yea or nay, the extent, the power, the motives and the methods of the seditious movement in Ireland. All the elements of disafection have shown their hand. The State has struck, but its work is not yet finished. The surgeon's knife has been put to the corruption in the body of Ireland, and its course must not be stayed until the whole malignant growth has been removed. In the verdict of history weakness to-day would be even more criminal than the indifference of the last few months. Sedition must be rooted out of Ireland once and for all. The rapine and bloodshed of the past week must be finished with a severity which will make any repetition of them impossible for generations to come....

But it was left to William Martin Murphy's paper, the *Irish Independent*, to carve a niche of its own into the record of 1916 with a tirade of vituperation against the Rising that lasted throughout the period of the executions. On 4 May it thundered: 'No terms of denunciation that pen could indite would be too strong to apply to those responsible for the insane and criminal rising of last week...' On 10 May when only Mac Dermott and Connolly of those executed were still alive (and how many more were to be shot was still unknown), the *Irish Independent*, published a picture of Connolly with the caption: 'Still lies in Dublin Castle slowly recovering from his wounds' ... and an editorial which, after twelve men had already been shot, said 'Let the worst of the ringleaders be singled out and dealt with as they deserve'[148].

The rather grandiloquent question of Yeats's: 'Did that play of mine send out Certain men the English shot?' might be more accurately and terribly adapted and applied to the newspapers of the period. That such shrill screams for bloody vengeance had about them the nervousness, in the first case, of the Protestant ascendancy (for *The Irish Times* was the organ of the Protestant community), in the second that of the now dishevelled and discredited Irish Party, and in the third of the general establishment and monied classes, there can be little doubt. That these demands for retribution, coming from the principal Irish newspapers, may have influenced Maxwell and confirmed his own judgement is speculation. That he was aware of them is hardly in question.

Yet, within days, as understanding of what those who took part in the Rising and what they stood for and tried to do spread, the mood across the country began to change. Divorced from the hysteria and distortions of the loyalist press, the people came to assess what had occurred. They began to see the Rising for what it had been and to recognise that, at whatever remove, those who took part in it had acted in their name, and they began to endorse that action in great and ever increasing numbers.

The revolutionary climate of thought necessary to win support from the people once the rising of those subject to an alien rule has begun and its purpose has become evident, had been created. The Rising was the beginning of the active phase.

In taking account of the general atmosphere of the times one thinks of a society without TV, without home radios and with very little cinema which, in any case, was both silent and almost exclusively for entertainment purposes. Popular mass entertainment consisted of the music-hall/theatre and musical evenings at home. There was much more pedestrian street activity. Popular movements attracted people, both the dedicated and the simply curious, in far greater numbers from much smaller local populations than is the case to-day. Newspapers were usually — and correctly — perceived as political voices. That being the case, allowances were automatically made in respect of whatever was being pontificated upon in the editorial columns. Word of mouth was the most common — and ultimately in small communities the most reliable — means of disseminating information.

As soon as he could after the Rising Dillon advised Redmond to stay in London, as 'if you were here you would be held more or less responsible for all done by the Castle and military authorities ... you should urge strongly on the Government the *extreme* unwisdom of any wholesale shooting of prisoners. The wisest course is to execute no one for the present ... If there were shootings of prisoners on a large scale the effect on public opinion might be disastrous in the extreme. So far feeling of the population in Dublin is against Sinn Feiners. But a reaction might very easily be created ... ' (Denis Gwynn, *The Life of John Dillon*, London, p.474-5). This extract, though its emphasis on the feelings of the population being against the 'Sinn Feiners' is suspect and probably no more than an anxiety to reassure his leader, does indicate Dillon's insight into the moods and feelings of the impoverished and deprived people, far removed though he was himself from their condition.

Dillon's perceptive advice to Redmond was an uncommon trait in the Parliamentary Party at that time. The reality was that already amidst the rubble that had been the centre of Dublin and throughout the country, the allegiance and support of the people was swinging dramatically away from the Irish Party which, within a matter of three years, would be demolished at the polls to be left to linger in some sort of political Limbo until, ironically, it — or its former members and adherents — could return to political power and influence following the signing of the Anglo-Irish Treaty in December, 1921. This was a direct consequence of the Rising. But, even if the Rising had not taken place, the writing for the Irish Party was writ large on the wall of the Irish national movement once the watered-down Home Rule was shelved. When Redmond gave his allegiance to Britain in the war and urged the Irish Volunteers to go and fight, it copper-fastened its demise. The executions, when they began, stirred something very deep in the people, race-memory, perhaps, and the hidden shape of self-image, shocked into wakefulness by a greater realisation of what the Rising was all about.

The first executions took place four days after the Rising, on Wednesday, 3 May. The news was conveyed to the public by the following statement issued by British HQ:

Three signatories of the notice proclaiming the Irish Republic, P.H.Pearse, T. MacDonagh, and T.J.Clarke have been tried by the Field General Courts-martial and sentenced to death. The sentence having been duly confirmed, the three above-mentioned men were shot this morning.

The executions continued over the next two weeks at daily, or slightly longer, intervals. On 4 May Joseph Plunkett — married to Grace Gifford in his cell hours before his death — Edward Daly, Willie Pearse, Michael O'Hanrahan. On 5 May Major John MacBride. On 8 May Eamonn Ceannt, Michael Mallin, Con Colbert, Sean Heuston. On 9 May Thomas Kent — Ceannt, no relation — (in Cork). On 12 May James Connolly — seriously wounded, in great pain and strapped to a chair to which he had been lifted from his stretcher, because he was unable to stand — and Sean MacDermott. Fifteen men in all were shot during those weeks. On 3 August Roger Casement was hanged in London.

On 11 May 1916, the day before Connolly and Sean MacDermott were killed, Dillon, since Redmond did not do so, appealed in the House of Commons at Westminster for an end to the executions. 'If there be a case of cold blooded murder, by all means try the man openly before a court martial if you like, but let the people know what the evidence is and prove he is a murderer, and then do what you like with him. But it is not murderers who are being executed; it is insurgents who have fought a clean fight and a brave fight', he was interrupted by a howl of protest from the Tory benches. Angered, he went on '— and it would be a damned good thing for you if your soldiers were able to put up as good a fight as did these men in Dublin: three thousand against twenty thousand with machine-guns and artillery'. And, as we know, the odds were more than twice that.

According to Lawlor (op. cit., p. 9, citing the Asquith papers), Asquith in a letter to King George on 6 May claimed that Maxwell had been instructed that the capital sentence was 'not to be carried out on any women' (which might explain Countess Markievicz's sentence being commuted to life imprisonment), that it was not to be inflicted 'except upon ringleaders and murderers' and that he was to 'bring the executions to a close as soon as possible'. There is no other confirmation of these alleged instructions, written to the king when eight men were still to be killed. It reads like an attempt to ameliorate for the king the severe fall-out that was already being felt. Asquith was in Dublin a few days later, while the final executions were taking place.

For all Dillon's experience and Redmond's squirming the Irish Parliamentary Party was in disarray; their policies had disintegrated and it was only a matter of time until their political power and prestige was taken from them. (It is a strange fact that those years after the Easter Rising saw in both Britain and Ireland not simply the collapse, but the total disappearance of two great political parties; the English Liberal Party and the Irish Parliamentary Party, both brought down, essentially, for the same reasons — their Irish policies).

There were 160 courts martial after the Rising before the proceedings were stopped by political intervention from London, rightly alarmed at the effect the protracted executions were having on world opinion. There were in all 97 death sentences, before the killing was halted. The remaining 82 were sentenced to penal servitude for various terms, from three years to life. In all 122 people were sentenced. But, in addition, thousands were rounded up and deported without trial to prisons and prison camps — Reading Jail, Frongoch and elsewhere — in England and Wales.

Lyons (op. cit., p. 365) takes the view — which the leaders of the Rising themselves shared — that they 'condemned' themselves: 'The decision which the prime movers of the insurrection had taken on Sunday — that they would start the rising on the morning of Easter Monday — condemned them, as they well knew, to an enterprise that was doomed to disaster before it had even begun'.

But his use of the word 'disaster' is interesting, since that interpretation is very much an open question. In terms of failing to destroy the enemy or capture his materiel it was certainly a failure. But, while a military operation, the Rising was not conceived in those terms, and it is strange that, even still, it is thought to have been. The military objective was Clausewitz's *third* aim of war; to gain public opinion, and **that** objective was achieved.

It is sometimes argued that had the executions not taken place everything would have returned to its cosy complacency and there would have been no War of Independence. Greaves (op. cit., p.35) comments:

It is worth dealing with the frequently made speculation that had Maxwell not introduced the white terror the revolution which followed 1916 would never have taken place ....This line of thought leads to fantasy. Once the act of defiance had been committed, provided that imperialism remained imperialism, that Ireland remained a subject nation, that the crisis of the world war was there and bound to develop further — granted these concretely existing conditions, there was no course of action British imperialism could adopt which would not serve to strengthen the national liberation movement.

As the attitude and activities of the prisoners in Frongoch and elsewhere throughout the remainder of 1916 show, together with the response of the general public and supporters at home at both social and political levels, there is no doubt that the intention to continue to some conclusion what was begun in 1916 was no longer confined to the IRB and some of the Volunteers, but was rapidly gaining ground amongst the people as a whole.

They began to see the Rising, and those who led, it as part of the process that had brought about 1798, 1803, 1848 and 1867 and, indeed, the Land War of the 1880s. In addition to the brutality of the executions, wholesale arrests and the maintainance of Martial Law contributed to this process and encouraged the public to view the Rising with a different and more understanding eye.

The change was quite rapid, from Spring 1916 to a nationwide expression of national will by mid 1917. But then, as we have noted, the nature and character of the British administration of what they still thought of (at least in principle) as part of the United Kingdom, also underwent a profound and drastic change. That change was itself an acceptance and admission — acknowledged or not — that the end of the Union was in sight. It was, or should have been, clear at this time that the Union could no longer be preserved by coercion, yet this remained unacknow-ledged by the British. The British had not been aware of the role of the IRB in organising the Rising, but with the execution of the 1916 leaders they unwittingly struck the IRB a severe blow. All its leaders were gone and many of its 2,000 rank-and-file members were in jail in England. The task of rebuilding the organisation began amongst these prisoners at the 'University of Frongoch', as it was called — giving rise, indeed, to some differences of opinion amongst the prisoners, between those who supported the IRB, and those who believed that future progress should be conducted more openly. Prisoners were also scattered in other prisons throughout England, those alleged to be 'most dangerous' (including the author's father) being transferred from Frongoch to Reading Jail. In August the Keating branch of the Gaelic League resumed activities. A new provisional Supreme Council of the IRB was formed. Sean O Muirthile, who became its secretary, wrote: 'The Gaelic League again proved useful, and under the guise of Gaelic League work we were able to hold frequent meetings throughout the Autumn' (Mulcahy papers). Contact was resumed with Devoy in America and steps were taken to resuscitate the Volunteers, re-named the Irish Republican Army (IRA) during the Rising[149]. Cathal Brugha was released from hospital in September and a representative meeting of Volunteers from all over the country met in Fleming's Hotel in Dublin under his chairmanship. 'By December 1916, therefore, a start had been made to revitalise the two organisations most involved in the Rising — the IRB and the Irish Volunteers, and a connection had been established with the Clan in America' (Murphy op. cit., p.70).

Aftermath

Paradoxically, and in a species of political mindless reflex, the Rising gave an unexpected — and unavailing — boost to Home Rule. In the weeks following the

Rising the British government clumsily sought to negotiate with Redmond 'whereby Redmond was offered immediate Home Rule over most of Ireland, provided that he agreed to the exclusion of the six north eastern counties'(John H. Whyte, *1916 — Revolution and Religion; Leaders and Men of the Easter Rising:Dublin 1916*, p.224). It must have been clear that Asquith's Home Rule proposal — as strange a proposal as the circumstances which produced it — was hopeless. On the one hand Asquith was desperate to save both his party and his political future, both in extreme distress, and as a means of reviving them, trying to negotiate the impossible with, on the other hand, John Redmond, already further down the slope of political oblivion than himself. Redmond, now evidently panicking, supported Asquith's proposal thereby effectively hammering the last nail into his own political coffin. Such a storm of protest was raised throughout Ireland that he withdrew his support and the proposal was abandoned. This had one unexpected effect. As Whyte says,

> it was hardly possible to condemn the resort to arms without, by implication, supporting the constitutional action of the Irish Parliamentary Party. Now [because of the foregoing] the Irish Party ... gave great offence to some of those clerics who had been among its staunchest supporters'

since the proposal to partition the country, now being supported by Redmond, 'was violently opposed by the bishops and clergy of the area involved'.

But Asquith's immediate purpose — to allay anxiety in America as to British intentions regarding Ireland — **was** achieved. The offer had been a mere whitewash — a cynical exercise in showing cause — designed to offset the powerful reaction of Irish-Americans to the executions. Lloyd George, the brilliant and unscrupulous realist who was to succeed Asquith, said to William O'Brien at the time: 'The Irish-American vote will go over to the German side, they will break our blockade and force an ignominious peace on us, unless something is done, even provisionally, to satisfy America' (*The Irish Revolution and how it Came About*, William O'Brien, London, 1923, p.273)[150].

The British still laboured under the delusion that the Rising had been something other than it was, which may help to explain the crude and brutal execution policy of Gen. Maxwell. That such executions might contribute powerfully to ensuring the achievement of the Rising's purpose was either overlooked, ignored or, more likely, never considered. The well-polished jack-boot is a law unto itself that seldom considers other options and, in that sense, Maxwell may be said to have contributed handsomely to what he was committed to preventing. The British concluded — a combination, perhaps, of wishful thinking and continued misreading of Casement's and German involvement — a/ that it 'was not' an Irish rebellion (Birrell to Asquith, 29/4/1916), and b/ was 'nothing more than a Dublin row' (Augustine Birrell, *Things Past Redress*, London, 1937, p.220)

Asquith, however, more alive to the political implications than his generals (and no doubt equally conscious of the problems caused by those same generals a mere two years previously), wrote that Maxwell should be reminded that wholesale executions might 'easily cause a revulsion of feeling in Britain and lay up a store of future trouble in Ireland' (O Broin, op., cit.,p.130). Lord French, then Chief of the Imperial General Staff, advised Maxwell along these lines, adding that there was no intention to interfere with his freedom of action or initiative (French, Gerald, *Life of Field Marshal Sir John French*, London, 1931, pp. 340/1). John Dillon was rightly appalled by this and advised Redmond, who seemed less concerned. Nevertheless, urged on by Dillon's prompting, Redmond protested to Asquith, asking him to intervene, and stating that 'his military men had gone too far and had dragged out the executions intolerably'. The total number executed was small compared with the daily casualties in the war which ran into thousands, but to the Irish people it was 'as though they watched a stream of blood coming from beneath a closed door'(O Broin, op. cit., p.131).

On 9 May Maxwell replied to Asquith defending his policy.

In view of the gravity of the rebellion and its connection with German intrigue and propaganda and in view of the great loss of life and destruction of property resulting therefrom, the General Officer Commanding in Chief, Irish Command, has found it imperative to inflict the most severe sentences on the organisers of this detestable Rising and on the Commanders who took an actual [active?] part in the actual fighting which occurred. It is hoped that these examples will be sufficient to act as a deterrent to intriguers and to bring home to them that the murder of His Majesty's subjects or other acts calculated to imperil the safety of the realm will not be tolerated.

This is a relatively simple military response and it is significant, particularly in view of the war situation and the German successes, that it is the German connection that receives initial attention in it. The 'hope' of the executions acting as a deterrent displays an ignorance of both political wisdom and of domestic Irish history seemingly typical of the English military mind of the period.

Also on 9 May, when eleven executions had already taken place over the previous week, the Irish Party tabled a resolution which, unintentionally, encapsulates their amphibolous and feeble position: 'The continuance of the military executions, carried out against persistent protests ... has caused rapidly increasing bitterness amongst the large majority of the Irish people who had no sympathy with the Insurrection ... in the interests of the Empire, as well as of Ireland, no further executions should be allowed to take place ... and martial law [be] immediately withdrawn'. Martial law, of course, seriously affected trade and commerce throughout the country.

Asquith sent his private secretary with a message to French — not to Maxwell — expressing his surprise and perturbation at the execution of 'so many' Irish leaders.

Eighty-two more death sentences were passed and, on 21 May, Asquith secured an undertaking from Maxwell that no sentence of death would be confirmed without reference to him (O Broin op. cit., pp. 132/3). When Asquith visited Ireland Maxwell availed of the opportunity to give the prime minister the benefit of his political views on the Rising, which, he said, was undoubtedly fomented by German promises and propaganda.

Had the enterprise of Sir Roger Casement succeeded the whole of the west of Ireland including Cork (sic!) would have risen and I deliberately think that we have narrowly missed a most serious rebellion. One danger must not be lost sight of ... the younger generation is likely to be more revolutionary than their predecessors...(Asquith papers, 44. Maxwell to French, 13.5.1916, Bodleian)

He went on to make a second prophecy: 'I think I can, however, assert that recent events have proved to the extremists that rebellion without ample arms and organisation cannot succeed, and that they have no chance of success against trained soldiers ... There is a strong recrudescence of Sinn Feinism...Though the Irish rebellion **was** condemned, it is now being used as a lever to bring on Home Rule, **or an Irish Republic**'.

In a post-Rising summary for Asquith of the events leading up to the Rising, Maxwell had underscored Nathan's views (10 April, to the Adjutant General) that he did not believe that the Sinn Fein leaders intended insurrection or that the Volunteers had sufficient arms even if the leaders did mean it. Nathan's statement, he said, prevented the military taking action against the Volunteers in the pre-Rising as they had intended. On 22 March the Director of Military Intelligence, Maj. Gen G.M.W. MacDonagh 'whom Winston Churchill regarded as the best intelligence officer in Europe' (O Broin, op. cit., p.144) informed French that he had absolutely reliable information that a rising was intended in Ireland 'on 22 April' and that the Irish were in contact with Germany with a view to obtaining assistance. Arms and munitions were to be provided by Germany to Limerick by that date.

This, as we know, was based on the wireless messages between the German Embassy in Washington and the German Foreign Office, intercepted by the British Navy almost from the outbreak of the war.

Eoin MacNeill, anticipating reprisals, had approached Maxwell on 1 May before the executions began. Instead of a hearing with Maxwell and, in spite of his known opposition to, and non-participation in, the Rising he was arrested and court-martialled. He was sentenced to penal servitude for life. Citing the MacNeill papers, O Broin comments that a particularly good example of how little the Government knew of how the Rising occurred, and of the military's distrust of some of the Irish Party leaders, emerged during MacNeill's interrogation by Army Intelligence [Major Price], when the latter attempted to get MacNeill to involve John Dillon and Joe Devlin of the Irish Party in the Rising.

This curious ineptitude of the British is also demonstrated in a communication from the secretary of the Army Council, to French dated 28 April 1916. O Broin writes (op. cit p.145):

Even before the Rising was suppressed, the Council were concerned with disciplinary issues. They had been informed that on the day the disturbances commenced Friend was in England, and that certain officers attended a race meeting at a distance from their stations and were reported to have been taken by the Insurgents and held hostages. 'On 22nd March, 1916' Brade [secretary to the Army Council] went on, 'a secret memo. on the state of Ireland was sent from the War Office to your Irish staff, *and ... was communicated to Friend* [O Broin's italics]. There is further reason to believe that on 16 April Friend received information from General Officer Commanding Queenstown

(Stafford) ... that two submarines and a vessel containing arms had left Germany for Ireland. In connection with these two events ... it is noted that Sir Roger Casement was arrested on 20 April and the vessel sunk on the 21 April'. French was asked to report fully the circumstances under which, in view of the very serious warnings that had presumably been received by him, Friend was not present in his command [he was in London], and the officers were allowed to absent themselves from their stations.

French defended Friend, pointing out that his military dispositions were adequate in the circumstances, that, following the arrest of Casement and MacNeill's countermanding orders, the possibility of a rising was very small; that it was doubtful if there were any foundation for the rumours of one.

A Royal Commission report on the rising issued at the end of June (1916) said ... that the main cause of the rebellion was an unchecked growth of lawlessness, and the fact that Ireland for several years had been administered on the principle that it was safer and more expedient to leave the law in abeyance, if collision with any faction could thereby be avoided. Such a policy was the negation of the cardinal rule of law which demands that the enforcement of law and the preservation of order should always be independent of political expediency.

If the events leading to the Rising took place surprisingly quickly and in secret, those which followed and led, openly, to the War of Independence, were even more startling — not alone in their rapidity but, more spectacularly, in their widespread public acceptance. Within a few weeks of the Rising the Volunteers of 1916 were being hailed as heroes and martyrs. A few weeks after the Rising, Maxwell felt it necessary to defend his execution policy even more strongly than before.

Certainly the executions played a large part in harnessing public opinion against the British administration, as did the brutal and callous demands in the *Irish Times* and the *Irish Independent* for vengeful reprisals. But, as subsequent events indicate, it was the Rising itself that was the essential catalyst. It achieved to the full its objective in arousing in the lethargic people a fury for justice and an active protest against the indignity under which they were being forced to live. The Rising erased the verbiage and euphemisms of half-hearted constitutional nationalism so that it was really no longer possible to blinker the people and occlude the bottom line — Nationality and Freedom — with comfortable pedantry.

From the ashes of the Rising grew and spread a national unity of purpose more powerful and single-minded than anything — with the possible exceptions of the Land movement in the 1880s and Catholic emancipation ninety-four years earlier — that had preceded it. The feeling was like a wind across the barley; widespread, directional and visible. The accumulated outrage of national identity was unlocked and became active.

Causes were combining to make the idea of independence, of an Irish Republic, a possibility — no mere unattainable dream. All over the world the tide of democracy was rising. President Wilson, in his pronouncements, was giving the ideal of international equity inspiration and form (Macardle, op. cit. p. 199).

In September, only four months after the executions, a group — mainly from the north — established an 'Irish Nation League' to oppose partition. The League was later described, more or less accurately, as 'a place where some souls suffer for a time before they enter the republican movement'.

The executions, the virtual death of Home Rule, martial law, the hanging of Casement and the effects of the 'University of Frongoch' all contributed. The returning prisoners — most of whom were released at Christmas and who were greeted with torchlight processions and bonfires — were the leaven that raised the national spirit and channelled it into a national movement.

Lloyd George became prime minister of England on 6 December 1916 — a day of the month that would, within a few years, feature twice again in Irish history.

1917.

In January 1917 a by-election arose in Roscommon and the emergent 'national' movement decided that this was the platform from which they would spring politically. A representative committee was formed and it selected Count Plunkett, father of the executed leader Joseph, as their candidate. It was a 'safe' Irish Party seat and it is a measure of the changed times that, in spite of this, Plunkett was elected — narrowly, but decisively.

Two additional events of importance then occurred. Bearing in mind that there had not really been an electoral platform other than to put Plunkett forward and take the Irish Party seat, a formal meeting was convened to decide, *post factum*, what in fact the vote had been for. Delegates from public bodies all over the country attended and, after a heated meeting, it was agreed to form a National Council. The National Council (not to be confused with Lloyd George's 'National Convention', below) declared Ireland to be a separate nation and bound itself to use every means in its power to attain complete liberty for the country. It demanded representation for the nation at the post-war Peace Conference.

To this unexpected move by the Irish electorate the new British Government reacted in a new and different way. Lloyd George was a very different kettle-of-fish to his predecessor. Possessed of extraordinary political insight, he read the message of the Roscommon by-election with clarity. He then proceeded to act with the deviousness for which he became no less renowned. 'Heavy American pressure was exerted in the spring of 1917 to bring about ... a satisfactory form of self government for Ireland' (Lyons, op. cit., p. 285). Lloyd George set about doing his best to put a smooth face on Britain's position *vis-a-vis* Ireland — which had received a battering internationally after the Rising. He appeared to oppose conscription for Ireland. At the same time he:

> ... with characteristic adaptability, was now taking a new tone in his references to Ireland, employing a combination of disarming frankness and subtle mis-representation which was exceedingly successful in detaching sympathy from the Irish cause (Macardle, op. cit., p.210).

In particular, **knowing it would be rejected** — and that is worth remembering — he, too, offered immediate Home Rule, but with partition. Lloyd George's motive in going to such unlikely lengths to have Home Rule back on the British-

Irish agenda was not prompted solely by an anxiety to improve Britain's international image regarding Ireland, nor yet by the events of Easter Week. The war was not going well for England. Conscription was still in the air. In spite of the war situation he put conscription on 'the long finger' for the moment, but eventually would resolve 'to press the proposals for conscription "with all the support at our command, on the ground that the military need is overwhelming"' (Lawlor, op. cit., p. 20).

Lloyd George's immediate purpose was to focus international attention on the 'reasonable generosity' of Britain and the 'intransigence' of the Irish. But his proposal for Home Rule was rejected by Redmond. He at once made a second 'reasonable' proposal and one, curiously enough, originally floated by Redmond. Lloyd George 'seized on a suggestion of Redmond's that a conference or convention of Irishmen should be held in the hope that they might be able to work out their own salvation', as Lyons somewhat ambiguously puts it (Ibid.). After some to-ing and fro-ing the Irish National Council suggested terms for their participating in this 'Convention of Irishmen'. But as these terms would have ensured the defeat of Lloyd George's purpose, and as he had no intention of running the risk of getting 'recommendations from his Convention which would reveal the strength of the Irish demand for independence and unity' (Macardle, op. cit., p. 218), he ignored the National Council's terms and unilaterally announced his own composition of the Convention. It was to have one hundred and one 'hand-picked' members. Fifteen were to be nominated by the Crown. It would have forty-seven mayors and chairmen of public bodies (all of them elected before the Rising and therefore unrepresentative of contemporary national views). The remaining thirty-nine members would consist of representatives from Chambers of Commerce (the commercial Establishment), the Churches, organised labour and political parties. Sinn Fein was offered five seats, but Sinn Fein, organised labour and other bodies refused to participate. This unrepresentative Convention met in Trinity College in July. Its only significant achievement was the release of prisoners, which was to have an important effect on the development of Sinn Fein and, ultimately, on the War of Independence.

The mirage was now becoming the reality as Sinn Fein (to which so much had been, incorrectly, attributed in the past), expanded to fit the image imposed on it. But this was not accomplished without considerable difficulty and struggle, essentially between Plunkett, Brugha and other militant republicans on the one hand and Griffith, Sean Milroy and William O'Brien on the other. It was a clash between militant nationalism and active socialism with a common objective, but with differing views as to how that objective might be achieved.

The evidence is clear that in the debate on the future constitution of Sinn Fein, Arthur Griffith defended his partiality for a 'king, lords and commons' structure for an independent Ireland to the last. Dr Thomas Dillon, who was secretary to the provisional standing committee of Sinn Fein, expressed the view that 'Griffith was a strong theoretical monarchist and would have preferred at the time to have the King of England as King of Ireland, with a completely independent parliament, to an Irish Republic'.

Brugha, of course, held the opposite view. At a meeting in June at his house in Rathmines, the differences were compromised and a committee was formed to draft a new constitution for a reconstituted umbrella Sinn Fein.

The Castle's answer to the by-election successes was to arrest and deport visible leaders of national organisations of all sorts[151]. It was not just Griffith's Sinn Fein, or the separatist movement, that was now generally known by that name (indeed some Volunteers[152] and other active separatists resented the 'Sinn Fein' label pinned on them by the British and the Press). For that reason alone (and there were others), they were not all that well disposed to Griffith or his organisation. But the label stuck, and virtually everyone in any way Irish in outlook and who was not an obvious supporter of the rapidly declining Irish Party became a 'Sinn Feiner' by, as it were, a process of national osmosis. A sense of outrage at moral injustice was aroused, even in the most unlikely people, and from then on proceeded to strengthen under that label.

But even disaffected Irish Party supporters whose latent national outlook had been stimulated by the events of the previous year, now began to identify with Sinn Fein. The National Committee decided to contest a by-election in Longford, the second in a sequence of popular victories. Joe McGuinness, then a prisoner in Lewes jail in England, was selected as candidate with the slogan 'Put him in to get him out' (a validly elected member of the British parliament could not be sent to prison unless convicted of a crime). Simultaneously, however, with the accelerated constitutional activity the Volunteers 'were warned against abandoning physical force' (Murphy, op. cit., citing F. O'Donoghue, *Re-organisation of the Irish Volunteers 1916-1917*, Capuchin Annual, 1967, p. 382).

Lloyd George had made partition an issue once again, and, compounding its already substantial litany of errors, the Irish Party, evidently in a misguided endeavour to recover ground after the Roscommon fiasco, came out obliquely in support of partition by supporting Lloyd George's new Home Rule proposals. Joe Devlin blared that the issue was 'whether they were in favour of a self-governed Ireland or a hopeless fight for an Irish republic. There could' he said, 'be no half-way house'. But this was a species of 'bottom-line' mistake, of the sort parties and party leaders commit when they imagine the electorate is too stupid to understand what they're saying. The misrepresentation deceived no one, especially not an intelligent electorate. The Irish Party was, indeed, asking them to vote for a half-way house. But it wasn't just simply that Home Rule had been watered down to less than genuine self-government. The people were being asked to vote for an Ireland partitioned, and they knew it and were having none of it.

Two days before the election eighteen Irish bishops issued a manifesto against partition, giving Sinn Fein an unexpected boost. Although the register was old and excluded thousands of young people who might have been expected to support Sinn Fein, McGuinness won with a small majority. The second victory in a row for Irish separatism, this one was clearly and decisively a Sinn Fein victory. There were celebrations all over Ireland. The pro-British *The Irish Times* said that the mere hint that the Parliamentary Party was ready to accept partition had helped defeat it (the Party). 'After the bishops' manifesto partition is as dead as a doornail and any government which should try to resurrect it would show itself incredibly ignorant or insanely contemptuous of the solitary conviction which now unites all political parties in Ireland.' One after another, with increasing majorities, Sinn Fein won each by-election — five in all — between January and September. De Valera was selected as candidate, either virtually as he was released from Pentonville Jail in England where he had been serving the life-sentence he was given after 1916, or immediately he arrived in Dublin a few days later; it is unclear which. He polled more than two and a half times the votes of his opponent in East Clare[153]. That victory, in particular, was considered the most signal political victory for Sinn Fein. De Valera was the last surviving Commandant of Easter Week and he had emerged in the interim as a leader of character and considerable charisma. Macardle writes (p.223): 'A Dublin Castle official told an English journalist that "this [the East Clare] was the most important election that had ever taken place, or ever will take place, in Irish history"' (*Daily Telegraph*, 10 July). Certainly it stunned the British establishment, as their reaction showed. Sinn Fein 'has swept the country like a tidal wave and blotted out the Irish Party completely and, apparently, irretrievably' (*The Daily Express*).

The British found de Valera's characteristic detached yet distinctive deliberate pragmatism, allied to uncompromising principle, extremely dangerous. In an election speech which was almost a prelude to the formula he proposed (See p. 188 below) to reconcile what had seemed irreconcilable differences at the Sinn Fein Convention in October, he said:

We want an Irish republic because if Ireland had her freedom, it is, I believe, the most likely form of government. But if the Irish people wanted to have another form of government, so long as it was an Irish government, I would not put in a word against it.

De Valera's victory acted like a torch to oil. All over the country meetings and rallys supported the surge of separatist republicanism that lifted the people in its swell. Many of these meetings were attacked by police and, at at least one — at Ballybunion — a man was shot dead by a policeman.

If there was indifference or apathy in the people towards the Rising when it occurred, that had changed in the following twelve months. If the Easter Rising of 1916 had not been nationwide, by Easter 1917 a nationwide expression of national feeling, under the generic name 'Sinn Fein', was amply evident. By the summer the whole nation, with the exception of the unionist north, was under brutal martial law and the people openly supported the movement for national sovereignty. But in April the United States, provoked by Germany's unwise declaration of unrestricted U-Boat warfare in the Atlantic[154], declared war on Germany, and this, to some extent, relieved pressure on Lloyd George about Britain's image in America on Ireland.

All over the country that Easter popular demonstrations commemorated the previous Easter, with people wearing tricolour ribbons mounted on black. The Proclamation of the Republic was reprinted and pasted on walls everywhere and the tricolour was flown in every town and village. Public meetings were prohibited, but took place nevertheless. In the streets the people were met by police and soldiers. Perhaps most poignant of all on this first anniversary of the Rising, the tricolour was seen to be flying at half-mast above the ruins of the GPO in Dublin. The authorities had difficulty removing it because of the danger involved.

It became clear that the time had come to coordinate and direct the as yet unorganised national energy which had surfaced in the past year. Sinn Fein was the obvious choice. In October 'new' Sinn Fein held its annual convention. It was attended by representatives of many organisations besides Sinn Fein, including the IRB and the National Council formed after Count Plunkett's election. A new constitution was adopted which reconciled the aspirations of the separatists and the constitutionalists in common cause. The formula (provided by de Valera after bitter argument and near collapse of the convention), was:

Sinn Fein aims at securing the international recognition of Ireland as an independent Irish republic. Having achieved that status the Irish people may, by referendum, freely choose their own form of government.

The name Sinn Fein was retained for what now embraced many hitherto diverse, even confrontational, shades of opinion, from the republican separatist to the constitutional nationalist, in a more or less homogeneous national organisation committed to 'securing the international recognition of Ireland as an independent Irish republic'. The preamble to the new constitution also declared that Sinn Fein would, in the name of the sovereign Irish people:

(a) deny the right and oppose the will of the British parliament and the British crown *or any other foreign government* to legislate for Ireland;

(b) make use of any and every available means to render impotent the power of England to hold Ireland in subjugation by military force or otherwise (preamble to Sinn Fein Constitution, of 25 October, 1917. See Appendix Four).

According to O'Hegarty (op. cit., p.715) the new constitution was a cause of some disagreement, though, because of his partisanship, he must be considered somewhat unreliable on this point. He maintained that the disagreement was between the 'old' Sinn Feiners and the 'new' and that most of the leaders would have been content with the old constitution, that it was a separatist constitution which authorised acceptance of a settlement based on the Constitution of 1782 and the Renunciation Act of 1783. But that the new Sinn Feiners rejected this.

Making a similar point (op. cit., pp. 390/1) Lyons takes the view that the newly released prisoners from England, bringing with them 'an aura of 1916', took over the reconstructed Sinn Fein.

But there is here a double irony, namely that it was partly the (false) association of Sinn Fein, mainly by the British and their supporters, with the Rising that enabled Sinn Fein to be restored 'to health'.

The reconstituted Sinn Fein was a coalition held together by one common cause, namely an independent republican Ireland. David Fitzpatrick (*Politics and Irish Life*, Dublin, 1977) argues that in the 1916 Proclamation (of the Republic) Pearse and Connolly outlined a new society of equal social and economic opportunity — what to-day might be called a society with an egalitarian base — but that this had little appeal for those who, in 1917, began to support Sinn Fein. It is an argument which, while it has the merit of being provocative and to some extent 'new', strains to make a case. Connolly himself made the obvious point when he advised his troops to keep their weapons in the event of a victory since 'those who are our comrades to-day we may be compelled to fight tomorrow' (O'Neill, op. cit., p. 90). O'Neill also (Ibid. p. 89) points out: 'Easter Week was **not** a proletarian revolution...' There was a social input by both Connolly and his Citizen Army[155] which reflected not simply the need for social improvement in Ireland, but was part of the social revolutionary movement which swept Europe during the previous twenty years. It was, however, very much subordinate to the republican thrust and whatever about the opinions of some individuals involved the Rising could not be considered to have been primarily a social revolution.

In fact what was happening in the following year, 1917, was that the natural progress of revolutionary change was taking place. The active phase (phase 2), of the revolutionary process was developing and attracting a broader cross-section of the population than had been evident during the creation of a climate of opinion (phase 1), or than participated in the initial part of phase 2, (the Rising). It was now clear, beyond doubt, that Home Rule involved partition, that that was unacceptable to a majority of the people and that Redmond and his party were politically outcast in Ireland because of his support of it. For instance in June the Rural District Council of Ennis in the constituency of Redmond's brother, Major Willie (killed a few days later in France), passed a resolution calling on John Redmond and the Parliamentary Party to 'resign their seats in Parliament as they no longer represent the views and wishes of the Irish people either at home or abroad' (Macardle, op. cit., p. 220).

The Sinn Fein successes were also evident in other ways, all of which alarmed and enraged the British authorities. Tricolour ribbons and badges were worn by women, engravings and photographs of the executed leaders were sold by the tens of thousands, the ranks of the Army swelled. In July, uniforms and carrying 'weapons of offence or articles capable of being used as such unless carried solely with the object of being used for some lawful employment or pastime' were banned under DORA (the Defence Of The Realm Act) by General Sir Bryan T. Mahon, who had succeeded Maxwell as military governor of Ireland, so the Army paraded with sticks and hurleys instead of weapons. But even these were then brought under the terms of the Act.

In June there were extraordinary scenes when, in a remarkable about-face by the British, Irish political prisoners were released from English jails and sent home. Traffic was brought to a standstill in Dublin, and 'all work was suspended and all traffic sidetracked while the prisoners were driven in cars between ranks of people cheering and shouting their welcome and delight' (Macardle, p.221). The prisoners were officially welcomed home by a group of Dublin Aldermen.

De Valera emerged as the perceived leader of both Sinn Fein and the Volunteers. In October he was unanimously elected president of Sinn Fein and, in November, president of the Volunteers, 'thus blurring the differences between the political and the paramilitary movements' (Lee, op. cit., p.38), but, more accurately, reconciling the aims and objectives of the 'old' and the 'new' Sinn

Fein. It thus became the powerful, homogeneous organisation it would remain for the next five years. This reconciliation between the separatist and constitutional movements was of fundamental importance (though, curiously and significantly, the IRB again secured election to a majority of leading positions on the Volunteer executive). After his election to the presidency of Sinn Fein de Valera referred to its aim of 'Securing international recognition of Ireland as an independent Irish Republic', saying: 'That is what I stand for and it is because I stand for that that I was elected here'. In spite of the DORA prohibition, he advised Volunteers to wear the Volunteer uniform as their habitual dress and to carry sticks always, which they continued to do and for which many of them were jailed.

Everywhere throughout the country republican separatist sentiments and support were expressed by the people, endorsing the fact that the new Sinn Fein movement was the legacy of the Rising.

The situation at the end of 1917 was strikingly different to that immediately after the Rising. As late as November of 1916, while preparations were being made for a West Cork by-election, William O'Brien had (rightly) claimed that Sinn Fein did not exist. At that time it meant different things to different people; there were physical force Sinn Feiners, constitutional Sinn Feiners and ordinary people who resented English actions over Easter Week, who were all called 'Sinn Feiners'.

By the end of 1917 these disparate elements, under the common name Sinn Fein, had formed a well-organised alliance which enjoyed the backing of a revitalised military organisation — (Murphy, op. cit., p. 96).

De Valera's coordinated leadership of both the political and military separatist movements in Ireland was a new phenomenon of great concern to the British. The deliberate tone of his speeches, for instance that at Hospital in Limerick on 26 August, when he said: 'Sinn Fein have a definite policy and the people of Ireland are determined to make it a success; that is, to make English rule absolutely impossible in Ireland', was something new and frightening so far as they were concerned. What made it particularly alarming was the new, and homogeneous, environment in which it was was taking place. This environment did not seem to present them with any opportunity to 'divide and conquer' as they had done in the past when the Irish Parliamentary Party dominated the Irish political stage and the separatists were sidelined. Now that the constitutional and separatist movements spoke with a single, strong, republican, voice, that was no longer possible. Lloyd George asked in the British House of Commons, 'How can the Government treat speeches of that kind as if they were the sort of excitable speeches delivered by people of no consequence which would end in nothing?'

Home Rule with partition as proposed by the British Government was rejected by a majority of the Irish people and the Union had failed. In one form or another something had to replace it, and there were only four choices:

1/. Enforced Home Rule excluding all or part of Ulster.

2/. A reconsidered, national, Home Rule proposal which **might** be acceptable to all but the Ulster unionists.

3/. Some form of sovereign independence.

4/. Military governorship and enforced rule.

Each of these was unacceptable to one or more parties. The first was unacceptable to a majority, some eighty per cent., of the people. The second was unacceptable to a unionist minority, perhaps twenty per cent. (of whom Lyons, p.386, writes: 'The time had surely come to realise that Ulster Unionists were not bluffing and that when they said they would not be a party to any scheme of Home Rule they meant precisely what they said'). The third was unacceptable to the British, viz. —

There is a great deal of talk among Sinn Feiners which ... means complete separation ... it means secession. The words which are used are 'sovereign independence.' This country could not accept that under any conditions — Lloyd George, House of Commons, 23 October 1917.

And the fourth was unacceptable to practically everyone except, at the time, the Ulster unionists.

Nevertheless that was the option chosen by the British who did not seem to understand, or did not care (and the reason became obvious in 1918), that a return to the *status quo ante* the Rising was simply not possible. Renewed threats of conscription re-emerged and were a powerful factor in the growth of Sinn Fein, and the Sinn Fein clubs that sprouted, like shamrock, all over Ireland.

Throughout the summer and autumn the campaign of shooting, arrest and imprisonment of 'Sinn Feiners' on blatantly spurious charges increased. In August alone eighty-four republicans were arrested. One of those jailed (he had been arrested in August under DORA for making speeches 'calculated to cause disaffection') was Thomas Ashe, who had led the action at Ashbourne and who had been sentenced to death, commuted to life imprisonment, the previous year (he was released with others as a result of the activities of the otherwise ineffective National Convention of Irishmen). When he, and other prisoners, demanded to be treated as prisoners of war, not as criminals, the demand was refused. Ashe, who was deprived of clothing and bedding, went on hunger-strike and was forcibly fed, under which he died. He was given what amounted to a state funeral, lying in state in the City Hall with a guard of honour from the Army. 'Thousands filed past the coffin to pay their tribute to his memory and allegiance to his cause' (Macardle, p. 228). More than thirty thousand people followed his funeral 'and countless thousands lined the streets wearing the forbidden tricolour badge'(ibid). The death of Ashe from forcible feeding while still in prison, was a bitter reminder of the executions the previous year, and triggered an upsurge in support for Sinn Fein. This was enhanced by the presence of Archbishop Walsh at Ashe's funeral. 'Irish observers felt that the death of Ashe had transformed the national scene. Shrewd British commentators frankly admitted that that was the case' (Murphy, op. cit., p. 92). It became the most significant political demonstration since the rising. Volunteers paraded armed and in uniform, with neither police nor troops intervening. They fired three volleys over the grave 'and two sentences were spoken by a young man still unknown to the world at large. The young man was Michael Collins ... The prominence of Collins on this occasion has a double significance ...(Lyons, p. 387).

Collins had been an IRB member since his days in England before 1916, and he now persuaded the IRB to accept a group he had formed in Frongoch prison camp in Wales (Merionethshire) as a full branch. As their leader this gave him a place in the Centre. At about the same time he became secretary of the National Aid Organisation — one of the organisations formed to assist prisoners and their families, and around which the 'new' Sinn Fein grew — and through it he made vital contacts throughout the country.

But the IRB — perhaps in part due to its excessive secrecy about the Rising and its plans — was no longer in favour with all shades of separatist leadership. Cathal Brugha, for instance, who had been an IRB member, now opposed the brotherhood. After his release from hospital in 1916, and while the IRB and Volunteers were being revived, it seemed to some of his old comrades that Brugha had lost some of his old faith in the IRB (See O Broin, *Revolutionary Underground*). Certainly, like de Valera and Denis McCullough, President of the IRB, he felt that the organisation had served its purpose with the Rising and should be disbanded. According to O Broin, O Muirthile, on the other hand, held that on his return from imprisonment Collins dedicated himself to restoring the IRB. He goes on: 'In origin, therefore, the renewal of the IRB and the Irish Volunteers contained within itself the seeds of discord, and the grounds for the personal animosity that developed between Brugha and Collins (O Broin, op. cit. p.179)[156].

In the combination of Collins with his genius for organisation, the IRB, and the developing opposition to it, may lie the origin of some of the differences which later became unhappily more pronounced, particularly as the IRB was again infiltrating the army, as it had the Irish Volunteer movement before the Rising. While political differences could have been expected to arise anyway in the normal course of political development, these were deeper and darker shadows. Collins made the IRB — of which he would soon become Head Centre — his power-base. In this, and in the IRB's control of the Volunteers in 1916, but more significantly in Collins's persistence in the view that the President of the Supreme Council of the IRB remained the President of the Republic, it may be possible to discern a source of rivalry between himself and de Valera, the politician, now president of both Sinn Fein and of the Volunteers. Collins also consistently opposed the Army being brought under the political control of the Dail (which in fact finally occurred on a proposal from Brugha). He was not, of course, opposed to its being under the control of the IRB, and many Army officers were — and remained — IRB men.

Particularly interesting is the fact that, even later in 1919, the IRB did not relinquish its claim that its president was President of the Republic. In that connection General Sean MacEoin, one of the most distinguished veterans of the War of Independence and subsequently a TD and minister, made a significant statement in his contribution to *With the IRA in the Fight for Freedom*, which, regrettably, does not provide a date, but is certainly in the early to mid 1950s. He wrote (p. 15): 'From the date of the Proclamation of the Republic in 1916 until assembly of the First Dail in January 1919, the Government of the Republic was in the hands of the Supreme Council of the IRB to whose president (Collins) *all members had sworn obedience and allegiance as the Titular Head of the Republic.*' MacEoin goes on: 'An entirely new situation arose with the assembly of the First Dail and its re-affirmation of the Declaration of the Republic and its acceptance of the social principles embodied therein. There was then in existence an established government appointed by the legally elected representatives of the people, and to that Government the Supreme Council of the IRB at once voluntarily ceded all its powers except one. *The President of the IRB continued to be regarded by the Brotherhood as the President of the Republic until 1921*, when ... Eamon de Valera was nominated and elected to succeed him' [as President of the Republic]. The Supreme Council of the IRB did not dissolve until 1924, and 'As long as the struggle continued, there was danger that the elected government and Dail might, at any moment, find themselves extinguished by enemy action, and, should this happen, *the Supreme Council held itself in readiness to carry on the fight as a "caretaker" government'* (author's italics). It does not appear that these very important statements have received from historians the obvious attention they require, clearly demonstrating a basis of confrontation between constitutionalist republicans like Brugha and de Valera, and Collins and the IRB. They equally clearly demonstrate the extent of Collins's power-base in the IRB and, finally, the extent to which the IRB is likely to have influenced events up to 1924.

While de Valera was in the United States in 1919 and 1920 Collins was in a position to strengthen his IRB power-base enormously. He became Director of Organisation of the Army and other IRB officers acquired similar prominent positions. Diarmuid Lynch became Director of Communications and Sean McGarry General Secretary. Cathal Brugha who was Chief of Staff was deeply opposed to the principle of secret organisations like the IRB. De Valera and others were also opposed to secrecy, holding that the new movement should henceforth be an open one and that no one who accepted responsibility as an elected representative ought to be subject to secret control' (Macardle, op.cit., p. 231). It was a difference in attitude that, in the post-Rising period, concerned many who had not been troubled by the question before.

External events also influenced the Irish situation at that time, including President Woodrow Wilson's address to Congress the previous January on the Monroe doctrine, which included the following:

> No nation should seek to extend its polity over any other nation or people, but [that] every people should be left free to determine its own polity, its own way of development, unhindered, unthreatened, unafraid, the little along with the great and powerful ... I am proposing government by the consent of the governed ... No peace can last, or ought to last, which does not recognise and accept the principle that Governments derive all their just powers from the consent of the governed, and that no right anywhere exists to hand peoples about from sovereignty to sovereignty as if they were property ...

For the people in Ireland these fine words offered a real promise and stimulated even more intense national effort. Inherent in them, they believed, was an assured and rewarding hearing at the post-war peace conference. Referring to an earlier speech of Wilson's in similar circumstances, Lyons points out (p. 385) 'such language, though perhaps more concerned with Wilson's need to get re-elected ... than with the realities of Irish politics, was music to the ears of the ... Irish'.

There had been a revolution in Russia while the war was in progress. Following the subsequent collapse of both the Russian army and Kerensky's new government after the battle of Riga, Russia was no longer a belligerent, the treaty of Brest-Litovsk being signed between the opposing forces in November. Germany was then able to transfer troops to the west.

1918.

For republicans, therefore, 1918 began with the hope, if not the prospect, of Ireland's claim to sovereignty being heard at the peace conference after the war. The end of the war, following America's entry into it, was now indisputably — though as yet indecisively — not too far ahead . The Irish leaders felt that their claim for a hearing before the peace conference now had every hope of being supported whichever side won the war. Although Germany was far from beaten, she was effectively surrounded and cut off from both imports and international markets. In March three enormous German guns bombarded Paris from a range of seventy-five miles. In the same month General Erich von Ludendorff, together with General Paul von Beneckendorff und Hindenburg, the German strategists and commanders-in-chief, launched their massive attack *Plan Michael* (otherwise, and briefly, called *Kaiser-schlacht*, or Emperor's Battle, for the purposes of the pre-attack conference attended by the Kaiser), calculated to bring about such a German victory that it would enable them to sue for a satisfactory peace. It all but succeeded. Even at that stage an Allied victory was not a foregone conclusion.

In Ireland Sinn Fein's position continued to strengthen. A Sinn Fein cumman (or club) in every parish was the immediate goal. At the same time as this great organisational offensive was taking place, a policy of passive resistance to British rule was adopted.

Nevertheless, throughout the country, but especially in the south, there was a feeling that another — and this time more militarily effective — rising should be undertaken. It was a 'gut' feeling, unstructured and, in view of the now substantial jittery British military and police presence no less than the state of unreadiness in the army generally, impractical. And both the Sinn Fein Council and the Army Executive — besides the IRB — were against it at that time. But it reflected one extreme of popular feeling.

The extent to which Sinn Fein had become a power in the land may be gauged from the fact that when exports of food from Ireland to Britain threatened serious food shortages in Ireland, Sinn Fein took steps to conserve food supplies by successfully imposing a system of compulsory tillage on large estates. It was, in one sense, a revival of the period of land agitation in the previous century. However, the Army — or Volunteers — were forbidden by their executive to take part in such actions. Foster somewhat misleadingly (since he does not stress the food situation giving rise to it), writes: 'The movement subsumed the more earthy concerns of local agrarian agitators, so much so that by the end of the year the organization of cattle-drives by local Sinn Fein branches was attracting adverse comment, and was disavowed by the leadership in the following months (p.488).'

Coercion again became an implement of British policy in Ireland. In February Clare was proclaimed a military area, with 'passports' necessary to leave or enter and with postal censorship. The following month there were two hundred and thirteen arrests under DORA. When prisoners went on strike they were released under the Prisoners' (Temporary Discharge for Ill-Health) Bill of 1913, (introduced in England during the suffragette campaign when a Miss Lillian Lenton, having been force fed while she was on hunger-strike, almost died). It came to be known as the 'Cat-and-Mouse' Act and was used extensively in Ireland from this time onwards.

During March there were raids on police barracks for arms and some volunteers were killed by the RIC. Police were shot in Tralee. These events are categorised as 'unauthorised' (Macardle, p.244) local initiatives. Meantime British military and the police continued to raid Sinn Fein meetings and arrest members.

Lloyd George's Convention reported in April, but was signed by less than half its members. It proposed a form of national Home Rule in which 40% representation would be given to the unionists (representing less than 20% of the population)[157]. The report marked the end of the Convention and was overshadowed by a revival of the threat of conscription. 'The report of the Irish Convention reached Lloyd George on 8 April. Whether he ever read it remains in doubt. When the House of Commons reassembled on the following day he announced the terms of the new Manpower Bill by which conscription[158] could be applied to Ireland ... at any time' (Macardle, p.248).

Towards Crisis

Lloyd George hoped that Home Rule would resolve the conscription issue. To put, as the British incredibly seemed to see it, sugar on the pill, they proposed to introduce Home Rule with partition at the same time as the Manpower (conscription) Bill, a proposal that enraged even the Irish Parliamentary Party which warned the British Government that this amounted to 'a declaration of war against Ireland'. They stated that it would take three army corps to get one in Ireland, and went on to say that the Irish Party could not prevent the conflict that would inevitably ensue.

For the remainder of the year, in one way or another, the threat of conscription, and resistance to it, coloured events until the extraordinary general election of December.

In the face of the British decision a national conference, which brought together Sinn Fein, the Irish Parliamentary Party, Labour and other interests, convened in Dublin to oppose conscription in what Lyons (p. 393) describes as 'the most massive demonstration of nationalist solidarity that had been seen since the beginning of the war'. It issued a declaration which echoed the statement of the Irish Party in Westminister that 'The passing of the Conscription Bill by the British House of Commons must be regarded as a declaration of war on the Irish nation'. It also produced an anti-conscription pledge drawn up by de Valera —

Denying the right of the British Government to enforce compulsory service on this country, we pledge ourselves solemnly to one another to resist conscription by the most effective means at our disposal.

Plans were made by Sinn Fein 'to formulate a national policy to defeat this menace' (Sinn Fein Standing Committee, 10 April, 1918). An anti-conscription campaign which would have paralysed the country to an extent far greater than the Dublin general strike and lockout of 1913, and a boycott of English goods, were prepared. In spite of continuous pressure from Irish, southern, unionists such as Lord Midleton and from members of his own cabinet, the opposition of the Irish people to conscription persuaded Lloyd George to hesitate.

Anti-conscription strikes and demonstrations culminated in a nationwide pledge and general strike on 23 April. It was made evident that the people of Ireland would not support the British proposal in either of its aspects — diminished Home Rule or conscription. Moreover they had now clearly rejected the Union and were indeed, within a year, to place themselves outside it *de facto* and, so far as they were concerned, also *de jure*. In spite of the clear mood of the population the British Government decided to enforce conscription anyway and, as a preliminary step, appointed Field Marshal Lord French as Lord Lieutenant and Governor-General. French, in turn, swept the existing administration clean and appointed his own, which was hostile and bellicose. Sir Henry Wilson, by this time confidante of Lloyd George and Chief of the Imperial General Staff, noted in his diary: 'Lloyd George impressed on Johnny (French) the necessity of putting the onus for the *first* shooting on the rebels...'(author's italics.)

One of Casement's old Irish Brigade, a man called Dowling had landed from a U-Boat in Galway (on 12 April) and was captured. He had, it is true, been sent by the German authorities to try to make contact with Sinn Fein and the Volunteers, but they knew nothing about either him or his purpose[159]. But it was a godsend for French. Sweeping arrests followed on 17 May in which all senior Sinn Fein and Volunteer figures were arrested and deported to English jails without trial. As explanation the Castle proclaimed that a 'German Plot' had been unearthed.

A by-election in Cavan was won by Griffith, now in jail, and the victory celebrations were broken up by the RIC. A number of people were injured. In June much of Munster, the west and part of the Midlands became 'proclaimed districts', which meant that people charged in these areas could be removed and tried, by special juries, in another area more suitable to the purposes of the administration. Three days later some of these areas were 'upgraded' and became 'special military areas', and on 4 July Sinn Fein, the Volunteers, Cumann na mBan and the Gaelic League were all proclaimed illegal. People attending their meetings were liable to prosecution by a court of summary jurisdiction. On 5 July all public meetings, assemblies or processions, including sports meetings, were banned (See Macardle p. 255 et seq; Lyons, p. 396, etc.). In three months over a thousand arrests were made under French's programme of, futile, coercion.

In November Bonar Law circulated a letter which he had received from Lloyd George in October, in which the latter emphasised that he 'can support no settlement which would involve the forcible coercion of Ulster' and that he had a right to bring a settlement into effect based on ... Home Rule with the exclusion of six counties of Ulster'. Here is the active genesis of the subsequent Government of Ireland Act and partition. Lloyd George's letter testifies both to his pragmatism and, if such were needed, is an additional proof of his guile. A point that must be borne in mind is that it does more than that. His political prescience made it clear to him that popular opinion in Ireland was for independent sovereignty. It will have been equally clear to him — especially with an election looming — that the British people, no less than the British Government would not tolerate such a concession at that time. From the British point of view Ireland, Britain's first colony, was part of the United Kingdom. The most that could be conceded had already been offered.

Parnell had stated in Cork thirty-three years before that they, meaning the Irish people, could not ask for, or expect, less than Grattan's Parliament. He went on to coin his famous phrase, but 'No man has the right to fix the boundary to the march of a nation; no man has the right to say to his country — this far shalt thou go and no further.' Lloyd George understood that what was on offer was much less than Grattan's parliament and that, even if it were accepted, it would not halt the move towards independence. But he was doing what all politicians must do; try to deal with conflicting facts in the immediate context and produce a compromise which would hold the support of a majority of the electorate. He could not, therefore, reveal, his purpose in full. To do so would damn him in the eyes of too many voters. With hindsight his purpose is clear and it is, perhaps, surprising that it wasn't clear to more people at the time. The letter emphasises Lloyd George's determination to ensure the retention of part of Ireland within the United Kingdom.

Since it was written while he still led a war cabinet and while the war — though all but concluded — was still on, it may be assumed that strategic reasons were among his priorities. He was determined to introduce the Government of Ireland Act as a *de jure* basis for the subsequent introduction of partition, in spite of the will of the Irish majority. It may also be assumed that the strategic priorities had not lessened three years later when he deliberately misled the Irish treaty delegates on the issue of partition. The Irish, to their cost, were not in a position to establish any similarly effective *contra de jure* position, whatever the *de facto* will of the people was.

The general election took place in December. In spite of the fact that most of its leaders and workers were in jail, that much of the country was under martial law, that republican papers were suppressed and others censored, that 'the whole election machinery and the post office were under British control' (Macardle, p. 262), and Sinn Fein itself banned, Sinn Fein was now so powerful that it was able to contest every constituency in the country except Trinity College and, by accident, North Down. Its election manifesto echoes the 1916 Proclamation and was uncompromisingly republican, citing the points made in the preamble to its new Constitution (p. 188 and Appendix Four).

The manifesto went on to promise the establishment of a constituent assembly, included an appeal to the Peace Conference and re-asserted the principles of the Proclamation of the Provisional Government of Easter, 1916,

The authorities frustrated the Sinn Fein campaign as much as possible. This manifesto was heavily censored (curiously the sentence 'Sinn Fein aims at securing the establishment of that Republic' remained after censorship). The Sinn Fein director of elections, Robert Brennan, was arrested three weeks before polling day, leaflets warning 'against voting Republican were scattered from aeroplanes...raids, arrests and seizures directed against Republicans were incessant and the polling booths on 14 December were watched by military as well as police' (Ibid 263/5). Forty-seven of the seventy-three Sinn Fein candidates were in jail.

In all there were one hundred and five seats, four of which were university seats. Before the election Dillon's Party held sixty-eight seats, the unionists held eighteen, independents held ten and Sinn Fein had seven.

The election results, on 28 December, shook the United Kingdom to its foundations and may be said to have signalled the threat to the British empire that was to materialise over the next three years. Sinn Fein secured a seat for every one of its seventy-three candidates (some of whom ran in more than one constituency). The university seats returned three Unionists and one republican. The remaining one hundred and one seats for which the general electorate voted were returned as follows: Sinn Fein (republican), 72; Unionist, 23; Irish Parliamentary Party, 6. Nothing like it had ever happened in a general election before.

The unionist historian, Ronald McNeill (Lord Cushendun), wrote:

The general election of 1918 revealed that the whole of Nationalist Ireland had gone over with horse, foot and artillery, with bag and baggage, from the camp of so-called Constitutional Home Rule, to the Sinn Feiners, who made no pretence that their aim was anything short of complete independent sovereignty for Ireland.

Three days after the result of the election Mr. Edward Shortt, French's Chief Secretary for Ireland, said that the Irish question would be settled 'peacefully or bloodily within six months' (See Macardle, p. 267). O'Hegarty (p., 725) wrote: 'It is one of the most unchallengeable self-determinations on record, whichever way it is taken ... On the principles enunciated by the Allies, the victors in the war, Ireland's claim to complete independence was unanswerable'. The Irish Party had been virtually wiped out by Sinn Fein. But that did not mean that constitutionalism was gone. In fact an extraordinary thing, still not fully recognised, had taken place. For the first time since 1798, out of the separatist movement had come a new constitutional movement; separatist and constitutionist had come together under a single national banner with a common purpose — Independence: Not Home Rule, not partition, not simply a castrated Irish parliament subject to the dubious largesse of Whitehall, but an honest-to-God, straightforward independent and sovereign republic such as was envisaged from 1798 onwards, and as proclaimed in 1916. Excluding O'Connell's Catholic emancipation movement, not for over three hundred years, since the terms of a nation-state had been redefined in the 18th century, had the nation been of such single-minded national purpose.

But there was also an important social ingredient. In spite of one or two individuals, the leadership of the Irish Party had been from the wealthier middle or professional classes, usually, but by no means always, Catholic. From amongst the masses they drew a following, but few challengers for leadership or public office. In that sense there was an element of social stratification involved in the 'constitutional national movement', an acknowledgement that from 'here' came the leaders and representatives, and from 'there' came the support.

One of the features of Sinn Fein's success was that it offered a befuddled electorate, outraged by the effects of British military rule after 1916, an alternative constitutional framework, and one that also had a powerful national voice, a militant separatist base and a more egalitarian structure. It was inevitable that, in the climate of the time, it would appeal to the popular vote. 'Nothing would ever be the same again,' (Lyons p.399).

PART THREE

The blood-red blossom of war ...Tennyson

Chapter 8

Towards Independence
The War

THE WAR OF INDEPENDENCE WAS very different from the Rising of 1916. Unlike the Rising it was conducted under the authority of an elected (if proscribed) government. It was a protracted campaign of incident and purpose with a specific political object, part of which was to continue striving for a hearing at the peace conference — a hope, though diminished by the victory of the Allies, that nonetheless placed confidence in President Wilson's pledges to the principles of national sovereignty — but it had little visible strategic pattern. The war was supported by an overwhelming majority of the people, and became a 20th century prototype for guerrilla warfare. Excluding the build-up period outlined in the previous chapter, it lasted for two years and shook the edifice of the British Empire, which had already seen the empires of Austria, of Germany, of Turkey and of Russia shattered and broken, to their foundations.

1919

The year 1919 was no less momentous than the three immediately preceding it. It saw the establishment, in January, of the first Dail, the ratification of the Republic declared in 1916 and the reading of Ireland's Declaration of Independence and, in September, that Dail's suppression; the first wholesale attempt by the British in the 20th century to rule Ireland by coercion and military force; and a new, and now utterly impossible, Home Rule Bill. Before the year was out it also heard exchanged the first shots of the War of Independence.

The question hanging over a potential reservoir of cannon-fodder in Ireland which might be conscripted for Britain had been resolved with the end of the Great War. But once the war ended, the 'Irish Question' emerged as a factor of great immediate importance in English domestic politics. The overwhelming demand by the Irish electorate, in the 1918 election and afterwards, for independence was ignored in England. Lloyd George's British cabinet signalled a continuation of coercion and military rule when it decided to leave Lord French in Ireland. The Irish were again engaged in what John Mitchel, in a savagely ironic description of the Young Irelanders from a British viewpoint, called a 'criminal conspiracy to set their country free'.

Soon after the December 1918 election Sinn Fein decided to summon the elected representatives and form an Irish government to act in the name of the people. Accordingly, on 21 January 1919, the first Dail Eireann — Assembly of Ireland — met at the Mansion House, Dublin, at 3.30 in the afternoon. Both de Valera and Griffith (together with thirty-four other republicans — just half those elected), were in jail in England. It was, therefore, proposed that Brugha preside. None of the elected representatives from the other parties turned up and, accordingly, the first Dail was constituted from the twenty-seven republican deputies able to attend. The proceedings were conducted largely through Irish. The Declaration of Independence (Appendix Five) was read and this was followed by an aspirational 'Democratic Programme'. Lyons (pp. 401/2) is, with some justification, critical of the latter document on the grounds that, while 'echoing Pearse (but significantly avoiding any mention of Connolly) ... it anticipated a whole series of social and economic reforms' without indicating how these might be achieved.

Between them the Declaration of Independence and the Democratic Programme sought to establish a link between the Republic proclaimed in 1916 and the newly created Dail Eireann[160]. It has been suggested that if de Valera or Griffith had been present the documents might have been modified. The evidence supporting such a thesis rests largely on de Valera's later *cri-de-couer*, made in different circumstances and in the context of the Treaty and looming civil war, about 'the strait-jacket of the republic'. A perhaps stronger argument, which I am not aware of having been put forward elsewhere, is de Valera's established dexterity in coining admirably precise and flexible compromises as, for instance, at the Sinn Fein Convention a few months earlier, and during his election campaign. Had he been at the first meeting of the Dail he might, had circumstances seemed to warrant it, have sought, in these documents, a greater degree of political flexibility. But there were no seriously conflicting views requiring reconciliation expressed at the meeting, and there is no evidence that any such serious conflicts, particularly in relation to the Declaration of Independence, existed at that session of the First Dail. Brugha was in the chair and Lyons, somewhat surprisingly, is back-handedly critical of him on the above score, describing him as '*an enrage* (a fanatic or mad extremist) if ever there was one'. Yet, neither then nor later — until it became a divisive issue during the Treaty debates — were criticisms of the republican nature of the Declaration of Independence seriously voiced. Nor is there any doubt that the issue of sovereignty, on which scorn has also been lavished, was given universal support. This was to be expected; clairvoyance was not. Before the adoption of the Declaration of Independence,

Brugha told the assembly: 'You understand from what is asserted in this Declaration that we are now done with England?'

This Dail also appointed three delegates to the Peace Conference in Paris. They were Griffith, de Valera and Count Plunkett. The French historian, M. Yann Morvran Goblet (pseudonym of Louis Treguiz) realised the significance of what occurred and that it was inspired by the Rising of 1916: 'And those who knew it' he wrote, 'partisans or adversaries, divined that a new epoch was beginning, and one that would be terrible' (See *L'Irlande dans le Crise Universelle*, 1914-1920, Paris, 1920, pp. 356/7).

On the second day, in private session, Brugha was elected acting president (priomh-aire ag gniomhu) — hardly something that would have happened had there been any serious division on policy — on the understanding that de Valera would be elected to the office of president (priomh-aire) when he was released from prison[161]. Sean T. O'Kelly was accredited to Paris as an envoy of the Government of the Irish Republic with instructions to press for a hearing for Ireland at the Peace Conference. This was to no avail[162]. 'The Irish envoy in Paris was early forced to realise that British influence at the Peace Conference was militating powerfully against a hearing of Ireland's claim' (Macardle, p.278).

A bitter division in the ranks of American support for Ireland resulted in the Irish lobby there being split, even becoming counter-productive. This split lasted for years and badly soured relations between activists in America and at home; even more seriously, some Irish/American organisations alienated President Wilson, a WASP with an Ulster background, a man of high-minded principle who was crucial to any prospect of Ireland being able to secure a hearing at the Peace Conference. In fact the prospect of Ireland — or Dail Eireann, whichever way one wishes to look at it — obtaining a hearing at the peace conference was remote at this stage: Ireland's main hope had been for a German victory or advantageous peace, either of which would have presented the optimum conditions. Following an Allied victory Irish hopes, in diminishing order, were for i/ Wilson's principles being universally and forcefully adopted by the other Allies, especially Britain; ii/ support from sufficient number of the Allies to persuade Britain to agree. Neither of these conditions existed. Wilson is reported to have said that Ireland could have no voice in the Peace Conference at present, since the Irish question was a matter between England and Ireland (See Macardle, p. 278, n., citing Reuters).

However in March the Congress of the United States — by a 261 to 41 majority — passed a resolution: 'That it is the earnest hope of the Congress of the United States of America that the Peace Conference now sitting at Paris will favourably consider the claims of Ireland to self-determination'. Although Macardle (p.294) writes: 'The American people had instructed their president to support Ireland's claim' the careful phraseology of this resolution was not, and could not be thought to be, support by Congress for a hearing for Ireland at the peace Conference. It was an expression of hope that the conference would favourably consider Ireland's claims, not that it should give Ireland an opportunity to present and elaborate those claims before the Conference. Nevertheless it was a diplomatic set-back to the British government for Ireland's case to be thus raised and approved in the United States Congress. And in June the United States Senate passed a more specific resolution with but one dissenting vote. This read: 'That the Senate of the United States earnestly requests the American Peace Commission at Versailles to endeavour to secure for Eamon de Valera, Arthur Griffith and George Noble Count Plunkett, a hearing before the Peace Conference in order that they may present the case of Ireland. And further, the Senate of the United States expresses its sympathy with the aspirations of the Irish people for a government of their own choice'.

Here was something more concrete and precise. In March O'Kelly had written to the French prime minister, Georges Clemenceau, President of the Peace Conference, and to every delegate at the conference, detailing Ireland's case for a hearing. He received no reply. A factor which may have had some bearing on this, and to which I can find no previous reference in this context, was Clemenceau's intransigent hatred of Germany. Bearing in mind the British-inspired so-called 'German plot' of the previous year and the association between the Irish separatists and Germany in 1916, it is possible — even likely — that Clemenceau's hatred of Germany was manipulated by the British to their advantage.

In February de Valera, Sean Milroy and Sean McGarry, using a key made from a wax impression, escaped from Lincoln Jail with the help of Collins and Harry Boland. The following month most of the remaining political prisoners were released. Yet, at the same time, the British authorities in Ireland were behaving with great provocation, as if looking for an excuse to bring about a confrontation. One writer expressed it: 'The army authorities are hoping against hope for a bit of a scrap' (R.M. Anthony, *English Review*, July 1919). The arrival of de Valera in Dublin, where he was to be greeted by a civic reception, was seen as a possible flashpoint. Accordingly the civic reception was cancelled. Nevertheless there were considerable celebrations throughout the capital.

> ...the Government response became more and more heavy-handed; displays of military force were excitedly noted by, for instance, the American Commission for Irish Freedom on their visit in May, 1919, and random and pointless imprisonment of activists helped swing support towards the IRA line (Foster, op. cit., p. 495).

De Valera was duly elected priomh-aire at the second meeting of the Dail in April, at which he appointed a number of ministers. In order to raise revenues the Dail approved the issue of Republican Bonds to the value of £250,000 (the equivalent of about £10m to-day), and Michael Collins, as Minister for Finance, was given responsibility for this. When the loan was advertised all the papers which carried the advertisement were 'immediately suppressed by order of the British military authorities', (Macardle, p.285). A week after the second meeting of the Dail de Valera was elected president of Sinn Fein. He was now in a position of very considerable and widespread power right across the spectrum of the national movement; priomh-aire of the Dail, president of Sinn Fein and president of the Volunteers.

About this time the British authorities, very conscious of Sinn Fein's extra-ordinary victory the previous December (which had been on the straight-vote system), decided to introduce proportional representation for Ireland only. They saw this as a means of limiting the effect of the Sinn Fein vote. The move back-fired. Sinn Fein welcomed proportional representation, de Valera saying:

> whether it benefitted us or not I would be in favour of the principle because it is founded in justice. We know the object for which it was designed. It was a crooked object. Let us meet it in a straight way. That is the principle guiding us the whole time.

By adopting this consistently principled approach Sinn Fein continued to hold the moral highground, which was to be its strongest strategic weapon in the war to come. The public expression of integrity also helped to emphasise the vital point that the leadership of the nation had passed, decisively, to the Dail.

Although the incident was not recognised at the time for what it was, what have come to be considered the first shots in the War of Independence were fired at Soloheadbeg, County Tipperary, the same day the first Dail met — 21 January 1919. It was an ambush by nine young men, three of whom became legendary figures of the War of Independence which followed (See Lyons, p. 409). They were Dan Breen, Seamus Robinson, O/C, and Sean Treacy of the 3rd Tipperary Brigade. Their objective was a cartload of explosives being escorted by RIC men, and not their deaths. According to Breen (*My Fight for Irish Freedom*), the police were called on to surrender, but resisted and were shot. This incident also high-lights the fact that the RIC were one of the most immediately available sources of arms and munitions for the IRA.

Once the Dail was established it was vital to bring the Army — up to then not only an independent organisation, but the most formidable separatist movement in the country — under its control. Clearly this presented difficulties for both organisations. Brugha, as Minister of Defence and former Chief of Staff of the Army (a post to which Dick Mulcahy was appointed when Brugha became minister), worked assiduously to find a solution. In-mid 1919 the Dail approved an oath of allegiance to the state which would be common both to deputies and to Volunteers. The Army also accepted this oath, but, because of the risks associated with trying to hold an army convention, the oath was taken individually and was not formally ratified by the Volunteer Executive. But, from then on, the Army was considered to be the army of the republic, and it was from then that 'Irish Republican Army', or 'IRA' came, universally, to replace 'Volunteers'.

It was always a policy of British rule in restless colonies to provoke a situation that would enable them to stamp out resistance with brute force. That an armed conflict was in the making in Ireland in 1919 was abundantly clear. That sooner or later the British policy of military coercion must provoke action was equally clear. It was only a question of time. The will of the people was unmistakable. Thousands of men had been arrested over the previous three years. The spirit and temper of the land was such that the distress resulting from military rule could not continue without the confrontation the British seemed willing, even anxious, to provoke. In January, after the first meeting of the Dail, the Bishop of Killaloe, Dr. Michael Fogarty, said (in Clare, long under martial law and where de Valera won his important electoral victory): 'The fight for Irish freedom has passed into the hands of the young men of Ireland ... and when the young men of Ireland hit back at their oppressors it is not for an old man like me to cry "foul".'

Throughout the spring and summer the army concentrated on trying to secure arms. A number of police and military posts were attacked and weapons and ammunition obtained. There were some casualties on both sides.

> What should be noted about these events is that they were sporadic; that after March they had been conducted against the express orders of the Executive; but that that executive had, as early as 1917, alluded to completing 'by force of arms' the 1916 'work'; and that some, though by no means all of those involved in these sporadic incidents may have been looking to such an armed struggle (Lawlor, op. cit., p.6)

In fact the extent to which, after January, such events were conducted against 'the express orders' of the Executive is limited. As already noted the Army Executive forbade members of the army to engage, in that capacity, in the neo-Land War activities of Sinn Fein. In Tipperary the police adopted a policy of seizing and terrorising children in order to obtain information from them. An eight-year-old boy was questioned at length in a shed as to the whereabouts of his father and, in February, another young boy named McGrath was virtually kidnapped by the police from his house and brought to Dublin where he was held incommunicado for some days. In response Seamus Robinson posted a proclamation stating that, after a certain date, people in South Tipperary supporting the British were in danger of being shot. The Executive condemned *this* and issued orders that it was not to be put into effect. It may be to this that Lawlor refers.

A number of dramatic incidents of the kind that were to become almost commonplace over the following two years also occurred, notably the rescue of Sean Hogan from a strong RIC guard at Knocklong railway station in County Limerick, in spite of the fact that Limerick was under martial law with a curfew and a heavy military presence. Other clashes occurred. By May martial law had been extended to most of the country, which was in a state bordering a perpetual state of war.

Criticism for the shooting of members of the RIC at this time has been made. Such shootings must be placed in context. 'The government were determined' as Eoin MacNeill declared in the Dail, 'to make the police supreme in Ireland.' It is important to bear in mind that the RIC was more of an auxiliary military force than a police force, and was armed as light infantry. Its members spied on the community and were responsible for most of the wholesale arrests taking place, for provoking attacks on innocent bystanders and for shooting incidents. 'It was the British propagandist device to refer to these men as "policemen", a very misleading term; and when people abroad were told of "policemen" being shot, it suggested the lawless violence of bandits ... The RIC were never policemen in the proper sense of the term ... They were a military force, armed with rifles and living in barracks, whose task it was to hold the country in subjugation to England ...

It was obvious that the RIC was the most essential component of the machinery of British administration in Ireland, and that action must first be taken against that force' (Piaras Beaslai, *The Anglo-Irish War*, With the IRA in the Fight for Irish Freedom, p. 6).

The main threat to Sinn Fein and to the army from the RIC was their information-gathering. In the Dail de Valera proposed that a policy of social ostracism should be directed against the RIC. He said: 'Their history is a continuity of brutal treason against their own people. They must be shown and made to feel how base are the functions they perform and how vile is the position they occupy' (Dail Eireann, Minutes of Proceedings to April 1919, p.47). This policy of ostracism was implemented throughout the country and produced an effect, particularly on recruitment. There were also some resignations, but not as many as would later occur. '...The RIC' says Lyons (p.410), 'stood full in the path of the revolutionaries and must expect to bear the brunt of the coming storm.'

Meantime O'Kelly in Paris had maintained the pressure to have Ireland's case heard, but without result. Nevertheless Ireland's case was attracting international attention at another level. The Second International (Labour) meeting in Amsterdam in April affirmed the right of the Irish people to independence and declared: 'the principle of free and absolute self-determination shall be applied immediately in the case of Ireland.' It further asked that the Peace Conference make good this claim (see Macardle p.293). Pressure from Ireland and America on President Wilson and other members of the Peace Conference continued throughout the summer to no avail. Meanwhile the coercion continued.

In July *The Manchester Guardian* wrote:

> It cannot be denied that women and men have been arrested and detained for long periods without trial, that the imprisonment fatally broke the health of a few of them and destroyed the reason of others, that scores of other political prisoners sentenced by court martial have been in conflict with the prison authorities, that police truncheons, firemen's hoses, handcuffing behind the back for several days (including days of solitary confinement in punishment cells) have been used to reduce them to subjugation, that the conflict still goes on and the end is not in sight ...

Irish hopes of a hearing at Paris were finally dashed when, in July, Wilson admitted that there was an agreement among the Committee of Four (The United States, France, Britain and Italy), that no small nation should appear before it without the unanimous consent of the whole committee. Of course Britain vetoed Ireland's claim.

In June, having been elected president of the Dail, de Valera went to America in that capacity. Griffith became acting president in his absence. More and more, Ireland began to resemble a war-zone. *The Freeman's Journal*, (10 June 1919) commented:-

> Soldiers with fixed bayonets, wearing trench-helmets, paraded the streets; a machine-gun post commanded Liberty Hall; military cordons with armoured lorries surrounded whole districts of Dublin while military and police carried

out raids. They saw, in June, the Dublin quays 'jammed with tanks, armoured cars, guns and motor lorries, and thousands of troops, as if the port was the base of a formidable expeditionary force'.

British civil administration of Ireland had completely broken down, and the military administration was ineffective and counter-productive. It 'could no longer succeed in governing Ireland, it could only prevent her governing herself' (Goblet, op. cit., p. 360).

The paradox with which England was now struggling in Ireland was one it had in the past successfully managed for many years, there and elsewhere; namely to present to the world the face of enlightenment and moral integrity, while at the same time plundering her colonies. While international communications and literacy were poor and the principle of *laissez-faire* was dominant, this was not too difficult. With the universal onset of rapid communications and literacy in an increasingly equitable political climate, it became more difficult for Britain, convincingly, to express concern for the small nations of Europe, while trampling the rights of the Irish people under her own jack-boot. It was a problem the British were unable to come to terms with or find a solution to. Accordingly they followed their established pattern of ruling by force and hoping that this would restore the *status quo ante*.

In June the Dail approved the establishment of local courts. In a remarkable civil victory for the nation and in spite of the outlawing and hounding of individuals at every level of the *de facto* national republican administration, these republican courts took over from the British courts in many parts of the country. A republican police force was established some time later and the two arms of the law operated closely. A land bank was established and a national loan floated.

In August the issue of the role of the army vis-a-vis the Dail again arose on foot of a proposal by Brugha for an oath of allegiance to the Republic and the Dail to be taken by all members of the administration, legislature, judiciary and army. The proposal was supported by Griffith, but opposed by Collins, who argued that the oath to the Republic was enough. Collins at this time had become President of the Supreme Council of the IRB and was, therefore, not simply President of the 'secret' IRB Government, but also 'President of the Republic', in accordance with the 1873 declarations of the Supreme Council of the IRB. To what extent this affected Collins attitude to Brugha's proposal is conjectural.

Brugha, now opposed the secret organisation, was himself an ex-IRB man who knew much of its plans and methodology. Consequently, whatever the reason for Collin's reluctance to bring the army directly under the control of the Dail, it is obvious that the position of IRB men giving allegiance to both the republican Dail and 'the sole government of the Supreme Council' was, to say the least of it, anomalous. However the army agreed to take the oath and, on 25 August Collins wrote to de Valera: The Volunteer affair is now fixed'. The IRB, however, remained separate and secret.

Now Collins's influence began to be felt. A man of enormous energy and self-discipline, he poured both into his work. In addition to being Minister of Finance and President of the IRB's Supreme Council, he was also Director of Organisation and Director of Intelligence of the Volunteers. He devoted enormous interest to intelligence work, agreeing with the principle that not only is good intelligence worth three divisions, but also that to deny intelligence to the enemy was worth as many more. To that end he was ruthless and resourceful, and soon had a network of agents in what the British considered to be their most secure areas — the British army, the RIC, the Civil Service (of which Nathan wrote before 1916; 'for some reason which I am unable to fathom a large proportion of the people treasonable to England are to be found in the lower ranks of the government service'), even in Dublin Castle itself. His men had 'colleagues among engine-drivers, ships' crews and stokers, post-office clerks, office cleaners, domestic servants — in every position where information of enemy plans might conceivably be obtained' (Macardle, p. 306).

Collins himself wrote about his espionage and counter-intelligence operations in a series of articles in the *New York American* in 1922.

> England could always reinforce her army. She could replace every soldier that she lost. But there were others indispensable for her purposes which were not so easily replaced. To paralyse the British machine it was necessary to strike at individuals. Without her spies England was helpless ... Without their police throughout the country, how could they find the man they 'wanted'? ... Spies are not so ready to step into the shoes of their departed comrades as are soldiers to fill up the front line in honourable battle ...
>
> We struck at individuals, and by so doing we cut their lines of communication, and we shook their morale. And we conducted the conflict, difficult as it was, with the unequal terms imposed by the enemy, as far as possible, according to the rules of war. Only the armed forces and the spies and criminal agents of the British Government were attacked. Prisoners of war were treated honourably and considerately, and were released after they had been disarmed.

At the same time as Collin's people infiltrated the enemy sanctum the Army began to adopt the guerrilla tactics against the British regular forces that were to become the hallmark of the War of Independence[163]. But, throughout 1919, shortage of arms and munitions continued to be a problem. Jailbreaks on a large scale by republican prisoners were also to become a feature of the period[164]. In Fermoy, Co. Cork, in September, an exchange took place which was to set a pattern for some of the more brutal activities of the British forces during the following two years. A party of British troops on Church parade, but armed, was attacked by units of Cork No. 2 Brigade. One soldier was killed. Next day some two hundred British soldiers from Fermoy barracks on the hill above it descended on the important market town astride the River Blackwater, sacked and looted shops and roughed-up passers by. No attempt was made either to control or discipline the troops involved or to make reparation. It was not the first act of terrorism by British forces against the civilian population, but it was the first 'organised' reprisal by mobs of armed troops. It set a precedent which, though in itself extreme, would appear insignificant compared with some of those that were to follow[165].

As to the war, which, by September was clearly underway, Macardle (p.308) describes it accurately. In doing so she points up not just the dilemma facing the British in Ireland, but a significant difference between the armed protest now underway and and the Rising of 1916:

It was with a popular revolution, not with an armed rising, that the British administration had to deal.

It had, as Lyons points out, three phases. During the first phase, essentially confined to 1919, the pattern which the war would follow emerged. The second phase, in 1920, saw a further escalation of British terror tactics with the introduction of two new special forces, the Black and Tans and the Auxiliary Cadets, after which open warfare and terror became a norm. The third phase was the successful development of advanced guerrilla tactics and actions by Irish Army flying columns which lasted until the truce of July 1921.

The result of the 1918 election, the establishment of the Dail and international support for Ireland, reinforced the fact that Britain now had only two choices so far as Ireland was concerned; either to grant Ireland its independence — which they would not do — or try to reconquer it. They made the latter choice. As a first step, on 10 September, the Dail was prohibited and suppressed. Apart from strategic considerations, the new and uneasy British Government was clearly motivated by a fear of what the electorate's reaction might be to what would have been perceived — and trumpeted by the Tories — as the first step towards a break-up of the empire had they moved towards independence for Ireland. Though the break-up of the British empire came eventually, it could not, in 1919, have been foreseen by the British as the inevitability it was.

Once the British had declared war on the independent Irish Parliament, (the First Dail), every nationalist element in the country rallied to its support. Side by side with Sinn Fein stood Labour, the Irish Parliamentary Party and the Ancient Order of Hibernians (Gen. Sean MacEoin, The Constitutional Basis of the National Struggle, *With the IRA in the Fight for Freedom 1919 to the Truce*, Tralee, no date). On the suppression of the Dail, Macardle (p.309), notes:
[It] gave incalculable impetus to the Irish campaign in the United States. In ... American cities ... de Valera had explained the conflict at home, shown that the right of the Irish people to a government of their own choice was being denied ... by a violent military regime. No single act of the British administration could more strikingly have demonstrated the truth of his statements.

In the United States, de Valera's official objects were to gain general sympathy for the Irish cause, to seek recognition of the Irish Republic by the United States, to obtain a favourable relationship with the United States in matters relating to the nascent League of Nations if America decided to join (which, in the event, she did not, thus weakening its purpose of international cooperation), and to promote Dail loans. These were to some extent affected, even at times overshadowed, by his attempts to heal the bitter divisions amongst the Irish/American organisations. Nevertheless he raised $5,000,000 with a bond-drive in one year, half the quota.

While in America (in an interview with the *Westminster Gazette*, February, 1920), he made a far-reaching suggestion, namely that Britain and Ireland should declare a sort of Monroe doctrine (a trans-Atlantic *entente cordiale* between the United States and Cuba under which Cuba undertook not to allow herself to be used by foreign powers against the United States). The importance of this suggestion was that it focussed on Britain's security **after** Irish independence. It had another historic significance in that 'from it may be discerned the germ of the doctrine of external association of which so much was to be heard during the next thirty years' (Lyons, op. cit.), forming the basis of the association, in particular, between independent India and Britain.

De Valera's visit was a success. Everywhere on his trans-American journey he was greeted with huge crowds, State governors, mayors and civic receptions including motorcades and a flypast (in Columbus, Ohio), on a scale appropriate to a visiting head of State. When news of the suppression of the Dail reached New York a protest meeting in the Lexington Avenue theatre overflowed into the street outside.

In Ireland the suppression of the Dail was seen as a declaration of war by England. It was followed by an acceleration of military aggression against the civil population — a preamble to the reign of terror that would come in a few months — confirming this view. By December England deployed some forty-three thousand troops in Ireland in addition to the para-military RIC. Assemblies of any sort, including sports meetings, lectures and so on were raided and banned, the homes of private citizens were also raided and many people were arrested[166]. The urge to provoke was evidently strong in Dublin Castle. But to provoke what? If it were a military confrontation — as it probably was — then with whom? The views of the people were well-known by now and, even if it was intended to jail most of them, their views would not alter. Blindly the British seemed bent on a course that must lead to terrorization on a grand scale. The original Dublin Castle staff had been replaced wholesale by hardliners intent on subduing Ireland. There was a current view that Lord French's object was to provoke another rising, giving a pretext for widespread terror and executions (See Macardle p. 317).

Property also — in an era, it should be remembered, when property rights still often had a value greater than human ones — became a target. The troops that had sacked Fermoy the previous September were transferred to Cork where they sacked and looted Patrick street in November. Kinsale and Athlone were given similar treatment. More sinister, people now began to be shot indiscriminately — one of them, in Mayo, a boy of fourteen.

Somehow, in spite of intimidation and arrests and of the heavy military presence, the Dail and the Courts managed to function. Consulates were opened in Europe and the Americas. Collins continued to strengthen his intelligence organisation. He formed his famous 'Squad', a chief function of which was the elimination of British spies and informers. Although any Press in Ireland in the smallest way sympathetic, let alone favourable, to the republicans had been banned and suppressed, an official Bulletin, edited initially by Desmond Fitzgerald (later by Erskine Childers, both of whom ran the Dail Department of

Publicity), was issued several times a week to confront British propaganda and give the facts on British terrorism.

World opinion was reacting strongly to events in Ireland and, in England, moderate and liberal forces were distressed. A former British cabinet minister, Sir Herbert Samuel, said in a speech at St. Alban's that December:

> ... if what is now going on in Ireland had been going on in the Austrian Empire, all England would be ringing with denunciations of the tyranny of the Hapsburgs and denying people the right to rule themselves.

Even *The Times* of London (13 December 1919), the long-established mouthpiece of British establishment thinking, went so far as to permit a special correspondent to write: 'The citadel of Sinn Fein is in the minds of the young. The prospect of dying for Ireland haunts the dreams of thousands of youths to-day — you can neither terrify nor bribe Sinn Fein'. In October an unsuccessful attempt was made by Collins's Squad and units of the 3rd Tipperary Brigade to assassinate French. In the same week the RIC — the police — were issued with hand-grenades.

On 22 December Lloyd George introduced the 'last' Home Rule Bill — to which he gave what, in the circumstances, can only be described as the euphemistic title 'Better Government of Ireland Bill'. 'Totally divorced as it was from the realities of political life in Ireland, Lloyd George's offer had no effect whatever on the deadly struggle then moving towards its climax in the south' (Lyons, p. 414). It proposed partition with separate parliaments for six north-eastern counties and the other twenty-six, with powers to create a council of representatives of both Irish parliaments. In effect it was the previous Home Rule Bill dressed up, like a Christmas tree, with lights and gee-gaws. Few people in Ireland showed any interest. It was a preamble to the year-and-a-half of terror that lay ahead. The Ulster Unionists accepted this proposal, but the rest of Ireland rejected it. The Bill became law in December 1920, accompanied by an extension of martial law, and a new legal base was created.

1920

The shock of Sinn Fein's 1918 general election victory was followed by a further jolt by the results of the Municipal and Urban elections in January 1920. In spite of the introduction of proportional representation with the intention of restricting the effect of the Sinn Fein vote, Sinn Fein was again extraordinarily successful.

Sinn Fein candidates carried eleven of the twelve Irish cities and boroughs, the odd one out — not surprisingly — being Belfast. Twenty-three out of forty-five towns in Ulster elected nationalist majorities, decisively demonstrating that Ulster was far from being a unionist province. Of two hundred and six Councils in Ireland, one hundred and seventy-two returned nationalist majorities. It was clear that the 1918 general election successes were no mere flash-in-the-pan. The result also put Lloyd George's recent Bill and his so-called 'six unionist counties' into perspective, amply demonstrating the false basis of his proposal. Of the six counties which it was proposed to exclude on the grounds that they were 'unionist', two, Fermanagh and Tyrone, returned a Sinn Fein majority. Derry city also brought in a nationalist majority.

A resolution from Dublin Corporation was typical. It demonstrated how the combined constitutional and separatist republican programme had spread. From being the preserve of the dedicated few it had become the acknowledged right of the many. The resolution read:—

That this council of the elected representatives of Dublin hereby acknowledges the authority of Dail Eireann as the duly elected Government of the Irish people, and undertakes to give effect to all decrees duly promulgated by the said Dail Eireann insofar as the same affect this Council. That copies of this resolution be transmitted to the Governments of Europe, and to the President and Chairman of the Senate and the House of Representatives of the U.S.A.

In Cork the election brought to the office of Lord Mayor a man whose name, like that of his colleague the Mayor of Limerick, Michael O'Callaghan, would become synonymous with atrocity by Crown forces. He was Tomás MacCurtain. His deputy, Terence MacSwiney, was a man of rare vision and distinction whose courage and name were to enter the international records of endurance in the name of an ideal for the sake of truth and justice[167].

The fact that MacCurtain and MacSwiney were Lord Mayor and deputy Lord Mayor of Cork was an example of a recent phenomenon that resulted from the Sinn Fein electoral successes and the British response to them. Civic leaders elected on the Sinn Fein ticket were targetted by the authorities. 'Everywhere' says Macardle (p.328), 'Republicans elected to responsible positions took the precaution of instructing others in the duties of their office, knowing that in accepting election they had designated themselves for arrest'. This must represent one of the most extraordinary civic responsibilities in the history of modern democracy until the event of Nazi-occupied Europe. In the cases of MacSwiney and McCurtain the above quotation is slightly disingenuous in that at that time McCurtain was also brigade commandant of the First Cork Brigade and MacSwiney was brigade vice-commandant and on these grounds — but, it must be emphasised, no more than their election on the Sinn Fein ticket — they were in most danger of arrest. The dual roles filled by MacCurtain and MacSwiney were not uncommon.

After the elections in January the campaign of coercion intensified. The county Tipperary town of Thurles was sacked by British military and, as part of a concerted nationwide sweep the principal targets of which were republican representatives elected to local office, the chairman of the town council, together with four other republican councillors, was arrested and deported to jail in England.

Over sixty ... were arrested and deported to England as a result of the first sweep-up on the last day of January, 1920 — Gen. Sir Nevil Macready, British GOC in Ireland, *Annals of an Active Life*, vol 11. p.439.

In March the United States Senate again passed a resolution 'sympathising' with the Irish demand for self-government, ' a consummation' it hoped was at hand, and stating that when it came about Ireland should be admitted to the League of Nations[168].

For the first four or five months of this year, in which the war entered its most active phase, both sides were, one might say, 'jockeying for position' — but for very different positions. The Irish Army was still preoccupied with the problem of arms and munitions, still in very short supply. This was so even in west Cork, one of the most active areas[169], and the position elsewhere was worse. In general at the beginning of 1920 a battalion of the 3rd (West) Cork Brigade of which Liam Deasy was at that time adjutant (later brigade commandant), might expect to have a few old rifles, possibly miniatures (.22), some shotguns and a few revolvers with, or without, ammunition. But during the year the character of the war altered radically, from being one of minor, almost defensive, engagements with the enemy to one of significant confrontations in which the Army took the offensive. This change was the result of two important factors. The first was an improved, though still ludicrously small, availability of arms and munitions which strengthened the materiel resources of units, for instance from four shotguns and one rifle for a company of 130 men, to perhaps, in the best of situations, fifteen or twenty rifles. Ammunition remained an even more critical problem, four or five rounds a weapon being average. Such increases were mainly the result of the minor engagements referred to above. Secondly was the effect of training by experienced officers like Tom Barry and Dick McKee. To these important factors was added the all-important confidence resulting from experience gained under fire. Initially attacks tended to be mounted with small groups of five to eight men, half of whom might be armed, the object being to obtain arms and ammunition. By mid June, and from then on following a meeting of brigade commanders and staff officers in GHQ, Dublin, the Army took the initiative.

We '[the brigade]' began the year with twenty-nine rifles, a collection of shotguns — better suited to farmers and others who wished to enjoy a day shooting game than soldiers engaged in real warfare — a few revolvers, and a very limited supply of ammunition. We ended the year with one hundred and twenty rifles, sixty revolvers, a supply of mills bombs and home-made bombs, over a ton of gun-cotton, and about thirty-thousand rounds of ammunition (Liam Deasy, *Towards Ireland Free*, Cork, 1973, p. 189).

As part of their campaign of destabilisation the British military authorities decided that the most effective way of dealing with the widespread constitutional expression of nationalism and support for Sinn Fein was to step up the campaign of provocation against the civilian population and the rural economy. Arbitrary arrests and harrassment became a daily practice. Rewards of up to £10,000 were offered for information when a member of the RIC was shot. During January there were more than 1,000 raids by the British and over 250 arrests. In February the number of raids rose to over a thousand a week, more than four thousand for the month, with 260 arrests. Curfew facilitating the raids was imposed over most of the country including Dublin. Considerable effort and manpower was devoted to trying to locate and seize republican funds, but with limited success.

Besides the nightly raids with tanks and armoured cars in the cities by battle-dressed soldiers, the military governors conducted a campaign calculated to sabotage the country with a combined programme of military terrorism and economic disruption. Fairs and markets were suppressed. This was a body-blow to an agriculturally dependent country. As a result the cost of living, especially in rural areas, shot up. Farmers bringing produce to a sale were arrested, charged and sentenced — in one notorious case, in Tipperary, to eight months imprisonment.

But by now the Church in Ireland was openly condemning these acts of violence against the people. The Bishop of Cloyne, Dr. Robert Browne, said that the policy of the British government 'seems to be to make use of every means and every opportunity to exasperate the people and drive them to acts of desperation'. Nonetheless coercion intensified. Towns continued to be shot up and looted. The campaign against the economic life of the country was extended and 'this' as Macardle (p.333) says, 'was a logical part of the British attempt to destroy the Republic'.

On 19 March occurred an incident which, while by no means the first British counter-productive action of the war, was to prove the first of a number that were disastrously so. At the same time it proved enormously — if tragically — strengthening from the Irish point of view. At about one-thirty that morning police and military, together with a number of men in civilian clothes, surrounded and isolated the district where Tomas MacCurtain, the Lord Mayor of Cork, lived with his wife and five small children. Macardle (p.334) describes what then happened:

> Shortly afterwards Mrs. MacCurtain heard a knock at the door of the house; she looked out of her window and saw a group of men with blackened faces; before anyone could open the door they had burst in. Some of the men seized Mrs. MacCurtain while others rushed upstairs and shot Tomas MacCurtain at the door of his room. He died in a quarter of an hour. The men left and about half an hour later military entered the house and raided it ...

The murderers were subsequently identified as being members of the RIC and a coroner's jury — even though selected by the police — brought in a finding that MacCurtain was 'wilfully murdered under circumstances of most callous brutality; that the murder was organised and carried out by the Royal Irish Constabulary officially directed by the British Government'. A verdict of wilful murder was returned against Lloyd George, French, MacPherson, the chief secretary, and members of the RIC. One of the RIC officers named by the jury, District Inspector Swanzy, was later shot by the Army.

When news of the atrocity reached New York a picket, which continued for three weeks, was placed on the British Embassy in Washington by Irish-Americans. Similar murders of elected republican representatives by military and police occurred from then on from time to time. Terence MacSwiney succeeded MacCurtain both as Lord Mayor of Cork and as brigade commandant of Cork No. 1 Brigade.

As one might expect the British 'reprisal' policy did not meet with universal approval throughout the British administration. French himself is claimed to have disapproved 'of methods used by some of his colleagues in Dublin Castle'. And, while there were 'members of the British cabinet who believed that a solution lay in provoking another rising in Ireland', there were others who were taken aback by the methods being employed. There were yet others who, anticipating a prolonged guerrilla war, believed that 'only by terrorising the civilian population into submission could the reconquest of Ireland be achieved'. And it was they who had the decisive word. As to the political policy behind this imperialistic approach, Macardle (See pp 336/7) provides an illuminating summary:

Among all this confusion Lloyd George was pursuing a patient and politic course. Clearly, he had made up his mind that the solution of the Irish question lay in Partition. With six counties secured for the Empire as a garrison, the resistance of the twenty-six counties could more easily be worn down; even though it might become necessary to give these a measure of self-government, Ireland partitioned would be unable to achieve a position of prosperity or influence. To reduce the Irish people to a condition in which they would be ready to consent to Partition and renounce the Republic was the task entrusted to the Administration in Dublin Castle. The Prime Minister would not hamper the Executive or its forces by inquiries into the methods they might find it necessary to use; he relieved Lord French of obstructive personalities sent him reinforcements, and proceeded with the passing through Parliament of his 'Bill for the Better Government of Ireland'.

But the Bill, passed without any reference to the Irish electorate, was the worst sort of political compromise. There was no longer any pretence that it offered Irish self-determination. Insofar as it served any interests, these were, primarily, the British strategic one of a foothold in Ireland, and secondly those of a reluctant Carson, who accepted it on the grounds that it provided a six-county (Unionist) statelet. It was Sir Walter Long, chairman of the Irish Committee who proposed two separate parliaments for Ireland, one for six of the Ulster counties where Unionists could remain entrenched, the other for the twenty-six remaining counties. This proposal was based on Lloyd George's earlier assurance to Carson that 'We must make it clear that at the end of the provisional period Ulster does not, whether she wills it or not, merge in the rest of Ireland' (Murphy, op. cit., p. 57). It was this pledge, ensuring the support of the Ulster loyalists, that enabled the Bill to be passed. (See also Robert Kee, *The Green Flag, A History of Irish Nationalism*, 1972, p. 583)[170]

In order to prepare the ground for this Bill — which, if it was passed would establish partition as a legal principle so far as Britain was concerned — it was essential to stabilise and coordinate administrative and military activity in Ireland, which, up to mid-March, was chaotic and conflicting. The administration had 'lost its grip on the civil government of Ireland and the military were left to their own devices ...the Castle administration does not administer'" (Murphy, op. cit., p. 112 and citing the investigative report of Sir Warren Fisher of May, 1920). Lloyd George rapidly installed a new, tough administration which was to lay the groundwork. A key figure in this regime was Alfred (Andy) Cope, a direct conduit to Lloyd George who became an extraordinarily powerful, influential and controversial figure and about whom, and whose activities, there is yet much to discover. He is said to have formed a close relationship and reached a meeting of minds with Collins at a relatively early stage. 'Stories about Cope's influence on Collins were rife both before and after the Treaty. Collins, naturally enough, was extremely sensitive about them' (Murphy, p.111). But the suggestion, for instance, that there was a reward of £10,000 on Collins dead or alive, though used by Griffith (*The Freeman's Journal*, 5 January, 1922) two days before the crucial vote in the Dail on the Treaty, is thought to have originated with Cope, who might, at that time, have been considered to be the Treaty party's 'spin-doctor' *par excellence*. The relevant Griffith quotation is illuminating:

> When the fight was on Mr. de Valera and Mr. Erskine Childers fell accidentally into the hands of the military. They were immediately released. That was at a time when there was a £10,000 reward for the corpse of Michael Collins. The Irish people must stand up, and begin their freedom by giving their fate into the hands of their countrymen.

The latter reference is to observations made earlier in the same article that de Valera 'has not the instinct of the Irishman in his blood' and that Childers was 'an Englishman who has achieved fame in the British Intelligence Service' — unworthy remarks, particularly in view of Cope's influence at the time on Griffith's own party.

> Cope was particularly friendly with Martin Fitzgerald, the owner of the *Freeman*, and through him could influence the contents of the paper. Sturgis had no doubt on the matter ... Cope, himself, admitted an ability to control the paper (Murphy, op.cit., p. 123).

Cope was a former detective and was well-suited to his role of acting as Lloyd George's personal envoy and trying to establish contact with the Irish leaders. His power evidently became enormous. Murphy suggests that it was due to Cope's influence that both Collins and one of his men in the Castle, David Neligan, were protected, and that Cope's influence over the military and police forces in matters pertaining to Sinn Fein was absolute. 'The Army chiefs, Sturgis' [Mark Sturgis, Assistant Under-Secretary at Dublin Castle under the new regime] 'noted "regard Andy as a complete Shinn, and treat him in much the same way as they would Michael Collins' (Murphy, op. cit. p. 124 and citing Sturgis's diary).

As to why the full nine Ulster counties were not included, Carson himself explained that '... if we were saddled with ... these three counties ... while you would leave out 70,000 [protestants] who are in [them] ... you would bring from these three counties in the northern province an additional 260,000 Roman Catholics' (House of Commons debate, 18 May 1920). It did not serve the interests of the Irish people as a whole in any way, Lloyd George himself observing: 'If you asked the people of Ireland what plan they would accept, by an emphatic majority they would say: "We want independence and an Irish republic". There is absolutely no doubt about that. The elected representatives of Ireland now, by a clear, definite majority, have declared in favour of independence — of secession'. (The House of Commons, 31 March 1920)

In March General Sir Nevil Macready was appointed British Commander-in-Chief, Ireland, and at the same time a new force was recruited in England for service in Ireland. They were the Black and Tans, as they came to be called from their uniforms of khaki military trousers and almost black police tunics. 'The whole new organization was being camouflaged' because money could be obtained in England for police operations in Ireland, but not on the military vote, (W. F. P. Crozier, *Impressions and Recollections*, p.251). To put it bluntly it was a piece of political finagling to enable this terrorist military force to be raised outside the military vote. The feeling was that a police operation would appear less objectionable than a military one in the eyes of the world, particularly at a time when Britain was still, during an American election campaign, trying to impress the United States with her good will towards Ireland.

In the event the plan back-fired, mainly because as Macardle correctly points out (p. 340):

> The despatch of this new force to Ireland helped relieve England of a very dangerous type of unemployable — men of low mentality whose more primitive instincts had been aroused by the war and who were now difficult to control.

This accurate, if somewhat highly-coloured, description is not greatly different from that of Richard Bennet (an Englishman and former British Army officer) in his book (*The Black and Tans*, p. 38):

> They never looked and behaved like policemen. Their only service experience had been in trench warfare which had a brutalising ... effect, a training quite useless against the Irish Republican Army's tip-and-run campaign. Their morale had not been improved by months of unemployment ... The full force of Black and Tan violence and indiscipline did not break out until later in the year.

A second and even deadlier force was also recruited for Ireland in June. They were the so-called Auxiliary Cadets who were paid the substantial sum of £1 a day, twice as much as the Black and Tans[171]. The Auxiliaries, who were in effect a mercenary body, were a separate command under neither military nor police discipline. They were not amenable to trial by civil courts. The British Army in Ireland and these two special forces were supported by reinforcements of a further eight regular infantry battalions, fully equipped with supply and transport. The 'Auxies', about 1,500 strong, consisted exclusively of ex-officers of the British Forces. In general they wore a sinister black uniform with Sam Browne belt and Tam O'Shanter caps. But, except for the Tam O'Shanters, frequently wore whatever military gear came to hand, often leather 'wind-breakers' or, like their opponents in the IRA, trench coats. Initially they were regimented in fifteen companies — at Inistioge, Co. Kilkenny, Macroom, Co. Cork, Gormanstown and in Cork and Dublin cities. Later they became a strike force attached to many military and police barracks throughout the country.

The Irish Army and the Dail had one overriding objective which, for the duration of the war, gave to both the Army and the nationalists a common purpose. This was to make it so costly for the British to try to govern Ireland that they would withdraw. The tactics employed were those which, ironically, the British learned so thoroughly that they were able to pass them on to the Resistance in Nazi-occupied countries during World War Two.

Roads were trenched to leave a margin that would allow a farm-cart to pass beside a pit into which a military lorry travelling at speed would crash. Bridges were blown up, railway tracks damaged and telephone lines cut, in order to destroy the communications of the British military. Captured barracks all over the country were systematically burnt to the ground; the districts in which they stood could thus no longer be occupied by the Crown forces.

The size of the Irish Army operating against the British at this time is an indication of how effectively a small, dedicated guerrilla force can not alone pin down an enemy vastly superior in numbers and fire-power, but actually take the initiative. Apart from the Black and Tans and the Auxiliaries the British initially deployed upwards of 45,000 regular troops in the country, not counting Navy and Marine personnel or police. Strength was later increased to approximately 55,000 troops in all. The Irish Army numbered about five thousand poorly armed effectives, but with a very considerable back-up force which extended into every area of community life in the country. In addition they had the element without which no guerrilla force, however well-armed, can hope to succeed for long; the goodwill and support of the people at large.

By the summer the Army had made considerable progress. 'Authorisation', says Deasy (pps. 81 et seq)

> was granted to conduct attacks on barracks in West Cork from the beginning of the ... year. Hitherto the three principal methods used to acquire arms and ammunition had been raids on loyalist houses, attacks on RIC barracks and ambushes of police and military patrols ... and GHQ had not openly advocated attacks on enemy forces as a matter of general policy.

In The Field

The War of Independence, while nationwide, was essentially in the hands of local commanders. For different reasons it was more active in some areas than in others. But all had a common purpose and also tended to have similar objectives and methods. For these reasons, rather than attempt to give even a sketchy account of the armed struggle right across the country as it developed, it seems more practical to give an outline of the campaign in one area. As it was the most active I have selected West Cork to serve as a general guideline on the course of the war, with reference to major actions elsewhere as appropriate.

> ... The southern counties, Cork in particular, took the lead in military activity and remained in the forefront until the bitter end. Cork put more men in the field than any other county, undertook the biggest and most costly engage-ments in the war, maintained an unbroken offensive against the enemy and suffered more intensively than any other area at his hands (Donal O'Kelly, *Ordeal by Fire*, With the IRA in the Fight for Freedom, p. 31).

Deasy's Kilbrittain company had attacked the British military post at Rathclarin, in June 1919, and from the beginning of 1920 attacks of this kind became frequent. The following May attacks also began on coastguard barracks defended by marines. Deasy points out that as their military patrols and barracks were attacked, the RIC began to withdraw both from the barracks and the areas they were in. The districts thus left without even a semblance of British law enforcement were administered by the IRA until the formation of the republican police in June, 1920.

It was at about this time that a significant move, which was to have a decisive effect on the campaign in general and here in particular, was made by the field officers in West Cork.

> In the face of the rapidly-changing pattern of the war, towards the middle of 1920, a new need made itself felt, namely, that of forming fighting columns to provide mobile striking forces that would help us maintain the initiative in our campaign (Deasy, p.141).

A Brigade Council meeting (of the 3rd Cork Brigade) was held at a place called Coppeen, the brigade having been in continuous service for the previous four weeks. It was decided to establish an independent Brigade Flying Column; battalion columns had already been in operation for some weeks, and it was decided to retain these as well[172]. Tom Barry, who had been a sergeant with the British Army during the World War, was appointed its commander. He had already provided invaluable training courses in the brigade area.

> The Column took part in practically every major engagement in the ensuing months. It ranged through five of the seven battalion areas of the Brigade bringing help to weak districts, and everywhere raising the morale of the people. Gradually it achieved its main objective: it took the initiative from the enemy and became an attacking rather than a defensive force (Deasy).

In many parts of the country towns and villages had been cleared of the RIC who were now concentrated in larger barracks heavily defended with sand-bags, barbed wire entanglements, machine-gun emplacements and bombs. Even as late as December, 1920, when the RIC had been driven from many of their barracks and these reduced to rubble, it was possible for Liam Deasy to write (op. cit., p. 189): 'somehow we did not, at this time, or at any later period, consider the military, or the Auxiliaries, or even the notorious Black and Tans such formidable foes as the R.I.C., for to our way of thinking, they were the eyes and ears of the enemy forces in Ireland.'

According to the *The Irish Times* (1 May 1920) the king's government had virtually ceased to exist south of the Boyne and west of the Shannon. 'The forces of the Crown' it said, 'are being driven back to their headquarters in Dublin by a steadily advancing enemy'. Any vestige of support for a continuation of British rule or Home Rule amongst the public in general was not just long since gone; in the previous year and a half or so it had been replaced with positive support for the republic. When, in April, republican prisoners in Mountjoy jail, Dublin, went on hunger-strike, the Irish Labour Party and the Trades Union Congress called a general strike in support. In those days of no security of tenure, the strike was undertaken in spite of the risks of loss of money and dismissal. The secretary of the Irish Women Workers' Union, Miss Louie Bennett, testifying before the American Commission on Conditions in Ireland, 1920-21[173], said: 'I can speak for my own trade union women; there was not a single case in which the workers objected to refuse to work'. Three days after the general strike the prisoners were released. They had been on hunger-strike for ten days. The release of the prisoners and the end of the general strike was a cause for celebration everywhere. But at Miltown Malbay, County Clare, while the crowds were singing and dancing around celebratory bonfires, police and military arrived and fired into the crowd, killing three people and wounding nine.

In May there was another strike by the Irish Transport Workers' Union. 'In the late spring Ireland was full of troops. . . in war equipment. When armed soldiers or Black and Tans boarded a train the engine-driver would refuse to start. By 22 May railwaymen as well as dockers were refusing to handle munitions of war. The strikers were supported by a fund voluntarily subscribed, amounting to a sum of over one hundred and sixteen thousand pounds. Their resistance lasted until the end of the year' (Macardle, p. 347).

The republican police force which was formed in June was largely voluntary, in that its members were for the most part unpaid. They were generally unarmed and were successful in maintaining order and carrying out the edicts of the republican Courts, especially in areas which had been cleared of the enemy. Besides the Land Courts already established, Arbitration Courts and Courts of Justice were also created so that the whole machinery of law and law enforcement was established and functioning at this time. Hugh Martin, correspondent for the English Conservative paper the *Daily News*, wrote:

> Sinn Fein has accomplished an amazing work in producing law and order in those parts of Ireland in which it is in power. Sinn Fein law has a sanction behind it such as no other law in Ireland has had for generations.

Side by side with the rising effectiveness of the Sinn Fein Courts and law-and-order, the British military rule of Ireland continued with terror as one of its principal methods, the paradoxically macabre purpose being to 'restore order'. In Counties Cork and Limerick that June when republican police took criminal prisoners, British military and police intervened, released the prisoners, and shot dead the unarmed republican police.

More local elections were held in June, this time for County Councils, Rural District Councils and Boards of Poor Law Guardians, and again republicans swept the boards. The Sinn Fein successes in January and fourteen months earlier in the general election were reinforced. Republican majorities were returned in one hundred and seventy-two of the two hundred and six councils in the country. This included thirty-six of the fifty-five Rural District Councils in Ulster.

During June and July the Irish stepped up the pace and intensity of the campaign, twenty-four attacks taking place in June and over thirty in July, including one on government offices in Dublin in broad daylight. From June onwards the war atmosphere became universal and unmistakable. The British attorney-general for Ireland, Denis Henry, said in the House of Commons on 22 June that British troops in Ireland had been instructed to behave as if on a battle-field. Macardle describes the situation graphically (pp. 354-6), pointing out that the battlegrounds of these troops were the homes of the Irish people and their behaviour not that of disciplined soldiers. In Dublin sections of the city were frequently cordoned off with barbed wire, the troops supported by military vehicles and tanks. As these armoured columns trundled through the streets at night searchlights played across house-fronts. When a lorry stopped in a street residents rushed from bed to the doorways to open them and avoid their being broken in. This would be followed by the soldiery rushing in and storming through the house from attic to cellar, threatening the occupants, and frequently smashing their way through cupboards, furniture and floorboards and ripping clothing, cushions and matresses to bits. They were frequently drunk and often fired their weapons through the walls and ceilings from inside, looting any valuables they found. Men were in danger of being shot out of hand or 'while attempting to escape'.

In parts of the north, cementing the shaky relations with the British, northern unionists did much of the terrorist work elsewhere in the country carried out by the British army and police. This helped to establish a relationship between them on the essentially impermanent grounds of sectarian and political favouritism. It was a relationship further sustained on the grounds that 'nationalist' and 'Catholic' were synonymous terms — a variety of 'Home Rule is Rome rule'. Violence and prejudice against the Catholic community was its hall-mark. Derry, because of its sizeable Catholic population a severe irritant to local unionists, was, like Belfast, a flashpoint[174]. On 19 July armed Protestant mobs attacked Catholic areas, looting and firing houses and shops. Nineteen people were killed and fifty injured in four days of fighting. The British military did not intervene until the republican army had done so to protect the Catholic community — and then they attacked the IRA.

Belfast followed. On 21 July Catholic workers were driven out of the shipyards with great ferocity and over the following days and nights armed attacks on the Catholic areas of the city were intense. Hundreds were killed, wounded and left homeless. Workers were threatened with death if they returned to their workplaces. The military did not intervene to protect the Catholic community. This appears to have been part of a calculated unionist programme to clear the six proposed partition counties of 'Fenians' before Lloyd George's Bill came into effect.

The events of 1913 were forgotten. Unrestrained by police or military Orange mobs, essentially Carson's UVF, drove Catholics from their homes, towns and cities. Sectarian murders of Catholic men, women and children — most of whom had nothing directly to do with the national movement — became a characteristic of unionist activists. Five thousand Catholic workers were driven out of the shipyards. An English reporter from *The Daily News* wrote an account of Belfast at this time (Hugh Martin, *Ireland's Insurrection London, 1921*). It includes:

In other directions the war on Catholics — indiscriminately dubbed 'Sinn Feiners' by the Orange majority — was being systematically and ruthlessly pressed. The entire Catholic population of Lisburn and Banbridge, about 1,000 in each case, had been successfully 'evacuated' — that was the military term universally employed — and the Orange army was dealing section by section, night by night, with Belfast. Two thousand men women and children had been evacuated from the Ballymacarrett district, and on the night of my arrival the attack upon the Catholics of the Crumlin road district began 'according to plan' as the saying goes ... Since the early days of the German invasion of Belgium, when I witnessed the civil evacuation of Alost and the flight from Ostend, I had seen nothing more pathetic than the Irish migration. Over 150 families, numbering 750 people in all, were dealt with in a single day at one of the Catholic receiving centres, St. Mary's Hall, and it was to the credit of the afflicted Catholic population of the city that every family found a refuge before nightfall.

Most of the refugees were from Lisburn, where not a single Catholic was left...I found two mothers, who, each with a family of five small children, had tramped eight miles from Lisburn to Belfast, coming by the solitary road over the Black Mountain for safety's sake. They had slept on the hills, and gone without food from Friday afternoon till Saturday midday. In two cases the husbands had for days been fruitlessly searching for their wives, just as happened during the invasion of Belgium (op. cit., p.167 et seq.).

That same week an organised attack, in which sixteen people were shot dead, began on the Catholic areas of Belfast. Over one million pounds damage was caused and by the time it was over in mid October almost sixty Catholics had been killed. These attacks were organised principally by the UVF which had threatened civil war in 1914.

In spite of these events, and in one of its more extraordinarily stupid or cynical moves, the British Government decided to enrol Carson's UVF and the Orange mobs as a new force of Ulster Special Constabulary, the A, B and C Specials, of which the B Specials would become the most notorious. Simultaneously obstructions were put in the way of Catholics who tried to remain in any of the six of the nine Ulster counties designated as 'partition' counties — Antrim, Armagh, Derry, Down, Fermanagh and Tyrone. Political tests of loyalty were imposed, and all were forced to sign a declaration of loyalty to the British government before being given promotion or employment.

The hideous politicisation of sectarianism[175] had reached its apogee with fearful and enduring consequences for both sides. The response of the Dail was impressive and illuminating. Concerned lest Catholic employers and employers sympathetic to Sinn Fein throughout the country might retaliate by dismissing or by otherwise harrassing Protestant workers, it issued a decree prohibiting similar tests as a condition of employment or promotion.

All over the country in March orders had been issued requiring the RIC to accompany the military in armoured cars or tanks, armed with machine-guns and loaded with 120 gallons of petrol and 120 hand-grenades. Suspected members of the 'Sinn Fein movement' were stood in front of their houses and machine-gunned. The petrol and grenades were for burning the houses. As a result of such policies of atrocity and of the pressure they were under from the Irish army, resignations from the RIC became increasingly frequent. During the two months of June and July there were 556 such resignations. But there were resignations from another, and more surprising, quarter, further reinforcing the *de facto* position of the republic. During the same period 313 magistrates also resigned, the magistrates of Cork doing so *en masse* on 22 July, having passed the following resolution:

> That having regard to the unalterable opinion of the vast majority of our fellow-countrymen, and with whom we cordially agree, that Ireland is entitled, like other oppressed nationalities, to that form of government chosen by the people, and that, as this was the basic principle underlying the great European War to crush militarism, we consider it our duty to surrender our commissions sanctioned by British law.

In Kerry the RIC mutinied against orders they were given. The following is a shortened version of an account by one of the RIC taken from *The Irish Bulletin*, July, 1920:

> The men were addressed by Col. Smyth, Divisional Police Commissioner for Munster: — '... if a police barracks is burned or if the barracks already occupied is not suitable, then the best house in the locality is to be commandeered, the occupants thrown out in the gutter. Let them die there — the more the merrier. Police and military will patrol the country at least five nights a week. They are not to confine themselves to main roads, but make across the country, lie in ambush and, when civilians are seen approaching, shout "Hands up!" Should the order not be immediately obeyed, shoot and shoot with effect. If the persons approaching carry their hands in their pockets, or are in any way suspicious looking, shoot them down.
>
> 'You may make mistakes occasionally and innocent persons may be shot but that cannot be helped, and you are bound to get the right parties some time. The more you shoot, the better I will like you, and I assure you no policeman will get into trouble for shooting any man.
>
> 'Hunger-strikers will be allowed to die in jail — the more the merrier. Some of them have died already and a damn bad job they were not all allowed to die. As a matter of fact some of them have already been dealt with in a manner their friends will never hear about'.
>
> At the close of this speech Mr. Smyth addressed the first man in the ranks of the assembled constables, saying: 'Are you prepared to co-operate?'
> The man referred him to the spokesman [they] had chosen. This constable replied; 'By your accent I take it you are an Englishman and in your ignorance forget that you are addressing Irishmen'. The constable then took off his cap, belt and bayonet and laid them on the table saying;
>
> 'These, too, are English. Take them as a present from me — and to hell to you — you are a murderer.'
>
> Colonel Smyth then ordered the arrest of the spokesman; the other constables swore that if a hand was laid on him the room would 'run red with blood'.

Smyth was shot in Cork by the Army shortly afterwards. Even allowing for any element of exaggeration, the general thrust of this blood-chilling account was verified as authentic. Not all the RIC reacted to their orders as did those in Kerry and throughout the country in June and July homes and businesses were wrecked and burned and a number of civilian men and women were murdered by the police.

In June, too, there occurred the famous mutiny of three hundred and fifty men of the Connaught Rangers in India, out of sympathy with what was happening in Ireland. One was executed and the others were sentenced to penal servitude for terms of up to twenty years.

By July it was clear that part of the objective of the Dail and the Army had been accomplished; English government of Ireland was impossible by any civilised means. The next step was to bring about the government of Ireland by the Irish. On 29 June the Dail met in secret with Griffith presiding. It passed a number of important votes including empowering 'the President [de Valera] to expend a sum up to $1,000,000 to obtain recognition of the Irish Republic by the Government of the United States'. Diplomatic appointments were made and it was agreed to send a diplomatic mission to the new Government of Soviet Russia. A sum of $1,000,000 was voted to the Department of Defence from funds subscribed from America. The collection of income tax was authorised and the Internal Loan of £250,000 was closed having been over-subscribed by £40,000. It was at this meeting that courts of justice and equity were decreed. Judges were appointed by Austin Stack, Minister for Justice. From today's standpoint, when issues of equality of rights are prominent, it is noteworthy that in the case of an appeal by an unmarried mother for medical expenses, the judge, James Creed Meredith, First President of the Supreme Court, held that English law was retrograde in this respect and applied the old Irish Brehon code, finding in favour of the girl.

Except in parts of the North the courts operated throughout the country, manifestly validating existence of an independent Irish administration and leaving the English assizes and courts empty. Accordingly in July attempts to suppress them began. Of eighty republican courts held in July, five were broken up. As the year progressed these raids increased. Court officers, including judges, were arrested and imprisoned and documents were seized. But the republican courts continued with the support of the republican police, and enforced and carried out the law so that English courts everywhere except in the north of Ireland, fell into disuse.

The combined military and civil resistance together with a national executive and legislature all supported by the vast majority of the people provided unassailable evidence of the will of the people. In no arm of administration, civil or military, on no political platform — save in the unionist north — nor in any public forum, were the British able to find a supportive voice, much less a majority. Torture of republican prisoners and suspects, which up to then had tended to be reactive and haphazard, now became routine and commonplace.

A campaign against creameries was part of the plan to destroy Irish commercial life. In August mills and bacon factories were also attacked. George Russell (AE), the founder of the great co-operative movement of which the creameries were part, wrote (*Irish Homestead*, August 1920): 'creameries and mills have been burned to the ground, their machinery wrecked; agricultural stores have been burned, property looted, employees have been killed, wounded, beaten, threatened or otherwise ill-treated...'

In August Dr. Daniel Mannix, Archbishop of Melbourne, and a supporter of Sinn Fein, was arrested at sea. He was on a journey to visit his mother in Ireland, and his ship, the *Celtic* was stopped by a British destroyer off Cobh (Queenstown), Mannix was arrested and transferred to the destroyer and brought to England. He was not permitted to visit Ireland.

From this point onwards the republican movement in Ireland, in both its constitutional and military aspects, was not only fighting for the republic and self-determination for Ireland, was not simply warring against the enforced Union with England and British forces in Ireland; it was clearly opposing the British Empire and the entire concept that this represented. It is a point perhaps not always sufficiently put in context. This awareness lay at the heart of much of the hard-nosed opposition in England to what was clearly and unmistakably the will of the majority of the Irish people. The empire, after all, had been visibly weakened by the recent World War. It would take enormous effort to recover from that. To be further — and severely — wounded on the doorstep of the mother-country, and by the first colony, was unthinkable. But that is what seemed to be happening. It must not be allowed. It must be stopped, at all costs. Limited Home Rule without military, fiscal or diplomatic rights together with partition enabling the retention of a stronghold in northern Ireland was as far as it was possible to go. If that didn't satisfy them, then, as Lord Birkenhead would put it in a matter of a few months, 'the resources of civilisation were not exhausted'. The re-conquest of Ireland with all that that entailed was not out of the question; but an independent republic was. Absolutely!

The difficulty from the British point of view was obvious. They had no clearcut policy in relation to Ireland or what was happening there. They had not, even yet, understood the effect of the 1916 Rising on the Irish people. The British Government, while pursuing a vague Home Rule 'Irish' policy — which, since it was inherited from its own statute book, it felt obliged to do — was under no illusion that it was acceptable to either the republicans or the unionists. As a consequence partition had been introduced through the back-door as a species of political subterfuge to keep a British government from collapsing, to prevent civil war by the unionists and to maintain a powerful hold on Ireland. It was this, and not Home Rule, that had become the essential platform of the British Government's Irish policy. It was spelled out in Lloyd George's 'Better Government of Ireland Bill'. And it was a proposal that satisfied no one. But it continued the pattern of English policy in Ireland which appears to have been based on the proposition that any proposal that, for different reasons, fails simultaneously to satisfy a second and third party must be correct.

The Better Government of Ireland Bill was to bring about a partitioned Ireland. But it did more than that, it institutionalised political sectarianism in a manner that had never been done before, in effect legislating for a 'protestant', unionist, statelet. Large areas, indisputably nationalist, would be separated from the remainder of nationalist Ireland, and isolated within this statelet. Neither unionists nor nationalists accepted the Act as equitable. The unionists opposed the recognition of any form of Irish nationalism (which, with signal irony given the 18th century Irish view of political and religious freedom being synonymous, they persisted, with the inherited loathing of sixteenth century reformationists, in seeing as a form of Papistry), and the nationalists, of course, were strongly opposed to any attempt to partition the country for any reason. The British were patently motivated by two, conflicting, main considerations; the force of world opinion and the age-old strategic imperative represented by Ireland on her western doorstep. In an attempt to reconcile the unionists' civil war threat, the republican aspiration, international pressure and her own interests, the partition Bill was cobbled together as a face-saving make-weight.

Meanwhile the British Government provided the military administration in Ireland with a free hand to deal with the war. And an utter mess they were making of it so far as the politicians were concerned. The military administration itself was restricted only financially and by a refusal to allow them to settle the matter with overwhelming force, which is what they wanted. Hence they felt considerably frustrated and, while successfully provoking the 'Shinner' enemy with coercion, provocation and harassment of the public, were not permitted to follow up and destroy him. Consequently they found themselves holding the unpleasant end of the stick and winning no laurels for it, while the enemy encroached and consolidated his position militarily, politically and morally. It was an unenviable position for the military to be in and was one which could have only one foreseeable conclusion. However the Government in London was led by one of the most astute and unscrupulous politicians of this century. He, too, foresaw the inevitable. But he was determined to shape it to his own ends.

Extending the protective umbrella over the activities of British forces in Ireland, the Defence of the Realm Act (DORA) was reinforced by the Restoration of Order in Ireland Act, 1920. This gave extraordinary powers and immunity to the British military and police. It aroused considerable opposition in the House of Commons in London, but came into force nonetheless. As a result anyone connected, even remotely, with a proclaimed organisation — the Gaelic Athletic Association and the Gaelic League, for example, no less than Sinn Fein — or who supported the Dail, was guilty of a crime punishable by trial by secret court without legal representation. Coroners' inquests, which had returned many verdicts of murder against British police and military, could be suppressed and substituted by military enquiries. This became common, and coroner's courts were seldom employed thereafter in cases involving British forces.

> The British preparations for the final phase of the reconquest of Ireland were almost complete; the Irish nation had been outlawed; members of the Government's forces had been indemnified in advance for excesses against Republicans; their campaign of terror had been categorically legalised (Macardle, p.381).

On 12 August Terence MacSwiney, Lord Mayor of Cork, was arrested while presiding at a meeting in the City Hall. Ten others were arrested with him. Taken to Cork jail, they all went on immediate hunger-strike. On the third day of his strike Mac Swiney was deported to England.

I was in London making attempts to get permission from the German police to spend a year in Munich to study music when a telegram from Mary [Mac Swiney] told me that Terry had been transferred to an unknown English prison. I tried to find out which. Mary and Annie [MacSwiney] came over and after a day or so we were told he was in Brixton (Geraldine Neeson, unpublished memoirs)[176].

MacSwiney died on 25 October, the seventy-fourth day of his hunger-strike, having, by his extraordinary fast-to-death, attracted the attention of the world to his country's plight.

English attitudes to Mac Swiney ranged from that of an individual who sent a little bottle of strychnine 'to finish the brute off', to a letter from an ex-sergeant major who was prepared to wait at the gate of Brixton prison all day and every day to donate pints of blood for Terry when he was released. I saw him shortly before he died. His face hadn't changed much except for the waxen pallor. He was quite lucid and spoke clearly, but in a whisper (Ibid.).

In County Cork, particularly West Cork, the war intensified to one of classic guerrilla proportions, setting a standard for guerrilla campaigns against foreign domination for much of the century, not to be superseded until weapons technology after World War Two imposed major changes on guerrilla tactics. (Thereafter the moral supremacy which was such a powerful factor for the Irish Army in the war of independence was increasingly subordinated to that of terrorism as an overt tactic).

The reasons for this change are complex and, since terrorism by those on the republican side was isolated and incidental, need not concern us here except in one respect. That is to refute the unthinking and ill-informed charges sometimes made that the IRA in the War of Independence adopted terrorist tactics of this later kind, which is simply untrue. Irish policy was exactly the opposite as the statements and orders of Irish commanders of the time demonstrate. It would, moreover, have been counter-productive since it would have put the hard-won moral superiority at risk. When acts of terrorism by Army personnel did sometimes occur, the Army command was usually the first to seek out and punish the offender. It was a specific axiom of Dail and Army policy not to employ the terrorist methods of the enemy.

Some indication of the problems facing the Army in this most active area may be gauged from the fact that in August the three Cork brigades, numbering between them some 10,000 men, could then command a total of only 200 or so rifles. Attacks on the enemy, some of them dramatic, helped to improve this situation. Tom Barry (*Guerrilla Days In Ireland*) states that the Army in Cork never had more than 310 riflemen in the field at any one time 'for the very excellent reason that this was the total of rifles held by the combined three Cork Brigades. The only other IRA arms (excluding shotguns) within the county were five machineguns and some 350 automatics and revolvers. Even this small armed force could not be mobilised for a major operation likely to continue for a day, as its ammunition did not exceed fifty rounds a rifle, two fills per revolver and automatic; and a few full drums for each machinegun'. At this time, according to Maj. Gen. E.P.Strickland, GOC the British Sixth Division in Cork, there were twelve thousand six hundred British troops there on a war-footing, excluding naval and marine personnel.

In a battle at Kilmichael on 28 November, eighteen Auxiliaries from Macroom, which was outside the third brigade area, were killed and their arms captured. Three Irish soldiers were also killed[177]. It is worth quoting from Tom Barry's account of this battle (Auxiliaries wiped out at Kilmichael in their first clash with the I.R.A., *With the IRA in the Fight for Irish Freedom*, Tralee):

Revolvers were used at point-blank range and at times rifle-butts replaced rifle-shots. So close were the combatants that in one instance the pumping blood from an Auxiliary's severed artery struck one attacker full in the mouth before the Auxiliary hit the ground ... Once I got a side glimpse of Flyer's [John Nyhan) bayonet being driven through an Auxiliary, whom I thought dead as I passed him, but who had risen to fire and missed me at four yards range ... A second tender of Auxiliaries were lying in small groups on the road firing back at No. 2 section ... Waiting only to reload revolvers and pick up an Auxiliary's rifle and some clips of ammunition [four of us] ... ran crouched up the side of the road. We had gone about fifty yards when we heard the Auxiliaries shout 'We surrender'... Firing stopped, but we continued, still unobserved, to jog towards them. Then we saw three of our comrades of No. 2 section stand up, one crouched and two upright. Suddenly the Auxiliaries were firing again with revolvers. One of our three men spun round before he fell and Pat Deasy staggered before he, too, went down.

When this occurred, we had reached a point about twenty-five yards behind the enemy party and dropped down as I gave the order, 'Rapid fire and do not stop until I tell you'.... Some of the survivors of our No. 2 section had again joined in and the enemy, sandwiched between the two fires, were again shouting 'We surrender'.

Having seen more than enough of their surrender tactics I shouted the order, 'Keep firing on them until the Cease Fire'.

By mid-autumn local authorities throughout the country had severed connection with Dublin Castle and now acted under the authority of the Dail Minister of Local Government, W.T. Cosgrave.

In autumn, too, attacks by military, police, Black and Tans and Auxiliaries on towns increased. Tuam, Carrick-on-Shannon, Drumshanbo, Galway city, Lahinch, Ennistymon, Miltown Malbay were all attacked over the three nights of 20-22 September in what was clearly a coordinated effort by local units in the Clare, Galway and mid-west regions. But the attacks were not confined to the west. On 20 September a large section of the small town of Balbriggan in County Dublin was virtually razed to the ground by Auxiliaries from their camp three miles away. Twenty-five houses were destroyed and one of the two village hosiery factories was burnt out. The people of the village fled as the Auxiliaries rampaged through it — except for three young men who were killed, two of them bayonetted in the street.

The war was now being carried to the ordinary people by the British forces. In the following weeks Trim and Mallow were similarly attacked by the Auxiliaries and military, and all over the country the same type of attack and destruction occurred on a smaller scale. People were driven to living in stables and barns.

But these things did not go unnoticed by the world outside. 'In England intellectual leaders like Gilbert Murray, H.G.Wells and C.P.Scott gave strong expression to their indignation on Ireland's behalf' (Macardle, 391). The Irish bishops issued a pastoral, much quoted abroad, that if there was anarchy in Ireland the British Government were its architects[178]. In a letter to *The Times* on 4 October Asquith wrote of Lloyd George's policy: 'Its only logical sequence is to take in hand the task of re-conquering Ireland, and holding her by force — a task which, though not, perhaps, beyond the powers, will never be sanctioned by the will or the conscience of the British people'.

He was not alone in his view. Many members of parliament, and the Labour Party as a whole, were opposed to the British Government's policy on Ireland. The Labour Party put forward a proposal for the withdrawal of the British Army of occupation, relegating the question of an Irish government to an Irish constituent assembly elected by proportional representation. It sought constitutional protection for minorities, and that Ireland would not become a military threat to Britain — a variant of de Valera's 'Monroe Doctrine' proposal.

The Irish Labour movement supported this policy, and a British Labour Party Commission of enquiry reported that reprisals by members of the Crown Forces fell under these main heads; general terrorism and provocative behaviour, arson, the wilful destruction of property — otherwise than by fire — looting, cruelty to persons, and shooting.

On 17 October one of the men arrested with MacSwiney, Michael Fitzgerald, died of his hunger-strike in Cork jail. MacSwiney, in London, died on 25 October. The others, also in Cork, at the request of Griffith the acting President, ended their strike. All had been close to death.

There was an extraordinary irony about MacSwiney's funeral. The ordinary people of London stood in respect as the coffin, draped in the tricolour, was accompanied by a guard of honour of Irish soldiers[179] and was followed by thousands of Irish people and, as Macardle notes: 'That passing through London would have been remembered as an example of magnanimity in the English but for what happened at Holyhead'.

What happened at Holyhead was prompted essentially by British anxiety to prevent MacSwiney's body being brought to Dublin. The family had decided on Dublin in view of the national figure MacSwiney had become. The British decided otherwise, as they anticipated a demonstration there on an unprecedented scale, and insisted on the coffin being brought to Cork. At Holyhead the principal mourners, including the MacSwiney family, were taken from the train by force and the coffin was shipped direct to Cork. This action was the result, it transpired, of Sir Henry Wilson's intervention. He had 'stormed' about the proposal to permit the funeral to pass through Dublin. The handling of the matter was as clumsy as might be expected and is perhaps best described by one of those affected:

It was decided that the women of the party would assemble around the coffin when we reached Holyhead. We were to make a token resistance, but not allow ourselves to be hurt. On arrival we followed this plan and after an ignominious scuffle found ourselves on the quayside...The colour of dark grey always brings back that scene to me... It had been raining and the ground was grey and wet in the lamplight; the uniforms of the soldiers and Black and Tans who were in a semi-circle around us seemed grey; the kneeling women appeared grey in that light. So, too, appeared the brown habit of Father Dominick as he stood holding the crucifix aloft, reciting loud enough to quell the sneers of the troops: 'I bless the body of Terence MacSwiney', as the ship moved out over the still water (Geraldine Neeson, op. cit.)[180].

MacSwiney was buried in Cork on 31 October.

In November an eighteen-year-old Irish soldier, Kevin Barry, was hanged following an ambush on British military in Dublin. He had been tortured by British soldiers while in prison. Throughout that month a number of indiscriminate fatal shootings of civilians took place — one of them a woman nursing her baby while in her garden; another a child of eight, one of a group of children; another a priest in County Galway. In all thirty-three innocent men and women 'other than Volunteers killed in action' died in November (Macardle, p.400). Torture was common.

On 21 November Collins's Squad eliminated the so-called 'Cairo Gang' of some fourteen British agents brought into the country — some from Egypt, hence the name — specifically to 'get' Collins. Collins got them first. That afternoon the British exacted a frightful revenge. Some seven thousand people were attending a football match at Croke Park, Dublin, when the stadium was surrounded by troops. Suddenly the Black and Tans and the RIC drove up in lorries and opened fire on the crowd, killing twelve and wounding sixty people. The firing continued for upwards of ten minutes. Following this the ground was searched for arms. None were found[181]. That night Dick McKee, brigade commandant of the Dublin Brigade, Peadar Clancy, vice-commandant, and Conor Clune, a civilian and a nephew of the Bishop of Perth, were arrested by British troops and taken to Dublin Castle, where they were first tortured by Auxiliaries and then murdered in the guardroom.

A plot described by Brigadier F.P.Crozier[182] (See Crozier, *Ireland for Ever*, London, 1932) to murder the outspoken Catholic Bishop of Killaloe, by drowning him in the Shannon in a sack, was thwarted when the Auxiliaries involved raided the bishop's house while he was absent in Dublin.

An important step was taken by the Dublin brigade when, for similar reasons to the establishment of Tom Barry's Flying Column in West Cork, they formed the Active Service Unit. This was a permanent, paid force of fifty men which would engage the enemy on a continuing basis. Similar units were formed in Cork city and Belfast. But, for the moment, the confrontational war was essentially localised in rural areas, particularly in the west, mainly West Cork, and in a battle between Collins's intelligence units and the intelligence arm of Dublin Castle, in both of which the Irish were more than holding their own. Irish agents were active in most administrative departments and were particularly useful in the Post Office where they were in positions to monitor and control vast amounts of information intended for the British authorities, providing copies to the IRA. As the *Irish Press* (14 June 1933) put it:- 'they placed the service of the British Post Office at the disposal of the Republican Government'.

The supply of arms improved considerably, purchases being made through Robert Briscoe (later the first, and very popular, Jewish Lord Mayor of Dublin), in Germany and elsewhere on the Continent as well as from captured arms. The Army made plans for action in England against communications, the economy, spies and the auxiliary corps, but with limited results.

That same month Lloyd George clarified British policy to partition Ireland. On 11 November the Government of Ireland (Partition) Bill was passed in the House of Commons. Ironically enough even the four unionist members refused to vote for it and walked out, so that: 'This Bill for the Government of Ireland was thus made law in spite of the opposition of every Irish Representative. It was carried and imposed upon Ireland wholly by British votes' (Macardle, p.402). It became law on 23 November.

On 25 November Arthur Griffith, Acting President of the Dail and of the Republic, was arrested and Michael Collins became Acting President — a measure of how far this young man (just thirty) had come since 1916.

In that bleak month of November a new note was heard through the smoke of terror and gunfire. For the first time peace feelers — vague and unofficial though they might have been — weaved unsteadily by way of several sources from Downing street to Dail Eireann. They contained mention neither of the partition on which Lloyd George was determined, nor of the now defunct Home Rule. Their unacknowledged significance appeared to be a recognition by the British that Dail Eireann was the representative body of the Irish people and that de Valera was the leader acknowledged and empowered by them to act on their behalf. It seemed just possible that something worthwhile for both countries might result from these overtures. But in response to his tentative and informal peace feelers and, as can tragically happen in a crisis at such delicate moments, Lloyd George's prescient political 'nose' evidently misled him on this occasion and he picked up the wrong signals from the wrong sources. These led him to misread the situation in Ireland and to reach the erroneous conclusion that the Irish were weaker than in fact they were. He concluded, wrongly, that a majority of the Irish people would accept his proposals. He therefore announced that he was willing to negotiate on the basis already stated by him and that in the meantime the campaign against Sinn Fein would be heightened. Martial law was extended and the war intensified. Lloyd George now required the surrender of all arms on penalty of death, a penalty also to apply to those guilty of 'the aiding, abetting and harbouring of rebels'.

His preconditions for negotiation were thus 1/ partition to stand, 2/ no secession of any part of Ireland from the United Kingdom, and 3/ nothing to be agreed that [in the opinion of the British Government] detracted in any way from the 'security of these islands, and their safety in days of war'(Lloyd George in the House of Commons, 10 December 1920). For the Irish these unacceptable and impossible pre-conditions were a clear indication of the extent to which Lloyd

George misread the reality in Ireland. But, even so, both Macready and Wilson opposed a truce of any kind and pressed for an intensification of the war.

On the day Lloyd George made this speech martial law was imposed on the whole of County Cork. On the following night, with curfew in operation, the Auxiliaries burned the entire centre of Cork city, and the city hall over half a mile away.

> As I rode down Patrick street [on 19 December] in the midwinter dawn I saw the burnt-out portion of the city was still smouldering; smoke was still rising from the ruins caused by the fire that was set alight on the night of 11-12 December (Deasy, op.cit., p.179).

Thousands of people were thrown out of work. The background to the burning of Cork is clear even if some of the details are less so. It was obviously something that had been planned in advance and was the culmination of gross outrages that had been practised on the citizens of the city for some time by 'K' company of Auxiliaries stationed in Victoria (Collins) Barracks. The 'K' company

> had indulged in raids on houses, holding up and searching civilians in the streets, robbery and insulting behaviour. In November and December their drunken aggressiveness became so pronounced that no person was safe from their molestations. Age or sex was no protection. Poor women were robbed of their few shillings in the streets by these 'gentlemen' in broad daylight. After their raids on houses articles of value were frequently missing. Whips were taken from shops with which to flog unoffending pedestrians. Drink was demanded at the point of a revolver.

The IRA determined to put an end to this intolerable situation. Ambushes were laid at various points in the city over a period of several weeks, and that at Dillon's Cross on the night of the eleventh of December was the first to come off. (Florence O'Donoghue; The Sacking of Cork City, *With the IRA in the Fight for Freedom 1919 to the Truce*, Tralee, p. 131)

It has been argued that the conflagration was precipitated by the ambush that evening at Dillon's Cross, a few hundred yards from the barracks, of some lorry-loads of Auxiliaries. But that is so unlikely as to be impossible. The fact that the ambush occurred on the same night may well have added fuel to the outrage, if the pun is permissible, but the timing of the events appears to have been coincidental. It is very doubtful if an operation as elaborate as the wholesale arson involved could have been mounted literally within minutes without pre-planning.

The ambush took place at almost exactly the same time that Black and Tans were clearing the streets of the city below, that is between eight-thirty (2030) and nine. At least one Auxiliary was killed and twelve wounded (it may well be that they were en route to participate in the burning when they were ambushed.) The Irish party of six got away unscathed. Houses at Dillon's Cross were afterwards fired by Auxiliaries and Black and Tans, but by that time the centre of the city was already ablaze.

The report of the British Labour Commission stated:

> The Commission was impressed by the sense of impending disaster which overhung the city of Cork during the time it was staying there. The uncertainty

was ended by the tragic occurrences of Saturday, 11 December when the Regent street of Cork was destroyed by incendiaries.

Shortly before 9 p.m. on Saturday, 11 December Auxiliary Police and 'Black and Tans' appeared in large numbers in the streets of the city, and at revolver point (before actual firing took place) drove people to their homes earlier than the curfew regulations required.

This was regarded by the citizens as ominous ... the streets were soon entirely deserted and the work of destruction begun ... Eye-witnesses ... state positively that the incendiaries were agents of the British Government ... In some cases explosions occurred. Others, again, saw them engaged in looting ...

We would point out that the fires occurred after the Crown Forces had driven the people indoors, and that during the greater part of the time that outbreaks of fire took place the Curfew regulations were in operation. We are of the opinion that the incendiarism in Cork during the night of 11-12 December was not a 'reprisal' for the ambush which took place on the same date at Dillon's Cross. The fires appear to have been an organised attempt to destroy the most valuable premises in the city, and we do not think that the arrangements could have been carried out if they had been hastily made after the unfortunate occurrence at Dillon's Cross (Report of the Labour Commission, op. cit., p.32 et seq).

Firemen were obstructed and fired on by police and military as they attempted to deal with some of the fires, and at least two were wounded. Looting was on a staggering scale. Afterwards the Auxiliaries in Cork wore burnt corks in their caps as a derisive gesture of contempt. But it was a gesture which, in fact, served only to show how out of control this force was. By the end of December British forces (mainly Black and Tans and Auxiliaries) had killed 203 unarmed men women and children — apart from Irish soldiers — in this year alone.

The report of the British Labour Commission referred to above, issued on 29 December, is a detailed, authenticated and documented record of destruction, arson, looting, terrorism and murder by these forces, recording, amongst others, these killings. It also states the view of the Commission that what was in progress was 'the wanton destruction of economic Ireland ... ' and that the Black and Tans and Auxiliaries were 'compelling the whole Irish people — men, women and children — to live in an atmosphere of sheer terrorism' (op. cit., Appendix V., p.101).

The British Government refused to publish the report on the burning of Cork submitted by Strickland. The London *Daily News* of 19 January, 1921, said: 'The report is so damning that public opinion would demand the removal of Sir Hamar Greenwood' [Permanent Secretary in Dublin castle). Sir John Simon said, in Sunderland, ten days later: 'A system of vengeance has been established in Ireland, and after what had happened there, I beg to hear no more about what the Germans did in Belgium'.

Asquith also spoke out strongly: 'I say deliberately that never in the lifetime of the oldest amongst us has Britain sunk so low in the moral scale of nations ... things are being done in Ireland that would disgrace the blackest annals of the lowest despotism in Europe...'

The year 1920 ended with the introduction of the new regulations announced by Lloyd George, for breach of which the penalty was death.

1921

The new year opened with a new twist to the British military policy of reprisals (a policy reminiscent of that which received international condemnation with the reprisal destruction of the Czech village of Lidice in June, 1942, twenty-one years later). Seven householders in Midleton, Co. Cork, were given notice by the British military that they had one hour to evacuate their homes after which these were to be destroyed. They might remove personal valuables only. The reason given was that an ambush had taken place in the neighbourhood and the local community had 'neglected to give information to the military and police' (The *Cork Examiner*, 8 January 1921)[183]. The homes were destroyed in accordance with the notification. Except for the north most of Ireland was now under martial law and *habeas corpus* did not operate. At this time Strickland, military governor of Munster, issued a number of proclamations directed mainly against the civilian population, one of which stated baldly: 'Any attitude of neutrality is quite inconsistent with loyalty and will render those adopting it liable to trial by military courts' or be 'dealt with summarily'. Another proclamation required every householder, lodging-house owner and hotel to display on the doors of their premises the names, ages, sex and occupation of every occupant. Changes had to be reported to the police within three hours. All houses were obliged to keep a current list of male occupants posted outside. The first 'execution' under the new regulations was on the first of February when a young Corkman, Con Murphy, was shot for possession of a revolver. In what is surely one of the most mendacious misstatements published during the war, the official *Weekly Summary* (issued by Hamar Greenwood, Chief Secretary for Ireland) reported this 'execution' under the heading '*Potential Murderer Shot*'.

In the same month internment camps capable of holding thousands of prisoners were established in various parts of the country. The new phase of the British campaign moved ahead. Even though a state of war was acknowledged by both the British administration and the [British] High Court in Ireland, prisoners continued to be tortured and killed in defiance of the provisions of the Hague Convention. These shootings and hangings aroused the public in much the same way as had the executions in 1916 and, from the British point of view, were, accordingly, counter-productive.

In Dublin curfew was at 8 p.m., leaving the streets free to the British military, the Auxiliaries and the Black and Tans. Large areas were systematically cordoned off and ransacked for men and 'incriminating' evidence. Looting by these forces was widespread. (According to their one-time commanding officer, Brigadier Crozier, a depot was later opened in England from which the proceeds of looting by Auxiliaries in Ireland were sold. Crozier resigned his command because of the behaviour of the Auxiliaries). Hospitals were raided in searches for wounded Irish soldiers.

By now the Auxiliaries, instead of being the intended 'strike-force', were an undisciplined, uniformed mob given to excesses, atrocity and looting. When, in

February, fifteen Irish soldiers surrendered with their hands up after a battle at Clonmult, Co. Cork, the Auxiliaries fell on them, beat nine of them to death, badly injured five more and looted the bodies. One man escaped. About the same time, in Dublin, they took from the Castle two youths who had been arrested, stood them against a wall in a field, put buckets over their heads and used the buckets as targets. When, on occasion, some of these 'Cadets' were suspended, they threatened to make public details of similar incidents on a substantial scale involving the whole force. This the authorities could not permit, and enquiries were dropped.

Lloyd George now fired the same cannon he had primed ever since he became prime minister, and had fired many times during the previous twelve months. In the House of Commons 'They [the Irish people] must have an Irish Republic, an Irish army, an Irish navy. They won't get it', he declared.

The risk of taking public office was again highlighted in March when the Mayor of Limerick, George Clancy, his predecessor, Michael O'Callaghan and another leading citizen, were, like Tomas Mac Curtain in Cork almost exactly a year before, murdered in their beds during curfew by mysterious strangers understood to be either police or Auxiliaries.

That same Brigadier Gough (by then Major-General) who had done all in his power to sustain and defend the mutiny of British troops at the Curragh, was so appalled at conditions in Ireland that, echoing Asquith a few weeks before, he wrote:

> Law and order have given place to bloody and brutal anarchy in which the armed agents of the Crown violate every law in aimless and vindictive and insolent savagery. England has departed further from her own standards, and from the standards even of any nation in the world, not excepting the Turk and Zulu, than has ever been known in history before (cited Macardle, p.432).

The daily newspapers published casualty lists in which civilians of both sexes featured prominently. The mutilated bodies of those who had been arrested, or 'shot while trying to escape', turned up in increasing numbers all over the country, with an average of a murder every day by British forces.

The hardships which the people endured at this time were not, however, confined to murder, torture and savagery. The policy of wrecking the economy and so forcing the people to withdraw their support from the Dail and the Army intensified. The houses of alleged republican families were stripped of everything of value, and often burned. All over the country families whose houses had been destroyed were living in stables and barns;

> Women and children, driven at night out to fields and bogs, were dying as a result of exposure; old people whose sons had been murdered before their eyes were dying from shock and grief; with increasing frequency babies were born dead. For the devastation wrought by the military and Black and Tans in martial law areas, the plundered and starving people were forced to pay. British Courts of Justice were prohibited from hearing claims for compensation against the Forces of the Crown for destruction done in the areas under Martial Law (Macardle, p.434).

Irish and international relief organisations, including some in Britain, contributed funds enabling the people to continue to support the Irish authorities. By far the most important of these was the Irish White Cross fund which, by August, 1922, had collected £1,374,795 (See *Report of the Irish White Cross*, Martin Lester, Dublin). A committee of American relief delegates opened offices in Dublin. The Pope sent £5,000 and an apostolic benediction to the people of Ireland being subjected to 'devastation and slaughter'.

That spring of 1921 was the most critical period of the war. The previous November the Auxiliaries had come face to face with the Brigade flying column at Kilmichael in West Cork. Now it was decided to tackle them head on. In Deasy's words (op. cit. p.198):

> The reign of terror which began in mid-December with the arrival of the Auxiliaries in Dunmanway had continued into the New Year, but now the column was in the field again under the inspiring leadership of Tom Barry, we felt that the Auxiliaries' worst efforts could be successfully countered, and that we could strike again with devastating effect as had already been done at Kilmichael. Soon the indiscriminate raids and nocturnal visits organised by the Auxiliaries ceased almost entirely, and they rarely moved out of barracks except in full strength in convoys of lorries or tenders.

Attacks on military and police strongholds were carried into towns in the Brigade area and those at Bandon, Inishannon and Skibbereen were all attacked, in some cases more than once.

A difficulty in the West Cork Brigade area, and one that, sometimes, long after the events, became controversial, was that of spies and informers who threatened the lives of Irish soldiers and the very existence of the Brigade itself. It was, for instance, an organisation called the Anti-Sinn Fein Society in Bandon which was responsible for the cold-blooded murder of two brothers called Coffey in their beds in Ahiohill. But the Army took immediate action after these murders; two members of the murder gang were tried and shot and a third fled the area. Of particular interest is the fact that the accused were 'invariably given every opportunity to defend themselves, and sentence was passed only when the evidence against them was conclusive ... A case to illustrate this ... involved a farmer who lived in Drimoleague ... he was tried by the local Battalion staff and sentenced to death. As the sentence could not be carried out without Brigade sanction, and as the evidence of the prisoner's guilt, though strong, was not conclusive, the Brigade opened an appeal court. As there was still some doubt after the second trial the prisoner was acquitted and set free' (Deasy op. cit., pp. 200/1).

One particularly interesting case involved a seventeen-year-old girl, daughter of a farmer near Bandon. She had written to the commanding officer of Bandon Barracks giving the names of sixteen officers and men of local companies. The letter was intercepted by an Irish Army intelligence agent and handed over to the local battalion headquarters. Officers called to the girl's home and found the blotting paper she had used in writing the letter which still compared with its contents. The evidence was beyond doubt. Deasy comments:

When questioned she admitted writing and posting the letter, but in her defence she said she had acted as she did because a local Volunteer whose bicycle had broken down while he was on despatch duty, had commandeered hers to complete his mission and left her his broken one. She resented this action so much that she had written the letter to take revenge. In the circumstances the officers felt that drastic action should not be taken, but instead they ordered the girl and her family to leave the country within twenty-four hours. The sentence was considered to be suitable punishment, and a necessary protective action (op. cit. p.210).

A point Deasy does not emphasise in this context is that Bandon and district was a stronghold of pro-British and unionist sympathy.

An indication of the resilient strength of the Army organisation, and of the fact that it was far from being the haphazard structure sometimes suggested, may be gauged from one incident that occurred in the Schull, Co. Cork, area in January when a sweep by British military and Auxiliaries — acting on supplied information — resulted in the capture of the captains of two companies of the Schull battalion, as well as other officers and men. By the following day these officers and men had been replaced without disruption or interruption of operations.

Of course not all encounters with the enemy were victories. The attack on a force of British troops, which had been estimated at about fifteen to twenty in number, at Upton station on 15 February is one example. It resulted in three Irish soldiers being killed and three wounded, including the loss of the Battalion engineer and the serious wounding of the Brigade Commander, Charlie Hurley, out of an attacking party of fourteen. There was a number of British casualties also, and six civilians were killed and five wounded. What had happened was that the train with the original enemy group had picked up half a company of troops from Kinsale en route and, although the attempt was made, it was not possible to alert the attackers to this in time.

> The engagement at Upton was undoubtedly the most serious reverse suffered by the Brigade, and what was particularly unfortunate about it was the loss ... of so many civilian lives as well as the loss of three outstanding Volunteers ... (Deasy, pp.221/2).

The British cabinet policy of intensified military terror and of dragging Ireland towards partition was beginning to have an effect, Deasy continues, saying that all-in-all February can be recorded as Cork's Black Month, and West Cork had no monopoly of the reverses and disappointments that were a feature of the period. On 27 January a column of the Donoughmore Battalion was surprised at Dripsey, five being captured, four of whom were executed, the fifth dying of his wounds. On 20 February the Midleton Battalion suffered the losses at Clonmult. At Mourne Abbey on 15 February the Mallow battalion column lost five killed in action and two captured and executed. And there were other reverses. But these served to inspire the Army and their civilian supporters to greater efforts.

The most important and successful engagement of the war in the area took place on Saturday, 19 March at a place called Crossbarry on the Cork/Bandon road, some fifteen miles from Cork, twenty or so from Macroom, and about eight miles from Bandon[184]. The decision to mount this attack was, says Deasy, the most momentuous decision in the whole campaign in West Cork. The largest fighting column so far put in the field, one hundred and two men, was assembled on 17 March to attack a convoy of the Essex regiment, units of which had a particularly bad reputation, at a place called Shippool on the Bandon River between Inishannon and Kinsale. The Essex, however, in a remarkable irony, decided to celebrate St. Patrick's Day by not sending out a convoy, and the Irish column marched to Crossbarry where it was hoped to ambush five or six lorries of British troops believed to travel in the area. The battle started around 0700 on the morning of the 19th and continued for about twelve hours all told. It was quickly obvious that the British had been informed of a column (probably while they lay in wait at Shippool), and were deploying considerable forces estimated at between 500 and 1,000, including regular troops and Auxiliaries, in an encircling movement.

Enemy movements, approaching from the west, were sighted by Irish scouts at 0230 and positions were prepared before dawn with the column in seven sections, two of them guarding the rear and flanks. The other five sections occupied the ambush site, which was not ideal, consisting in large part of open ground. But the sections dug in and camouflaged their positions. By daybreak they were ready. A burst of fire about 0700 from where Charlie Hurley was laid up, wounded, was the first indication that the enemy were also to the north and east. They were now approaching from the west, south and north east.

The Irish attacked the first convoy, destroyed it, and then, over a period of several hours in a prolonged fire-fight, denied the enemy the high ground and an opportunity to encircle them. Holding open a passage to the north they performed what became a classic fighting withdrawal without loss (though Charlie Hurley, who was wounded and lying in a house a mile or so distant from the action, was captured and killed). They inflicted considerable casualties on the enemy and captured an amount of ammunition and arms, including a Lewis gun. As they retired they encountered a strong unit of Auxiliaries crossing their path. Unseen, the column changed direction leaving three volunteers to delay the Auxiliaries. The small unit took up positions and opened fire on the Auxiliaries at close range, killing both their commanding officer and his second-in-command with the first volley, whereupon the others turned and ran. An interesting aspect of this lengthy Crossbarry battle is that the Assistant Brigade Adjutant, Flor Begley, made an important and significant contribution to the fighting spirit and morale of the Irish troops (and may, indeed, have had the opposite effect on the enemy), by playing the war-pipes during the action.

Deasy, who was Brigade Adjutant at the time (he did not become Brigade O/C until May), took part in the ambush under the command of Tom Barry. He wrote afterwards:

> We had encountered a better trained, more numerous and far better armed
> force than our own, and had acquitted ourselves remarkably well ... Two years
> — indeed even one year — earlier we could not have put up anything like the

fight at Crossbarry, and the main reason for the change was acquisition of arms (op. cit. pp. 248/9).

The interesting point of view is sometimes encountered that it was 'unfair' of the Irish to oppose British terrorist tactics with ambushes. When de Valera, as President, was asked in March by a foreign journalist if he considered the ambushing of British forces justifiable, he replied:

> Certainly. If the Irish nation and the Irish Republic as a State directly founded upon the consent and will of the people is not entitled to use force to defend itself, then no nation or state is entitled to use force. The English forces are in our country as invaders, on a war-footing as they themselves have declared; in fact actually waging war upon us not only an unjust but a barbarous war. Protected by the most modern war-appliances they swoop down upon us and kill and burn and loot and outrage — why should it be wrong for us to do our utmost to see that they will not do these things with impunity?
>
> If they may use their tanks and steel armoured-cars, why should we hesitate to use the cover of stone walls and ditches? (Press interview, U.S., March 1921).

By the end of April the Army had succeeded in destroying or irreparably damaging more than 800 enemy barracks and strong points. In Britain in April English church leaders wrote to Lloyd George protesting that government policy in Ireland was 'causing grave unrest throughout the Empire' and was resulting in 'the hostile criticism of even the most friendly of the Nations of the World'. Lloyd George's reply was consistent with his policy. He said: 'So long as Sinn Fein demands a republic the present evils must go on'.

Everything was to be subordinate to the strategic value of Ireland to British imperial long-term interests, even if this meant protracted war and a policy of continued terror in Ireland. But while this was so it was also the case that, sooner or later, there must come an end. The question was on what terms would it end? World opinion was now turning decisively against the British campaign in Ireland.

By March it was obvious that a solution — and not simply an imposed, unilateral solution by England — was inevitable. Clearly what Lloyd George was trying to achieve in the first five months of 1921 was not simply a crushing military victory (though that would do), and a return to things as they were before 1916, which was no longer an option. Now, astute and far-sighted politician that he was, he sought to create the conditions to enable him to make the best deal he could. That was clearly to yield as little as possible beyond the provisions of the recent Government of Ireland Act, due to come into effect in May. Once that happened he would be negotiating from a strong position. He would, in fact, have carved up Ireland and created the laws to support such action before any settlement was achieved. He must hang on until May, when the will of the Irish to resist might also have been broken. Thereafter, he could afford to negotiate. But until the Act was in place, secured by general elections, he could not afford the risk of open negotiation. If, before then, he could crush the Irish Army, demoralise and weaken the people so that they capitulated, so much the better. If not, the fight must continue.

In the meantime, as an additional way of creating the climate of opinion most favourable to him — at home and abroad — and of probing for some sign of weakness on the Irish side, Lloyd George encouraged unofficial peace moves. Archbishop Clune — uncle of Conor Clune, murdered in Dublin Castle the previous November — was one of the more important intermediaries, but his efforts were unsuccessful. There were other similar unofficial attempts to bring about a Truce. Writing on behalf of the fighting men, Deasy (op.cit., p.195), says:

> Our attitude was very sceptical in regard to these moves. Suggestions that the British Cabinet was anxious for a Truce to end hostilities were indeed interesting, but we were not in the least enthusiastic about them. Neither were we in any way perturbed by them, nor did we accept them as an indication of weakening on the part of the enemy in the field. We faced the future with a confidence that we felt was fully justified.

In April the strange and shadowy figure, A.W. 'Andy' Cope, nominally Assistant Under-Secretary for Ireland, was specifically charged by Lloyd George to explore the possibility of negotiations[185]. Behind-the-scenes discussions took place in the established British tradition. Supported by rumour and innuendo, this useful manoeuvre is usually intended to create a climate of opinion in favour of 'Peace'. If successful any kind of opinion may then be exploited to advantage. It does not always work, especially if clumsily handled. On 21 April the most significant approach yet made came to de Valera through Lord Derby who indicated that the British Government was prepared to offer a modified form of Dominion Home Rule. The offer was rejected. Then Lloyd George, for the first time, raised a crucial question — was de Valera insisting on the principle of complete independence as a pre-condition to negotiations? De Valera responded with a counter question: 'Will [the British Premier] not consent to meet me or any representative of the Government of Ireland unless the principle of complete independence be first surrendered by us?'

There was no immediate response, but in an interview with an American journalist on 11 May Lloyd George stated his willingness to meet without pre-conditions on either side. Before it was possible to follow this suggestion up, the general elections which would, according to English law, give effect to the partitionist Government of Ireland Act were held. The Act had come into force on 3 May and the respective parliaments of Southern and Northern Ireland were summoned to meet in June after the elections, which were held respectively on 19 and 24 May. The Southern Parliament was to have 128 members, the Northern 52. The South was entitled to send 33 members to Westminster, the North 13.

The Dail decided to regard these elections as elections for the Second Dail[186]. Prior to the election every nationalist party agreed to support Sinn Fein and the Republic and republican candidates won all of the contestable 124 seats, the other four being those allotted to Trinity College[187].

In the North, in spite of serious sectarian riots, republicans 'won twelve of the fifty-two seats, an insignificant return measured against the sentiments of the populace. Nevertheless, the Unionists said that "too many Sinn Fein votes had been cast" — in spite of the measures they had taken to prevent it, and that "they would drive Sinn Fein, bag and baggage, out of the Six Counties". Almost immediately a pogrom of murder and violence began in which more than a hundred victims, many of them women and children, were murdered and thousands were driven from their homes' (Neeson, *The Civil War, 1922-23*). Some indication of the effectiveness of this intimidation may be gauged from the fact that at the time nationalist representation in the area was in the region of 34%.

During a pogrom between 10 and 15 June, six Catholics were killed by the forces of 'law and order' in the newly partitioned-off Northern Ireland, eleven others died during riots and about 150 Catholic families were driven from their homes (See Andrew Boyd, *Holy War in Ulster*, pp. 181-195, whose graphic account of this time when sectarian violence reached extraordinarily violent levels with armed mobs roaming the streets murdering, looting, shooting and burning, is by far the best modern account).

The election results were recognised as a sweeping victory for Sinn Fein and a virtually unanimous repudiation of the Government of Ireland Act. Nevertheless from the British viewpoint the Act was now law in Ireland, to be enforced with violence in proportion to the Irish people's detestation of it, (See Macardle, p.455).

The British Government now had in place the perverse legal mechanism they required. The Government of Ireland Act was law. It placed in the hands of the British a *de jure*, if fraudulent, legal advantage which they would later exercise with a high sense of moral justification. In addition to being grossly sectarian and a perversion of the democratic principle, it was — and indeed remains — one of the most hypocritical political acts of this century. 'From that moment,' wrote Churchill, 'the position of Ulster became unassailable' (cited Macardle, 455/6).

Towards Truce

By now the people of Great Britain, appalled by what was happening in Ireland in their name, were making their voices loudly heard. In the face of public opinion Lloyd George was forced, in June, to concede that 'Two thirds of the population of Ireland demand the setting up of an independent Republic in that island. At a recent election they reaffirmed that demand. Every effort I have made, publicly and otherwise, to secure a modification of that demand has failed. They have emphatically stated they will agree to nothing else'.

Cope, Generals Macready and Wilson — the latter with considerable advocacy — pointed out to the Government in London that they must either replace with fresh troops and commanders the army of 80,000 men in Ireland and stage an all-out war of extermination, or reach a settlement. All were agreed, however, that the English people were unlikely to support the first course of action. Churchill, Chairman of the Cabinet Committee on Irish Affairs and Secretary of State for the Colonies, estimated the logistics of such an operation:

A hundred thousand new special troops and police must be raised, thousands of motor cars must be armoured and equipped; the three southern provinces of Ireland must be closely laced with cordons of block-houses and barbed wire; a systematic rummaging and questioning of every individual must be put in force ...

He said the alternatives were a greater measure of self-government for the twenty-six counties of Southern Ireland, or 'the most unlimited exercise of rough-handed force — a tremendous onslaught' (House of Commons, June 1921).

But on 24 May the British Government adopted a modification of this course. Troops in Ireland were to be reinforced and, if the Southern Parliament was not in operation by 12 July — a singular repetition of this significant date in Irish history — then martial law would be strengthened. There were already thousands of republicans in internment camps with another fifteen hundred serving terms of penal servitude.

In this uncertain climate both the Army and the Dail were confident in the justice of their cause and seemed equally — perhaps excessively — confident of a just outcome. In March, while being interviewed by foreign correspondents, de Valera had outlined the establishing of the Republic, its status, mandate and title. In the course of this interview he made the following succinct statement:

> The Republic of 1916, provisional and liable to question before the elections of December, 1918, was by these elections placed on a foundation of certitude unassailable either in point of fact or of moral right. Those who question the moral validity of the Republic must challenge the foundations of democracy and the constitutional rights of peoples everywhere...

In the Army a major reorganisation was taking place in preparation for continuance of hostilities. Towards the end of March Deasy was summoned to a conference in GHQ in Dublin. On his return he was appointed Brigade OC of the Third (West) Cork Brigade, and on 24 April a staff meeting of officers from the three Cork, the three Kerry, the two Waterford and the west Limerick brigades was convened near Millstreet, Co. Cork, to put into effect a directive from GHQ to form the First Southern Division, as part of the expanding organisational structure of the Army. At that time Deasy's own brigade of seven battalions mustered about 5,000 volunteers and 500 Cumann na mBan. Liam Lynch, then Commandant of the Second Cork Brigade and also Divisional Centre of the IRB for South Munster, was appointed Divisional Commandant[188]. But, as stated above, the total number of IRA effectives did not exceed 5,000 men.

Divisional HQ were set up near Ballyvourney in West Cork. There was a plan to send experienced officers and men in columns to weaker areas to extend the range of military activity. According to Deasy (pp. 267/8) such an extension to new areas of conflict would relieve pressure on active areas. This would enable training, the treatment of wounded, and rest for the more active units. Only a Division formation, it was felt, under an experienced GOC and staff, could achieve this.

The Army was confident at the time, feeling 'the tide of battle was definitely turning in our favour' (Deasy. p.264) and that they were in a strong position to intensify an offensive in the coming months. 'The republican guerrilla campaign proved too determined, too resilient and too resourceful to be put down by the military force which was employed against it,' (See Charles Townsend, *The British Campaign in Ireland*).

A serious problem with which they had to deal was the official execution of volunteers captured with arms in their possession, 'now a settled policy in the enemy's terror campaign' (Ibid.), and the frequent unofficial execution of volunteers captured with or without arms. It was decided to counter with reprisals against all British armed forces in the Brigade area if these policies continued, and the British GOC in Cork, Strickland, was so informed.

Another problem, and one which later gave rise to extraordinary exaggerations, was the British policy, which had become very widespread, of burning down the houses of those suspected of being republican sympathisers. Accordingly it was decided to burn the houses of British supporters in retaliation. The Army GHQ issued an order to this effect on June 22 in which it was stipulated (1) that formal notice should be served on the person whose house was to be destroyed; (2) that the property for the destruction of which this was a reprisal should be specified and (3) that 'no persons shall be regarded as enemies of Ireland, whether they be described locally as Unionists, Orangemen, etc., unless they are actively anti-Irish in their actions'.

British supporters in County Cork were so alarmed that they sent a telegram to Lloyd George ... appealing to him to end the policy of burning nationalists' houses as the ones now most affected were the loyalists in southern Ireland. The effect was immediate and the British policy of burning houses came to a virtual end.

About this time the British began a policy of trying to cripple army communications by seizing all the bicycles in the area. However after the initial seizures the brigade collected all available bicycles, and had them safely hidden.

On 14 May more than twelve daylight attacks were made on enemy positions in the brigade area, including the barracks in Bandon, Dunmanway, Inishannon, Kilbrittain, Courtmacsherry, Clonakilty, Drimoleague and other places. The moral boost to the people and the Army itself was immense.

> The enemy . . . who were not killed took to their heels . . . and did not reappear until after our forces had left the scenes of action. In no case did we suffer any casualties, and everywhere our men . . . carried out their duties with efficiency and courage (Deasy p. 277).

In Dublin, on 25 May, the Dublin Brigade fired the Custom House, thereby striking a severe blow at British administration in Ireland. All Local Government records as well as much of the tax records for the country were destroyed in the conflagration. But the brigade suffered substantial casualties, over eighty men being arrested.

The Irish military view as expressed by Barry (*Guerrilla Days in Ireland*), Lynch (*No Other Law*) and Deasy was one of confidence.

> Everywhere we sensed a great spirit of optimism. We could see no other outcome of the long struggle but victory, and though we did not know when the hour of liberation would come, we felt that its coming was now inevitable (Deasy, op.cit., p.290).

Already there were large areas of the country completely cleared of British forces and known as 'Free Republic' areas. From the political viewpoint — particularly in Dublin — the situation was not quite so clear. The people had sustained — and were continuing to sustain — great hardship; the economy was in ribbons; the Government and its members were proscribed, imprisoned or on the run and the Dublin Brigade had been decimated in the Custom House attack. Continuance of a frightful war, whether one of attrition or a massive onslaught, seemed inescapable. The question that troubled them was, therefore, not primarily whether the Army could continue to sustain such a war, but whether the country and the people could do so.

Habeus Corpus had long been suspended. On 16 June a hearing brought by an Irish King's Counsel was opened before the Law Lords in England seeking a Writ of Prohibition against Courts Martials on the grounds that they were illegal. The decision was in favour: Courts Martial and executions were deemed to be illegal. Lloyd George continued to send out feelers to try to find out if slightly improved measures of autonomy over those in the Government of Ireland Act would be acceptable to the Republicans. De Valera took the view that 'The best line to pursue is to indicate that they are going on the wrong tack, that the right way is to propose a treaty with Ireland regarded as a separate state. Irish representatives would then be willing to consider making certain concessions to England's fears and England's interest, that there is no other way' (Letter to Art O'Brien, Dail London representative, 14 June 1921).

The Northern Ireland parliament was due to be formally opened on 22 June by King George V. The King, in an extraordinary personal move made in conjunction with General Smuts of South Africa, revised the speech which had been prepared for him. The revision was approved by the Cabinet, but with evident reluctance, because its thrust and tenor virtually rendered out-of-the-question any possible 'tremendous onslaught'.

King George said:

I speak from a full heart when I pray that my coming to Ireland today may prove to be the first step towards the end of strife among her people, whatever their race or creed. In that hope I appeal to all Irishmen to pause, stretch out the hand of forbearance and conciliation, to forgive and forget, and join in making for the land they love a new era of peace, contentment and goodwill.

It is my earnest desire that in Southern Ireland, too, there may, ere long, take place a parallel to what is passing in this hall; that a similar occasion may present itself, and a similar ceremony be preformed. For this the parliament of the United Kingdom has in the fullest measure provided the powers. For this the parliament of Ulster is pointing the way[189].

The future lies in the hands of my Irish people themselves. May this historic gathering be the prelude of the day in which the Irish people, North and South, under one parliament or two as these parliaments may themselves decide, shall work together in common love for Ireland upon the common ground of mutual justice and respect.

That same day de Valera was arrested in Dublin in a surprise raid. Twenty-four hours later, to the bewilderment of both himself and the Irish people, he was released without explanation. That came two days later in a letter from Lloyd George asking him to come to London for a conference with himself and Sir James Craig, the new prime minister of the new Northern Ireland, 'to explore the possibilities of a settlement'[190].

This letter was the carefully phrased opening-shot of what both men knew must become negotiations for peace, and it was fired by Lloyd George in his own time having, as we have seen, first carefully sited and primed his battery on ground of his own choosing. Partition was not only a pre-condition of these discussions, it had now both a *de jure* and *de facto* existence. The letter spoke, more in sorrow than in anger, of Ireland as a disruptive but continuing part of the Empire, and it referred to ending the 'ruinous conflict which has for centuries divided Ireland', which was nonsense.

De Valera replied to Lloyd George on the day the Southern parliament was supposed to meet. Of the one hundred and twenty-eight representatives, only four — those from Trinity College — turned up; of the sixty-four senators, only the fifteen appointed by the Governor General attended. It was a farce. It adjourned *sine die* after fifteen minutes which in effect meant, since the statutory number of members did not attend, that the Southern parliament lapsed (though, as we shall see, a strange further meeting was summoned for an equally brief session the following year).

De Valera replied to Lloyd George:

> Sir,
> I have received your letter. I am in consultation with such of the principal representatives of our nation as are available. We most earnestly desire to help in bringing about a lasting peace between the peoples of these two islands, but we see no avenue by which it can be reached if you deny Ireland's essential unity and set aside the principle of national self-determination.
> Before replying more fully to your letter, I am seeking a conference with certain representatives of the political minority in this country.
>
> Eamon de Valera
> Mansion House, Dublin.

The meeting de Valera mentioned was held in the Mansion House. Of the five people invited four, besides himself, attended. They were the Earl of Midleton, Sir Maurice Dockrell, Sir Robert H. Woods and Mr. Andrew Jameson. Sir James Craig, securing his position as prime minister of Northern Ireland, refused to attend. De Valera had written to them saying

> The reply which I, as spokesman for the Irish Nation, shall make to Mr. Lloyd George will affect the lives and fortunes of the political minority on this island, no less than those of the majority ... therefore I would like to confer with you ... to learn ... the views of a certain section of our people of whom you are representative ... I am confident you will not refuse this service to Ireland ...

This conference lasted from 4 to 8 July and on that day de Valera telegraphed his willingness to meet Lloyd George in London on 14 July. In Dublin a truce was agreed between both sides and was signed in the Mansion House on behalf of their respective forces by Gen. Macready, Colonel J. Brind and W.S.Cope; and by Commandant R.C. Barton, T.D. and Commandant E.J. Duggan, T.D.

The following statement was then issued:

On Behalf of the British Army it is agreed as follows:

1 No incoming troops, R.I.C., and Auxiliary Police and munitions, and no movements for military purposes of troops and munitions, except maintenance drafts.

2. No provocative display of forces, armed or unarmed.

3. It is understood that all provisions of this truce apply to the martial law area equally with the rest of Ireland.

4. No pursuit of Irish officers or men or war materials or military stores.

5. No secret agents, noting descriptions or movements, and no interference with the movements of Irish persons, military or civil, and no attempts to discover the haunts or habits of Irish officers or men.

6. No pursuit or observation of lines of communication or connection.

NOTE: — There are other details connected with courts martial, motor permits, and R.O.I.R.[191] to be agreed later.

* * * * * *

On behalf of the Irish Army it is agreed that:

(a) Attacks on Crown Forces and civilians to cease.

(b) No provocative displays of forces, armed or unarmed.

(c) No interference with Government or private property.

(d) To discountenance and prevent any action likely to cause disturbance of the peace which might necessitate military interference.

These terms became effective at noon on Monday, 11 July.

The country heaved a collective sigh of relief. In one sense the Truce had a more profound effect on the civilian population, right across the board, than the Treaty would have five months later[192].

Nevertheless this 'uneasy truce between the Volunteers and the British Forces ... tottered unsteadily beneath the threat of "might is right"' (Neeson, *The Civil War*, p.53), and was not welcomed everywhere, especially in some army quarters.

We received the news in ... a dazed silence ... Had I been asked my opinion beforehand, I should have opposed a cessation of hostilities at this time, unless a clear and definite assurance of a satisfactory outcome were part of the arrangement. . .

But . . . the gap between the terms of peace we sought were so far removed from the terms the British Government was prepared to accept that we saw no immediate prospect of a peace settlement. In consequence we viewed the Truce as a mere breathing space, a stage on the journey towards our goal ... (Deasy, op. cit., pp. 312/3/4).

Furthermore there was felt to be an insidious downside. The relaxation of the active service standards which accompanied the Truce would inevitably affect discipline. So long as the war continued excellent standards existed. But in the absence of wartime discipline resolve might well weaken. There would be, in addition, the great difficulty of trying to restore it if hostilities were renewed. Deasy feared that there was a danger that the military efficiency that had been built up with such effort might be seriously impaired by the time the Truce came to an end.

He summed up the nationwide war-effort with a tribute to the brigades and men and what they achieved in two years' hard fighting from one end of the country to the other. And then says:

> Briefly, my knowledge of the internal organisation of the Volunteers through-out the country, of the efficiency of the movement as a guerrilla army ... led me to be optimistic as to its capability of exacting from the enemy, in the end, the terms of peace on which we had set our hearts, namely, the complete independence of Ireland in its totality, and the establishment of an Irish Republic.

One of the strongest arguments put forward in support of acceptance of the Treaty has been that the Army could not have held out against an all-out British onslaught. That is possibly true. But the argument depends primarily on three things: firstly, what is meant by an 'all-out onslaught', secondly the capability, not only in terms of logistics, but also in the face of world opinion, of the British to mount and sustain such an onslaught and, thirdly, the attitude and ability of the Army and the people to resist.

An 'all-out onslaught' was, at that time, probably not within the capacity of the British. It would have taken, as we have seen from their own estimates, more than 100,000 fresh troops to secure and hold the country, and even that would not have eliminated guerrilla and underground warfare. Such warfare was not, in those days, a war in which civilians are the major casualties. They would undoubtedly have suffered hardship and the terror would have continued, perhaps even on an intensified scale. But the object of the British at that time would not have been to destroy the civilian population, but the Army. However it is unlikely that they would have been able to mount such an offensive, and would have been reduced to continuing the campaign with what fresh troops they might muster on much the same unsuccessful basis as before. A 'massive all-out campaign' would not have compared realistically with, say, the warfare on the Western Front during the Great European war, with masses of ranked artillery, barbed wire entanglements and entrenched troops, or anything like that. It would, at worst, have meant an intensification of military repression and terrorism.

Secondly, so far as logistics went, the British had their hands full elsewhere, in India, in the Middle East and in Russia, to name but three areas. Fresh troops were needed in Ireland: 'I am convinced that by October, unless a peaceful solution has been reached, it will not be safe to ask the troops to continue there' [in Ireland] 'another winter under the conditions which obtained during the last' (Gen. Macready, memorandum to the Cabinet, 23 May, 1921; cited Murphy, op. cit., p. 130). The cost of raising these fresh troops or running the risks Macready feared, whatever they were, would have been enormous. The possibility of employing

Flying Columns and using the Navy existed, but that would merely have extended a war of attrition. International public opinion, and that in Britain itself, would have been very much opposed to a continuation, much less an extension, of the type of terrorist tactics in Ireland which had received such world-wide publicity. On the whole the likelihood of the British mounting a massive all-out campaign in Ireland in the second half of 1921 seems very unlikely and Lloyd George's threat a substantial bluff. The report presented to the British Cabinet on 24 June, written by a military assessor who had been sent to Ireland for the purpose, included this telling sentence: 'The British army in Ireland is besieged' and unless more fresh troops are made immediately available 'we shall be beaten' (Murphy, op. cit., p. 130). That they would, and could, have rattled the sabre, producing an immediate post-negotiation-break-down display of force, cannot be doubted. But that is a very different thing from a massive all-out war of repression which could only have been counter-productive.

Thirdly there is the question whether the Army and the people could have held out. According to Collins, in particular, the Army could not have carried on the fight. This point of view has been repeated by other voices. But was it so? Deasy is not alone in taking the opposite view. Tom Barry, Florie O'Donoghue and Tom Maguire all agreed that the Army in the field was strong and powerful and that morale was high.

Townshend (Charles Townshend *The British Campaign in Ireland 1919-1921* p. 193), says:

> It was commonly said after the Truce, and is often accepted now, that the IRA was reaching the end of its tether. Such a conclusion ... seems exaggerated. There is no reason to doubt that, given time, strength, and public support, the British forces could have reduced rebel operations to negligible proportions. But these quintessential conditions were missing.

And here there are two points worth making. The first is that the outlook from Dublin — where the Castle authorities operated a powerful and influential network through Cope, where the Dublin Brigade had been decimated in May after the burning of the Custom House and where the Tans and Auxies patrolled the streets by day and night, terrorising the citizenry — was very different from that in the combat areas in the south and west. And, of course, Collins was in Dublin. Secondly, Collins was not in control of the Army. Brugha was Minister for Defence and Mulcahy was Chief of Staff. It was through them that the effective chain-of-command ran. The fact that Collins was primarily concerned with intelligence and financial matters, in addition to his relationship with Cope and the IRB, may have coloured his view pessimistically.

One of the historically most enduring — though often enough forgotten — features of the Irish War of Independence is the fact that its success spelled the beginning of the end of the great British Empire, which had, for so long in the name of civilization, spattered both the maps of the world and the world itself with red. Probably the empire was ready to collapse within a few decades anyway, but the War of Independence hastened the process.

Following the Truce four meetings took place, on 14, 15, 18 and 21 July, at 10 Downing street, London, between President de Valera and Prime Minister Lloyd George. On July 20 Lloyd George sent de Valera 'Proposals of the British Government for an Irish Settlement' (*Official Correspondence relating to the Peace Negotiations June-September, 1921*, Dail Eireann, 1921 -pp. 6,7,8). These proposals, which offered less than Dominion status, were rejected by de Valera and the Dail in a reply (in Irish) to Lloyd George on 10 August (ibid.). This elicited a very interesting letter from Lloyd George (13 August, 1921), in the course of which he emphasised the importance attached — by both sides — to the question of the Crown, and also stated what may be taken as the 'definitive' word on the question of the so-called 'British Isles' when the term is used, erroneously, to include Ireland:- '.. we must direct your attention to one point upon which you lay some emphasis and upon which no British Government can compromise — namely, the claim that we should acknowledge the right of Ireland to secede from her allegiance to the King. No such right can ever be acknowledged by us. The geographical propinquity of Ireland to the British Isles is a fundamental fact ...'

Unsatisfactory correspondence was exchanged thereafter until it indeed began to look as if there would be a resumption of war. However, while also stating the British position clearly and unequivocally, on 29 September Lloyd George issued another invitation to a fresh conference. This was worded in such a way as to be without preconditions and was accepted on that basis by de Valera.

Perhaps it is not inappropriate to leave the final word on the War of Independence to an historian who has made a signal contribution to the record of Irish history.

The itch to fight, to hold on, to contend with almost insuperable difficulties and almost impossible odds, had its roots in a tradition of insurrection and a spirit of resistance which, however irrational, were too strong and too deeply implicit in the history of the country to be ignored. The embers of Irish identity had been subdued; they had not been extinguished; and out of them, as dedicated and desperate men blew on the glowing coals, rose once more the phoenix of independent nationality (Lyons, p.32/3).

The hand that signed the treaty bred a fever — Dylan Thomas

Chapter 9

Truce and Negotiations

THE TRUCE PERIOD MAY BE DIVIDED into two main parts. The first of these was during the early summer months of 1921 when the Irish and British leaders were concerned with trying to find a formula, acceptable to both sides (and, indeed, to Northern Ireland), which would make it possible for negotiations to begin. The second, which began in the autumn, was devoted to the negotiations themselves. The whole period ended on 6 December 1921 with the signing of the Treaty (more correctly called Articles of Agreement Between Great Britain and Ireland: See Appendix Nine).

Each side, while anxious to begin negotiations, was naturally unwilling to compromise or to accept preconditions which would weaken its position. The British, having secured Northern Ireland, were prepared to offer the remainder of Ireland something slightly more than the Government of Ireland Act, but considerably less than free dominion status, let alone an independent republic. The Irish did not accept the reality — much less the validity — of partition and, supported by conviction and the mandate of the people of Ireland as a whole, sought a republic. Before discussions on the issue could begin it was necessary to find a formula that would enable the respective sides to meet without compromising their positions. Both sides realised that if an enduring peace was to be achieved, compromise of some sort was necessary. From the Irish viewpoint it was unfortunate that the hierarchy, meeting in Maynooth on 21 June, rejected de Valera's appeal to them to recognise the Republic. Some authorities take the view that Cope, who had seen Cardinal Logue and other bishops shortly before, had some input into influencing this decision.

On 14 July de Valera, together with Austin Stack, Griffith, Count Plunkett, Robert Barton and Erskine Childers, met Lloyd George and Sir James Craig at 10 Downing street, London. The meeting was cordial, but after separate talks with Lloyd George, Craig issued a statement which said 'that it was only necessary for Mr. de Valera and Lloyd George to come to terms regarding the area outside that of which I am Prime Minister'. This statement, with its clear implication that partition was final and a precondition to any negotiations, drew a strong protest from de Valera to Lloyd George, in which he said: 'If peace is to come the negotiations must be conducted between nation and nation.'

But this was not Lloyd George's view. His treaty proposal consisted of an invitation to Ireland 'to take her place in the great association of free nations over which His Majesty reigns.' The proposal then proceeded to put considerable limits on that 'freedom'. It demanded naval, air and military facilities, rights of recruitment, restrictions on Irish armed forces, a contribution from Ireland to Britain's war debt, full recognition of the Six-County parliament and an oath of allegiance to the King of Great Britain. This offer, which was not even dominion status, was rejected.

Lloyd George then pointed out that the alternative to this was war. Nonetheless the Dail cabinet confirmed rejection of the English proposals and Lloyd George did not pursue his threat. The Irish rejection of the British proposals enabled Craig to state publicly that he would not have any further discussions with de Valera or any other representative of Dail Eireann — until the dubious Northern parliament was recognised. This, of course, the Republican Dail felt it could not do. The mandate they had been given by the people did not allow for compromise on partition.

At a meeting of the Dail on 16 July, two days after his meeting with Lloyd George in London, de Valera stated that their first duty was to make the Republic *de facto* as well as *de jure*. In this he was strongly supported by Griffith who said that they 'were all absolutely united and ready in their efforts to secure a sovereign Republic ... and prepared to negotiate on these principles'. This reaffirmation of the Republic brought from Lord Birkenhead ('Galloper' Smith) a threat of 'hostilities on a scale never hitherto undertaken by this country against Ireland', notwithstanding which the Dail rejected the British offer.

Two questions may be asked. The first, of course, is why, in the face of international and domestic criticism and the clear will of the Irish, did the British make an offer which was certain to be rejected? The second is why did the Irish not, at that stage, indicate a greater willingness to compromise?

From the outset the positions of the two parties were at odds in respect of status and terms of reference. The Irish position was that they were negotiating on the basis of 'nation with nation'. The British position was that they were conceding certain powers of local autonomy to an integral part of the United Kingdom, not even a colony. Accordingly the question of an Irish nation, or national rights or will, did not enter into British considerations of negotiations — *except, and notably, insofar as Northern Ireland was concerned*. Given that position their approach was based primarily on the normal principle of negotiations, namely that of conceding as little as possible. Moral questions such as 'right' or 'wrong' did not arise, except, as pointed out, in relation to Northern Ireland. And here was the irony — hypocrisy, if you will. Their stated position on Northern Ireland was (and remains) one of moral standing; support for the will of a majority of the people living in that area. But this, as we have seen, is a nonsense, since there was (and is) a nationalist majority in two and a half of the six counties involved. In fact their concern was simply strategic; a determination to retain a powerful, totally British-dominated, land-base in Ireland, using the old Roman technique of 'Divide and Conquer' they had adopted so well.

The argument that a modest local majority, a minority of the total, has rights of autonomy and of self-determination based on sectarian grounds in an ancient and established nation is so fallacious as to need no further comment. It is, nevertheless, the argument put forward by successive British governments since 1912 in defence of this so-called 'right' of the Unionists to do just that.

From the British perspective the Irish demand for national independence in republican terms was a threat to the empire; moreover it was a threat on the doorstep of the mother-country. Imperialism was still a way of life — though the collapse, only three or four years before, of the German, the Turkish, the Austro-Hungarian, the Russian and, almost visibly, the Chinese, empires, and the emergence as world powers of great republics like the United States and the USSR, had sent a shudder of apprehension through the British establishment. Where next? Canada? India? Mesopotamia? Even Australia? And here was this tuppenny-halfpenny little country, forever restless and hostile, at England's very back-door, discontented with the privilege of being named British, demanding the impossible. Issues of great principle and matters of great concern to British interests were at stake.

Moreover, from the immediate British political point of view, much hung on the outcome of these discussions with the Irish. Who would remain in office after any settlement of the Irish question, for instance; the present coalition government, or something else? And the something else would, of course, be a Conservative government. There was no other alternative at that time. For the Irish the prospect of dealing with a Conservative government was hardly, at the time, an improvement. Both sides were well aware of this as they stood restlessly on the starting blocks. The English attitude may be summarised as having both strategic and political considerations, to both of which retention of the North, in some form or another, was so fundamental that it could not be affected by questions of right or justice.

For the Irish the considerations were different. They had, by their own efforts and with the support of a huge majority of the people, reasserted their national identity and demanded in its name their proper place and rights as a nation, in common with younger nations for whose identical rights the late war was supposed to have been fought. Thus their position was not one of negotiable interest, but of inalienable right not subject to barter. As to the political structure comprising the Dail, it was at once simple and complex. It was a uni-party government. The Irish Party was moribund, or at least in political limbo. There was a Labour movement, but no Labour Party nor any Labour representative. Sinn Fein, the great national party, was the only party in the Dail. Nonetheless Sinn Fein comprised representatives whose views spanned much of the spectrum of democratic political dynamics. It was united and homogeneous on one issue and one issue only, the realisation of an independent Irish Republic. Once that great goal was achieved it was understood — and de Valera referred to this on 20 July — that democratic procedures would produce alternative parties and a constitutional Opposition.

On 26 August a new Dail cabinet was elected, with de Valera as President and Griffith, Stack, Brugha, Collins, W.T.Cosgrave and Robert Barton as cabinet ministers. Count Plunkett, Kevin O'Higgins, Desmond Fitzgerald, J.J.O'Kelly, Countess Markievicz, Ernest Blythe, Art O'Connor and Sean Etchingham were appointed ministers outside the cabinet.

Britain refused to meet on the basis of 'nation and nation' and, pointing out that Irish leaders in the past had asked less than Britain had already offered, renewed the threat of force. The Irish responded that historical references were misleading and the present was the reality with which they had to deal. Only on the basis of 'government by the consent of the governed' they said, was there any hope of progress. This problem, of trying to establish a mutually acceptable basis from which to begin negotiations, persisted through August and September.

When it began to look as if a resumption of the war was inevitable, Lloyd George, from his holiday home at Gairloch in Scotland, came up with the following formula:

How the association of Ireland with the community of nations known as the British Empire may be best reconciled with Irish National aspirations.This proposal, which became known as the Gairloch Formula, was, from the Irish point of view, capable of an interpretation which surrendered nothing of the republican position; neither did it commit Britain to recognition of the Republic. The proposal was accepted by President de Valera on 30 September 1921.

It was now a matter of appointing Irish delegates to negotiate with their British counterparts. The Irish prepared proposals for a settlement based on the concept of external association for Ireland with the British Commonwealth, which became known as 'Draft Treaty A' (See Appendix Six).

De Valera was recognized as a skilful negotiator and it was assumed by many that he would be part of the Irish negotiating team. De Valera disagreed, making the point, in keeping with his views mentioned in endnote 184, that the place of the head of State was in reserve[193]. Criticism of this decision is, for the most part, based on the assumption that by adopting this attitude de Valera was conceding advantage by not, as the foremost and most persuasive Irish leader, going as a negotiator. Such criticism is academic and *post factum*. The cabinet, Griffith and Kevin O'Higgins in particular, supported de Valera's views and it was agreed that the delegation would keep in close touch with Dublin where any final proposals were to be agreed.

Five delegates were chosen. They were Michael Collins; Arthur Griffith and Robert Barton, together with two legal advisors, George Gavan Duffy and Eamonn Duggan. Secretaries were Erskine Childers, Fionan Lynch, Diarmuid O'Hegarty and John Chartres. They were given the following credentials:—

In virtue of the authority vested in me by Dail Eireann I hereby appoint Arthur Griffith, TD[194], Minister for Foreign Affairs; Michael Collins, TD, Minister for Finance; Robert C. Barton, TD, Minister for Economic Affairs; Edmund J. Duggan, TD and George Gavan Duffy, TD, as Envoys Plenipotentiary of the *Republic of Ireland* to negotiate and *conclude on behalf of Ireland*, with the representatives of His Majesty George V, a treaty or treaties of settlement, association and accommodation between Ireland and the community of nations known as the British Commonwealth. In witness whereof I hereunder subscribe my name as President.

Eamon de Valera

The delegates were also given the following written instructions:

(1) The Plenipotentiaries have full powers as defined in their credentials.
(2) It is understood, before decisions are finally reached on a main question, that a dispatch notifying the intention to make these decisions will be sent to members of the Cabinet in Dublin, and that a reply will be awaited by the Plenipotentiaries *before the final decision is made*.
(3) It is understood that a complete text of the draft Treaty about to be signed will be submitted to Dublin, and a reply awaited.
(4) In the case of a break, the text of the final proposals will be similarly submitted.
(5) It is understood that the Cabinet in Dublin will be kept regularly informed of the progress of the negotiations (*author's italics*).

It is sometimes argued that the credentials and the written instructions to the plenipotentiaries were contradictory; and that the words 'conclude on behalf of Ireland' meant that the delegates had authority to act on their own, whereas their instructions contradicted such an interpretation. This argument does not survive close examination. The plenipotentiaries were given the credentials to *conclude on behalf of Ireland*, with the representatives of His Majesty George V, a treaty. What this means is that they had the authority to do this. It does not mean that they had the authority to do so in spite of, or in defiance of, any other or additional instructions which they received. This would become a point of bitter debate. It might also be noted that they were nominated as 'Envoys Plenipotentiary of the Republic of Ireland'. In fact, and in spite of the bitterness they aroused in the heated Treaty debates early the following year, the credentials were never presented. In the crisis the delegates did not observe points (2) and (3) of their written instructions.

The Irish and British delegates met for the first time at 10 Downing street on 11 October 1921. One of the remarkable aspects of the Treaty negotiations is the role played by partition. For the Irish delegation it was — or became — both the issue on which they should break, if break there was to be, and a non-issue. They were eventually persuaded by the British that only four counties would, in the event, be affected and that these would prove to be an uneconomic and politically non-viable unit. When that occurred, the argument went, they would be forced to join with the rest of Ireland.

For the British, on the other hand, partition was of paramount importance. It dominated their thinking and purpose from the outset. And yet they managed to keep it off the agenda in any critical sense. From the outset they sought to wrong-foot the Irish over the question of Northern Ireland by adopting a Pontius Pilate approach. Lloyd George said that he proposed to adopt an attitude of 'benevolent neutrality' on any efforts of the Dail to induce 'Ulster' to unite with the rest of

Ireland. And he continued to negotiate on the basis that dominion status alone was what was on offer (See Thomas Jones, *Whitehall Diaries*, Oxford).

Most of the next two weeks were concerned with manoeuvring by both sides. The British, clearly aware of a hostile Conservative Opposition in the Commons led by Carson and Bonar Law, and still with dominion status in mind, tended to try to head discussion into comparatively minor matters of detail as if the superior issue were settled. From their point of view — teetering as they were on a political tight-rope — any excessive concessions to Ireland, in particular any weakness in relation to Northern Ireland, might precipitate a general election. This was well understood by the Irish delegation. Even if it had not been, they were made well aware of it by Lloyd George during the course of the negotiations, when one scenario presented for their consideration was the prospect of negotiating with a Conservative government under Bonar Law, probably with Carson in the Cabinet. It is a virtual certainty that British strategy in these negotiations was, in the broad sense, a result of cross-party consultations and that there was considerable Tory input. Of one thing there is no doubt, and that is that the British cabinet team were not acting from a position of political strength. Whether, if they had been, their attitude would have been more conciliatory is anybody's guess, but it is unlikely.

The Treaty

The British refused to negotiate on the basis of 'nation and nation' and the Irish maintained the *de jure* existence of an all-Ireland Republic. Yet it was clear that an independent, sovereign and totally separate republic was, at that time, unattainable. The Irish introduced the interesting formula of 'external association'. With it they sought to put forward an acceptable *via media*, such as Cuba then had with the United States[195].

On 24 October, before a three-day adjournment, Lloyd George said that 1/ they [The British] must know whether the king was to be repudiated by the Irish representatives, 2/ was Ireland prepared to be associated like the other dominions within the British Empire and 3/ was Ireland prepared to grant the naval facilities which England required. On 24 October, the Irish presented their first proposals. Neither side had altered its position regarding Northern Ireland.

The Irish proposals contained a new offer of a subordinate parliament for Northern Ireland with local government powers besides guaranteed representation in an All-Ireland Parliament. It was pointed out to the British that so long as the British failed to realise that Ireland was an independent nation and neither a colony nor a dependency, the negotiations could not produce a result. Ireland was not seeking dominion status and, in any case, the British proposals did not offer even that. The Irish maintained that their proposals offered a solution which met Britain's principal requirement, namely the security of her Empire, while also meeting Ireland's resolve to achieve freedom. (See Appendix Seven).

In continuing discussions the British insisted on allegiance to the Crown, inclusion in the Empire and naval facilities. The Irish insisted that there 'could be no question of asking the Irish people to enter into an agreement which would make them subject to the Crown or demand from them allegiance to the King'

(Letter from de Valera to Griffith, 25 October, 1921), and were firm against partition. The compromise of the external association proposal was, in the circumstances, remarkably constructive. The suggestion that the problem of the North could be met on the basis of local autonomy and representation in an All-Ireland parliament, though moving further from their own position than the other side was willing to do, remained unacceptable to the British. The British ignored the external association idea, which might have provided the basis for a lasting and dignified relationship between the two countries, and reiterated their basic demands.

The Dublin cabinet were satisfied that the proposals they had given to the delegates represented limits beyond which they could not go. The fear — reinforced by this ignoring of the external association formula — was that the British would fail to move to meet them. They feared a renewal of the war, but were prepared to face it if there was no alternative. On 28 October de Valera made a speech at the Mansion House, Dublin, in which he said: 'Ireland's representatives will never call upon the people to swear allegiance to an English King, but they would, perhaps, be forced to call on them to face an "abomination of persecution again"' He went on: 'I believe that if ... differences of opinion arose and were carried to the country it would mean disaster. As sure as the nation is divided, the nation will be tricked.'

Lloyd George again shifted his ground, this time tactically, and it is perhaps worth a few lines of consideration. First and foremost, of course, is the principle of divide and conquer, the most recent and outstanding example of which was the creation of the statelet of Northern Ireland a few months previously. Now, like it or not so far as the Irish were concerned, it played a role in the negotiations. Lloyd George could be reasonably sure that he had mollified the unionists and satisfied the Conservatives on partition; reassured world opinion that he was making a genuine effort to reconcile the 'differences' in Ireland (whereas he was in fact exacerbating the problems); and had wrong-footed and out-manoeuvred the Irish before negotiations with Dublin began. Now his tactic was simply to split the Irish delegation so that they would disagree amongst themselves.

> He proposed that he and Winston Churchill meet Griffith and Collins in private conference. He chose the most dynamic and impressionable of the Irish delegation for this purpose. The Irish delegation never again sat in the conference room as a delegation until the Treaty was signed (Neeson, Civil War., p.58)[196].

In adopting this tactic Lloyd George was assisted by one vital fact which was, paradoxically, the apparent homogeneity of the Irish parliament. He, more than most, would have been well aware that political all-party consensus in time of war leads, inevitably, to divergence and political realignment in the peaceful aftermath. He knew, as did most of the Irish leaders, that whatever Treaty resulted from the negotiations would mean division in Sinn Fein. Any Treaty would be capable of two interpretations, one most favourable to England and one most favourable to Ireland. A point would be reached where negotiations could be brought to a halt. At that point Britain would stick. By favouring the group which then supported the Treaty, Britain could maintain a hold of some description over Ireland. Such were the tactics.

Lloyd George was himself walking the uneasy political tightrope of a wartime government trying to hold together in time of peace. Early in November he was faced with a serious political crisis from several quarters, mainly over his handling of the 'Irish' question. He persuaded Griffith to give him certain personal assurances on the Crown, 'free partnership with the British Commonwealth', and facilities for the British navy on the Irish coast, which would enable him to meet this crisis, in return for which he would subsequently use his influence on behalf of Irish unity. Now, while Griffith had always felt strongly on the question of unity, his feelings on the Crown — as his old nickname 'Kings, Lords and Commons' suggests — were less strong, and the phrase 'free partnership with the British Empire', containing a hint of external association, together with the alternative prospect of an English government led by Bonar Law, may have persuaded him. He gave the personal assurance Lloyd George asked for to help him weather his political storm (which included a vote of censure in the House of Commons; See Appendix Eight for text of Griffith's undertaking).

This letter of assurance, no less than de Valera's reluctance to be a delegate, has been the subject of considerable uninformed controversy. Whatever about the circumstances in which he signed the Treaty, the letter itself is so written and qualified that it would be difficult to interpret it as undermining the Irish position to the extent often suggested in the subsequent Treaty debates, except in one, vital, respect; namely Griffith's extraordinary and unqualified concession on the question of the six partitioned counties of Ulster.

The Irish delegates had been instructed that if a break was to come, then it must come on the question of a united Ireland. The British now found the wedge they sought to insert in this position, splitting the Irish delegation. On 5 November, Thomas Jones, one of the British secretaries — but hardly, it is correct to point out, acting on his own initiative — suggested a boundary commission to determine the size of the unionist majority area. The clear implication was that this rendered at least flexible the area already decided on for Northern Ireland. Craig had already rejected the Irish proposal for a Northern Parliament subordinate to an All-Ireland one, put to him, clearly with tongue in cheek, by Lloyd George. Now here, in this boundary commission proposal, emerged Lloyd George's snare, that the unionist north could be reduced to an uneconomic unit of four counties which would thus be forced to join the rest of Ireland. Griffith wrote to de Valera: 'This would give us most of Tyrone, Fermanagh, part of Armagh, Down etc.'

Jockeying for final position between Lloyd George, Griffith/Collins, and Craig, continued through November.

It is hard to avoid the suspicion of collusion between Lloyd George and Craig — a suspicion subsequent events would seem to reinforce (Neeson, *The Civil War*, p.62.).

On 25 November, at a cabinet meeting in Dublin attended by Griffith and Collins, a formula was hammered out which it was thought would resolve the problem of the Crown to which the British attached so much importance. It was: 'Ireland shall recognize the British Crown for the purposes of the Association (with the Commonwealth) as the symbol and accepted head of the combination of Associated States' (but see Griffith's letter of November 2, Appendix Six).

The final British counter-proposals resulted in a critical cabinet meeting in Dublin on 3 December. Far from being a modification, or move towards meeting the Irish, the British proposals included an oath of allegiance to the King as Head of State, coastal defence to be exclusively British, Britain to have whatever facilities she required in wartime; Northern Ireland, if the new parliament there wished, to be excluded from the Irish Free State (title of the new state). Now Lloyd George's carefully placed wedge took effect. The solid front of the delegation began to crack.

> Already, because of the private nature of the discussions between Collins, Griffith and their British opposite numbers, Gavan Duffy, Barton and Duggan were uneasy. Childers, once a British diplomat himself, was frantic and is said to have felt that the Republic was almost irretrievably compromised (Ibid., p.63).

The delegation was already divided when the Dublin cabinet began consideration of the British proposals. Griffith was in favour of acceptance. He said he did not like the document, but he did not think it dishonourable. Duggan favoured acceptance, believing that more concessions could be obtained. Collins thought the document should be recommended to the electorate; that concessions could be won; that non-acceptance of the oath should also be recommended. Duffy was against acceptance, believing that the Irish proposals could yet succeed. Barton was against acceptance since there was no guarantee against partition. Erskine Childers, who was consulted, was against acceptance as the proposals offered Ireland no national status and made neutrality impossible. The cabinet rejected the proposals.

Barton appealed to de Valera to join the delegation in London for the concluding negotiations, pointing out that it was unfair to Griffith to expect him to lead a delegation which might have to recommend war, when he himself was already satisfied. De Valera was inclined to agree. But Brugha intervened, saying to Griffith: 'Do you realize that to sign such proposals would split the nation?' Griffith then gave an undertaking that he would not accept the Crown as a symbol of the Head of State and would not sign an acceptance of allegiance to the king. He would not sign anything without referring it to the Dail and, if necessary, to the people. Regarding de Valera's not going to the negotiations: It was decided at that meeting that 'The President shall not go to London at this stage of the negotiations'. Clearly, and what is often overlooked, is that implicit in this decision are (i) that further negotiations were anticipated, and (ii) that de Valera would likely attend final negotiations. That opportunity did not arise. Neither de Valera, nor anyone else on the Irish side, could have known that the negotiations would conclude when and in the way that they did.

A further not so well-known point is that, for all practical purposes leadership of the delegation had during the negotiations, passed from Griffith to Collins.

Griffith was ill and uneasy and, like Collins, the focus of concentrated and isolated attention from the British. Within the delegation comradeship was so fractured that Barton, Duffy and Childers returned to London by a different route to Griffith, Collins and Duggan.

It seems clear that the Irish delegation believed that rejection of the British proposals could mean war, but were divided in opinion as to whether the end of bargaining had been reached. Griffith, Collins and Duggan felt that it had while Duffy, Barton and Childers — supported by the cabinet as a whole — felt that further progress was possible.

The issue before the delegates was by no means clear-cut. They had instructions to break, if a break came, on the Six Counties. But they had not been directed what to do if these instructions could not be carried out. They were not able to break on the Six Counties. Britain, as was expected, again dismissed the idea of a Republic. The delegates were given no time to return to Dublin for further consultation. On 4 December, the day after the cabinet meeting in Dublin, Childers, Barton and Duffy prepared a fresh draft of the Irish proposals as outlined in Dublin (Appendix Seven).

Collins and Griffith, in spite of the instructions they had received from the cabinet and dissatisfied with proposals which they were sure would be rejected, refused to present them. They were supported by Duggan. They said it was for those who wanted a break to present them. Finally Griffith, realizing the danger of Barton and Duffy going alone, agreed to accompany them. The proposals were treated by the British as hopelessly inadequate, even though Griffith fought for them and defended them tenaciously. The Irish delegation returned to their headquarters convinced the negotiations had finally broken down.

Lloyd George met Collins the following morning and felt that he 'had resigned himself to the duty of war' (Frank Pakenham, *Peace By Ordeal*, London, 1972 edn., p.283). Lloyd George believed that Collins would accept dominion status in preference to war, and proceeded to try to reassure him on the Six Counties, the Oath, Defence and Trade. He succeeded in persuading Collins to have another plenary session that afternoon on the basis of dominion status for Ireland, in the belief that Collins and Griffith would accept the British terms in the last resort. The meeting was at 3 p.m. 'From the first moments the clouds of impending war hovered over the Council Chamber and weighed down the spirits of all' (Churchill *Aftermath*, London, 1929).

Collins had drafted a form of oath which, he felt, was ambiguous enough to satisfy English demands and Irish aspirations. With minor alterations, it eventually became the Treaty oath[197]. But that was as far as the Irish were prepared to go. They remained firm in their determination that, if a break must come, then it must come on the partition question. What, then, brought about a change?

When the Irish determination became clear to Lloyd George he had 10 Downing street searched for the written undertaking Griffith had earlier given at the time of his own political crisis a month earlier. This was produced to Griffith and Lloyd George, though the undertaking had been given in a different context, reminded Griffith that he had promised not to let him down. For whatever reason, blind to his overriding undertaking to the Republic, Griffith said: 'I have never let a man down in my life and I never will'. He then agreed to abandon the position of breaking on partition. Lloyd George pressed this advantage and said that the British could concede no more and debate no further. 'The Irish delegates must settle now'.

'Griffith replied: "I will give the answer of the Irish delegation tonight at nine; but, Mr. Prime Minister, I will personally sign this agreement and recommend it to my countrymen."

'"Do I understand Mr. Griffith', said Lloyd George, "that though everyone else refuses to sign you will nevertheless agree to sign?"

'"Yes, that is so, Mr. Prime Minister", replied this quiet little man of great heart and purpose.

'Michael Collins rose, looking as though he were going to shoot someone, preferably himself. In all my life I never saw so much passion and suffering in restraint...'(Churchill, *Aftermath*).

Lloyd George, too, felt and recorded the charged atmosphere: 'Both Michael Collins and Arthur Griffith saw the shadow of doom clouding over that fateful paper ...'(*Is It Peace*, London, 1923).

Dublin was already awash with rumours that the negotiations had broken down. In anticipation of a renewal of the war and in breach of the Truce, Auxiliaries and Black and Tans swaggered about the streets threatening and harassing civilians. The country waited uneasily.

Having engineered and brought into the open the split in the Irish delegation, Lloyd George proceeded to press it. He warned the Irish that he had a special train standing by with steam up, ready to race to Holyhead to catch a destroyer which would make for Belfast with his emissary, Geoffrey Shakespeare, on board. Shakespeare would bring with him to Craig one of two letters. One letter read: 'Peace, the negotiations are successful'. The other read: 'War in three days, the negotiations have failed'.

Peace, at a price — or war. These were the final alternatives for the Irish delegation in the British ultimatum given at five o'clock in the afternoon on 5 December, 1921.

How can one begin to appreciate the minds of the Irish delegates at that point? They had been negotiating for two months with one of the most experienced and cunning teams of political manipulators of this century; they had been split, they had been worked on and their inexperience showed. Not all the dedication and commitment they could command was equal to the combined shrewdness and vast experience available to the other side. Griffith who, two days earlier, had given an undertaking to the Dail cabinet that he would not sign anything without referring it to the Dail, had subordinated that promise to an undertaking he had given to the enemy leader a month earlier in a completely different context. Later when challenged in the Dail as to why he had gone so far and not just recommended acceptance, he replied:'We have got to deal with people. We have got to remember that they are flesh and blood. We have got to remember that we were not sitting at a table playing chess with Mr. Lloyd George'. But by that time the signatories were locked into defensive positions not really of their own making.

Following the English ultimatum Collins — and it is notable that it was Collins who did so — asked for four hours in which to consider. But it was more than seven hours later, after midnight, that the Irish returned to Downing street. In the interval discussion and argument among themselves had been strong, sometimes violent and bitter. First Duggan, then Collins, agreed to sign with Griffith. With that the position of Barton and Gavan Duffy became hopeless. Barton agreed to sign rather than be responsible for bringing renewed war to Ireland. Gavan Duffy — though he believed the threat of war to be bluff — could not take sole responsibility. He, too, agreed to sign. Why, it has been asked repeatedly, did they not telephone Dublin? Why did they not stall? Why did they sign without carrying out their instructions to submit the draft treaty to Dublin and await a reply? There are no clear-cut answers.

The Treaty was signed by the delegates at 0215 on the morning of Tuesday, 6 December 1921. One of the factors that persuaded Collins and the others to sign may have been the belief encouraged by Lloyd George that, if Northern Ireland rejected the principle of eventual unity with the rest of Ireland, a boundary commission would bring about a boundary revision of the Six County area which would enable 'Tyrone, Fermanagh, parts of Derry, Armagh and Down' to be retained in the Irish Free State and leave 'Northern Ireland', reduced to an uneconomic and non-viable political unit which would, with England's persuasion, become part of a united Ireland. Collins was doubtful of the ability of the Army to continue the war, but this may well have had more to do with his unhappiness at the public position he found himself in, far from the secret arenas in which he had formerly been so successful[198].

There is no doubt that Collins, who became one of the most charismatic and legendary figures of the civil war, intended, whatever settlement was reached, to see it greatly amplified in Ireland's favour as soon as possible. A famous sentence of his during the Treaty debate in the Dail is: 'The Treaty gives us freedom, not the ultimate freedom that all nations desire and develop to, but the freedom to achieve it'.

While Griffith was the first to agree to acceptance of the Treaty, it would hardly have been accepted by either the cabinet or the Dail on his recommendation alone. It was Collins who was the final arbiter. Without his agreement neither Barton nor Gavan Duffy would have signed; without his vote a majority of the cabinet would not have recommended the Treaty to the Dail, and without his recommendation the Dail would not have voted in its favour. It is virtually certain that, were it not for his influence, the IRB — which really decided the issue, and of which he was Supreme Head Centre at the time (and President of the alternative government, remember) — would have rejected it.

But the fact of the matter was that the Republic, and the Treaty which had been signed, could not co-exist in the same state.

While peace had been the aim of the negotiations, the Treaty did not bring peace with it to Ireland. Speaking in the House of Commons on 14 December Winston Churchill said:

Sinn Fein demanded an independent Sovereign Republic for the whole of Ireland, including Ulster. We insisted upon allegiance to the Crown, partnership in the Empire, facilities and securities for the Navy, and complete option for Ulster. Every one of these conditions is embodied in the Treaty.

As soon as it was signed it was decided in London to publish details of the agreement without further reference to the Irish cabinet. Accordingly, before the Irish president or his cabinet knew what they were, these details were published simultaneously in London and Dublin and the Irish Cabinet first learned what had been signed from the Press (See Appendix Eight).

So far as the British were concerned the Treaty was a development of Home Rule, the spectre of which had hung in the background of events since 1914. From the outset they had envisaged partition which, although it was a vital subject, was not — or was not allowed to become — an issue of any significance during the negotiations. The Irish, on the other hand, had long put Home Rule behind them and believed the British when they 'guaranteed' reduction of the partitioned area to a non-viable four-county statelet. Viable or not the British had no intention of abandoning a foothold in Ireland. This was not out of love or concern for the Unionists, or for any other moral consideration — but purely for strategic reasons which did not diminish until 1991/2. It is worth remembering that, in the context of 1922, these northern counties, because of the unionist strength there, offered the safest and most secure base for Britain in Ireland. Moreover British strategists would at that time have anticipated a relatively easy military take-over of the south again, from the north, should circumstances seem to justify it.

Never come such division 'tween our souls... Shakespeare, Julius Caesar

Chapter 10

The Split

THE ANNOUNCEMENT THAT A TREATY HAD been signed was the signal for tremendous rejoicing in both countries. The Press hailed the settlement and praised the Treaty. The public was ecstatic; peace was assured, Ireland was 'A Nation Once Again'.

Consequently when de Valera issued a statement saying that he could not recommend acceptance of the Agreement, there was shock, confusion and consternation.

> The Treaty, [wrote Frank Pakenham], signed as it was, must always have divided Ireland with bitter discord, torn her with conflict between cruel existing loyalties and so preserved her for a space for the British Commonwealth with an economy of British lives (*Peace By Ordeal*).

After the Treaty details were published the Irish delegates were summoned by telegram to Dublin for a cabinet meeting. There can be no doubt that they anticipated a stormy meeting and an eventful Dail session. There can be little doubt either that they prepared for both.

Though it had been signed, the Treaty had not been approved by the Dail, which was entitled to reject it — as, indeed, was the British parliament. What the outcome might have been had matters been allowed to rest with the Dail for a final decision without propaganda and misrepresentation is anybody's guess. As it was, perhaps compelled to try to justify his decision, Griffith began to defend and consolidate his position as far as possible even before the details were published. This may be why he agreed to publication of the details of the Agreement before his own cabinet had seen them. He certainly understood, as did the other delegates, that as a peaceful — if inadequate — solution, it was bound to win enormous support from the Irish establishment, the Press and from a large section of the Irish public, as well as in Britain and internationally. Before coming to Dublin for the cabinet meeting Griffith issued a statement calculated to win support for the Agreement both at home and abroad. It concluded· 'These proposals do give Ireland control of her destinies. They put the future in our own hands —

enable us to stand on our feet, develop our own civilization and national distinctiveness. In short, we have won liberty after the struggle of centuries.'

Some of the most compelling support for the Agreement came from the rump of the defunct Irish Parliamentary Party. As matters developed over the next weeks and months these experienced politicians and their supporters, who had been in a political wilderness for over two years, were enabled to return to active politics and bring to bear in support of the Treaty all their accumulated influence and expertise.

When de Valera learned details of the Agreement he asked the cabinet to repudiate it and remove from the cabinet those who had signed it. He was persuaded to wait and allow the delegates to explain their actions.

At a five hour Cabinet meeting the seven-member Cabinet was sharply divided. For acceptance were Collins, Griffith, Cosgrave and, because he had signed, Barton; de Valera, Brugha and Austin Stack ... were against. Griffith and Collins ... said that, apart from the ultimatum, there was no moral obligation that prevented signing. The circumstances of the signing were debated over and over. Griffith would not admit duress in signing. Collins admitted 'the duress of the facts' (Neeson, op. cit p. 72.[199]).

After this meeting de Valera announced that a public session of Dail Eireann would be held on the following Wednesday to consider the Agreement. The statement concluded: 'The greatest test of our people has come. Let us face it worthily, without bitterness and above all without recriminations. There is a definite constitutional way of resolving our political differences — let us not depart from it, and let the conduct of the Cabinet in this matter be an example to the whole nation'.

In any serious consideration of this period it is important to remember that the Irish people, following two years of war, had now known peace for nearly six months. The anxiety to continue this peace was, understandably, strong; the fear of further war great. Both sides were well aware of this.

When the Truce came into effect six months earlier it had seemed to many people that the peace it brought was virtually permanent. It produced a species of false euphoria. The mass effect was profound. Few, except the realists among the soldiers and politicians, considered a resumption of the war a real possibility. The news that agreement had been reached and signed was the signal that this hope was confirmed. Rejection of the Agreement by a substantial number of the cabinet, including the President, came as a gross shock. The reality now was that just when peace had seemed so secure, resumption of the war became an unexpected possibility. It is hardly to be wondered at that so many citizens rejected that possibility and those who postulated it, no matter what the cost to the republican ideal or to the Republic itself.

This 'Peace even at a Price' feeling swayed many dismayed and bewildered people to support of the Treaty. When the establishment as a whole, the Churches, the professions, the middle-classes, those in trade and commerce, the Press, home and domestic, massively came out in support of the Agreement, the people in general found little to disagree with in their opinions. Nevertheless the view of those in the cabinet who repudiated the Agreement because it repudiated the Republic was supported by surprisingly large numbers, particularly in the Army which would have to do the fighting if the war resumed. But for de Valera and his supporters, the delay before the next cabinet meeting was disastrous. During that week public opinion, under pressure from the Churches, the Press and vested interest pressure groups, hardened against them.

The public were edgy and receptive, tired of war, afraid of a renewal. Into this unsettled situation came a torrent of influence in favour of the Treaty from a very broad spectrum of interests, many of which had played little or no part in the struggle for independence. These included those who had been pro-British during the hostilities, members of the former Irish Party, respected and influential individuals who received Press space. Above all in the Churches, always at Christmas full to overflowing, sermons calling for peace were heard everywhere. The year 1921 closed in Ireland with a clamour for acceptance of the Treaty and a continuance of peace. Almost the entire middle-class supported the Treaty. Peace on the Treaty terms was, over the Holy Season, powerfully advocated as an acceptable alternative to the Republic which had acquired both *de facto* and *de jure* status. Those opposed to the Treaty, without the support of such moulders of public opinion, lost ground during the ten-day recess. Yet, for the benefit of that wider public, little real attempt had been made to analyse the Articles of Agreement in relation to the Republic, as would be the case with 'Document Number Two' (See Appendix Ten).

The split that had been latent in Sinn Fein came into the open. Divisions in what had been a movement united in the common purpose of driving the enemy out of Ireland, now accelerated. Common sense should have dictated that normal political allegiances would re-form under the democratic process and that a multi-party structure would emerge in conformity with de Valera's observation that: 'There is a definite constitutional way of resolving our political differences -'.

A majority of Irish bishops came out in support of the Treaty. The IRB Supreme Council permitted a free vote, but made its own position clear. 'The Supreme Council has considered the present situation, and, while it is of the opinion that it is to Ireland's interest that the Treaty should be passed, in the circumstances it makes no Order, but leaves every member free to vote and act according to his conscience (Communicated to the Circle of which the writer was a member and Michael Collins was Head Centre, by Collins, a few days after the Treaty was signed'— O'Hegarty, op. cit., pp.769/70). The significance of this statement, of course, is that it was 'communicated,'etc., *'a few days after the Treaty was signed'*. In other words the Supreme Council of the IRB, for whatever reason (and bearing in mind Collins's role and position as Head Centre and President of the 'alternative' government, such reason is not difficult to infer) had decided to support the Treaty *before* either the Treaty debates or the Dail vote on the issue took place.

A meeting of the Dail was called for 14 December. The breach was widening; opposing sets of opinion were hardening with, in the balance on the pro-Treaty side, the full and enormous weight of the Church, added to that of the Press of two nations. On 16 December the British House of Commons had ratified the Treaty. The House of Lords followed suit. Irish ratification was all that was now necessary. In spite of de Valera's exhortation to resolve their differences by constitutional means, the slide to civil war, which both sides strove mightily to avoid, was made easy.

The militarily and politically successful War of Independence had had little in the way of social content. On the political front, when the Truce was agreed the disparate political/social elements, which had hitherto subordinated their narrower commitments to the broader objective looked to their own interests, and began to ask 'What next? What kind of peace shall we have? Who will control it?' In addition, following the split in Sinn Fein on the Treaty issue, the opposition to Sinn Fein — increasingly dormant since the 1918 election — again began to participate actively in national affairs. In a curious take-over, as it were from Limbo, this group — particularly the former Irish Party — swamped and out-numbered the Sinn Fein Treaty supporters, and became a powerful force in the pro-Treaty movement. A third important point is that, largely because of his Irish policy, Lloyd George was himself in political trouble in Britain. His government hung by a thread. By encouraging dissent and possible civil war in Ireland he hoped to strengthen his position in a Britain beginning to see for what it was the first crack in the Empire structure (in fact he failed and fell to Bonar Law later that same year — but not before the outbreak of civil war in Ireland). When it appeared that de Valera and Collins had achieved a *via media* which would avoid civil war, Lloyd George issued an ultimatum to Collins which made it virtually inevitable.

Speaking in the Dail de Valera clarified his opposition to the Treaty. 'I am against this Treaty' he said, 'not because I am a man of war, but a man of peace. We went out to effect a reconciliation and we brought back a thing which will not even reconcile our own people'. From that meeting, when the Dail rose for Christmas, the Dail was already split into two increasingly bitterly opposed factions. Macardle (p. 617), points out that those who opposed the Treaty, looking at it from the [*rarified*] height of Republican idealism, saw it as loss, betrayal and degradation; those supporting the Treaty distorted and magnified it, representing it as giving more than it did (author's italics).

De Valera still believed that the External Association idea contained a formula which could provide a solution acceptable to both countries. He prepared a re-draft of the Irish proposals with the intention of having the Treaty rejected. He hoped, by means of some modifications, to make it possible for the Treaty as signed to incorporate also the substance of the External Association proposals already approved by the cabinet. But he had no opportunity to present this document (Document No. Two, See Appendix Ten) on 14 December. When he did so at a private session on 15 December it was opposed on the grounds that the signed articles were *fait accompli*. He then withdrew his proposal.

Those who accepted the Treaty advocated it in the Dail as an honourable settle-ment between nations, an entering into the Empire and becoming a Dominion by Ireland of her own free will — but in the face of the alternative of 'immediate and terrible war'. They pointed out that the Treaty gave Ireland full control of her economic affairs, her armies, her own flag; that acceptance of the Treaty at that time did not exclude the possibility of further advances towards complete independence. Collins said: 'I signed it because I would not be one of those who commit the people to war without the Irish people committing themselves to war'. He said they had the freedom to advance towards independence and a Gaelic state.

The counter arguments were that the Treaty had been forced on the people of Ireland; that what it provided had been fought against for generations and that, for the first time in history, the Irish people were committed by Treaty to voluntarily relinquishing their independence and becoming a satellite of Great Britain. The Treaty was a renunciation of the Republic proclaimed in 1916, established in 1919 and represented by the Dail; that the Dail as an elected republican administration had no authority to accept a Treaty denying existence of the Republic; there was no mandate for such a Treaty and it would have to go before the people to accept or reject it at an election. Some took the view of Dr. Patrick McCartan, who said: 'I see no glimmer of hope. We are presented with a *fait accompli* and asked to endorse it. I, as a republican, will not endorse it. But I will not vote for chaos'.

The debate was long and intense. It may be summarised in two quotations, the first by Gavan Duffy, one of the signatories; the other by Mary MacSwiney, brother of Terence, who had died on hunger-strike thirteen months previously.

I am going to recommend this Treaty to you very reluctantly but very sincerely because I see no alternative. The complaint is not that the alternative to our signing this particular Treaty was immediate war ... the position was this, that if we, every one of us, did not sign and undertake to recommend, fresh hordes of savages would be let loose upon this country to trample and torture and terrify it, and whether the Cabinet, Dail Eireann or the people of Ireland willed it or not, the iron heel would come down upon their heads with all the force which a last desperate effort at terrorism could impart to it. This is the complaint. We found ourselves faced with these alternatives, either to save the national dignity by unyielding principle, or to save the lives of the people by yielding to a *force majeure*, and that is why I stand where I do. We lost the Republic of Ireland in order to save the people of Ireland ...

Mary MacSwiney, speaking for those who opposed the Treaty, said:

I stand here for the will of the people, and the will of the people of Ireland is their freedom, which this so-called Treaty does not give them. The will of the people was expressed in December 1918. The will of the people was expressed in the [Sinn Fein] manifesto which sent every one of you here. And I ask any one of you voting for this Treaty what chance you would have had if on the twenty-fourth of last May [polling-day] you came out for Dominion Home Rule ... on the twenty-first of January, 1919, this assembly, elected by the will of the sovereign people of Ireland, declared by the will of the people the Republican form of Government as the best for Ireland, and cast off forever their allegiance to any foreigner.

She implored the Dail to throw out the Treaty and not commit 'the one unforgivable crime that has ever been committed by the representatives of the people of Ireland'. She recommended de Valera's re-drafted proposals.

Since it was the Army which would be expected to deal with a fresh British campaign if it came, many of those who were undecided looked to the Army chief-of-staff, Richard Mulcahy, for guidance. His position was that he could see no alternative to the acceptance of the Treaty. 'We have suffered a defeat' he said. His attitude was that acceptance was a matter of political and military expediency, not of principles or ideals. Curiously, however, in spite of this attitude of the chief-of-staff, a substantial majority of the existing Army, the very ones who were expected to renew the fighting if it came, and many experienced field commanders — for instance Deasy — opposed the Treaty.

The Dail was adjourned on 22 December until 3 January, all agreeing that in the interim there would be no canvassing of public support by either side. But this delay was unhelpful from the point of view of those opposed to the Treaty. While their political opponents maintained the agreement, all over the country religious, trade and commercial interests campaigned in support of the Treaty, so that when the Dail resumed there was a significant ground-swell of public opinion in favour of it. Without an election, of course, it was unmeasured and did not represent a new mandate replacing that given to the Republic. When the Dail rose on 22 December it is possible that a vote then might have favoured the opponents of the Treaty. Eleven days later things had changed.

> [An observer] will watch it [the Treaty] driving through the midst of the political leaders, and thence through every community, great or small, in Ireland, a deep penetrating wedge of resentment, alienation and suspicion; in such a way that from now on every motive and intention will be distorted, every act and gesture misconstrued (Pakenham, op.cit., pp. 334-5).

And it was this suspicion and alienation, and not any reasoned consideration on the merits of these great matters, that insidiously, but with great speed, began to dominate and polarise general attitudes and discussion into pro- and anti-Treaty positions. Acquaintances, colleagues, companions, friends, families separated and divided, often with astonishing intransigence and bitterness; new loyalties, allegiances and confrontation superseded the unanimity that had hitherto existed.

Principles Opposed

The distortion of motives and principles on both sides inhibited any real constitutional manner of dealing with the problem. Both sides agreed that acceptance of the Treaty and disestablishment of the Republic must be confirmed by the people in a general election. It was agreed that such an election would probably favour the Treaty, and the manner in which it would be canvassed and held. But this acknowledgement came to nothing. The results of the election (held on 16 June, 1922; the 'Pact Election') did favour the Treaty, but the agreed conditions were breached and it is therefore unclear whether the election, though favouring the Treaty, provided a mandate for disestablishing the Republic — though the majority treated the election as a valid mandate. The Dail divided (sixty-four for the Treaty, fifty-seven against) in January. After that the pro-Treaty members of the Dail (as outlined below) set up a Provisional Government to implement the terms of the Treaty and to disestablish the Republic. They held that the subsequent election validated, *post factum*, their doing so. The republican opposition did not treat the election as a valid mandate and repudiated the Provisional Government. The Provisional Government, claiming interests of public order, but under pressure of an ultimatum from Britain, attacked republicans who repudiated their authority. Thus began the civil war.

Resistance by the anti-Treatyites to the Provisional Government was not a revolt against legitimate authority as that term is normally understood; nor did the Provisional Government see their attack by themselves on the republican forces when it came as an attack on the Republic. Many of sober conscience, who would not normally sympathize with dissidents, joined and actively supported the anti-Treatyites. They claimed constitutional abuses by the Provisional Government, which the latter vehemently and sincerely denied. The pro-Treatyites held that since a majority of the people clearly (but before this was put to a vote) supported them, they had a mandate. The anti-Treatyites maintained that they had no mandate to disestablish the Republic and that the assault on it was being conducted in a treacherous and unconstitutional form.

By the time it went before the public in June the single issue from the Dail — maintenance or disestablishment of the Republic — was so obscured that it is doubtful if many knew what they voted for. To most it was more likely a simple 'war or peace' issue, hinging on the Treaty. What happened between January and polling day on 16 June shows how the eventful juggernaut of mutual distrust and suspicion acquired a momentum of its own, the appalling conclusion of which was civil war. In striving to avoid a renewed war with Britain, the Irish fell, bitterly, into war among themselves.

The nub of the constitutional problem was stated by Frank Fahy, later Cathaoirleach (chairman; speaker), in the Dail. He said: 'Had this instrument been submitted *unsigned* to Dail Eireann I feel convinced it would have been rejected by an overwhelming majority. The signing of it does not make it more acceptable, but we must base our arguments and decisions on a *fait accompli*. But', he went on, 'is not the declaration of the Republic also a *fait accompli*, or have we been playing at Republicanism?' Liam Mellowes, one of the most tragic figures of the months to come, said: 'Instead of discussing this Treaty here, we should be considering how we are going to maintain the Republic after that Treaty has been rejected and put on one side.'

Griffith, in response to such arguments, replied: 'When they charge and insinuate that we went with a mandate to demand a Republic and nothing else they are maligning us. If we got that mandate we would finish in five minutes in Downing street'. He went on

At a meeting of the Dail in August, President de Valera made a speech covering the ground on which they went there and saying, with reference to the form of Republican Government that they were not Republican doctrinaires as such, but were for Irish freedom and independence ... to attack us on the ground that we went to get a Republic and nothing else is false and maligning ground.

It is impossible to avoid the fact that that the delegates signed without reference to the Irish Cabinet and compounded this by immediately adopting strong positions of self-justification, agreeing to publication of the details before the Irish cabinet knew of them, for example. It is equally impossible to avoid the fact that, on the anti-Treaty side, there were some extremists who seemed unable to deal with the *fait accompli* in any except an outright condemnatory way. De Valera's Document Number Two — so-called by Collins — might have provided a via media had not ridicule and scorn made careful and dispassionate consideration of it by the Dail an impossibility.

Army Headquarters split evenly, six in favour and six against. This division went right through the Army commands, and feeling on both sides ran high. On 7 January de Valera, still President of the Republic, offered to resign as the cabinet was so sharply divided. Under protest he withdrew his resignation on condition that the motion to approve the Treaty be taken within twenty-four hours. He said:

> The Republic of Ireland still exists, its sovereign parliament still exists and the resolution recommending the ratification of a certain treaty is not a legal act. That will not be completed until the Irish people have disestablished the Republic which they set up with their own will.

Of de Valera and the anti-Treaty position at the time of the opening of negotiations three months before, Kevin O'Higgins — active on the other side — later wrote:

> Mr. de Valera, as President, did not instruct the Plenipotentiaries to seek recognition of the Irish Republic — he knew that the moment such a request was made the negotiations would be at an end. Speaking to Dail Eireann in private session on the day before his re-election as President, Mr. de Valera made it perfectly clear that he did not intend to embark on the negotiations on the basis of an existing Republic. He stated that if re-elected he would act, not as the nominee of any political party, but simply as one pledged to do the best he could for the Irish Nation in any circumstances that might arise. He dealt trenchantly with the question of the Republican oath taken by each member of Dail Eireann, stating that he never interpreted it as anything more than a pledge to the Irish Nation to do his best in the interest of the nation, that if he had considered it bound him irrevocably to any particular form of settlement he never would have taken it. Having listened attentively to this very clear and very honest exposition of his point of view Dail Eireann unanimously elected Mr. de Valera as President....'(Kevin O'Higgins, *Civil War and the Events Which Led to It*, p.12).

The vote on the Treaty was taken on 7 January with the result mentioned. By seven votes the Dail recommended the Treaty to the people.

Following the vote on the Treaty there was a vote on the Presidency. Griffith won by two votes, De Valera abstaining. A new Dail ministry of pro-Treaty members was formed. The anti-Treatyites now effectively formed an Opposition in Dail Eireann, but, as yet, did not have a separate party. It was, in fact, a division within Sinn Fein. But the new ministry and its supporters were committed to forming a provisional government in conformity with the terms of the Treaty.

De Valera said that when Griffith acted in his capacity as President of the Republic the anti-Treaty party would not stand in his way, but when he functioned as a member of another government they could give that government no recognition. The approaching situation seemed to be one in which the Executive of the Dail, the new Government, would be in revolt against the Legislature and the Judiciary.

The constitutional position was complex. The Republican Dail still existed; its members represented the combined total elected for the country (Unionists excepted), both pro- and anti-Treaty; its new president was Arthur Griffith. Acceptance of the Treaty would mean suspension of the Republic, of which the Dail and Cabinet were the parliament and government. Though divided, the Dail nevertheless represented the Republic and nothing else. The Treaty, however, did not recognize the Dail and required (Article 18) that the Treaty should be submitted forthwith to a 'meeting summoned for the purpose of the members elected to sit in the House of Commons of Southern Ireland' — the parliament that never sat. Having met, that assembly of elected members would then elect a provisional government to which the British Government would transfer 'the powers and machinery requisite for the discharge of its duties ... during the interval which must elapse' before the Irish Free State government was constituted. The Dail, clearly, could not carry out the work of a provisional Dominion and, in the process, disestablish itself. Accordingly the vote in favour of the Treaty left the Dail administration in a constitutional dilemma. While remaining the Government of the Republic until a general election was held, the Dail had to agree to the summoning of a rival — and unrecognized — parliament, largely consisting of its own members, whose main purpose was to render the Dail non-existent. As well as this rival government, it had also to recognize another government in Northern Ireland, the purpose of both being to disestablish and/or subvert the Republic.

Griffith, in his capacity as 'Chairman of the Irish Delegation of Plenipotentiaries' and in accordance with the provisions of the Treaty, summoned the elected representatives of Ireland — excluding those elected in the Northern Six Counties — to a meeting on 14 January to elect the Provisional Government. He did not invite the representatives from the Northern Ireland area as this was intended to be a meeting of the 'Southern Parliament'. Neither de Valera nor any of his anti-Treaty supporters attended on the grounds that they did not recognise the 'Southern Parliament'. This body met and held its one and only session on 14 January at which it passed a motion approving the Treaty. It was attended by sixty pro-Treaty members of Dail Eireann and the four representatives from Trinity College. A Provisional Government of the Irish Free State (the name to be given to the new state) to administer for the southern twenty-six counties, was elected; its chairman was Michael Collins, who was also Minister for Finance of Dail Eireann. There were twelve other ministers, of whom five were also officers of the Dail. On the same day, the British formally handed over control to the Provisional Government. Evacuation of British forces from the twenty-six county area began before the end of the month.

It is difficult to see from whom, or from what source, the Provisional Government derived any legal authority. The only satisfactory explanation is that given to the author by Ernest Blythe, Minister for Trade and Commerce in the new Dail, '— in a crisis, those who have the power also have the authority'. The Provisional Government consisted of pro-Treaty deputies only. The cabinets of both Dail Eireann and the Provisional Government overlapped; yet the Provisional Government, lacking a specific mandate from the people, was committed to the disestablishment of the Dail, which did have such a mandate and which its members (pro- and anti-Treaty alike), had taken an oath to protect. Here lies the essential weakness of the pro-Treaty position. The bringing into existence of this provisional government stung the anti-Treatyites to anger. They held that actions by it would be unconstitutional and an abrogation of the rights of the people. 'No executive that was not Republican could be formed from Dail Eireann' said Mary MacSwiney.

The failure of the anti-Treaty leaders, during the period from 14 January to 28 June, to establish a political centre to which the people could rally should the need arise was extraordinary. The argument is that Dail Eireann was still in existence and they could not subvert it. But it had been subverted already once the Provisional Government came into existence, and it was impractical and unrealistic to expect that its members had any intention of summoning a meeting of Dail Eireann in which they might be defeated on a division. The consequences of this omission became evident within a few months when, for want of such a political nucleus, the conduct of the civil war, so far as the anti-Treatyites were concerned, was left solely in the hands of anti-Treaty military leaders with inadequate appreciation of political and social requirements, leading to the inevitable outcome[200]. In fact the civil war was less a war between the respective armies of a divided Sinn Fein than a war of a politically directed army, the pro-Treaty side (supported by other elements), against the army of the anti-Treatyites acting on its own without recourse to adequate political guidance, even though this was available.

The attitude of the pro-Treaty supporters may be summarised: No matter what the people wanted two years ago when the Republic was established, they now — whether or not there has been an election to demonstrate the fact — want the Treaty. Mulcahy, the Minister for Defence, gave an assurance that the Army would 'remain the army of the Irish Republic'.

The road to civil war was strewn with confusion, blind conviction, personal loyalties, friendship, envy, even the accident of location, rather than with understanding and rationale. For many it was a question of the oath they had taken, and what it required of them. A considerable number took the pro-Treaty side not on the merits of the Treaty, but on the question of [assumed] majority rule, not questioning majority right; many took the other side for precisely the opposite reason, scrupulously questioning [assumed] majority right. Neither side took sufficient account of the fact that the people, majority or minority, had not spoken at an election, or that the voices of those in the northern six counties were no longer to be heard on the matter. Moreover throughout the whole confused period both sides were being nudged closer to civil war by Lloyd George, who stood to gain from such an outcome, politically, possibly in terms of apparent moral rectitude.

The people, insofar as they willed anything, willed the Treaty, but they did not will civil war. That became a private fight between two wings, and the anti-Treatyites turned it into a fight of the people against themselves by alienating the populace and arousing the enmity of the people (Lt. Gen. M.J.Costello to the author).

It is true that during the course of the civil war the anti-Treatyites alienated large sections of the public, but this was more because of the inept manner in which they conducted the campaign than from a rejection of their principles. In the post-civil war election, when many anti-Treaty supporters were detained and their electioneering was limited and subject to interference, they nevertheless returned a surprisingly large poll. It would appear that though the people wanted peace, they did nor like the price they had to pay for it and in the aftermath of the civil war came a powerful feeling of regret, if not guilt.

The time is long overdue when the divisive issues of the Treaty and the Civil War were put into perspective. Here is no right and wrong (though one must exclude some individual acts which occurred in the course of events). To believe otherwise is to believe that the honourable were dishonourable, that the dedicated were unpatriotic and that those who had fought as companions in arms for justice and liberty were no more than time-serving opportunists. The truth of the matter is painful in its simplicity and starkness. And what it amounts to is a/ inexperience in the murky arena of international statesmanship, where — as Griffith discovered at great cost — the word of a gentleman is of no value beside national and political self-interest and where the Irish delegation were faced with some of the most able, ruthless and cold-blooded negotiators of this century; b/ intransigence on both sides in the face of errors of judgement for which both de Valera and Collins might, amongst others, be cited; c/ political manoeuvring — for it was clear that Sinn Fein, unified and homogeneous on the issue of national independence, would fracture Right, Left, and perhaps Centre, once it was achieved; d/ personality. There was also e/ the effects of some or all of these factors on the public at large in the heady emotional climate of the times, when rumour and mis-information often carried many times the weight of fact, and when personal loyalties were enough to win the allegiance of strong and powerful men and women.

It is hardly accidental that there was considerable difference of opinion between de Valera and Collins, between Collins and Brugha, for instance, no less than between members of the Treaty delegation itself. Such differences are natural and to be expected. The larger, more democratic and more homogeneous an organisation, the greater likelihood of such tensions, often healthy and necessary. The leaders on both sides were men of common allegiance, aim and experience who differed essentially in matters of means and method, but not in matters of principle. Left to themselves the differences would not, one is forced to conclude, have overridden the superior principle. But there is a point at which, even in a conservative society, the tension is so powerful that it creates its own momentum all but impossible to halt. The point may be reached when this momentum, like a torrent, carries all before it, tossing flotsam to either side upon one committed bank or the other. Deeply felt principle can thus be in opposition to itself about the same issue. Right and wrong are no longer seen objectively as relevant, but as relative, terms.

Three external critical factors exercised profound influence on these events and on the leaders. In addition to the support of the Churches, the middle-class establishment (in particular former members of the Irish Party), who entered the ring with tremendous moral and pragmatic influence immediately following the signing of the Treaty, former, demobbed, British soldiers became an important element of the quickly established Provisional Government (later Free State) forces. The third element was, of course, the British Government whose interests were strategic and political expediency. On the establishment of the Provisional Government all three brought such concerted influence to bear that, even now, it is impossible to say if the pro-Treaty element of Sinn Fein remained dominant in the conduct of affairs, or whether it was subsumed by external powers, the most formative of them the moribund Irish Party. But it is clear that the Provisional Government became subjected to intense pressure and manipulation for reasons much removed from the national interest.

I am tired and sick of war ... War is hell... General W. T. Sherman.

Chapter 11

Civil War

FROM JANUARY 1922 THERE WERE, discounting the IRB, three governments in Ireland:- the Government of the statelet of Northern Ireland, still part of the United Kingdom; Dail Eireann, Government of the Republic, which, *de jure* by the people's mandate, exercised authority over the entire country, and the recently created instrument of the Treaty, the Provisional Government.

However one looks at it it was a situation fraught with uneasiness and distress. The accepted view is that because of the Treaty Sinn Fein divided and there was a civil war to see who was right. That is not alone a gross oversimplification, it isn't even correct. The so-called 'split' in Sinn Fein existed before the War of independence, let alone the Treaty, but an overriding unity of purpose maintained a uniformity during the struggle against English rule. As we saw in the previous chapter the source of the 'split' is evident enough, and it comes down to the rapid and extensive increase in support for the Treaty on the one hand, and the changes in the Sinn Fein Constitution on the other. 'While it would be wrong to stress unduly the signs of division in the Sinn Fein party — one can detect differences about the ultimate goal of the organisation as early as 1917 — The attempt to reconcile the republican aims of Count Plunkett with the non-republican proposals of Griffith was, he '[Fr. Michael O'Flanagan] 'felt, the source of all future controversies and of personal conflict' (Murphy. op. cit., p. 104). Fr. O'Flanagan was a dedicated republican who, between 1904 and 1927, exercised a very considerable influence on republican national affairs. During the Downing street peace-feeler period between March and May, 1921, he was one of the few intermediaries on whose views de Valera felt he could depend. It is abundantly clear that whatever Treaty came back from London in 1921, the least that would result politically in an Ireland under a new governmental regime was a constitutional opposition. But for the intervention and ultimatum of England that is all it might have been (if one excepts the North). It is, therefore, somewhat academic to seek, in that context, to trace the origin of the split in Sinn Fein.

Griffith, a principal architect of the Treaty, was now President of the Republic he was committed to abolishing, while the Opposition in the Dail were those equally committed to its preservation. Five ministers of the Dail were also ministers in the Provisional Government; every pro-Treaty member of the Dail was also a member of the Provisional Government. It is understandable that the anti-Treaty members and their supporters found it impossible to distinguish between actions by the pro-Treaty representatives intended to be on behalf of the Government of the Republic, and those meant to be on behalf of the Provisional Government. They, therefore, and understandably, treated everything done by 'government' with suspicion and distrust. Even though it was the effective national executive, the Provisional Government *did not have a legislature*, which continued to be Dail Eireann.

> The maintenance of Dail Eireann as the Irish Republic and the parade of loyalty to it was, in fact, whether sincere or otherwise, the master-stroke of pro-Treaty policy...the Dail became, after 7 January, the matador's cloak; the quite impotent focus of loyalty and hope; the facade behind which the Provisional Government gathered the Empire reins of control into its own hands and massed its strength (Florence O'Donoghue, *No Other Law* p.202, Dublin, 1954).

Jockeying for power, which had been more cautious up to then, began in earnest right across the country and in all organisations of influence between the pro- and anti- Treaty supporters once the decisive vote was taken in the Dail on 7 January. Perhaps the most significant propaganda aspect of the pro-Treaty campaign was the promise to the people that the new constitution of the Irish Free State would not be inconsistent with republican aspirations. It was not explained how this was to be achieved without violating the terms of the Treaty; the constitution, which had to be introduced before an election, would be subordinate to the Treaty[201]. In the event the constitution was not published until the morning of the inconclusive June election so that there was no time for the public to consider it, much less pass judgement on it, before voting[202].

It is unrealistic to think that internal rivalries between powerful and ambitious individuals, even when committed to the same purpose, are uncommon. It is unhelpful to any understanding of past events to believe, as often seems to be the case in relation to the leaders of this period, that they were all motivated by an identical purpose, sustained by the same commitment and anticipated a similar successful result. It is just as misleading to exaggerate and distort such internal rivalries; they are a normal part of the democratic political process.

The relationship between Collins and Griffith underwent a change and this needs to be understood. From being an extreme pacifist, Griffith became a vehement advocate of initiating hostilities against those opposing the Treaty on the grounds that the sooner such hostilities were over and done with, the better.

Collins, on the other hand, remained republican in outlook — even though that outlook was now, to coin a phrase that meets the case, 'republican gradualism'. This was expressed in his 'Stepping-Stone' formula through which he hoped, while accepting the Treaty, to use it as a base from which to move towards a republic. Griffith, like others, shared no such view and was not prepared to entertain proposals such as de Valera's Document Number Two or Collins's Stepping-Stone formula. Accordingly Collins and some of his closer associates, in the post-Treaty turbulence, found themselves allied with Home Rulers, and opposed to most of those with whom they had fought alongside and with whose republicanism they sympathised. As the country seemed heading towards civil war, Collins's position seemed increasingly ambivalent.

The Stepping-Stone formula, and what it implied, was a main cause of the growing differences between himself and Griffith. The irony was that Griffith, President of Republican Dail Eireann, was committed to implementing the Treaty as the final achievement. Collins, Chairman of the Provisional Government set up to disestablish the Dail, was not. Had their roles been reversed, with Collins President of the Dail, Griffith Chairman of the Provisional Government, civil war might have come even sooner. In that event, Collins, as President of Dail Eireann, might well have seen his role in a different light. As it was the burden on Collins was immense at this time. As Chairman of the Provisional Government it was his responsibility to take over from the British and on him fell the additional responsibility of trying to maintain administrative continuity. It was a formidable burden, even for one of his capacity. Griffith, President of the Republic, convinced that civil war was inevitable and anxious to get it over with as soon as possible, brought a number of cabinet ministers with him in this view. Ironically it was Collins who was anxious to negotiate and who would not succumb to pressure from other ministers so long as he felt there was still hope of a compromise with the anti-Treaty element of Sinn Fein.

Towards the end of February a serious situation arose in Limerick, when opposing forces occupied barracks and buildings. Tension was high, and an outbreak of fighting was averted only by the joint efforts of Liam Lynch and Oscar Traynor on the anti-Treaty side and (acting on the instructions of Collins) Mulcahy and Eoin O'Duffy on the other.

There were three opinions in government circles at the time. To the military leaders an armed clash was undesirable since they anticipated that it would encourage many volunteers to join the anti-Treatyites, and because their own forces were small and unreliable. On the other hand Griffith and several of his cabinet were anxious for what they foresaw as the inevitable to begin as soon as possible. Then there were those, including Collins, who hoped for a settlement. At a cabinet meeting in early March, when the Limerick crisis was at its height, Griffith at last succeeded in persuading Collins of the need for immediate action. Despairing of successful negotiations, Collins reluctantly agreed. At that point Mulcahy entered the room with the announcement of the settlement in Limerick. Collins was delighted. For him the successful avoidance of hostilities was a matter for rejoicing, but it led to sharp differences of opinion in cabinet between himself and Griffith.

The pro-Treaty side seemed to be more pragmatically aware of the implications of the power-struggle underway in spite of the best and most sincere efforts by some of those on both sides, and of the possibility of civil war, than were their opponents. Through the Provisional Government and the wealth of support it commanded throughout the country, they took contingency steps. These included the establishment, on 31 January, of a uniformed armed force which, from its headquarters at Beggars' Bush Barracks, was initially known as 'the Beggars' Bush Force'. It attracted pro-Treaty supporters from the Army (of the Dail) and later, in considerable numbers, former soldiers from disbanded Irish regiments of the British army.

During this period the anti-Treaty leaders, who claimed to be guarding the rights of the people as vested in the Republic, made a major error of judgement. At a time when the evolving situation demanded practical and coordinated political and military steps, the anti-Treaty leadership faced a dilemma which was a major obstacle to planning. The Army, which had voluntarily placed itself under the authority of the Dail in 1919, rejected that authority as represented by Griffith and his cabinet, but did not give allegiance to de Valera's opposition. The anti-Treaty political and military elements, therefore, had no common regulatory bond and were at one only in that they opposed the Treaty. The military, in particular, appear to have been preoccupied mainly with legal and constitutional dialectic. They were surprisingly casual about important military dispositions and planning, and had no means by which to coordinate military and political purpose. The Republic was under threat of either peaceful disestablishment or of armed attack. In either case the anti-Treaty element intended to resist, yet, though they claimed to act in defence of the people and of the Republic, their preparations were concerned more with argument than with disposition of forces or establishment of an alternative administration.

The Pact

While maintaining their moral position, and while their opponents prepared for foreseeable events, the anti-Treaty side did not make practical provision for the possibility of civil war, or for winning it if it came about. The charge may be fairly made that if they believed they carried responsibility for the Republic then they did not protect it adequately. Similar ineptitude was evident during the course of the civil war itself and this protracted inadequacy reduced their moral right to conduct a civil war. It should be borne in mind that it was the Army Executive, not the politicians, who, on the anti-Treaty side, directed the civil war.

In February the senior anti-Treaty officers of the Army had decided to revert to their own Executive and remove control of the Army from the Dail and/or the Provisional Government. In order to ratify this move an Army convention, at which it was calculated the anti-Treaty element would have a majority, was required. It would also re-affirm the Army's allegiance to the Irish Republic. Mulcahy, Minister for Defence, temporized, but agreed that the convention would be held on 26 March. On 30 March an Act of the British parliament was to pass appropriate power to the Provisional Government.

By 14 March the delegates to the Convention had been selected from all Army brigades. On 15 March, however, when it had become obvious that the convention would show that the Army was largely anti-Treaty, with consequent embarrassment to the Provisional Government, the Dail reversed its decision and banned the convention. Mulcahy issued a proclamation together with an order stating that any officer who attended the convention would be, ipso facto, dismissed. Of course this order increased the likelihood of an open Army split. In spite of the ban 211 anti-Treaty delegates claiming to represent 200 brigades and 80% (an estimate of about 95,000 men overall), of the Army, went ahead with the convention and elected an Executive with Liam Lynch as Chief-of-Staff.

Collins and de Valera, the two outstanding figures of the period, one on either side, had one very important difference between them. As well as being Chairman of the Provisional Government, Collins was also responsible for the Beggars' Bush Force, later becoming commander-in-chief of all the pro-Treaty forces, stepping down — in appearance only — as Chairman of the Provisional Government. W.T. Cosgrave became acting Chairman, but Collins never relinquished his dominance of the Provisional Government[203]. De Valera, on the other hand, had no influence whatever over the anti-Treaty forces. Indeed, once hostilities began he was, because of his anxiety to make peace, considered by the anti-Treaty military leadership to be an embarrassment. Liam Lynch, Chief-of-Staff of the anti-Treaty forces, was the man of critical importance in this context.

The new Army Executive was politically naive, divided and lacking in policy. Discussion frequently veered off military matters and became involved in social, economic and political theory. The extreme republican element led by Rory O'Connor occupied the Four Courts, seat of the judiciary, and some other buildings which they fortified.

During the latter part of March and April the situation deteriorated further. Political, military and personal allegiances divided the Army everywhere, and the respective GHQs were unable to exercise adequate control over all their scattered and overwrought troops. Tempers rose and nerves were strained. Several armed clashes occurred. Eight were killed, forty-nine wounded. Civil war, the horror most had been striving to avoid, began to loom unmistakably over the country.

In April Maj. Gen. George Boyd, GOC British troops in Dublin, received secret orders to reoccupy Dublin if the republicans overthrew the Provisional Government (see British documents on the period released in November 1993).

Three matters, each of them critical, helped to maintain an uneasy balance of peace. First was the constitution of the Irish Free State. While subordinate to the Treaty it would, according to pro-Treaty sources (who were drafting the Irish version), nevertheless be capable of an interpretation sufficiently broad to encompass and satisfy republican objectives.

Second was the Collins-de Valera Pact, which offered an internal political solution acceptable to both sides including preservation of Republican Dail Eireann. For precisely that reason, which in their eyes fundamentally breached the Treaty, it was bitterly opposed by, and totally unacceptable to, the British.

Third was the serious view taken by the British of the Army garrison in the Four Courts. They, rightly, believed it to be supplying weapons to the Army in Northern Ireland, though they do not seem to have been aware of Collins's complicity in this. ('He [Collins] was a natural conspirator — that was his great strength as the IRA's Director of Intelligence during the War of Independence' Michael Farrell, *Irish Times*, 15 December, 1982).

The Pact looked like being the answer the whole country sought. It was Collins's idea: '... I approached de Valera with a suggestion that he and I find a way out of this impasse. Out of our conference came what has been called the Collins/de Valera Pact' (Haydon Talbot, quoting Collins, *Michael Collins' Own Story*, London, 1923, p. 182 — See Appendix Ten).

The Pact was hammered out over 18, 19 and 20 May. In essence it provided that Sinn Fein — the original undivided party — would put forward a panel of candidates for election. A government would be formed of both pro- and anti-Treaty representatives in proportion to the respective numbers elected. From those elected would come Griffith as President, Mulcahy as Minister for Defence and five pro- and four anti-Treaty ministers. The Minister for Defence was to be approved by the Army Executive, ministers to be allocated by the President. It would be the Third Dail Eireann, not the Provisional Government. It was a not inconsiderable 'step' in Collins's stepping stones, and was a formula that satisfied de Valera. It looked as if the country was united again and that civil war was averted. The nation took heart. But the British were furious.

'Collins' writes Farrell (op. cit.) 'told the Dail that the Pact was more important to him than the Treaty'. He went on: 'It looked for a few days at the end of May and the beginning of June, 1922, as if Collins was close to breaking with the British Government and throwing in his lot with the opponents of the Treaty'. Collins himself, in a letter to Paddy Daly in April, wrote: 'I am in sympathy with a majority of the IRA. I wish to continue now and finish the fight. To postpone the struggle for fifteen or twenty years would be a forlorn consolation. The 'Big' businessmen and politicians will come forward when peace is established and perhaps after some years gain control. Their interests will never demand a renewal of war' (Mulcahy papers).

In Ireland opposition to the Pact came mainly from two very opposite sources. These were Griffith and his pro-Treaty Cabinet, and the extreme republican militant wing headed by Rory O'Connor. In Britain the Pact threw Whitehall into a frenzy. The evacuation of British troops from Ireland was halted. Since the Treaty had already been signed and any Dail resulting from the Pact election would, nonetheless, be required to abide by it, why were the British so upset? The most likely explanation for their view that it breached the Treaty lies, curiously enough, in Britain's own constitutional position. Britain did not, and does not now, have a written constitution. Accordingly governments can, and do, repudiate agreements made and undertakings given by their predecessors. This has been the position in England for centuries and has coloured the thinking of their statesmen and politicians. According to this view a new Irish republican government could — and might — repudiate the terms of the Treaty.

But, whatever their long-term aspirations, such thinking was not that behind the Pact from either side. What divided the anti- and pro-Treaty elements at this time was not acceptance or rejection of the Treaty, but how what had been signed might be brought to accommodate the republican point of view (hence, for instance, Document Number Two). A vote on the Treaty issue — which is what the British wanted — was something both sides in Ireland wished to avoid since it would copper-fasten the Treaty.

British opposition to the Pact is open to other interpretations. The Irish leaders in 1916, when the Republic was declared, had sought assistance from Germany. It was the republic, then declared and subsequently ratified, that was at issue. The concern of the British at the prospect of such an independent republic on her western flank in the 1920s and 30s, even under an 'interpretation' of the Treaty, can not be doubted. There were also immediate political considerations of importance to a shaky government. The Pact was perceived as a threat to the survival of the administration, to the future unity of the empire, and to strategic considerations. Accordingly the British set out to shatter it, employing again their most reliable tactic.

Lyons writes:

> To adopt a constitution which did not square with the Treaty would mean trouble with Britain; yet to adopt one which did not square with the concept of external association would mean trouble with de Valera...
>
> This Pact to which Collins no doubt put his name with the best of intentions, was by any odds a deplorable document ... No one summed up its likely consequences better than Churchill in a report to the British Cabinet ten days later: 'It prevented an expression of opinion on the Treaty; it gave the Provisional Government no further representation of strength or authority from the Irish people; it left the Government in its present weak and helpless position; it ruptured article 17 of the Treaty' (op. cit., pp. 456-8, et seq.).

Lyons's summary is misleading, particularly the quote from Churchill. While an agreed Sinn Fein panel was undoubtedly a democratic and electoral curiosity, its purpose was not to maintain the Provisional Government, but to maintain the republican Dail in some sort of harness with the Treaty. Secondly the Provisional Government was not trying to 'adopt a constitution which did not square with the Treaty', but was endeavouring to frame one which would *both* conform to an interpretation of the Treaty and be acceptable, however reluctantly, to de Valera and his followers. As far as Churchill's summary of the likely consequences of the Pact is concerned, it, too, is demonstrably one-sided and misrepresentative. A basic purpose of the Pact was precisely to avoid a public expression of opinion on the Treaty; the statement that it ruptured article 17 of the Treaty is simply not correct. Article 17 of the Treaty required 'that every member of such Provisional Government [administering the country until the Irish Free State came into formal existence] shall have signified in writing his or her acceptance of this instrument [the Treaty].' That issue had not then arisen. It is possible — though unlikely — that it might have arisen in respect of anti-Treaty members of the proposed Sinn Fein coalition Dail. On the other hand the point could have been overcome in the same manner as de Valera later overcame it when Fianna Fail went into parliament in 1927.

Having heard the views of the other ministers in cabinet, Lloyd George argued that to oppose the Pact directly would mean making an issue of Northern Ireland. But, he pointed out, the new constitution of the Irish Free State was still in the process of being drafted (by the Irish). Clearly, he said, the Irish would present for agreement a constitution which would be most favourable to themselves. And here, he argued, was the ground on which the Pact could be defeated

By refusing to accept the Irish draft and by insisting on a constitution which was radically British in interpretation, they could produce a document which the anti-Treatyites would be unable to accept. Thus there could be no coalition and so the Pact would be broken. And that, in effect, is what happened. (See British Cabinet minutes, esp. CAB 30/22(3) of 30/5/22). Clearly the British distrusted Collins, the man with whom, as Chairman of the Provisonal Government, they most had to deal at this time. Collins made no secret of his views, which would have been well known to A.W.Cope. Collins did not want civil war; he deplored the split in Sinn Fein and the Army; he was endeavouring by every means to heal it. He, too, was, caught in a strait-jacket — that of the Treaty. It was now — through its Irish adherents — using him as he had hoped to use it. His personal view may be summed up in his words to an officer, Eamon Horan, then neutral, to whom he said about this time: 'Support me now and I guarantee you'll have a republic in four years' (*The Civil War*, p. 63). The British also insisted that the Provisional Government 'deal with' the Four Courts element of the Army. The ironic trigger which set off these twin attacks on the Pact would be Field Marshal Sir Henry Wilson, a so-called 'anti-Irish Irishman.'

The British, well aware that a vote on that issue would favour it, wanted the election to be on the Treaty. If the Treaty were not the issue, the Sinn Fein vote would not split and the outcome would be the Pact coalition and a Dail again committed to republican interests and so, by definition, unfavourable to British ones. At a Cabinet meeting on 16 May, Churchill deplored that: 'there appears to be little chance of a free election being held' — by which he meant an election in which the Treaty would be the issue. He continued: 'There is really none too much difference between the Free State and the Republican parties and there is a general reluctance to kill one another...' On the Pact Churchill went on: 'I understand that the Provisional Government have entertained the idea that an agreed election should be held. I have written to Mr. Collins and pointed out to him that such an election would be received with world-wide reprobation...'

In the House of Commons, as Minister with direct responsibility for Irish affairs, he made the position of his government quite clear:

> If the republicans were to become members of the government without signing that declaration [of allegiance], the Treaty is broken by that very fact, at that very moment, and the Imperial government resumes such liberties of action, whether in regard to the resumption of powers which have been transferred [to the Provisional Government] or the reoccupation of territory, as we think appropriate to the gravity of the breach ... In the event of a setting up of a republic it would be the intention of the government to take Dublin as one of the preliminary and essential steps for the military operations'[204].

Meanwhile in the Four Courts an interesting situation existed. Liam Lynch, Chief-of-Staff of the now independent Army, together with most of the Army itself, was prepared to await both the election results and the new constitution. He did not join his extremist comrades in the Four Courts, but had his own headquarters in the Clarence Hotel across the river. Lynch, a senior member of the IRB, was also in constant communication with the Beggars' Bush HQ and drew up with them an agreement for joint control of a unified Army.

> When on the 24th of January, 1922, the Irish Provisional Government's constitutional drafting committee[205] began deliberations, it was involved in a twofold mission. The manifest purpose of its work was to follow Michael Collins' orders to produce a racially independent Irish constitution that would mention neither the British Crown nor the Anglo-Irish treaty. The latent purpose was to prevent an Irish civil war by reconciling most of the anti-treaty leaders to the Free State (D.H. Akenson and J.F. Fallin, *The Irish Civil War and the Drafting of the Free State Constitution*, Eire-Ireland, St. Paul, Minnesota, summer, 1970, p.42).

After the Pact was announced the British summoned Collins and Griffith to London for an explanation. There were renewed threats of reoccupation and war. It was made known that there were fresh troops in the North and that plans for a naval blockade of the South were on the drawing board. Collins, defending the Pact, said that only enemies of Ireland were displeased with it.

The Irish pointed out that the Pact had been agreed by both sides in the conviction that civil war might thus be averted. To the disgruntled British this was one of its most unsatisfactory aspects. They also understood the Irish hope for a constitution favourable to Ireland's point of view, with a united government and a united army in support. The Irish constitutional committee had drawn up such a constitution. In early June the draft was submitted to the British for their approval. In accordance with Lloyd George's strategy this was refused.

Modern scholarship is satisfied that Lloyd George's threat of 'immediate and terrible war' was bluff; neither in the face of world opinion nor in their ability to do so were the British prepared to go so far. That the door for further negotiation was still open, though untried, is generally accepted now. Birkenhead, in the House of Lords, said in 1923 that the British Government would not have been able to crush a united Volunteer force with less than 200,000 men, and it would not have been possible for them to put into Ireland enough troops to overcome an undivided Sinn Fein. He added: 'Parliament would not have granted the money [for war] and the country would not have given the volunteers'. The irony is that the pro-Treatyites agreed to the Treaty essentially from the fear that rejection would mean a resumption of the war with Britain; yet, in implementing it, brought about war with their own comrades. Compounding the situation was the fact that those who in the Dail accepted the Treaty on the basis of Collins's 'Steppingstone' principle, were much closer in spirit to their anti-Treaty opponents than they were to those who provided the overwhelming bulk of their support.

At about this time Lynch wrote to his brother, Fr. Tom Lynch: 'If we can force the Treaty party to draw up a Republican Constitution we are A1 again. This I consider quite possible'. Quite possible it was and it is what the Treaty party tried to do, only to be frustrated by the British.

Lloyd George and his cabinet refused to consider, much less accept, the Irish draft. They amended it radically and of the results the *Sunday Times* wrote:

'Instead of weakening the Treaty, as was generally expected in Ireland, it underwrites the Treaty, and underscores Treaty in a most emphatic manner. The English victory is plain.' Publication of the constitution was, 'for purely technical reasons' according to Lyons, delayed until the morning of polling day, 16 June. The purely tchnical reasons were the amendments by the British. There were, even in Britain, protests that the Irish people — who still believed the constitution would give a republic in all but name, albeit within the confines of the Treaty — were not to have the opportunity of seeing their constitution before voting. Two days before the election Collins made a speech in Cork in which he called on the public to vote pro-Treaty, and which has been interpreted as a repudiation of the Pact. On the morning of polling day the constitution was published in Dublin, but in most areas of the country it was not seen at all that day. Nowhere was there time for consideration of it. The result of the election, however, is interesting. Pro-Treaty, fifty-eight seats; anti-Treaty, thirty-six; Labour, seventeen; Farmers, seven; Unionists [Trinity College] four; Independents, six. The results did not become known until 24 June.

Even before the results became known the split in the Army had deepened. The Four Courts garrison, having proposed — and narrowly lost — a motion to end the Treaty and resume the war with Britain within seventy-two hours (which they believed would re-unite the country against the common enemy), barricaded themselves even against their more moderate colleagues in the Clarence Hotel. After election-day, 16 June, events moved swiftly and dramatically to a climax. While the anti-Treatyites interpreted the election as a vote in support of the Pact and peace, the pro-Treatyites appear to have forsaken the Pact and to have taken the result as a mandate for the Treaty. Prior to 28 June no invitation was extended to de Valera to join the Pact coalition assembly, due to meet on 30 June.

At the time Collins was deeply concerned with the situation in the north, where the Catholic population was being subjected to a vicious pogrom. Thousands were driven from their homes, killings and arson, frequently by the so-called 'forces of law and order' was wholesale against Catholics. The situation was so grave that for a time it seemed as if the Volunteer split might heal in the face of this brutal provocation and that they might, as Tom Barry proposed, strike against the newly created puppet northern sectarian statelet.

Then, on 22 June, Field Marshal Sir Henry Wilson — military advisor to and friend of Lloyd George's — was shot and killed in London by two London-based IRA men, Reginald Dunne and Joseph O'Sullivan. The order for his execution was issued by Collins largely, it is believed, because of Wilson's involvement in the northern pogroms, but possibly also because of his position as military advisor to the Northern Government which Collins, there can be little doubt, intended to attack sooner or later[206]. Lloyd George, having successfully diluted the constitution and smashed the Pact, now found to his hand the perfect lever to precipitate an attack on the Four Courts.

He immediately wrote to Collins insisting that the republicans in the Four Courts were responsible for Wilson's death and that failure to take strong and prompt action against them would be considered a breach of the Treaty. Collins's reply, in the light both of his own knowledge of events and what happened a week later, is particularly interesting. He asked what proof Lloyd George had that the shooting of Wilson had been the work of the anti-Treatyites. Lloyd George would not be deterred. Here was a golden opportunity to secure the Treaty, with beneficial political fall-out. He summoned General Macready from Dublin to London and asked him if he could capture the Four Courts at once (curiously, that same day — 23 June — a conference on the same question took place between Griffith and British officers in Dublin). On 24 June Macready, back in Dublin, received orders to attack the Four Courts next day[207]. But before the attack was launched, probably at least partly because of the election results which the British had expected would show much stronger support of the Treaty, those orders were countermanded. An ultimatum was issued instead to the Provisional Government to mount the attack.

The new assembly was due to meet five days hence and form the coalition Pact cabinet. Instead of following that course, the Provisional Government decided to accept the British ultimatum and stamp out extremist anti-Treaty armed opposition. On 27 June, pro-Treaty General 'Ginger' O'Connell was captured by anti-Treaty troops in retaliation for the pro-Treaty capture of an anti-Treaty officer, Leo Henderson. This incident was used as the excuse for the attack. About 0200 hours on the morning of 28 June the streets around the Four Courts filled with troops and armoured vehicles, some of which were driven against the doors of the great building to block them. The garrison held its fire, Rory O'Connor insisting the other side must fire first. At 0340 the pro-Treaty forces demanded surrender by 0400. This demand was rejected and at seven minutes past, four field guns acquired from the British opened fire. The civil war had begun[208].

Collins's own views will never now be known, but something may be gleaned from an understanding of what is known about his complex character. Since, as he himself stated, he sympathised more with the republicans than with his own supporters, and strove, given time and opportunity, to bring about a Republic, why did he give in to the British ultimatum?

He was faced with the following choice; attack the Four Courts, or it would be attacked by British troops. Since no Irish government could permit such a thing that would mean, in effect, a resumption of hostilities with England. It was therefore a resumption of war with Britain or civil war, hideous and prolonged — Ah! But would it be prolonged? Would it even be civil war? Was there not a split in the anti-Treaty forces? Were not those in the Four Courts merely a small group of extremists, isolated from everyone else? Was it not the case that it was simply this one small garrison which had to be dealt with? And that that might be done reasonably gently?

Such, certainly, seemed to be the case. And it may be that it was thus that Collins saw a solution to the immediate problem; it may well have seemed to him possible to secure the conditions he wanted at moderate cost.

But what Collins did not know — could not have known — was that the rift between the Four Courts and the main anti-Treaty forces was healed. In fact Liam Lynch left the Four Courts only a few hours before it was attacked. Following publication of the Constitution which did not fulfil the promise of meeting their aspirations, and following Collins's election speech in Cork, the anti-Treaty Army Executive was once again united. Civil war was thus a certainty if the Four Courts was attacked by Provisional Government forces.

* * * * *

The civil war fell into three more or less distinct phases. First came the attack on the Four Courts, and the battle that spread from there through the centre of Dublin between 28 June and 5 July. In that battle, for the second time in six years, the city's O'Connell street was reduced to rubble. The second phase was the 'field war' which in the main consisted of advancing Provisional Government troops attacking and capturing towns — mostly in Munster and Leinster — held by the anti-Treaty, or Army Executive, forces. This phase lasted from 28 June until mid-August. The third phase was a guerrilla campaign throughout the country from August 1922 to the Cease Fire on 24 May 1923.

The following points are worth bearing in mind in relation to the civil war: Firstly, it need not have happened. Secondly, it achieved nothing that could not have been achieved by constitutional means. Thirdly, once begun, it need not have lasted so long. Fourthly, the responsibility for its outbreak rests with the pro-Treaty element and for its duration with their Army (Executive) opponents. The Provisional Government assumed authority, and the responsibility for launching the attack on the Four Courts two days before the national assembly was due to meet rests with them. The Army Executive, on the other hand, prolonged the civil war when their own political adherents wanted to stop it and long after it was clear that they had lost both the war and the sympathy of the population, who suffered as a result. (For convenience the words 'anti-Treaty' and 'pro-Treaty' are used below to describe the opposed sides.)

The period of civil war, and that immediately preceding it from the signing of the Treaty onwards, is very complicated at several levels. The rapidity and extent of the changes taking place were — and remain — confusing and disturbing. They are not easy to identify with accuracy and clarity.

The Treaty exacerbated differences between often incongruous and diverse individuals and groups bound together with a common purpose during the War of Independence. The Treaty exacerbated and produced powerful and involved constitutional, executive and emotional conflicts, with which many of those affected were, for many reasons, ill-equipped to cope, particularly since dissension was exacerbated by outside forces that proved impossible to counter.

It would be convenient to accept that it was simply a question of 'for or against the Treaty'. But it wasn't so. That wasn't even the main issue. The Treaty negotiations opened on the basis of 'how the association of Ireland with the community of nations known as the British Empire may best be reconciled with Irish national aspirations'. The important word here is '**best**', and it is on an interpretation of it that the whole question turned. It is worth noting that Lloyd George's phrase refers to 'Ireland', not to 'Southern' and 'Northern' Ireland, the division he had worked so assiduously to bring about. For a time it even looked as if Lloyd George was seeking a formula for Ireland which would not involve secession by the North, and which would retain a satisfied Ireland within the British Empire (See *Treaty (Confirmation of Supplemental Agreement) Bill*, Dail Debates, Oct. 15. 1924, pp. 2519-2534).

There were on both sides individuals with extreme views unwilling to compromise — extremist republicans and committed Home Rulers, those opposed to what had been signed and those in favour of it. But so far as the vast majority of the Dail, of the Army and the public at large were concerned, the split was not because of what the Treaty **was**; it was because it had been **signed**. In fact but for a couple of vital points, the Treaty issue was capable of resolution. The great majority would have accepted the Treaty with limited, but significant, modifications, the main one being the question of the oath of allegiance to a British king. This was fundamentally unacceptable. Division on the issues was unavoidable. The civil war was not. The widening breach, almost healed by the Collins/de Valera Pact, was reopened by the threat of war from London.

Yet, in spite of all that had happened since the previous December, neither side was really prepared for civil war when it burst amongst them. Up to a day or two before the Four Courts attack it looked as if hostilities would be avoided. The people had closed their minds to thoughts of further bloodshed, and the election, the results of which were only four days old, seemed, with finality, to end such an awful prospect. True, there were the 'die-hards' in the Four Courts; true, the published constitution was neither what was hoped for, or promised; true, the Army was still reserving its position; true, de Valera and his political supporters waited to be called on to participate in the Pact 'coalition' Dail Eireann. While none of these things were satisfactory solutions in themselves, they did not necessarily mean war.

But with the breach between the 'die-hards' in the Four Courts and the rest of the Army healed, it was certain that an attack by Provisional Government forces on one would be perceived by the other as an attack on the entire Army. Accordingly when the Four Courts was shelled by Commandant Emmet Dalton and Commdt. Tom Ennis, on 28 June, it was responded to as an attack on the Army Executive as a whole, and not simply on the Four Courts garrison. What might Collins have done had he known the true position? On his record and stated views, both public and private, it seems likely that he would have resisted the British pressure, even any attempt by them to carry out their threat. In which case he would, of course, have had the whole country and a united Army and Sinn Fein behind him. Ironically, as their own records show, it now seems likely that the British threat was bluff and that they would have backed down for want of resources and in the face of world opinion before attemping to renew a major war-effort in Ireland where — it was possible to argue — the elecorate had ratified the Treaty only a few days earlier.

The anti-Treaty military forces no longer accepted the authority of the Dail. Even though they acknowledged Dail Eireann as the legitimate government of the country, they distrusted its president, Arthur Griffith. Nor did they owe allegiance to de Valera's hastily formed new party, *Cumann na Poblachta*, though they grudgingly acknowledged him as leader of a constitutional anti-Treaty movement, for which they had scant regard.

The Army of the Provisional Government, the Beggars' Bush Force, was at all times under political control, with according responsibility. That force soon mushroomed with an intake of huge numbers of former British soldiers and unemployed. But, initially, the anti-Treaty forces outnumbered the pro-Treaty forces (then thought to number about 10,000 men) by four or five to one. A surprising number remained neutral. But armaments, of course, were another matter. The anti-Treaty forces had augmented their arsenal with the dramatic capture of the British ship Upnor in the spring (see *The Civil War*), but they still relied exclusively on line weapons and munitions.

When hostilities began, the anti-Treaty forces had two positive military options. The first was an immediate and overwhelming direct assault by road and rail on Dublin from the south and west, with the First and Second Southern Divisions from Cork and Tipperary, and the Second, Third and Fourth Western Divisions from Galway, Roscommon, Mayo and Sligo reinforcing the anti-Treaty Dublin No. 1 and South Dublin Brigades, to take Dublin and convene the Dail. Units of Earnan O Maille's (Ernie O'Malley) Second Southern Division did advance to Wicklow, but in the absence of any co-ordinated plan of action then fell back with other withdrawing Dublin, Wicklow and Kildare units. The second option was an immediate withdrawal to the hills and mountains, guerilla warfare, without exposing the civilian population to the rigours of field warfare. A third possibility might have been a concerted attack on the North, with the hope that it would win the support of the pro-Treatyites. In the event the anti-Treatyites chose to form a static line of defence from Limerick to Waterford, behind which lay the so-called 'Munster Republic'. Here they waited to be attacked and rolled up — probably the weakest military option short of surrender open to them.

If the anti-Treatyites were horrified by the attack on the Four Courts, the Provisional Government were shocked when anti-Treaty officers in the Clarence Hotel HQ returned to their units to mobilise (or, in some cases, tried to join the Four Courts garrison). Oscar Traynor, O/C of Dublin No. 1 Brigade occupied positions in Dublin city centre and Liam Lynch, Chief-of-Staff, took control of the Army and returned to his First Southern Division. This was the single biggest unit, consisting of some 40,000 men, not all battle-hardened, and many of whom stayed neutral. When the shelling began, so certain were the people that civil war had been averted that many thought it was British warships that were shelling the city. The battle lasted for a week. The Four Courts garrison consisted of about 180 men under the command of Commdt. Pat O'Brien, together with several members of the Army Executive. De Valera issued a statement in which he said: 'At the bidding of the English, Irishmen are today shooting down in the streets of our capital brother-Irishmen — old comrades in arms'. De Valera then reported to his old battalion of the Dublin Brigade, the third, and was attached as staff-captain to brigade HQ staff in the Hammam Hotel in O'Connell street, beside the present-day Gresham Hotel. He continued in that position for some days.

Traynor occupied positions in Dublin not dissimilar to those held in 1916, but further east, forming a triangle with Moran's Hotel, Talbot street, the now vanished Nelson's Pillar and Barry's Hotel in Parnell square as the angles. Other positions were also occupied throughout the city, but this triangle was the principal anti-Treaty stronghold. Traynor, outnumbering the pro-Treaty forces, hoped to hold on until reinforcements arrived from the country. None arrived.

The Four Courts was under fire with shell, machine-gun and small arms fire for three days, by which time the city was like any other under siege. There were few civilians in the streets, rifle and machine-gun fire was continuous, armoured cars and searchlights swept the streets, shops had their shutters up. Communication with the rest of the country was at a standstill. On 30 June, Saturday, the day the elected assembly was to meet, the Four Courts caught fire from the shelling. Hand-to-hand fighting took place in the building. About midday there was a huge explosion when the anti-Treaty magazine in the cellars exploded. At the same time O'Brien received an order from Traynor to surrender, saying it would help him carry on the fight outside. At 1530 the garrison threw its arms into the flames and surrendered to Ennis's troops. Forty or so were dead or injured and the remaining hundred and forty were marched to Mountjoy jail. En route six, including Earnan O Maille, escaped.

Having inspected the ruins of the Four Courts and the Records Office which, with its precious contents, had disappeared, General Eoin O'Duffy, Chief-of-Staff of the Provisional forces, announced that the 'revolt' was all but over so far as Dublin was concerned, and that the provinces showed no signs of following the example put before them, reinforcing what was Collins's likely view that there was only the Four Courts to deal with. He was mistaken on both counts. There was a brief lull after the firing stopped on Saturday, but on Sunday afternoon a clash took place between anti-Treaty forces in Moran's hotel and pro-Treaty forces in an armoured lorry — part of a cordon being thrown around the centre-city anti-Treaty position.

On that Saturday, too, the parliament was prorogued to 15 July. This presented a curious constitutional position. The Four Courts had been attacked following the elections on 16 June and before the new parliament met. According to the election Pact that parliament was to be a Dail Eireann coalition and not the Provisional Parliament. De Valera and his followers had not been invited to join the new parliament, which was due to meet that day, Saturday 30 June. But neither had they been informed that they would not be so invited. What, then, was the parliament that was prorogued that day? If it was the Provisional parliament, it ignored both the provisions of the Pact and the platform put before the electorate. If it was Dail Eireann the constitutional anti-Treaty element had not been invited to attend[209]. Whichever it was, it was the Beggars' Bush Force of the pre-election Provisional Parliament that attacked the forces of the Army Executive.

There was sporadic fighting throughout Sunday as the pro-Treaty forces moved into position around the anti-Treaty city-centre. It was five days since the Four Courts had been attacked. Where were the anti-Treaty reinforcements? Basically, lack of adequate command structure ensured that absurd delays were caused by lack of information and communication, and interminable battalion, brigade and divison 'conferences' before decisions were made. Then it was unwisely decided to form the Limerick-Waterford line. Units of O Maille's Second Southern

Division under Commdt. Michael Sheehan, together with units of the mid-Kildare Brigade under Commdt. Paddy Brennan, met at Blessington with the intention of advancing on Dublin.

The Conflict Spreads

The Provisional Government force, though numerically weak, was compact and reasonably well armed, although the leadership privately expressed doubts about its strength and reliability. Political and military leadership was in harness and there was a clear, active chain of command — reinforced the previous day in both spheres. It had a clear policy, a visible purpose, united leadership and gradually increasing public support. The Army Executive anti-Treaty forces lacked precisely these qualities of policy, purpose and leadership. At the outset they lost the initiative and — except for minor set-backs — the pro-Treaty authorities never let it out of their hands until the war was over.

The Army Executive was ill-fitted on its own to lead a military campaign, much less give the all-embracing political leadership which the people had a right to expect. De Valera and Brugha were simply the leaders of the anti-Treaty group in Dail Eireann, though both rejoined military units when the fighting broke out. But de Valera, in particular, soon opposed anti-Treaty military policies and tactics and sought an end to the war so that differences might be dealt with on a constitutional basis. The purely military — and, therefore, dictatorial — anti-Treaty military leadership ignored him. Their want of foresight in neglecting to fully provide for the possibility of civil war now cost them dear. A shadow cabinet, a military council, an operational plan held in readiness against such an eventuality, would have cost them little and might have won them public support, if not the war.

At the government meeting on Saturday, Collins made several important announcements. Mulcahy, Minister for Defence, was moved to Portobello Barracks where he took over command as Chief-of-Staff. Collins himself would act as Minister for Defence. On 12 July a 'war council' consisting of Mulcahy, O'Duffy — GOC south — and Collins was appointed. At the same time Collins took up duty as Commander-in-Chief, announcing that he would not act in his ministerial capacities until further notice. There have been allegations that Collins was moved out of his position as Chairman of the Provisional Government and given the post of Commander-in-Chief to reduce his authority and get him out of the way. This is nonsense. The suggestion that he become Commander-in-Chief came from Collins to Griffith[210]. Cosgrave became acting Chairman in Collins's absence, but Collins retained his authority and looked on himself as 'Chairman' throughout, even issuing instructions to Cosgrave in that capacity from time to time.

Traynor's positions in O'Connell street, including his headquarters in the Hammam Hotel, came under increasingly heavy fire on Sunday afternoon. When, on Monday, 3 July, he found himself surrounded and without reinforcements, he began to evacuate his positions. That Monday he and most of his troops, including de Valera and Austin Stack. 'To our astonishment' (de Valera in a private conversation with the author), 'we successfully passed through the surrounding cordon'. Cathal Brugha with seventeen men remained as a rearguard to continue fighting as long as possible. During the next couple of days the fighting intensified. The mood was measured by incidents such as the capture of an anti-Treaty armoured car named 'The Mutineer' which was pressed into service by its captors and renamed 'The Ex-Mutineer'.

By Tuesday afternoon the centre of Dublin was once again a shambles. Right and left, the buildings that had been the hotels and commercial centres of the city lay in ruins. Called on to surrender, Brugha replied: 'Níl aon chuimhneamh agam ar leithéid do dhéanamh — I have no such intention'. When ordered, by runner, from Traynor to surrender, he also refused, though the Hammam Hotel, was in ruins and on fire. A final attack was launched at 0300 and by daylight the hotel was nothing but black and smoking ruins. Brugha and his force held on until evening when he ordered his men to surrender. Brugha, Nurse Linda Kearns and Dr. J.P. Brennan remained behind. Then Brugha appeared in a doorway, a pistol in his hand. It is not known whether or not it was loaded. He started forward in spite of appeals to halt and fell under a hail of bullets aimed at his legs. His femoral artery was severed. He was driven to hospital, but died two days later. The first of the great figures of 1916 and the War of Independence had fallen in the civil war.

That same day (5 July) the Provisional Government opened recruiting for five Dublin battalions in Dublin, and local commanders throughout the country were authorized to accept recruits. In Dublin, on the first day of recruitment, recruiting officers were unable to deal with the number of applicants. This was due in the main to huge unemployment, and to ex-British soldiers anxious to continue a life to which they were accustomed. Recruiting was at the rate of almost 1,000 a day and continued until there was an army of over 60,000 men in the field.

It will be readily realised that a large proportion of the criminal element found its way into the Army ... and needless to say the Government service on account of the pay involved was the more attractive. Old soldiers, experienced in every kind of military wrong-doing, were placed under the command of officers necessarily inexperienced and the resulting state of discipline is not to be wondered at (Michael Hopkinson citing Mulcahy's testimony at an Army Enquiry in 1924, *Green against Green*, Dublin, 1988, p. 137).

This indiscipline would later produce appalling results in the conduct of elements of the Pro-Treaty forces.

At the end of eight days the fighting in Dublin ended for the moment. Sixty were dead and more than three hundred had been wounded. The city centre was in ruins, the cost estimated at £6,000,000 — some £200,000,000 today. The reinforcements Traynor had been waiting for were still in Blessington, where the escaped O Maille took charge. He decided to go to Wexford and supervise the withdrawal of anti-Treaty troops from Enniscorthy in a strongly held pro-Treaty county. The Kildare and Wicklow units of the anti-Treaty forces in Blessington, reinforced by Sheehan's Tipperarymen, fought a delaying action southwards with pro-Treaty forces advancing on them. On Monday, 2 July, in broken and unpleasant weather, pro-Treaty forces converged on Blessington along a twenty-mile front. They took Ballymore-Eustace *en route* and soon afterwards were enveloped in a heavy mist. This both impeded their advance and gave their opponents the opportunity to withdraw under cover. The anti-Treaty rearguard of fifteen men was captured after a five hour fire-fight.

The capture of the Blessington/Ballymore Eustace position by the pro-Treaty forces meant that the main anti-Treaty stronghold in Munster was open to assault without danger of attack from the rear. The attack followed at both extremities, Waterford and Limerick, within days of each other. Communications were poor, in some cases all but non-existent. But once hostilities began, the pro-Treaty forces, in contrast to their opponents, took the initiative where they could. Waterford was attacked on 28 June by Commdt. John T. Prout, who had fought with the U.S. forces in the World War. Dundalk, held by units of Frank Aiken's[211] Fourth Northern Division which, though neutral, was a potential threat to the pro-Treaty rear, was attacked at the same time. Limerick was attacked on 2 July. There a curious situation developed.

The South

Liam Lynch and his senior staff arrived at Mallow, Co. Cork, on 29 June. Next day Lynch issued a statement in which he appealed to his troops to maintain discipline and not to interfere with the civilian population more than was necessary. On the same day he moved his headquarters to Limerick, his immediate priority being to try to secure the First Division area against internal threat. The only two pro-Treaty posts in First Division territory, Skibbereen in Cork and Listowel in Kerry, were attacked that day and quickly captured. In Limerick Liam Deasy, First Division GOC, reached an extremely one-sided agreement with his opposite number on the pro-Treaty side, Commdt. Gen. Donnchadha Hannigan[212]. Next day, 2 July, Commdt. Gen. D.A.MacManus of the pro-Treaty forces arrived from Dublin and immediately rejected this agreement. However officers from both sides continued to try to find a solution and a further joint agreement was reached on 7 July. Disapprovingly MacManus agreed, in the interests of trying to avoid country-wide conflict, to let it stand. However, at 0500 the following morning pro-Treaty troops in William street barracks fired on their opponents in the Ordnance barracks and the murmur of agreement was lost in the clatter of gunfire. While Lynch, like Collins, may have hoped that the fighting could be confined in and about Dublin, by keeping his troops in Munster he may have done the very thing that prevented this[212]. The defence of Munster seems to have been the only tactic the anti-Treaty Army Executive considered. But it should surely have been a *coup d'etat* or nothing.

The Provisional forces quickly appreciated that the main area of action was going to be in the south, and to that all other commitments were subordinated. In a fairly orderly manner strength was massed for an attack on both flanks of the anti-Treaty position in Munster. The capture of Limerick would drive a deep and strong wedge between the anti-Treatyites in Munster and those in the West. It would also open a gateway to counties Cork and Kerry, where anti-Treaty support was strongest.

Hardship resulting from the fighting was soon experienced. In places food became so scarce as to reach starvation levels. Both sides tried to alleviate distress, but their efforts were complicated by the need to feed the armies, and by profiteering, which was dealt with severely by the military on both sides. In Mungret College in Limerick two priests and five lay brothers tried to cater for 500 women and children, some of whom were already casualties. There was little food.

The fighting in Limerick lasted for nearly three weeks, but almost from the outset the conclusion was obvious. After a week (on 11 July) Lynch moved his headquarters to Clonmel (where de Valera — briefly — joined his staff). But the demoralizing effect of a war-policy wanting in aggressiveness was not helped by shifting HQ about. No army acting purely on the defensive can hope to succeed. The initiative passes to the other side and this, combined with the adverse effect on the morale of the troops, amounts to an increase of up to 50% in the enemy forces in the field.

Parliament was again prorogued on 12 July and the republican courts, which had operated so successfully since 1918, were suspended in favour of the old, British-established, judiciary which had been handed over to the Provisonal Government. On 18 July the pro-Treaty forces in Limerick, now heavily reinforced, began the concluding battle, which lasted for two days. The anti-Treaty forces withdrew from their positions under, what became a decisive factor in almost all similar cases — artillery fire. Much of the city was on fire or in ruins. The main anti-Treaty body fanned out to the south-west, blocking and mining roads and blowing up bridges as they withdrew to Bruree and Kilmallock, where they dug in.

The simultaneous attacks on Waterford, Limerick and Dundalk were part of a pro-Treaty overall strategy to quickly neutralise the most effective, or uncommitted but potentially dangerous, Executive forces. Though numerically smaller at this stage than their opponents, they were coordinated, mobile, and better armed. Moreover when the war began they held a number of key positions which only needed to be reinforced to act as bases from which to attack the anti-Treaty forces — Nenagh against Limerick, Athlone against the Midlands and the north-west, and Kilkenny against Waterford. They were supported by civil and ecclesiastical institutions and by the Press, and they were paid and could pay for supplies. The moral licence thus acquired, and denied their opponents, cannot be overestimated. They, clearly, understood that the first principle of good generalship is logistics.

The anti-Treaty forces exhibited extraordinary ineptitude. This may have been due more to their reluctance to be involved in a civil war than to anything else. But, once the fighting started, there was no further place for such reluctance. Units were allowed to act on their own without coordination or direction from above. They offered little in the way of adequate civil or civic administration and it was this, in the long run, which told most against them. Had they wooed public support instead of flouting it; taken the initiative instead of waiting to be attacked; cooperated with their political colleagues, and moved quickly against Dublin, the outcome of the war might have been different. At that time Dublin was not only the key to the whole situation, it was the only one of the four principal southern cities not in anti-Treaty hands.

Kilkenny, with ten main roads radiating from it like the spokes of a wheel, was the key to the Provisional attack on Waterford. And, from here, the Provisional forces made a second main thrust against the anti-Treaty line. The anti-Treatyites in Waterford sat and waited. The Provisional forces intention was to roll the anti-Treaty line up as far as Clonmel where they would join up with troops moving south from Nenagh.

Throughout July responsible bodies in the country repeatedly called for the meeting of the (coalition) Dail which had been summoned for 30 June. It remained unclear whether it was this Dail, or not, that had already been twice prorogued. There was no response from Dublin.

The Provisional commanders became increasingly confident as the war progressed. It looked as if there was every likelihood of winning it quickly. Four of the leading anti-Treaty Executive leaders (Rory O'Connor, Tom Barry, Liam Mellowes and Joe McKelvey) had been captured and Cathal Brugha, one of the great architects and advocates of the Republic, was dead. All this within a week. They had arms, supplies of ammunition, transport, financial resources, recruits and benedictions — all of which were denied their opponents.

Prout decided to attack Waterford across the River Suir from the heights known as Mount Misery, overlooking the city. The danger of an attack from Carrick-on-Suir, on their own right flank, nearly materialised, but for an error of judgement by an anti-Treaty officer. The anti-Treaty defenders had not taken the elementary precaution of securing Mount Misery, and Prout occupied it without difficulty, opening fire with an eighteen-pounder field gun from the reverse slope on 19 July. The gun was quickly moved forward to fire on the city Infantry Barracks, the Jail and the Cavalry Barracks over open sights. On the night of Thursday, 20 July, Provisional troops crossed the river and infiltrated the town. Fighting continued for the next twenty-four hours when the anti-Treaty defenders withdrew towards Carrick-on-Suir, twenty miles north-west.

By mid-July the anti-Treaty position was clear. Except for parts of the west and most of Munster, the principal military posts in the country were in the hands of pro-Treaty forces. Furthermore, any prospect of the anti-Treaty forces being able to defend what they held was very questionable. From holding three of the four main southern cities, the anti-Treatyites now held only one, Cork city, and it now became the focus of Provisonal attention. With Waterford, Limerick and Dundalk in pro-Treaty hands, it was possible for the leadership to concentrate on two primary objectives. The first was to roll up the line of the 'Munster Republic' from both ends and the second was to attack Cork and Kerry with the intention of bringing hostilities to a speedy end. For the anti-Treaty Executive forces all hope of defending the 'Munster Republic' had disappeared. The pro-Treaty pincers closed on the 'line' — a description which suggests a continuous front of fortified positions, and is misleading; in reality it consisted of occupied towns and villages with some outposts, where it still held, from Tipperary town to Carrick-on-Suir, with Clonmel in the centre.

So quickly had the situation developed in pro-Treaty favour that there was now no possibility that the anti-Treatyites could gain victory by force of arms alone. In spite of that and, almost paradoxically, in spite of their initial hesitancy and reluctance to become involved, the anti-Treaty military leaders did not contemplate ending the struggle — possibly because they envisaged this as a concession of principle. De Valera, on the other hand, was anxious to bring hostilities to an end as soon as possible. The Third Dail had not been summoned and he hoped that a constitutional solution and way forward might yet be found. Unfortunately the Provisional demand, possibly influenced by Griffith, was for unconditional surrender. Interestingly Collins, in a manner highly reminiscent of his earlier attitude, was far more conciliatory towards his erstwhile colleagues, and was anxious to bring about an end to the fighting in a way that would not involve any sacrifice of principle on their part. With some justification the pro-Treaty authorities believed the war to be nearly over[213]. The position of the prorogued government remained very obscure. It seems to have acted as either, or both, the Provisional Government or the Dail as required.

In a peculiar sense the Civil War was Dublin against the rest. This statement is not strictly accurate because, for instance, the Dublin Brigades of the Army were opposed to the Treaty, as were numbers of the civil population, and because there were important centres like Kilkenny and Nenagh in pro-Treaty hands when the war broke out. Nevertheless, since the Dail and the Provisional Government as well as their Army Headquarters were all in Dublin, that is how it was seen, and it is an abridgement of the general position. The onset of hostilities took place in Dublin. The vast bulk of pro-Treaty troops, and their HQ, were in Dublin. The anti-Treaty Executive forces withdrew from Dublin to the south, west and north and blockaded themselves in various places. The feelings of those who, in areas occupied by the anti-Treaty forces, supported the Provisional Government (and later the Free State Government) soon came to be shared by a majority of the people; they waited to be relieved from hunger, economic blockade and the threat of warfare in the sure and certain knowledge that this would happen and that they would return to life under the rule of government and effective administration, however they might disagree with what it stood for.

Tipperary town was attacked on Saturday, 29 July by troops from Thurles and Limerick. The battle for the town lasted for twenty-four hours. Golden and Bansha were also attacked and taken. The pro-Treaty advance, westward from Waterford and south and east from Nenagh, Thurles and Limerick, was interrupted all the way by clashes with the enemy, but the advance was not seriously affected, artillery as usual being the decisive factor. The anti-Treaty forces had no artillery and against it they had no effective defence. Nor did they have the essential logistic support — organized transport, supply services and communications — vital to warfare in open country. Withdrawal to the countryside and to mountain fastnesses, the familiar tactic of the War of Independence, and successful operations from such bases, depended on the support of the civilian population which the anti-Treaty conduct of the war seriously eroded. Moreover the pro-Treaty troops were familiar with the terrain and with the anti-Treaty leaders, knowing both where to look and who to look for.

With the capture of Tipperary a wedge, similar to that separating the anti-Treaty forces in Cork/Kerry from their fellows in Clare/Galway, was driven into south

Tipperary, splitting communications between the south Tipperary anti-Treaty positions and the Kilmallock salient. Clonmel was isolated and the Kilmallock flank was open to attack. Cashel, surrounded on three sides by pro-Treaty forces, was untenable and the anti-Treaty garrison withdrew on Monday. A further major blow to the anti-Treaty position at this time was a proclamation by the Irish Hierarchy condemning their action.

From the point of view of an attack-base Carrick-on-Suir lay in relation to Waterford as did Tipperary to Limerick. The pro-Treaty advance against Clonmel from Waterford could not proceed while Carrick-on-Suir was in anti-Treaty hands. There food was short and business was at a standstill. For the anti-Treaty forces military communications with Clonmel and Fermoy were open, but unsatisfactory. Other types of communication were almost impossible.

The civil population of Munster, the seat of republicanism, was being rapidly alienated by the forces of the anti-Treaty Army Executive. Commerce in the province — and in that of Connacht, the second anti-Treaty stronghold — was at a standstill and commercial communication with the rest of the country, especially Dublin, was almost non-existent. Orders were issued that when road and railway bridges were destroyed such destruction must aim at being permanent. Not surprisingly this was interpreted by the civil population, farmers and merchants, as being more of an attack on them than on the Provisional forces. The truism that it is a people and not their army who make a cause democratic was ignored behind the anti-Treaty lines. Ironically, the Provisional Government had taken power on a reversal of the same truism. But, then, Sinn Fein had effectively dominated political and military activity in the country with little reference to the people since 1918.

On Monday 31 July, Prout advanced on the outlying towns and villages around Carrick-on-Suir, and on 1 August opened the attack, with artillery. This lasted until 3 August, when the defenders withdrew under cover of darkness. The way was now open to Clonmel eleven miles to the west. Tralee had been taken, by a seaborne landing, the previous day.

The situation in which the Fourth Northern Division — Armagh, West and South Down and Louth — found itself was typical of many Army units. Aiken, its GOC, decided not to support either the Army Executive or the Provisional Government, but to remain neutral under the Dail Minister for Defence. He moved his Divisional HQ to Dundalk and occupied the barracks there with about 300 men. He informed Mulcahy that he would fight on neither side because the fight would 'only ruin the country without gaining any ground for the Republic'. He ordered his men to dump arms. In the early hours of 16 July he awoke with a revolver at his head and men of the pro-Treaty Fifth Northern Division, under Commdt. Gen. Dan Hogan, in possession of the town. Aiken protested to Mulcahy, saying that the civil war was being 'waged by eight Irishmen without a mandate from the people [by which he meant the Provisional Government] and without consulting the representatives of the people, to force Irishmen to take an oath of allegiance to a foreign king', but to no avail. On 27 July the remainder of Aiken's men attacked from outside and Aiken and his fellows in captivity were freed. Aiken then became active on the anti-Treaty side and, in one of their more successful engagements, recaptured Dundalk on 14 August, releasing the remainder of his HQ force and many other prisoners captured in the meantime. He issued a proclamation the same day, that the people wanted an immediate end to the fighting and a reaffirmation of the sovereignty of the Irish people; failing that a new election with the constitution as the issue. The proclamation was, of course, ignored by the Provisional authorities.

By the beginning of August the cities of Dublin, Waterford, Limerick and Galway and the towns of Carrick-on-Suir, Tipperary, Castlebar, Ballina, Dundalk, Wexford, Tralee and Sligo had been taken by Provisonal forces. The anti-Treaty forces were effectively hemmed-in in the twin counties of Cork and Kerry. North Cork, south Limerick and north Kerry include some of the richest and most prolific land in Europe. This green and fertile undulating country is drained by broad salmon rivers. Hills are low, green and cultivated. East of Tralee, the mountains of south Kerry and west Cork begin. These were the battlements to which some of the anti-Treaty forces now wished to retire. But they still held Cork and the approaches to it and, for the moment, Clonmel.

The Provisonal troops were cheerful and lighthearted in this 'summer campaign' and in almost every town were greeted as deliverers by an enthusiastic populace who welcomed not just the troops, but also the reopening of communications and commercial activity. Head offices in Dublin sent frantic demands for information, and equally frantic requests for supplies went in the other direction. Hundred of young men joined the victorious advancing troops as 'local recruits'. But as the anti-Treaty forces were driven from position to position they became more and more obdurate.

On Tuesday, 8 August, pro-Treaty troops moved out of Carrick-on-Suir to attack Clonmel, which was captured three days later. Tipperary was now entirely in pro-Treaty hands. There were simultaneous seaborne landings in the anti-Treaty rear in both Cork and Kerry. From then on, so far as the anti-Treaty forces were concerned, it became a guerrilla war against a now well-established enemy. For the Provisional (later Free State) forces it became an increasingly bitter campaign, as the fighting they expected to see brought to an end with the capture of the towns and cities of the 'Munster Republic'[214] dragged on in that most venomous of all wars, a guerrilla-based civil war. The anti-Treaty army was denounced from various pulpits throughout the country in accordance with the May pastoral letter and the recent denunciation by the hierarchy. In some extreme cases prisoners, so long as they upheld the Republic, were denied access to the Sacraments and the rites of the Church. Formal excommunication would be pronounced in an October pastoral letter. But this involved only the ordinary and secular clergy in each diocese, and excommunicated republicans were frequently and promptly absolved by the monks and friars of religious orders outside the jurisdiction of the bishops.

With Clonmel in pro-Treaty hands on 11 August, Cork being attacked on the Kilmallock front and from the rear by sea, Tralee captured and Kenmare under attack, Liam Lynch left his HQ — again back in Fermoy — ablaze, and took to the mountains. 'He was once more the leader of a guerrilla army without barracks or bases, stores or supplies' wrote O'Donoghue (*No Other Law*). He might have added 'without government', which was the greatest handicap of the Army Executive.

After the fall of the Four Courts, O Maille had gone to Wexford. There there was strong pro-Treaty feeling, except in Enniscorthy which was occupied by elements from both sides. The town changed hands between 2 July and 7 July, when a strong force of pro-Treaty troops approached and the anti-Treaty forces withdrew. The situation there was similar to that which developed in Galway and other towns. Those of the Midlands, the west and north-west were rapidly in pro-Treaty hands. Since there was no hostile population to contend with there was no need for the Provisional leaders to expend useful fighting troops in holding conquered territory.

In mid-August, far too late, the anti-Treaty forces decided to counter-attack in Dublin. To this end they mounted two operations. The first was to be the capture of Baldonnel (now Casement) military aerodrome where there were friendly troops, followed by, improbably, the bombing of Leinster House and Dublin barracks from the air, and, secondly, the isolation of Dublin by blowing up all the bridges across the canals and the River Liffey surrounding the city. Both attacks were abortive, and resulted only in the capture of some anti-Treaty troops. Firing did continue in Dublin throughout the night of 15 August, but without significant incident.

The main anti-Treaty forces were now concentrated between the rivers Lee and Blackwater, north and south, and between the Clonmel/Youghal line and the Tralee/Kenmare line, east and west. At Kilmallock they waited for what they believed would be the inevitable attack on Cork from the north. In fact when it came the main attack on Cork was by sea, and the anti-Treaty leadership there, in spite of previous similar landings in Kerry and at Westport, were unprepared for it. In the meantime the Kilmallock triangle, contained by the towns Bruff, Bruree and Kilmallock, was a natural defensive position covering the Cork-Dublin railway line and seven major roads. It was occupied by a strong force of anti-Treaty troops with, behind them, the bulk of their support.

Supply and communications lines could not easily be cut. The battle, which was probably the most prolonged of the war, lasted from Sunday, 23 July to Saturday, 5 August. The weather was poor with wind and sometimes driving rain. It was a to-and-fro battle, with both sides capturing and losing tactical positions more than once. Bruree was captured by the Provisional forces on Sunday, 30 July, after some tough fighting there and in the surrounding district. The Provisional forces estimated that over a thousand seasoned anti-Treaty troops were facing them — 'the best fighting material the Irregulars[215] can muster' according to O'Duffy, who was attacking them. There was a minor armoured battle between armoured cars from both sides in Bruree during an anti-Treaty offensive on Wednesday and Thursday, 26-27 July, intended to push the enemy back. But on Wednesday the pro-Treaty forces had landed at Fenit, the port for Tralee, in the anti-Treaty rear, and when the news reached the Kilmallock front it threw the anti-Treaty offensive out of kilter. A large proportion of the Kilmallock anti-Treaty force was made up of men from the Kerry Brigades who were immediately ordered to return to Kerry and fight in their own localities. Troops from the Cork Brigades held the line to cover their retreat. On Friday the pro-Treaty troops, under Generals Slattery and Murphy, counter-attacked and the anti-Treaty forces fell back on Charleville. Kilmallock was entered by Provisonal forces on Saturday afternoon, 5 August.

The landing at Fenit met with small local resistance, principally because local anti-Treaty troops were at Kilmallock and there was little more than a handful at Fenit and Tralee. The defences were quickly overrun — marked to-day by a line of small crosses from Fenit to Tralee — and the town was in pro-Treaty hands by nightfall of 2 August. The anti-Treaty rear was now exposed. Another miniature armoured battle took place in Tralee when several armoured cars from either side fought each other through the streets of the town. Simultaneously with the landing at Fenit, a sweep through the rich lowlands of north Kerry took place when Provisional troops crossed the Shannon at Tarbert and drove south to Listowel and Ballylongford. From this time onwards action in north Kerry by the anti-Treaty forces was limited to guerilla attacks on pro-Treaty positions.

Cork city was the 'capital' of the 'Munster Republic'. The principal city of the south, it was, and is, an important commercial and administrative centre. Relations between the anti-Treaty forces and the civic and commercial leaders were not cordial. It looked as if pro-Treaty policy would bring about an economic blockade of the south; unemployment, already high, rose rapidly as workers and office staffs were laid off and production and distribution came to a standstill. Many, even republican sympathizers, longed for peace. Many more were active pro-Treaty supporters. But such opposition as there was to the anti-Treaty forces was entirely political and came principally from the merchant and professional classes. The city did not have to contend with the raids and attacks on opposing forces that occurred daily elsewhere in the country, including in Dublin. But there was hardship: the banks were short of money and had been ordered by their head offices to close down; water was rationed; food was not expected to last more than three weeks.

The anti-Treaty defence of the city was based on the assumption that the attack would come by land from the north. Munitions were being manufactured and other preparations made, but resources were limited. As elsewhere, there was neither established war-policy, republican government nor effective central authority. The war continued to be conducted on the sole authority of the Army Executive.

Near to midnight on Wednesday, 8 August, a dark ship sailed unannounced through the harbour and upriver for about five miles, to anchor off Carrigaloe, near Passage East. It was *Arvonia*, and she brought Generals Emmet Dalton and Tom Ennis with over five hundred picked Provisional troops from Dublin. These troops landed and prepared to advance on the city ten miles away. On Thursday *Lady Wicklow* arrived with reinforcements, and the combined force advanced against scattered opposition, the bulk of the anti-Treaty troops being in

Charleville. Under this attack the anti-Treaty forces decided to abandon the city rather than submit the civilian population to the trials of a defence which they were, in any case, in little position to effect. They burned the military barracks before evacuating the city. From now on the anti-Treaty army would have temporary headquarters only. The troops moved west to where the war against the British had been most successful and where the hard-core of civilian supporters was to be found.

There was now no central rallying point from which the anti-Treaty forces might be directed. Throughout Munster they made for the mountains in preparation for a guerrilla war. To men like Lynch surrender of the ideal for which he was in arms was unthinkable.

Pro-Treaty Major-General Emmet Dalton took command in Cork and ended the economic blockade. Having done so on a number of occasions throughout July, de Valera again called on the anti-Treaty forces to lay down their arms, saying that the republican ideal had been sufficiently well defended and that there had been enough bloodshed. He was again ignored by the Army Executive command. These events took place on, or close to, Saturday, 12 August, 1922. On that day in Dublin, Arthur Griffith, President of Dail Eireann, died in Dublin of a cerebral haemorrhage.

There were those on the anti-Treaty side who still hoped that an honourable settlement could be reached. The republican ideal had been defended in arms, but the anti-Treaty Army Executive forces were now, demonstrably, defeated in the field and out of favour with the people. It did not follow — as the election of 1923 demonstrated — that the people were equally opposed to the anti-Treaty constitutional position. Continued fighting would achieve nothing, peace and constitutional methods might achieve something. This was also the view of some of those on the other side, including Michael Collins. Together Collins and de Valera might have worked out a solution, as they had so nearly done three months earlier with the Pact.

It was not to be. Fate intervened and as a result the war was prolonged and became increasingly bloody and bitter. On 22 August, while he was actually *en route* to a cross-representative meeting of IRB officers in Cork with, it seems clear, the intention of seeking a way to end the war, Michael Collins was killed in an ambush not far from his own family home at a place called Beal na mBlath in West Cork. He was, at that time, the only man with enough weight and authority to bring about a truce. That such was his intention is hardly in doubt. He was thirty-one years of age.

Collins had earlier set out on a tour of the south, but had returned to Dublin for Griffith's funeral. He then resumed his tour, reaching Cork on 20 August. The ambush in which he was killed was not conducted by an anti-Treaty column. It was planned, laid and manned by senior officers, including the brigade staff of Cork No. 3 brigade, officers from the five brigade battalions, and several division officers, who had come together at Beal na mBlath for the first major policy conference after the fall of Cork. It was an extraordinary, and tragic, coincidence.

As Collins's convoy passed through Beal na mBlath in the morning, he was seen and recognised by the anti-Treaty sentry outside the meeting place. The meeting decided that he would return by the same route and the ambush was laid accordingly about eight hundred yards from where the meeting was being held. After lying all day in wait the ambush was stood down and the bulk of the ambush party went towards the meeting-place, leaving six men behind to dismantle barricades and a mine. While they were engaged in this, Collins's convoy reappeared and one of the anti-Treaty covering party fired a warning shot, principally to alert his comrades on the road so that they would not be surprised by the convoy. Contrary to good military sense the convoy (apparently on Collins's explicit order) stopped and engaged the small party of enemy. During an engagement lasting about forty-five minutes Collins was killed, the result of a wound to his head. From this point on (though it seems to have been the case earlier), a system of 'dual-government' involving the Dail and the Provisional Government operated — 'what', as Gavan Duffy observed in Leinster House on 9 September 'they call in America an inter-locking directorate'.

Collins's personality had dominated the Provisional Government (and latterly the Dail) when he was alive. When Griffith died he had, for ten days, what amounted to unlimited power in his own hands with the unswerving allegiance of the cabinet. His declared policy was speedy victory and a solution to the war which would enable the enemy to lay down their arms, but preserve their integrity and principles. Virtually his last words of significance were about what he intended to do to bring about peace. His last journey was *en route* to a meeting to that end. After that things changed.

One by one the small towns of Munster were occupied by pro-Treaty forces. Sometimes towns changed hands again, but from mid-August onwards the whole character of the war altered. Guerrilla tactics, which had had startling success against the foreign army of occupation, were useless against a domestic army of local troops supported by the public and by a powerful government. By adopting guerrilla tactics the anti-Treaty forces were acknowledging that they were beaten in the field, but that they would not stop fighting. Although the towns were in the hands of the pro-Treatyites, it became difficult for their troops to move outside without being ambushed. Lynch had his headquarters in the Glen of Aherlow and refused to acknowledge the impossibility of his situation. De Valera, who was still opposed to the Treaty as it stood, believed that satisfactory revision could be obtained along the lines of his 'External Association' formula. He was more than ever opposed to a continuation of hostilities, but he did not have the authority to influence matters.

The refusal of the anti-Treaty forces to face the fact that they could not win, the continuance of the war, and the bitterness that was the outcome of the ambushes, brought about a new and ruthless campaign of terrorism from Provisional authorities in parts of the country, with consequent demoralization among some of the troops involved. General unrest and lack of discipline amongst the Provisonal forces contributed to the excesses, which occurred on a scale too wide-spread to have been isolated incidents. Nowhere did this fearful aspect of the war become more apparent than in Kerry, though it manifested itself everywhere.

The war had become a hunt. Sometimes Provisional forces did not take prisoners. When they did, they were liable to summary execution before or after torture without trial. In the spring of 1923 brutality reached a climax when, on 7 March, nine anti-Treaty prisoners, all battered, one with a broken arm, another with a broken wrist and one unable to walk as a result of spinal injuries, were brought to Ballyseedy Cross outside Tralee. Their hands were tied behind them and each man was roped to the man beside him so that they stood in a ring facing outwards. In the centre of the ring was a landmine. The soldiers who tied them took cover and exploded the mine. Eight men were blown to bits but, unknown to his captors, one man, Stephen Fuller, was blown clear. He escaped. The remains of the eight men were put into nine coffins.

The official explanation was that the men were killed while clearing mined barricades put up by their fellow anti-Treatyites. The story might have been believed were it not for Fuller, and had another man not also been blown clear in a precisely similar mass 'execution' at Countess Bridge, Killarney, on the same day, where five men were blown up. At Cahirciveen, five days later, five more prisoners were killed in the same way, but this time their captors took precautions; they shot each man in the legs before exploding the mine. A Provisional officer resigned and published an account of what had happened.

Largely as a result of such events, Colonel Fred Henry was appointed Provost Marshal of the Provisional forces. But a policy of official reprisal executions developed; these were met with counter-reprisals from the anti-Treaty Executive forces. As a result bitterness and hatred increased. Unscrupulous individuals on both sides took advantage of the situation to exploit the public and its property, sometimes claiming to do so in the name of a principle.

The anti-Treaty forces clung to the hope that, sooner or later, they would provoke the British to an attack and that public opinion and military tempers would be then sufficiently roused to restore national unity and purpose. In the circumstances it was a foolish and forlorn hope. The British post-Treaty Irish policy was as self-interestedly intelligent as their pre-Truce policy had been, from their own point of view, foolishly counter-productive. Macready's orders to attack the Four Courts had been quickly countermanded, the evacuation of British troops had been hastened and further significant involvement avoided once the Treaty vote in the Dail was taken.

The second phase of the civil war ended with the meeting of the parliament on 9 September. This was the meeting which had been twice previously prorogued and which, according to the Pact, was to have been the coalition Sinn Fein parliament and government[216]. The question therefore arose was it the Provisional parliament (still without a legislature), or the Dail? It was a question which understandably concerned de Valera and his constitutional anti-Treaty supporters. The anti-Treaty representatives were not summoned to attend, but one, Laurence Ginnell, did so. It became quickly clear that this was not a meeting of the Third Dail Eireann on the Pact platform, as intended. At that meeting the Labour Party brought up the matter of murder and torture by the Provisional forces.

Prior to the meeting of the parliament a secret meeting had taken place on Wednesday, 6 September, in Dublin between de Valera and Mulcahy to discuss the situation and seek, if possible, some means of accomodation. The meeting proved fruitless. De Valera was unable to persuade Mulcahy to accept the terms of the Collins/de Valera Pact before the assembly met on the following Saturday. When Ginnell attended as a 'test-case', he was ruled out of order on a procedural ruse, and the assembly emerged, with Cosgrave at its head, as the parliament of the Provisional Government. In his statement of policy Cosgrave said:

> It is my intention to implement this Treaty as sanctioned by vote of the Dail and the electorate *in so far as it was free to express an opinion*; to enact the constitution; to assert the authority and supremacy of the parliament; to support and assist the national army in asserting the people's rights; to ask parliament, if necessary, for such powers as may be deemed essential for the purpose of restoring order.

Both sides were now locked in extreme positions of 'principle' to be rigorously defended. In each case the principle involved was outside the realm of strict reason and logic and required considerable — and often passionate — special pleading. The Executive of the Army were defending the proclaimed and affirmed sovereign Irish Republic (which was not attainable from the Treaty negotiations even if External Association were accepted), while the Provisional Government were defending not so much the Treaty as its signing, claiming, as Cosgrave did, that the signing was 'sanctioned' by the Dail and the electorate. This was not the case unless the *post-factum* votes are taken as being 'sanction'.

Following this session of parliament the anti-Treaty constitutionalists, satisfied that this governing assembly was neither 'dual government', nor yet the Second Dail Eireann which had not been dissolved and to which they owed allegiance, nor the Third Dail Eireann, again became politically active. De Valera referred to the 'illegal junta called the "Provisional Government"'(letter to VC O'M, Dr. Conn O Murchadh, deputy for South Dublin, 6 September, 1922). In a document written the following day he stated that they (the constitutional anti-Treatyites) were justified in taking positive political steps to preserve the Second Dail, elected the previous January. He stated that the 'Provisional parliament' was an unconstitutional assembly which the anti-Treatyites should not attend. He felt that since he had been prepared to abide by the terms of the Pact which had been rejected by Mulcahy, he was now in a position to act.

The situation was then a curious one. The British Government of Ireland Act, 1920, had provided for two Irish parliaments in a partitioned — but not necessarily separated — Ireland. From this time on the pro-Treaty leaders treated their opponents with increasing ruthlessness and intransigence, refusing to consider their point of view at all. Gone was Collins's approach to let them lay down their arms, but keep their principles. Pro-Treaty unswerving allegiance to rigid policy converted that policy into an end in itself. Collins's 'Stepping-Stone' was submerged. Thus the policy served Britain's Government of Ireland Act as it had emerged (with an obdurate North) rather than anything else. The split in Sinn Fein and the hostilities that resulted must have seemed like a godsend to the Ulster unionists. It is not, perhaps, going too far to say that the civil war copper-fastened partition in a way that little else might have done.

De Valera came under pressure from his own supporters to form an alternative assembly, but he declined on the grounds that it would not be possible to maintain such an assembly without the support of the Army Executive. He had no sooner made this statement than, within a few hours, he received a letter from Liam Lynch which infuriated him because of its tone and content. The tone was that of a supreme commander to a somewhat tiresome civilian who had to be endured, and the content suggested that not only was the Executive unlikely to give allegiance to a new political authority, but that it considered itself the only proper anti-Treaty administration.

However, support for a constitutional republican party came from a surprising quarter. Liam Mellowes and other influential anti-Treaty prisoners smuggled from jail a call for a republican administration to be formed and for greater cooperation between the Army and de Valera. Mellowes, with justification, was in fact critical of the Army conduct of affairs. In October the Army agreed to give allegiance to a government under de Valera's presidency and this was formed — six months too late — on 25 October by anti-Treaty members of the Second Dail meeting in Dublin. It had a twelve-man council of state which could now do little more than issue statements of anti-Treaty policy from time to time.

In October, the constitution of the Irish Free State became law. The Labour Party, which now sat in the assembly, protested at some of the provisions being introduced, in particular those for military courts, special powers for the (Provisional) army and the death penalty for a variety of offences, saying that the parliament was being asked to consent to the establishment of a military dictatorship. The military courts began to operate from 15 October. From that date, apart from excommunication by the hierarchy, every anti-Treaty soldier faced death if captured. Thus the pro-Treaty forces were given, at once, a political and a moral licence.

From this time on ill-treatment and murder of anti-Treaty prisoners of war became notorious, and the subject of protests and enquiries. These things did not deter the Provisional authorities who, following the introduction of the military courts, introduced an executions policy. The first executions occurred on 17 November. A most unsavoury aspect of this policy was that prisoners who had been captured in the Four Courts six months before these Draconian measures came into existence, including some of the most important leaders on the republican side, were executed in reprisal executions[217]. The anti-Treatyite Executive forces responded by collectively condemning all those representatives who had voted in favour of the execution Bill — '*The Murder Bill*' — and issued instructions that they should be shot on sight. The practice became commonplace of sentencing anti-Treaty prisoners to death, but suspending the sentence, to be carried out if pro-Treaty troops were attacked in the prisoner's home area. The civil war had reached the nadir of bitterness.

On Wednesday 6 December, 1922 the Irish Free State came into official existence, exactly one year after the signing of the Treaty. The following day, 7 December, the Northern Ireland government exercised its right under the Treaty of seceding from a joint all-Ireland parliament[218]. Shortly before this Lloyd George had been toppled from his prime-ministerial perch in Downing street just as each warring side in Ireland marooned itself on islands of implausible principle. In considerable part his fall was due to his handling of the Irish question. Bonar Law, diehard unionist, formed a new government.

Ambushes, raids, attacks and counter-attacks were taking place all over the country, daily in the cities. The guerrilla war reached a pitch of intensity as great as, if not greater than, that against the British. It has been suggested that this indicates that the Army would have held its own against any renewed British war-effort and, coupled with the likelihood that the British threat was bluff, this is not implausible.

But as winter settled on the land and Christmas approached, the anti-Treaty position grew steadily worse. There was no possible hope of a successful outcome to the war for them. Defeat was only a matter of time and morale was low. They appealed to Rome against the imposition of excommunication by the Irish bishops, and were rewarded by the visit of a special papal envoy.

By the spring of 1923 the anti-Treatyites were in a bad way. Their position was hopeless; the number of dead and wounded, the number of prisoners in jails and internment camps, grew. Disease, hunger and fatigue were rampant and supplies — food, clothing and equipment — were almost unobtainable. The end was inevitable, but they continued to fight on. On 16 March, eleven members of the Army Executive met de Valera in south Tipperary to discuss his peace proposals. Nothing came of the meeting, but a proposal from Tom Barry that further armed resistance would not further the cause of the independence of the country was defeated by only one vote.

Liam Deasy, First Division GOC, had been captured on 18 January and sentenced to death. There is no doubt that the sentence did not influence Deasy, but he was satisfied that hostilities should end and asked his Free State captors for permission to contact his Army Executive colleagues. A stay of execution was ordered and he was granted permission to make contact, but only on condition that the Free State authorities wrote the appeal for unconditional surrender which Deasy would sign. As the only means at his disposal of helping to end the war, Deasy agreed on 29 January[219]. Similar requests for contact with the anti-Treaty leadership came from other prisoner sources. Lynch, who now seemed to have adopted the role of Commander-in-Chief rather than Chief-of-Staff, did not believe the anti-Treaty cause to be doomed, and rejected Deasy's document and the other approaches[220]. On his own authority he refused to convene Executive meetings, as he feared they might vote for surrender. He was finally forced to convene the meeting attended by de Valera in March. A second meeting was arranged for 10 April, to be held in the Knockmealdown mountains on the Waterford/Tipperary border. However a sweep of Free State troops was taking place in the area — whether as a result of being informed of the meeting, or not, is uncertain — and Lynch and some of his aides were seen and pursued. Lynch was killed in an exchange of fire.

With his death the will to continue the pointless struggle any longer left the anti-Treatyites. Lynch's death spurred the Free State forces to intensive action and, over the next few days, blow after blow fell on their opponents. Several more of their senior officers were captured or killed. On 20 April the adjourned anti-Treaty meeting was reconvened at Poulacapple in Tipperary. Aiken became Chief-of-Staff. With one dissentient the meeting agreed to negotiate for peace on the following terms:

(1) The sovereignty of the Irish nation and the integrity of its territory are inalienable.

(2) Any instrument purporting to the contrary is, to the extent of its violation of the above principle, null and void.

A week later de Valera issued a proclamation of the terms and at the same time called for a suspension of aggressive action by the anti-Treaty troops. This opened the way for negotiations. Cosgrave refused to negotiate himself, but agreed to Senators Andrew Jameson and James Douglas as intermediaries. Negotiations lasted for over a week, but final agreement could not be reached. De Valera sought agreement that elected representatives should be allowed to take their seats in the Dail without the obligation to take the oath of allegiance to the King of England. This could not, without breach of the constitution and the Treaty, be conceded by the Free State Government. The Free State, on the other hand, required all arms held by the anti-Treatyites to be handed over to them, together with strict adherence to the constitution, which included acceptance of the oath of allegiance.

The negotiations having failed, the Executive Army Council and republican cabinet met on 13 and 14 May. A decision was taken to order the anti-Treaty troops in the field to 'dump arms' and 'cease fire' as and from 24 May 1923. The civil war was over.

In his address to the anti-Treaty Executive army de Valera made the speech he had been anxious to make the previous July:

Soldiers of the Republic, Legion of the Rearguard ... the Republic can no longer be defended successfully by your arms ... military victory must be allowed to rest for the moment with those who have destroyed the Republic ... Much that you set out to accomplish is achieved. You have saved the nation's honour and kept open the road of independence. You have demonstrated in a way there is no mistaking that we are not a nation of willing bondslaves. Seven years of intense effort have exhausted our people. . .

The Free State rounded up thousands of prisoners, adding them to the 15,000 or so already interned or in jail.

None of the problems which the Treaty brought had been solved when the civil war ended. The pro-Treaty party — now the Free State government — emerged the stronger, and in power. The anti-Treatyites were defeated militarily, but with their purpose intact. A Public Safety Act was passed in June so that anti-Treatyites might be arrested and detained without trial, and it was decided to hold a general election in August.

The republicans were grievously handicapped in their electioneering. All their principal leaders were dead, in jail or open to arrest or imprisonment without trial. Campaigning was, therefore, a matter of great difficulty. They put forward eighty-seven candidates on the Sinn Fein ticket, most of them on the run[221]. The results of the election were a painful shock for the Free State Government. Out of a total of 153 seats, the government won only 63. In spite of the difficulties they faced in the campaign and with thousands of their supporters still behind bars, anti-Treaty Sinn Fein nevertheless won forty-four seats. The remainder were divided between a Farmers' Party, Labour and Independents. The vote showed that, whatever about the effect of the Treaty and the civil war, a strong minority of the electorate still supported the anti-Treaty position. The prisoners were released over the next two years. After the end of the civil war there was a period of political instability and considerable unemployment. The new government of the Irish Free State had a difficult time establishing civil order, trying to stabilise the economy and develop the country's resources. By virtue of the oath to the British king republicans were excluded from participation in running the country — much as the Irish Party had been between 1918 and 1921. The Boundary Commission established in 1924 was an ignominious betrayal of the undertakings given by the British leaders during the Treaty negotiations. The largely nationalist/Catholic counties of Fermanagh, Tyrone, south Down and south Armagh did not, as proposed, become part of the Irish Free State, but were coerced into the Northern statelet, where they have remained. It is very indicative that these were 'highly disturbed' areas from 1969 on.

In 1924 the so-called Army mutiny occurred. This was brought about because the Army was far too large for a peacetime establishment, but also, and more significantly, because many officers and men who had supported the principle of Collins's 'Stepping-Stone' policy, and who had fought in the Civil War against old comrades on that issue, felt betrayed by a government which had, in their eyes, abandoned this principle.

De Valera founded a new political party, Fianna Fail, and entered the Dail in 1927 stating that he and his supporters were not swearing an oath but mouthing a formula. In 1932 Fianna Fail took office and held it for sixteen years. The move to constitutional politics within the Free State alienated many republicans from Fianna Fail and, from then onwards, the militant IRA remained outside constitutional frameworks in the country.

They are ill discoverers that think there is no land,
when they can see nothing but sea . . . Francis Bacon.

Chapter 12

Personalities: the Ambush at Beal na mBlath

ROGER CASEMENT IS ONE OF THE MOST interesting, enigmatic and controversial figures of 1916. He is praised and vilified; condemned as traitor, pervert and degenerate, extolled as man of high principle, integrity and deep spirituality; lauded as a committed and active patriot, censured as an unrealistic romantic. He was hanged for high treason in London by the British on 3 August, 1916. The account of his involvement with the Rising has already been given in Chapter Five. He was the victim of a scurrilous plot designed to blacken his name and destroy his character. He'd been captured in Ireland and brought to England under a false name. The trial received immense international publicity, but with an extraordinary and unexpected 'spin', created by the circulation by the British of typed and photographed copies of extracts from the so-called 'black' diaries to influential sources, including the Press and diplomats, at home and abroad. These extracts purported to contain accounts of gross homosexual perversions indulged in and recorded by Casement over a number of years. The originals were said to have been found, compiled and 'edited' by a trio of senior British officials, the ultimate 'spin-doctors' of the day. They were F.E. Smith, Attorney General (formerly 'Galloper' to Lord Craig as commander-in-chief of the Ulster Volunteers, and legal advisor to Carson's short-lived, and treasonable, Provisional Government of Ulster and, for obvious reasons, no friend of Casement's); Captain W.E.Hall, head of British Naval Intelligence, who was responsible for intercepting the messages between New York, Dublin and Germany prior to the Rising; and Sir Basil Thomson, then Assistant Commissioner of police and head of the CID at Scotland Yard, and who is alleged (see debates in the British House of Commons, May 1956 and also Alfred Noyes, *The Accusing Ghost or Justice for Casement*, London, 1957) to have had the diaries deliberately faked. Lt. Col. Montgomery Hyde, Unionist MP for Belfast North, stated in the House of Commons (May 3, 1956), that 'it has been suggested that that the diaries are deliberately faked by Sir Basil Thomson, who intermingled some Casement genuine diaries with the obscene Putamayo diaries of Armando Normand.' Two independent sources (Mr. Terry Conneally, an English-born journalist and Mr.

Eoin O Maille) have stated that they are aware from those who worked closely with him, that it was Hall who orchestrated the forgeries. An important bearing on this is contained in the published transcript of German Gestapo chief Heinrich Müller by the American CIA, in which Müller volunteered the information that he had used a Swiss, named Zwingleman, who, Müller claimed, told the Gestapo that he had forged the 'Black Diaries', on Hall's instructions. (See *The Barnes Review*, Vol. iv, No. 2, 1998)

More than any of the real leaders of the Easter Rising of 1916, Casement was hated, reviled and despised by the British Establishment. The plot against Casement was intended to blacken his name and destroy his character; firstly, in order to alienate sympathy from him during his trial, particularly in America, at a crucial period of the war and, secondly, because the British believed, erroneously as we know, that Casement's role in the 1916 Rising was of greater importance than was in fact the case. The latter was a natural error given the atrocious level of British intelligence concerning events in Ireland in the pre-Rising period and given also Casement's high international and Establishment profile and what was known and learned of his activities in America and Germany before the Rising.

However wrongheaded and blinkered, the British Establishment attitude to Ireland and the Irish (the native, southern and mainly Catholic species, that is), was at the time, but especially after the Rising, essentially one of having been scurrilously betrayed. Nor could they bring themselves to believe that such a major event as Easter 1916 was planned and executed by mere bog-trotting peasants <u>unless</u> — and this is the essence of it — unless it was conceived and led by a prominent leader already known to themselves through the intelligence network which was their pride, their joy, their eyes and ears — and, at least in this instance very inadequate.

The British considered Casement to be an extremely dangerous man. It was partly for that reason, but more particularly because of the high Establishment status he had enjoyed; because of his international reputation and because of his public repudiation, in America, of Britain at the outbreak of the First World War, that he was considered to be so dangerous, that he became victim of sustained and ruthless character assassination and that he was accorded by them a role in the 1916 Rising of far more importance than he had. .

Leon O Broin states (*Dublin Castle and the 1916 Rising*), 'the (British) military shared the government view that Casement was the key man in the whole business'.

A second purpose of the hostile propaganda was to alienate sympathy from Casement and the movement for Irish independence with which he was associated, especially in America, during his trial at a crucial period of the war when Britain was seriously considering negotiating for peace. This helps explain the unprecedented scale with which the campaign was conducted.

It is reminiscent of Parnell and the forged Pigott diaries from the failure of which the forgers evidently learned. It has been suggested that extracts, either from the diaries of the South American murderer and degenerate, Armando Normand, (a copy of whose diaries Casement, in his own hand, had translated and submitted to the British Foreign Office some years earlier as evidence of his investigations in the Putamayo region), or material of a similar obscene nature, were interpolated in Casement's genuine diaries for the appropriate years. These had been brought to Scotland Yard after Casement went to New York in 1914. Bulmer Hobson noted: 'He '[Casement] 'told me that this man's [Normand's] private diaries recorded *details of the most unnatural and abominable crimes. He said that he had sent the diaries to the Foreign Office and had kept a copy of it.* I cannot clearly recollect now whether the diaries went in with his report or subsequent to it, or whether it was the diaries went in or the copy. But at any rate there is no doubt that there was an extant copy of this diary in Casement's handwriting, and that this was either at the Foreign Office or amongst Casement's own papers' (document in the National Library of Ireland; see also Alfred Noyes, The Accusing Ghost, p. 106). Denis Gwynn confirms the details. Dr. H.S.Dickey, who knew Casement in Peru and who had accompanied him on one of his expeditions, was convinced that the diaries were forgeries and that 'if Casement was one of those unfortunates (a homosexual), I am a rotten diagnostician' (Noyes wrote):

> Dr. Dickey had no particular reason to feel friendly towards Casement, for the unexpected publication by Casement of certain information ... which he had received from the physician made it necessary for the latter to throw up his appointment. He had no motive in making his affidavit (in 1936) except to clear Casement.

Almost everyone who knew Casement well was struck by his integrity and the sense of high-minded chivalry that evidently emanated from him. 'Moreover' wrote Noyes (op.cit. p. 162), 'the *kind* of testimony they [those who knew him] give has never in history been given to a man of bad moral character... It is not' he continues, 'the language of that ambiguous tolerance indifferent to all moral considerations. It is the sincere language of men and women profoundly aware of those moral considerations and profoundly indignant at the charges brought against a man whose mind was like an open book to them.'

The evidence of a plot to discredit Casement is, of course, circumstantial, but what evidence there is is strong and Noyes states the case admirably. One can only conclude either that Casement, in a manner beyond belief, was capable of deceiving friends, colleagues and critics all his life and in the most impossible circumstances, or that he was deliberately framed. Clearly the evidence that he was framed, circumstantial or not, is so considerable as to be all but incontrovertible. Those who accused him were known forgers, liars, manipulators and experts in mis- and dis- information. They had made political forgery into an effective tool of war and had experts and an office for that specific purpose. It was in their interest (or in the interest of their government) that Casement be publicly demolished. Both Casement's Putamayo diary, and his handwritten copy of Normand's diary, had been in their possession for years. There was a blatantly 'managed' trial which both the judge and the Attorney General manipulated as they saw fit, even to the extent of breaching the law. The Home Secretary pursued Casement to the grave, insisting that his body be buried in quicklime within the prison walls — a fate by law confined to those convicted of murder, but which was wrongfully applied to Casement though the crime with which he was charged was treason. The allegations against him were incomprehensible to anyone who knew him. 'He seemed to me', wrote Stephen Gwynn (*Recollections of a Literary Man*), 'one of the finest looking creatures I had ever seen; and his countenance had charm and distinction and a high chivalry.'

In the context of the trial Noyes put the matter clearly and succinctly:- 'At the precise psychological moment ... for the defeat of the petitions [for clemency] and to prevent Casement being regarded in Ireland as a patriot-martyr, a "diary" recording unnatural offences was alleged to have been found among his effects. On the advice of Sir Ernley Blackwell (the legal advisor to the Home Office) officially typed copies and photostatic extracts were circulated behind the scenes of the trial, through London clubs, among members of parliament and others, who might be thought to influence public opinion.

'The methods used were admittedly disgraceful, and for forty years now there has been a growing suspicion that this "diary" is as wicked a forgery as the notorious Pigott letters in the Parnell case' (Noyes op. cit., p.11).

* * *

Casement was born in Sandymount, County Dublin, in 1864 and was hanged in London in 1916 after a trial during which the noblest and highest example of justice and humanity evident was contained in his own speech from the dock — of which, in a remarkable tribute, F.E.Smith's son, the second Lord Birkenhead, wrote: 'His ... words were woven into rare beauty and pathos, and their richness and passion are hardly less moving than the last speech of Strafford three centuries ago' (the Earl of Birkenhead in his father's biography *Frederick Edwin, Earl of Birkenhead*).

In 1910 Casement was sent by the British Foreign Minister, Sir Edward Grey, to carry out an investigation into alleged atrocities in the area of the Putamayo river (a Peruvian tributary of the Amazon) by agents of the Anglo-Peruvian Amazon Rubber Company, registered and with offices in London. He was accompanied by five commissioners appointed by the company against which the charges were being brought (see Noyes, op. cit., pp 47/8) and who might have been expected to view any and all of Casement's activities — especially his fitness for the task — with a critical eye. They were with him throughout his investigation — precisely the period attributed to the 'black' diaries.

> It is hard to credit that if the offences attributed to Casement in the spurious diaries really occurred 'daily' at this very time, there should not have been a whisper of it in such a company (Noyes, op. cit., p.48)

It is also an extraordinary fact that, supposing the diaries to have been genuine, not a single one of Casement's friends — or enemies — had the slightest hint of his 'daily' degenerate behaviour until the 'diaries' were produced during the trial. It can be argued — with the example of Oscar Wilde not long before him — that he was devious and concealed his activities. But the sheer volume of tributes, from a great variety of sources, to his unusual nobility of character cast doubt on this. When allied to the evidence of collusion and deliberate misrepresentation by Thomson, Hall and Smith and to that of Heinrich Müller, there is really no alternative but to accept the obvious, which is that Casement was entirely innocent of the events in the so-called diaries.

> People who knew Casement ... among them Mr. William Cadbury ... take the view that these documents are spurious ... Mr. Cadbury, and others like him, take the view that these documents, or at any rate certain portions of them, are the diaries of a scoundrel and pervert named Armando Normand, whom Casement came across when investigating the rubber atrocities in the Putamayo for the Foreign Office, and that Casement translated these diaries from the Spanish in which they were originally written and kept a copy in his own handwriting, as he considered that they could not be entrusted to a typist — (Montgomery Hyde, House of Commons, May, 1956).

When, initially, Noyes was shown extracts from the so-called 'diary', he was horrified. For a time he was very hostile towards Casement, only afterwards changing his opinion in the light of greater information. In a letter to the *London Times* of 1 May 1956 he wrote: 'There has been an accumulation of evidence ... which has forced me to the conclusion that the documents are spurious'.

In 1916 while the trial was in progress, Sir Ernley Blackwell, legal advisor to the Home Office, submitted a memorandum to the British cabinet containing, *inter alia*: 'so far as I can judge, it would be far wiser from every point of view, to allow the law to take its course and by *judicious means* to use these diaries to prevent Casement from attaining martyrdom'. Blackwell may, or may not, have been a party to any plot by Thomson and Hall to forge the 'Casement diaries', but there is no doubt that he gratuitously read his memorandum to Thomson on July 21, only three days after he had submitted it to the British cabinet (see biography of Sir Basil Thomson, London, 1939).

Ben Allen, of Associated Press, was one of the journalists to whom the 'diaries' were shown in 1916. In keeping with the traditions of AP he asked if he could confront Casement — whom he knew — with the document, but was repeatedly refused. Nor was any independent and expert authority permitted to examine the originals together with all the related evidence.

There are many testimonies to Casement's innate goodness of character, but of them all his own words — perhaps in the fidelity of 'by their fruits ye shall know them' — speak plainest. In his report to Sir Edward Grey dated 17 March, 1911 (published by the British Government and presented to both Houses of Parliament July 1912) Casement presents a gruesome picture of the conditions to which the Putamayo Indians were submitted by the agents of the Anglo-Peruvian Rubber Company. It was commonplace for them, particularly women and children, to be beheaded at the whim of an overseer for a fault such as being unable to keep up on the march; for failing to speak Spanish; for crying; simply for being in the way. Men were shot and tortured, beaten to death by having their genitals repeatedly smashed with clubs ... and the killers were themselves often Indians who acted through fear of what would happen to them if they did not cooperate. In this report Casement writes:

> The tribes of the Putamayo in the hands of good men could be made into good men and women, useful and intelligent workers under an honest administration. Trained to be murderers, with the worst example men ever gave to men daily held up for imitation, with lust and greed and cruelty so often appealed to, I daily wondered that so much goodness still survived among the remnant we encountered ...

These are scarcely the words of a moral degenerate. And he goes on in his authentic diary: 'The thing that we find here is carrion, a pestilence, a crime ... a moral disease that religion and conscience and all that is upright in us should uncompromisingly condemn... God help the poor beings! Only He can help them! ... I wonder where that Heavenly Power can be that has so far allowed these beautiful images of Himself to be thus defaced and shamed in the name of a great association of English gentlemen' (the Anglo-Peruvian Rubber Company — Casement's Putamayo diary, National Library of Ireland).

> It would be difficult, writes Noyes (p. 58), to reconcile the tone of this, his real Putamayo diary, and also the circumstances in which it was written, with the daily offences alleged against Casement by the political enemies who determined to hang him.
> How, he asks (p.88), are we to account for the fact that in all the voluminous writings of Sir Roger Casement there is no trace of the propensities attributed to him except in the documents which passed through the hands of Sir Basil Thomson...?

The justification, no doubt, of these enemies was that any means was fair and proper against a wartime traitor guilty of high treason. That this particular 'traitor' was an avowed Irish patriot was of no consequence to them.

In 1912, E.D. Morel wrote of Casement: 'I have never known such personal magnetism ... it is not the physical gifts which are the primary cause, [Casement was six feet four inches tall, and strikingly handsome by all accounts], rather the mental unuttered conviction that is instantly formed that this man is the soul of honour' (*London Daily News*, 20 July 1912).

The priest who was with him at the end and was the sole mourner at the graveside, and who heard his last confession, spoke movingly of him thirty years later: 'Though thirty years have passed, the years have not dimmed the memory of a noble — gentle, lonely soul... He was a saint. We should be praying to him rather than *for* him.'

> No one who really understands what is possible and what is impossible language at such a time, writes Noyes (op. cit. p. 158), in the mouth of a Catholic Prison Chaplain of great experience, can doubt that they confirm the innocence of Roger Casement on the moral charge. To those who cannot accept the words of a priest about the nature of this man, the words of Ellis, the executioner, may perhaps convey a gleam of what was utterly beyond the comprehension of his calumniators: The impression will ever remain on my mind of the composure of his noble countenance, the smile of contentment

and happiness, as he willingly helped my assistant ... Roger Casement appeared to me the bravest man it fell to my unhappy lot to execute.

Throughout Casement's writings are constant and clearly heartfelt references to the Almighty totally inconsistent with the degenerate depicted in the 'diaries' and at his trial. The fact is that Casement had committed the ultimate 'sin'. He, a member of it, had publicly betrayed the British Establishment and their very curious 'code of ethics'. This was a much graver offence than betraying one's country — as the Curragh mutiny also demonstrated — and for this he was targetted as early as 1914 when, en route to Germany that year, an attempt was made by the British Minister in Norway — a man called Findlay — to subborn Casement's manservant, who was offered £5,000 to murder him. All this is documented in Casement's diary of the period (see Noyes p. 82 et seq.) It is hardly to be supposed that Mr. Findlay acted on his own initiative. The incident also raises the interesting, if secondary, question of an anxiety on the part of the British to discredit not alone Casement, but his diaries, the existence of which were well-known to Casement's associates.

Two trunks belonging to Casement were brought to Scotland Yard (where Thomson was head of the CID) more than *sixteen months before his trial.* The 'diaries' are alleged to have been fortuitously found in one of these as his trial began. It is astonishing that no other 'evidence', either before or after — for instance from Germany — exists of Casement's supposed degeneracy. It is also convenient — if not surprising — that the sections of the alleged diaries which were disseminated cover *only* the years 1903 and 1910/11, precisely the years for which Casement's genuine diaries for these periods, his reports etc. of the Putamayo investigations, *and* his translation of Normand's diary were available to Thomson during the sixteen months prior to Casement's arrest (And here it might be noted that Casement evidently had so much time on his hands in the Putomayo that he was not alone able, in the space of a few months, to complete his arduous mission **and** keep a 250,000 word open daily diary — See *The Amazon Journal of Roger Casement*, Angus Mitchell, ed., Lilliput — but also, according to his accusers, he had time to engage daily in the degenerate behaviour they alleged, keeping these activities secret from his constant companions many of them seriously hostile, while in addition keeping a second, secret, diary detailing these obscene activities. A Superman beyond question!).

Thomson later publicly lied about when the trunks were brought to Scotland Yard, saying that they were not acquired until *after* Casement was captured and brought to London for his trial (see article in the *Times*, 21 November, 1921; also Noyes p. 96). The British, as we have seen, believed Casement to be head of the Irish separatist conspiracy, a traitor in Germany and a dangerously influential man. To diminish him and blacken his name was imperative. They had sixteen months of access to his diaries before his capture. They had a copy of Normand's diary in Casement's own handwriting. They had three unscrupulous and ruthless men in Smith, Hall and Thomson (himself arrested later for indecency in Hyde Park) in control of events leading to his capture, and of Casement himself afterwards, and of the evidence to be presented against him. The results were predictable.

The purpose which at the time seemed important to the manipulators of propaganda was as far as possible to alienate sympathy from the movement with which Casement was associated, especially among Irish-Americans who were supporting him financially as well as politically. This is the only explanation of the unprecedented scale on which the smear campaign was conducted.

It is hardly co-incidental, but is instructive, that on April 15/16, 1916, a week before Thomson claimed he had first heard of Casement's trunks, known to have been in Scotland Yard for the previous sixteen months, the London *Daily Mail* published a totally false report that Casement had been arrested in Germany for unnatural vices. From this it might appear that the 1914 plot to 'get' Casement, culminating in the attempt to have him murdered in Norway, was re-activated before the Rising. It is also illuminating to know that when Casement was first being interrogated after his arrest he was informed that his trunks were in Scotland Yard, but locked, to which he replied: 'Break them again'. (See British Public Records documents HO 144/1639.)

It is ironic that the British Attorney General who appointed himself Crown Prosecutor against Casement, was the same F.E. Smith who, a mere three years earlier had, openly, vigorously and treasonably, incited the Ulster unionists on a grand scale. In his capacity as Attorney General he, and he alone, had the power to certify, on a point of law of public importance, the case going before the House of Lords on appeal. But Smith refused.

Casement's own speech from the dock includes the following:

> I did not land in England; I landed in Ireland. It was to Ireland I came; to Ireland I wanted to come; and the last place I desired to land was in England. But for the Attorney General of England there is only 'England' — there is no Ireland, there is only the law of England — no right of Ireland; the liberty of Ireland and of Irishmen is to be judged by the power of England ... it is by Irishmen, and by them alone, that I can be rightfully judged... I hope I shall be acquitted of presumption if I say that the Court I see before me now is not this High Court of Justice of England; but a far greater, a far higher, a far older assemblage of judges, that of the people of Ireland. Since in the acts which have led to this trial it was the people of Ireland I sought to serve — and them alone — I leave my judgement and my sentence in their hands... the faculty of preserving through centuries of misery the remembrance of lost liberty, this is surely the noblest cause that man ever strove for, ever lived for, ever died for. If this be the cause I stand here to-day indicted for, and convicted of sustaining, then I stand in a goodly company and a right noble succession.

Noyes (p. 161) writes of the trial: 'Through all the difficulties and complexities of his actual trial, there is not a single recorded instance of his having spoken a word that was not fearlessly true. On the other hand, the record of the other side is one long chain of trickery, evasion and falsehood, where if their acts had been honest, nothing would have been easier than to give a straightforward account'.

The Belfast writer, Robert Lynd, wrote: 'Even those who, like myself, have been diametrically opposed to his recent policy, can never lose our admiration and affection for everything in him that was noble and compassionate.'

Finally, it needs to be stressed that, although copies of the alleged diaries were widely circulated by the British where they thought it would do most good, all efforts by Casement's legal representatives (Gavan Duffy and Serjeant Sullivan) to be allowed to see the diary (or diaries) were frustrated. 'Casement (through Gavan Duffy on his behalf) wrote a letter from ...prison to the Secretary for Home Affairs asking permission to answer these false and malicious insinuations, and for information as to the contents of this "diary". This letter was never answered. We later enquired from the secretary of Mr. Herbert Samuel, who was the Secretary for Home Affairs, and Mr. Samuel's secretary denied ever having received such a letter. Up to the time he died, Roger Casement never saw this "diary" or any part of its alleged contents' — (Michael Francis Doyle, an American attorney retained on Casement's defence team in a letter to Noyes, 12 December, 1956).

There are six questions:- i/ was Casement a traitor; ii/ was he a patriot; iii/ did he have homosexual tendencies; iv/ did he put these into practice; v/ was he a corrupt degenerate (not necessarily the same thing); vi/ were the diaries forged? Of these only two, v/, and vi/, receive sustained attention.

The answers to i/, was he a traitor, and ii/, was he a patriot, are obvious — No and Yes. Was he a homosexual? No one who knew him believed the allegations and are unanimous as to his extremely high sense of moral integrity. Other than the suspect 'diaries' there is no evidence from any source suggesting otherwise. The virtual impossibility of his practising the gross degeneracies at all, let alone with the frequency alleged, is demonstrable. On the other hand the opportunity, the motive, the will and the means for the British to have forged the diaries were there in abundance and the available evidence all points to it. No one who knew Casement, suspected — or, when alleged, believed — the charges.

* * * * *

COLLINS AND DE VALERA

The two dominant figures of the civil war, one on either side, were Michael Collins and Eamon de Valera and of the two Collins was, during that period at least, by far the more influential and powerful.

They were curiously alike in some ways; very different in others. The differences between them — of personality, character, background and outlook — have been so exaggerated and distorted by prejudice and partisanship that the similarities have been forgotten, but they were there. There was one very important difference between them at this time: besides being Chairman of the Provisional Government, Collins was also acknowledged as being responsible for the pro-Treaty armed forces, of which he later became Commander-in-Chief. He stepped down, in appearance only, as Chairman of the Provisional Government. When he did so, W.T. Cosgrave became acting Chairman. De Valera, on the other hand, had no influence whatever over the anti-Treaty forces, by whose leadership, indeed, he was, because of his attempts to make peace, considered an embarrassment once hostilities began.

But the principal area of difference was one of both background and outlook. Collins was a committed IRB officer: '...he almost wrecked his own cause by trying to capture a young and fast growing national movement by secret devices. He had great faith in the secret conclaves of the few, as if he despised the intelligence of the many', (Robert Brennan *Allegiance*, p. 153; see also Murphy, op. cit., pp. 97/98).

The IRB was the real power base for the influence that Collins exercised...Despite the objections of de Valera and Brugha, Collins was resolved to pursue his ambitions for Ireland within the IRB (Murphy, op. cit., p.97).

De Valera believed that the IRB was counter-productive. He was opposed to it as a vehicle for national progress, and he encouraged the Volunteers as an alternative power-base to that of the IRB. To what extent he was influenced by his realisation of the IRB's infiltration of the Volunteers before the Rising is speculative, but de Valera's respect for MacNeill never diminished. He was also concerned 'over Collins's high and even dominant position in the IRB ... Between the arrest of Griffith and the arrival of de Valera in Ireland (November to December 1920) Collins was acting president at a time when he was looked on in the IRB as their effective leader. De Valera was under the impression, in later years, that a strong element of the IRB would have preferred Collins to be President instead of himself' (Longford/O'Neill, p. 148). And, of course, in their eyes Collins, according to IRB policy, was the effective caretaker President of the Republic. This difference in attitude, dating from at least 1917, indicates that while such differences could be subordinated to a superior issue — independence — when that was achieved there would be, at least, powerful differing political forces under any new regime.

Nevertheless, during the civil war, Collins was probably closer in thinking and outlook to de Valera than to anyone on his own side (a point also made by Conor Cruise O'Brien, with whose idiosyncratic observations the author would normally find himself at odds — *Irish Times*, 4 December, 1981). This further indicates that the alliance between Griffith and Collins was one of power-expediency rather than principle. In a commentary at the McGill Summer School (August, 1985), Sean MacBride said: 'Collins and de Valera shared the leadership. Nobody dreamed of anybody else'. These two important comments have great bearing on any explanation of the Pact and its purpose.

Both were complex personalities. Collins, the 'born conspirator', was also a very physical man, intellectually and physically domineering, who achieved dominance by stealth and in secrecy (and was manifestly disturbed when these tools of which he was such a master were denied him), and by brute force (See Tom Barry's description of wrestling with Collins, *Guerrilla Days in Ireland*). He was enormously energetic and attracted intense loyalty as well as dislike that was almost as intense. The loyalty is easy to understand, the dislike less so. He could be very abrasive, not always with justification. Apart from this abrasiveness, often camouflaged by his great abilities, Collins's deviousness and capacity — amounting almost to a mania —

for intrigue and secrecy, alienated many. At times his attitude was the not uncommon one of great achievers, 'if you are not with me, then you are against me', even in matters beyond his authority and competence.

For much of his adult life he wore an aura of power and success — except, perhaps, for the period between September 1921 and June 1922. His character, both irritating and inspiring, won him hostility no less than friendship. When he was killed all were at one in acknowledging the loss of a great Irishman and patriot. In his book (*A Journey Through Ireland*), Peter Golden (a relation of Terence MacSwiney and by no means well-disposed to the pro-Treatyites), wrote: '... he was the only man sufficiently big and strong on the Free State (sic) side to compel his associates to carry out his ideas however inimical to his associates those ideas might be'.

During the civil war, in particular, Collins's relationships with Griffith, Brugha and de Valera — and to a lesser extent, Liam Lynch — were conflicting and critically important from time to time. For one period of ten days, between the death of Griffith on 12 August, 1922, and his own death on 22 August, Collins was far and away the most powerful and influential figure in the country, the only man who might have succeeded in bringing the civil war to an end. During that period he committed himself, as he himself said, to the quest for peace and was on his way to a meeting of his original power-base, the IRB, in Cork for that purpose when he was killed. Had he not been killed — who knows? Almost certainly the civil war would have ended sooner with less bloodshed and far less bitterness. Perhaps the Pact coalition Sinn Fein government would have emerged. Very likely the debacle of the Boundary Commission would have been avoided and the Northern Ireland statelet reduced to the four counties proposed to Collins by the British. A more cohesive national policy regarding the North would probably have existed, and, almost certainly, the divisive character of Irish politics during the twenties and thirties would have been much less.

De Valera was also powerful, though his strength was principally intellectual and he could be extremely subtle; so subtle, indeed, that there is sometimes a tendency to attribute artifice rather than precision to some of his thinking. Overall, of course, there is no doubt. Both men were, at that time, inexperienced in matters of statesmanship and political manoeuvring, particularly at international level. Contrary to the opinion sometimes advanced, de Valera disliked casuistry involving principle, though he could be very precise. For him a principle was important in itself. He might almost — but not truly — be said to have the motto '*principia, non homines*'. For him the appearance of fact could have little substance unless it agreed with the principle to which it was subordinate. Hence, for instance, his position over the oath of allegiance.

His consistency may be readily gauged. In 1915, as Adjutant of the Dublin Brigade and Commandant of the 3rd Battalion, de Valera was concerned to discover that some of his battalion officers, all IRB men, seemed to know more about HQ plans than he did. He took the matter up with Thomas MacDonagh, the Brigade Commander, and at his invitation joined the IRB when he learned that it controlled the Volunteer Executive. But he refused to attend IRB meetings.

In the run-up to the civil war de Valera was deeply conscious, not only of British intimidation and threats of war, but of the genuine dilemma facing the people as a result of the Treaty. There had been no election to give a mandate to the Treaty or to disestablishment of the Republic. Nevertheless he understood that a majority supported the Treaty. He later expressed it: 'The conflict between the two principles, majority rule on the one hand and the inalienability of the national sovereignty on the other, that was the dilemma of the Treaty' (See Eamon de Valera, *A National Policy*, Fianna Fail pamphlet No. 1, pp. 9-10). Even conceding that status to a local so-called 'majority' in Northern Ireland, that is precisely the constitutional dilemma there. During the civil war de Valera had little influence on the anti-Treaty Executive forces: '... the Republican part of the Army went on their way with complete indifference to any views of his'. (Longford/O'Neill, p.187).

The Irish Free State constitution, released on the morning of the 1922 election, created a constitutional problem for de Valera and the anti-Treatyites since it was far from being, as was promised by the Provisional Government, acceptable to republican principles. De Valera hoped that, by challenging parts of it before the Courts, it might be possible to prove the unacceptable clauses invalid, and proceed with the Pact coalition. But the call to help form a government never came. The civil war began two days before the new Dail was due to meet. When the Provisional Government did in fact meet the following 9 September it was clear that it was not the Third Dail and that it derived, not from the Second Dail, but from British Acts of Parliament.

In 1933, as head of the Irish Free State Government, de Valera gave an important statement of Ireland's position to the British Dominions Secretary, J. H. Thomas, in which he wrote: 'The Irish people have never sought membership of the Commonwealth. Their association with Great Britain and the Commonwealth has never been on their side a voluntary association. In every generation they have striven with such means as were at their disposal to maintain their right to existence as a distinct and independent nation, and whenever they yielded to British rule in any form they did so under the pressure of overwhelming material force' (Eamon de Valera to J.H. Thomas, 29 November, 1933, cited Longford/O'Neill, p. 303). He pointed out that the Treaty settlement and Partition had been imposed by force and could not be a basis for lasting friendship between the two countries.

Contrary to recent popular conditioned opinion, de Valera emerges as the leader with most common sense. He was not, as he stated 'a doctrinaire republican'. He certainly was not, like Griffith, a monarchist, nor was he prepared to unduly compromise on principle or purpose. What, then, did he stand for? The republic had been declared in 1916 and was adopted in 1919. Brugha was a dedicated republican. For Griffith, the monarchist, a republic was less than desirable. For Collins a republic was an objective — if it could be attained (and in this Collins and de Valera were alike). De Valera realised that a republic was one, but not the only, expression of a free democratic people. It was in that context of keeping options open that he stated that he was not a 'doctrinaire republican' and that once freedom was attained the Irish people might choose whatever system they wanted. This did not mean that he was not a republican. It did mean that he understood and accepted that there were alternatives. More importantly he understood that by acknowledging this when he did he was gaining freedom of movement. In this speech (Dail Eireann, 16 August, 1921) he also said: 'Irish independence could not be realised at the present time in any other way so suitably as through a Republic.'

For Collins principles were (in certain circumstances) subject to expediency, though perhaps not to the extent of Mulcahy's famous 'finessing with honour' approach. This was in accord with IRB tradition and, when considering Collins and his motives for doing what he did, it is always advisable to bear in mind that the IRB had, to a great extent, moulded his political and military outlook. It was the base on which he developed his strength and it had been, since 1919, very much his instrument. John Devoy always supported Collins (though this may have been as much for personal reasons as because of their common IRB heritage). And de Valera had long since rejected the IRB as 'unnecessary'. In fact, as he told the author in a private conversation, he had come to consider it a constitutional danger. And here, clearly, are grounds for a fundamental difference between himself and Collins.

Collins's approach might be summarised: he did not demur at expediency when he considered it necessary, if to do otherwise would — *in his opinion* — endanger substantial real gains, even though the latter were not in accord with the principle involved. And he did not mind if this were known. So, while these two men shared a common objective and a common principle relating to it, differ they would fundamentally, in certain circumstances, with regard to the means by which this objective might be achieved.

There was also, of course, a large element of personal rivalry between the two, exacerbated by Collins's inherent suspicion of those in a position to challenge his power and by de Valera's irritation with someone, however powerful, who challenged his position at a critical time.

Collins's relationship with Cathal Brugha became strained during the War of Independence due, in the main, to Collins's resentment of interference, however justifiable, from others in what he considered to be his own concern. As Director of Intelligence of the Army he was subordinate to Brugha (Minister for Defence and Chief-of-Staff of the Army[222] but could not tolerate Brugha's seniority — more correctly, the authority which his position invested in Brugha — and relations between them grew steadily more strained. Eventually they each tended to act unilaterally in some important matters, rather than cooperatively. And the want of adequate co-operation between them led to each, from time to time, trying to get his own way by means of *fait accompli* and reaction. But the tension between them, as in the case of de Valera and Collins, appears to have originated because of their conflicting attitudes to the IRB. It must be remembered that Collins was also at this time Head Centre of the IRB (until 1919 still of the view that it was the legitimate government of the Republic) and considered himself to be, in secret, president of that government as well. His extraordinary relationship with the extraordinary position of the IRB is, therefore, crucial to any appreciation of Collins and his sometimes apparently contradictory behaviour, particularly

from the signing of the Treaty onwards. He was also, of course, Minister for
Finance and, therefore, wore a ministerial hat equal to Brugha's. Accounts written
by devotees of Collins tend to place the blame for a deterioration in their relationship on Brugha and exonerate Collins. An objective assessment of the period,
of their respective positions and what was happening hardly supports such a one-
sided view. Although Minister for Finance Collins, as Director of Army
Intelligence, was subordinate to Brugha in that capacity; he was younger; he was
committed to a policy of — even internal — secrecy; he was both ambitious and
an opportunist and he was extraordinarily energetic and able.

Brugha, who had been a member of the IRB, was now opposed to it as a secret
organisation. He worked energetically to bring the Army under the control of the
Dail, a move to which Collins, in his turn, was opposed. It could mean a lessening of
IRB influence in the Army. Both of these things would have been reason enough for
strong disagreement between them. So, although they were committed to a
common objective, they saw its achievement in different ways. But there was also
an undeniable clash of personalities.

Murphy devotes some space to this, but also to the evident reasons for 'an
uncritical admiration of Collins which manifests itself in an antipathy to Brugha
and his part in the national movement' (op. cit., p.101). Murphy points out that
Brugha, Plunkett and Father Michael O'Flanagan were leaders among those
committed to the republican ideal as proclaimed in 1916 on which — to an
increasing extent and in the following order — de Valera, Collins and Griffith
were prepared to compromise. That is not to suggest that the others were
intransigent 'doctrinaire' republicans unwilling to accommodate any other
political viewpoint. It is, however, to say that that is how they have been
inaccurately portrayed. If they had not forced the issue of the Roscommon by-
election in 1917 with Plunkett as candidate, that critical win would have been
missed. Again, as Murphy points out, 'if they had not defended the Republic in
the debates before the Sinn Fein October convention the constitution may well
have reflected, to an even greater degree, the monarchical views of Griffith'
(ibid.).

With regard, specifically, to the relationship between Brugha and Collins he
reinforces what has been said above. He argues, convincingly, that the uncritical
adulation of Collins, but particularly the 'bad press' Brugha has received, is:

> In large part ... a reflection of the treatment accorded Brugha in the Beaslai
> biography of Collins (*Michael Collins and the Making of a new Ireland*, 2
> vols., 1926) ... Having been sworn into the IRB by Brugha ... Beaslai
> committed himself to Collins after the Rising. He questioned the judgement
> of Brugha [by then opposed to the principle of the IRB]; characterised it as
> 'sheer wrong-headedness'; and was critical of his 'taurine obstinacy'.
> Personal prejudice against Collins, Beaslai felt, had distorted Brugha's clarity
> of thought. Countless biographers of Collins have reproduced this damning
> picture of Brugha without justification. Brugha was critical of Collins because
> he refused to submit the secret organisation of the IRB to the democratic process
> after 1916. Brugha wanted the IRB to be disbanded: Collins resolutely

supported the reconstitution of the IRB as a separate entity from the Irish Volunteers. Brugha wanted the Volunteers to take the oath to the Republic and Dail Eireann. Collins did not. While it is reasonable to engage in debate as to the effectiveness and propriety of the means adopted — arguments for the democratic as opposed to the secret development of the nationalist movement — it would appear altogether unreasonable to attribute Brugha's dislike of Collins to merely personal considerations (Ibid.).

The growing differences of opinion between Collins and Griffith because of the Pact, and Collins's reluctance to start a shooting-war with his old Army friends and companions, demonstrate another facet of these tension-riddled relationships. There is little doubt that Collins was unsympathetic to Griffith's 'Kings, Lords and Commons' idea. But he had committed himself to the Treaty by signing it, and he could not make significant use of the IRB without also having the support of one or other constitutional group. In one sense the period from January to June, and the Pact which emerged from it, might be seen as an accommodation between the Head Centre of the IRB and the democratic republican constitutionalists.

Collins's relationship with Griffith also indicated the extent to which he could differ from his colleagues and at the same time influence them. There can be little doubt that Collins had much less in common with the vast bulk of pro-Treaty civil support than with his former comrades. Tom Barry has paid tribute to the genius of Collins in his book (op. cit.), but he also made this observation: 'Big hearted and generous, as I was personally to experience, this energetic and restless man seemed to be forever battling with something or someone, even with himself ...'

MacBride made a strong case that Collins was engaging in activities of which some of his Provisional Government colleagues disapproved. Above all, like Brugha before them, they were understandably irritated by his tendency to act unilaterally on his own initiative. Few of his government colleagues approved of the Pact.

Three critical matters bore on the outbreak of civil war. First was the Pact, which offered a solution acceptable to both sides in Sinn Fein, but which was opposed by the British. Second was the Constitution of the Irish Free State, subordinate to the Treaty, but yet — according to the provisional authorities — capable of an interpretation sufficiently broad to encompass and satisfy essential republican objections. Third, and perhaps most significant, was the British hostility to the Army garrison in the Four Courts which, they evidently (and wrongly) believed, constituted the principal source of opposition to implementation of the Treaty and also the most likely source of a republican administration should the provisional government be overthrown. They also, correctly, believed that the Four Courts garrison was supplying weapons to Army units in the north, though they may not have been aware of Collins's involvement in this. In addition there were incidents such as the shooting of Wilson that provided the 'excuse' for the attack on the Four Courts.

Having achieved the Pact with so much effort and in the face of so much powerful opposition, why did Collins break it? Clearly he did so under, on the one hand, the threat from London that the British would attack the Four Courts if he did not and, on the other, in the belief that he could limit hostilities to a local action against that garrison and so preserve control. That he anticipated nation-wide civil war as a result is most unlikely.

As far as I am concerned, I accept that Collins regarded the Truce as merely a pause in the war [against the British] and that the fighting would resume as soon as we were ready and had replenished our armoury. I do think that this was also Michael Collins's view and that at that period he was seeking to retrieve the ground that he had lost by signing the Treaty (Sean MacBride, private conversation, August 1987).

Had the constitution been published ten days before the election, the uproar in Ireland when it was learned that it was much less favourable to the republic than indicated might have reinforced the Pact, rather than anything else.

Collins met Lloyd George in London on the day before he made the Cork speech breaking the Pact. He was unmistakably, by now, in the straitjacket of the Treaty. The only positive option open to him, and one that was in character, was to acquire as much power and control as possible in order to reunite the country on a republican front within the confines then limiting him. This appears to be what he tried to do. In this situation, and instead of the coalition which might have staved it off, began the series of events which precipitated civil war and which led to Collins's death at Beal na mBlath less than two months later.

Beal na mBlath

Collins set out from Dublin on 20 August 1922 on his renewed inspection tour of the south, interrupted by Griffith's death and funeral. *En route* he called into Portlaoise (then Maryborough) Jail to see Tom Malone[223] an anti-Treaty prisoner, and then continued his journey. Clearly, as may be judged from the above footnote, it was his intention to try to make contact with Tom Hales (IRB man and anti-Treaty Brigadier, 3rd Cork Brigade), and he had instructed Brigadier Sean Hales of his own forces (Tom's brother), to try to make contact with his brother to that end.

On the morning of August 22 he set out from Cork for Macroom. He had arranged a meeting for that night in Desmond's Hotel in Cork which would, he hoped, be attended by neutral IRB officers and IRB officers from both sides, including Tom Hales. He had also instructed Colonel Frank Thornton to contact Liam Lynch (also an IRB man), but Thornton was ambushed on his way south. That same day a meeting had been called of officers from the First Southern Division of the Executive forces. It was the first divisional staff meeting to have been held since the fall of Cork twelve days earlier and it included division, brigade and other staff officers. The venue was the house of Mrs. Murray in Beal na mBlath. It was officers from this meeting, and not a line column, which attacked Michael Collins's convoy later that day.

From that point onwards until Collins was killed there was a strange and mordant series of coincidences related to this major one. About 0900 that morning Collins's convoy of motor-cyclist, Crossley tender (or according to some reports two such), open touring car and armoured-car, passed the house of Denis Long, where some of the anti-Treaty officers had spent the night, stopping outside to ask a pedestrian (who happened to be an Executive sentry) the route to Bandon. The sentry had hidden his rifle when he saw the convoy approaching. He recognised Collins. When he reported the incident a decision was taken to set up an ambush for the convoy on its return journey. The ambush was planned for ten hours before it took place; it was directed against one particular column and it had one particular objective, to kill or capture Collins, preferably the latter.

The twenty-five or so men who comprised the ambush party occupied a bohereen (minor roadway) on the western side of the Beal na mBlath/ Newceston road and running parallel to it over distances ranging from one hundred to two hundred and fifty yards and at an elevation of between thirty and eighty feet. They had a good field of fire. The extended U-shaped bohereen connected with the road at two points about eight hundred yards apart. The officers lay waiting in their positions throughout the day, but nothing happened. As dusk approached Brigadier Tom Hales arrived late and immediately stood down the ambush *before consulting with his own superiors*, who had laid the ambush. On the face of it it was an extraordinary thing to do. Hales also ordered the officers to return to Murray's, where Lynch was, to resume the meeting.

Jim Hurley and Tom Hales were walking towards Beal na mBlath when they discovered the ambush. Hales criticised the ambushers and ordered them off. They continued on their way towards Murrays. They met Deasy and Hales and Hurley returned to help clear the road block. Shortly afterwards the men on the road heard shooting (Lt. General M. J. Costello, who later, with Tom Barry, made a detailed examination and survey of the ambush site, in a private conversation with the author).

This is an important statement. Hales arrived late and may not have been in the vicinity earlier. It suggests that he was either unaware of the Beal na mBlath meeting that morning (highly unlikely), or that he was otherwise occupied on something he considered of greater importance. It also suggests either that he was unaware of Collins's anxiety to contact him for the Cork meeting or that he was going to the Beal na mBlath meeting first with the intention of a briefing on, and being briefed for, the Cork meeting. What is abundantly clear is that he must have had a very strong reason for overriding his superior officers and standing the ambush down. Moreover he displayed a sense of urgency about this, as he hurried back to help clear the road-block.

There are three possible reasons why Hales might have ordered the ambush to stand down. Because he

(a) disagreed with it in principle,

(b) wanted to get on with the meeting; or,

(c) did not, for important and pressing reasons, want it to take place and run the risk of Collins being either captured or killed.

It is hard to credit that a soldier, even a brigadier, would, on foot of either (a) or (b), countermand the orders of his superiors who were close by without first consulting them.

Except for six — the four who remained to dismantle a mine and a road-block, and Hales and Hurley — all the men retired. They never resumed the meeting. Firing from the rear broke out before they reached Murrays. Collins's convoy had reappeared and the men on the hill fired the warning to alert those on the road that they were in danger from it. Thus began the encounter at Beal na mBlath.

There are three eye-witness accounts of the ambush from the pro-Treaty side — by General Emmet Dalton, M.B.Corry, driver of the touring car (a Leyland-Thomas straight-eight-cylinder), and John O'Connell — and two accounts from the anti-Treaty side, from Pete Kearney and Tom Kelleher/Liam Deasy[224]. All have appeared in print before. There are differing versions of the first three, which differ among themselves. Meda Ryan (*The Day Michael Collins was shot*, Dublin, 1989) gives a very detailed account of the ambush. Some of what she asserts is unsourced and is at variance with existing accounts, but, if what she claims is correct, it throws some interesting additional light on the action .

The men left behind to cover the rear and dismantle the road-block and mine (according to a statement shown by Tom Kelleher to the author many years ago and published by J. Anthony Gaughan (*The Irish Times*, August 20, 1988), were Kelleher himself, Dan Holland, Denis 'Sonny' Neil and John O'Callaghan, joined by Hales and Hurley.

When the motor-cycle outrider of the convoy came round a bend on the road he saw the dray which had been used to block the road and immediately skidded to a halt. He was wounded in the subsequent exchanges. The convoy stopped on Collins's command and the action continued for some time. There are some discrepancies in accounts given many years later, in particular with respect to Ryan's very detailed account. The author was the first to publish (in 1966) an account of the engagement from the anti-Treaty side. It is virtually certain that the shot which killed Collins was fired by Sonny Neil, who was an ex British Army marksman. His statement, given to the author independently by General Costello, Tom Barry and Tom Kelleher, emphasises that not all six men were able to get involved in the action because the constant heavy fire made it difficult to get their heads up to fire, let alone get off an aimed shot, but that he (Neil) was able to do so and he fired an aimed shot at what he thought was a head coming out of the turret of the armoured car.

In fact what he saw was the round[225] turret of the armoured car rising as McPeake, the machine-gunner, cleared his weapon. This is consistent with most accounts and the lull thus caused enabled Neil to take aim and fire at the 'head'. McPeake later deposed to the anti-Treatyites that as he raised the turret-lid a bullet struck it. 'I raised the hatch-cover to get some air and as I did so, whang, a bullet hit a lug on the cover and blew it off'[226].

By this time Collins was to the rear, that is to the south, of the armoured-car, and facing the enemy. He was, nevertheless, struck behind the right ear. This seems an impossibility unless a) he turned his head so far round as to be looking behind him at the other side of the road, where there was a small cliff; b) he was shot from that direction or, c) he was struck by a ricochet. Given the description of the wound by, amongst others Dr. Oliver St.John Gogarty, who expressed his belief that it was a ricochet wound, "c" seems the most likely explanation. As to whether it was the bullet itself or the lug blown off the turret is an open question. Kelleher's statement says that Neil's shot first struck the road, but Neil does not mention this and McPeake's testimony is pretty conclusive as to the shot having struck the armoured car[227]. Of the six men in the ambush position only four managed to engage the enemy with any consistency.

The initial action lasted about twenty minutes. Then there was a lull, but not a complete cessation of fire. The reason for the lull is twofold. Of the six men on the hill, two were re-loading, two were withdrawing in a direct line across country and two were trying to give covering fire. From the other side the reason for the 'lull' was the stoppage of the Vickers gun, which, apart from a change of belt, might have been caused by any one of four generally accepted stoppages[228].

It is a fact that Collins was discovered dead shortly after several of those present on both sides claim to have heard a single shot. This fact gives rise to two questions.

1. What was the source of the shot? and

2. Could it have been the shot which killed Collins?

The answer to the second question is that it could and probably was. It was not, as is sometimes alleged, the last shot in the action by a long way. So far as the answer to the first question is concerned all the available evidence points clearly to only one conclusion, the one we have already surmised; that it was Sonny Neil's shot which ricochetted off the armoured car and killed Collins.

There are six, and only six, possible sources for the fatal bullet — excluding the bizarre notion that Collins took his own life. These are:
That he was shot either (a) deliberately or (b) accidentally

1. By the enemy

2. By McPeake

3. By some other of his own unit.

It is virtually beyond doubt that he was shot by the enemy and that while it was an aimed shot, it was neither aimed at Collins, nor did the anti-Treatyites know the bullet had hit Collins. It is also established that at this point a bullet — very probably the same (there is no evidence of any other shot from the anti-Treatyites at that point) — hit the armoured-car turret and blew a lug off it.

An autopsy was carried out in Shankiel Hospital in Cork. The body was examined by Drs. Leo Ahearn and Michael Riordan. Ahearn states (Meda Ryan, op. cit., p. 139): 'The wound was a large gaping wound to the right of the poll. There was no other wound. There was no exit wound ... only the large entrance wound. There was definitely no wound in the forehead ... It was important for me to check the wound, and to establish the cause of death...'. Dr. Riordan maintained: 'There was no exit wound. I'm certain there was only one, deep wound ... part of the head was blown off...' The medical report itself appears to have been destroyed, perhaps when Collins documents were destroyed at the first domestic change of government in 1932[229], an appalling destruction of unpublished documents relating to Collins.

During the lull Collins had moved twice. He left the first position he took up and where he had been for up to twenty minutes, and moved some distance (estimated at between fifty and a hundred yards) back to the armoured car from the cover of which he observed the enemy positions. After some minutes at the armoured car he moved again, about fifteen yards (according to Dalton). He was now alone and at the extreme eastern end of his force. He was in this position, lying down, when he was shot. Why Collins made these unnecessary moves is open to conjecture.

Where was de Valera during this time? He, too, had stayed near Beal na mBlath the previous night hoping to see Lynch and Deasy to try to persuade them to come to terms. He spent the night at Sullivan's of Gurranreacht with his aide, Jimmy Flynn, Sean Hyde and Liam Deasy. During the morning he heard that Collins had passed through Beal na mBlath before he reached there. Recalling that morning he said[230]; 'My impression is that he was in a car with a driver and that we were the stronger party.' Asked what he would have done had he met Collins at Beal na mBlath, he said: 'We could have come to some arrangement. I would have taken him with me,' meaning he would have taken him as his prisoner. He was not then aware of the armoured car and the considerable escort.

De Valera then retraced his steps to Ballingeary where he crossed the River Lee at about 11 a.m., travelling from there to Ballyvourney where he crossed the River Sullane. From there he went to Mourne Abbey where he stayed with the Creedons of Clogheen, Lashabuidhe. Next day he went on to Ballyhooley with George Power's column and from there to Glanworth where he stayed with the Barrys. It was here, on the night of the 23rd, that he learned of Collins's death. The man who brought the message was pleased with his information. The shock brought de Valera to his feet. 'It's come to a very bad pass' he said, 'when Irishmen congratulate themselves on the shooting of a man like Michael Collins.'

After Collins's death a shock-wave that the civil war did nothing to diminish hit the country. The unspoken reality beforehand had been that he was the one man who might have been able to bring an end to hostilities. His death changed all that.

Appendix One

THE NORTH BEGAN
Eoin MacNeill
(From *An Claidheamh Soluis* 1st November, 1913, p.6)

A WONDERFUL STATE OF THING HAS HAS COME TO PASS IN ULSTER. Three distinct parties, each too weak to be of much force in politics, have ranged themselves against Home Rule. These are the Orange industrial workers, mainly Church of Ireland Protestants; the Presbyterian rural community; and the remnant of the feudal aristocracy. The first two elements have been drawn together by what is called the 'No-Popery' sentiment. This fact has been turned to account by the third element, and, when dual ownership, land purchase, and the abolition of Grand Jury government had, apparently consigned Feudalism to the incurable ward, a combination of landlords, land-agents, land-lawyers, and their adherents, in return for conferring the stamp of 'respectability' on 'No-Popery' sentiment has managed to secure the control of the an alliance of wage earners and rent-payers. That this is literally true may be verified by anyone who consults the newspaper files for (1) the names of those who took the initiative in the organisation of the Ulster 'Unionist Clubs', and (2) the names of the numerous personnel of the Ulster 'Provisional Government'. To attain such an ascendancy seems almost a miracle of political adroitness, but there is another side to the picture.

The Parliament Act deprived Irish Feudalism of what hitherto had been its chief resource, the effective support of British Feudalism in the legislature. Then the masters of the Ulster triple alliance decided on an extraordinary step, the enrolment of a Volunteer force manned by their 'allies,' the 'Unionist' wage-earners and rent-payers. Of the three 'allied' forces, one only, the managing element, is really 'Unionist'. Intermarriage, social intercourse, and self-interest, unite the decaying Feudal aristocracy of Ireland to the still opulent Feudal aristocracy of Great Britain; but history shows and observation confirms that the Orange democracy and the Presbyterian rural party are home rulers in principle and in essence. The loyalty of Orangemen to the 'Crown,' the 'Constitution,' the 'Empire,' and the 'Union,' arise out of the notion that these entities secure them in possession of Home Rule and a little more. But whenever any abatement of that little more seems likely to come from Constitutional developments, loyalty and affection instantaneously put on a different face. The Presbyterian country party, as its history shows, though slower to move and understand, is not less radically attached to Home Rule than the Orange party.

The skill of the Feudal element in obtaining the lead is more than counterbalanced by their fatuity in starting among the essential Home Rulers of their present following the most decisive move towards Irish autonomy that has been made since O'Connell invented constitutional agitation. The Ulster Volunteer movement is essentially and obviously a Home Rule movement. It claims, no doubt, to hold Ireland 'for the Empire'; but really it is no matter whether Ireland is to be held for the empire or for the empyrean, against the Pope, against John Redmond, or against the Man in the Moon. What matters is, *by whom Ireland is to be held*. Lord Lansdowne, speaking recently against Home Rule, spoke fine old medieval words, 'We have Ireland and we mean to keep her.' The Ulster Volunteer reply, '*We* are going to hold Ireland — of course *for* your Lordships.'

The true meaning of this extraordinary development is dawning painfully on English Unionists. They are beginning to understand that Sir Edward Carson has knocked the bottom out of Unionism. To add to their comfort, a Mr. Arnold White has been proving in elaborate detail that the the present available resources of the British army are not sufficient to put down the Volunteer movement in four of the thirty-two Irish counties. In any case it appears that the British Army cannot now be used to prevent enrolment, drilling, and reviewing of Volunteers in Ireland. There is nothing to prevent the other twenty-eight counties from calling into existence citizen forces to hold Ireland 'for the Empire.' It was precisely with this object that the Volunteers of 1782 were enrolled, and they became the instrument of establishing self-government and Irish prosperity. Their disbanding led to the destruction alike of self-government and of prosperity, and the opportunity of rectifying a capital error of this sort does not always come again to nations.

The more responsible section of English Unionist opinion has taken alarm and is tentatively drawing away from the two-edged sword of 'Ulster.' But even the rashest English Unionists are clearly in great uneasiness; and while they threaten with Ulster, they are openly beseeching the other side to find them a way out of their mess. Dick Steele's creditors once sent him a deputation, as they said, 'to discuss his difficulties with him.'; 'Pardon me, gentlemen,' was his remark, 'your difficulties, not mine.' Sir Edward Carson proclaimed that, in launching his new Ulster policy, he had not counted the cost. It looks like it.

The moral of the story is that, in public movements, every element of sham and insincerity is a mortgage given to destiny. I do not say that Sir Edward Carson is insincere. Probably he, too, like the Orangemen and the Presbyterians, is at heart a Home Ruler, and thinks that the sort of Home Rule that he wants is best guaranteed by the semblance of government from outside. His English allies, however, hoped that his master-move would do effective electioneering work for them, and the fact that, since he 'drew the sword' in Ulster, he has devoted most of his energies to a political tour in Great Britain shows that he has lent himself to the game. That does not pay. In Ulster, too, the local managers, the Feudal Remnant, who have good reason not to be earnest when they make a military array of wage-earners and rent-payers, thus mounting and loading a machine gun whose mechanism they cannot hope to control, have shown their hand and been found evidently bluffing. Their 'Provisional Government', with its pompous detail of phantom departments, put on paper in secret session at a Belfast club, is the most ridiculous piece of political histrionics ever staged. A parcel of schoolboys would be ashamed to own it. In order to pretend strength they arranged to hold reviews in such overwhelmingly Nationalist districts as Omagh, Raphoe, Armagh, Newry and Kilkeel, but perhaps the crowning shame was the announcement of an insurance fund of £1,000,000. The real insurance fund for real war is fighting material, men, arms, ammunition, transport, ships, fortifications; and those who are in earnest about war will not devote a penny to any other sort of insurance. All this shows that Feudalism in Ireland is doating as well as decaying, and that the cheap cuteness that can play successfully upon religious fanaticism is no proof of any form of any higher intelligence.

English Unionists realise, explicitly or instinctively, that the Ulster Volunteers have scuttled the ship; some of them, sooner than admit their discomfiture, are hankering after the separation from Ireland of what they are pleased to call 'homogeneous Ulster,' namely the four eastern counties. Not a single responsible man and no assembly of men in Ireland has authorised this proposal. All Nationalist opinion and any Unionist opinion that has been expressed is strongly hostile to it. And for very good reason. *There is no 'Homogeneous Ulster.'*

It is impossible to separate from Ireland the city that Saint Patrick founded, the city that Saint Columba founded, or the tombs of Patrick, Brigid and Columba. They would defy and nullify the attempt. It is impossible to separate from Ireland the 'frontier town' of Newry, the men of South Down, Norman and Gael, the Gaelic stock of the Fews that hold 'the Gap of the North,' the glensmen of South Derry, or North Antrim. If there were any possibility of civil war, if civil war were assured, not to speak of its being insured, these districts alone would hold immovable all the resources of General — I believe — Richardson. There are besides the 100,000 Nationalist Home Rulers of Belfast, and others, Protestants, Catholic, Orange and Presbyterian, in every corner of the four counties, who under any change of government are certain to 'revert to type.' With what facility they have fallen in with the idea of holding Ireland — for the Empire!

It is evident that the only solution now possible is for the Empire either to make terms with Ireland or to let Ireland go her own way. In any case, it is manifest that all Irish people, Unionist as well as Nationalist, are determined to have their own way in Ireland. On that point, and it is the main point, Ireland is united. It is not to follow, and it will not follow, that any part of Ireland, majority or minority, is to interfere with the liberty of any other part. Sir Edward Carson may yet, at the head of his Volunteers 'march to Cork.' If so, their progress will probably be accompanied by the greetings of ten times their number of National Volunteers, and Cork will give them a hospitable and memorable reception. Some years ago, speaking at the Toome Feis, in the heart of 'homogeneous Ulster,' I said that the day would come when men of every creed and party would come and join in celebrating the Defence of Derry and the Battle of Benburb. That day is nearer than I expected.

EOIN MAC NEILL

Appendix Two

Casement's open-letter from New York.
New York, 17 September 1914

A S AN IRISHMAN and one who has been identified with the Irish Volunteer movement since it began, I feel it my duty to protest against the claim now being put forward by the British Government that, because that Government has agreed with its political opponents to 'place the Home Rule Bill on the Statute Book' and to defer its operation until after the war and until an 'Amending Bill' to profoundly modify its provisions has been introduced and passed, Irishmen in return should enlist in the British Army and aid the allied Asiatic and European powers in a war against a people who have never wronged Ireland. The British Liberal party has been publicly pledged for twenty-eight years to give self-government to Ireland. It has not yet fulfilled that pledge. Instead it now offers to sell, at a very high price, a wholly hypothetical and indefinite form of partial internal control of certain specified Irish services, if, in return for this promissory note (payable after death), the Irish people will contribute their blood, their honour and their manhood in a war that in no wise concerns them. Ireland has no quarrel with the German people or just cause of offence against them ... Ireland has no blood to give to any land, to any cause but that of Ireland. Our duty as a Christian people is to abstain from bloodshed, and our duty as Irishmen is to give our lives for Ireland. Ireland needs all her sons. In the space of sixty-eight years her population has fallen by far over 4,000,000 souls, and in every particular of national life she shows a steady decline of vitality. Were the Home Rule Bill all that is claimed for it and were it freely given today, to come into operation tomorrow, instead of being offered for sale on terms of exchange that only a fool would accept, it would be the duty of Irishmen to save their strength and manhood for the trying tasks before them, to build up from a depleted population the fabric of a ruined national life.

Ireland has suffered at the hands of British administrators a more prolonged series of evils, deliberately inflicted, than any other community of civilized men. To-day when no margin of vital strength remains for vital tasks at home, when its fertile fields are reduced by set design to producing animals and not men, the remnant of our people are being urged to lay down their lives in foreign fields, in order that the great and inordinately wealthy communities may grow greater and richer by the destruction of a rival's trade and industry. Had this war the highest moral aim in view, as its originators claim for it, it would still be the duty of Irishmen to keep out of it.

If Irish blood is to be 'the seal that will bring all Ireland together in one nation and in liberties equal and common to all' then let that blood be shed in Ireland, where alone it can be righteously shed to secure those liberties. It was not Germany who destroyed the national liberties of the Irish people, and we cannot recover the national life struck down in our own land by carrying fire and sword into another land.

The cause of Ireland is greater than the cause of any party; higher than the worth of any man; richer in its poverty than all the riches of Empire. If to-day we barter that cause in a sordid bargain, we shall prove ourselves unworthy of freedom — a dwindling race of cravens from whose veins the blood of manhood has been drained. If to now fight is our duty, then let us fight on that soil where so many generations of slain Irishmen lie in honour and fame. Let our graves be that patriot grass whence alone the corpse of Irish nationality can spring to life. Ireland will be 'false to her history, to every consideration of honour, good faith and self-interest' if she now willingly responds to the call of the British government to send her brave sons and faithful hearts to fight in a cause that has no glint of chivalry or gleam of generosity in all its line of battle. If this be a war for the 'small nationalities', as its planners term it, then let it begin, for one small nationality, at home.

Speaking as one of those who helped to found the Irish Volunteers, I say, in their name, that no Irishman fit to bear arms in the cause of his country's freedom can join the allied millions now attacking Germany in a war that at best concerns Ireland not at all and that can only add fresh burdens and establish a new drain, in the interest of another community, upon a people that has already been bled to the verge of Death.

Roger Casement

Appendix Three

Proclamation of the Republic, 1916

POBLACHT NA h-EIREANN
The Provisional Government
of the
Irish Republic

To the People of Ireland

IRISHMEN AND IRISHWOMEN: In the name of God and of the dead generations from which she received her old tradition of manhood, Ireland, through us, summons her children to her flag and strikes for her freedom.

Having organized and trained her manhood through her secret revolutionary organization, the Irish Republican Brotherhood, and through her open military organizations, the Irish Volunteers and the Irish Citizen Army, having patiently perfected her discipline, having resolutely waited for the right moment to reveal itself, she now seizes that moment and, supported by her exiled children in America and by gallant allies in Europe, but relying first on her own strength, she strikes in full confidence of victory.

We declare the right of the people of Ireland to the ownership of Ireland and to the unfettered control of Irish destinies, to be sovereign and indefeasible. The long usurpation has not extinguished the right, nor can it ever be extinguished except by the destruction of the Irish people. In every generation of the Irish people they have asserted their right to national freedom and sovereignty; six times during the past three hundred years they have asserted it in arms. Standing on that fundamental right and again asserting it in arms in the face of the world, we hereby proclaim the Irish Republic as a Sovereign Independent State, and we pledge our lives and the lives of our comrades-in-arms to the cause of its freedom, of its welfare and of its exaltation among nations.

The Irish Republic is entitled to, and hereby claims, the allegiance of every Irishman and Irishwoman. The Republic guarantees religious and civil liberty, equal rights and equal opportunities to all citizens and declares its resolve to pursue the happiness and prosperity of the whole nation equally and oblivious of the differences carefully fostered by an alien government, which have divided a minority from the majority in the past.

Until our arms have brought the opportune moment for the establishment of a permanent National Government, representative of the whole people of Ireland, and elected by the suffrages of all her men and women, the Provisional Government, hereby constituted, will administer the civil and military affairs of the Republic, in trust for her people, We place the cause of the Irish Republic under the protection of the Most High God, Whose blessings we invoke upon our arms, and we pray that no one who serves that cause will dishonour it by cowardice, inhumanity or rapine. In this supreme hour the Irish nation must, by its valour and discipline and by the readiness of its children to sacrifice themselves for the common good, prove itself worthy of the august destiny to which it is called.

Signed on behalf of the Provisional Government, *Thomas J. Clarke, Sean Mac Diarmada, P. H. Pearse, James Connolly, Thomas Mac Donagh, Eamonn Ceannt, Joseph Plunkett.*

Appendix Four

The Sinn Féin Constitution
(As adopted by the Ard-Fhéis which met in Dublin on October 25th, 1917)

I

1. The name of this organisation shall be Sinn Féin.

2. Sinn Féin aims at securing the International recognition of Ireland as an independent Irish Republic.

Having achieved that status the Irish people may be referendum freely choose their own form of Government.

3. This object shall be attained through the Sinn Féin Organisation.

4. WHEREAS no law made without the authority and consent of the Irish people is or ever can be binding on their conscience.

Therefore in accordance with the Resolution of Sinn Féin adopted in Convention, 1905, a Constituent Assembly shall be convoked, comprising persons chosen by the Irish Constituencies as the supreme national authority to speak and act in the name of the Irish people and to devise and formulate measures for the welfare of the whole people of Ireland.

Such as:
(a) The introduction of a Protective System for the Irish industries and Commerce by combined action of the Irish County Councils, Urban Councils, Rural Councils, Poor Law Boards, Harbour Boards and other bodies directly responsible to the Irish people.

(b) The establishment and maintenance under the direction of a National Assembly or other authority approved by the people of Ireland of an Irish Consular Service for the advancement of Irish Commerce and Irish interests generally.

(c) The re-establishment of an Irish Mercantile Marine to facilitate direct trading between Ireland and the countries of Continental Europe, America, Africa, and the Far East.

(d) The industrial survey of Ireland and the development of its mineral resources under the auspices of a National Assembly or other national authority approved by the people of Ireland.

(e) The establishment of a National Stock Exchange.

(f) The creation of a National Civil Service, embracing all the employees of the County Councils, Rural Councils, Poor Law Boards, Harbour Boards, and other bodies responsible to the Irish people, by the institution of a common national qualifying examination and a local competitive examination (the latter at the discretion of the local bodies).

(g) The establishment of Sinn Féin Courts of Arbitration for the speedy and satisfactory adjustment of disputes.

(h) The development of transit by rail, road and water, of waste lands for the national benefit by a national authority approved by the people of Ireland.

(i) The development of the Irish Sea Fisheries by National Assembly or other National authority approved by the people of Ireland.

(j) The reform of education, to render its basis national and industrial by the compulsory teaching of the Irish language. Irish history and Irish agricultural and manufacturing potentialities in the primary system, and, in addition, to elevate to a position of dominance in the University system Irish agriculture and economics.

(k) The abolition of the Poor Law System and substitution in its stead of adequate outdoor relief to the aged and infirm, and the employment of the able-bodied in the reclamation of waste lands, afforestation and other national and reproductive works.

II

A special meeting of the Executive may be summoned on three days' notice by the President on requisition presented to him signed by six members of the Executive specifying the object for which the meeting is called.

In case of an urgent emergency the President shall call all members of the Executive to an urgency meeting, and may take acton in the name of the Executive in case he secures the approval of an absolute majority of the entire Executive. The action taken is to be reported for confirmation at next ordinary meeting of the Executive.

III

That where Irish resources are being developed, or where industries exist, Sinn Féiners should make it their business to secure that workers are paid a living wage.

The the equality of men and women in this Organisation be emphasised in all speeches and leaflets.

Appendix Five

The Declaration of Independence

DECLARATION OF INDEPENDENCE

Whereas the Irish people is by right a free people:

And whereas for seven hundred years the Irish people has never ceased to repudiate and has repeatedly protested in arms against foreign usurpation;

And whereas English rule in this country is, and always has been, based upon force and fraud and maintained by military occupation against the declared will of the people;

And whereas the Irish Republic was proclaimed in Dublin on Easter Monday, 1916, by the Irish Republican Army, acting on behalf of the Irish people;

And whereas the Irish people is resolved to secure and maintain its complete independence in order to promote the common weal, to re-establish justice, to provide for future defence, to ensure peace at home and good will with all nations, and to constitute a national policy based upon the people's will, with equal rights for every citizen;

And whereas at the threshold of a new era in history the Irish electorate has in the General Election of December 1918, seized the first occasion to declare by an overwhelming majority its allegiance to the Irish Republic;

Now therefore, we, the elected Representatives of the ancient Irish people in national Parliament assembled, do in the name of the Irish Nation, ratify the establishment of the Irish Republic and pledge ourselves and our people to make this declaration effective by every means at our command;

We ordain that the elected Representatives of the Irish people alone have power to make laws binding on the people of Ireland, and that the Irish Parliament is the only Parliament to which that people will give its allegiance;

We solemnly declare foreign government in Ireland to be an invasion of our national right which we will never tolerate, and we demand the evacuation of our country by the English Garrison;

We claim for our national independence the recognition and support of every free nation in the world, and we proclaim that independence to be a condition precedent to international peace thereafter;

In the name of the Irish people we humbly submit our destiny to Almighty God Who gave our fathers the courage and determination to persevere through long centuries of a ruthless tyranny, and strong in the justice of the cause which they have handed down to us, we ask His Divine blessing on this the last stage of the struggle we have pledged ourselves to carry through to freedom.

Appendix Six

Irish Draft Treaty 'A'

THIS IS THE ROUGH DRAFT of the External Association Proposal, embodying ideas and principles agreed upon by the Republican Cabinet, which formed the basis of the Irish offer during the London Conference in 1921.

(Outlines for *ideas* and *principles* only. Wording tentative and rough. Expert draftsmen will be engaged for the wording and form when the principles are agreed upon.)

Recital. Great Britain having, in the name of the British Commonwealth, invited Ireland to enter into association with her and the other states of that Commonwealth, and Great Britain and Ireland being equally desirous to end the ruinous secular conflict between them and to secure the mutual benefits of concord and amity, have resolved to conclude a Treaty of Settlement, Accommodation, and Association, and for that purpose have appointed, the Government of Great Britain ... the Elected Government of Ireland ... who, after communicating to each other their respective full powers, found in good and due form, agree upon the following:

Article I. Great Britain and the partner states of the British Commonwealth recognize Ireland as a sovereign independent state and Great Britain renounces all claims to govern or to legislate for Ireland.

Article II. Ireland agrees to become an external associate of the states of the British Commonwealth. As an associate Ireland's status shall be that of equality with the sovereign partner states of the Commonwealth and Ireland shall be so separately represented in British Imperial Council – Great Britain, Canada, Australia, etc. – and shall be so recognized by those several states.

Article III. In virtue of Ireland's association with the states of the British Commonwealth, citizens of Ireland shall enjoy in each of these states the same rights and privileges as if they were natural born citizens of these states, and reciprocally the citizens of each of these states shall enjoy in Ireland the rights of natural born Irish citizens.

Article IV. Irish citizens resident in the states of the British Commonwealth, and reciprocally citizens of these states, resident in Ireland, shall be excepted from all compulsory service in the military, naval of police forces of the states in which they are resident and from all contributions which may be imposed in lieu of personal service.

Article V. Ireland accepts and the British Commonwealth guarantees the perpetual neutrality of Ireland and the integrity and inviolability of Irish territory; and both in its own interest and in friendly regard tot he strategic interests of the British Commonwealth binds itself to enter no compact, and to take no action, nor permit any action to be taken, inconsistent with the obligation of preserving its own neutrality and inviolability and to repel with force any attempt to violate its territory or to use its territorial waters for warlike purposes.

Article VI. Financial article, to be drafted by *Minister of Finance.*

Article VII. Trade article, to be drafter by *Minister of Economic Affairs.*

Article VIII. Constitution and Ulster Question – to be drafted by Mr. Griffith.

Article IX. Within fourteen days of the signing of this Treaty, the British Government shall evacuate from Ireland all Military forces and all 'auxiliary police' and all members of their police forces in Ireland recruited since the 1st day of January, 1919.

Article X. This Treaty shall be ratified. It shall be submitted on the side of Ireland to *Dáil Éireann*, and on the side of Great Britain to the Parliament of Westminster. Should ratification not ensue, or should either Parliament so determine, it shall be submitted to the peoples of the respective countries, and if the Treaty shall be approved by a majority of the electors, it shall be deemed to have been ratified by the peoples of these respective countries.

For the ratification by the states of the British Commonwealth other than Great Britain, this Treaty shall be communicated by the Government of Great Britain, to the Governors of the Dominion of Canada, Commonwealth of Australia, and the Dominion of New Zealand, the Union of South Africa, and the Colony of Newfoundland, for transmission to the Parliament of these respective states. Refusal or failure, however, of any of the states to ratify shall not effect the general validity of the Treaty.

Article XI. As soon as ratification of this Treaty shall have been exchanged, the British Government shall communicate the text of Articles to all states with which it entertains diplomatic relations, and the text of the Treaty as a whole to the President and Council of the League of Nations.

The British Government engages to support the securing of the formal recognition of Ireland's perpetual neutrality by the United States of America, by Germany, and by Russia, and by other States with which Great Britain entertains diplomatic relations and which are not members of the League of Nations.

The representatives of the British Commonwealth in the League of Nations engage to support the formal recognition of Ireland's neutrality, integrity, and inviolability by the League of Nations in conformity with the similar guarantee in favour of Switzerland recognized by Article 455 of the Treaty of Versailles of June 28th, 1919, and to support an application that may hereafter be made by Ireland for inclusion in the League of Nations.

Appendix Seven

<hr/>

Amendments Proposed by Irish Delegates
4 December, 1921

THESE ARE THE COUNTER-PROPOSALS drafted by Barton, Gavan Duffy and Childers, as altered at the instance of Griffith and Collins, and presented at Downing Street on December 4th, 1921.

1. The Legislative, executive, and judicial authority of Ireland shall be derived exclusively from the Elected Representatives of the Irish people.

2. Ireland will agree to be associated with the British Commonwealth for all purposes of common concern, including defence, peace and war, and political treaties, and to recognise the British Crown as Head of the Association.

3. As a token of that recognition, the Irish legislature will vote an annual contribution to the King's personal revenue.

4. In matters of common concern, the rights and status of Ireland shall be in no respect less than those enjoyed by any of the component States of the British Commonwealth represented in the League of Nations. There shall be between Ireland and these States such concerted action, founded on consultation, as the several Governments may determine.

5. The Oath to be taken by members of the Irish Parliament shall be in the following form:
I do swear to bear true faith and allegiance to the Constitution of Ireland and to the Treaty of Association of Ireland with the British Commonwealth of Nations, and to recognise the King of Great Britain as Head of the Associated States.

6. Ireland shall assume liability for such a portion, if any, of the Public Debt of Great Britain and Ireland existing at the date hereof and of the war pensions existing at that date as may be fair and equitable, having regard to any just claims, if any, on the part of Ireland by way of set-off or counter-claim, the amount of such sums being determined in default of agreement by the arbitration of one or more independent persons being citizens of the British Empire.

7. (1) As an Associated State, Ireland recognises the obligation of providing for her own defence by sea, land, and air, and of repelling by force any attempt to violate the integrity of her shores and territorial waters.

(2) For five years, pending the establishment of Irish Coastal Defence forces, facilities for the coastal defence of Ireland shall be afforded to the British Government as follows:

(*a*) In time of peace such Harbour and other facilities as are indicated in the Annex A hereto, or such other facilities as may from time to time be agreed between the British Government and the Government of the Irish Free State.

(*b*) In time of war such harbour and other facilities as the British Government may require for the purposes of such defence as aforesaid.

8. With a view to securing the observance of the principle of international limitation of armaments, if the Government of the Irish Free State establishes and maintains a local military force, the establishment thereof shall not exceed in size such proportion of the military establishment maintained in Great Britain as that which the population of Ireland bears to the population of Great Britain.

9. No protective customs duties shall be imposed in Great Britain on Irish goods nor in Ireland on British goods, but this provision shall not be construed as preventing the imposition of customs duties designed against dumping or other unfair competition nor as preventing the Irish Government from taking measures for the encouragement of infant industries and for the economic development of Ireland.

10. A Convention shall be made between the British and Irish Governments for the regulation of civil communication by air.

11. The Government of Ireland agrees to pay fair compensation on terms not less favourable than those accorded by the Act of 1920 to judges, officials, members of Police Forces, and other public servants who are discharged by it or who retire in consequence of the change of Government effected in pursuance hereof.

Provided that this agreement shall not apply to members of the Auxiliary Police Force or to persons recruited in Great Britain for the Royal Irish Constabulary during the two years next preceding the date hereof.

The British Government will assume responsibility for such compensation or pensions as may be payable to any of these excepted persons.

Appendix Eight

Griffith's Undertaking to Lloyd George – November, 1921.

The Right Hon. David Lloyd George,   22 Hans Place,
10 Downing Street, London   London, S.W.

Sir,

In our personal conversation on Sunday night you stated that three things were vital - our attitude to the British Commonwealth, the Crown and Naval Defence. You ask me whether, provided I was satisfied on other points, I would give you personal assurances in relation to these matters.

I assured you in reply that, provided I was so satisfied, I was prepared to recommend a free partnership of Ireland with the other States associated with the British Commonwealth, the formula defining the partnership to be arrived at in a later discussion. I was, on the same condition, prepared to recommend that Ireland should consent to a recognition of the Crown as head of the proposed association of free states.

As to Naval Defence, I noted the assurance contained in your memorandum of October 27th to the effect that:

The objects of the British Government in regard to the Navy and the Air Force are and will remain purely defensive. None of their stipulations is intended in the smallest degree to afford either armed occupation or political control of any part of Ireland'; and I agreed consequently to recommend that the British Navy should be afforded such coastal facilities as may be necessary pending an agreement similar to those made with the Dominions providing for the assumption by Ireland of her own coastal defence.

I stated that this attitude of mine was conditional on the recognition of the essential unity of Ireland. As to the North-East of Ireland, while reserving for further discussion the question of area, I would agree to any necessary safeguards and to the existence of existing parliamentary powers, and would agree that its industrial life should not be hampered or discriminated against in any way.

With reference to the question of financial relations between the two nations, I am willing to let the adjustment of this matter rest in the hands of the agreed arbitrator.

Arthur Griffith

Appendix Nine

Articles of Agreement as Signed
on 6 December 1921

1. Ireland shall have the same constitutional status in the Community of Nations known as the British Empire as the Dominion of New Zealand, and the Union of South Africa, with a parliament having powers to make laws for the peace, order and good government of Ireland and an Executive responsible to that Parliament, and shall be styled and known as the Irish Free State.

2. Subject to the provisions hereinafter set out the position of the Irish Free State in relation to the Imperial Parliament and Government and otherwise shall be that of the Dominion of Canada, and the law, practice and constitutional usage governing the relationship of the Crown or the representative of the Crown and of the Imperial Parliament to the Dominion of Canada shall govern their relationship to the Irish Free State.

3. The representative of the Crown in Ireland shall be appointed in like manner as the Governor-General of Canada and in accordance with the practice observed in the making of such appointments.

4. The oath to be taken by Members of the Parliament of the Irish Free State shall be in the following form:
   I…do solemnly swear true faith and allegiance to the Constitution of the Irish Free State as by law established and that I will be faithful to H.M. King George V, his heirs and successors by law, in virtue of the common citizenship of Ireland with Great Britain and her adherence to and membership of the group of nations forming the British Commonwealth of Nations.

5. The Irish Free State shall assume liability for the service of the Public Debt of the United Kingdom as existing at the date hereof and towards the payment of war pensions as existing at that date in such proportion as may be fair and equitable, having regard to any just claims on the part of Ireland by way of set-off or counter-claim, the amount of such sums being determined in default of agreement by the arbitration of one or more independent persons being citizens of the British Empire.

6. Until an arrangement has been made between the British and Irish Governments whereby the Irish Free State undertakes her own coastal defence, the defence by sea of Great Britain and Ireland shall be undertaken by his Majesty's Imperial Forces. But this shall not prevent the construction or maintenance by the Government of the Irish Free State of such vessels as are necessary for the protection of the Revenue or the Fisheries.

The foregoing provisions of the Article shall be reviewed at a Conference of Representatives of the British and Irish Government to be held at the expiration of five years from the date hereof with a view to the undertaking by Ireland of a share in her own coastal defence.

7. The Government of the Irish Free State shall afford to His Majesty's Imperial Forces: (a) In time of peace such harbour and other facilities as are indicated in the Annex hereto, or such other facilities as may from time to time be agreed between the British Government and the Government of the Irish Free State; and (b) In time of war or of strained relations with a Foreign Power such harbour and other facilities as the British Government may require for the purposes of such defence as aforesaid.

8. With a view to securing the observance of the principle of international limitation of armaments, if the Government of the Irish Free State establishes and maintains a military defence force, the establishments thereof shall not exceed in size such proportion of the military establishments maintained in Great Britain as that which the population of Ireland bears to the population of Great Britain.

9. The ports of Great Britain and the Free Irish State shall be freely open to the ships of the other country on payment of the customary port and other dues.

10. The Government of the Irish Free State agrees to pay fair compensation on terms no less favourable than those accorded by the Act of 1920 to judges, officials, members of Police Forces and other Public Servants who are discharged by it or who retire in consequence of the change of Government effected in pursuance hereof.

    Provided that this agreement shall not apply to members of the Auxiliary Police Force or to persons recruited in Great Britain for the Royal Irish Constabulary during the two years next preceding the date hereof. The British Government will assume responsibility for such compensation or pensions as may be payable to any of these excepted persons.

11. Until the expiration of one month from the passing of the Act of Parliament for the ratification of this instrument, the powers of the Parliament and the Government of the Irish Free State shall not be exercisable as respects Northern Ireland and the provisions of the Government of Ireland Act, 1920, shall so far as they relate to Northern Ireland remain of full force and effect, and no election shall be held for the return of members to serve in the Parliament of the Irish Free State for constituencies in Northern Ireland, unless a resolution is passed by both Houses of the Parliament of Northern Ireland in favour of the holding of such election before the end of the said month.

12. If before the expiration of the said month, an address is presented to His Majesty by both Houses of the Parliament of Northern Ireland to that effect, the powers of the Parliament and Government of the Irish Free State shall no

longer extend to Northern Ireland, and the provisions of the Government of Ireland, Act, 1920 (including those relating to the Council of Ireland) shall so far as they relate to Northern Ireland, continue to be full force and effect, and this instrument shall have effect subject to the necessary modifications.

Provided that if such an address is so presented a Commission consisting of three persons, one to be appointed by the Government of the Irish State, one to be appointed by the Government of Northern Ireland and one who shall be Chairman to be appointed by the British Government shall determine in accordance with the wishes of the inhabitants, so far as may be compatible with economic and geographic conditions, the boundaries between Northern Ireland and the rest of Ireland, and for the purposes of the Government of Ireland Act, 1920, and of this instrument, the boundary of Northern Ireland shall be such as may be determined by such Commission.

13. For the purpose of the last foregoing article, the powers of the Parliament of Southern Ireland under the Government of Ireland Act, 1920, to elect members of the Council of Ireland shall after the Parliament of the Irish Free State is constituted be exercised by that Parliament.

14. After the expiration of the said month, if no such address as is mentioned in Article 12 hereof is presented, the Parliament and Government of Northern Ireland shall continue in exercise as respects Northern Ireland the powers conferred on them by the Government of Ireland Act, 1920, but the Parliament and Government of the Irish Free State shall in Northern Ireland have in relation to matters in respect of which the Parliament of Northern Ireland had not power to make laws under that Act (including matters which under the said Act within the jurisdiction of the Council of Ireland) the same powers as in the rest of Ireland, subject to such other provisions as may be agreed in manner hereinafter appearing.

15. At any time after the date hereof the Government of Northern Ireland and the provisional Government of Southern Ireland hereinafter constituted may meet for the purpose of discussing the provisions subject to which the last foregoing article is to operate in the event of no such address as is therein mentioned being presented and those provisions may include:
   (a) Safeguards with regard to patronage in Northern Ireland;
   (b) Safeguards with regard to the collection of revenue in Northern Ireland;
   (c) Safeguards with regard to import and export duties affecting the trade or industry of Northern Ireland;
   (d) Safeguards for minorities in Northern Ireland;
   (e) The settlement of the financial relations between Northern Ireland and the Irish Free State;
   (f) The establishment and powers of a local militia in Northern Ireland and the relation of the Defence Forces of the Irish Free State and of Northern Ireland respectively;

and if at any such meeting provisions are agreed to, the same shall have effect as if they were included amongst the provisions subject to which the Powers of the Parliament and Government of the Irish Free State are to be exercisable in Northern Ireland under Article 14 hereof.

16. Neither the Parliament of the Irish Free State nor the Parliament of Northern Ireland shall make any law so as either directly or indirectly to endow any religion or prohibit or restrict the free exercise thereof or give any preference or impose any disability on account of religious belief or religious status or affect prejudicially the right of any child to attend a school receiving public money without attending the religious instruction at the school or make any discrimination as respects state aid between schools under the management of different religious denominations or divert from any religious denomination or any educational institution any of its property except for public utility purposes and on payment of compensation.

17. By way of provisional arrangement for the administration of Southern Ireland during the interval which must elapse between the date hereof and the constitution of a Parliament and Government of the Irish Free State in accordance therewith, steps shall be taken forthwith for summoning a meeting of members of Parliament elected for constituencies in Southern Ireland since the passing of the Government of Ireland Act, 1920, and for constituting a Provisional Government, and the British Government shall take the steps necessary to transfer to such Provisional Government the powers and machinery requisite for the discharge of its duties, provided that every member of such Provisional Government shall have signified in writing his or her acceptance of this instrument. But this arrangement shall not continue in force beyond the expiration of twelve months from the date hereof.

18. This instrument shall be submitted forthwith by His Majesty's Government for the approval of Parliament and by the Irish signatories to a meeting summoned for the purpose of the members elected to sit in the House of Commons of Southern Ireland, and if approved shall be ratified by the necessary legislation.

On behalf of the British Delegation.	On behalf of the Irish Delegation.
Signed.	*Signed.*
D. Lloyd George.	*Art Ó Griobhtha.*
Austen Chamberlain.	*Michael Ó Coileáin.*
Birkenhead.	*Riobárd Bartún.*
Winston S. Churchill.	*Eudhmonn S. Ó Dúgáin.*
L. Worthington-Evans.	*Seorsa Ghabháin Uí.*
Hamar Greenwood.	*Dhúbhthaígh.*
Gordon Hewart.	

December 6th, 1921.

Appendix Ten

Document Number Two

THE FOLLOWING IS THE COUNTER-PROPOSAL drafted by President de Valéra as an Amendment to the motion for Approval of the Articles of Agreement. He intended to move the Amendment on January 4th, 1922.

"The inasmuch as the 'Articles of Agreement for a treaty between Great Britain and Ireland', signed in London on December 6th, 1921, do not reconcile Irish National aspirations and the Association of Ireland with the Community of Nations known as the British Commonwealth, and cannot be the basis of an enduring peace between the Irish and the British peoples, Dáil Éireann, in the name of the Sovereign Irish Nation, makes to the Government of Great Britain, to the Government of the other States of the British Commonwealth, and to the peoples of Great Britain and of these several States, the following Proposal for a Treaty of Amity and Association which, Dáil Éireann is convinced, could be entered into by the Irish people with the sincerity of good-will":

Proposed Treaty of Association Between
Ireland and the British Commonwealth

In order to bring to an end the long and ruinous conflict between Great Britain and Ireland by a sure and lasting peace honourable to both nations, it is agreed

Status of Ireland

1. That the legislative, executive, and judicial authority of Ireland shall be derived solely from the people of Ireland.

Terms of Association

2. That, for purposes of common concern, Ireland shall be associated with the States of the British Commonwealth, viz: – The Kingdom of Great Britain, the Dominion of Canada, the Commonwealth of Australia, the Dominion of New Zealand, and the Union of South Africa.

3. That when acting as an associate the rights, status, and privileges of Ireland shall be in no respect less than those enjoyed by any of the component States of the British Commonwealth.

4. That the matters of "common concern" shall include Defence, Peace and War, Political Treaties, and all matters now treated as of common concern, amongst the States of the British Commonwealth, and that in these matters there shall be between Ireland and the States of the British Commonwealth "such concerted action founded on consultation as the several Governments may determine."

5. That in virtue of this association of Ireland with the States of the British Commonwealth, citizens of Ireland in any of these States shall not be subject to any dis-

abilities which a citizen of one of the component States of the British Commonwealth would not be subject to, and reciprocally for citizens of these States in Ireland.

6. That, for purposes of the Association, Ireland shall recognise His Brittanic Majesty as head of the Association.

Defence

7. That, so far as her resources permit, Ireland shall provide for her own defence by sea, land and air, and shall repel by force any attempt by a foreign Power to violate the integrity of her soil and territorial waters, or to use them for any purpose hostile to Great Britain and the other associated States.

8. That for five years, pending the establishment of Irish coastal defence forces, or for such other period as the Governments of the two countries may later agree upon, facilities for the coastal defence of Ireland shall be given to the British Government as follows:–
(a) In time of peace such harbour and other facilities as are indicated in the Annex hereto, or such other facilities as may from time to time be agreed upon between the British Government and the Government of Ireland;
(b) In time of war such harbour and other naval facilities as the British Government may reasonably require for the purposes of such defence as aforesaid.

9. That within five years from the date of exchange of ratifications of this Treaty a Conference between the British and Irish Governments shall be held in order to hand over the coastal defence of Ireland to the Irish Government, unless some other arrangement for naval defence be agreed by both Governments to be desirable in the common interest of Ireland, Great Britain and the other Associated States.

10. That, in order to co-operate in furthering the principle of international limitation of armaments, the Government of Ireland shall not
(a) Build submarines unless by agreement with Great Britain and other States of the Commonwealth;
(b) Maintain a military defence force, the establishments whereof exceed in size such proportion of the military establishments maintained in Great Britain as that which the population of Ireland bears to the population of Great Britain.

Miscellaneous

11. That the Governments of Great Britain and of Ireland shall make a convention for the regulation of civil communication by air.

12. That the ports of Great Britain and of Ireland shall be freely open to the ships of each country on payment of the customary port and other dues.

13. That Ireland shall assume liability for such share of the present public debt of Great Britain and Ireland, and of payment of war pensions as existing at this date as may be fair and equitable, having regard to any just claims on the part of Ireland by way of set-off or counter-claim, the amount of such sums being determined in default of agreement, by the arbitration of one or more independent persons, being citizens of Ireland or of the British Commonwealth.

14. That the Government of Ireland agrees to pay compensation on terms not less favourable than those proposed by the British Government of Ireland Act of 1920 to that Government's judges, officials, members of Police Forces and other Public

Servants who are discharged by the Government of Ireland, or who retire in consequence of the change of government elected in pursuance hereof:

Provided that this agreement shall not apply to members of the Auxiliary Police Force, or to persons recruited in Great Britain for the Royal Irish Constabulary during the two years next preceding the date hereof. The British Government will assume responsibility for date hereof. The British Government will assume responsibility for such compensation or pensions as may be payable to any of these excepted persons.

15. That neither the Parliament of Ireland nor any subordinate Legislature in Ireland shall make any law so as either directly or indirectly to endow any religion or prohibit or restrict the free exercise thereof, or give any preference or impose any disability on account of religious belief or religious status, or affect prejudicially the right of any child to attend a school receiving public money without attending a religious instruction at the school, or make any discrimination as respects State aid between schools under the management of different religious denominations, or divert from any religious denomination or any educational institution any of its property except for public utility purposes and on payment of compensation.

Transitional
16. That by way of transitional arrangement for the Administration of Ireland during the interval which must elapse between the date hereof and the setting up of a Parliament and Government of Ireland in accordance herewith, the members elected for constituencies in Ireland since the passing of the British Government of Ireland Act in 1920 shall, at a meeting summoned for the purpose, elect a transitional Government to which the British Government and Dáil Éireann shall transfer the authority, powers, and machinery requisite for the discharge of its duties, provided that every member of such transition Government shall have signified in writing his or her acceptance of this instrument. But this arrangement shall not continue in force beyond the expiration of twelve months from the date hereof.

Ratification
17. That this instrument shall be submitted for ratification forthwith by His Britannic Majesty's Government to the Parliament at Westminster, and by the Cabinet of Dáil Éireann to a meeting of the members elected for the constituencies in Ireland set forth in the British Government of Ireland Act, 1920, and when ratifications have been exchanged shall take immediate effect.

ANNEX
1. The following are the specific facilities referred to in Article 8 (*a*):

Dockyard Port at Berehaven
(a) British Admiralty property and rights to be retained as the date hereof. Harbour defences to remain in charge of British care and maintenance parties.

Queenstown
(*b*) Harbour defences to remain in charge of British care and maintenance parties. Certain mooring buoys to be retained for use of His Brittanic Majesty's ships.

Belfast Lough
(*c*) Harbour defences to remain in charge of British care and maintenance parties.

Aviation

(*e*) Facilities in the neighbourhood of the above Ports for coastal defence by air.

Oil Fuel Storage

(*f*) Haulbowline and Rathmullen { To be offered for sale to commercial companies under guarantee that purchasers shall maintain a certain minimum stock for British Admiralty purposes.

2. A Convention covering a period of five years shall be made between the British and Irish Governments to give effect to the following conditions:

(*a*) That submarine cables shall not be landed or wireless stations for communications with places outside Ireland be established except by agreement with the British Government; that the existing cable landing rights and wireless concessions shall not be withdrawn except by agreement with the British Government; and that the British Government shall be entitled to land additional submarine cables or establish additional wireless stations for communication with places outside Ireland.

(*b*) That lighthouses, buoys, beacons, and any navigational marks or navigational aids shall be maintained by the Government of Ireland as at the date hereof and shall not be removed or added to except by agreement with the British Government.

(*c*) That war signal stations shall be closed down and left in charge of care and maintenance parties, the Government of Ireland being offered the option of taking them over and working them for commercial purposes subject to British Admiralty inspection and guaranteeing the upkeep of existing telegraphic communication therewith.

(The following addendum concerning N.E. Ulster was to be proposed as a separate resolution by the President.)

ADDENDUM
NORTH-EAST ULSTER

Resolved:

That, whilst refusing to admit the right of any part of Ireland to be excluded from the supreme authority of the Parliament of Ireland, or that the relations between the Parliament of Ireland and any subordinate Legislature in Ireland can be a matter for treaty with a government outside Ireland, nevertheless, in sincere regard for internal peace, and in order to make manifest our desire not to bring force or coercion to bear upon any substantial part of the Province of Ulster, whose inhabitants may now be unwilling to accept the national authority, we are prepare to grant to that portion of Ulster which is defined as Northern Ireland in the British Government of Ireland Act of 1920, privileges and safeguards not less substantial than those provided for in the Articles of Agreement for a Treaty between Great Britain and Ireland signed in London on December 6th, 1921.

Appendix Eleven

The Pact

THE PACT
Between Collins and de Valera 20 May 1922

We are agreed:

(1) That a National Coalition panel for this Third Dáil representing both parties in the Dáil and in the Sinn Féin organization be sent forward on the ground that the national position requires the entrusting of the Government of the country into the joint hands of those who have been the strength of the national situation during the last few years, without prejudice to their present respective positions.

(2) That this Coalition panel be sent forward as from the Sinn Féin organization, the number from each party being their present strength in the Dáil.

(3) That the candidates be nominated through each of the existing party Executives.

(4) That every and any interest is free to go up and contest the election equally with the National-Sinn Féin panel.

(5) That constituencies where an election is not held shall continue to be represented by their present deputies.*

(6) That after the election the Executive shall consist of the President, elected as formerly; the Minister for Defence, representing the Army; and nine other ministers — five from the majority party and four from the minority, each party to chose its own nominees. The allocation [of office] will be in the hands of the President.

(7) In the event of the Coalition Government finding it necessary to dissolve, a general election will be held as soon as possible on adult suffrage.

---

* A provision to accommodate representation in the six north-eastern counties.

NOTES

INTRODUCTION. Pp 1 - 19

[1] The following is some indication of the strength and endurance of republican thought and action in parts of the country:'[in Wicklow] the resistance movement under the leadership of Michael Dwyer continued for five and a half years (1798 to 1803), unquestionably encouraged and sustained by the reconstituted United Irish Directory until the hope of French intervention had been finally relinquished', Charles Dixon, *The Wexford Rising in 1798*, p. 181.

[2] English politicians and the establishment as a whole, the Press and to a large extent public opinion, expressed two main concerns about Home Rule. Firstly, they were opposed to legislative independence for Ireland under any circumstances. Secondly, Ireland should not be 'allowed to protect her manufactures (such as they were) at the cost of those of England' (Parnell *Speeches and Letters*, p.351). No question concerning the position of the Ulster Unionists arose in England at the time, and did not until the Conservatives, in 1885, made it their platform. Parnell (Ibid., p. 353), goes on: 'Whatever chance the English may have of drawing to themselves the affection of the Irish people, lies in destroying the abominable system of legislative union between the two countries, by conceding fully and freely to Ireland the right to manage her own affairs. It is impossible for us to give guarantees, but we can point to the past, we can show that the march of English rule is a constant series of steps from bad to worse, that the condition of English power is more insecure and unstable at the present moment than it has ever been.'

He went on to cite the example of Hungary and Austria that Griffith was later to take up in more detail and with more effect.

[3] *The Master.*

[4] Indeed it is interesting that the overflow meeting at the Rotunda in November 1914 at which the Volunteers were formed was the subject of some disruption by trade union activists, though whether or not these were from the Citizen Army, formed a short while before, is difficult to say.

CHAPTER ONE. Pp 21 - 32

[5] Recent genetic studies have contributed to this conclusion. Research by Professor Hilary Hoey of Trinity College, Dublin, revealed significant differences in growth and puberty patterns between Irish and British children. She attributed these differences largely to racial distinctiveness, the Irish racial distinctiveness being based on Celtic ancestry. the English on a racially mixed ancestry — See Irish Times, 25 February, 1995.

[6] Leading figure in the country by 1914. He was born in Glanarm, Co. Antrim in 1867, and was educated at St, Malachy's College, Belfast. He was a founder member of the Gaelic League (1893). He became Professor of Early Irish History at University College,

Dublin. He was 49 when the Rising took place. Until his part in the formation of the Volunteers he was considered a conservative, even a Home Ruler, in politics. Became chairman of the provisional committee of the Volunteers in 1913.

[7] 'An Irishman will soon be as scarce on the banks of the Shannon as a Red Indian on the banks of the Delaware' Times of London, 1856.

[8] It is interesting to note an original — and marked — difference between the Wild Geese regiments of France and those, formed some hundred years earlier, of Spain — the *Irlanda*, the *Ultonia* and the *Hibernia*. (There was originally another Spanish regiment called the *Tir Eoghan*, Tyrone). The Spanish regiments, both officers and men, were made up in the main of Gaelic Irish and owed no allegiance to the Stuarts. The relationship with Spain, while having a religious content due to the counter-reformation, was very old and, though old, was primarily anti-English at that time. The situation of the Wild Geese regiments in France was quite different. While there was a religious content the regiments were, in the main, raised by Old English leaders who provided much — but by no means all -of the officer corps as well. They were supported by the Stuarts, while the other ranks were Gaelic Irish. Initially they were what remained of James Stuart's — Seamus a Cac — Irish armies that fought in England and Ireland. This was the beginning of the Irish/French alliance which superceded the Irish/Spanish one in the 17th and 18th centuries. In the main the wars of the 18th century in Ireland were not wars of the people. They were not even to do with Ireland, but with what was happening in England and in Europe beyond it. The Flight of the Earls and the regiments in Spain and France that developed after that were followed 83 years later by the Flight of the Wild Geese. The one involved the departure — the virtual extinction — of the old Irish system with its structure and ideals. The other had little to do with that, though history has enabled it to absorb some of the mystique of the former and acquire, as a result, a romantic image of Gaelic chivalry. The Wild Geese became mercenaries. In France they originated with the remnants of the Irish armies of the Stuart kings, and had nothing, except by association and the provision of cannon-fodder, to do with the old order. The French brigades were raised by aristocratic, in the main old (but sometimes new — FitzJames, Bulkeley) English, supporters of the Stuarts, to whose cause they clung. They did little, and cared less, for the people of benighted 18th century Ireland whom they pillaged for recruits and whom they left without hope, without ideal and without leadership.

[9] More than 1,000,000 served with France alone during the hundred years to 1791; that is a mean intake of 10,000 men a year — implying a huge casualty rate. This takes no account of those who served with Spain, Austria, Russia and elsewhere, including Great Britain.

[10] An article in *The Irish Times* in December 1993 asserted that Northern Ireland Protestants commonly hold the view that Catholics are not Christians.

[11] In fact the situation in Ireland was one of the first, and certainly the most enduring, example of that extraordinary and brutal racial and religious bigotry that has, across the globe — in the southern United States, in Australia, in South Africa and, of course, in Northern Ireland — characterised administration by certain fundamentalist protestant settlers claiming Anglo-Saxon and Anglo-Dutch origins.

[12] 'When we find a hardy, industrious race transplanted to a country under the sanction and by the authority of the Crown, protected and favoured by the laws and ruling authority of the State, placed under fostering landlords who exhibit a paternal care, and then permitted to hold of their farms under a custom which practically gave them a lease in perpetuity it would be a strange thing, indeed, if prosperity were not the result' — Dardis, *The Occupation of Land in Ireland*, London, 1902.

[13] Lazare Hoche was a distinguished French general who had defended Dunquerqe against the Duke of York, drove the Austrians from Alsace, and commanded the attempted landing of a French army in Ireland in 1796. When Hoche's expedition appeared off Bantry Bay, in December, 1796 ... Had [his] army corps (consisting of about 15,000 men) landed, as there was then no English force in Ireland, nothing could have prevented them marching on Dublin and establishing there a provisional government. Everywhere he would have been joined by the people...As to men, a hundred thousand could have been enrolled at once... The country possessed all the resources necessary for this great undertaking... the Protestant counties of the North were all organized and ready to shake off the English yoke. The United Irishmen and the Presbyterians, whether they were United Irishmen or not, were all republicans. They knew that Hoche came not for conquest, but to afford them an occasion for declaring their right to self-government; therefore all the north would have joined him at once...' Miles Byrne, *Memoirs: Notes of an Irish Exile of 1798*, Dublin — no date — pp. 3/4. Byrne was a Wexford man who was 'out' in '98 and subsequently fled the ensuing terror to France, where he served with Napoleon's Irish Legion, reaching the rank of colonel and becoming a member of the Legion of Honour.

[14] Not all Catholic clergy — even those who wished to do so — benefitted from being pro Establishment and anti republican, as the following shows: 'The priests did everything in their power to stop the progress of the United Irish; particularly poor Father John Redmond, who refused to hear the confessions of the United Irish and turned them away from his knees. He was ill-requited afterwards for his great zeal and devotion to the enemies of his country; for, after the Insurrection was all over, Earl Mountnorris brought him a prisoner to the British camp at Gorey, with a rope about his neck, hung him up to a tree, and fired a brace of bullets through his body ... Both Redmond and the parish priest ... were on the best terms with Earl Mountnorris, dining frequently with him at his seat, Camolin Park, which Father Redmond prevented being plundered during the Insurrection. This was the only part he had taken in the struggle' — *Memoirs of Miles Byrne*, Dublin, no date.

[15] A less often referred to aspect of 1798 and the republican ethos is the effect that it had on the relationship of the Catholic masses — a majority — who supported it, and the Catholic clergy, who did not. After it was officially recognised by the English administration in 1775 and permitted to practice, the Church was understandably reluctant to offend the Establishment of which it had become part by giving political offence to the British authorities, thereby threatening its newly-won (if still very restricted) concessions. It was, for instance, pointed out to the French Minister of Religion by Dr. John Baptist Walsh, superior of the Irish colleges in Paris during the Revolution and after, that: 'Maynooth would be tolerated for a certain time but that its future was in no way assured due to the "changing policy of the British government which held the Irish bishops in its hands ..."' and that they were '" forced, no doubt, by the British government, who compels them to say yes or no depending on its whims"'Swords, op.cit., p 204. It should be borne in mind that at the time of writing Walsh was trying to reassure the French (Napoleonic) government about the future of the Irish colleges in Paris, which had been adversely affected by the establishment of Maynooth, and was simultaneously seeking elevation of his post as superior to that of bishop *in partibus*. The view of the Irish bishops was one that was reinforced by the support, albeit cautious, of the Pope, even if that support was based on a different premise. And it is that premise that tends to be overlooked — namely that the republican movement in Ireland was most influenced by the republican movement in anti-clerical France and that '98 occurred a mere three years after Napoleon's defeat of the Pope at the Battle of Lodi. The Irish bishops — who had in the past relied strongly on the

Irish colleges in France — were acutely conscious of the compound threat from irreligious, republican France. Having struggled free of Penal repression they had no intention of jeopardising that freedom by encouraging, even condoning, political activity hostile to the English administration, particularly any materialising from an irreligious environment. Accordingly 'henceforth its [the Irish hierarchy's] influence was thrown broadly in favour of the English connexion, and against any efforts to weaken or break that connexion'(O'Hegarty, op.cit. p.50).

[16] The great parliamentarian of the eighteenth century. Born in Dublin of a mixed marriage (Protestant father, Catholic mother) he was educated at Trinity College. He became an M.P. in 1765, but, because he was 'an Irish adventurer' and a suspect Catholic, he was kept from high office all his life. He was a remarkable orator and liberal thinker. Throughout his political career he was much concerned about the plight both of Ireland and of its Catholic population.

[17] Quoted by O'Connell at the Dublin Corporation Debate on Repeal, March, 1843.

CHAPTER TWO. Pp.33 - 61.

[18] Sir Robert Peel, English prime minister, House of Commons, 1843, quoted Gavan Duffy, *Young Ireland*, vol 1, pp.81/2, cited O'Hegarty, op.cit., p.134.

[19] It is said that Mahatma Gandhi invented the phrase 'passive resistance'. It is not to detract from the achievements of the Mahatma to say that O'Connell's speeches during the Repeal movement are clear examples of passive resistance being articulated and preached in the ideas — almost the very words — expressed by Gandhi a hundred years later. The speech in Cork on 20 May, 1843, is a good example. John Mitchell used the following phrase '...in short, to offer a passive resistance universally...' in his *Last Conquest*, 1861, p.224., cited O'Hegarty op. cit., p 331.

[20] William Edward Hartpole Lecky (1838-1903), major Irish historian. Born Dublin, educated at Trinity. His major work is *History of England in the Eighteenth Century*, almost one half of which is devoted to Ireland, specifically to refuting the calumnies of his contemporary James Anthony Froude, whose *English in Ireland in the Eighteenth Century* roused Lecky's anger.

[21] This dilemma was also contributed to by the leadership 'takeover' by the Old English monarchist leaders who supported the Stuarts, particularly James 11, after he reverted to Catholicism.

[22] The double irony — and pointed success of British policy — is that these recent republican allies were not only opposed to one another in religion and, now, in politics; they were both rendered additionally vulnerable and insecure by virtue of the delicately balanced nature of their separate aspirations.

[23] 'The United Irishmen and the presbyterians, whether they were United Irishmen or not, were all republicans. They knew that Hoche had come not for conquest, but to afford them an occasion for declaring their right to self-government: therefore all the north would have joined them at once ... I shall never forget it, the mournful silence, the consternation of the poor people at the different chapels on Christmas Day on the following Sunday, after learning that the French had not landed and that the French fleet had returned to France', wrote Miles Byrne, *Notes of an Irish Exile of 1798*, pp 4/5. Throughout Byrne makes the clear distinction between presbyterianism and 'infernal' Orangeism. 'The first members of the Orange order were lower-class protestants ... as Lecky observed "the most worthless protestant if he had nothing else to boast of, at least found it pleasing to think that he was a member of a dominant race"'(Robert Shepherd, *Ireland's Fate, the Boyne and After*, London 1990, p.208). On page 207 Shepherd makes the point that, in the north, 'The alliance between the (Catholic) Defenders and the mainly Presbyterian United

Irishmen' gave the government 'concern to break the link between the northern Presbyterian radicals and Catholics' and 'gave them (the government) an interest in the continuation of sectarian division'.

[24] Winston Churchill, while writing a biography of his father, Randolph, found a note to Lord Justice Fitzgibbon dated 16th February 1886, which underlines the political cynicism employed to destroy the Liberals and, coincidentally, encouraged the monster of Unionist bigotry which has bedevilled relations between Ireland and England ever since: 'I decided some time ago that if the G.O.M. (Gladstone) went for Home Rule, the Orange card would be the one to play. Please God it may turn out the ace of trumps and not the two', Dangerfield p. 88).

[25] This is not as far-fetched as contemporary liberalist thinking might suggest. Famine, the Third Horseman of the Apocalypse has always been an instrument of war, as we see all too clearly in parts of the world to-day. Moreover the nineteenth century was notorious for deliberate policies of famine as a means of exterminating unwanted populations — in the United States, in Australia, in Tasmania, in South America and in Africa induced famine was common. It would not, therefore, be exceptional if this belief, common in Ireland at the time (See Gerald Keegan's *Famine Diary*, ed. J.J.Manghan, Dublin 1997), were correct.

[26] Before the famine of 1847-9 the population of Ireland approached nine million, that of England being about twenty-five. On that basis it is arguable that, had there not been a famine —or had it been contained — the population of Ireland to-day might reasonably be expected to be in the region of 15,000,000, with all the resulting associated benefits.

[27] It is a curious fact that while Gladstone preached to the Ascendancy classes in Ireland that 'property has its duties as well as rights', a hundred years later, in a sovereign, democratic republic, social and political observers are aware of the need to preach to the public at large in Ireland that there is no liberty without a corresponding level of responsibility. That wheel, like so many others, seems to have gone full circle.

[28] Report of the Commission on the Trial of John Sarsfield Casey 1877.

[29] It involved a limited Irish legislature. Lord Salisbury, leader of the Conservative Party, acknowledged that something, though not a parliament, was an unavoidable consideration for Ireland. The principle was explored at highly secret meetings between Lord Carnarvon and Parnell, but with no definite outcome. Any result would certainly have involved even less than the derisory limitations of the Liberal Home Rule Bill and would, accordingly, have been unlikely to recommend itself to Parnell. On the other hand, coming from the Conservative Party, it would have had a far better chance of a passage through the then decisive House of Lords. In any case the overtures fell by the wayside in 1886 in a matter of months.

[30] During this period the word 'Boycott' entered the English language as a pejorative verb meaning to ostracise, when an agent by that name evicted tenants for non-payment of rent and was 'Boycotted' for his pains with much local violence and and national attention.

[31] The ambush was intended for W.E.Forster (much hated by nationalists because of his policy of coercion and Draconian methods) who preceded Lord Frederick Cavendish as Chief Secretary for Ireland. Forster in fact resigned in protest at the so-called 'Kilmainham Treaty' under which Parnell was released from that prison following his agreement with Gladstone to recognise the latter's controversial Land Act in settlement of the land question. It was both a matter of political and personal expediency on Parnell's part to recognise the Act, which was far from acceptable to many of his associates, especially those in the Land League. Forster was incensed, but for entirely different reasons, feeling

that his coercive policies — which had an appearance of immediate effect — were being undermined by the 'treaty'. Cavendish had arrived in Ireland only the day before he was murdered in the Phoenix Park where he was evidently being briefed by Under-Secretary Burke. Since the assassination had been planned by The Invincibles for some time it seems unarguable that the intended victim was Forster and not Cavendish. The *ex-officio* aspect of the killing has the appearance of being a *post-factum* addition, particularly in view of the nature and character of The Invincibles.

[32] It is interesting that, although the British cabinet of the day (1921) was a coalition led by Lloyd George who might have been expected to follow the Gladstonian line, in fact so tenuous was his position as prime minister at that time that the nuts and bolts of his Irish policy were fitted and tightened by the Tories. Lloyd George evidently hoped that appeasement on the Irish question would enable his tired war-time coalition cabinet to survive. Ireland, therefore, became a critical factor in British domestic politics of the time, over which it could exercise no influence. Lloyd George's attitude was, in one so politically astute, a vain hope. But when his government collapsed under the Tory onslaught in 1922, the damage to Ireland was already done.

[33] 'The Orange Order, which had come into being at the end of the eighteenth century as an instrument of defence (or of aggression, according to your point of view) against Catholics, had languished for some seventy years after the Union ... with its parades, its banners, its pounding drums, it injected into Ulster life ... an element of political hysteria not essentially different from, though unhappily more permanent than, the religious hysteria to which the province had shown itself so prone' — Lyons, op.cit., p.25.

[34] Parnell, Portsmouth, June 25, 1886.

[35] Kate was in line to inherit a fortune which, provided they were still married, he might lay claim to. Her relationship with Parnell threatened this inheritance. O'Shea's prospects existed only so long as it remained secret.

[36] It is an accurate description of Ireland between 1922 and 1960, but an incorrect attribution of the reasons for it. The civil war, the prolonged economic war with Britain throughout the 1930's, the burden of land annuity payments to Britain, the Local Loan Fund and other impositions of the financial settlement associated with the Treaty of 1921, are among the more significant reasons for the slowness with which development occurred after independence. These were followed by the Second World War (the Emergency), and their accumulated and stultifying economic consequences are extremely significant in this context.

CHAPTER THREE. Pp. 63-83

[37] In a speech that year, when the question of some form of legislative independence for Ireland was a highly emotive electoral issue in England, Lord Salisbury, for the Conservative Party, did not reject the question out of hand and, for the first time, indicated that it was one for consideration. About the same time he made a speech reiterating the Conservative traditional position on Ireland, but leaving the door open. In the course of this speech he made an observation intended, at the time, as a warning of the possible consequences of local autonomy in a country where the majority/minority divergences and dissentions were so extreme. He, of course, had in mind a situation where the majority would be Catholic and the minority Protestant or Dissenter. The words of this prophetic Tory went unheeded and very much 'out of mind' when his successors deceitfully brought about Partition and created the puppet area of Northern Ireland some thirty-seven years later. Salisbury had written: 'I fully recognise that, in the case of local institutions especially, there is one element of consideration which in the state of Ireland you cannot

leave out of mind. Local authorities are more exposed to the temptations of enabling the majority to be unjust to the minority when they obtain jurisdiction over a small area than is the case when the authority derives its sanction and extends its authority over a wider area. It would be impossible to leave out of sight, in the extension of any such local authority to Ireland, the fact that the population is on several subjects deeply divided and that it is the duty of every Government on all matters essential to justice to protect the minority against the majority.'

[38] The name is said to have been coined by Douglas Hyde, though this is disputed. Sean O Luing points out (op.cit.,p. 59) that 'The National Library has a letter in which Griffith gives Maire Butler the credit for suggesting the title *Sinn Fein*. Sinn Fein is described by Brian Murphy, (op. cit.,p.26) as being 'moribund in 1916; resurrected as a term of abuse to describe, first, the Irish Volunteers, and, second, the participants in the Easter Rising — such was the level to which the Sinn Fein ideal had sunk. Where, it is reasonable to ask, is to be found the revolutionary dynamic so confidently identified by recent historians?' Judge Kingsmill Moore, according to the State Papers of Ireland and also cited by Murphy, observed that: 'Sinn Fein, if not very successful,managed to avoid extinction and survived as a a somewhat languishing and enfeebled organisation, familiar to few and kept alive only by the rugged courage and resource of Arthur Griffith. The name Sinn Fein was so euphoniously encompassing that in fact it came to be a blanket term applied to some organisations that never used the term, some — at least three — that did and by the British, indiscriminately, to everyone and everything that seemed even vaguely national, let alone rebellious — e.g. the 'Shinners' rebellion, the 'Shinner', Michael Collins, etc. When Sinn Fein was founded in 1900 it was stipulated by Griffith that members should declare themselves 'advocates of an Irish republic'.

[39] Amongst Orange toasts are the following: — 'The crown of the causeway on road or street, and the Papishes under my feet'; 'And may all Croppies be rammed, jammed and dammed into the great gun that is in Athlone, and may I be standing by with a lighted torch to blow them into innumerable fragments over the Hill of Blastation...'; and, perhaps the daddy of them all, that of the oath of the Aldermen of Skinner's Row: 'The glorious, pious and immortal memory of the great and good King William, not forgetting Oliver Cromwell, who assisted in redeeming us from popery, slavery, arbitrary power, brass money and wooden shoes. May we never want for a Williamite to kick the arse of a Jacobite! And a fart for the Bishop of Cork!' — a protestant prelate who had unwisely expressed views not entirely condemnatory of Taigs and papists. It goes on: 'And he that won't drink this '[toast]' whether he be priest, bishop, deacon bellows-blower, grave-digger, or any other of the fraternity of the clergy — may a north wind blow him to the south, and a west wind blow him to the east! May he have a dark night, a lee shore, a rank storm and a leaky vessel to carry him over the Styx! May the dog Cerberus make a meal of his rump, and may the devil jump down his throat with a red-hot harrow, with every pin tear out a gut, and blow him with a clean carcase to hell — Amen!'

[40] He in fact spoke publicly in support of Home Rule and the Irish Party as late as 1912.

[41] Later, during the First World War, he was falsely accused by British of being a spy. This accusation was based on the logic that, since he was German, he must be a spy. In a similar frame of mind the Dublin City Council rescinded the Freedom of Dublin it had bestowed on him for his scholarly work on Irish literature.

[42] The uncomfortable irony is that, since Independence — but especially since the 1960s — and evidently voluntarily, the country seems to have become more Anglicised in manner, habit, speech, outlook and lifestyle than the English were able to impose in 400 years of occupation. Whether this is due to mass communications and the universal cult

of the lowest common cultural denominator — the barbarous Mittel Atlantische Kultur referred to elsewhere — to a residual 'slibhinism' producing a proliferation of vulgarisms such as placenames like 'Devon Downs' and 'Tudor Courts' — to migratory trends, a North-European and American Anglo-Saxon degenerated protestant culture, or to a combination of these and other factors, it is impossible to say. What is apparent is that we seem to have developed very rapidly an iconoclastic disregard for, and loss of pride in, our great heritage, a lack of interest in our national self-image, and are so over-anxious to appear 'reasonable', 'liberal' and, God help us, 'enlightened', that we sometimes appear to encourage libertinism instead of liberty and to 'tolerate' ourselves out of existence.

[43]   Born County Leitrim 1884, joined the Gaelic League; member of the IRB from 1906; stricken with polio, 1912; signatory of the Proclamation of the Irish Republic; executed 12 May, 1916.

[44]   Born Waterford 1886; post-office clerk; joined Volunteers in 1913; second in command to Thomas Ashe in 1916 at the Battle of Ashbourne; interned 1916; elected for Clontarf in 1918 election. TD from 1923-61; supported Treaty; became commander of the pro-Treaty forces after the death of Collins in August, 1922. Held several ministerial appointments in Fine Gael coalitions. Leader of Fine Gael 1944-59.

[45]   Born Tipperary in 1879 and became a teacher. Early on he became involved in the Gaelic revival and joined the Gaelic League in 1901. Helped Pearse establish St. Enda's in 1908. In 1911 became assistant lecturer in UCD. He wrote a number of plays and was a poet of promise. In the aftermath of the 1913 riot and lockout he developed an interest in military matters and was a founder-member of the Irish Volunteers. He later became a member of the IRB. He was a capable organiser and was involved in the organisation of the Howth gun-running and the huge demonstration at O'Donovan Rossa's funeral where Pearse made his renowned oration. Was considered to be a hard-headed pragmatist. He may have been responsible for the publication of the so-called 'Castle Document' before the Rising. He was one of the signatories of the Proclamation of the Republic. Shot, Kilmainham Jail, 3 May, 1916. Michael Collins considered him his mentor in military matters.

[46]   Born Galway, 1881, son of an RIC officer; clerk in Dublin Corporation; joined Gaelic League, 1900. Joined Sinn Fein 1908; founded the Dublin Piper's Club, 1910. Was a founder member of the Volunteers. Member of the IRB Supreme Council. Signatory to the Proclamation of the Republic, executed 8 May 1916.

[47]   The difference in wages for 'an ordinary labourer' in 1883, for instance, was: England 2/6d to 4/-; Scotland 2/6d to 3/4d; Wales 2/4d to 2/10d; Ireland 1/6d to 1/10d — *Journal of Forestry* 1883, Vol.7, p.126 (attached table). By the turn of the century there had been little relative change. Lyons points out (pps 99/100) that there was a significant and important difference between Protestant and Catholic incomes and that "these differ-ences may well have reinforced religio-political rivalries by a sense of deprivation among Catholics, and of privilege among Protestants". He cites the work of Professor E. Larkin (*Economic Growth, Capital Investment and the Roman Catholic Church in Ireland*, American Historical Review, April 1967), to show that it is possible to assume "for the first half of the nineteenth century a subsistence figure of £5 a year for the individual ... throughout that period the Catholic population *as a whole* fell regularly below that amount... The Protestant minority, on the other hand never came remotely within sight of the subsistence border-line and their income per head ... was generally triple, sometimes quadruple, that of the Catholic majority" (my italics).

[48]   Son of the sixth Lord Dunsany, launched the cooperative campaign in 1889; Unionist MP; convened the famous Recess Committee of 1895; became a Home Rule

supporter; knighted in 1903; became a member of the Irish Senate in 1922; home burned in 1923 and he left Ireland then.

[49] This was the favoured solution for Griffith, and one he never really abandoned.

[50] Edward Carson was born in Dublin in 1854. He studied law at Trinity and quickly achieved prominence. He was a man of saturnine appearance and melancholy, but fervid, disposition. He became associated with Balfour, then Chief Secretary, and they worked well together. He moved to London in 1893, and brought his growing reputation with him where it increased. He was leading prosecuting counsel in the trial of Oscar Wilde. He was, it is claimed in spite of his hair-raising and treasonable speeches between 1910 and 1914, 'more liberal in his politics than the Unionists whom he later led -' by no means a difficult achievement. 'He stood far to the Left of those Ulster Unionists whom he was to lead for so long... He had only a limited amount in common with those same Ulster Unionists...' (Lyons, op. cit. p.300). Maintenance of the Union was, as he put it, 'The Guiding star of my political life... in his strategy the aim of Ulster resistance [to Home Rule] should not be to secure some special status for the north, rather to make Home Rule impossible for any part of Ireland. Time was to bring him to a cruel understanding that his vision of Irish Unionism as a seamless robe was not shared by those on whom he most relied'(Ibid.) This rather lenient picture, however, is hard to reconcile with the facts or with the demagogue who spoke as he did at Coleraine on September 20th, 1912.

James Craig was born in Belfast in 1871, the son of a wealthy whiskey distiller. He served in the Boer war and became an MP for Down in 1906. He was a very different character from Carson. His vision was more limited and brutal, and was very much an Ulster Unionist, bigoted and narrow-minded, brave and unbending and prepared, 'if necessary, to go into armed rebellion ... to preserve the character and integrity of the Ulster he knew and loved'(Lyons, op.cit., p.300). He was Chief of Staff of the Ulster Army, the UVF and became Treasurer of His Majesty's Household in December, 1916.

[51] The Ulster Covenant; 'Being convinced in our consciences that Home Rule would be disastrous to the material well-being of Ulster as well as the whole of Ireland, subversive of our civil and religious freedom, destructive of our citizenship, and perilous to the unity of the Empire, we, whose names are underwritten, men of Ulster, loyal subjects of his gracious Majesty, King George the Fifth, humbly relying on the God whom our fathers in days of stress and trial confidently trusted, hereby pledge ourselves in solemn Covenant in this our time of threatened calamity to stand by one another in defending, for ourselves and our children, our cherished position of equal citizenship in the United Kingdom, in using all means which may be found necessary to defeat the present conspiracy to set up a Home Rule Parliament in Ireland; and in the event of such a Parliament being forced upon us, we further solemnly and mutually pledge ourselves to refuse to recognise its authority. In sure confidence that God will defend the right, we hereunto subscribe our names, and further, we individually declare that we have not already signed this Covenant'.

This document, signed by nearly half a million people, with its clear emphasis on 'material well-being' and 'civil and religious freedom' and, above all, equal citizenship in the United Kingdom, confirms in their own words the point emphasised in Chapter One — namely the nature of the benefit of the Union to the Dissenters as a whole and to the Presbyterians in particular.

[52] It is important to remember when talking about the Ulster Volunteer Force and the Irish Volunteers, which were formed a little later, that one is not comparing like with like

either as to arms, manpower or representation. The UVF reached full mobilisation with about 90,000 men. They were well armed and represented about 800,000 (maximum) northern unionists, in other words about 12% of the northern population. The Irish Volunteers, on the other hand, except for a brief period after the Bachelor's Walk massacre, never exceeded about 18,000. They were poorly armed, some not at all, and at that time represented perhaps 25% of the population (within a few years, of course, that picture altered so radically that Sinn Fein and nationalists represented approximately 92% of the population after the 1918 general election, and the unionists about 8%). Redmond's National Volunteers — the break-away group that bloomed and then faded after Bachelor's Walk — mustered about 130,000. That the representation by the Irish Volunteers, and the Citizen Army (about 200), was so small before 1916, is not an indication of lack of support (which mushroomed rapidly after the Rising), but of indifference and complacency.

[53] Further prohibitions on the import of arms were later introduced on 7 December 1913, but were directed primarily at the Irish Volunteer Force, formed the previous month.

[54] With the selection by Field-Marshal Roberts of General Richardson to command the Ulster Volunteers the ground was prepared for what was seen as 'the worst case' — the imposition of Home Rule on all Ireland. Carson took immediate advantage and, in a speech at Antrim, said: 'We have pledges and promises from some of the greatest generals in the army that , when the time comes and if it is necessary, they will come over to help us keep the old flag flying and defy those who dare invade our liberties'(Dangerfield, op. cit., cited p. 135). One of the 'greatest generals' he referred to was undoubtedly Major-General Sir Henry Wilson then Director of Military Operations at the War Office — an Ulsterman of sanguine temperament and considerable gifts '(who)' sat spinning a contradictory web in which the army should be ... rendered so mutinous in temper that it would refuse to obey the government in any gesture against Ulster... the War Office, with Sir Henry Wilson's help, was slowly being honeycombed with Tory intrigue' (Ibid. p.136).

[55] He would later become Lord Birkenhead. A leader of the Tory party, on 12 July, 1912, he informed a meeting of Orangemen at Belfast: 'If the Unionists could not keep all of Ireland ... at least they could keep Ulster; and no Home Rule Bill would be acceptable unless it contained a provision that Ulster would be excluded. What could be more reasonable?' (Dangerfield, op. cit., p.104). Smith was later to play an influential part in the Treaty negotiations during which he evidently made a considerable impression on Michael Collins. He acquired the nickname 'Galloper' when he became galloper to General Richardson, commander-in-chief of the UVF. He was one of those who were involved in the 'forged diaries' controversy over Roger Casement and was Attorney General during his trial, which he prosecuted himself.

CHAPTER FOUR. Pp 85 - 108

[56] There is no doubt that Carson and his supporters brought about a real threat of civil war, including the possibility of a German protectorate in the north, but to say, as has been asserted by some historians, that they were a primary cause of the Easter Rising is going too far. It suggests that the IRB would not have acted in pursuit of independent sovereignty if it had not been for the opposition of Carson and the Ulster Unionists to Home Rule, which contradicts both logic and all that the IRB stood for.

[57] The usual estimate is 40,000 rifles and 3,000,000 rounds of ammunition landed at Larne. The amount varies from source to source. But, since there were landings elsewhere in Ulster besides Larne, this may have given rise to the confusion. Certainly there were not less than 20,000 rifles and 3,000,000 rounds landed at Larne. It would, therefore, seem that something in the region of another 20,000 rifles with appropriate ammunition were

landed at other points, as Colonel Hickman indicated. It is, perhaps, of some interest to note that there is to-day in Northern Ireland a para-military terrorist force also called the Ulster Volunteer Force dedicated to the preservation of 'Protestant Ulster'.

[58] Were it not for the hostility of Tom Clarke and Sean McDermott following Hobson's vote in favour of accepting Redmond's ultimatum in 1914, Hobson would almost certainly have been a signatory of the Proclamation. Before the crisis in the IRB brought about by the decision of the Volunteer Committee to accept Redmond's ultimatum (by 18 votes to nine), but under duress, Hobson's position had been one of great influence in the IRB. He was a member of the Supreme Council, was Leinster Centre, editor of the IRB magazine *Irish Freedom* and chairman of the Dublin Centres Board. He had also played a major role in the organisation of IRB military training before the formation of the Volunteers, the formation of the Volunteers themselves and the landing of the guns at Howth and Kilcoole. In short his exclusion would, had the internal split not occurred, have been extraordinary (Hobson's reasoning that to have refused would have meant a split in the Volunteers was not accepted by Clarke and McDermott).

[59] 'For the rest, England, which during the last two years Germany has been trying, not without success, to detach from France and Russia, is paralysed by internal dissentions and her Irish quarrels' — despatch from *Baron Beyens, Belgian Minister at Berlin, reviewing the situation as it appeared to German officials, July 26, 1914.*

'Dr E.J.Dillon, one of the best informed journalists in Europe, telegraphing from Vienna on July 26, 1914, gave five reasons why Austria expected a free hand in dealing with Serbia. The third in order of importance was as follows: — "It was a moment when the cares of the British Government were absorbed in forecasting and preparing for the fateful consequence of its internal policy in regard to Irish Home Rule, which may, it is apprehended, culminate in civil war"' — Horgan, op.cit, p 39.

The situation was so evident that the *Daily Telegraph* wrote in October, 1913, that 'any attempt to break the loyalists of Ulster by the armed forces of the Crown will probably result in the disorganization of the army for several years'.

[60] Campbell was Legal Assessor to the Ulster Provisional Government and, later, to be, of all things, Attorney General for Ireland (1916); Lord Chief Justice for Ireland, and Lord Chancellor for Ireland, (1918).

[61] These Orders read: 'I am commanded by the Army Council to *inform* you that in consequence of reports which have been received by His Majesty's Government that attempts may be made in various parts of Ireland by evil-disposed persons to obtain possession of arms, ammunition, and other Government stores, it is considered advisable that you should at once take special precautions for safeguarding depots and other places where arms or stores are kept, *as you may think advisable.* It appears from the information received that Armagh, Omagh, Carrickfergus, and Enniskillen are insufficiently guarded, being specially liable to attack. You will, therefore, please take the necessary steps, and report to this office' — War Office to General Sir A. Paget, the General Officer Commanding in Chief for Ireland, dated March 14, 1914 (*author's italics*).

[62] 'They had pledges and promises from some of the greatest generals in the army that, when the time comes, and if it is necessary, they will come over to help us to keep the old flag flying, and to defy those who would dare invade our liberties -' Carson, speaking at Antrim, September 20, 1913. The signals for the army to mutiny were crowned with a speech by Bonar Law, the Canadian Orangeman and leader of the Opposition, in Dublin, in November, when he said: 'There is another point to which I would specially refer. In order to carry out his despotic intention, King James had the largest paid army which had ever been seen in

England. What happened? There was a revolution and the king disappeared. Why? Because his army refused to fight for him...' This was the most extraordinary incitement to any British Army to treason in modern history, and it has received little enough attention — or been dismissed, together with the 'mutiny' itself, as not being treason or mutiny at all, but something else, unspecified. 'A more extraordinary appeal to the army had never been made, it is safe to say, by any Opposition leader'. Dangerfield, op.cit. p.137. Wilson was to become Chief of the Imperial General Staff. He was assassinated in London in 1921 (see infra). A bigoted Ulster Unionist of whom Asquith wrote: 'He was voluble, impetuous and an indefatigable intriguer. As his Diaries, which the misplaced devotion of his friends have disclosed to the world, abundantly show, he was endowned by Nature with a loose tongue, and was in the habit of wielding a looser pen -' Oxford and Asquith, The Earl of, *Memories and Reflections*, vol.11, p.185.

[63] For all that turbulent events in England had been the first preoccupation of government since 1911, what was happening in Continental Europe was sufficiently dark and threatening to have alerted key members of the cabinet — including Churchill — to the possibility of war. He proposed, for instance, to spend the then astronomical sum of £52m on refitting the British navy with new dreadnaughts.

[64] Gough, in an interview with the *Daily Telegraph*, stated 'I got a signed guarantee that *in no circumstances* shall we be used to force Home Rule on the Ulster people. If it comes to civil war I would fight for Ulster rather than against her'(Daily Telegraph, March 25th, 1914).

[65] According to Hobson (See *Foundation and growth of the Irish Volunteers 1913-14*, p. 44 by Bulmer Hobson, *The Irish Volunteers 1913-1915*, ed. F.X.Martin) who is the most reliable source, MacNeill was in touch with Redmond prior to Redmond's take-over bid seeking his cooperation regarding the Volunteers. Evidently the discussions (described by Hobson, p.45) led Redmond to the conclusion that it was imperative to 'take over' the Volunteers, hence his ultimatum of 9 June — one day before the convening of the First Volunteer Convention intended to elect a national executive. MacNeill was evidently unaware of Redmond's plans at this stage. What is most significant is that MacNeill was acting on his own without the knowledge of his fellow Volunteer officers, thus highlighting the tendency — however well-intentioned — to ill-advised unilateral action which seems to have played a part in Irish affairs almost as great as loose talk and informers. Casement, according to Hobson, also displayed a tendency to unilateral action. Hobson writes (p.47): 'Although I was in no way a party to MacNeill's negotiations and had no desire to see Redmond in a position to control the Volunteers, I clearly saw that it was necessary to accept this ultimatum (of 9 June) if the Volunteers were not to be split into two opposing camps.

'I was as much opposed to this action on the part of Redmond as those who disapproved of my attitude. I recognised even then that Redmond's aim was the destroying or curbing of a growing national organisation which he had hitherto bitterly opposed; but I realised equally that if his request, which was in fact an ultimatum, were not acceded to it would lead to a disastrous and, indeed, a fatal split in the Volunteers and in the country as a whole.'

It is interesting to compare this assessment with the writer, James Stephens's — who could not in any way be called a separatist, much less a republican — acerbic contemporary (1916) comment on Redmond: '... the leader of the Irish Party (Redmond) misrepresented his people in the English House of Parliament. On the day of the declaration of war between England and Germany he took the Irish case, weighty with eight centuries of history and tradition, and he threw it out of the window. He pledged Ireland to a particular course of action and he had no authority to give this pledge and he had no guarantee that it would be met. The ramshackle intelligence of his party and his own emotional nature betrayed him, and us and England ... he pledged his country's credit so deeply that he did not leave her even one National rag to cover herself with ... Mr Redmond told the lie and he is answerable to England for the violence she had to be guilty of, and to Ireland for the desolation to which we have had to submit ... Ireland must in ages gone have been guilty of abominable crimes or she could not at this juncture have been afflicted with a John Redmond.' (James Stephens, *The Insurrection in Dublin*, Dublin, 1916).

[66] Jointly by Hobson and The O'Rahilly, who was managing director of *An Claideamh Soluis* and who, in the first place, had asked MacNeill to write the article 'on matters of general public interest' (Lyons, op. cit., p.320). Bulmer Hobson, acting for the IRB, then asked O'Rahilly, who <u>was</u> <u>not</u> an IRB man and was not aware of IRB long-term plans, to approach MacNeill. T. Desmond Williams — *Eoin MacNeill and the Irish Volunteers, Leaders and Men of the Easter Rising: Dublin 1916*, ed. Martin — writes (p. 139) 'Within a week of the publication of this article, MacNeill was visited by Bulmer Hobson and the O'Rahilly'. There is some minor confusion as to whether Hobson went with The O'Rahilly to see MacNeill. Hobson himself (op.cit. p.24) writes; 'At my suggestion he [O'Rahilly] asked MacNeill if he would preside at a committee meeting to discuss the formation of a Volunteer body. Next day he said that MacNeill was quite willing to take the chair'. This clearly indicates that O'Rahilly put the question to MacNeill on his own and in the absence of Hobson. On the other hand Mac Neill writes:' A few days after its publication the O'Rahilly came again to my house, accompanied by Bulmer Hobson. They referred to this article of mine and asked me did I mean it in earnest ...' (*How the Volunteers Began*, an extract from unpublished memoirs of Eoin MacNeill, Martin; *The Irish Volunteers 1913-1915*, p.71). This is ambiguous. Both accounts appear to have been written fifteen or more years later. On balance Hobson, the IRB man, who was probably the most immediately concerned, is most likely to have remembered the sequence correctly. MacNeill goes on to make the following interesting comments: 'I had no doubt in my mind that both these men came to me from the old physical force party whose organisation was the I.R.B. [He was wrong in this insofar as The O'Rahilly was concerned], and I also had little doubt of the part I was expected to play.

'By this time, through the Gaelic League activities, I had come to be known to people in nearly every part of Ireland and I was regarded as a man of moderate views. The appeal of the physical force party had always been limited, and a person like me who stood well with many who did not belong to that party, including many of the clergy, might well be able to recommend a programme of action, which would be regarded askance if it came forward from those who were called extremist. I have no doubt that first and last this was the view of the physical force tradition. Personally, I was no doctrinaire, whether on behalf of physical force or against it.'

[67] But Lyons, op.cit. p. 322 says: — 'of the ten men who participated in that meeting, four were members of the IRB'. In this Lyons is borne out by Hobson, who arranged the meeting. Those present were MacNeill, W.J.Ryan, Joseph Cambpell, The O'Rahilly, P.H.Pearse, Pierce Beaslai, Sean McDermott, Eamonn Ceannt, James A. Deakin, the latter four being IRB. Hobson himself did not attend: 'I was generally regarded as an extreme nationalist, and thought it better at this initial stage to absent myself from Dublin ... that evening' (Hobson, op. cit., p. 25). O'Hegarty may possibly be confusing the inaugural meeting with the subsequent committee of 30 members, of which twelve were IRB, four were Members of the United Irish League, an offshoot of the Irish Parliamentary Party, four of the Ancient Order of Hibernians, and the remaining ten not affiliated with any party.

[68] A body of local Volunteers, later absorbed into the Irish Volunteers, is said to have been formed in Athlone even before the Irish Volunteer Force. But the existence of this body is open to question, according to The O'Rahilly (*The Secret History of the Irish Volunteers*, Dublin, 1915, p.3), who states that the organisers of the Irish Volunteers 'absolutely failed to discover any Volunteers either in Athlone or the Midlands until long after the Wynn's Hotel meeting'.

[69] Larkin was born in Liverpool 1876 of Irish parents, Larkin's background was similar to that of Connolly in many ways. Physically a very powerful man, he had a big presence — Big Jim — and an even bigger voice which allowed him to dominate vast meetings even in the open air. In 1908 he founded the Irish Transport and General Workers' Union. In 1913 Larkin organised the dockers and won for them a substantial wage increase. He then turned his attention to the Dublin Tramway company, one of William Martin Murphy's enterprises. Before he could open negotiations Murphy forestalled him. He had founded the Employers' Federation (1911) and now declared that the company would recognise neither Larkin nor his union. Larkin called the tramwaymen out on August 26 during Horse Show week. The strike spread, there was considerable violence and the Employers Federation decided to break the strike by a lock-out of all employees who belonged to Larkin's union. This dreadful strike lasted from August 1913 to February 1914, when the wretched workers resumed work.

William Martin Murphy was one of the wealthiest magnates in Dublin, with many interests at home and abroad. He pioneered tram and railway services in several countries and owned the Metropole Hotel, Department stores, the Independent Newspaper Group. Given the existing political tension with Home Rule and the Unionists, and the series of strikes and outrages that had rocked parts of England and the Continent since 1910, the 1913 lockout, which was essentially a struggle between Larkin's trade unionists and Murphy's employers' federation, and therefore a social and class struggle, had a profound effect right across the Irish social spectrum. It even began to look as if 'Ireland might dissolve into civil war, dragging Britain after her into the abyss'(Lyons, op.cit. p.284).

[70] Initially it was armed with hurleys and its particular function was to protect the Fintan Lalor pipe band which was formed by the Transport Workers' Union to lead demonstrations. Accordingly it was normally in the forefront when the police attacked. On March 22, 1914, the Citizen Army adopted a constitution and uniform, which was dark green with a slouch hat turned up on the right hand side.

[71] Connolly was born in Edinburgh in 1868 of emigre Irish parents. Came to Ireland in 1896, married at 21, self-educated, carter employed by Edinburgh corporation. Connolly was one of the greatest socialist thinkers of his generation. For him the 'Irish question' was basically an economic one, but political action provided the 'readiest and most effective means' of preparing to deal finally with it.

[72] The origin of the plan giving rise to this idea, and the subsequent gun-running, curiously enough had little to do with the IRB. The plan was devised by Casement, Bulmer Hobson, The O'Rahilly and MacNeill, only one of whom — Hobson — was an IRB man, and he wasn't brought into the plot until the landing was imminent.

[73] Eoin MacNeill was not, at least as late as 1913, a republican in outlook, which explains the attitude of Pearse and the other IRB men towards him. It is possible that, following Redmond's take-over bid for the Volunteers in 1914, he altered his views somewhat, but, according to J.J. Horgan, Mac Neill told him 'to allow Mr. Redmond to know in the best way you can, that I pledge myself against any use of the Volunteer movement to weaken his party, *which is also my party*' (Horgan, *Parnell to Pearse, some*

recollections and reflections, Dublin, 1948, p.228), author's italics. That was in December, 1913. MacNeill was undoubtedly later disillusioned by Redmond's attitude and the split he caused in the Volunteers, but his prevarication in 1916 becomes more understandable in the light of this statement. It also reinforces the reasoning behind his Volunteer policy. He held the view that the Volunteers were not a revolutionary army, but a defensive organisation, a power-base to be used at a later date to ensure the introduction of Home Rule. The only circumstances in which they might become involved in hostilities were if they were themselves attacked or conscription was introduced. It is interesting that when he was asked in later years how the revolution came about in Ireland, his answer was 'Mainly by Carson'.

[74] Whatever his motive, it is open to question. One likelihood is that, because of the impending situation in Europe, Redmond came under pressure from England to render the Volunteers harmless or, preferably, have them inducted into the British army; by no means beyond the bounds of possibility given that large numbers of the Volunteers were ex-soldiers of both commissioned and non-commissioned rank.

[75] It was primarily in an effort to buy time in this regard (if not to completely offset it) that the Home Rule Act was rendered so feeble. The British saw the Unionists as a major threat (politically, also, of course, but that, too, they misread). And in trying to ameliorate that danger, as they saw it, they had no hesitation in reducing the Home Rule Act to a cosmetic exercise which became unacceptable, very quickly, to the Irish populace in general. In short, for political considerations, they sold out Home Rule and the expectations of the majority to placate the Unionist minority. The clear inference is that they expected — and indeed had every reason to expect — trouble from the Unionists. They did not expect it from the nationalists.

[76] Knighted by the British for his work in exposing atrocities in Africa and South America, Casement was one of the most important — if not influential, and that is debatable — and enigmatic figures of the whole Irish separatist movement from 1900 onwards. He was eventually captured on Good Friday 1916, after landing from Germany by submarine in Tralee Bay. For a variety of reasons the British were under the erroneous impression that he was the key figure in any foreseeable Irish uprising and, with his capture, coupled with the sinking of the German arms ship, *Aud*, evidently concluded that no such danger any longer existed. Casement was particularly reviled by the British because of his status and position, both of which lent substance — and therefore the greater danger — to his views. During Casement's subsequent and notorious trial the infamous British 'dirty-tricks' brigade produced what purported to be a set of Casement's diaries showing him to be a sexual pervert, and widely publicised and circulated extracts from these. It is a — perhaps not unrelated — fact that during his investigations in South America Casement uncovered examples of gross sexual abuse and perversion there and translated the diary of one degenerate from Spanish into English. This he submitted to the British authorities. It is argued that extracts from this were interpolated in his own diaries in order to destroy his character and diminish his standing (See chapter 12).

[77] Dangerfield (op. cit., p.417), says that a secondary purpose may have been to prevent Redmond gaining excessive control over the Volunteers. But, given the sequence already outlined, this seems like reasoning a *posteriori*.

[78] Not to be confused with Conor Cruise O'Brien, an entirely different individual.

[79] The ammunition for these rifles has been a matter of uncertainty. There are two main types of military round, ball, or general-purpose ammunition, coated (that is fully-hard-metal-jacketed), and, usually half-coated, ammunition. (Special-purpose ammunition for small-arms includes armour-piercing, tracer, incendiary, blank, grenade and spotting

cartridges. Explosive cartridges are not used). The Howth rifles were Mauser military rifles for which the ammunition was supplied. According to Hobson the rifles were 'Mauser rifles with which the German Army was re-armed after the Franco-Prussian war' (op.cit., p.33), mainly the 9.5mm 1887 Mauser. Ammunition for these weapons was both coated and half-coated, but the latter was discouraged and eventually discontinued as it tended to foul barrels. The British themselves, certainly, were using — and continued to use — soft-nosed ammunition throughout the war on certain fronts. Virtually all revolver ammunition is soft-nosed. Lee (op. cit., p. 25) refers to 'the explosive bullets landed in the Howth gun-running'. It should be made quite clear that they were definitely **not** explosive bullets, which had long been banned. These were then a rare and highly specialised ammunition certainly not in common military use in the decade prior to 1914, and unquestionably were not landed in the Howth gun-running. Explosive bullets were developed from about 1825, but did not become popular until Colonel (later General) John Jacob developed explosive bullets which were used in the Indian Mutiny (1857-1859). Explosive bullets were outlawed at an international conference held in St. Petersburg shortly after the American Civil War, in which both sides used them. It is also sometimes alleged that the Howth ammunition was 'dum-dum' — a name derived from the factory at Dum-Dum, Calcutta, where Jacob's bullet was produced. Such references are equally misleading. At the period, 1914, when explosive bullets had long been outlawed, 'dum-dum' usually meant rounds which had been individually 'flattened' or hollowed or had the hard-metal jacketting partly removed. This was not the case with the Howth ammuniton. It is also of interest that, according to Meda Ryan (See *The Day Michael Collins was Killed*), some of the rounds used at Beal na mBlath by the anti-Treaty side were 'doctored' rounds that had been captured from the British. It is, therefore, completely wrong to claim a/ that the ammunition for the Howth rifles was 'explosive', which is ridiculous, or b/ uncoated i.e. 'dum-dum', which, though possible, is at best speculative and is, in any case, unlikely to have applied to the whole ammunition consignment.

[80] However, it is hardly to be supposed that the national fervour which exhilarated the mass of the people following the murders at Bachelor's Walk disappeared of its own accord. It certainly diversified and, perhaps, diminished. But, taken together with the chicanery relating to the Home Rule Bill and the general mood of unease and revolt, north and south, that undeniably existed, it is not unreasonable to conclude that the climate of change towards separatism was well underway.

[81] It is barely conceivable that this experienced politician had some vague thought of reconciling the Unionists with the majority opinion in Ireland. If so, it was about as impractical a notion as might be imagined. In any case it went completely awry.

[82] Indeed, if one wants to make a case for the Volunteers being betrayed and deceived, here is an example, more deliberately callous and certainly more anti-national, than any species of deception that might be alleged to have been perpetrated on the Volunteers by the IRB, who were motivated solely by the desire for national independence.

Conscription was not the only aspect of the war that concerned Irish leaders ... or indeed their English counterparts. In England thousands of young men of military age had to be exempted from duty because they were skilled workers; the Irish, for the most part, were technologically unskilled, and would therefore make ideal cannon-fodder. There was also the economic compulsion to join.

[83] There is an interesting hypothesis (advanced by D.W. Miller, *Church, state and nation in Ireland, 1898-1921*, pp. 308-310 and Lee, op. cit., p.21) that there were 'strong tactical' reasons for Redmond's support of Britain's war effort 'even from a separatist viewpoint'. This was that the war was expected to 'be over by Christmas' and that a post-

war election in 1915 would favour an Ireland that had stood by England in her hour of peril. It is certainly a thesis worthy of consideration. Redmond had already shown an unpolitical tendency to put all his eggs in one basket, coupled with a regrettable propensity to fly in the face of the abundant evidence and place his trust in the British. On those grounds, and the grounds that his political judgement was — if not at that time actually impaired — under very considerable influence, it is an interesting speculation. However, even such a man clinging desperately to the hope of leading a parliament of whatever sort, must also have taken into account the fact that its merit rested not alone on the war being over by 1915, but also on an English — or at least an Allied — victory, which was far from likely throughout 1915 and 1916 up to the Rising. The IRB's contemporary attitude, even without the benefit of hindsight, seems to have been rather more realistic — namely to plan for a rising before the war ended and a place at the post-war peace conference table. In the context of these two opposed policies it is significant — as Lee says (p. 24) — that it was initially hoped that a rising would take place in September 1915. He seems to be confusing a declaration of intent, 1915, with the actual planning. So far as it is possible to assess, no specific plans for a rising were made other than those prepared by the Military Council of the IRB for 1916 unless one takes Casement's activities in Germany to possess more substance than they had. On the whole the IRB planners demonstrated the better strategy, linked as it was to their acute perception — wished-for or not — that the mood of the people was swinging decisively away from the Parliamentary Party. It would certainly have made more political sense for Redmond to have heeded the voices from his own grass roots, which were reasonably clear after the dilution of the Home Rule Bill in 1912; to have recognised the intransigency of the northern unionists to Home Rule and to have taken steps to win the allegiance of the increasingly powerful 'Irish-Ireland' movement, rather than cast his bread upon the waters of the British war effort and trust in a bountiful return.

It is also interesting to note that even before Redmond's offer at Woodenbridge or in the House of Commons, Captain Maurice Talbot Crosbie, at that time Chief Inspecting Officer of the Cork Volunteer Corps, on his own initiative and without consulting any other members of the Cork Military Council of the Volunteers, sent a telegram to the British Secretary of State for War on the day war was declared offering the services of the Cork Corps to Britain. He was subsequently relieved of his duties, but he provoked a split in the Cork Volunteer Corps which preceded the national split brought about by Redmond's action by some three weeks, and with similar results.

[84] Born Dublin in 1879 in Great Brunswick street (now Pearse street) his father was an English monumental sculptor who was married for the second time. Brother William and two sisters. Ed. Christian Brothers. Took his BA and was later called to the Bar. His real interest was education and he was an advanced thinker and writer on the subject, which he combined with practical application. Committed to Irish language revival. At 17 started the New Ireland Society to popularise language, poetry and folklore. Founded St. Enda's school in 1908 to 'instil into the rising generation a love for their own past and for their language and literature.' Described the British system of education as a Murder Machine. Joined the Gaelic League and edited their paper An Claideamh Soluis 1903-9. Became a speaker 'of extraordinary power and magnetism'(Lyons, op. cit., p. 333). His oration at the grave of O'Donovan Rossa (1913) was probably, for Pearse, the turning point from being moderate to militarist. Before that he had spoken in support of Home Rule. He was a man of high principles and ideals and wrote: 'I am old fashioned enough to be both a Catholic and a Nationalist'(P.H.Pearse, *Political Writings and Speeches*, Dublin 1922). Joined the IRB in December 1913, and went immediately to America to

raise funds. There was, undoubtedly, an element of theatricality about him, but it was not unusual at the time and was so allied to integrity and directness that it did not diminish, rather reinforced, the substance of his idealism and the reality to which he was committed. Theatricality in people in the public eye (and Pearse had been in the public eye for some time), in an age without wireless or TV, was normal enough. Moreover Victorian romanticism was by no means solely an English phenomenon. It was universal and Tennyson had his counterparts everywhere — Rilke, Poe and so on. In Ireland Yeats, AE and others were caught up in the heady surreal and mystic movements. And theatricality went then, as to some extent it does now, hand in hand with idealism, bloodshed and slavery. 'We may make mistakes in the beginning and shoot the wrong people; but bloodshed is a cleansing and a sanctifying thing, and the nation which regards it as the final horror has lost its manhood. There are many things more horrible than bloodshed; and slavery is one of them'(Pearse, ibid). This quotation is often used argumentatively and out of context. In its complete form it is clearly less a glorification and justification of bloodshed than a condemnation of national servitude and means, in effect, that if bloodshed be the necessary means of escape from slavery, then it is justified.

[85] Joseph Mary Plunkett was born in Dublin in 1887. His father was a papal count, a supporter of Griffith's Sinn Fein and director of the National Museum. Joseph suffered from ill-health and spent much of his youth abroad in warm climates. He was interested in philosophy, poetry and generalship. Co-founder of the Abbey Theatre; member of the Supreme Council of the IRB; met McDonagh in 1910 and the two became friends. He had, according to some sources, a deceptive theatricality about him. Together with MacDonagh, Pearse and Connolly he was one of the military planners of the 1916 Rising. Signatory to the Proclamation; he was married hours before his execution in Kilmainham jail on May 4, 1916.

[86] In one of his last essays Pearse wrote the following, enunciating a social and political philosophy far-removed from a romantic 'blood-sacrifice' and close to the teaching of Connolly. Like much of Pearse's writing it captures a similar clear-headed vision to that of Wolfe Tone, Davis and Mitchell. Tone had appealed to 'that numerous and respectable class, the men of no property' and in that gallant and characteristic phrase he had revealed his perception of a great historic truth, namely, that, in Ireland, 'the gentry (as they affect to call themselves) have uniformly been corrupted by England, and the merchants and middle-class capitalists have, when not corrupted, been uniformly intimidated, whereas the common people have for the most part remained unbought and unterrified. It is in fact true that the repositories of the Irish tradition, as well as the spiritual tradition of nationality and the kindred tradition of stubborn physical resistance to England, have been the great, splendid, faithful, common people ...'

[87] 'Had they' meaning the Liberals, wondered Dangerfield, 'discovered that Redmond cared more for Home Rule than for Ireland?' op. cit p.110.

[88] O'Hegarty, op. cit., pp 666/7. Yet, when, during a speech in Scotland — where Orangeism was prevalent — in which ambiguity and judicious caution (a formula he was much at home with) were carefully mixed, Winston Churchill made a case for special treatment for north-east Ulster, Redmond responded quickly: 'Irish Nationalists can never be consenting parties to the mutilation of the Irish nation'- F.S.L.Lyons, *John Dillon*, pp 332-4.

[89] 'The Irish were regarded not as different to the English, but inferior'(Martin, op.cit. p.249).

CHAPTER FIVE. Pp 109 - 135

[90] There is some confusion about this. There were in fact two Supreme Council meetings, as Devoy's meeting in New York with the German Ambassador makes clear. It was at the first of these that the critical decisions were taken. This was followed by Devoy's meeting in New York which, interestingly, occurred shortly after Pearse had been in New York and in contact with Devoy and other Clan na Gael members. Devoy was able to inform the ambassador that a decision for a rising in Ireland had been taken and asked for German help. The second meeting was held in September and other nationalists, including William O'Brien and Connolly were invited with a view to forming a nationalist coalition committee, but the idea was not pursued. The Military Council had been formed in the meantime.

[91] Sean T. O Ceallaigh, *An Phoblacht*, April, 1926.

[92] Macardle, Dorothy, *The Irish Republic*, p.126. There is slight confusion as to who in fact were the first members of the Military Council (committee). Macardle says it was 'Thomas Clarke, Sean MacDermott, Joseph Plunkett and Padraic Pearse'(ibid.). O'Donoghue, however, states specifically that the first members consisted *only* of Pearse, Plunkett and Ceannt, 'none of them at that time members of the Supreme Council [of the IRB], but all were Volunteer commandants and members of the Volunteer Executive'. Donagh MacDonagh, son of Thomas, says 'The Committee originally consisted of Plunkett, Pearse and Ceannt, with [Tom] Clarke and [Sean] MacDermott as *ex officio* members...' (*Plunkett and MacDonagh; Leaders and Men of the Easter Rising: Dublin 1916*, ed. F. X. Martin, p. 167), while David Thornley in an essay — *Patrick Pearse — the Evolution of a Republican*, in the same publication — is more specific, stating that Pearse, Plunkett and Ceannt were appointed members of a three-man mili-tary committee set up in May 1915. 'This committee later became the Military Council and was widened in 1915 to include Clarke and MacDermott, *ex officio*'. Kevin B. Nowlan in his essay, *Tom Clarke, MacDermott, and the I.R.B.*, has a slightly different version; 'The first members were P.H.Pearse, Joseph Plunkett and Eamonn Ceannt and from the beginning they worked in close co-operation with the two dominant members of the Executive, Sean MacDermott, the Secretary, and Tom Clarke, the Treasurer. In effect these five constituted the original military council of the I.R.B.' All-in-all the consensus is that it was originally three, later became five and later still six and then seven. It is probable that the original three-man military committee of Pearse, Plunkett and Ceannt was expanded to the Military Council of five with the addition of Clarke and MacDermott, as is suggested by O'Donoghue (op.cit., p. 196), who was in a position to know, being himself an IRB officer: 'In the absence of Plunkett on his visit to Germany from April to July, and again from September to November when he visited the United States on a mission to Clan na Gael in connection with the rising, Pearse and Ceannt worked alone until September when Sean MacDermott was released from jail. From that date he and Clarke joined the Military Council. From mid-January 1916 Connolly was a member and in April Thomas MacDonagh was co-opted. These seven were the signatories to the proclamation.

[93] There is some doubt about Devoy's attitude — but then, there often was doubt about Devoy's attitude with respect to one thing or another. Regarding Casement, in particular regarding doubts which had been cast on his reliability, Devoy wrote to the German authorities on November 12, 1915 saying that the Irish Nationalist leaders in America had the fullest confidence in Casement, and that he was their duly accredited 'Envoy'. The letter concluded 'We hereby certify to the German Government that Sir Roger Casement has authority to speak for and represent the Irish Revolutionary Party in

Ireland and America' — See Mackey, op. cit., pp. 77/78.It is, of course, possible that Devoy was making the best of what he considered to be a bad situation.

[94]   'The Irish Revolutionary Directory' (cf. Spindler) plans (from America) to the German General Staff included the following:

A. In Ireland, Beginning of February 1916.

1. *On England's Side:*

a) British troops, roughly .... 30,000 strong

poorly trained, few competent officers, no trained non-commissioned officers, little artillery and few machine-guns, all of old pattern.

Location: 3-4 training camps for recruits, remainder in small garrisons, In Dublin 3,000, in Limerick 1,000 soldiers (all recruits).

b) Irish Police................10,000 strong

efficient, all armed with rifles [read carbines], distributed in quite small detachments throughout country.

Total   40,000 strong.

11. *On the Side of the Revolutionary Directory:*

a) *Assured:* Irish Volunteers .....40,000 strong

Trained as efficient as the American National Guard; having 10,000 rifles various pattern, mostly Lee-Enfields with 200 rounds apiece. (They can further obtain possession of a further 20,000 rifles of inferior quality but practically without ammunition). There is a lack of superior officers.

b) *Anticipated:* Redmond Volunteers 50,000 strong

scattered, not well trained. It is reckoned that practically all of them will join the revolution.

c) *Probable:* Many thousands of unorganised Irishmen, provided they can be armed.

B. Support in the form of persons and arms from America is impossible.

C. *Proposition:*

Support from Germany:

25,000 to 50,000 rifles with cartridges, proportionate number of machine-guns and field artillery as well as a few superior (sic!) officers to be sent on transport ship to Limerick taking northern route and escorted by submarines. (Even for 100,000 rifles the necessary number of men would be obtainable). (Source, *Spindler,* pp 246/247).

It is obvious — bearing in mind, for instance, the 1,500 guns landed at Howth — that Irish resources were considerably over-stated. For what reason, other than to make the Germans think that the proposition was more viable than it was in reality, is unclear.

[95]   As later events proved MacNeill's concept of guerrilla warfare was, in the prevailing circumstances and in practical military terms, a realistic view of the optimum strategy for a sustained campaign, if the necessary conditions existed, which they did not. But a sustained campaign was not the intention of the IRB planners. In the event MacNeill's calamitous prevarication significantly weakened the military effectiveness of the Rising.

[96]   It may be seen that three active elements — the Irish Party and their 'Home Rule' following, Sinn Fein and the IRB — all sought to control the Volunteers. The Home Rulers were by far the largest group, followed by Sinn Fein and both operated, more or less, in the public eye. Certainly, long after he had lost the confidence and support of any activist group, political or otherwise, in Ireland, Redmond was still seen from Whitehall

— as myopic as ever when it came to Irish affairs — as the populist Irish leader. The IRB, by far the smallest group, also operated in secret, and single-mindedly. Membership of these groups overlapped.

[97] The oath of the IRB was also a subject of minor controversy, presumably because of the secrecy and distances involved. This is Stephens's original oath of 1858 (note the significant reference to the Irish Republic): 'I, AB, in the presence of Almighty God, do solemnly swear allegiance to the Irish Republic now virtually established; and that I will do my very utmost, at every risk, while life lasts, to defend its independence and integrity; and finally, that I will yield implicit obedience in all things not contrary to the laws of God to the commands of my superior officer. So help me God. Amen'. A later version went as follows: 'In the presence of God I.... . do solemnly swear that I will do my utmost to establish the national independence of Ireland, and that I will bear true allegiance to the Supreme Council of the Irish Republican Brotherhood and the Government of the Irish Republic and implicitly obey the Constitution of the Irish Republican Brotherhood and all my superior officers and that I will preserve inviolable the secrets of the organisation'.(Hobson, Bulmer, *Ireland Yesterday and Tomorrow*, p.104).

[98] Thomas J. Clarke was born in England (Isle of Wight), of Irish parents in 1857. Soon after his parents went to South Africa, but returned to Dungannon in 1868. He went to America in 1881 and returned in 1883 as part of the Clan na Gael bombing campaign in Britain (betrayed by the English spy Henri le Caron). Clarke was arrested and sentenced to penal servitude for life. He served almost sixteen years, being released in September 1898. He went to America the following year, but returned to settle in Dublin in 1907 where he ran a tobacconists/newsagents shop in Parnell street which became an IRB centre. He became immediately active in the IRB, encouraging the younger men to take over and revitalise the organisation. He was the first signatory to the Proclamation of the Republic in 1916 and fought in the GPO. He was shot in Kilmainham Jail on May 3rd, 1916. He was in his sixtieth year, but looked older. He was a man who, though of enormous energy and willpower, looked frail. It is said of him that he was the driving force behind the IRB and its plans for a Rising.

[99] It is worth bearing in mind that intelligence gathering, interpreting and dispensing for great combined armed forces, were still, in those days, relatively primitive and uncoordinated and there is little basis for comparison with the extraordinary facilities and resources available and employed to-day.

[100] Just prior to the Rising the following was the political/military line up on the Irish side:
1. Irish Nationalists, mainly Home Rulers, which included the Irish Party and Redmond's National Volunteers also under Redmond's leadership. Not involved in the Rising.
2. Sinn Fein, as yet not significantly politically active; cultural groups, the Gaelic League, GAA, etc.
3. The Irish Volunteers under MacNeill's nominal leadership. They would be involved in the Rising, mainly in Dublin, and less than 1,500 in all out of a national total of approximately 16,000.
4. The IRB, which had penetrated all the above, especially 3.
5. The labour/socialist movement based in Liberty Hall and the Citizen Army, both led by James Connolly, and
6. The IRB and its military council which planned the Rising in total secrecy from any of the others.

[101] Lee (op. cit., pp. 25/6) says 'In the event, the Rising had turned into a blood sacrifice. But it had not been planned that way from the outset ... however profusely blood sacrifice sentiments spatter the later writings of Pearse and MacDonagh, and however retrospectively relevant they appeared to be in the circumstances, it seems unhistorical to

interpret these sentiments as the basis of the actual planning of the Rising ... On Easter Monday morning many of the leaders must have felt ... that they were going out to be slaughtered. But that does not justify the presentation of the Rising in purely blood sacrifice terms'.

[102] The relative strengths given by Lyons are as follows: British army on active service in Ireland, about 6,000 effectives, to which should be added a considerable number of war-wounded; 9,500 of the para-military Royal Irish Constabulary, 1,000 of the unarmed Dublin Metropolitan police. However, the establishment of British troops in Ireland as given by Leon O'Broin (Dublin *Castle and the 1916 Rising*, p.117), which may be taken as being more accurate, was different: — 17,000 infantry, 3,149 cavalry, 1,000 artillerymen plus a thousand Royal Marines, batteries of machine-guns (as they were then mobilised) and artillery (at Galway) and a thousand Royal Marines, besides the 59th division, in Easter Week itself. The number of troops was rapidly augmented from England during the course of the Rising. On the Irish side there was an establishment of about 16,000 Volunteers throughout the country, most of them unarmed, and 200 members of the Citizen Army in Dublin. Only the latter and about 1,500 Volunteers all told (800 or so in Dublin) took part in the Rising.

[103] It is not only characteristic, but symptomatic, of most of the leaders of 1916 — and, indeed, of most of those who led the War of Independence — that they were motivated, and sometimes racked, by profound moral considerations. Idealism had not then been displaced by material cynicism and the success of 1916 and, more particularly because it was a prolonged and successful campaign, the War of Independence, was due in no small measure to the fact that the Volunteers and later the IRA captured, and held, the moral high ground throughout. The fine moral edge between what is right and what is expedient sometimes, (as with MacNeill and the morality of a rising, prior to the event), caused some heart-searching. But it was not until the Civil War that this fine line came more sharply into focus.

[104] Casement brought back from his Putumayo investigations the diary of a man called Armando Normand, whom he described as 'a man of whom nothing good can be said' and who committed the most fearful crimes and debaucheries against the Indians ... wrapping the Peruvian flag around a young girl, soaking it in paraffin and setting it on fire, then shooting her, because she refused to sleep with one of his men; leaving Indian men and women in the stocks until they starved to death and decomposed; burning alive an Indian, beheading his wife, dismembering the bodies of their children and throwing the remains on the fire; ordering one of his young (14-18 years old) catamites to behead Indian prisoners; ordering these 'cholitos' and 'muchachos' to spreadeagle and batter Indians on the genitals until they were dead, and so on ... Casement translated this monster's diary into English and submitted it as evidence to the British Foreign Office. Both Bulner Hobson and O'Hegarty have testified to the fact that Casement read or showed them parts of this appalling diary, of which he said he had kept a copy (see Chapter Eleven; also Mackey, op. cit., and Denis Gwynn, *The Life and Death of Roger Casement*, London, 1930). Casement's contemporaries, and early biographers, do not credit his alleged homosexuality and degeneracy. The rumour that he returned to Ireland to 'stop' the rising (which, in spite of all the contemporary real evidence to the contrary, seems to have sprung into existence only in the work of some recent historians) is also false; but it makes more 'interesting' reading. The two are not, of course, related, and proof of one in no way affects the other. Certainly the circumstantial evidence that the British undertook a major 'dirty-tricks' campaign against Casement and successfully alienated many influential people in Britain, Ireland and, by no means least at that juncture in the war, America, who would

otherwise have supported a plea for clemency for Casement, far outweighs any available proof that Casement was a homosexual degenerate.

[105] Other writers, including Roger McHugh — *Casement and German Help, Leaders and Men of the Easter Rising: Dublin 1916*, ed. Martin, p. 182 — and Tim Pat Coogan — *Michael Collins*, p. 52 — repeat this.

[106] Casement's prison manuscript includes the following: 'I want to make it very plain that I approve of the Rising — failure and all — in one sense. As a man of "travelled mind and understanding" I should never have sanctioned it had I been in Ireland, but since those there were bent on it, I, too (like the O'Rahilly) *would certainly have gone with it.*'

[107] Given that these two men, Casement and Plunkett, were, to say the least, romantic in appearance and unconventional in manner, the erosion of German confidence in the Irish leaders of a proposed rising is not entirely to be wondered at. The fact that Plunkett was, in fact, a skilled military theorist was not enough to offset this. Indeed it is alleged that he raised the indignation of more than one member of the German High Command staff by seeming to advise **them** on how to conduct the war.

By the time of the arms shipment responsibility for the supply as well as the transportation of arms to Ireland had passed from the German Foreign Office to the Imperial German Navy. The official German naval history of the war (translation in *An t-Oglach*, the Army Journal, July, 1926) sets out the German interest in the Rising, which, not surprisingly, was based on how a rising might affect military and strategic considerations so far as the conduct of the war was concerned. The official German view was that a rising in Ireland would i/ affect British morale, ii/ divert British forces from the western front and iii/ make available submarine bases or depots on the west coast of Ireland.

[108] Count Plunkett may also have contributed to the confusion about the timing. In this note, forwarded to Casement through Georg von Wedel of the Imperial Foreign Office and dated 'Berne, 5th April, 1916', Plunkett included the following as one of four points, the first of which was that the rising was fixed for the evening of next Easter Sunday: 'The large consignment of arms to be brought into Tralee Bay must arrive there *not later than the dawn of Easter Monday*'(author's italics).

[109] Beverly — real name Baily — later betrayed his companions to save his own neck.

[110] 'A diver later recovered some rifles which bore evidence that they had been manufactured in Orleans in 1902 and had been captured by the Germans in the Russian retreat at the beginning of the war'(O Broin, op. cit. p. 150), which, no doubt, accounts for the pertinacious rumour of the Germans sending 'old Russian guns'.

[111] The secrecy and effectiveness of this intelligence operation were to some extent mutually exclusive, as we have seen. This was not helped by the fact that the British appear to have placed more reliance on military, rather than naval, intelligence, which was evidently, at least in this case, less reliable. There was a need for absolute secrecy about their successful interception of German transmissions. According to O Broin (149): 'Admiral (sic) Hall was most careful that the means he was employing should not become known. He would have preferred that the rebellion in Ireland should succeed than that Britain should lose what his biographer described as "our most valuable weapon against Germany"' (The *Eyes of the Navy*, William M. James, London, 1955).

[112] This telegram was from Washington stating that the arms were to be landed *between* 20th and 23rd April.

[113] Later Uachtarain na hEireann, President of Ireland.

[114] O Broin (Ibid, p.148) comments: 'In the particular sequence of messages intercepted between 10 February and 21 March, 1916, the agreement for collaboration between the revolutionary groups in Ireland, working through the Clan na Gael leader,

John Devoy, in New York, and the German Government was uncovered. This radio correspondence continued right up to the Rising, but by 21st March the intention to rise, the date of the Rising, the nature of the German contribution and the place of landing were firmly known to the British, although there were variations later in points of detail'. These variations were the confusion that arose between John Devoy and the Germans about the actual day and Devoy specified Limerick, not Fenit, as the place of landing. For whatever reason the British military paid so little attention to the information 'from an absolutely reliable source' as to ignore it completely. They certainly never converted this information into intelligence.

[115] In April, 1922, Cathal Brugha published a summary of the plan for Dublin in the Easter edition of *Poblacht na h-Eireann*, as follows: 'Connolly it was who prepared the plan for the defence of Dublin. Strong positions between the city and the various military barracks that almost surrounded it were to be seized by the Volunteers. The one in the city itself (Ship street) was to be dominated by the seizure of certain strong buildings in its vicinity. A human chain was to link up such strongholds with others. There was to be an open chain from the Liffey to Clontarf and Fairview up to Phibsboro', over this space a mobile force was to be concentrated. The defence was to be carried out by the Volunteers and the Citizen Army acting together. The successful holding of the city for a certain time was based on the assumption that at least 1,500 would participate. Arrangements were made in various parts of the country to rise simultaneously.' Of interest are two points, the first and most significant being the statement that the plan was prepared by Connolly. If this is so it immediately raises the question of 'When?'. The obvious answer is during the days that he spent in January with the Military Council of the IRB and about which he was so secretive afterwards. If that is so then, of course, it was not his input alone that produced the plan, which is more likely. The second point is Brugha's statement that the plan was based on the assumption that 'at least 1,500 would participate'. In view of the accepted military view that it would have required between 3,000 and 4,000 men to make the plan effective, this seems to be a mistake. Moreover Connolly did not have 1,500 men at his disposal in the Citizen Army.

Of interest, too, in this context is the German attitude, as expressed in the official German naval history of the war (1914-1918, translation in *An t-Oglach*, the Army journal, July, 1926). It is also relevant to point out that by the time the arms left Germany for Ireland in 1916 responsibility for their supply, as well as for the transportation of the arms to Ireland, had passed from the German Foreign Office to the Imperial German Navy. The German interest in the Rising was, not surprisingly, based on how the Rising might affect military and strategic considerations so far as the conduct of the war was concerned. The view was that such a rising would i/ affect British morale, ii/ divert British forces from the Western front and iii/ make available submarine bases or depots on the west coast.

CHAPTER SIX. Pp. 137-172

[116] In a letter to Birrell dated Easter Saturday Nathan informed his superior 'I see no indications of a "rising"'. He was also unaware of the IRB cadre in the Volunteers. After the event when he , rightly, placed responsibility on the IRB, he did not know 'of the dominant position that Pearse, Plunkett, McDermott and Ceannt' held. 'He, and his police advisers, had their eyes still on the old men, on T.J.Clarke of Dublin and John Daly of Limerick, what they called "the small knot of violent men"', who had been sentenced to penal servitude in 1883 in connection with the dynamite outrages of that time. These men, Nathan said, worked in great secrecy, never appearing on public platforms or in the press, or making themselves amenable to the law, all of which is true; but '[with the exception

of Clarke]' the initiative had long passed to other and younger men whose writing and speeches in favour of revolt were so common that they had come to believe that the Castle thought nothing of them'(See O Broin, op. cit., p. 83 et seq.)

[117] O'Hegarty describes the RIC thus: 'It was, in fact, not a police force at all, but a Janissary force. The Turkish Janissary, used to keep down his own people, is the only parallel in history to the Royal Irish Constabulary man. His duties were military duties, and not police duties... "The police in Scotland cost £400,000, in Ireland £1,300,000"'. Insofar as it has been common, from time immemorial, for a conqueror to raise a special force from the conquered people to subdue their own, this is something of an overstatement, but that in no way diminishes the point being made. (Op. cit., p 401 and p. 403 citing L. Paul Dubois).

[118] Ryan (p. 42) tells us that Pearse, 'in conversations at St. Enda's before the Rising ... '[said]...'that "Germany had pledged her word that if this blow" [a rising] "were struck during the war, Ireland would come into the peace terms as a belligerent"'.

[119] Indeed it may be that it is because it is a focal point as well as an historic event that 1916 attracts so much — and so much of it vexed — attention. To attempt to treat 1916 as if it were merely an historic event is rather like a great family trying to treat a critical marriage simply as an episode of some importance in their lives and leaving out the formative social, economic and emotional factors altogether, to say nothing of consequential ones.

The argument that the Rising was not an inevitability is sometimes put forward, supported by statements such as 'It need never have happened because Home Rule was on the Statute Book', 'Small nations were going to be recognised sooner or later, anyway', 'The people didn't want it' and the like. Such arguments provide a useful academic stimulus, perhaps, but that is all. It is worth considering the requisite facts in context. Leaving the IRB aside for the moment, there had not been an armed insurrection (if one excludes the Land War activities) in the name of the nation for forty-nine years, more than a generation. There was, therefore, unquestionably a strong undercurrent of separatist energy available.

Secondly the unionists were preparing for war. They had arms and an army and had the backing of the Kaiser.

Thirdly even if MacNeill had not provided the opportunity for the formation of the Volunteers under the hidden hand of the IRB, someone else would have done so before long. Any such force would also, sooner or later, have attracted Redmond's attention. If that happened, and Redmond followed the course he actually did, a similar split, emphasising the increasing public face of separatism, would have taken place.

Fourthly there is no reason to suppose that the Citizen Army, which was outside the sphere of influence of the IRB, would have acted differently, or that Connolly would not have goaded any other group of volunteers in the same way.

Fifthly, even if the IRB had not acted as it did, or did not exist, Clan na Gael and John Devoy in America certainly did and would undoubtedly have plotted for a Rising.

Sixthly it is agreed that a majority of the people did not support the Rising and were not in favour of one beforehand. The raison d'etre of the Rising, as repeatedly stated by leader after leader, was to revitalise a sense of separate national identity in the people. Thus, to point out that the Rising did not have the support of a majority of the people in advance is an inapplicable nonsense.

The essential questions are:

1. Could what 1916 achieved have been otherwise achieved than by a rising?

2. If the Rising had not taken place in 1916, would there have been a rising at all?

Leaving theories and rationalisations aside the answer to these questions has to be, respectively: 'No' and 'Yes'.

The constitutional/separatist pendulum that affected Irish political outlook, behaviour and manners throughout the 19th century — since the establishment of the Union, and before it — did not simply go away with the new century in 1900. When, in 1914, Home Rule died on the stocks, as it were, the uneasiness of the people was quite different from the apathy of ten or twelve years earlier, and the social agitation of the previous year. There was confusion, there was energy with a national tinge to it, there was a growing sense of betrayal and, most importantly, of dissatisfaction with the constitutional party. More and more political and national energy became focused in what was collectively — and incorrectly — dubbed Sinn Fein activities; the Volunteers, the Citizen Army, social unrest, the GAA, the Gaelic League, cultural revival, Sinn Fein itself and other activities were all infiltrated by the IRB. It was a small, but potent, recipe for change, and the change — however and whenever it came — would be in the direction of separatist nationalism, by force if necessary. As we know the main differences between MacNeill and the IRB were philosophic and tactical, rather than ones of principle (even allowing for the fact that MacNeill was a constitutionalist; as he points out he 'was not doctrinaire, either on behalf of physical force or against it'). Given so much, in the climate of the times, it is clear that a Rising must have taken place sooner or later. As it happens the IRB's was the plan that preceded and gave rise to the War of Independence which was supported by the vast majority of the people. Home Rule was dead. In any case, although it was law, it was both suspended indefinitely and was to have partition imposed upon it. By Christmas 1914 faith in Home Rule was no longer widespread. 'The Home Rule Act was dead and out of date and the political theory behind it that Irish self-government was something which England was entitled to give or withhold, no longer commanded any support'- O'Hegarty. The Irish Party, too, had lost credibility, though Redmond had succeeded in sending thousands of former Irish Volunteers to die needlessly in Europe in a war meaning nothing to them. Accordingly, to the first question 'Could what 1916 achieved — proclamation of the Republic, the declaration in arms of its justification and a resurgence of nationalist spirit?' — have been otherwise achieved than by a Rising', the answer must be 'No'. As to the second question, 'If the Rising had not taken place in 1916, would there have been a rising at all?', the answer — as intervening events have clearly demonstrated -is 'Yes'.

[120] *The Making of 1916*, ed. Kevin B. Nowlan, is probably the best and most incisive compilation of comment and observation on the Easter Rising, especially the contributions of Maureen Wall, Hayes-McCoy and the overview Introduction by Nowlan.

For those who find the speculation of interest that the Rising was pointless and that Home Rule would have materialised anyway, the following might be borne in mind:-

1. Home Rule was discredited. There was no guarantee that it would ever get beyond the Statute Book; if it did partition of the country was an inevitable concomitant.

2. The IRB, committed to a rising, would have remained alive and active.

3. A rising during the 20s, or more likely the 30s, was a distinct possibility had one not already taken place, Home Rule or no.

4. Without a doubt, had one not already taken place, a rising would have occurred during the course of the Second World War.

It is not, therefore, a question of whether or nor a rising had merit or did not have merit, but whether the Rising that did take place was adequate as to purpose, timing and effect. Writing on this question Brian Murphy says:-

In this ... English denial of Home Rule one finds the source of justification for the action of Pearse. Ireland had not received, and could not expect to receive, fair treatment from England

... Ireland, alert and awake to its national destiny, was about to enter the promised land (Home Rule); Pearse was wrong to interfere with the expected inheritance. What, however, if the promises were not to be trusted, and the land itself to be divided? That, indeed, was the reality of the situation in 1916. The Rising may not have been wanted, but it was needed if the promised land of Ireland's historic aspirations was to be secured — (op. cit., p.58).

It should also not be overlooked that, had the Rising not pre-empted the intended British swoop and arrests that same week, as planned, a rising, if reactive, would have been inevitable anyway in accordance with Volunteer policy to resist any such attempt.

[121] O'Donoghue, op. cit., p. 200, points out that 'commandants throughout the country received a series of conflicting orders over the week-end, not all delivered everywhere, and not always in the sequence in which they had been issued. The result was a state of confusion, uncertainty and frustration which largely immobilized the country commands'.

The limited — in the purely military sense of the word — nature of the plan is reinforced by the fact that, so far as the rest of the country was concerned outside Dublin, city, town and rural areas alike, there was no alternative plan to that of mobilisation to offload and distribute the arms from Aud in any of the Brigade areas involved. The broad plan for the country related solely to that and to the subsequent holding position on the Shannon. Even in Cork city there was no plan to fight in the city, or any other related contingency plan. 'There was not, and never had been, an alternative plan for the Cork Brigade ... There was not at any time a resolve to fight in the city, and no plans had been made for such a contingency.' (Florence O'Donoghue, *Tomas Mac Curtain — Soldier and Patriot*, Tralee 1955, pp. 85/6).

An important point raised with me by Major Gen. P.F. Nowlan, Assistant Army Chief-of-Staff, was :- What rations did the Volunteers muster with? In other words how long did they expect to be in the field.

So far as I can ascertain the (different) mobilisation orders to the Volunteers and Citizen Army specified *either* two, or three, days *field rations*. What it probably boiled down to was that each man was told to bring enough food for himself for the specified period, possibly with an indication as to what this should be. I can find only one reference as to what that was, and that does not indicate a standard: -'ate his whole three days' ration, and emergency Oxo cubes...'(*WAR BY THE IRISH*, John McCann, pp.49/50). 'Companies were to parade with all arms, ammunition and equipment, rations for two days, overcoats and blankets ... carried food and cooking equipment... rations for two days...' O'Donoghue, op. cit. pp. 74, 89, 94; 'three-day manoeuvres planned ...' *THE IRISH REPUBLIC*, Macardle, p. 156; 'We'll hold Dublin for a week and save Ireland...' Sean MacDermott to P.S.O'Hegarty, *A HISTORY OF IRELAND UNDER THE UNION*, O'Hegarty, p.700; 'parade with three-days field rations', is generally accepted in most books on the period so far as Dublin is concerned.

Logistically, so far as munitions and commissariat facilities were concerned, it seems that little provision was either made or was possible.

The Dublin Volunteers were restricted to front-line ammunition. In the countryside, especially south and west, reliance, so far as arms and munitions were concerned, was principally on what was expected from the arms ship. Of course, the rising was initially intended to be in Dublin only (O'Hegarty, p.700).

Therefore, if one accepts 'three days' field rations as being probable (and it has a substantial foundation in that the Rising was based on orders for three-day manoeuvres similar to those carried out a year earlier), then it seems likely that a Rising lasting perhaps three, possibly four, days is what was envisaged.

The alternative is that a longer rising would rely on forage. Even allowing for the fact that Boland's Bakery and Jacob's Biscuit factory were occupied, while this might have been feasible in rural areas, it would have been a problem in Dublin.

Given the basic nature of the plan, the restricted supplies and what we know of the mobilisation orders, it is probably safe to conclude that the Rising was planned to last three days in Dublin, followed by withdrawal westward, and further resistance for an unspecified period in the Shannon region for as long as possible. In the event the Rising in Dublin surpassed all expectations of logistics and manpower while the rest of the country, because of the confusion and lack of arms, rose only in an isolated and unco-ordinated way.

[122] Falkenhayn's plan had gone awry — not because of failure, but, ironically, because of too much success. His limited force of nine divisions broke through more rapidly, and further, than anticipated, enabling the French to re-group and counter-attack in a see-saw engagement that — lasting from February until June — became, until then, the longest battle of the war.

[123] Notably Arthur Griffith, but the idea had little support and, even at the time, was generally considered to be unrealistic. 'Mr. Griffith's perverse high Tory demand for an Irish King, Lords and Commons was openly repudiated' (George Dangerfield *The Strange Death of Liberal England*, p.359). Griffith's proposal envisaged inviting some European prince to 'accept' the throne of Ireland. O'Connell, during his 'Repeal' agitation, also referred to a future 'Irish king', but this was possibly mere rhetoric. The notion may be said to be bizarre in the sense that it was very much out of touch with both the mood and outlook of the ordinary people who had had no effective experience of native aristocratic leadership since the beginning of the eighteenth century, and, for want of it, had suffered greatly in the meantime, and with the republican commitment of the IRB and the Volunteers. By and large, in spite of the proclaimed, and often bitter, differences between the separatists such as the Young Irelanders, the Fenians and the IRB, and the Constitutionalists such as O'Connell, the Home Rule party and the Irish Party, the people managed to fuse the essence of both in a visionary amalgam by which religious and political freedom became synonymous under a republican banner — comparable to the dual vision that sustained them during the dreadful years of the eighteenth century. An Irish puppet king, given the temper of the masses, could, at best, have provided a short-term solution. But as recently as 1993 (*Irish Times*, May 29, 1993 — *Our Republicanism is more recent than we realise*) the economist and former Taoiseach (1981/2; 1982/7), Garret FitzGerald, son of Desmond — a member of the GPO garrison in 1916 — in a better position than most to know the facts, resurrected the notion of a king for an independent Ireland (specifically, in this instance, Prince Joachim, sixth son of Kaiser Wilhelm). In support of this thesis Fitzgerald offered a carefully worded argument purporting to show i/ that:- 'Contrary to some of our myths (*sic!*) there is little evidence that before independence Irish people in general were specifically *republican* in sentiment — as distinct from being, as to a majority, separatist'. This generous sentence, focusing on the word 'evidence', is one of meticulous ambiguity. On it it is possible to base almost any proposition of political allegiance one likes. For instance there is little evidence that Irish people in general were specifically monarchical or, for that matter, dictatorial or socialist, or anything — Home Rule being effectively dead — except Sinn Fein.

The timing of the argument may have some significance. It was published at a time when concern to bring about a ceasefire in Northern Ireland was mounting (the Hume-Adams agreement and the Irish/British joint declaration for peace came soon afterwards).

But the simple fact is that republicanism was the core of Irish separatism since 1798. Robert Emmet sought to continue the republican movement of '98. A generation later the Young Irelanders were motivated by republican ideals, as were the Fenians a generation later than that. The IRB became the republican source which, whether one likes it or not, inspired future separatist action.

The people voted overwhelmingly for Sinn Fein in 1920 and Sinn Fein adopted republicanism and declared a republic following the general election of 1918. 'It had established this as a *de jure* republic and it claimed authority also as a *de facto* one' (P.S.O'Hegarty, *A History of Ireland under the Union*). If the ballot box isn't evidence of what the people's sentiments were before independence, what is? Contentions to the contrary, especially from a source such as Garret FitzGerald, can seriously distort the correct perception of historical development.

It is, however, true that the idea of an Irish monarchy was promulgated by a few individuals between 1910 and 1916. When it is understood that the proposal was for a son of the German Kaiser to be offered the post (which he could not, in fact, under the German constitution, have accepted), the reason for doing so becomes clear. The IRB were committed to rising against English rule in Ireland when and if England was involved in a greater struggle. From 1911 onwards the most likely opponent of Great Britain in a looming international conflict was Germany, which already outstripped her in steel production, rivalled her navy and looked fair to becoming the world's leading power. It made some sense for the Irish leaders to consider every means of strengthening bonds of friendship with a potential wartime ally. However cock-eyed the 'King of Ireland' proposal might seem at first sight, not to have considered it at all would have been negligent.

So far as an independent monarchy is concerned, the question of an Irish king in the tradition of the Irish kingdoms that flourished until the thirteenth century, did not, apparently, arise. The idea was for a king who accommodated to — and would be drawn from — the current European mould, a kind of Ruritanian, off-the-shelf wholesale king who had nothing to do with Ireland. Those proposing the idea may have felt that an 'Irish' king (more correctly, presumably, a 'king of Ireland') might, by some legal contrivance, manage to retain a position within the English constitutional system yet be subordinate to the English king — hardly an enticing prospect for most European princes at the time. The argument appears to have been that in this way an Irish parliament might be re-created which, while remaining subordinate to that of England and lacking fiscal independence, would nevertheless acquire a measure of legislative authority and independence. It was a silly concept at best and no serious nationalist gave it a second thought. Griffith, its main proponent, acquired the derisory nickname 'Kings, Lords and Commons' because of his fervour in the matter.

There had not been an Irish king for over six hundred years. Then the process of selection was entirely different. Primogeniture was unknown under the Irish system, which, while confining kingship to members of a ruling minority, was nonetheless elective. A king, or ruler, was elected by his peers from amongst five generations of appropriately qualified families. It was hardly a broad-based democratic process in the modern sense of the term, but kingship was certainly not confined to a single family group, let alone a dynasty (except by *force majeure* as in the case of the Ui Neil which sept, though complying with this procedure, nevertheless dominated the kingship of Ireland almost uninterruptedly for five hundred years, until their hold was broken by Brian Boru between 980 and 1014). Since then such kingship-at-a-remove as there was had been foreign and frequently hostile. Nevertheless, even in the imperialistic world of Griffith's time with its efflorescence of kings and kingships in Europe and elsewhere (and but two major republics in the world, France and the United States), the idea of a king in Ireland remained far-fetched.

Contrary to what Garret FitzGerald suggests the republican link is clear and indisputable. From another source FitzGerald's argument might have been readily dismissed as simply that of yet another 'barrack-room historian' who selected what facts he/she wanted and hammered them into the shape of the preferred theory. Coming from the source it did, however, it could not be so lightly dismissed and required to be considered in the light of who the author was and the effect his words might have. Judged in that way one must, however reluctantly, conclude that the author was not serious and, perhaps, enjoyed the feel of his tongue in his cheek; either that or he had some other, less obvious, purpose. What might such a purpose be? His father, Desmond, was one of those — and it is by no means clear that there were any others — who supported Griffith's curious desire for an Irish monarchy, yet he argues that the question was considered by those who planned the 1916 Rising. This appears to be true, for the reasons mentioned above. But it is also true that it was rejected.

[124] However Brian O'Higgins (*Wolfe Tone Annual*, 1946, pp.23/24) writes: 'Six years after the Rising of 1916, and a few months before his own heroic last fight in which he was shot down ... Cathal Brugha revealed the fact that the plan of operations in Dublin was drawn up by James Connolly'. If this is correct it might help explain *both* the three-day period in which Connolly was thought to be 'kidnapped', and his subsequent reticence about it. Both he and the Military Committee must, by then — January 1916 — have had plans for Dublin in the event of a Rising. Welding them together into one would certainly require a minimum of three days. As to Brugha's alleged statement and any authority he might have had for making such a dogmatic assertion, it is now impossible to verify. It is, however, extremely unlikely that Connolly *did not* have an input into the plan. Interestingly, in the same issue of the *Wolfe Tone Annual*, Brian O'Higgins publishes extracts (p.98) from an unpublished document by Liam Mellowes (executed during the civil war, 1922) which contains the following: 'As to the projected plans, it is obvious that the present time is inopportune to disclose them. Suffice it to say that they were carefully prepared months ahead, every detail that would ensure success and co-ordination being worked out'. It is correct that the 1916 leaders had extended plans to include many aspects of civil government, including the issue of stamps.

[125] The importance of this last point was recognised by the British and by the Provisional Governments in 1922, as noted in a secret memorandum to General Boyd, GOC British Forces in Dublin, when armed opposition to the Provisional Government seemed possible and Boyd was given contingency orders.

[126] 'The Proclamation of the Republic stressed the historic right of the Irish nation to independence ...The Rising was to be in defence of that right, against continued aggression and so this object was to be achieved, not by attacking the British garrisons directly, but by seizing certain points openly in the name of the Irish nation, and defending them openly against the inevitable British attack' (Eoghan O Neill, op. cit., p.214).

[127] While the Volunteers had attained a fair state of training and discipline, all were not armed. In the best armed brigades outside Dublin not more than one man in five had a service rifle; shotguns were the commonest weapons in most of the country units; some were almost entirely unarmed. In the whole force there was not a single machine-gun or heavier weapon', (O'Donoghue, op. cit.,, p.192).

[128] The secrecy imposed on them by the plans to which they were committed led these men into a number of actions which they justified to themselves on the grounds of military necessity. All of these were aimed at their colleagues in the Volunteer Executive.

Pearse, availing of his position as Director of Organisation, and others conveyed secretly to the principal Volunteer officers in the country, many of whom had been previously sworn into the IRB, instructions for military dispositions to be taken up'- O Broin, op. cit, p.38.

[129] On Palm Sunday Connolly had lectured to his men: "'I'm going to fight the way I want, not the way the enemy wants" he announced'. 'It'll be a new way, one the soldiers haven't been trained to deal with. We'll use the roof-tops for a start. But remember this; if you do snipe your man, don't get enthusiastic and stand up and cheer, for if you do it'll probably be the last cheer you'll ever give'" (O'Neill, cited p. 40).

[130] It should be borne in mind that, until 1916 — but especially until 1919, and then, usually, only amongst 'those-in-the-know' — the term 'Irish Republican Army' was a vague title that had been applied intermittently to a variety of military organisations at home and abroad since the Rising of 1798. Right up to the Truce the more commonly used term, both in Britain and elsewhere, for the collective political and military forces of Ireland was 'Shinners', or 'Sinn Fein' itself (which may contribute to the lack of ability in some quarters to distinguish between the two organisations today). In spite of the adoption of the term in 1916, 'IRA' only came into gradual use after the Sinn Fein convention of 1919, when the Volunteers voluntarily placed their organisation under the control of the Dail.

[131] Born 1868 in London, Constance Gore-Booth of Lissadell, Sligo. Married Count Casimir, 1900. Joined Sinn Fein, but disliked Griffith — the distaste appears to have been mutual — because of his pacifism. Helped Maude Gonne's women's organisation, Inghinidhe na hEireann, and founded Fianna Eireann — Irish Boy Scouts — in 1909. Joined the Citizen Army (a move that precipitated Sean O'Casey's resignation) and was sentenced to death, commuted, because she was a woman, to penal servitude for life, for her part in the Rising. Became president of Cumman na mBan in 1917. Elected on the Sinn Fein ticket in 1918 (the first woman to be elected to Westminster). Minister for Labour in the first and second Dail Cabinets. Supported the anti-Treatyites in the Civil War. TD (Dail Deputy — TD Teachta Dala) 1923 until her death in 1927. She had a deep compassion for the poor who loved her for it to the end of her days. 'She sheltered Larkin before he made his famous speech from the balcony of the Imperial Hotel...She was not easy to work with — voluble, seemingly arrogant .. and as the years went on, becoming more and more bitter and intense ... she had many of the attributes of a soldier and her fondness for uniform was not mere exhibitionism'(Lyons, op. cit., p. 286).

[132] The precise number is impossible to calculate as small groups of Volunteers, and individuals, came (and went). For instance, as the lancers charged in O'Connell street a small contingent from Rathfarnham arrived at the GPO seeking admission. Similarly at St. Stephen's Green a number of men climbed over the railings to join those inside. Similar accretions to the original force occurred elsewhere and throughout the week. But the total number on Monday was between 700 and 800 men and never, during the remainder of the week, exceeded 1,100.

[133] Besides not having sufficient men to implement the prepared plan (which called for 3,000 Volunteers) or press home the attack on Dublin Castle, for the same reason the Volunteers were unable to take the vital telephone exchange in Crown Alley. Even if they had the authorities were able to re-route telegraph and telephone cables through private circuits bringing them to Aldborough House in Amiens street (see O Broin op. cit., p. 98), thus neutralising the loss of the telegraph office in the GPO. Post was, of course, impossible, though the Volunteers had prepared special stamps overprinted "Rialtas Sealachais na Heireann" — (Provisional Government of Ireland).

[134] The attackers did not know that it was held that Easter Monday by a mere handful of men and could have been easily taken. Even if they had known, however, they did not have enough men to hold it.

[135] Max Caulfield, *The Easter Rebellion*, London, 1964. Caulfield's book is a colourful 'factional' account of the Rising (much of it in a Paddy-whackery begorrah and bejabers style). It contains an amount of detail not elsewhere recorded. However, because of his free exercise of imagined conversations and evident bias it can not — except where it is possible to verify accounts and incidents — be taken as a reliable source. His Dublin geography and orientation are also unreliable in some important instances. The present writer did some research for Caulfield in the 1950's and was startled by the cavalier treatment the material provided received. In his account the 'courageous' British on the whole display the virtues of the *Boys Own Paper*, being 'staunch old warriors', and 'stern and quite superbly martial', while the unstable Irish tend to behave with predictable Hibernian peasant ineptitude. The startling thing is, of course, not that they acted as they did, but that they managed, in the face of British gallantry, to organise sufficiently to act at all!

[136] Because of their para-military status the RIC occupied 'barracks' as distinct from police stations, and it is interesting that as a result, to this day, Garda Siochana (Civic Guard) stations in Ireland are often, and erroneously, still referred to as 'barracks'.

[137]   Brigadier W.F.H. Stafford, the same who had passed upwards the information he had himself received from Admiral Sir Lewis Bayly about *Aud*, took command of operations in the South of Ireland and Brigadier Hackett-Paine, assumed command in Ulster.

[138]   General Friend returned to Dublin from London, and as reinforcements became available to him, established a line from Kingsbridge (now Heuston) railway station to Trinity College 'which divided the insurgent forces in two providing a safe line of advance to troops extending operations to the North and South [of the city] and despatch rider communication with some of the commands' (O Broin op. cit. p 117). By Saturday it was obvious that the Rising was on the point of collapse. Birrell, who had also returned to Dublin — for the first time in a considerable period, having been detained in London due to the cabinet crisis there — wrote to Asquith that Pearse 'the wretched "commandant" of the insurgents had been before the general' (Maxwell) (O Broin, citing Asquith papers, Birrell to Asquith 29.4.1916) and that Pearse's surrender was the result of Maxwell's tactic of maintaining the barrage all the previous day and night thus demoralising the enemy and 'reducing them to despair'. Maxwell, he said, anticipated that 'the whole pack of them' would surrender unconditionally before the day ended. Birrell went on to describe the centre of Dublin in ruins, that certain parts of the provinces were 'very jumpy' and that 'The horrible thing proves how deep in the Irish heart lies this passion for insurrection'(See O Broin, op. cit. pp.117-20).

 The British were of the opinion that the Rising was something other than what it was and this, perhaps, explains Maxwell's brutal executions policy — four on May 4th; one on May 5th; four more on May 8th; one on May 9th; two on May 12th — that ensured the Rising would achieve its purpose and bring about the very thing they were most anxious to prevent. They decided — a combination, perhaps, of wishful thinking and the continuing misreading of Casement's and German involvement — that 'it was not an Irish lion' (Birrell to Asquith, op.cit) and was 'nothing more than a Dublin riot' (Augustine Birrell, *Things Past Redress*, London 1937, p.220).

[139] O'Neill gives many of his quotations, such as this one, without specific attribution. It reads like part of a newspaper report, and is, perhaps, abstracted from one of the many newspapers he cites as references at the end of his book.

[140] According to Peter de Rosa, *Rebels; The Irish Rising of 1916.* p. 308, the artillery 'blasted everything in their path'. De Rosa's account is often inaccurate and unreliable, consisting largely of imagined conversations. It is in a similar fanciful style to Caulfield's earlier book, only more so.

[141] O'Neill wrote: '...no printing plant was seized, except for the *Daily Express* offices, and here *the printers were turned out of the building at the point of a bayonet* (his italics). . . Had every available printing plant been employed through Monday night in running off revolutionary newspapers, manifestos, leaflets in thousands, Dublin on Tuesday would have rung with the call to the struggle and substantial reinforcements would have been assured, even if it were too much to expect the whole city to rise. The recruits (*sic*) who at all points on Tuesday were slipping through the British cordons to join the various revolutionary commands were an indication of the response a broadcast appeal might have ensured' — op. cit., p.46. But this reads like wishful thinking and hindsight. Most of those who 'slipped through the British cordons' were Volunteers who had obeyed MacNeill's order and could not be said to be recruits representative of what might have happened had there been widespread publicity. That is not to say that propaganda on a large scale might not have made a valuable contribution, as the author well knows*. In 1916 propaganda, though as yet an imperfectly understood weapon, was certainly given a minor role, *per se*. On Tuesday *The Irish War News*, a four-page paper, appeared carrying news of the Rising and its purpose and 'a little later' a broadsheet was issued containing a manifesto and calling for help from the citizens of Dublin (See Macardle, op. cit., p.171). However what was critical was to try to counter the effect of MacNeill's published advertisement.

In the original plan for the Rising, had it been possible to execute it, it was planned to establish radio communications with the United States, Germany and other countries. Internally a nation-wide rising would have been self-generating as regards publicity. Therefore, O'Neill's criticism is relevant *only* in the context of the restricted action that occurred. But then how, in that context, would a massive publicity effort have been conceived, written and mounted between Sunday and Monday? How would the 'revolutionary newspapers, manifestos, leaflets in thousands' have been distributed, even if it had been possible to produce them? Who would have organized these things and, more to the point, where was the manpower with which to do it? If all of this had proved successful and produced a response such as O'Neill suggests, how would the 'substantial reinforcements' without arms or leadership, have successfully penetrated the British cordons? They might, if trained and under well organised leadership, have established an outer cordon, or outer strongpoints, and attacked the British in the rear. But there was no such plan. The leaders were all within the cordon and, more significantly, there were no arms — or ammunition — available outside the British cordon, and precious few, and little, inside it.

It is one of the few observations in O'Neill's otherwise admirable book on the Rising that is incomplete. It is relevant, too, to point out that when Griffith learned about the Rising he got a message through to the GPO leaders asking to be allowed to join them. But they refused his offer on the grounds that he would be more useful outside as a writer and propagandist.

*The author, then Director of the Government Information Bureau, organized, controlled and directed the Irish Government international information and publicity campaign, 1969/73, to counter the world-wide propaganda of the British and Northern Ireland Office in relation to the horrendous events which, in the summer of 1969, erupted and continued in Northern Ireland. It was the first such internationally focused government campaign since the foundation of the State, and successfully achieved its objectives.

[142] With the exception of the Battle in the South Dublin Union, the Battle of Mount street Bridge is remembered as probably the single most celebrated battle of the week. There are several detailed accounts of both, the most reliable being Desmond Ryan's (*The Rising*). Caulfield gives a lengthy and colourful version, but, while it is very readable, it contains so many inaccuracies as to render its overall validity highly dubious. For instance, at the most elementary level, he gratuitously increases the Irish garrison in Clanwilliam House and 25 Northumberland road to seventeen men, whereas in fact it was nine, and contracts the length of the battle from over nine hours to five(op. cit., p. 235).

[143] The exact number is in doubt. Some accounts give the number as twenty, others slightly more. The maximum given is twenty-six.

[144] Ryan, op cit. p. 256. De Rosa (op. cit.,p. 360) doubles this number, without attribution. However, his book is inaccurate throughout. O'Neill (p. 77) says that the *total* number in the combined garrisons of the GPO and the Four Courts were about 400 at surrender.

[145] This particular *canard*, that the Irish troops were reviled and disowned by the people of Dublin, has been promoted quite strongly in recent years. Certainly there were some expressions of hostility. In the main these appear to have come from the more 'respectable' areas and from women whose husbands were serving in the British army. Like the blind man holding the elephant's tail and describing the pachyderm as a small snake, the usual description is distorted as the following eye-witness accounts amply demonstrate. ... it is clear that there was also much sympathy for the rebels, at least while there appeared to be some hope of success. James Stephens reports few of those feelings of "detestation and horror" which Redmond attributed to Irish public opinion in his House of Commons statement on 27 April. Redmond was at that stage in no position to know what Irish public opinion was' (Lee, op. cit., p. 31). Indeed he might have made the point that Redmond had seemed to be out of touch with Irish public opinion for some time. General Maxwell himself noted that when 'we tried to get the women and children to leave North King street. They would not go. Their sympathies were with the rebels.' (*Irish Independent,* May 19, 1916).

[146] It must be borne in mind that the R.I.C. were a well-armed para-military force, normally equipped with both carbines and revolvers. They also had access to heavier weapons and had recently been issued with hand-grenades as standard equipment and were a formidable force.

[147] There is some confusion about this, Ryan stating (op. cit., pp.226/7) that Ashe was offered safe conduct to see Pearse in Kilmainham and that Mulcahy went instead — but to Arbour Hill. Certainly Pearse was in Arbour Hill for a while — as his own letter to Macready shows. But his trial was in Richmond Barracks and his execution was at Kilmainham. So it is quite possible that Mulcahy was brought to Arbour Hill.

CHAPTER SEVEN. Pp. 173-199

[148] But Murphy, privately to Tim Healy, said that he was responsible for neither the leading article nor the photograph and would not have allowed them to be published had he known about them — T. M. Healy, *Letters and Leaders of My Day*. The very fact that the *Irish Independent*, the organ of William Martin Murphy who had been so bitterly opposed to Larkin and the workers in 1913 and the subsequent lockout, was so condemnatory of the Rising and its leaders suggests the possibility that many Dublin workers would have sympathised with the Volunteers for that reason alone.

[149] Since the late 1920's some writers, and most governments here, have been coy about using the term Irish Republican Army in connection with 1916. This is because of the

usurpation of the term by successive waves of activist nationalists, mainly in Northern Ireland, who have increasingly adopted the tactics of terrorism and — with counter-productive logic — tried to make of them something nationally legitimate. The strongest weapon in the armoury of the IRA between 1916 and 1921 was that they took, and held, the moral high ground — an impossibility if terrorist tactics are employed. Nonetheless to euphemise the title of those who fought in 1916 and the War of Independence is to belittle them and what they achieved and, to their shame, this is what successive governments here have succeeded in doing instead of claiming for the people, and standing over, the rightful ownership of the name and title The Irish Republican Army. In failing to do that they have contributed in no small way to a confusion of self-image and sense of history.

[150] The previous year, on 7 May, the Cunard liner *Lusitania* had been torpedoed by a U-Boat and sunk off Kinsale. The allegations are that she was carrying war material, including explosives as well as passengers. It has even been suggested that details of her manifest were deliberately leaked by Churchill so that she would be attacked with the object of provoking American intervention on the side of the Allies. So far these rumours remain unproven. Following the sinking of the ship the Cork Coroner, J.J.Horgan, brought in a verdict of murder against the German Government and the Kaiser.

[151 Including Terence MacSwiney and Tomas MacCurtain from Cork.

[152] There seems to be some confusion about the terminology used by the Irish army during this period. It seems, in some cases, to have reverted to the pre-1916 terminology of 'Irish Volunteers', rather than 'Irish Republican Army', which was the specific title used during the Rising. But this may be a later gloss by such writers as Macardle and O'Hegarty, anxious to divorce the 1916-1922 military organisation from the organisation of the same name, IRA, which was subversive of the State after its foundation in 1922. It certainly resumed the name Irish Republican Army and the abbreviation IRA during the War of Independence. On the other hand the confusion may arise simply because it sounded more euphonious, and was more convenient for writers to write, for instance, 'some Volunteers' rather than 'some members of the Irish Republican Army'.

[153] Thomas Ashe was the alternative candidate to de Valera. Ashe, the leader of the successful action at Ashbourne in 1916, was also at the time president of the IRB. But he stood down in favour of de Valera for fear of creating a split in the ranks. Here, it is suggested, may again be seen the differences between the IRB, who supported Ashe (and later, of course, Collins) and the Volunteers who supported de Valera. As significantly may be discerned at this time differences between de Valera and Griffith, who ignored the republican significance of the Clare election and claimed it to be a victory in support of his own policy based on the 'Kings, Lords and Commons' idea. It should be borne in mind that the election occurred during the most difficult period of negotiation between the Brugha/Plunkett element of the 'new Sinn Fein' and the Griffith/Milroy one of the 'old' Sinn Fein — But see Murphy, op. cit., pp. 89, 96/97 for greater detail and elucidation.

[154] Unwise, perhaps, but it should not be overlooked that the United States was supplying Britain with huge quantities of materials vital to their war effort and that this was the reason for the German action.

[155] In his essay defending the 1916 Rising, Lenin wrote 'A blow delivered against the British imperialist bourgeoisie by a rebellion in Ireland has a hundred times more political significance than a blow of equal weight would have in Asia or Africa.' In writing this he was, of course, looking at the Rising primarily from the viewpoint of a social, not a political, revolutionary. While it was a point of view which would certainly have been shared by Connolly and some of the other leaders, Mellowes, perhaps, it would not have been the primary point of view of all.

[156] The suggestion that the renewal of the IRB and the Volunteers in 1916 had 'within itself the seeds of discord' to a greater extent than any similar effort might have had, would appear to go too far. Such differences might have been resolved. The question of personalities, and their actions, was another matter.

[157] A curious event had taken place in Boston in January, 1918, when F.E.Smith bluntly revealed Lloyd George's 'Convention' for what it was, an expedient to mollify American opinion about what was happening in Ireland and assist in influencing America's decision to enter the war.

[158] The objective was to raise the equivalent of an Army corps, 150,000 men, by conscription at a time when men of 50 to 55 were being impressed in England. 'For several weeks the cabinet threshed about in an effort to get the 150,000 men they so badly wanted from Ireland without at the same time creating a major political crisis in that country' — Lyons, op. cit., p.p.392/3.

[159] By co-incidence this event unknowingly resurfaced, if I may be forgiven the pun, in the *Irish Times* on April 15, 1998 in its *Times Past* column, headed *German submarines and Irish fishing craft,* which reproduced a paragraph with that heading from its issue of April 15, 1918. The paragraph in question demonstrated clearly one of the early uses of disinformation propaganda. Shortly thereafter the Castle authorities used the capture of Dowling as an excuse to proclaim a 'German Plot', the purpose of which was to arrest and deport as many Sinn Fein leaders as possible. This paragraph, published three days after Dowling's capture, about 'Irish fishermen and skippers' (of 'yawls!') off the west coast is pure propaganda and scene-setting of the most obvious kind and the lurid statements of each of the four entirely anonymous 'fishermen' quoted as having been in (usually violent) contact with U-Boat officers are blatantly fictitious. Evidently these officers, who threatened and stole from them, and who boarded them from mysterious (and extraordinarily invisible) submarines all spoke excellent English (or, of course, Irish); either that or that the Irish skippers and fishermen of these 'yawls' were fluent in German.

CHAPTER EIGHT. Pp. 201-250

[160] It has been succinctly described by General Sean MacEoin, who was one of those present. 'The Consititution for the Dail was submitted and approved. The Declaration of Independence proclaimed in 1916 was confirmed and was published in a new form, in Irish, French and English. Delegates representing the Irish nation were appointed to the Peace Conference in Paris, and a message of peace and goodwill was sent to all the free nations in the world. A democratic programme was enacted and in the report of that programme is the first official recognition of the President of the Republic. It is given on page twenty-two of that first session which contains the phrase: "We declare, in the words of the Irish Republican Proclamation, the right of the people of Ireland to the ownership of Ireland, and to the unfettered control of Irish destinies, to be indefeasible, and, in the language of our first President, Padraig Mac Piarais, we declare that the nation's sovereignty extends not only to all men and women of the nation, but to all its material possessions, the nation's soil and all its resources" — *The Constitutional Basis*, WTI-ITFFF, pp. 13/14.

[161] Under the Constitution of the Dail the office of priomh-aire combined the functions of president and prime-minister. Constitutionally it more closely resembled the executive/presidential role of the President of the United States than the purely ex-political and non-executive role of the President of Ireland to-day, which is why de Valera was being treated in such a capacity in America later in 1919.

[162] The presenting of Ireland's case concerned a question of international law. Ireland's claim to be heard at the Peace Conference was, as Griffith pointed out at the Sinn Fein Convention of 1917, 'based on a doctrine of international law, the doctrine of suppressed sovereignty. We can not ... secure belligerent rights unless we become, *de facto*, master of the country'. The claim, which was a good one, he continued, could only be heard on two conditions. First, that the representation in the English Parliament was destroyed. 'The very *existence* of that representation in the English Parliament denies Ireland's claim to sovereign independence ... In addition we must, *before the conference meets*, have a constitutional assembly chosen by the people of Ireland...'.

Here is the reason for the policy of abstention on which Sinn Fein swept the board at the general election of 1918. Here, also, is the genesis of the First Dail, formed immediately afterwards. The voice of the electorate was clear and unequivocal. They wanted the Sinn Fein abstentionist candidates to represent them and they wanted what those Sinn Fein candidates stood for. It was a message to the world that was unmistakable, but, as it turned out, to no avail so far as the peace conference was concerned.

[163] Some of the tactics employed by the IRA during the War of Independence became standard studies in military colleges as diverse as those of Sweden and Egypt, notably Tom Barry's actions at Kilmichael and Crossbarry in County Cork.

[164] One of the largest and so far as I know the first in Cork was, according to the late Lt. Gen. M.J.Costello, organised by the author's father.

[165] Fifteen towns and villages had been similarly sacked and/or looted in the six months between January and June. But the burning of Cork and the sacking of Balbriggan, which came later, were by far the most serious.

[166] In 1917 450 people were arrested for subversive or similar activities; in 1918, 1,651 and in 1919, 15,818.

[167] MacSwiney, born in Cork in 1879, died on hunger-strike in 1920. An accountant by profession, he was also interested in drama. He helped to found the Cork Dramatic Society and a play of his, *The Revolutionist,* was performed by the Abbey Theatre (in 1921, after his death). He helped to establish the Volunteer movement in Cork in 1913. He was interned in Frongoch in 1916-17, and was elected to the Dail (for West Cork) in 1919. He was arrested on August 12, 1920 and went on immediate hunger-strike which lasted until his death seventy-four days later.

[168] The Irish Free State became a member of the League of Nations on 10 September, 1923. Eamon de Valera became President of the Executive Council of the Irish Free State in 1932, when he also became President of the thirteenth Assembly of the League of Nations.

[169] Even as late as the autumn of 1920 when the war was at its height, the three Cork brigades, numbering perhaps ten thousand men, had between them barely 200 rifles of mixed variety, a greater number of revolvers and shotguns. The latter were usually armed with cartridges which had been re-loaded and charged with black powder, notoriously prone to misfire as Volunteers often found out, and detonated with a powder of fulminite of mercury. At no time were there sufficient arms in the brigade to fully equip a standard military company with small arms. There were, however, considerable quantities of explosives — mainly gun-cotton — as result of successful raids on military and naval establishments. This was used for making mines of one sort or another, with mixed success, until an English deserter with mining experience improved the detonators.

[170] Keys's book, an extension of a necessarily superficial television series, is seemingly intended for casual non-Irish readership. It contains a patronising earnestness shy of permitting a fact to cloud a prejudice.

[171] The two tend to be confused in popular imagery, as for instance in the street-ballad commemorating the ambush of Auxiliaries from Macroom later in the year, which contains the line : 'The Tans they set out from Macroom'. The Black and Tans were entitled to a pension, but the Auxiliaries were not.

[172] Cork 'county was ... sub-divided into three brigade areas' [in 1918] 'and Cork City was an integral part of Cork No. 1 Brigade area, which extended from Youghal in the east, north to Donoughmore and Macroom and west to the borders of Kerry. The brigade consisted of ten line battalions, plus special services and of these the First and Second battalions were recruited from and operated mainly in the city and immediate suburbs. At the height of the struggle, in February, 1921, a separate city command, consisting of the two city battalions and the Active Service Unit drawn from their ranks was formed, but this was a formation within the Brigade and subordinate to the Brigade O.C.' — O'Kelly, *Ordeal by Fire*,p 31.

O'Kelly's account is perhaps overstated in places. In March 1921 Liam Deasy, then Brigadier-elect of Cork No. 1, reported to Mulcahy that the brigade 'had in our seven battalions almost five thousand Volunteers and an active Cumann na Mban membership of over five hundred'. The Irish troops, with the exception of the small active service units, were, by and large, 'part-time soldiers', who deserve all the more credit on that account.

[173] This was a commission nominated by a committee of American citizens. The committee included senior clergymen from the main Christian churches, including Cardinal Gibbons and seven leading episcopal bishops, five State governors, eleven senators, thirteen congressmen and so on, in all numbering more than one hundred distinguished people. They formed the commission of five members and requested witnesses to attend. Lord French was one of these, but neither he nor any other British witness accepted.

[174] As it would again become in 1969.

[175] Politically manoeuvred sectarianism, as I called it in *The Civil War in Ireland.*

[176] Geraldine Neeson (nee Sullivan), the author's mother, was a close friend of Muriel Murphy, daughter of the Cork brewing family, who became Mac Swiney's wife. Mac Swiney and the author's father, Sean Neeson, met and became friends in Frongoch. The families of both women disapproved of the prospective husbands, wanting their daughters to marry people of their own social background. The MacSwiney wedding took place in 1917, in England, where Mac Swiney was detained. He was married in his uniform of vice-commandant which had been smuggled to England for the purpose by the bridesmaid, Geraldine Sullivan. This caused some confusion amongst some of the locals who thought him to be a colonial officer of some sort. To the amusement of the wedding party they were invited to a garden party at the local manor house, but declined politely. Richard Mulcahy was best man. Geraldine saw MacSwiney shortly before his death when, barely able to speak, he whispered to her: 'I know you have a trouble, Geraldine, and I am praying for you'. The 'trouble' was the attitude of her own family to her future husband.

[177] The funeral of these three soldiers took place at 0200 a few nights later at Castletownkenneigh cemetery about five miles from Inchigeela. It was conducted by Fr. O'Connell, the parish priest of Enniskean and was attended by many local people as well as his comrades. They draped the three coffins in the tricolour and fired a volley over the graves. In his address to the mourners Fr. O'Connell said — 'whether as soldiers or civilians the future destiny of our country was in our hands, and must be regarded as a sacred trust by all. He reminded us that every man had but one life and if the freedom of his country demanded it, then he must be prepared to sacrifice it willingly' — (Deasy, op. cit. p. 177).

A significant feature of the volunteer republican army everywhere was the sense of natural devotion that never left it. Before action priests were called to hear confessions and/or give general absolution. Mass was attended whenever possible, and a simple ceremony such as 'my mother's parting gift to us as we left was her blessing accompanied with a liberal sprinkling of holy water' (Ibid.) indicates how much, in peace or war, their faith and its practice permeated the lives of the people. It undoubtedly contributed in no small way to the capture and seizure of the 'moral high ground' that was for them so strategically significant.

[178] It is sometimes argued that in this the bishops were motivated because they were Catholic, Irish and nationalist. This simplistic view — which accorded with that of the Orange unionists — ignores the fact that irrespective of what the bishops may or may not have been as individuals, torture, murder and rapine of innocent Irish people and their property were occurring on an increasing scale and on a daily basis by the British forces in Ireland. Furthermore the Irish hierarchy, far from having a tradition of republican nationalism, had, as a group, since 1798 consistently expressed its fundamental opposition to both it and separatism. They could not remain blind to the evils perpetrated by Crown forces within their jurisdiction and, in these circumstances, had a duty to speak out and condemn the atrocities.

[179] 'Proudly' as Macardle says (p.392) 'wearing the prohibited uniform' of the Irish Volunteers. Macardle writes: 'These deaths set England in the dock The English people were themselves shaken by them to compassion — London citizens lined the route in respectful silence'.

[180] The loss of a sense of colour is a known phenomenon in some people in moments of stress or anger. It may be genetic. Whether that is the reason for Geraldine's monochrome recollection is now impossible to say. The author has experienced it himself occasionally.

[181] Bennet in his *'The Black and Tans'* claims otherwise, and that several revolvers were found, but gives no authority for this statement which is contradicted by Macardle and other sources.

[182] Who resigned command of the Auxiliaries in protest at their barbarities.

[183] The first three of these houses were those of Paul McCarthy, Jack O'Shea and Edmund Carey. Carey was a member of Sinn Fein. The notices were listed alphabetically and were dated 1 January, 1921. They were signed by 'Brigadier General H.W.Higginson, Military Governor, O.B.E., D.S.O.', and read as follows: 'NOTICE 'A', 'B', 'C' etc., TO:- name, MIDLETON, WHEREAS attacks by unknown rebels were made on the Forces of the Crown on the 29th December 1920 at MIDLETON and near GLEBE HOUSE MIDLETON of CORK, and whereas it is considered that you being in the vicinity of the outrages were bound to have known of the ambushes and attacks and that you neglected to give any information to the Military or Police Authorities, now therefore I, Brigadier General. H.W.Higginson, O.B., (*sic*) D.S.O. Commanding 17th Infantry Brigade and Military Governor have ordered the destruction of your property. Signed at CORK this first day of January 1921.'

[184] There are several accounts available of this important action, notably those of Tom Barry, who was in command, in *Guerrilla Days in Ireland*; Deasy, op. cit.; *With the IRA in the Fight for Irish Freedom*, Macardle and others.

[185] Cope is said to have become intimate with Collins and to have influenced him and events in Ireland at this time to an astonishing degree. He is still a shadowy figure in many respects, but that his power over the military, police and civil authorities was phenomenal is clear (See Murphy, op. cit.).

[186] O'Hegarty writes: 'Sinn Fein had, following the general election of 1918, declared a Republic. It had established this as a *de jure* republic, and it claimed authority also as *de facto* one... One would expect that something like the sinister import of this Act of 1920

would have penetrated to the minds of the Dail members....' (but)' it entirely escaped them that this Act would, in fact, partition Ireland. They could have declared the Act *ultra vires*, as being an act of a parliament which was not an Irish parliament and whose authority had been repudiated in a most unmistakable manner by the Irish people. They could have proclaimed the whole business of the elections as illegal, and they could have prevented the elections taking place at all outside the Six Counties. But what they did do was allow the elections to be held, and, not only that, but to legalize them'.

Whether or not it is the case that the significance of the Government of Ireland Act regarding partition escaped the notice of the Dail members, as O'Hegarty says, is impossible to say; it seems somewhat far-fetched to think that this was the case. On the other hand there is no doubt that the Act, and the subsequent elections, copper-fastened partition long before it became a negotiating issue and, when that time came, Lloyd George was able to negotiate from a strong position on this point.

[187] Interestingly even the remnant of the Irish Parliamentary Party — now led by John Dillon following Redmond's death in 1918, and bitterly as Dillon opposed Sinn Fein, agreed not to contest seats against Sinn Fein. The Nationalists of Ulster under Joseph Devlin came to the same agreement and, indeed, Devlin signed a contract to that effect with de Valera. In a letter to the Press on May 9 Dillon wrote: 'The policy and proceedings of the British Government for the past three years make it practically impossible for a Nationalist Irishman to fight Sinn Fein at this election'.

The effect of the overwhelming republican victory virtually wiped the Irish Parliamentary Party off the political map for the better part of the following twelve months when, in a new guise and in a totally different context, it returned in most decisive fashion.

[188] 'Commandant' was a broad-spectrum title rather than rank in itself and acquired the substantive ranking with the associated command; for instance Battalion-Commandant, Brigade-Commandant, Divisional-Commandant — corresponding with Lt. Colonel, Colonel/Brigadier, and Maj. General respectively.

[189] It is notable that, although only six of the nine counties of the province of Ulster were subordinate to this parliament, King George, like many of his later fellow country-men, referred to the 'parliament of Ulster', which, of course, it was not.

[190] The full text of Lloyd George's letter is as follows:

'Sir,

'The British Government are deeply anxious that, so far as they can assure it, the King's appeal for reconciliation in Ireland shall not have been made in vain. Rather than allow yet another opportunity of settlement in Ireland to be cast aside, they felt it incumbent upon them to make a final appeal, in the spirit of the King's words, for a conference between themselves and the representatives of Southern and Northern Ireland.

'I write, therefore, to convey the following invitation to you as the chosen leader of the great majority in Southern Ireland, and to Sir James Craig, the Premier of Northern Ireland:

(1) That you should attend a conference here in London, in company with Sir James Craig, to explore to the utmost the possibility of a settlement.

(2) That you should bring with you for the purpose any colleagues whom you may select. The Government will, of course, give a safe conduct to all who may be chosen to partici-pate in the conference.

'We make this invitation with a fervent desire to end the ruinous conflict which has for centuries divided Ireland and embittered the relations of the peoples of these two islands, who ought to live in neighbourly harmony with each other, and whose co-operation would mean so much not only to the Empire but to humanity.

'We wish that no endeavour should be lacking on our part to realise the king's prayer, and we ask you to meet us, as we will meet you, in the spirit of conciliation for which His Majesty appealed.

'I am, Sir,

'Your obedient servant,

'D. Lloyd George.

E. de Valera, Esq.'

[191] Restoration of Order in Ireland Act, 1920.

[192] 'Hegarty's description of the Truce is valuable for more than one reason. He writes:

'The state of public opinion at the time (1920-22) has been distorted out of all semblance to its actuality, both in regard to the people, the rank and file of the Sinn Fein Movement, and the members of the Dail, by the unreal post-Truce bellicosity, and by such propagandist fanciful writing as Miss (Dorothy) Macardle's *The Irish Republic*.' Unfortunately his own work on the period, *A History of Ireland Under the Union*, is itself marred by what some would consider to be even stronger examples of prejudice such as he criticises in Macardle, particularly in respect of de Valera and the *de jure* Republic. The point he makes about public opinion, however, is valid and important and is a view that was shared, in fact, by many who opposed the Treaty. To that end the first part of the sentence, while perhaps somewhat over-emphatic, does portray an aspect of the heady atmosphere of the Truce period. Regrettably the accumulated and evident bitterness of the Civil War survived to blemish O'Hegarty's account, as is evident in the concluding part of the same sentence. Here, as elsewhere in his accounts relating to events and individuals to whom he was politically and dialectically opposed, an element of a *posteriori* reasoning, and prejudice, detracts from a book otherwise important and meritorious, especially in its historical analysis and explication of the interactions of social and political forces and motives during the 19th century. It is not until he comes to later events that his evident embitterment prompts him to such as the following: 'This (de Valera's) reply, it will be seen, was ambiguous, argumentative, theoretical and tendentiously dialectical, as were the whole of his letters' (op. cit. p.750), a verbal barrage that is, paradoxically, more self-revealing than accurate.

CHAPTER NINE. Pp. 251-263

[193] When rejecting the British terms, and on being nominated for re-election as President, de Valera said that he was no longer to be regarded merely as a party leader. As President he would keep himself free to consider every question as it arose and would act as the head of government of any country would act. 'My position is that, when such time comes, I will be in a position, having discussed the matter with the Cabinet, to come forward with such proposals as we think wise and right. It will then be for you to either accept the recommendations of the Ministry or reject them. You would then be creating a definite active opposition.'

The full text of Lloyd George's 'Gairloch Formula' telegram is rarely given. Since, besides issuing the unconditional invitation to a conference which the Irish accepted, it also sets out the British position, it is worth reproducing in full.

Gairloch

Eamon de Valera, Esq.   Sept. 29th.

Mansion House, Dublin.

Sir,

His Majesty's Government have given close and earnest consideration to the correspondence which has passed between us since their invitation to you to send delegates to a conference at Inverness. In spite of their sincere desire for peace and in spite of the more conciliatory tone of your last communication, they cannot enter into a conference on the basis of this correspondence. Notwithstanding your personal assurance to the contrary, which they much appreciate, it might be argued in future that the acceptance of a conference on this basis had involved them in a recognition which no British Government can accord. On this point they must guard themselves against any possible doubt. There is no purpose to be served by any further interchange of explanatory and argumentative communications on this subject. The position taken up by His Majesty's Government is fundamental to the existence of the British Empire and they cannot alter it. My colleagues and I remain, however, keenly anxious to make in co-operation with your delegates another determined effort to explore every possibility of a settlement by personal discussion. The proposals which we have already made have been taken by the whole world as proof that our endeavours for reconciliation and settlement are no empty form, and we feel that conference not correspondence is the most practical and hopeful way to an understanding such as we ardently desire to achieve. We, therefore, send you herewith a fresh invitation to a conference in London on October 11th, where we can meet your delegates as spokesmen of the people whom you represent with a view to ascertaining how the association of Ireland with the community of nations known as the British Empire may best be reconciled with Irish national aspirations.

I am, Sir,
Yours faithfully,
D. LLOYD GEORGE

Most, if not all, the guile is gone from this bald statement which indicates both Lloyd George's anxiety for a settlement and his confidence in the outcome of a conference on his home ground.

In a revealing post-Treaty letter to Joe McGarrity de Valera stated the reasons why 'against the will of the majority of the other members of the Cabinet, I decided to stay at home myself. My reasons being (amongst others):

1. To avoid compromising the Republic, of which being head I was a symbol, by even a word or a suggestion over the conference table. To get the best results it might be necessary to dissimulate a little in dealing with Lloyd George, and my position would handicap me in that respect.

2. I wished to remain here as a reserve against the tricks of Lloyd George, such as he played on the other Irish leaders, bad faith etc. I could best rally an united nation by not being mixed up myself.

3. If the proposal of external association were to be accepted by the British, I would need all the influence I could command here to get those republicans who desire isolation to consent. My influence with men like Brugha and Stack, and women such as Mrs. Clarke, would be greater if I were not directly in the negotiations myself.

   Having decided that I should remain at home, it was necessary that Collins and Griffith should go. That Griffith would accept the Crown under pressure I had no doubt. From the preliminary work which Collins was doing with the IRB of which I had heard something, and from my own weighing up of him, I felt certain that he too was contemplating accepting the Crown, but I had hoped that all this would simply make them both a better bait for Lloyd George leading him on and on further in our direction. I felt convinced on the other hand that as matters came to a close we would be able to hold them from this side from crossing the line.

[194] Teachta Dala — Deputy of Parliament, title of a member of the Irish Parliament.
[195] The concept of External Association, which was hailed by the Irish cabinet in July 1921 when de Valera developed it, later became a subject of bitter controversy and ridicule

during and after the civil war. Nonetheless it was a remarkable conception of political interrelationships. It was later given serious consideration by British legislators and was successfully employed by them as a basis for later forms of related independence, as in the case of India's relationship with the British Commonwealth from 1947, for the Cypriot agreement in 1959 and for the Association between Britain and South Africa. It was, perhaps, before its time in 1921, misunderstood by the British and abused by its Irish opponents.

[196] There are two schools of thought about the dividing of the Irish delegation. The most common one is that the delegation was split by the British by inviting Griffith and Collins to side talks, which they attended. Another less common and clearly wrong view, advocated in the main by those who hold Collins responsible for an unsatisfactory outcome to the negotiations, is that Collins initiated the side-talks having been suborned by a combination of drink, high-living in London, Lady Lavery and the mysterious Cope.

[197] 'I ..... do solemnly swear true faith and allegiance to the constitution of the Irish Free State as by law established and that I will be faithful to His Majesty King George V, his heirs and successors by law, in virtue of the common citizenship of Ireland with Great Britain and her adherence to, and membership of, the group of nations forming the British Commonwealth of Nations.'

By contrast the Republican oath taken in 1919 by every deputy, officer and clerk of the Dail and later by every Volunteer and member of the IRB, was:

'I ..... do solemnly swear that I do not and shall not yield a voluntary support to any pretended Government, authority or power within Ireland hostile and inimical thereto, and I do further swear that to the best of my knowledge and ability I will support and defend the Irish Republic and the Government of the Irish Republic, which is Dail Eireann, against all enemies foreign or domestic, and I will bear true faith and allegiance to the same, and that I take this obligation freely and without mental reservation or purpose of evasion, so help me God.'

[198] The Government of Ireland Act allowed for a council of members from both the northern and southern parliaments. The underlying idea was that the council would be an intermediary body until both parliaments coalesced. From both this and Lloyd George's precarious political position at the time it is evident that the emergence of the northern Ireland six-county statelet as a more or less permanent entity had less to do with intent than with political expediency.

CHAPTER TEN. Pp. 265-276

[199] A detailed account of the period between this cabinet meeting and the outbreak of the civil war may be found in the author's *The Civil War.*

[200] Anticipating the necessity de Valera did form a new political group, *Cumann na Poblachta* (Republican Party), but it did not attract the support he hoped for.

CHAPTER ELEVEN. Pp. 277-309

[201] Richard Mulcahy, one of the most pragmatic on the pro-Treaty side, said that such a promise was necessary in the circumstances, *and was not without hope of realisation.* There is no doubt that the Provisional Government fought with great tenacity to achieve this almost impossible goal, but were thwarted in the end. Ironically they might have had more hope of success had Collins and de Valera not agreed the 'Pact' in May, details of which are given in the appropriate place. It was this Pact, to form an agreed coalition government, that infuriated the British. Like the Treaty, either of two constitutions was

possible; one favouring an Irish interpretation of the Treaty and one favouring an English interpretation. Following the Pact the British slammed the door on any interpretation favourable to Irish interests and issued the Provisional Government with an ultimatum leading to civil war.

[202] This was the election which was, under the Pact, intended to elect a coalition Sinn Fein Cabinet. Sinn Fein returned 94 seats, 58 pro-Treaty, 36 anti-Treaty. In addition there were 17 Labour, 7 Farmers' Party, 6 Independents and the 4 Unionists from Trinity College. How the Dail might have divided is open to speculation. Some Independents would, presumably, have supported the anti-Treaty element. If the Sinn Fein coalition did not take office, a minority pro-Treaty Government might have been formed with support from the Farmers' Party and Unionists and the anti-Treaty deputies and others forming an Opposition.

[203] Mr. Liam T. Cosgrave, former Taoiseach and son of W.T., said in a private conversation (November, 1985): 'I always understood my father's role to be *acting* Chairman and Minister for Finance'. Confusion over this point has led to some curious misinterpretations. The fact that Collins, while Commander-in-Chief, also retained control of the Provisional Government, and that Cosgrave's position was that of acting Chairman only, throws an important light on subsequent events.

[204] A warning and cautionary note the anti-Treatyites might have paid more attention to.

[205] The committee included (at various times), Darrel Figgis (chairman); Professor Alfred O'Rahilly; James Douglas; Professor James Murnaghan; James MacNeill; Hugh Kennedy; John O'Byrne and C.J.France. In addition 'AE' — George Russell, George O'Brien and Tim Healy, and perhaps others, were called upon as consultants. There was some dissent in the committee and there were at least three drafts — known as Draft A, Draft B and Draft C — before the final draft was brought to London.

[206] Sean MacBride told the author (1987) that he was satisfied the order was issued by Collins and that he 'was well aware of it'. It is a sad comment on the tragic roller-coaster of events that MacBride, though a member of the Four Courts garrison, was working for Collins on the joint arms-for-the-North plan and had been in conference with him on this on the evening of June 27, the night before the attack on the Four Courts.

[207] British documents on the period released in November 1993 indicate that the British were, in fact, to a large extent bluffing with regard to a major re-occupation of Ireland and instead favoured support (even, as we noted above, military support in Dublin) of the Provisional Government. 'Secure the personnel of the usurping government '[in the event of a republican *coup d'etat* or, presumably, if the Pact government sat] '... and employ flying columns and a special striking force which would be landed from England', Major Gen. Sir William Thwaites, Director of Military Operations (Wilson's old posting), War Office. Macready, however, favoured an economic blockade of Ireland, his experience having satisfied him that military measures 'would be utterly useless as a means of producing a settlement of the Irish question'.

[208] Cope, though he tried, according to Murphy (op. cit., p.127) to defend the Pact to his political masters, was also instrumental in obtaining the field guns from the British which were used against the Four Courts. 'Through representations to London by Cope I received instructions to hand over two 18-pounder field guns to the Provisional Government with a reasonable supply of ammunition (Macready, *Annals of an Active Life*; see also Murphy, op. cit., p127). Cope was also involved in supplying arms for the Provisional Government in association with Frank FitzGerald (uncle of Garret), who had been paid, by the military authorities in Dublin (essentially Collins), '£10,000 to buy arms, ammunition and chemicals in London

which were to be used by the Northern Division of the Army in Ulster'. This not only agrees with MacBride's statements of co-operation between the anti- and pro-Treaty forces in this respect, but shows the devious hand of Collins clearly at work. Fitzgerald was detained in London and was subsequently censured by the Dail Public Accounts Committee 'for the impropriety of his business dealings. He was found to have made profits which were "grossly excessive"' (ibid.)

[209] To prorogue — to discontinue meetings for a time without dissolution. Given this interpretation it may be taken that the Provisional Government adopted the view that it was the Provisional Government, and not the Third Dail Eireann, that was being pro-rogued. But this was not a universally held view.

[210] 'It would be well, I think, if the Government issued a sort of official Instruction to me nominating the War Council of Three, and appointing me to act by special order of the Government as Commander-in-Chief during the period of hostilities' — Mulcahy Papers P7/B/177. What is particularly interesting about this is that it is a memorandum from the Chairman of the Provisional Government to the President of Dail Eireann. It suggests that the position in respect of the two bodies following the election was not seen as clearly then as was later suggested.

[211] Born Armagh, 1898. Sinn Fein organizer Armagh, 1917. Commdt. 1919-1921. TD for Louth, 1923-73. IRA Chief-of-Staff, 1924. Founder member of Fianna Fail, 1926. Cabinet minister in every Fianna Fail government until 1973. Tanaiste, 1965-69. Represented Ireland at the United Nations.

[212] O'Donoghue says it represented the hopes of such officers on both sides that by limiting the area of conflict some solution to the Army problem would be found. It was an unrealistic hope.

[213] 'If the republicans had concentrated on Dublin and on finishing the fight there, instead of consolidating themselves in the south, the end might have been very different. There is every likelihood that if they had come up from the south during the ten days of fighting in Dublin to reinforce the Dublin Brigade that the Government forces would have been contained and, eventually, beaten in the capital'- F. O'Donoghue in a note to the author. There is a view that the 'Republic of Munster' was de Valera's idea. But that is not in accordance with the known facts. It was essentially Liam Lynch's policy for which he was criticised by, amongst others, O'Malley, who wanted to attack Dublin.

[214] To some extent this belief reinforces the earlier — and also erroneous — view that it was only the Four Courts garrison with which they had to deal.

[215] One of the names given to the anti-Treaty forces by their opponents. In late 1922 a directive was issued by the Free State Government that all anti-Treaty soldiers were to be identified by this title.

[216] Dr. Seamus Fitzgerald, one of the Cork anti-Treaty leaders, later told the author: 'If a constitutional assembly had met on Saturday, 30 June, as intended, it would have solved the Four Courts problem'.

[217] Including Erskine Childers, convicted and condemned for having in his possession a small pearl-handled pistol which had been given to him by Michael Collins. Childers was executed while his appeal was pending. An official bulletin (*The Free State*, October 12, 1922), stated: 'If prisoners are taken they must not be released until they are incapable of further harm. If executions are necessary they must be carried out with no fear of the chimera of popular reaction'.

[218] On 5 December the Irish Free State Constitution Act and the Irish Free State (Consequential Provisions) Act became law in England. On 8 December four prisoners, Rory O'Connor, Liam Mellowes, Dick Barrett and Joseph McKelvey, who had been

captured from the Four Courts at the beginning of July, were executed by the Provisional Government.

[219] 'I have undertaken for the future of Ireland to accept and aid in the immediate and unconditional surrender of all arms and men and have signed the following statement: — I accept and will aid an immediate and unconditional surrender of all arms and men as required by General Mulcahy. Signed, Liam Deasy'.

There was an addendum.

'In pursuance of this undertaking I am asked to appeal for a similar undertaking from the following: E. de Valera, Liam Lynch, T. Barry and the other members of the Republican Executive, and for the immediate and unconditional surrender of themselves after the issue by them of an order for surrender of those associated with them together with their arms and equipment.'

The inclusion of de Valera's name and the use of the phrase 'of the Republican Executive', are interesting. Bearing in mind that the wording was that of the Free State authorities, it seems probable that the intent was to lump together in some vague, blameworthy and discreditable way both the constitutional and military leaders of the anti-Treaty movement.

[220] 'His appreciation' says O'Donoghue, 'of the military situation was more optimistic than the facts warranted.'

[221] 'Police, military and intelligence agents were used to dislocate the election work of Sinn Fein. Election offices were raided ... many chairmen and speakers were arrested ... beaten ... fired on and one man was shot dead' (Macardle, p.833).

CHAPTER TWELVE. Pp. 311-330

[222] There is some disagreement about Brugha's position as Chief-of-Staff. Michael Hayes (*Sunday Independent*, 5 January , 1969, in a review of the author's *The Life and Death of Michael Collins*), stated that 'Brugha was not Chief-of-Staff, but Chairman of the Resident Executive of the Irish Volunteers and was the obvious choice for Minister for Defence, which he became in 1919'. P.S.O'Hegarty (op.cit., p. 737) says that Brugha was 'Secretary for Defence'. Both these writers were pro-Treaty. Dorothy Macardle, who may be said to have been anti-Treaty in outlook, states unequivocally that Brugha was appointed Chief-of-Staff in 1917 (op. cit., p. 235). Later and uncommitted writers may be more reliable. Foster (op. cit.p.508) is specific, stating that Brugha was IRA Chief-of-Staff, October 1917-April 1919, while Lyons (op. cit., p. 392) puts it like this:

> Just as the IRB had moved rapidly into key positions in the original Volunteer head-quarters staff, so now [1917] they did precisely the same thing with the reconstituted executive. Thus Collins became Director of Organisation, Diarmuid Lynch, Director of Communications and another IRB man, Sean McGarry, General Secretary. On the other hand, since Cathal Brugha, now a convinced opponent of the IRB, was Chief-of-Staff, there was obvious scope for future friction.

[223] According to General M.J.Costello, who was on duty at Portlaoise at the time, Collins came out and said to him: '"The three Toms will end this thing", meaning the three anti-Treaty officers, Tom Malone of Limerick, Tom Barry, then in Kilmainham Jail, and Tom Hales, brigadier of Cork No. 3 (West Cork) brigade in whose brigade area was a small cross-roads in a valley known as Beal na mBlath. A detailed account of the ambush may be found in *The Life and Death of Michael Collins*, Cork, 1968.

[224] See *The Civil War.*

[225] The original turret in the armoured car — Slievenamon, ARR 2 — was round. It was later replaced by a square turret. When the Vickers machine-gun in the armoured car

'stopped', the gunner, McPeake, had to depress the handles in order to clear it and he raised the turret to let out the cordite fumes at the same time.

[226] McPeake, a Scot and a former member of a Scots regiment (Argyle and Sutherland Highlanders), had been a machine-gunner. He was arrested in Glasgow in 1921 for IRA activities. On December 2, 1922, he deserted from the Provisional Forces, taking the armoured car with him (See *The Life and Death of Michael Collins*). Contrary to what is consistently alleged (by Hopkinson, for instance), he did not join the anti-Treaty forces, nor did he receive any money from them. But he was helped by them to return to Scotland. Because of his desertion he was suspected of complicity in the death of Collins. He was later brought back to Ireland and tried for stealing the armoured car. As recently as 1967 the author received an anonymous letter from New York stating as a 'fact' that McPeake shot Collins. McPeake's desertion had nothing to do with his having fired the fatal shot. But he felt that suspicion centred on him, that his life was in danger; he opposed the terrorist activities of some of the Provisional troops and these were the reasons for his desertion.

[227] The relevant portion of Kelleher's statement, as published by Fr. Anthony Gaughan in *The Irish Times*, is given here with his kind permission:

Tom Hales was engaged in dismantling the barricades when the motorcyclist was heard. I shouted to Tom Hales to run for cover and he had only scrambled over the barricade (singular) when Neill and I opened fire on the Free State (sic.) party.

The Lewis gun of the armoured car, handled by McPeak, was firing on the position held by me — the jamming of the machine-gun saved my life. The man nearest to me [Neil], a former soldier in the British Army, was a crack shot and one of his bullets hit the road near where Collins was lying, firing his rifle, and the ricochet of that bullet upwards hit Collins in the back of the head, fatally wounding him.

Apart from the question of the bullet striking the road, time or circumstance affected Kelleher's accuracy in this statement in some minor, but important, points. For instance the armoured car was not armed with a Lewis gun, but with a Vickers gun, an altogether more deadly and powerful weapon. There was, however, a Lewis gun in action with the troops in the Crossley tender, who were also armed with rifles and sub-machine (Thompson) guns. They had had a second Lewis gun, but left it at Macroom that morning when the O/C there asked for additional armament. In view of McPeake's own statement it may be taken that Neil's bullet — if it did hit the road — then went on to hit the turret. But taken together with Neil's own statement that he aimed at the 'head' coming out of the turret this is unlikely.

[228] Without going into too much technical detail it can be readily established that a Vickers gun does not 'jam' in the sense of siezing up, and that the immediate action taken to remedy any of the four stoppages, which have approximately eighteen sub-divisions amongst them, cannot result in the accidental discharge of a single shot. A round, or burst, from a Vickers gun cannot be fired until a minimum of three, and more often four, deliberate, routine actions are taken by the gunner. The question of McPeake having been responsible for Collins's death has long since been ruled out by the author in *The Life and Death of Michael Collins*, and subsequently by other authorities.

[229] This is claimed to have been done by Liam Tobin acting on the instructions of Desmond Fitzgerald, but, though the information was furnished by two impeccable sources (Sean MacEoin and Sean MacBride), it has been denied both by General Tobin's daughter, Mrs. Maura Tobin-Hand, and by the late Col. Dan Bryan (in a letter to *The Irish Times*, 14 February, 1969). Dan Bryan claimed to be one of three or four people who segregated and destroyed some documents at that time. He never saw or heard of General Tobin being connected with that work, nor did he notice any Collins documents in the few

he did not personally deal with. However, what my old friend Dan Bryan says boils down to this: He and three or four associates destroyed some (defence) documents at that time (he does not say on whose instructions); that he personally 'destroyed most of them'; that they 'did not include any documents which can now or in the future be a serious loss to historical research'; that he is sure that there was no Collins material in them and that Liam Tobin was not involved in that particular piece of work. For Dan Bryan, or anyone else, to have concluded from this that no Collins documents were destroyed by anyone else seems to me to be a pretty big step. He produced no evidence in support of his contention that this was not possible; even likely. One cannot help wondering what Dan Bryan, then a serving officer, might have done had he discovered important Collins documents amongst those he destroyed that 'did not include any documents which can now or in the future be a serious loss to historical research', and was ordered to destroy them. The balance of probabilities is that some significant documents are missing, presumably destroyed, irrespective of by whom. Gen. Sean MacEoin, who informed me that Tobin had done so, also held this view, as did both Dr. Dermot Keogh and Sean MacBride.
[230] Private conversation with the author.

Select Bibliography

(LAMER — Leaders and Men of the Easter Rising, ed F.X. Martin).
(WTIITFFF — With the IRA in the Fight For Freedom, Tralee).

Andrews, C.S., *Dublin Made Me*, Cork, 1979.
Barry, Tom, *Guerrilla Days in Ireland*, Tralee, no date.
Barnett, Corelli, *The Great War*, London, 1979.
Beaslai, Piaras, *Michael Collins and the Making of a New Ireland*, (2 vols), Dublin, 1926.
— *The Anglo-Irish War*, WTIITFFF
Bell, J. Bowyer, *The Secret Army*, London, 1970.
Berresford Ellis, Peter, *Irish Democrat*.
Bennett, Richard, *The Black and Tans*, London, 1959
Birrell, Augustine, *Things Past Redress*, London, 1937).
Blake, R., *The Unknown Prime Minister*, London, 1995.
Bowman, John, *de Valera and the Ulster Question, 1917-73*, London, 1972.
Boyce, D.G., *Englishmen and Irish Troubles*, London, 1972.
Boyd, Andrew, *Holy War in Belfast*, Belfast, 1970.
Breen, Dan, *My Fight For Irish Freedom*, Tralee.
Butt, Isaac, *The Famine in the Land*, London, 1847.
Byrne, Miles, *Memoirs*, Dublin, 1945.
Caulfield, Max, *The Easter Rebellion*, London, 1964.
Cavanagh, Michael, *Memoirs of General Thomas Francis Meagher*, Massachusetts, 1892.
Charteris, John, *Diaries*, Dublin.
Churchill, W., *Life of Lord Randolph Churchill*.
— *Aftermath*, London, 1929.
Clarke, Thomas, *Glimpses of an Irish Felon's Prison Life*, Cork, 1922.
Colum, Padraic, *Arthur Griffith*, Dublin, 1959.
Connolly, Joseph, *Memoirs*, courtesy Connolly Family.
Connolly O'Brien, Nora, *Portrait of a Rebel Father*, Dublin, 1935.
Coogan, T.P., *Michael Collins*, London, 1990.
Costello, Francis J., *Enduring the Most*, (Terence MacSwiney), Dingle, 1995.
Cronin, Sean, *The McGarrity Papers*, Tralee, 1972.
Crozier, W.F.P., *Impressions and Recollections*, London.
— *Ireland For Ever*, London, 1932.
Curtis, Liz, *The Cause of Ireland*, Belfast, 1994.
Dangerfield, George, *The Strange Death of Liberal England*, 1910-1914, New York, 1935.

Davitt, *The Fall of Feudalism.*

Deasy, Liam, *Towards Ireland Free,* Cork, 1973.

Denieffe, Joseph, *Personal Narrative of the Irish Revolutionary Brotherhood,* Limerick,, 1969.

De Rosa, Peter, *Rebels; The Irish Rising of 1916,* London, 1990.

De Vere White, Terence, *Kevin O'Higgins,* London, 1948.

Devoy, John, *Recollections of an Irish Rebel,* new edn, Shannon, 1969.

Dickson, Keogh, Whelan, *The United Irishmen,* (ed.) Dublin, 1993.

Duffy, Gavan, *The League of North and South,* 1886.

Duggan, John P., *A History of the Irish Army,* Dublin, 1991.

Dwyer, T.Ryle, *Michael Collins and the Treaty;His differences with de Valera,* Cork, 1981.

Elliot, Marianne, *Wolfe Tone,* London, 1989.

Fabry, J.G.A and Hanotaux, G., *The Life of Marshal Joseph Joffre,* Paris, 1921.

Feehan, John M.,*The Shooting of Michael Collins,* Cork, 1981.

Figgis, Darrell, *The Gaelic State in the Past and in the Future,* Dublin, 1917.

Fitzpatrick, David, *Politics and Irish Life, 1913-21,* Dublin, 1977.

Fitz-Patrick, W.D., *The Sham Squire,* Dublin, 1865.

Foster, R.E., *Modern Ireland 1600-1972,* London, 1988.

Fox, R.M., *James Connolly,* Tralee, 1946.

French, Gerald, *Life of Field Marshal Sir John French,* London, 1931.

Gallagher, Thomas, *Paddy's Lament; Ireland 1846-1847,* Dublin 1988.

Gallagher, Frank, *King and Constitution.*
     — *The Indivisible Island,* London, 1957.

Goblet, Yann Morvran, *L'Irelande dans le Crise Universelle, 1914-1920,* Paris, 1920.

Golden, Peter, *A Journey Through Ireland.*

Greaves, C.Desmond, *The Life and Times of James Connolly,* Dublin.

Griffith, Arthur, *The Resurrection of Hungary,* Dublin, 1918.

Gwynn, Denis, *The Life of John Dillon,* London, 1932.
     — *The Life of John Redmond.*

Gwynn, Stephen, *John Redmond's Last Years,* London, 1919.

Healy, T.M., *Letters and Leaders of My Day,* London, 1931 (2 vols).
     — *The Great Fraud of Ulster,* Dublin, 1917.

Hopkinson, Michael, *Green Against Green,* Dublin, 1988.

Hobson, Bulmer, *Ireland Yesterday and Tomorrow,* Tralee, 1968

Horgan, J.J., *The Complete Grammer of Anarchy,* London, 1918.
     — *Parnell to Pearse,* Dublin, 1948.

Hoy, H.C,. *40 O.B. or How the War Was Won,* London 1932

Ireland, John de Courcy, *The Sea and the Easter Rising,* Dun Laoghaire.

Irwin, Wilmot, *Betrayal in Ireland,* The Northern Whig, no date.

Jones, Thomas, *Whitehall Diaries,* Oxford.

Jenkins, R., *Asquith,* London, 1964,

Kee, Robert, *The Green Flag, A History of Irish Nationalism,* London, 1972.

Keogh, Dermot, *Twentieth-Century Ireland; Nation and State,* Dublin, 1994.

Kerryman, The, *With the IRA in the Fight for Freedom*, Kerryman, no date.
— *Rebel Cork's Fighting Story*, no date.
Koseki, Takashi, *Dublin Confederate Clubs and the Repeal Movement*, Tokyo, 1992.
Lawlor, Sheila, *Britain and Ireland, 1914-23*, Dublin, 1983.
Le Caron, Henri, *Twenty-five years in the Secret Service*, London, 1892.
Lecky, W.E.H, M.P. *History of Ireland in the Eighteenth Century*.
— *Leaders of Public Opinion in Ireland*, London, 1906.
Lee, J.J., *Ireland 1912-1985; Politics and Society*, Cambridge, 1989.
Longford, Earl of and O'Neill, T.P., *Eamon de Valera*, 1970.
Lowe, C.J. and Dockrill, M.L., *British Foreign Policy, 1914-1922*, (two vols.) London, 1972.
Lloyd George, David, *Is It Peace?*, London, 1923.
Lyons, F.S.L., *Ireland Since the Famine*, London, 1971.
— *The Fall of Parnell,* London, 1960.
— *Culture and Anarchy in Ireland 1890 - 1939*, Oxford, 1982.
Lyons, Dr. R.S., M.P., *The Forestry Journal*, February, 1883.
Macardle, Dorothy, *The Irish Republic*, Dublin, 1951 (new edn.)
— *Tragedies of Kerry*.
McCaffrey, Lawrence J.,*The Irish Question*, Kentucky, 1968.
McCann, John, *War By The Irish*, Tralee, 1946.
Mackey, Herbet O., *The Life and Times of Roger Casement*, Dublin, 1954.
McEoin, Sean, *WTIITFFF (1919 to the Truce)*, Tralee.
MacEoin, Uninseann, *Survivors,* Dublin, 1980.
McHugh, Roger, *Dublin 1916*, (ed), London, 1966.
MacNeill, Eoin, *Celtic Ireland*, Dublin, 1921.
Macready, General Sir Nevil, *Annals of an Active Life*, Hutchinson, London, 1924
MacSwiney, Terence, *Principles of Freedom*,
Martin, F.X. (Ed.), *Leaders and Men of the Easter Rising (LAMER)*, Dublin, 1967.
— *Eoin MacNeill on the 1916 Rising*; Memorandum II.
— (Ed.), *The Irish Volunteers 1913 - 1915*, Dublin, 1963.
Martin, Hugh, *Ireland's Insurrection,* London, 1921.
Miller, David, *Queen's Rebels*, London.
Mitchell, Angus (ed.), *The Amazon Journal of Roger Casement*, Dublin, 1997.
Montieth, Robert, *Casement's Last Adventure*, Dublin, 1953.
Morley, John, *Life of Gladstone*, 1908
Murphy, Brian P., *Patrick Pearse and the Lost Republican Ideal*, Dublin, 1991.
Murphy, John A. (Ed.), *The French are in the Bay*, Cork, 1997.
Neeson, Eoin, *The Civil War*, Cork, 1966; Dublin, 1988.
— *The Life and Death of Michael Collins,* Cork, 1968.
— *A History of Irish Forestry*, Dublin, 1991.
Neeson, Geraldine, *Unpublished Memoirs*.
Nowlan, Kevin B. (ed.), *The Making of 1916*, Dublin, 1969.
Noyes, Alfred, *The Accusing Ghost,* London, 1957.
O'Brien, William (Ed), *My Life in the Irish Brigade*, William McCarter, California, 1996.

O'Brien, Nora Connolly, *Portrait of a Rebel Father,* Dublin/London, 1935.
O'Brien, William, *The Irish Revolution and How it Came About,* London, 1923.
O Broin, Leon, *Revolutionary Underground,* Dublin.
 — *Dublin Castle and the 1916 Rising,* Dublin.
O'Connor, Frank, *The Big Fellow.*
O'Donnel, Peadar, *There Will Be Another Day,* Dublin, 1963.
O'Donoghue, Florence, *No Other Law,* Cork.
 — *WTIITFFF, (The Sacking of Cork City).*
 — *Tomas Mac Curtain,* Tralee, 1955.
O'Hegarty, P.S., *History of Ireland Under the Union, 1801-1922,* London, 1952.
O'Higgins, Kevin, *Civil War and the Events Which Led to It.*
O Luing, Sean, *LAMER (Arthur Griffith and Sinn Fein),*
O'Mahony, Sean, *Frongoch,* Dublin, 1987.
O'Malley, Ernie, *On Another Man's Wound,* London, 1936.
O'Neill, Brian, *Easter Week,* Dublin, 1936.
O'Rahilly, Aodogan, *Winding the Clock O'Rahilly and the 1916 Rising,* Dublin 1991.
Pakenham, Frank, *Peace by Ordeal,* London.
Pankhurst, Sylvia, *The Suffragette Movement,* London, 1977.
Pearse, P.H., *Manifesto,* Collected Works
Peterson, Harold L., *The Book of the Gun,* London, 1962.
Phoenix, Eamon, *Northern Nationalism,* Belfast, 1994.
Ryan, Desmond, *The Rising,* Dublin, 1949.
 — *Sean Treacy,* Tralee, 1946.
 — *The Study of a Success,* P.H.Pearse, (ed.), Dublin, 1917.
Ryan, Meda, *The Day Michael Collins was Shot,* Dublin, 1989.
Shepherd, Robert, *Ireland's Fate,* London, 1990.
Spindler, Karl, *The Mystery of the Casement Ship,* Berlin, 1931.
Stephens, James, *The Insurrection in Dublin,* Dublin 1916.
Stewart, A.T.Q., *The Summer Soldiers,* Belfast, 1995.
Sullivan, A. M., *Recollections of Troubled Times in Irish Politics.*
Sun, Tzu, *The Art of War,* Wordsworth edition, Trns. Hanzhang, Tao/ Stone Norman, 1994.
Swords, Liam, *The Green Cockade, the Irish in the French Revolution, 1798-1815,* Dublin, 1989.
Talbot, Hayden, *Michael Collins' Own Story,* London, 1923.
Tansill, Charles Callan, *America And The Fight for Irish Freedom,* New York, 1957.
Taylor, Rex, *Michael Collins,* London, 1958.
Townshend, Charles, *The British Campaign in Ireland 1919-1921,* London, 1975.
Vane, Francis, *Agin' the Government,* London.
Whyte, John. H., *1916 — Revolution and Religion; the Easter Rising*: Martin (ed).
Williams, T. Desmond, *Eoin MacNeill and the Irish Volunteers,* Martin (ed).
Wilmore and Pimlott, *Strategy and Tactics of War,* London.
Woodham Smith, Cecil, *The Great Hunger,* London, 1962.
Younger, Calton, *Ireland's Civil War,* London, 1968.

* * * * *

BOOKLETS, PAMPHLETS, ETC.,

Akenson, D.H. and Fallin, J.F., The Irish Civil War and the Drafting of the Free State Constitution, Eire-Ireland, September, 1970.

British Cabinet Papers, 1921/1922.

Collins, Michael, Arguments for the Treaty, Dublin, 1922.

Connolly Papers.

Dail Debates, 1922-1924.

Greaves, C.Desmond, 1916 as History; the Myth of the Blood Sacrifice, Dublin, 1991.

Ireland Yesterday and Tomorrow, Tralee, 1968.

Mulcahy Papers.

Official Correspondence relating to the Peace Negotiations
    June-Sept. 1921, Dublin, 1923.

Prospectus for The Nation included in Thomas Davis: Essays and Poems with a Centenary Memoir, Dublin, 1945.

Report of the Irish White Cross, Martin Lester, Dublin, 1922.

Wolfe Tone Annual, 1946.

* * * * *

Newspapers/Periodicals

The Irish Independent.

The Irish Press.

The Irish Times.

The Christian Science Monitor.

Sgeal Catha Luimnighe.

The Cork Examiner.

The Nation

The Irish People

The Irish Worker

The Freeman's Journal

The Sunday Review

INDEX